D1557313

MIRACLES AND SACRILEGE:
ROBERTO ROSSELLINI, THE CHURCH,
AND FILM CENSORSHIP IN HOLLYWOOD

Miracles and Sacrilege is the story of the epochal conflict between censorship and freedom in film, recounted through an in-depth analysis of the U.S. Supreme Court's decision striking down a government ban on Roberto Rossellini's film *The Miracle* (1950). In this extraordinary case, the court ultimately chose to abandon its own long-standing determination that film was merely a 'business' unworthy of free-speech rights, declaring that the First Amendment barred government from banning any film as 'sacrilegious.'

Using legal briefs, affidavits, and other court records, as well as letters, memoranda, and other archival materials to elucidate what was at issue in the case, William Bruce Johnson also analyses the social, cultural, and religious elements that form the background of this complex and hard-fought controversy, focusing particularly on the fundamental role played by the Catholic Church in the history of film censorship. Tracing the development of the Church in the United States, Johnson discusses why it found *The Miracle* sacrilegious and how it attained the power to persuade civil authorities to ban it. The court's decision was not only a milestone in the law of church-state relations, but paved the way for a succession of later decisions that gradually established a firm legal basis for freedom of expression in the arts.

WILLIAM BRUCE JOHNSON is an attorney and writer based in New York. He holds a PhD from the University of London.

WILLIAM BRUCE JOHNSON

Miracles & Sacrilege

Roberto Rossellini, the Church, and Film Censorship in Hollywood

UNIVERSITY OF TORONTO PRESS
Toronto Buffalo London

© University of Toronto Press Incorporated 2008
Toronto Buffalo London
www.utppublishing.com
Printed in Canada

ISBN 978-0-8020-9307-3 (cloth)
ISBN 978-0-8020-9493-3 (paper)

Printed on acid-free paper

Library and Archives Canada Cataloguing in Publication

Johnson, William Bruce
  Miracles and sacrilege : Roberto Rossellini, the church and film
censorship in Hollywood / William Bruce Johnson.

  Includes bibliographical references and index.
  ISBN 978-0-8020-9307-3 (bound)
  ISBN 978-0-8020-9493-3 (pbk.)

  1. Motion pictures – Censorship – United States – History.   2. Freedom of
speech – United States – History – 20th century.   3. Catholic Church –
United States – History – 20th century.   4. Rossellini, Roberto, 1906–1977
Miracle.   I. Title.

  BX1407.M68J64 2008   342.7308'53   C2007-903097-1

University of Toronto Press acknowledges the financial assistance to its
publishing program of the Canada Council for the Arts and the Ontario
Arts Council.

University of Toronto Press acknowledges the financial support for its
publishing activities of the Government of Canada through the Book
Publishing Industry Development Program (BPIDP).

For Madeleine

Contents

Illustrations follow page 136

MIRACLES AND SACRILEGE

Introduction

In *The Miracle of the Bells* (1948), Fred MacMurray plays Bill Dunnigan, a hardbitten Hollywood press agent who accompanies the body of actress Olga Treskovna back to her childhood home in Coaltown, Pennsylvania. Flashbacks recount how he had fallen in love with Olga, how he had convinced tough-as-nails producer Marcus Harris (Lee J. Cobb) to let her play the lead in *Joan of Arc*, how she handled the film's immolation scene so brilliantly that the cast applauded, but how a few days later she died of complications from the Pennsylvania coal dust she had inhaled as a child.

Harris refuses to release *Joan of Arc*, asserting that a studio can market a picture with a star who is dead, or a star who is unknown, but not with a star both dead and unknown. Undeterred, Dunnigan suggests a clever promotional idea: generate posthumous publicity for Olga by having every church in Coaltown ring its bells for three days prior to her funeral. The gimmick sparks a local religious revival and everyone in town attends the service. As it begins, the parishioners are amazed to see the statues of the Virgin Mary and Saint Michael rotate slightly, so that they are facing Olga's coffin. As everyone prays fervently, Father Paul (Frank Sinatra) takes a flashlight to the basement and finds that it is only the weight of the capacity crowd on the old pillars beneath the floor that has caused the statues to turn. 'The Church,' he tells Dunnigan, 'doesn't accept miracles without investigating them carefully.' But Dunnigan, deeply changed by everything that has happened, asks Father Paul not to reveal that this was no miracle:

> Maybe I wanted a miracle because I'm a press agent, but I'm not thinking of putting over a movie now ... I tell you Father, God was trying to say

Life's all right, it's not as bad as it seems, and I'm up here watching and trying to help. And if He didn't say it, if nobody up there said it, don't you see Father, it's been said. Because it's in their hearts now. It'll go out all over the world. And if God doesn't speak like that out of Heaven, He'll be speaking out of people's hearts, and what's the difference where He speaks from? ... The saints came to Joan of Arc because she believed in God and wanted to help serve ... the people of France. Olga believed in God just as much. She wanted to help the people of Coaltown just as much. Give her a chance, Father Paul.[1]

Back in Hollywood, when informed that Coaltown has witnessed a miracle, Harris derides it as just another of Dunnigan's publicity stunts, adding: 'Do you think for one moment God is interested in selling movies for me? I won't hear such bunk; it's sacrilegious.' But then on the radio he hears a live broadcast from Coaltown reporting that hordes of people are entering the town's churches and crossing themselves:

Every man, woman, and child here believes that the grace of God has touched them. To them a miracle has happened. What is a miracle? The word 'miracle' comes from the Latin and it means 'a wonderful thing.' Well, most certainly a wonderful thing has happened here. Something so wondrous, that it has torn the bitterness and the doubts from the hearts of the people and brought them back to God. Whether this is a miracle or not, that is up to the Church authorities to decide. But I do know this, when Olga Treskovna was brought home, a wonderful thing happened and everyone here is convinced that somehow divine providence has blessed Coaltown and the people in it.

Harris, himself now changed by what he has heard, flies to Coaltown and announces that he will build a local hospital for black-lung disease.

Just a few years earlier, Hollywood would not have dared give a film such a distinctly Catholic flavour. However, the positive public reception given *The Song of Bernadette* (1943) had demonstrated that an apparition of the Virgin Mary could be an acceptable movie premise, while *Going My Way* (1944) and *The Bells of St Mary's* (1945) had proven that a portrayal of Catholic life, even the kind found in gritty, urban parishes similar to the one in Coaltown, could be not only an unobjectionable but even an attractive subject for America's predominantly Protestant audience. *The Miracle of the Bells*, riding this wave of successful, pro-Catholic films, thus confidently invites members of the audience – whatever their religious views – to believe that miracles do somehow happen, to acquiesce in the notion that the Roman Catholic Church is the ultimate arbiter of which miracles are real, and to accept that through miracles God is telling those who will listen: 'I'm up here watching and trying to help.'

The Next Voice You Hear, released in 1950, is a sort of modern miracle play. Mary Smith (played by Nancy Davis) is due to have a baby. Her husband, Joe (James Whitmore), bursts into the kitchen saying he has just heard God talking on the radio about miracles. The next day, Joe's buddies down at the aircraft factory say they have heard it too, one suggesting that maybe it was some hoax like Orson Welles's radio show about an invasion from Mars. The cynical shop foreman mutters: 'I don't like that talk about miracles, not one bit.' But now men at the plant who had been sworn enemies are saying 'God bless you' to one another. The worn-out starter in Joe's old car now works fine. God in His next nightly program declares: 'I've noted many changes and they please me. Enjoy the miracles I have given you and the miracles you have made for each other.' News commentators report that God's voice has been heard on radios in a number of countries, each in its own language. Significantly, there are no reports from behind the Iron Curtain, because the Communist authorities deny God's existence. In the final scene, Joe paces nervously in a hospital waiting room, then peeks through the crack of a door, from where a baby's crying is heard. Mary is wheeled out on a gurney, coming directly toward us. 'Talk about miracles!' someone says, as if the everyday life of Joe and Mary in urban, post-war America has in some way reprised the miracle of Christ's Nativity.

These films, reaffirming God's benevolent intervention on earth, appeared at an odd, disquieting time. The Depression of the 1930s was now a fading memory. A righteous war against Fascism had been won, with unspeakable horrors exposed via stark documentary footage and war-crimes trials. The GIs were back home, most of them adjusting quite well, with wages up, consumer goods in abundance, and housing and college educations being underwritten by grateful taxpayers. The pent-up demand for family life could now be fulfilled, with Joe and Mary's infant joining what would confidently be declared a 'Baby Boom.' While the defeated peoples of Germany, Italy, and Japan were still suffering, the basic benevolence of the collective American heart had yielded massive economic aid, along with a healthy injection of American political principles.

And yet the understandable pride and happiness to be derived from a great victory against diabolical evil, followed by a new flowering of the Good Life, would soon vanish. The Soviet Union and China quickly emerged as America's new and virulent enemies, their combined threat being all the more distressing because the United States had done so much to save both from falling to the Axis. In August 1949 the Soviets detonated an atomic device. Mao Zedong's Communists, backed by the Soviets, drove the forces of Chiang Kai-shek off the Asian mainland and declared a Communist state totalling half a billion people. A year earlier, an admitted ex-Communist named Whittaker Chambers had appeared before the House Committee on Un-American Activities (HUAC) and accused Alger Hiss, a former high-ranking State Department official, of being a Communist and of copying State Department documents for transmission to Russia. The charges struck most observers as preposterous, in that Hiss's credentials and pedigree seemed unassailable. He had been a law clerk for the great Oliver Wendell Holmes. Among his character witnesses were two other Supreme Court justices, Felix Frankfurter and Stanley Reed. Yet in January 1950, he was convicted. If Alger Hiss was a Communist infiltrator, anyone might be. On 9 February, Senator Joseph R. McCarthy (R-WI) told the Republican Women's Club of Wheeling, West Virginia, that while he would not take the time to specify every State Department official who was a Communist spy, he did have in his hand a list of 205 names. That summer the FBI arrested a former Army employee named Julius Rosenberg and his wife, Ethel, on charges of providing Russia with the secret of the implosion mechanism for the atomic bomb. It appeared that disloyal elements had been working for years to undermine the United States from within, and that the Soviets could now annihilate America, using technology stolen by treacherous, pro-Communist Americans. As Chambers had flatly told HUAC, it was time for citizens to recognize that they were up against 'a secret, sinister and enormously powerful force whose tireless purpose is their enslavement.'[2]

Thus, at a moment when peace and prosperity were finally at hand, when America's system of free enterprise was back on its feet and functioning as it should, the Communists – foreign and domestic, known and unknown – were displaying the desire and ability not only to challenge the political, spiritual, and moral values people were now defensively calling 'The American Way of Life,' but to initiate Armageddon. As the nations of Eastern Europe toppled, new Communist regimes snuffed out all traces of representative government and individual rights. Contemptuous of religion, they arrested and tortured priests and nuns, threw them in jails and insane asylums, and forced them to renounce their parishioners and even their personal faith. God, these totalitarians were saying, was dead. Well might Americans yearn for some message from God acknowledging His existence and His sympathy. Well might Americans hope for and even pray for miracles.

On 12 December 1950, a film called *The Miracle* opened at New York's Paris Theatre on 58th Street. Directed by Roberto Rossellini, it concerns a homeless woman (played by Anna Magnani) living on charity in a southern Italian village. She encounters a stranger (played by Federico Fellini), whom she believes to be Saint Joseph. Confiding in him that the world she lives in is plagued by demons, she repeatedly begs him to kill her and take her away to heaven. Saying nothing, he offers her wine, which she drinks until she slips into unconsciousness. Some weeks later, she discovers that she is pregnant. When she declares that she is graced by God and will give birth to a divine son, a crowd derisively strews flowers in her path and 'crowns' her as the Virgin Mary by putting a wash-basin on her head. Months later, beginning her labour but afraid to return to the village, she wanders in the hills until, led by a goat, she comes upon a small mountain church. It is locked, but she manages to pry open the door of a storage room. In this crèche-like atmosphere, she gives birth.

Some critics hailed *The Miracle* not only as a tour de force by Magnani but as a reverent and even a 'Catholic' work. Francis Cardinal Spellman, the head of the Catholic Church in the United States, was not of that view, proclaiming that 'Satan alone' would make such a film. For many years the New York Board of Regents, that state's highest educational authority, had delegated to a panel of professional film censors the task of deciding which films should be granted licences for exhibition in movie theatres. Although these censors had approved *The Miracle*, the Regents, following Cardinal Spellman's accusation, overruled them, thereby forcing the theatre to stop showing the film. Since the early 1930s, the Catholic Church had been the dominant force in American film censorship, having successfully threatened a national boycott as a means to force Hollywood into strict compliance with the so-called 'Hays Code.' From the perspective of Spellman and his advisers, by getting New York State to ban *The Miracle*, they had vindicated the chastity of Mary and the miracle of the Virgin Birth at a time when these and other essentials of Catholic faith were being trampled upon by atheistic Communism. That Rossellini specifically intended to mock

Catholic values seemed to them particularly evident because of hearsay comments to the effect that he was a 'Communist,' and because he and Ingrid Bergman, beloved for her portrayal of a nun in *The Bells of St Mary's*, had recently had a highly publicized affair, resulting in a birth out-of-wedlock.

The *Miracle*'s American distributor, Joseph Burstyn, sued to get the Regents' ban lifted. For Burstyn and the few who espoused his cause, at issue was nothing less than the right of a great artist to create and of audiences to have access to that creation. These reciprocal rights, although today considered the cultural bedrock of any free society, had been flatly rejected by the U.S. Supreme Court, which in the *Mutual Film* case (1915) declared film-making to be merely a 'business' for which free-speech rights were irrelevant. Hollywood, for its part, did not welcome Burstyn's demand for freedom of the screen, seeing it as a threat to the *entente cordiale* the studios had previously reached with the Church. Moreover, when in 1947 HUAC had accused Hollywood of lacing its films with Communist propaganda, the studios fired and blacklisted a number of left-leaning writers, directors, and producers. And although Hollywood still virtually monopolized what American audiences saw, it considered Burstyn and the extraordinary films he imported (among them, Rossellini's *Open City* and Vittorio De Sica's *The Bicycle Thief*) as unwanted competition, at a time when the advent of television and a massive federal antitrust suit were already bringing down the curtain on Hollywood's 'Golden Age.' Thus, even though a victory for Burstyn would mean greater freedom of expression for all film-makers, many in Hollywood wanted Burstyn to lose.

How the *Miracle* litigation came to be, why the U.S. Supreme Court thought a purportedly 'sacrilegious' film worth its deliberations, and what the outcome of the case meant for American society, are matters worth exploring.

1 'A Business Pure and Simple'

In 1903 Justice Oliver Wendell Holmes warned that it would be 'dangerous' for persons trained only in law to declare themselves 'final judges' of the educational and aesthetic value of a work of pictorial art, since 'it may be more than doubted' whether the works of Goya or Manet 'would have been sure of protection when seen for the first time.'[1] That year a new visual medium, the motion picture, was evolving from the 'peepshow' Kinetoscopes and Mutoscopes of the amusement arcades to the projected format shown in converted storefronts, then in purpose-built 'nickelodeons.' While a few cities and states commenced film censorship bureaus to protect the public from unsavoury material, most instead deferred to the National Board of Censorship of Motion Pictures, a non-profit organization which screened and rated thousands of films.[2]

In 1914 Board founder Frederic Howe divided the public into three camps: those who believed that film – like newspapers – should be free of government meddling; those who thought film intrinsically malevolent, to be suppressed altogether; and a third group – by far the largest – which wanted to suppress all films dealing with subjects 'they do not wish to think about,' such as 'the baser passions,' 'the seamy side of life,' the 'sex problem,' and 'the social evil' (i.e., venereal disease). Such topics, already whittling away at Victorian reticence in major newspapers of the Progressive era as well as in several New York plays, soon also found their way into a film medium that could no longer draw audiences with train robberies and racing fire trucks.[3] Opposing government censorship of the nascent film industry, the *Independent*, a respected periodical, declared movies to be 'both journalism and drama, already the most popular form of the latter and likely to become of equal importance in the former field. To hamper this art in its infancy by shackles from which the older arts of representation have with diffi- culty freed themselves,' it argued, 'is to do untold harm to its future development.' Art historian Erwin Panofsky praised the new medium as a 'folk art,' while the poet Vachel Lindsay said films can exceed journalism in penetrating the 'social fabric.' W.P. Lawson, an official of the Board of Censorship, voiced a reluctance to censor films because, despite widespread warnings about their 'psychological effects,' no acknowledged expert had yet articulated what these effects were. Sit- ting in a theatre in Toledo, Ohio, watching an episode of Albert Capellani's *Les Misérables* (1913), Lawson noticed two couples, one mid- dle-aged, the other newly wed. The middle-aged man, who before the lights went down had chatted with his wife about this and that, leaned over to her during the film and asked: 'Who is this Jean Valjean?' She answered: 'I don't know, John, but Sarah told me it was a swell release.' When the film ended, he exclaimed: 'I gotta do more reading. I wouldn't have missed this – for a coupla bucks!' The newly wed woman had tears rolling down her cheeks. On her husband's face, 'as he walked out with head erect, was an expression of faint awe, while his chin had a resolute tilt that spoke well for the fitness of his spirit at that moment.' Lawson concluded:

> Now there is nothing here tangible, nothing that you can measure and weigh ... But if we could follow the thought planted in the minds of the four that night during its germination and development we might dis- cover that its eventual results would prove extremely tangible. That is the sort of influence we know as yet very little about but which I believe in time we will understand and direct for ethical ends. We can deal now in practice with only the more obvious effects of the motion picture in the field of morality, but our standards are dynamic and we are trying all the time to learn more and do more.[4]

Because of the logistics of film distribution, the films Toledo audi- ences saw had already been vetted by municipal censors in nearby Cleveland, although most of Ohio's towns had no film censorship and thus many of the state's 1,200 movie houses showed uncensored ver- sions. As censorship boards sprouted in a number of U.S. cities, several state legislatures considered whether film censorship might be an ap- propriate state function. So that everyone in Ohio would see the same thing, Ohio's legislature in 1913 enacted a law establishing a three-person State Board of Censors.[5] Governor James Cox thought it important that the Board include a woman, and soon the state announced the appointment of Maude Murray Miller, a newspaper columnist, feminist, and member of the Democratic National Committee. (She would later back Cox's run for the Presidency.) Her agenda included much stricter censorship than she had seen from the private Board of Censorship, whose refusal to come down hard on the film industry was evident in its decision to change its name to the 'National Board of Review.'[6] Journalist Norman Hapgood disagreed with her, putting the weight of *Harper's Weekly* behind an unsuccessful effort to repeal Ohio's new statute.[7] Meanwhile, Mutual Film Corporation, backed by the investment banking firm of Kuhn, Loeb & Co., decided to fight the Ohio law in court. Rather than appeal any one censorship decision regarding any particular film, Mutual's lawyers argued that Ohio had no legal authority to censor *any* of Mutual's films, and thus that Mutual should not be obliged to submit its offerings to the Board and pay its $1-per-reel fee prior to distributing them to exhibitors in the state. Mutual's complaint in Ohio federal court asserted, among other things, that film censorship violated the First Amendment of the U.S. Constitution.[8]

The First Amendment

In Federalist no. 84 (1788), Alexander Hamilton argued that since the new federal government would be one of limited and specified powers, the best way to protect free speech from intrusion by that government would be to say nothing about it in the federal Constitution, thus leaving the subject entirely to the state constitutions and statutes and to the 'common law,' an evolving set of legal principles derived from the published opinions issued by judges in thousands of individual cases.[9] The most influential summary of those principles was Sir William Blackstone's *Commentaries on the Laws of England*, first published in the 1760s. Blackstone declared: 'The liberty of the press ... consists in laying no previous restraints upon publications ... Every freeman has an undoubted right to lay what sentiments he pleases before the public; to forbid this, is to destroy the freedom of the press; but if he publishes what is improper, mischievous, or illegal, he must take the consequences of his own temerity.' Governments, that is, may not block the publication of a newspaper, pamphlet, or book, but if the published work contains 'improper, mischievous, or illegal' material (for instance, if it is libelous, seditious, obscene, or urges murder or mayhem), the publisher is open to civil lawsuits and/or criminal prosecution.[10]

The framers of the Constitution ultimately decided that free speech should be addressed, and thus provided in the First Amendment: 'Congress shall make no law ... abridging the freedom of speech, or of the press ...'[11] Little emerged by way of recorded legislative history. Most observers, consistent with their reading of Blackstone, understood the provision solely as prohibiting the new federal government from forbidding or blocking publications.[12] That it might offer some post-publication immunity to a publisher who has been sued for libel by a public official, or to an author writing earnestly about a sensitive subject, or to an artist attempting to capture some significant aspect of human experience, were notions still far in the future.[13]

In 1906 the *Denver Times* published several articles and cartoons alleging that members of the Colorado Supreme Court participated in a plot to oust duly elected Democrats from various state offices, and that two of the Republican judges on the court obtained their appointments as a part of the scheme. When the court reacted by issuing a contempt citation, the newspaper cited the First Amendment.[14] Although that provision by its terms bars only Congress from abridging press freedom, it had been construed as also applying to the executive and judicial branches of the federal government. On the other hand, the framers of the federal Constitution had rejected James Madison's proposed amendment barring *state* governments from infringing free-speech rights, and the U.S. Supreme Court in *Barron v. Baltimore* (1833) had established that none of the human rights enumerated in the first eight amendments to the federal Constitution were enforceable against actions taken by a state.[15]

Not that the *Denver Times'* argument was without colourable authority. In 1868 the nation ratified the Fourteenth Amendment, section 1 of which provides:

> All persons born or naturalized in the United States and subject to the jurisdiction thereof, are citizens of the United States and of the State wherein they reside. No State shall make or enforce any law which shall abridge the privileges or immunities of citizens of the United States; nor shall any State deprive any person of life, liberty, or property, without due process of law; nor deny to any person within its jurisdiction the equal protection of the laws.

Some suggested that this negated *Barron v. Baltimore* and thus protected all U.S. citizens against any state's attempt to abridge any of the rights listed in the first eight amendments of the federal Constitution. Whether that was so depended upon how one defined 'privileges or immunities of citizens of the United States.' Some concluded that the provision protected *several* of the rights specified in the first eight amendments against infringement by the states, but not *all*. Some argued that by establishing the concept of national citizenship, the provision was an adjunct to the Thirteenth Amendment abolishing slavery, and simply provided former slaves legal equality with other citizens.[16]

Additional ambiguity clung to the terms 'citizens,' 'persons,' 'liberty,' and 'due process of law.' While section 1 defines 'citizens' as '[a]ll persons born or naturalized' in the United States, 'persons' was construed to include citizens, non-citizens, and such artificial 'persons' as railroads, partnerships, and corporations.[17] If free speech was one of the 'privileges or immunities' of national citizenship, then a 'citizen's' free-speech rights were protected from state infringement in some absolute sense. Under that reading, a 'citizen' who wrote an editorial protesting oppression by a Colorado court would have the same federal free-speech rights that would be available if his editorial were criticizing Congress. But if this right to protest government oppression was *not* a 'privilege or immunity' afforded 'citizens' but instead a 'liberty' afforded 'persons,' then section 1 seemed to say that a state *could* infringe that right so long as it did so with 'due process of law.'[18] This latter term had a long history in British jurisprudence, commonly in the context of criminal procedure, often construed as a right to a fair hearing by a tribunal appropriately convened.[19] Although 'liberty' had traditionally meant freedom from 'mere physical restraint, as by incarceration,' in 1897 the Supreme Court stretched the word to mean 'the right of the citizen to be free in the enjoyment of all his faculties' and 'to use them in all lawful ways.'[20] In sum, neither the various terms used in section 1, nor its legislative history, nor the early judicial opinions construing it, offered a perspicuous guide as to what Congress actually intended.[21] It was with a Fourteenth Amendment so subject to a blurred mix of possible interpretations that the *Denver Times* and its owner, Senator Thomas M. Patterson (D-CO), appealed the Colorado Supreme Court's contempt citation to the U.S. Supreme Court.

Justice Oliver Wendell Holmes, writing for the Court, upheld the contempt citation. Applying Blackstone's narrow conception of press freedom as only a protection from prior restraints, Holmes reasoned that the free-press provision of the First Amendment did not alter the common law and that, as a matter of common law, the contempt citation, because it was issued only after the newspaper's accusations were published, could not be a prior restraint. Thus, the First Amendment would have afforded the *Denver Times* no protection even if it did apply to actions by a state. That being so, the issue of whether the Fourteenth Amendment caused the First Amendment to protect a newspaper against actions by a state court did not even need to be addressed. Holmes added that while the Fourteenth Amendment did afford the newspaper a federal right to 'due process,' the contempt citation complied with due process.[22] Thus – Holmes reasoned – once a statement was published, neither the Fourteenth Amendment's 'privileges or immunities' language, nor its term 'due process of law,' provided federal protection for that statement against suits or prosecutions by a state.

Ohio's film censorship law provided: 'Only such films as are in the judgment and discretion of the Board of Censors of a moral, educational or amusing and harmless character shall be ... approved.'[23] Mutual Film's lawyers argued that the provision comprised a prior restraint because it placed in the hands of three censors the decision as to what films Ohio citizens could see, much as if state censors forced a newspaper to delete certain news stories or editorials before the newspaper could be sold at newsstands. While Mutual Film's lawyers also contended that the First Amendment should be applied to strike down the Ohio film law, Holmes's recent *Denver Times* decision left little chance for success with that argument. So they also asserted that film is protected by the free-speech provision of Ohio's own state constitution. That provision contained essentially the same Blackstonian conception of free speech found in the constitutions of a majority of U.S. states: 'Every citizen may freely speak, write and publish his sentiments on all subjects, being responsible for the abuse of the right; and no law shall be passed to restrain or abridge the liberty of speech, or of the press.'[24]

Since Ohio's censors could ban films only if they were not 'moral,' 'educational,' or 'amusing and harmless,' Mutual vouchsafed that none of the movies it offered, including 'dramatizations of standard novels and short stories and the performance of standard dramas,' would violate these standards. In 1911, Justice Holmes had described films as a form of 'drama.' But since neither dramas, nor novels, nor short stories had enjoyed blanket protection from censorship under either the First Amendment or the various state constitutions, Mutual could not reasonably have hoped to establish free-speech rights for films by making that particular analogy.[25] It therefore added that it also offered news-reels, projecting 'events of great historical and current interest as they occur throughout the world – the same events which are described in words and by photographs in newspapers, weekly periodicals, magazines and other publications ... depicted in motion pictures within a few days after they happen.' Because printed news had never been subjected to prior restraints – Mutual asserted – newsreels should not be.

This was Mutual's best argument. The title cards shown between the visual images of a silent newsreel were akin to newspaper headlines and copy, while the visual images themselves were 'news' in the same sense that the pictures in a newspaper were. When in October 1896 an audience of prominent Republicans cheered a film of presidential candidate William McKinley on his lawn in Canton, Ohio, McKinley became part of the same natural progression of media that had earlier enlivened newspapers and magazines with line illustrations and then photogravure.[26] Following the explosion which destroyed the battleship *Maine* in Havana Harbor, a film of men unloading the sailors' coffins would be the first newsreels many Americans would see, thus fuelling the American fervour for war. Shortly thereafter, Vitagraph's *Tearing Down the Spanish Flag!* (1898) was received with jubilant patriotism. Audiences were still so innocent regarding verisimilitude that when, two years before, Thomas Edison had projected a British film of waves breaking on a beach, it was reported that those in the front rows feared getting wet. Now watching Vitagraph's chauvinistic portrayal of a fierce naval battle in Manila Bay, the crowd had no idea that it was actually viewing miniature boats filmed in a tank of water on a Manhattan rooftop.[27] When the Pathé brothers commenced a newsreel service in the United States in 1910/11, a decade before the first news broadcasts on commercial radio, millions of people gained their first appreciation of significant world events by going to the nickelodeon. And in 1914 the great film pioneer Edwin S. Porter praised newsreels which recorded the U.S. skirmishes with Mexico, affording 'future generations' the chance to experience them 'with such realism and exactitude as the spoken or written word could never convey.'[28]

Nor was Mutual the first to analogize newsreels and newspapers in a legal context. In 1912, New York mayor William Jay Gaynor urged upon City aldermen the notion that the phrase 'the press' should include 'all methods of expression by writing or pictures,' thus making the censorship of newsreels an unlawful 'prior restraint.' 'I do not believe the people of this country are ready to permit any censor to decide in advance,' Gaynor argued, 'what may be published for them to read, or what pictures may be exhibited to them.' A student at Columbia Law School cogently observed: 'since moving pictures are instrumentalities for the transmission of thought, and actual words and sentences are often thrown upon the screen, such a form of publication would seem to merit as much protection as the printing of the same words or sentences on paper.'[29]

On 2 April 1914 a panel of three federal district court judges in Ohio rejected Mutual's claimed analogy between newsreels and newspapers, instead finding film's antecedents in various kinds of popular shows. States had always had the so-called 'police power' of requiring that theatres be licensed and that the plays and other entertainments shown in them be clean and wholesome. Since neither vaudeville nor – for that matter – legitimate theatre had any constitutional immunity from government regulation, film was in no better position.[30] Mutual appealed to the U.S. Supreme Court.

Civil authorities had always viewed as a common-law 'nuisance' any kind of public event that tended to attract riff-raff and no-accounts, who when brought together might at any moment become a violent mob. Given such people's ignorance, shiftlessness, and demonstrably low tastes, in seeking entertainment they would forgo a performance of *Così Fan Tutte* in favour of mountebanks, minstrels, or itinerant jugglers, the kind of exhibition which, as stated in a leading British case in the seventeenth century, draws a 'crowd of idle and naughty people,' including 'apprentices inveigled from their shops.' A simple way to eliminate such crowds was to ban the entertainments likely to attract them. Thus Connecticut in 1821 barred 'any company of players or persons' from 'exhibit[ing] any tragedies, comedies, farces or other dramatic pieces or compositions, or any pantomimes, or other theatrical shows whatsoever,' as well as 'any mountebank, tumbler, rope-dancer, master of puppet-shows ... or feats of uncommon dexterity.' Vermont's similar statute was violated by one G.H. Fox when, 'on the 4th day of July, A.D. 1842 ... at Burlington, aforesaid, [he] did exhibit comedies, farces and ludicrous compositions, to divers citizens,' the court approving the statute as a measure 'to prevent idle persons from inducing people to spend their time and money in practices of folly and dissipation.'[31]

By the turn of the twentieth century, Gustave Le Bon and others claiming expertise in the new social sciences were asserting that such outbreaks of mass lawlessness as the bloody Paris Commune of 1871 were subject to certain rules of crowd psychology. As nickelodeons proliferated, qualified observers came to believe that the typical movie venue was a place where trouble seemed to happen, either through the collective excitement a given film might generate, or merely because it was a place where anonymous strangers gathered, side by side, in the dark. A 1913 study of Cleveland's 131 theatres revealed:

> A young girl, 16 years of age, frequented a certain very poorly lighted motion picture theater ... A flirtation with a strange man considerably her senior ... sprang up. Soon they were daily ... sitting in the dark recesses of the room and embracing each other. Later an illegitimate child resulting from this association was thrown over the back fence by the [girl's] irate mother ... The girl who had always been known as decent up to the time she started on her downward path, became incorrigible and is now detained in one of our public institutions because of her gross immorality which she claims she cannot live without.

The study further revealed that of 8,245 children attending movies in Cleveland at a given moment, 4,290 were unaccompanied by an adult. A similar report from Chicago indicated that 'outside the theatres ... was always a crowd of children ... attracted by the lurid advertisements and sensational posters, and these crowds were often worked by evil-minded men, who are generally to be found where little girls congregate. The boys and men in such crowds often speak to the girls and invite them to see the show, and there is an unwritten code that such courtesies shall be paid for later by the girls.' Nellie Smith in her advice book for girls included movie shows with dance halls, amusement parks, and train stations as hang-outs for procurers. William Trufant Foster, president of Reed College, lumped movies with slot machines, vaudeville, comic operas, and exhibits by quack doctors as 'cunningly devised to excite sex impulses and at the same time to lower respect for women' by adolescent boys, even those who initially had only been seeking 'innocent recreation.'[32]

In *State v. Morris*, a 1910 Delaware case relied upon by Ohio's censors in *Mutual Film*, a statute provided that no one could operate a 'circus' without a licence. The defendant, a movie exhibitor, argued that his nickelodeon was not a 'circus' and thus that Delaware's circus statute did not apply. Unfortunately, the definitional section of Delaware's circus law could have been drafted by the March Hare, providing that 'every building, tent, space or area where feats of horsemanship, or acrobatic sports, or theatrical performances are exhibited, shall be deemed a circus.' Thus, in Delaware, in order to exhibit a film such as Giovanni Pastrone's masterwork *La caduta di Troia* (*The Fall of Troy*, 1910) or – for that matter – to mount a live stage production of *King Lear* or *Oedipus at Colonus*, arguably one first needed to obtain a circus licence. The trial judge explained to the jury that the defendant was in the business of 'exhibiting moving pictures upon a screen ... by means of a certain apparatus made for that purpose ... in a building known as No. 411 Market Street, Wilmington ... [S]aid moving pictures consisted of pictorial representations of scenes, persons, and things in motion, for the amusement and pleasure of the spectators assembled ... [also] exhibiting, by means of magic lantern, slides, and other proper apparatus sundry stationary pictures during the exhibition of which ... some person ... would sing songs which ... were then and there illustrated by said stationary pictures.' The court concluded that, as a matter of Delaware law, a film was a circus.[33]

The Ohio censors in *Mutual Film* also relied upon *Higgins v. LaCroix*, a case brought before the Minnesota Supreme Court in 1912. The village of Deer River had passed an ordinance requiring a yearly licence fee of $200 for 'every permanent theater, theater comique, vaudeville theater, electric theater, variety show, moving picture show, or other show of similar nature.' While such language might suggest that this northern municipality of a thousand souls enjoyed a bustling nightlife which generated substantial fees to swell the public coffers, in fact the town had but one theatre, its owner asserting that if this $200 tariff applied to him, he would have to close down. The court, holding that such an ordinance was plainly within the village's constitutional authority, sensed that this new form of entertainment required ample regulation:

> Moving picture shows are of comparatively recent origin but of rapid growth, springing up everywhere in the large cities and invading even villages and towns of modest size. While, as generally conducted, some educational value may be conceded to exist in these shows, it is nevertheless true that the chief aim is to furnish the sort of entertainment that will draw the most dimes. To furnish people with innocent and cheap entertainment is laudable, but experience teaches that, where amusements are furnished for pecuniary profit, the tendency is to furnish that which will attract the greatest number rather than that which instructs or elevates. To say the least, opinions are quite at variance as to the merits of moving picture shows as an influence for good or evil in a community. It must therefore be classed among those pursuits which are liable to degenerate

and menace the good order and morals of the people, and may therefore not only be licensed and regulated, but also prevented by a village council ... Common observation reveals the fact that crowds attend these picture shows afternoons and evenings every day in the week ... [T]he entrance ... is undoubtedly the rendezvous of the young and thoughtless, as well as the vicious. Police surveillance is likely to become a necessity.

In view of these factors, the court held that a yearly licence fee of $200 was legally appropriate.[34]

The Supreme Court in *Mutual Film* embraced these precedents, Justice Joseph McKenna declaring that the audiences films assemble, 'not of women alone nor of men alone, but together, not of adults only, but of children, make them the more insidious in corruption by a pretense of worthy purpose ... They take their attraction from the general interest, eager and wholesome it may be, in their subjects, but a prurient interest may be excited and appealed to.' In the same conservative spirit that had earlier banned exhibitions by mountebanks and jugglers, McKenna believed that if one recognized free speech for film, then one would have to extend it also to 'the theatre, the circus, and all other shows and spectacles.' This he would not abide, since 'some things ... should not have pictorial representation in public places and to all audiences.' As to Mutual's proffered analogy with newspapers:

The exhibition of moving pictures is a business pure and simple, originated and conducted for profit, like other spectacles, not to be regarded by the Ohio Constitution, we think, as part of the press of the country or as organs of public opinion. They are mere representations of events, of ideas and sentiments published and known, vivid, useful and entertaining no doubt, but ... capable of evil, having power for it, the greater because of their attractiveness and manner of exhibition. It was this capability and power ... that induced the State of Ohio ... to require censorship before exhibition ... We cannot regard this as beyond the power of government.[35]

Thus ended – in 1915 – the American film industry's attempt to establish itself legally as a legitimate communicator of ideas.

2 The Church, 'Modernism,' and 'Americanism'

The Holy See was a monarchy, ruling via an assertion of divine right substantially more ancient and compelling than any other European throne could claim. In the decades following the founding of the American Republic, Lyman Beecher, Samuel F.B. Morse, and numerous other Protestants argued that Catholics could never be fully American because they continued to bow to a foreign prince.[1] Conspiracies were periodically alleged between Rome and its 'docile' immigrants to take over America, culminating in a popular movement in the 1870s to reinforce the First Amendment's ban on an established religion by adding another constitutional amendment authorizing Congress to 'prevent the establishment ... of any foreign hierarchical power in this country founded on principles or dogmas antagonistic to republican institutions.'[2]

While many Protestants thus feared the growth of Catholic secular power, Catholic intellectuals saw things quite differently. Shortly before Pope Gregory XVI in *Commissum Divinitus* (1835) denounced the relentless drive throughout Europe to subject the Church to secular civil authority, Tocqueville wrote that it was erroneous to regard Catholicism as an enemy of democracy, when in his view it was, of the several Christian sects, 'one of the most favourable to equality of conditions.' Not that America's Catholic leaders needed to look to an admiring Frenchman for moral support. Although numerically insignificant during the American Revolution, Catholics were prominent among the Founding Fathers. The signatures of Daniel Carroll and Thomas Fitzsimmons appeared on the Constitution, those of Charles Carroll and William Paca on the Declaration of Independence, an independence due in no small part to the brilliant exploits of the Irish-born John Barry, 'the Father of the Navy.'

Although the subsequent exponential growth of the Catholic population triggered numerous anti-Catholic backlashes, in 1848–9, when it appeared that various secular forces might strip Pope Pius IX of his temporal rule over a huge swath of central Italy, several American newspapers proposed inviting him and the College of Cardinals to resettle in the United States, where they 'might live in perfect safety, attend to their religious duties, and restore the Catholic Church to the purity and moral influence which it ... enjoyed in the first centuries of its history,' that is, when it was a spiritual but not yet a political power. Orestes Brownson wished to syncretize Catholicism and Americanism, asserting that democracy is 'a mischievous dream' except under the guidance of the Catholic Church, since only Catholicism rules from above the fray, independent of all the wrangling that for decades had divided the various orthodox and liberal Protestant sects. Brownson had given the matter considerable thought. A Presbyterian at twenty, he had switched the next year to Universalism, then became a Unitarian preacher. Still unsettled, he dabbled in the scepticism of Frances Wright, an experimenter in the philosophy of 'free love' as well as the co-owner (with Robert Dale Owen) of a radical periodical, the *Free Enquirer*. Finally, in 1844, at age forty-one, Brownson found his spiritual home by converting to the Church of Rome (for which Ralph Waldo Emerson ended their friendship). Brownson proclaimed that the Transcendentalists' 'fatal mistake' is to worship the human creature rather than the Creator, just as the English Romantic poet errs by going into an 'ecstasy before a daisy,' thus making nature 'independent from God.'[3]

In the next generation, James Gibbons, whose father died in the Irish potato famine in 1847 when James was thirteen, and whose decision in 1855 to become a priest derived in part from the new thinking engendered by Brownson and others, repeatedly proclaimed that Catholicism was thriving in America's democracy and had benefited the nation substantially. While Irish and German Catholics quickly built political power bases in America's cities, they also became a force to be reckoned with nationally. In the fall of 1884, Republican James G. Blaine's presidential bid backfired because in his presence a Protestant minister had characterized Grover Cleveland's Democrats as the party of 'rum, Romanism, and rebellion.' Several days later, American Catholic prelates, despite initial disagreements, jointly declared that there was no antagonism between the 'laws, institutions and spirit' of the Church and those of the United States. John Lancaster Spalding, bishop of Peoria and American Catholicism's premiere intellectual, urged that in the United States the Church is 'almost for the first time in her history ... really free,' needing only the establishment of a university to make Catholicism 'a determining force' in the 'living controversies of the age,' in a nation above all others in 'good will,' 'readiness to help,' 'general intelligence,' and the 'sanguine faith in the ability of an enlightened and religious people.'[4]

Gibbons's friend, Bishop Denis J. O'Connell – born in County Cork in 1849, arriving in America in 1854, and rising to the rectorship of the North American College in Rome (1885–95) – and John J. Keane – born in Donegal, arriving in America in 1846 at age seven, and becoming rector of the new Catholic university Spalding had envisioned – similarly urged a playing out of some kind of Catholic/American exceptionalism. Even as Protestants formed two new major anti-Catholic organizations – the American Protective Association and the National League for the Protection of American Institutions – lay Catholic congresses in Baltimore in 1889 and in Chicago in 1893 reiterated the new sense of a synergistic relationship between Catholic faith and America's 'noble experiment.'

John Ireland, born in Kilkenny in 1838, arriving in America at age eleven as his parents escaped the Irish famine, would as chaplain to the Fifth Regiment of the Minnesota Volunteers see action in the Civil War, later becoming archbishop of St Paul. A founder of the Anti-Saloon League, a prominent Republican, and an intimate of McKinley, Theodore Roosevelt, and William Howard Taft, Archbishop Ireland stridently preached a Catholic version of Manifest Destiny in which 'Catholicism and Americanism commingle graciously their intertwinings when the Star-Spangled Banner is in peril. Let Catholics elsewhere, if they will, move on in old grooves, and fear, lest by quickened pace, they disturb their souls or ruffle their garments. Our motto be: "Dare and do."' Pope Leo XIII initially tolerated such nationalism, as when, dispatching a personal representative to Chicago to exhibit the Vatican's Renaissance maps at the World's Columbian Exposition of 1893, he ascribed the discovery of America to Columbus's Catholic faith, for which 'the whole human race owes not a little to the Church.'[5]

Isaac Thomas Hecker, raised a Methodist, spent time at Bronson Alcott's vegetarian experiment at Fruitlands and in the Transcendentalist enclave of Brook Farm, counting Hawthorne among his friends.

Under the influence of his mentor, Orestes Brownson, he converted to Catholicism in 1844, perhaps hoping also to convert Henry David Thoreau by suggesting to him a Franciscan pilgrimage across Europe, 'without purse ... depending upon the all-embracing love of God, Humanity, and the spark of courage imprisoned in us.' (Thoreau declined.) Like Brownson, he believed that democracy did not have a comfortable home in the disputatious world of conflicting voices initiated by Luther and Calvin and exemplified in mid-nineteenth-century America by dozens of mutually disdainful Protestant sects. Staunchly opposing the replication in the United States of Europe's tradition of sectarian Catholic enclaves, he wished to unite America's Irish, German, Polish, and French émigré parishes into one powerful Catholic entity which could then extend ecumenical ties to America's many Protestant factions. Hecker's was a prophetic vision of America's providential democracy, urging the Church to evangelize the nation and then disperse Catholic-inspired ideals of democracy and progress elsewhere, with the whole world ultimately reorganizing itself as a Catholic commonwealth. Among those coming under his influence was the future leader of the American Catholic Church, James Gibbons. In 1858 Hecker founded the Paulists as well as a periodical, the *Catholic World*, wherein he would later declare that the nation's priests embrace the conviction 'that American political institutions are in advance of those of Europe in helping a man to save his soul, and that they promise a triumph for Catholicity more perfect than its victory in medieval times.'[6]

Despite their collective exuberance, these articulate American clerics ultimately were not free to pursue such ideas in the to-and-fro of American debate. The Church was premised not only upon a set of substantive beliefs about Christ, but also upon the conviction of its own exclusive authority – through Peter's successors – to maintain, declare, and explain those beliefs. This was to be contrasted with the Enlightenment's secular philosophy, the entire enterprise begun with Bacon's call to abandon reliance on authority in favour of personal investigation, observation, experiment, and analysis. And it was Luther's challenge to papal authority with which the Protestant Reformation began. The United States was the offspring of the combined forces of the Reformation and the Enlightenment, concerning which Pope Pius IX in *Quanta Cura* (1864) categorically refused to accept any accommodation. Containing sixteen propositions critical of the political, social, and philosophical theories collectively called 'Modernism,' *Quanta Cura* was accompanied by a 'Syllabus errorum,' a catalogue of eighty separate disapproved developments, including such hallmarks of American culture as civil control of education and the separation of church and state. To many thoughtful American Catholics, *Quanta Cura* seemed to provide evidence for the charge by Protestant extremists that Rome was anti-American. Bishop William McCloskey of Louisville facetiously noted: 'It is consoling to think that Our Holy Father has in all his official acts a light of guidance from on High, for according to all the rules of mere human prudence and wisdom [*Quanta Cura*] ... would be considered ill-timed. It can hardly be doubted that it places us in a state of apparent antagonism, at least as far as our principles are concerned, to the [American] institutions under which we live – and affords a great pretext to the fanatics who are eager to get up a crusade against us. God knows best what is good for His Church.' Among the reasons the U.S. Senate in 1867 severed diplomatic relations with the Holy See was the senators' reaction to *Quanta Cura*, described as a 'sirocco blast' at which 'lovers of civil and religious freedom throughout Roman-catholic Christendom bent their heads in silence.'[7]

At the First Vatican Council in 1869–70, Pius IX asked the world's bishops to ratify his declaration that all papal pronouncements on matters of faith and morals were infallible. Although many wanted to ask pointed questions or even voice their objections, no opportunity was provided, not at least in the public sessions. Among the Americans, opposition was widespread, Archbishops John McCloskey of New York and Peter Richard Kenrick of St Louis, Bishop Bernard McQuaid of Rochester, and nineteen other Americans being among the eighty-eight bishops who found this declaration of papal infallibility to be 'inopportune.' As discussions went forward, Kenrick in March 1870 feared that Pius's real purpose was to turn the long list of anti-Modernist charges comprising the 'Syllabus errorum' into 'general laws of the Church.' Archbishop Martin John Spalding of Baltimore was similarly concerned, while Cincinnati archbishop John Baptist Purcell was reportedly appalled.[8] Although Hecker, there as an aide to Archbishop Spalding, worked to keep the infallibility question from coming to a vote, this was in vain. At 9:00 p.m. on Saturday, 16 July 1870, Georges Darboy, archbishop of Paris, urged Pius to insert in the operative document some temporizing language indicating that he would seek the advice of the world's bishops prior to making any pronouncement deemed to be infallible. Since the gist of infallibility was that it required no one's approval, Pius rejected the suggested amendment.[9]

The voting took place on Monday, 18 July. Since there was no doubt that the declaration would pass and that a recorded objection would thus be not only meaningless but uncollegial, most bishops chose to go along, although fifty-five, among them Peter Kenrick, tacitly registered their protest by packing up and leaving Rome early. The 18th began oppressively hot, followed by high winds and torrential rain. Far above the Pope's throne, a ceiling window shattered, its glass falling nearby, followed by a small circle of rain. As the voting went forward, lightning reflected off the polished walls, anti-infallibilists claiming it as a sign of God's displeasure, while others sensed a reprise of God's delivery of the Ten Commandments to Moses, with thunder-claps marking out a diapason for the final 'Te Deum.'[10] With 533 still present and voting in favour ('*placet*'), only two actually dared to record their objections ('*non placet*'). One was an Italian, the other, Bishop Edward Fitzgerald of Little Rock, Arkansas.[11] Gibbons, dubbed 'the boy bishop' because he was the youngest in attendance, prudentially omitted from his reports to an American Catholic periodical the widespread unease among the American bishops. Although Gibbons stayed for the vote and joined the majority, it was he who wittily expressed the argument against the pope's infallibility by noting: 'Well, the last time I saw His Holiness, he called me "Jibbons."'[12]

Three years earlier, in 1867, Italian legions under Giuseppe Garibaldi had attempted to take Rome from the pope, only to be repelled by French troops imported to defend the Holy See against the Kingdom of Italy. On 19 July, the day after the vote on papal infallibility, France declared war on Prussia, the Vatican librarian noting that the war was providential in that it would prevent liberal French and German bishops from joining together in a conspiracy against Pius. While that much was true, the French soon abandoned Rome to fight Prussia, and by September, Italian forces of Victor Emmanuel II were entering Rome, the Catholic kingdoms of Austria, Spain, and Bavaria having refused to come to Pius's aid. In Prussia, Bismarck used the declaration of infallibility as ammunition in his ongoing *Kulturkampf*, arguing that the pope had deprived German bishops of the right to think for themselves.[13] By May 1871, Italian forces had ended a papal monarchy that had ruled substantial portions of central Italy for 1,100 years. Not until 1929 would any of a succession of so-called 'prisoner popes' deign to enter into any treaty of peace with the Italian nation now surrounding them.[14]

The first Letter to Timothy ends: 'guard the trust and keep free from profane novelties in speech and the contradictions of so-called knowledge, which some have professed and have fallen away from the faith.'

Among the 'Modernist,' liberal ideas disapproved by Pius IX was the free expression of 'profane novelties' and 'so-called knowledge.'[15] Pius IX's successor, Leo XIII, although he thought *Quanta Cura* a grave mistake, nevertheless in his own *Immortale Dei* (1885) declared 'liberty of thinking, and of publishing' to be 'the fountain-head and origin of many evils ... Whatever ... is opposed to virtue and truth may not rightly be brought temptingly before the eye of man, much less sanctioned by the favour and protection of the law ... The Church of Christ is the true and sole teacher of virtue and guardian of morals.' As for the Reformation, Leo excoriated the sixteenth century's 'harmful and deplorable passion for innovation' which threw Christianity

into confusion ... and next, by natural sequence, invaded the precincts of philosophy, whence it spread amongst all classes of society. From this source, as from a fountain-head, burst forth all those later tenets of unbridled licence which, in the midst of the terrible upheavals of the [eighteenth] century, were wildly conceived and boldly proclaimed as the principles and foundation of that new conception of law which was not merely previously unknown, but was at variance on many points with not only the Christian, but even the natural law.

... Amongst these [false] principles the main one lays down that as all men are alike by race and nature, so in like manner all are equal in the control of their life; that each one is so far his own master as to be in no sense under the rule of any other individual; that each is free to think on every subject just as he may choose, and to do whatever he may like to do; that no man has any right to rule over other men. In a society grounded upon such maxims all government is nothing more nor less than the will of the people, and the people, being under the power of itself alone, is alone its own ruler. It does choose, nevertheless, some to whose charge it may commit itself, but in such wise that it makes over to them not the right so much as the business of governing, to be exercised, however, in its name.

Such ideas Leo saw as an anarchic deviance from centralized, temporal governance by the Church, albeit temporal rule had become – since the upheaval of 1870 – only a memory to be nostalgically espoused. While Catholic intellectuals in the United States envisioned a substantial degree of independence from Rome and a great new synthesis of Catholic and American ideals, Leo warned Bishop Keane in 1883 that the American bishops had failed to give Rome due respect. In *Longinqua oceani* (1895),

Leo declared that it would be 'very erroneous' to conclude 'that in America is to be sought the type of the most desirable status of the Church, or that it would be universally lawful or expedient for State and Church to be, as in America, dissevered and divorced ... [The Church] would bring forth more abundant fruits if, in addition to liberty, she enjoyed the favour of the laws and the patronage of public authority.'[16]

As early as 1877 there was talk of Rome's assigning an apostolic delegate to the United States, one of whose tasks would be to keep an eye on the demonstrably independent American hierarchy. Bishop McQuaid found the prospect distasteful, since it would subject any bishop who was not prepared to bow to the Vatican on all issues to the predations of 'spies, eaves-droppers, meddlers, and every contemptible species of humanity.' The proposal was successfully resisted until 1893, when Leo Francesco Satolli, archbishop of Lepanto, became the Holy See's first *de facto* apostolic delegate to the United States. Bishop John Lancaster Spalding dared criticize the appointment, arguing that American Catholics 'recognize in the pope Christ's vicar and gladly receive from him doctrines of faith and morals' (i.e., areas in which papal infallibility had been declared), but otherwise 'they ask him to interfere as little as possible.' Satolli, not surprisingly, called Spalding's statement 'a great and monstrous scandal.'[17]

Father Hecker died in 1888. In 1897 an abridged French version of Hecker's biography became a lightning rod for conservative bishops across Europe, alleging a radical-democratic 'heresy' by unspecified factions of American Catholicism, with Hecker becoming – posthumously – the personification of various Modernist/liberal notions now referred to scornfully as 'Americanism.' That Hecker, born a Methodist, had at Brook Farm and Fruitlands participated in significant developments in American cultural life, struck conservatives as questionable, even dangerous. Also under scrutiny by the Europeans was the independent-minded St Paul archbishop John Ireland, who had written a glowing introduction to the Hecker biography. Although Archbishop Ireland had initially responded positively to the Vatican's plea to help preserve peace between the United States and Catholic Spain, once war started, he was among those who embraced the Yankee chauvinism of Theodore Roosevelt and W.R. Hearst, openly proclaiming that a war with Spain was better for the United States than 'lowering ... its flag through disgrace abetted by cowardice.' When in short order the United States soundly defeated Spain and began bringing secular principles to the education of 7.5 million Filipinos, Europe's conservative episcopacy threw down the anti-Americanist gauntlet.[18]

Conservative French prelates, living uncomfortably in an environment of increasing secularism, viewed all modern, libertarian, democratic, and anti-monarchical ideas from the perspective of having witnessed the tumultuous Commune of 1871, in which Georges Darboy was murdered by the Communards, the third archbishop of Paris to die bravely and by violence since the initial insurrectional movement of 1848. In 1890 Abbé Villeneuve quantified the injury dealt Catholicism by Americanism, declaring that twenty million Catholic immigrants to the United States and their descendants had rejected their faith, seduced by America's overweening secular values. After Keane, Gibbons, and Ireland all chose to participate in Chicago's International Congress of Religions in 1893, Leo condemned further gatherings by priests with non-Catholic theologians.[19]

Rome came to consider Denis O'Connell too liberal to retain the rectorship of the American College in Rome, and in 1895 he was forced out. When Satolli had Keane ousted from the rectorship of Catholic University, Keane moved to Rome, where he and other liberals met in Denis O'Connell's apartment, which some called 'Liberty Hall.' For much of the European hierarchy, for Satolli, for other Thomists such as Cardinal Camillo Mazzella and Fathers Salvatore Brandi and Alberto Lepidi, it was important that Leo align himself with Europe's conservatives, and in 1899 Leo obliged, issuing an extraordinary letter to Gibbons, *Testem Benevolentiae*, in which he declared that the Church would not accommodate itself to modern political or cultural ideas, either to entice potential converts, or to lure back Catholics who had strayed into Protestantism or agnosticism. Among the 'Americanist' notions Leo now excoriated were 'the passion for discussing and pouring contempt upon any possible subject' and 'the assumed right to hold whatever opinions one pleases upon any subject and to set them forth in print to the world,' which had 'so wrapped minds in darkness that there is now a greater need of the Church's teaching office than ever before.' Lord Acton had called the doctrine of infallibility 'the common refuge of those who shunned' liberal tendencies. Leo's letter, construed by some as infallible, appeared to mean that papal teachings 'must be taken or left. Whoever accepts them in all their fullness and strictness is a Catholic; whoever hesitates, staggers, adjusts himself to the times, makes compromises, may call [himself] what name [he] will but before God and the church he is a rebel and a traitor.' A young seminarian in Boston construed *Testem* as the 'revenge of Latin ecclesiastics' for the U.S. victory over Catholic Spain. France's ambassador in Washington, Jules Cambon, having helped negotiate the end of that war, reported to his superiors in Paris that Leo had substantially toned down the draft originally co-authored by Cardinal Satolli, which had been intended as a public swipe at Archbishop Ireland.[20]

Confiding to Denis O'Connell, Gibbons found it 'very discouraging' that the enemies of what he and his colleagues had been trying to accomplish 'lie with impunity' and 'are listened to' in Rome. Gibbons frankly told Leo: 'This doctrine, which I deliberately call extravagant and absurd, this Americanism as it has been called, has nothing in common with the views, aspirations, doctrine and conduct of Americans.' Archbishop Ireland, having escaped being named in the document, wrote that the 'Americanism' Leo referred to had been 'conjured up' by the 'fanatics' who drafted it for Leo's signature. Historian Gerald P. Fogarty, S.J., has written that Rome viewed Catholicism in the United States as 'a Church of immigrants,' its primary task being the preservation of the laity's faith, in the hostile atmosphere of a culture dominated by Protestants and secularists. That the evangelical Catholicism envisioned by self-declared Americanist intellectuals like Hecker might offer some new, positive, and distinctively Catholic direction for the United States, and even the world, was simply lost on them. Meanwhile, Ambassador Cambon speculated that Leo's actual concern was not a disintegration of Catholic faith in the United States, but rather 'the contagion of these American ideas in other countries – particularly in France, where they could have consequences very different from those in the United States.'[21]

Despite *Testem Benevolentiae*, Archbishop Ireland continued his vocal love affair with America. 'In my earnest desire that the Catholic Church should be all that God intends it to be,' he said in 1901, 'may I be allowed to say to Catholics: Be, in the truest and best sense of the word, Americans – loving America, loving its institutions, devoted to its interests, slow to blame it, ardent to defend it ... I have unbounded confidence in American liberty and American justice.' Given such comments, as well as his misguided audacity in seeking a cardinalate by asking President Roosevelt to intercede for him in Rome, Archbishop Ireland lost his influence, as patriotic sentiments like his ceased being articulated by younger priests seeking preferment. Now the Vatican's apostolic delegate played a key role in choosing U.S. bishops, who in turn looked for approval not to Gibbons but to Rome. Gone were the peri-

odic national councils issuing progressive letters like that drafted by
Gibbons himself in 1884. Dennis P. McCann has called *Testem Benevolentiae*
a 'preemptive strike' against the kind of Catholicism the American
priests had wanted, forcing them to be 'unduly defensive in their approach to American institutions and cultural values' and 'curiously
ungenerous in their estimate of the moral aspirations and achievements
of the American people,' as well as 'strangely ambivalent in their attempt to bring a biblically prophetic perspective to bear on American
social and economic practices.' Father Andrew Greeley has claimed that
Leo's letter to Gibbons dealt 'a death blow to the creative liberalism of
American Catholicism,' while David O'Brien has gone so far as to claim
that because of the letter, 'American Catholicism' – as such – ceased to
exist.[22]

The Legacy of Pope Pius X

For over a century, German scholars had been engaging in substantial
historiographical researches in order to establish authoritative biblical
texts and to recover the historical milieus in which those texts were
composed. Some vouchsafed that their scientific research methods would
not be tainted by the assumption that the biblical texts were divinely
inspired, while others stressed that the Bible's claim to a divine source
would never be undermined by a scholarly piecing together of its
'natural,' sublunary history. Leo XIII opened the extensive Vatican Secret Archives to philologists of all faiths interested in comparing the
early scriptural texts, ordered a Pontifical Commission for Biblical Studies, and approved the efforts of Père Marie-Joseph Lagrange's École
Biblique et Archéologique Française in Jerusalem. On the other hand, in
Providentissimus Deus (18 Nov. 1893) Leo declared that 'nothing can be
proved either by physical science or archaeology which can really contradict the Scriptures,' then warned against the 'fallacious and impru-
dent novelties' of scholars who study the Bible without believing it to
be divinely inspired. In 1895 he awarded an honourary Ph.D. to John A.
Zahm, priest/scientist of the University of Notre Dame, but when
Zahm in *Evolution and Dogma* (1896) attempted to harmonize Catholic
doctrine with Darwin, Zahm's book was placed on the *Index Librorum
Prohibitorum*, thus forcing him to recant.[23]

The Supreme Sacred Congregation of the Roman and Universal Inquisition, the oldest of the nine congregations forming the Curial government of the Holy See, was established in the mid-sixteenth century

to regulate matters of faith and heresy. In 1907 it issued the decree *Lamentabili sane exitu*, also called *The Syllabus of Pius X* in imitation of Pius IX's famous indictment of *modernità* forty years earlier. *Lamentabili* listed and rejected sixty-five Modernist doctrines, arrogating to the Church the last word on biblical scholarship and on science, while purging the Pontifical Biblical Commission (as one Modernist put it) 'of all the scientific intellect it contained.' Some said Pius X invested the document with infallibility. In any event, once it was issued, essentially all one needed to know about the writers of Scripture was that they were inspired by the Holy Ghost.[24]

Pius X, known for his enforcement of doctrinal rigor and the catechetical method, in one year (1907) issued not fewer than fourteen warnings against Modernism. In the most famous of these, *Pascendi dominici gregis* (1907), he referred to the 'Modernists' in baroque terms as 'hid' in the 'very bosom and heart' of the Church, exercising their 'thousand noxious arts' to undo faith by declaring Church dogma to be subject to Darwin, to progress, to the needs of the individual, and to 'that most pernicious doctrine which would make of the laity a factor of progress in the Church.' Further, 'the error these [Modernists] are spreading is much more deadly than those of Luther ... they are trying to bring the Church to the world, not the world to the Church – reducing sacred things to a natural level, depriving religion of the supernatural.' Just as Gibbons had claimed several years earlier that there were no 'Americanists' of the kind Leo had attacked, now some said Pius had identified a Modernist conspiracy which did not exist as such, that he had imagined people 'join[ing] the Modernists much as they join a definite political party.'[25]

Doctrinaire 'Modernism' did exist, however, and while it was similar to and at times partially overlapped with Americanism, it was a European phenomenon. As Father Fogarty has written, Catholic scholarship in America was 'in its infancy,' tending only to reflect what was happening in Europe, thus making a distinctly American Modernism impossible. Many European Catholics identified themselves as Modernists, either by adopting modern methods of biblical study, or by otherwise seeking accommodation with modern culture, an enemy accusing them of lacking 'the most essential condition of membership in the Catholic Church, i.e. faith in the sense in which faith has always been required,' that is, 'accepting certain things as true, on the testimony of God,' who speaks through 'Revelation and its credentials, especially miracles and prophecies.'[26] Thus, at least in one iteration, if one did not believe in miracles, one was a Modernist and – therefore – not a Catholic. As bulwarks against Modernism, Pius now proclaimed:

- the exclusion from seminaries and universities of anyone 'who in any way' is imbued with it,
- a halt on the reading of anything 'infected' with it, bý banning all Modernist material from seminaries and universities,
- a ban on the laity's reading any such material, enforced by obliging Catholic booksellers not to stock it,
- a return to Aquinas and scholastic theology, and
- assigning to modern science a secondary place in Catholic studies.

In addition, the motu proprio *Sacrorum Antistitum* (1910) demanded that each newly ordained priest utter an anti-Modernist oath, averring, among other things: 'I accept ... the external proofs of revelation, that is, divine acts and especially miracles and prophecies as the surest signs of the divine origin of the Christian religion.' Winfred Ernest Garrison would write that 'with the funeral of Americanism' in Leo XIII's *Testem Benevolentiae* and of Catholic Modernism in Pius X's *Pascendi*, 'ended all reasonable hopes' that the Church would 'allow the modern spirit to have any influence upon its ideas, its attitudes, or its methods.' The 1907–12 edition of the *Catholic Encyclopedia* praised Pius IX's *Syllabus of Errors* (1864) for 'unmasking the false liberalism which had begun to insinuate its subtle poison into the very marrow of Catholicism.'[27]

Pius X's anti-Modernist marching orders coincided with his appointment of William Henry O'Connell as Boston's new archbishop. O'Connell immediately issued an anti-Modernist statement of his own, had it published in the secular press, sent copies to the Vatican as evidence of his ultramontane loyalty, and publicly scolded other bishops for not similarly declaring their admiration for Rome's new regime of intellectual insularism. That O'Connell should so quickly and so vocally align himself with the Vatican was hardly surprising, since he owed his meteoric success to his close friendship with Pius X's secretary of state, Rafael Merry del Val. San Francisco archbishop Patrick Riordan had accurately gauged Merry del Val's appointment as a sign that Pius would have no sympathy with 'Modernist' or 'Americanist' bishops. Pius X's subsequent appointment of William O'Connell as bishop of Portland, Maine, in 1901 came as a bolt from the blue, in that Rome had not deemed it necessary to consult with the New England episcopacy. In 1904 O'Connell saw fit to advise Merry del Val that Americanists among New England's bishops and priests were scheming to insure that one of their number would replace Boston's ailing incumbent archbishop, John Williams. Soon Rome was being told that the primary goal of this alleged Americanist conspiracy was to block William O'Connell's ascendancy, as if he personified *romanità* and thus to deny him preferment would be to favour Rome's enemies.

In 1906, again without consulting local bishops, Rome chose O'Connell as Boston's coadjutor, in line to succeed Williams. 'Rome has made her irrevocable decision,' O'Connell told a gathering of New England's five hundred priests. 'I believe as strongly as I believe that there is a God that that God has placed me where I am.' Gibbon was appalled. Riordan called O'Connell's appointment 'the most disastrous thing that has happened to religion in a century,' even wondering why American bishops should continue 'sending money across the Atlantic' when Rome chose to ignore their views and concerns. Within months, Williams was dead and O'Connell was archbishop. As if to seal the new anti-Modernist, anti-Americanist bargain with a duly chastened and reorganized American hierarchy, the Vatican finally ended the 'missionary' status in which the American Church had operated for over a century, giving it in *Sapienti Consilio* the status enjoyed by Europe's national churches.[28]

Lamentabili was issued in part to censure Antonio Fogazzaro, who in a novel had suggested that the Church return to apostolic simplicity. While numerous Protestant sects were known for their resistance to hierarchical structures and their desire to imitate the primitivism of the early Church, Pius X had no such impulse. It was he who commissioned the compilation of the 2,414 articles comprising the *Codex Iuris Canonici*, a vast codification of centralized and hierarchical Church authority on dozens of matters. And while it was deemed impracticable for the Church simply to integrate the thousands of local Irish, Italian, German, and Polish parishes that had sprouted in thousands of America's ethnic enclaves, the new accent was on a uniform practice, supervised from Rome. Individual orders such as the Franciscans and the Ursulines were barred from building their own schools or inculcating their own doctrines, with power increasingly concentrated in a central diocesan structure reporting to the Curia. The American prelacy was now issuing unified messages on a variety of issues, not just from the pulpit but in the growing number of Catholic colleges and parochial schools as well as in such periodicals as *The Pilot*, purchased in 1908 by Archbishop O'Connell for the dissemination of centrally approved Catholic ideas.

He directed each parish priest to have each family subscribe, then to forward the list of subscribers along with a list of all families in the parish. The two lists had to match.[29]

Schools of theology fell in line. Priests began following a 'hush-hush' policy of never publicly criticizing the Church, preferring 'safe doctrine' to 'sorties into hostile territory.' Prominent among the victims of the new order was America's most learned Catholic periodical, the *New York Review*, which closed down following an article positing that Christ was not omniscient. 'There was no possibility of any form of dissent, even interior,' Father Paul Collins has noted, 'contrary to the traditional Catholic understanding of the role of conscience.' Several scholars protested the new regime by resigning the priesthood and marrying. Father Zahm, formerly both a scientist and an avowed Americanist, abandoned the controversies of empirical exploration in favour of composing travel books about South America. Father Fogarty has summed up the situation as 'The End of American Catholic Intellectual Life,' while some have gone further, calling anti-Modernism 'a reign of intellectual terror.'[30]

The young Francis Joseph Spellman learned Church politics during his studies in Rome from 1911 to 1916. In those years, the Holy See, no longer a major temporal sovereign, reduced to 108.7 acres, and surrounded by a united, secular Italy, continued to resent the political, social, and cultural developments it had always abhorred and could now observe – quite literally – at its doorstep. Senior Curial officials experienced the bunker mentality their predecessors had passed on to them, then fostered that mentality among younger colleagues. M.D. Petre wrote in 1914 of a 'spirit of suspiciousness and ... keenness for the denunciation of others':

The anti-Modernist profession is one in which place and use can be found for some of the basest qualities of human nature ... It is one element of its strength that its victims dare not complain, for to complain would be to render themselves liable to the suspicion of being, not what they really are, anti-anti-Modernists, but of having lapsed into Modernism itself. So bishops, and even Cardinals, suffer, in great part silently, the insolence and abuse of the sect; Catholic journalists endure the condemnations brought on them by their anti-Modernist rivals; ecclesiastics in positions of authority tolerate, in their close neighbourhood, the persons of those they know to be spies. Thus, a priest was more afraid of being called a Modernist than of being charged with carelessness in stimulating people to the spiritual life and rousing them to moral reform, rendering him like a shepherd too afraid of being bitten by sheep-dogs to have time to look after his flock.

Word spread that Vatican bureaucrats maintained confidential files on numerous priests. Blacklisting, surveillance of perceived heretical conspiracies, and dismissals from academic posts all came into play, as did scurrilous charges planted anonymously in cheap newspapers. A Sicilian bishop was dismissed after local ladies complained of his Modernism to a quasi-official secret society. When Giorgio La Piana, a promising young cleric travelling from Sicily to Rome in hopes of a significant Church appointment, found himself in conversation on the train with a priest who professed Modernist views, La Piana voiced his agreement. A few days later, he was ordered to go home to Palermo, the stranger on the train having been not a like-minded Modernist colleague but a representative of the Curia who had tricked La Piana into revealing his disapproved beliefs. The Church, Carlo Falconi has written, seemed to be 'devouring its own children.' Angelo Roncalli did not get access to his own file until 1958, when – installed as Pope John XXIII – no one could stop him from seeing it.[31]

With freedom of inquiry gone and the empirical study of primitive Christianity fraught with danger, those still interested in intellectual work reverted to the sure ground of the medieval period. In a book boldly entitled *The Thirteenth: The Greatest of Centuries* (1907), Fordham physician James J. Walsh purported to find in Saint Francis the true father of the Renaissance. The Church's intellectual fountainhead, however, was Thomas Aquinas, declared by Leo XIII in *Aeterni Patris* (4 Aug. 1879) to be the ultimate interpreter of all matters, sacred and profane. That encyclical, later underscored and 'enforced,' as it were, by *Pascendi*, meant that thinkers 'slipped more or less peaceably into a half-century's theological hibernation,' with Thomism institutionalized as the only correct method of Catholic thought, 'not so often read,' Mark Jordan has observed, 'as brandished.'[32] With innumerable priests thus intimidated into silence, there would be no trouble with the laity, from whom intellectual contributions were neither expected nor accepted. Although many Protestant sects were led by plainly dressed, untrained lay preachers and major denominations urged members to find their own individual, unmediated relationship with God, Pius X described the Church as 'essentially an *unequal* society ... comprising two categories of persons, the Pastors and the flock ... So distinct are these categories that with the pastoral body only rests the necessary right and authority for promoting the end of the society and directing all its members towards that end; the one duty of the multitude is to allow themselves to be led, and, like a docile flock, to follow the Pastors.' Although Pius X's successor, Benedict XV, called off the secret denunciations and spying, he also urged Catholics to 'shrink' from the 'errors' and the 'spirit' of Modernism, particularly its 'eager search[ing] after novelties.' Benedict's successor, Pius XI, despite a background in librarianship, continued his namesake's ban on Modernist reading matter.[33]

3 A Church of Immigrants

The Irish

In 1790, the United States was home to a small number of Catholics, pending the influx of a few more fleeing the French Revolution, then substantial additions following the acquisitions of French Louisiana in 1803 and Spanish Florida in 1821. In the following decades, French and Spanish Catholics, then Germans, would exert substantial influence in regions where their numbers were concentrated. But substantially stronger ties – national in dimension and reciprocal in effect – would bond the Republic with the Irish.

Beginning in the 1690s, the English had imposed on Ireland the infamous Penal Laws (e.g., a ban on Catholic education, either at home or on the Continent; the expulsion of priests; bounties on priests who remained; and a complex of vicious *de jure* discriminations in employment, intermarriage, and property), all in an apparent effort gradually to extirpate Catholicism. Although these were eventually abrogated and Irish Catholics were formally emancipated in 1829, Italian statesman Camillo Cavour dared say of British oppression in Ireland that he found it 'hard to resist' a desire to see a new day 'not only of justice but also of revenge.' Tocqueville, just after his sojourn in America, visited Ireland and noted the widespread poverty and hunger imposed on its Catholic peasantry by a predominantly English/Protestant aristocracy. 'The memory of the great persecutions is not forgotten,' he noted, 'and who sows injustice must sooner or later reap the fruits.' Tocqueville's collaborator, Gustave de Beaumont, observed in 1839: 'The declaration of American independence ... taught Ireland that a dependent people might become free, and taught England that it is perilous to refuse liberty to those who can take it.'[1]

Following the potato famine of 1845–9, the Irish had even more reason than before to wish revenge upon British Protestants, either their immediate Anglo-Irish landlords, or the English across St George's Channel, some of whom blithely considered the death of a million or more Catholic peasants and the forced migration of millions more to be only a rationalization of land tenancy, as beneficial as the disappearance of 'the Red Indian' from 'the shores of Manhattan.' In 1850, landlords evicted 20,000 families, a total of 100,000 people, many of whom just huddled in the road until they died. While such moral indifference was by no means universal in England, so tardy and misguided were arrangements for Irish relief that John Stuart Mill said the only good that might come of them was 'through excess of evil.' Relief efforts were often accompanied by proselytizing for Protestantism, even by demands to renounce the Virgin Mary as a condition for getting soup. Not surprisingly, Tocqueville observed of the Irish who had emigrated to America that they were – given their oppressive past – 'the most republican and democratic class ... in the United States.'[2] And while fleeing to America did not constitute the revenge Cavour had prophesized, it would eventually yield the Irish their due, suggesting what they would have accomplished and contributed had the environment at home been just.

After living (some dying) in what could be appalling conditions crossing the Atlantic, predominantly unskilled or strictly agrarian Irish labourers lacked the wherewithal to head inland and/or to buy freeholds, so that those not hired to dig the canals and coal mines or to build the railroads were consigned to America's East Coast ghettoes. Urban America struck Boston Congregationalist minister S.L. Loomis as two nations: Catholic workers and Protestant managers, a mild reprise of the old peasant/landlord relationship. 'Know-Nothings' and various other Protestant hate groups, as well as the everyday prejudice summed up in the words 'No Irish Need Apply,' thwarted Irish integration into American life, even as prominent Catholic thinkers urged a synergistic relationship between their religion and American democracy. By 1855 a quarter of New York City was Irish-born, the worst-off living in the infamous Five Points, an area sufficiently squalid to shock even the visiting Charles Dickens. Archbishop John Hughes called its inhabitants the 'most wretched population that can be found in the world – the scattered debris of the Irish nation.'[3]

Few Protestants voiced sympathy. George Templeton Strong, watching Irish women spontaneously 'keening' over the bodies of their dead husbands following a fatal construction accident, could offhandedly call the Irish 'as remote from us in temperament ... as the Chinese.' Edward Everett Hale, a Unitarian clergyman, thought Irish emigration 'the dispersion, after its last defeat, of a great race of men ... fugitives from defeat,' for whom neither God nor the world has any further use. Generations later, British novelist Evelyn Waugh would similarly write that the migration played out Ireland's historic destiny: 'They alone of the newcomers are never for a moment taken in by the multifarious frauds of Modernity. They have been changed from peasants and soldiers into townsmen. They have learned some of the superficial habits of "good citizenship," but at heart they remain the same adroit and joyless race that broke the hearts of all who ever tried to help them.'[4] Hale could not have been more wrong in believing that God had turned His back on these people. Waugh, too, was grossly mistaken: the Irish – despite everything – were far from joyless, and no one had seriously tried to help them.

While most readers warm to the Irish wit of Swift's *A Modest Proposal* (1729), that would not be true if one's children had starved to death. 'History is a nightmare' – Joyce's Stephen Dedalus proclaims in *Ulysses* – 'from which I am trying to awake.' Those seeking causes for that sense of doom other than in the nightmare of British rule in Ireland, might well infer a God that punished fallen humanity, an inference that would be natural enough in a people shaped by persecution and starvation. In 1839 Beaumont, looking back on the era of the Penal Laws, wrote that it was as if – for almost a century – Catholic Ireland had never existed. Yet, he added, the Irishman, stripped for decades of his civil rights and of lawful religious observances, came through this more Catholic than before, having 'reserved his soul' as 'an asylum for virtue.' At the time Beaumont wrote, just prior to the Hungry Forties, Irish Catholics could not have been uniformly observant, since the island had but one priest for every 3,000 Catholics and only one nun for every 6,500. In his travels through Ireland in 1842, Thackeray repeatedly noted Catholic churches that had been started but never finished, for lack of funds. Denied for generations the benefits of a formal Mass conducted in a church and led by an ordained priest, pre-Famine Catholics were devout, albeit – as Kerby Miller has suggested – their piety could revert to 'archaic, communal traditions which had originated in pre-Christian times' with 'only a thin veneer of medieval Catholicism.' As Patrick J. Corish has written, insofar as one seeks a 'strictly religious explanation' for the 'sad severity' of Irish Catholics living under conditions of repression, 'it may well be that a sense of personal relationship with God ... remained in the shadow of an essentially pagan notion of God as an arbitrary being waiting to punish.' Some scholars add that there was also the tincture of Jansenism, a set of austere principles stressing original sin, human depravity, contrition, and predestination. Priests would have absorbed the doctrine during their training in France or – when the French Revolution closed those seminaries – from the French émigrés and French-trained professors at Maynooth College in Kildare, opening in 1795. The Jansenist – Kurt Reinhardt has noted – is 'dry and cold,' 'anti-Franciscan,' suffering from 'extreme scrupulosity,' and rejecting all avenues of forgiveness and reward found in such popular forms of devotionalism as Marian veneration.[5] Then, just as successive graduates of Maynooth were re-establishing a formal religious infrastructure, the Famine hit. This conjunction of events allowed many to turn exclusively to Roman Catholicism at a time when the traditional Celtic deities – partially Christianized following the arrival of Saint Patrick – most glaringly failed to yield the bountiful harvests for which they had been traditionally responsible.[6]

Jansenism was no radical departure for Christianity but only an overlay on a Pauline/Augustinian tradition wherein sexuality is worldly, sinful, and dangerous. For Paul, and for the Pauline Christ, sexuality and generation were irrelevant, since resurrection and everlasting life were as imminent for the righteous, as was obliteration for the sinners. Sexual chastity became a fundament of the religion, featuring communal restraints on sexual activity and communal revulsion at sexual sins. In Ireland, sparse anecdotal records from the eighteenth century suggest a relative paucity of non-marital births, that is, a general custom of pre-marital chastity. Whether – as Thackeray suggested – this was because of the daunting prospect of confession (at least when and where there were priests to hear confessions), or merely because of village-level inhibitions more intense than similar inhibitions in other villages in other countries, in Ireland, premarital sexuality in Ireland appears to have been tightly controlled.[7]

The Famine would have reinforced that restraint. Among families trying to retain or expand rights in land, a young woman's reputation had to be kept intact if her family was to make for her a 'suitable match,' in a marginal economy in which many landlords wanted tenants 'cleared' to make way for pasturing. Thus, an early and thoughtless marriage, followed by a further subdivision of the leasehold with no strategic benefit, was thought a prescription for more misery if and when the mysterious potato blight returned. In such an economic environment, flirtations and dalliances were out of the question. Rates for non-marital births would thus remain low in post-Famine Ireland, despite the fact that women would be well out of adolescence when they married, and men were commonly in their thirties, in contrast to a pre-Famine world in which peasant youth married earlier and less thoughtfully. Between 1841 and 1851, the proportion of Irish women aged twenty-five to thirty-four who remained single rose from 28 per cent to 39 per cent. Between 1841 and the 1880s, the marriage rate dropped from 7 or 8 per thousand per year to 4, as if Irish peasants had sworn to abide by Malthus's prescription of moral restraint as the bulwark against the catastrophic laws of population. While 42 per cent of males aged twenty-five to forty-two were unmarried in 1841, that percentage increased every decade; by 1930 it had reached 72 per cent. A preoccupation with familial loyalty and chastity, leading to a late marriage derived solely from economic calculation, would have dovetailed with a religious regime of self-denial and a national psyche focused on the risks of eviction and starvation.[8]

Thus, the resurgence of Irish Catholicism of a Jansenist or at least a rigorist tincture, taking place amidst the sequelae of eviction and famine, and overlaid on centuries of religious oppression, could not have been a religion of pleasure.[9] Its culture of renunciation travelled the Atlantic, where many postponed marriage to finance the emigration of siblings or simply to send money home. William Laurence Sullivan, born in Boston in 1872, a year after his parents arrived from County Cork, recalled that 'sin and its punishment ... were the first clear ideas that grew into form out of the early formless grandeur impressed by Catholicism upon my childish mind.'[10] Insofar as a young man or woman failed to avoid lascivious thoughts, on either side of the Atlantic they could be confessed to the growing number of priests, each of whom was a moral exemplar in that he had succeeded not just in his doctrinal studies but in a celibate commitment. Thus were the penitent's wrongful actions and even his/her private thoughts and desires articulable to an agent of the Church and – ultimately – of God. To the degree one was sexually aroused, the priest was the instrumentality identifying and clarifying the inappropriate thought and prescribing avoidance and reform, through such means as invoking help by the Virgin Mary. Jay P. Dolan describes a Catholic 'economy of sin' in which 'mercy and forgiveness' are 'guaranteed' at confession, the expiation of guilt inevitably reaffirming the efficacy and wisdom of the representative and institution with which the subject was bound to share his/her darkest secrets. In 1910 Pope Pius X in *Quam Singulari* lowered the age of first confession to around age seven, thus making the Church the child's ultimate moral authority while also introducing some at an impressionable age to the attractions of a celibate religious vocation.[11]

It was natural to turn to Mary, the great post-classical exemplar of female chastity.[12] In Ireland, Bríg, originally a Celtic mother goddess, then transformed into Saint Brigid of Kildare, became retrospectively in the records of Christian monks a virginal sister or companion to Mary, and in some iterations a 'Second Mary' or domesticated 'Mary of Gael,' even a *Dei Genetrix*, until the Church in the eighth century assured a transition to Marianism by having festivals in Mary's honour take place on the same day as older pagan celebrations. Although evidences of Mary and Marianized deities float through the folklore of all northern as well as southern European countries, the relevant Irish history has been partially obliterated, since in 1639, and again in 1703, magistrates were ordered to destroy all Catholic shrines.[13] Since Protestants thought Marian devotion not just idolatrous but emblematic of Jacobite scheming, the destruction of her images in Ireland must have been substantial. Then, upon the defeat in 1745/46 of the Catholic Pretender to the British throne, official anti-Catholic prejudice lost some of its animus; thus began the process of easing – if haltingly and inconsistently – the persecutions that had been the hallmarks of the Anglo/Irish reign, even if in the 1770s it was still incumbent upon Nano Nagle, starting in Cork the first school of the Presentation Sisters of the Blessed Virgin Mary, to do so in secret.

In the county town of Tralee in 1842, Thackeray witnessed a Feast of the Assumption 'thronged with worshippers, such as one never sees' in England. As demonstrated by the thousands on their knees with rosaries that day, public devotionalism was already well established in Ireland when Pope Pius IX in 1854 officially declared Mary's Immaculate Conception a dogma of the Church. While Marian devotions intensified everywhere, the new era was most evident in Ireland, which saw the introduction of significant elements originated elsewhere, including novenas, shrines, scapulars, medals, and rosaries.[14] Rome's agent in working this great change was Archbishop Paul Cullen, who had shown his personal loyalty to Pius IX in 1848, when Pius avoided capture and assassination in Rome by escaping to the Kingdom of Naples in disguise. Cullen was rewarded with the primatial see of Ireland, under instructions to invoke 'Ultramontanism' – direct and absolute rule from

Rome – and to introduce the new Marian devotionalism prescribed by Pius as the surest antidote to secular ideas and Gallican influences. Thus could historian Michael Staunton posit that the 'familiar image of Catholic Ireland ... [as] a devout and somewhat puritanical people, strongly under the influence of their priests and bishops,' is a nine-teenth-century phenomenon.[15]

The chaste mother, devoted to her divine son, would have had par-ticular resonance in Ireland's post-Famine world of gender segregation and delayed marriages, in which many unmarried males worked their widowed mothers' farms for so many years that by the time the mother died, the son (still called her 'boy' – though he might be fifty-five or sixty) was too confirmed in his bachelorhood to marry at all. In 1879, as Cullen's new devotionalism was taking hold, Ireland had its first nota-ble Marian vision, at a church in An Cnoc, County Mayo, causing the town to be renamed Cnoc Mhuire, 'Mary's Hill.' While 'Brigid' re-mained a popular name, now a family's first-born girl was more likely to be christened 'Mary.' By 1900, following Ireland's construction and reconstruction of hundreds of churches and the training of tens of thousands of priests and nuns, the proportion of Catholics attending Mass exceeded 85 per cent, having in three generations attained such a thorough and punctilious custom of observance that people came to assume that things had always been that way.

Following Irish independence, Catholicism was transformed from a battle flag in the fight against Anglo-Protestant domination, into a badge of honour whose wearers could look down on the Protestant foreigners with contempt. Devotion to an interventionist, all-forgiving, crisis-solving Mary was now nearly universal, even if in the depths of the Famine times many would have dismissed her as having no more charitable efficacy than the midnight bonfires, Lughnasa feasts, and similar holdovers from old Celtic times, all of which had failed to stave off disaster. (Where Lughnasa had evolved into a celebration of digging up the first new potatoes, the Great Hunger would have turned that festival into a bitter joke.) Thus, it was Pius IX's Mary of the Immaculate Conception, invoked by Cullen during decades of larger land tenancies, yielding generally successful and more diversified crops, and burdened with feeding fewer mouths, who now stood near Christ, a second central figure in Christian redemption.[16]

Persecuted and downtrodden for centuries in their homeland, scarred by death, once in America, the Irish immediately set about helping themselves, led by the only authorities they had any historical reason to trust, their priests, under the ultimate leadership of the indomitable Archbishop Hughes. Although in its first decades the Catholic Church in the United States had been dominated by the French, between 1840 and 1896, 596 of the 1,407 priests trained at All Hallows College near Dublin were dispatched to the United States, among them John Glennon, future archbishop of St Louis. Of 107 priests in the New York diocese in 1845, 59 had been born in Ireland. Even in far-flung San Francisco, 64 of the archdiocese's 88 priests were Irish-born.[17] As beneficiaries of this substantial Irish missionary effort, three million Irish Catholics built a distinct and cohesive identity, making Catholics the largest communion in the United States, exceeding Methodists, Baptists, and Presbyterians, with a first- and second-generation population larger than that left behind. Between 1848 and 1900, Irish immigrants sent back to Ireland an average of $5 million every year, much of it to finance further emigration.[18]

Since Cullen's new devotionalism overlapped the great Irish migration, some embraced these pieties just as Cullen's hierarchy was introducing them, while others learned them in America, from the Irish priests sent there as missionaries, wearing Roman collars and black clerical dress – distinctive innovations also initiated by Cullen. Richard Cardinal Cushing recalled that both his parents brought with them from Ireland to South Boston the custom of praying the rosary every night. Not that the new Marian devotions obliterated the underlying sense of a transcendent God of Judgment. The Irish never lost their sense of His presence, and of humanity's fallen state. Waugh said the Irishman had only two ultimate realities: Hell and the United States. That is, humankind was either punished without release, or released from punishment by being exiled. Yeats described Ireland as 'That country where a man can be so crossed; / Can be so battered, badgered and destroyed / That he's a loveless man,' its 'Exiles wandering over lands and seas, / And planning, plotting always that some morrow / May set a stone upon ancestral Sorrow!' Clarence Darrow noted that when an attorney defends an 'underdog' charged with a crime, it is malpractice not to pick any Irishman who presents himself at jury selection: 'There is no reason for asking about his religion; he is Irish; that is enough. We may not agree with his religion, but it matters not, his feelings go deeper than any religion ... If he is chosen as a juror, his imagination will place him in the dock; really, he is trying himself.'[19]

Despite a history of rapid and multifarious achievements in what many considered a forced expulsion or 'exile,' memories of centuries of persecution, culminating in the Great Hunger, inevitably carried a lingering fatalism. But neither Jansenism, nor the Famine, nor forced emigrations, could eradicate a major feature of the Irish personality, its unsurpassed lyric wit, a glittering element so endemic as to be inseparable from the objective human condition upon which it was putatively a comment. 'God is good,' the Irish proverb says, 'but never dance in a small boat.' Parishioners typically approached God's various tests – including familial loyalty and postponed marriage – with commendable courage and a greater or lesser measure of ironic detachment. Some could endure life's trials only with whiskey, a common accompaniment and aggravating factor in depression, passing down the generations as a constant counterpoint to the brilliant wit. 'Drink is the curse of the land,' it was said. 'It makes you shoot at your landlord and it makes you miss.' A 1947 New York study of first admissions for alcoholism showed the rate among those of Irish heritage to be 25.6 per 100,000 of population, versus 4.8 among Italians, 3.8 for Germans. Although antidotes might include a happy married life, a long postponed and economically arranged nuptial could not be the most auspicious beginning. Every woman who became a nun also became a spinster, while also preserving some unknown man in his perennial bachelorhood. And in an Irish economy with limited opportunities for upward mobility, the smartest young men were commonly tapped to be priests, thus depriving them and an equal number of women from marital fulfilments. Andrew Greeley suggested that although people commonly think the personalities of priests to have been forged by Church doctrines and institutions, perhaps instead those doctrines and institutions were forged by the priests' personalities, including 'the self-hatred and inability to express emotion of so many Irish males – and the consequent proclivity to alcoholism.' Rosemary Radford Ruether wrote of going to Mass as a child in a Jesuit parish near Washington, which supplemented its staff 'with alcoholic theologians from [Georgetown] university. My childhood picture of the typical priest was one of an eloquent, silver-haired Jesuit around whom hung an indefinable air of tragic depression and who occasionally stumbled as he descended the altar stairs.'[20]

When John McCloskey became America's first cardinal in 1875, Cardinal Cullen told him that although he was sad to see multitudes leaving 'the Mother's breast' of Ireland, he 'rejoiced' that they were being transferred to the jurisdiction of 'one of our race ... a Prince of the Church whose love will be not less than our own, and under whose strong guardianship their souls will be in safe and holy keeping.' At a time when many American Protestants showed little by way of religious commitment, Catholics comprised almost a third of those who did, making it a 'virtual' majority if not a numerical one. Thus could Patrick Murphy, settling in New York in the 1880s, write home to his mother: 'there are plenty of good Catholic people, and no fear of losing our way, as Father Dwyer said.' In that decade the Knights of Columbus, an Irish-dominated fraternal organization, provided a vehicle for middle-class Catholics to establish (for themselves and for nay-saying Protestants) an aura of civic responsibility.[21]

Justice Joseph McKenna, author of the opinion in *Mutual Film*, was born in 1843, a year after his parents arrived from Ireland. Up to that time, he and another member of the Supreme Court who joined in the *Mutual Film* decision, Chief Justice Edward D. White, were the only Catholics to have served on the Court since the nation's founding, other than Chief Justice Roger Taney in the mid-nineteenth century. McKenna's nomination by President McKinley in 1898 comprised – French ambassador Jules Cambon noted – a recognition of Archbishop John Ireland's success in convincing Catholics to vote the Republican ticket in a tight race against William Jennings Bryan. But the simultaneous presence of two Catholics on the Supreme Court was not the only sign of Catholic progress. In East Coast cities, the Irish were no longer the 'foreigners,' Bernard Lynch noting in 1888 that on New York's streets the 'traditional Irish apple-woman' was giving way to 'the Italian corner fruit-vendor.' By 1900, with Catholics already constituting 18 per cent of the U.S. white population, the Irish had a rough socio-economic parity with the white Protestant majority – an extraordinary achievement that would have been unimaginable without brilliant ecclesiastical leadership.[22] With the 'lace-curtain' Irish thoroughly 'Americanized,' their priests now found themselves with a new responsibility, that of Americanizing a newly arrived Catholic immigrant group.

The Italians

Although its government was now entirely secular, Italy had been the centre of western Christianity for two millennia. Italian incumbents had monopolized the papacy since 1523, dominated the Curia, and in 1900 held about half the seats in the College of Cardinals. But because Italians had been only a tiny and quiescent minority during the formative period of the American hierarchy, they did not reach positions of authority.[23] To greet the 3.8 million Italian immigrants arriving between

1891 and 1920, most incumbents of the American episcopacy were Irish, with Germans and a scattering of French and Spanish reflecting local constituencies.[24] Having funded, constructed, and administered an organization from almost nothing, the Irish saw no reason to give way. Despite the overwhelming Italian influence at the Vatican, not until 1954 was an Italian American (Joseph Maria Pernicone) appointed to a U.S. bishopric.[25] Not until 1982 did an Italian American (Joseph Bernardin) become an archbishop.

At the parish level, too, Italians were under-represented. In 1900, with a reported 750,000 Italian immigrants in the United States, there were only sixty Italian priests. In Boston, of 1,519 men ordained as diocesan, secular priests (that is, not affiliated with religious orders such as the Jesuits, Dominicans, Capuchins, and Franciscans) between 1884 and 1945, only twenty were Italian-American. Of 1,164 ordained in Chicago between 1903 and 1939, there were only ten. While after 1887 Italian Americans were sent to Giovanni Baptista Scalabrini's special apostolic college at Piacenza for clerical training, there were never enough to service the influx of Italian immigrants. Nor could the shortage be allayed by the expedient of importing competent, experienced priests from Italy, since few wished to work in American ghettoes. Some who did come were deemed questionable characters, subject to rumours about drunkenness or other inappropriate behaviour, fiscal mismanagement, even the evasion of crimes in Italy. Fr. John T. McNicholas, assigned to a poor Italian-American parish, concluded that the Italian priests he observed had neither the training nor the personal qualities required for pastoral care.[26] A survey in 1917/18 indicated that of 410 diocesan priests from Italy, the Irish and German bishops chose to treat 330 as on permanent 'loan,' never granting them the 'incardination' by which priests obtained the prestige and security of a local appointment. Thus consigned to professional limbo, many drifted into apostasy, some resigning in favour of agnosticism, while others were lured into Freemasonry and other anticlerical commitments. Still others were proselytized by evangelistic missionary groups into becoming Protestant ministers, their first assignment being to persuade Italian Americans to reject Catholicism and join their respective congregations.[27]

Embracing Protestantism was not so strange, since many of those who came from southern Italy, the so-called *Mezzogiorno*, practised forms of Catholicism so disdained by America's Irish priests that the first visit to an Irish parish church would be mutually alienating. In so-called 'duplex' parishes, masses for the Irish (or Germans) were held in the church proper, for the Italians in the basement. If the God of the Jansenists was 'transcendent,' that of the southern Italian peasants, the *contadini*, was 'immanent,' their immediate environment being alive with divinity, to be contacted not just at Mass or with a votive candle but on the streets and in the fields, where numerous sanctuaries were bestrewn with offerings of flowers and gifts. Joseph Stella, whose paintings of the Madonna and of the Brooklyn Bridge form a brilliant transition between Italian Futurism and American Abstraction, recalled the hills around his village in Potenza, 'like a familiar face that one meets on the balcony of one's soul ... the reassuring smile of a DIVINE FRIEND-SHIP,' where one is 'bathed in the holy waters of baptism.'[28]

This palpable sacramentality did not lack a sense of delight. The famous Baltimore Catechism, commissioned by the predominantly Irish bishops in 1884 and used in virtually all parochial schools until Vatican II, recited: 'Q – "Why did God make me?" A – "To know Him, to love Him, and to serve Him in this life, and to be happy with Him forever in the next."' The Italians, however, saw no need to wait. Cardinal O'Connell described Boston's Italian North End as celebrating a 'theology of the streets,' while in New York in the mid-1880s, Archbishop Michael Corrigan banned Italian processions, reporting that of 50,000 Italians living in and near New York, not more than 1,200 attended mass. The Irish-born Fr. McNicholas, similarly, complained that his Italian constituents would not come to church except for marriages, baptisms, and *feste della Madonna*. The bishops hoped to purge these new immigrants of their pleasure in festivals, of their propensity for praying to a variety of local or specialized Madonnas and saints, of their superstitious preoccupation with the *mal'occhio*, the evil eye, and of such flamboyant penitential acts as 'tongue dragging,' in which women licked the floor of the aisle leading to the Madonna or other saint. In 1921 the prominent Augustinian scholar Aurelio Palmieri accused the Irish of 'reformatory puritanism,' an utter failure to understand – much less to respect – the rich, numinous religious traditions that the *contadini* had brought with them.[29]

'Pagan' derives from *paganus*, 'peasant.' Northern Europeans, including northern Italians, considered the south an Ur-Christian throwback, as when one of Camillo Cavour's generals reported back to him in 1860: 'This is not Italy! This is Africa!' Six years earlier, Alfred Maury wrote that a trip down Italy was a trip back in time: modernity in Turin and Milan, Renaissance Florence, medieval Rome, the pagan era around Naples, then Salerno, where 'the customs present themselves to you with all the native simplicity of ancient times.' 'We're not Christians,' declared the peasants in the hills east of Salerno in Carlo Levi's novel, because not even Christ penetrated this far inland.

The ubiquity in southern Europe of statuary portraying Isis suckling Horus indicated a strong affinity for this pair, lasting even to late Roman times. Since both mother and son were divine, such statues naturally came to hand among early Christians.[30] Other pagan deities could be similarly transposed, Yale sociologist Phyllis H. Williams noting among southern peasants 'the worship of ... statues and sacred relics, and the attributing of specific powers and qualities to individual saints': Mary's mother Anna for the travails of childbirth, Lucia for eyesight, Rocco for illness, etc. Although some early Christians had warned that an undue preoccupation with religious images, icons, and relics might constitute idolatry, the Second General Council of Nicaea (787) and the Council of Trent (1545–63), recognizing the inevitability of such devotionalism among Mediterranean peoples, permitted the veneration of sacred objects 'according to the pious custom of the ancients,' gently tolerated by all parish priests who were themselves locals. Williams described a shop in Palermo specializing in votive objects in the shapes of various body parts which customers could buy and pray to, the objects themselves metonymously called *miracoli*, 'miracles,' the shop's sign proclaiming: *Qui si fanno miracoli*, 'miracles are done here.' From the early sixteenth to mid-eighteenth centuries, miracles ascribed to saints and relics in the Kingdom of Naples totalled over three thousand.

Not that these traditions were encouraged by Rome. During the Counter-Reformation, some Church officials involved in missionary work around the world referred to southern Italy as 'our Italian Indies,' a place requiring missionary help in fully converting to Christianity. In 1911 a British traveller found it difficult 'to appreciate the doctrinal standpoint of a good Catholic who places implicit faith in a cimaruta or amulet ... or a coral on his watch-chain,' while another British traveller two years later, upon asking local priests whether Italian peasants believed in Church dogmas, came away with the sense that their religion combined superstition with scepticism or – at most – a simple belief in a divine being.[31]

In *Old Calabria* (1915), British novelist Norman Douglas wrote that the cult of the Madonna first emerged in fourth-century Italy, thereafter providing Christianity with what it lacked but the pagan Mediterranean had always provided: 'a female element in religion.' In 1944

Leonard Covello, relying heavily on Douglas's work, wrote that the *contadini* attended church, not because Rome told them to, but because such activity comprised 'a natural outgrowth' of the Hellenistic and Roman cults of their ancestors. Prominent among bishops opposing papal infallibility at Vatican I were four from southern Italy, one of them, Bishop Luigi Riccio of Cajazzo, joining Edward Fitzgerald of Little Rock in actually recording his objection. Refusing to embrace the particular Mariology developed up in Rome or by the Spanish occupiers of their region, the southerners tended to see Mary as a miracle-working mother who also had a mother's common concerns. Jesus was generally viewed as a *bambino* in her arms, since apparently they had no interest in worshipping an unmarried, childless adult male who had no job or abode.[32]

They prayed not to one Madonna but many, each associated with a particular district or with a miraculous power to cure some particular ailment, 'endowed with the qualities of the ancient deities they supplanted.' As Douglas wrote: 'An inhabitant of village A would stand a poor chance of his prayers being heard by the Madonna of village B,' nor would one's money worries be resolved by praying to a Madonna who specialized in weather. Even if one directed one's prayers appropriately, things could go wrong. Following the eruption of Vesuvius in 1906, many Madonna statues were discarded in ditches, once venerated but now declared useless because they had failed to fulfil a bargain in which 'so many candles and festivals' were supposed to yield 'so much protection.'[33]

Of almost four million Italians who arrived in the United States between 1890 and 1920, 75–80 per cent were from the *Mezzogiorno*. By 1920 New York City had absorbed 800,000. Van Wyck Brooks, sitting in some commodious spot along the Bay of Naples in 1915, watched as another shipload sailed off, 'to gain prosperity and to lose everything else ... How soon they forget,' he observed, 'that they were once delighted by a ribbon or a song!' Not that they left their culture behind. On East 115th Street in New York, the Pallottine order established Our Lady of Mount Carmel, a sanctuary containing an Italian-made statue of Mary, one of only three sanctuaries in the New World to be formally coronated by pontifical decree. In this respect, Our Lady of Mount Carmel became an Italian outpost amidst an Irish-dominated American Church, even as the Italians' traditional forms of Madonna worship haltingly began to assume a revised character.[34]

'Bum Catholics'

Ireland's pre-Christian religions, like Italy's, remained recognizable, despite centuries of transitioning into Christian channels. Nevertheless, these were no part of the theological curriculum at Maynooth, nor were Irish-trained priests free to sprinkle among the new ultramontane pieties imposed so effectively by Cardinal Cullen, any of the old Celtic elements they were supposed to replace. It would have been hard enough to make Ireland's own pre-Christian superstitions give way. Seán Ó Faoláin recalled asking a country woman in West Cork if she believed in fairies. 'No I do not,' she replied. 'But they're there.' While vestigial evidence of Irish paganism might be forgiven with a patriotic smile, tolerance for similar Italian traditions was unthinkable. When in 1860 New York's first Italian church was demolished, its parishioners petitioned Archbishop Hughes for another church 'where they might all unite to pray and worship the Lord, and preserve incontaminated and intact the rites as transmitted to us by our ancestors.' Hughes turned them down. As the Irish moved out of New York's Lower East Side, Italians became the dominant parishioners at St Brigid's, built by the Irish as shiploads of refugees from the potato famine arrived at the docks nearby. Such similarity of circumstance seemed not to inculcate any sense of comradeship. 'What Catholics these people would become,' Bernard Lynch declared in 1888, 'if they only had the qualities fitting them to be good Americans!'

Many Irish-American priests assigned to make the Italians 'good Catholics' and 'good Americans' were not pleased with the prospect. To begin with, the newcomers were all from the new secular Italian nation formed by Cavour, its huge central portion comprised of lands confiscated from Pius IX. As Leo XIII's special legate in the United States made clear in 1888, these immigrants had not come to the pope's defence. In fact, a plebiscite overwhelmingly rejected temporal rule. Cullen, on the other hand, had organized a thousand-man brigade of young Irishmen to fight for Pius, several dozen of whom had died doing so. Well might a reasonably informed Irish-American priest think of the Italian immigrants both as anti-pope and nationalistic. But, in fact, most of the southerners arrived not thinking of themselves in such terms, their perceptual horizon being that of the *campanilismo*, the political, cultural, and social world circumscribed by what was within earshot of the village bell tower. 'Having made Italy,' the patriot Massimo

D'Azeglio had proclaimed, 'we must make Italians!' Those arriving in the United States from the *Mezzogiorno* were 'foreigners' not only to America but to Rome. So inadequate were the transportation facilities of the south that as of 1860, 1,621 of 1,848 villages surveyed could not be accessed by road. A mere 2.5 per cent of the Italian population spoke literary-quality Italian as their everyday language, the rest employing a variety of dialects. For many, the Church had meant oppression from the north, and now secular nationalism meant the same. Any perspective beyond *il campanilismo* was negative: a long history of conquerors and would-be conquerors, military occupation, the absentee landlord, the itinerant tax collector, conscription. To the degree their views were 'nationalistic,' it was only in rebellion against the Bourbons. Although they had not suffered a major famine, they certainly had had their own *miseria*. While the new Kingdom of Italy had confiscated vast Church lands, only in isolated instances were those lands distributed to the poor. With confiscatory taxes, high interest rates, droughts, earthquakes, no system of crop rotation, and no capital investment by absentee landlords in irrigation, drainage, and fertilizer, the southern Italian of the 1880s was in essentially the same condition – Humbert S. Nelli has noted – as the Irish of the 1840s.[35]

Lynch called the southern Italians living around Mott and Park Streets 'the worst off in religious equipment of, perhaps, any foreign Catholics whatever,' many of them not knowing the Trinity, the Redemption, or the Incarnation, much less the Apostles' Creed. The similarly miserable condition of Irish immigrants in the same neighbourhood forty years before, seemed now quite forgotten. In 1915 Fr. Francis C. Kelley complained that while the first Irish, German, French, Polish, and Slavic immigrants were all 'self-supporting, both materially and spiritually,' the Italians were in his estimation no more 'Catholic' in the United States than they had been in Italy. 'Isn't it a pity, Richard,' one future priest's Irish-American mother told her son, 'that the pope always has to be an Italian. And they're such bum Catholics!' Fr. McNicholas wrote: 'shall we dispose of them in our self-asserting American fashion by saying, "Let the Italians take care of themselves"? If they do not appreciate sufficiently the birthright of their faith and the obligation of guarding it for their children, let us teach them.' Much like a Roman of the Counter-Reformation, McNicholas offhandedly referred to the priests' exertions with their constituents from the *Mezzogiorno* as 'missionary' work.[36]

Although the substantial efforts of the Scalabrinian missionaries on behalf of Italian emigrants are now recognized, and Maria Francesca Cabrini and her Missionary Sisters of the Sacred Heart of Jesus helped build sixty-seven orphanages, hospitals, and similar institutions in the United States and elsewhere, their extraordinary achievements were at the time grossly underpraised. And although the Irish-American hierarchy wisely rejected the vicious eugenic arguments being made against 'Mediterraneans' by prominent Protestants, they did not treat the Italians as their cultural equals. In 1917, the year of Mother Cabrini's death, B.J. Reilly, Irish pastor of Nativity Church in New York, wrote to the Irish-born New York archbishop, John M. Cardinal Farley: 'The Italians are not a sensitive people like our own. When they are told that they are about the worst Catholics that ever came to this country they don't resent it or deny it.' Lynch had found the Italians 'totally devoid of what may be termed the sense of respectability.' In addition to enjoying frequent *feste*, they refused to make the substantial donations demanded of them to support the Catholic infrastructure. Some refused because they did not plan to stay in America. Although among Irish immigrants the male/female ratio approached 1:1, of five million Italians who emigrated to the United States during 1890–1910, four million were male, many of them 'birds of passage' whose sole ambition was to make enough money to support them and their families back home, some sailing back and forth repeatedly in pursuit of that goal. Some, as Carlo Levi noted, originally intended to go back, but then chose to stay in America and start new families, leaving their wives to do the same with new husbands back in Italy. Others intended to stay but wanted above all to accumulate capital. Still others had no interest in funding churches in which they were deemed second-class citizens. The bishop of Trenton noted that if the Italian adults proved too intractable to turn into good Catholics, perhaps Italian nuns trained as teachers might 'attract, and teach, and save' the Italian children from their parents' allegedly negative influences. But Italian families tended to avoid parochial schools, many of which charged tuition, and some of which discriminated against Italian children by segregating them in the back of the room. A 1908 study of twenty-four U.S. cities revealed that 85 per cent of Italian children attended public schools. In New York, 60,000 Italians attended public schools, only 8,000 Catholic schools, while in Boston only a handful of Italian parishes built schools. In Chicago, while seven out of ten Catholic parishes had their own schools, in Italian parishes the figure was one out of ten.[37]

The gradual 'Americanization' of the Italians meant increased attendances at Mass and an offsetting diminution in the number of *feste*, with Mary becoming the link between the old Italian practices and the new. In the nineteen official Italian-American national parishes founded between 1921 and 1945, three had Jesus as their patron, while eight had Mary. Although Mary thus eased the transition and became the focal point for a multi-ethnic solidarity of the faithful, regular attendance at Mass did not entirely 'take,' and many Italian Americans drifted. Of eighty Italian-language newspapers in the United States in 1913, none had a Catholic orientation. In 1921 Philip Rose, pastor of Hartford's First Italian Congregational Church, hinted that in proselytizing Italian Americans, Protestant organizers would have less trouble with any ingrained Catholicism, more with a significant anti-religious impulse. By one estimate in 1939, one Italian American in six was lost to Catholicism, with another three 'doubtful.'[38]

4 A New Catholic-American Culture

Given England's many attempts to stamp out Catholic education in Ireland, no one could be surprised to find Cardinal Cullen agreeing with Pius IX that any educational system either dominated by Protestants, or stripped of religious content to avoid sectarian animosities, should be avoided by Catholics. In the mid-nineteenth century United States, public schools commonly required readings from the King James Bible. Its preface, written just six years after the Guy Fawkes conspiracy, referred to the pope as 'that Man of Sin,' hardly an invitation for Catholics to join in reciting this text in schools. A Boston boy's hands were whipped until they bled because he refused to participate, and anti-Catholic school boards, despite the warm sentiments about Christmas inculcated by Washington Irving and Charles Dickens, required all children to attend school on Christmas Day and punished Catholics who broke the rule. Archbishop Hughes saw in a public-school textbook the observation that America had become 'the common sewer of Ireland,' while another priest overheard a prominent Bostonian remark that 'the only way to elevate the foreign population was to make Protestants of their children.'[1]

Such vile prejudices suggested a separate system of Catholic education. Peter Kenrick's brother Francis, appointed bishop of Philadelphia in 1831, built a school for almost every parish in his diocese. By 1840 Catholics were conducting 200 parish schools nationally, and expanding that number dramatically to accommodate Irish and German immigration. 'Build the school-house first,' Hughes advised, 'and the church afterward.' Francis Kenrick was awarded the archbishopric of Baltimore in time to preside over the First Plenary Council's commitment to parochial schools in 1852. In 1884, the U.S. episcopacy having grown to fourteen archbishops and sixty-one bishops, the Third Plenary Council ordered nationally the ambitious goal Kenrick had achieved in Philadelphia: a parochial school for each parish. While the Church never actually approached that goal, by the 1890s 60 per cent of parishes had a school, and by 1910 some 4,845 Catholic schools enrolled 1.2 million students, an extraordinary achievement, with enrolment in some neighbourhoods exceeding that of the local public school. While the Ku Klux Klan and other anti-Catholic groups lobbied for state statutes barring parochial schools, the Supreme Court in 1925 declared such laws inconsistent with the traditional right of parents to direct their children's education.[2]

Although Protestant school boards of the 1850s could be criticized for using an anti-Catholic Bible, by 1900 the chief Catholic criticism of public education was that it had so retreated from teaching values – even Protestant values – that it retained no moral component. Added to this criticism was an equitable issue triggered by the constitutional separation of church and state, in that Catholics who opted for parochial schools were nevertheless obliged to pay taxes for public schools. The moral and financial issues might have been pursued more effectively by allying with the growing number of Protestant evangelicals and fundamentalists who held similar views. Yet Rome's disapproval of making common cause with Protestants, coupled with Catholic opposition to child-labour laws, to education about birth limitation and venereal disease, and to the evangelicals' major project, Prohibition, tended to make militant and articulate urban reformers like Margaret Sanger (who happened to be the daughter of a devout Catholic) view the Church, not as a potential partner in the ameliorative effort, but rather as part of the urban problem. Two decades of ongoing Catholic insularity continued in Pope Pius XI's *Mortalium Animos* (1928), which excoriated Protestant attempts at pan-denominational organizations and warned Catholics against any ecumenical dialogue. Not that Catholics avoided involvement in public education. Despite their distaste for moral anarchy in the public schools, in some cities Catholic control of taxed-based education constituted a political prize. First among edifices of Catholic municipal power was Boston, where O'Connell, despite substantial rhetoric about building parochial schools, in fact oversaw a situation in which eight of ten top administrative posts in Boston's school system in 1930 were held by Catholics, who also comprised half the school principals. Among political stereotypes of the period was the archetypical Irish ward healer, at times a legman for brilliant reformers like New York's John Purroy Mitchel and Al Smith, but more likely just a cog in corrupt but functional urban machines.[3]

The parochial system required not only substantial financial commitments from parishioners, but compliant, low-wage teachers, and by 1900 American nuns outnumbered priests four-to-one. Barred from receiving training in Catholic men's colleges, they nevertheless bore the labouring oar in most schools. Parochial schools featured the catechetical method, a series of questions to which – in contrast to the Socratic method – there was always only one right answer, known to the questioner, as a generation before it had been known to the catechist who had questioned him. This was also the method in training teachers, an ex-seminarian complaining of a 'cut-and-dried' Catholic academic curriculum which neither required nor permitted individual interpretation, 'a system little adapted to produce men of thought and individuality.' In the 1920s, the curriculum at St Anthony's Seminary in Santa Barbara featured liberal arts from the Catholic viewpoint, history from the Catholic viewpoint, Catholic scholastic philosophy, and patristic theology, with the Bible itself receiving scant attention. The course work at St Joseph's Seminary at Dunwoodie, New York, included no research papers, and the library was open only four hours a week.[4] John Cogley has written that while the Irish-American priests 'did not produce many front-rank theologians ... they were excellent catechism teachers' and, alongside equally punctilious nuns, cultivated among students 'an almost monastic view of the virtues of chastity and obedience to ecclesiastical superiors.' William Clancy recalled learning 'the standard things' in parochial school, 'all negative': 'Protestants reject the authority of the Pope; they do not honour the Virgin Mary; they deny the efficacy of good works ... Through eighteen years of Catholic education I heard nothing positive about Protestantism.' While such curricular elements comprised an understandable reaction to centuries of Protestant abuse, Flannery O'Connor called the Catholic education of her formative years 'vapid,' adding that eventually 'you have to save yourself from it ... or dry up.'[5]

While life in a parochial school could thus be narrow intellectually, it also could be spiritually auspicious, a 'dreamland' – a priest wrote in 1929 – 'bright, emotionally real, varied, and peopled by the most charming persons.' Daniel Callahan noted in the 1920s 'a great surge in more frequent communions, increased devotions to the Eucharist, a growth of devotions to the Sacred Heart, the Blessed Virgin and St Joseph.' Primary in appeal was Mary, the pupil's 'second mother,' 'a star-crowned

Queen' who is close to him via a scapular worn around his neck, comprising his claim on Mary's protection. He is taught stories illustrating its utility: 'Once upon a time two boys went out to swim. One of them was a good boy and wore his scapular. The other boy had forgotten to put on his scapular. Well, while they were swimming a great wave came and swept the boys out to sea. The boy who had his scapular round his neck was carried by a current to a rock and was saved. The other boy was drowned.'[6]

Narrow curricula and papal prohibitions on religious speculation did not inhibit Catholic higher education, and here America's so-called 'bricks-and-mortar' bishops performed brilliantly. By 1900 sixty-three Catholic colleges had emerged in the United States, followed by Catholic medical schools and law schools. These edifices, coupled with increased attendance by Irish-American Catholics in non-Catholic colleges, meant that by 1918 Catholics were receiving higher education and landing white-collar jobs at rates well above the national average for non-Hispanic whites. During 1900–20 Catholic graduate programs turned out eighty-one PhD's, while in the mid-1920s, sixty-four PhD's and 626 master's degrees were granted by forty-two Catholic institutions, with an average annual increase in enrolments in Catholic colleges of 19 per cent. Prominent among those committing themselves to an education centred on systematic philosophy were the Jesuits, who in 1930 taught 45,000 students at twenty-six universities and colleges as well as 15,000 students at thirty-six high schools. '[E]ducation,' Pius XI declared in 1929, 'belongs preeminently to the Church,' both because of Jesus' instruction to the Apostles to 'teach ye all nations,' and because the Church, 'spotless spouse of Christ, generates, nurtures and educates souls in the divine life of grace.' Not that Jesus himself became the object of study in the universities and high schools, any more than in the seminaries. Students surveyed at a Catholic college indicated that none had read through the New Testament, and only two in ten had read a biography of Christ. In a survey of eighty-four Catholic colleges in 1937, only three offered a major in religion.[7]

The lack of interest in Jesus did not make the education secular, since piety and mysticism, the breviary and the catechism, were not considered merely for children. George Bull, S.J., differentiated Catholic from Modernist thinking in that the Catholic can reach beyond the experience of his senses to 'an immaterial world' in which 'he is as sure of the existence of an angel, as he is of a tree.' For that reason, Bull argued, 'research' – at least, research into the world of sublunary facts – 'cannot be the primary object of a Catholic graduate school,' because research 'is at war with the whole Catholic life of the mind.' Of nineteen top American physicists working in 1930, not one was known to be Catholic.[8]

A Catholic Culture

The censorship and paranoia of the anti-Americanist, anti-Modernist ethos did not yield a climate of intellectual or aesthetic speculation, W.M. Halsey characterizing Catholic culture as 'an array of rear-guard actions to deny the realities and uncertainties of twentieth-century life.' Catholic intellectuals writing non-fiction in English about contemporary life were – like Brownson and Hecker in their day – converts who brought their intellectual proclivities with them. Although Catholic University's original importation of European scholars had been promising, that ended with the anti-Modernist regime. James J. Daly, S.J., began 'Catholic Contributions to American Prose' (1923) by announcing that he would not include any living writers, and although his stated reason was that he did not want to hurt the feelings of anyone he left out, perhaps instead he feared that those he might name were otherwise unknown to the general public. In 1927 *Commonweal*, a Catholic lay periodical inaugurated three years earlier to foster American-Catholic culture, complained that while Catholics comprised one out of six Americans, the first hundred entries in *Who's Who* included only two. If gaining admission to an Ivy-League college helped one reach *Who's Who*, anti-Catholic prejudice among admissions officers was a significant factor. In publishing, of fifty important religious books of 1928, only three were by Catholics, the secretary of the Catholic Book Club carping that of three books awarded prizes by the Catholic Press Association, two were written by Protestants, the third by a deceased Polish nun. Evelyn Waugh pointed out that of thirty-five prominent American Catholics featured in a book by apostolic delegate Amleto Giovanni Cicognani, thirty-one were born and educated abroad, and of the four American-born, two were converts. The theme of any 'typical' Catholic-American novel was the same theme inculcated by the hierarchy: the vindication of Catholic family values against materialistic philosophy, liberal sex mores, contraception, and divorce. Of notable American poets, only one, Joyce Kilmer, had been Catholic, and he had converted (in 1913, the year he published 'Trees'). *Commonweal* in 1926 complained that the Church could claim 'no John Dewey, no Elihu Root, no Ralph Adams Cram, no H.L. Mencken, no Edward Arlington

Robinson – and we have not seemed particularly to care about having them.' While Thomism remained available as a subject for approved intellectual endeavour, Aquinas's two great analysts, Etienne Gilson and Jacques Maritain, were both lay Frenchmen, the latter a convert, while lay Catholicism's other intellectuals – Hilaire Belloc, Karl Adam, and G.K. Chesterton – were also European.[9]

The primary victim of anti-Modernism in France had been Professor Alfred Loisy, who wished to obliterate the dichotomy between the natural and supernatural by positing that God is immanent in man and in the world. Dismissed from Paris's Catholic Institute in 1893, by 1903 Loisy had five major works on the *Index*, before being finally excommunicated in 1908. He analogized the intellectual atmosphere invoked by *Pascendi* and *Lamentabili* to 'breathing at the bottom of the sea,' elsewhere referring to 'a veritable orgy of fanaticism and senselessness.' A Congregationalist minister prophesized that somehow Loisy – despite his excommunication – would soon lead Catholics in an intellectual renaissance. Some looked for a new, specifically Catholic synthesis of the conservative and the creative, via some new Thomist intellectual system. But although three Thomist journals appeared between 1925 and 1940, the new crystallization did not occur. In 1923, William Inge, Anglican dean of St Paul's Cathedral, repeated to readers of the *Atlantic Monthly* what many Protestants had been openly saying for decades: that Catholic clericalism, 'more like a permanent conspiracy than a dominant power,' was 'condemned ... to fight a losing battle in the more advanced nations, and must content itself with the allegiance of peoples whom it can screen from contact with progress and enlightenment.'[10]

In his introduction to American culture, Denis Brogan in 1941 remarked that because of the Church's constant focus on the needs of successive waves of peasant immigrants, it 'has counted for astonishingly little in the formation of the American intellectual climate,' meaning that 'in no modern Western society is the intellectual prestige of Catholicism lower than in the country where, in such respects as wealth, numbers, and strength of organization, it is so powerful.' The issue seemed to haunt everyone. John T. McNicholas, an accomplished Thomist who rose to the archbishopric of Cincinnati, invigorated Thomistic study at the local seminary and dispatched over one hundred Cincinnati priests to study in various Thomist centres in Europe. As chairman of the Pontifical Commission for Ecclesiastical Studies, McNicholas accused the then-rector of Catholic University of trying to secularize the institution, that is, to make it 'a little Harvard.' After persuading Rome

to have the rector fired and transferred to Omaha, McNicholas continued to complain that neither priests nor the laity in the United States
had 'arrived as yet at the stage of producing outstanding scholars' –
presumably of the Thomistic kind. In 1940 George Shuster, president of
Hunter College and former managing editor of *Commonweal*, complained
that 'Catholic books can find no market' because the American Church
has 'no use for intellectuals.' In 1946 Willard L. Sperry, dean of the
Harvard Divinity School, dared to observe in his history of American
religion: 'we fail to find in Catholicism what we might expect, a common meeting ground for more meditative minds,' adding in mitigation
that despite the Vatican crackdown on Modernism, 'private conversation' with Catholics often uncovers 'a good deal of residual Modernism ... biding its time.' Boston archbishop Richard Cushing remarked in
1947 that the American-Catholic bishops, most of them born before
1900, all came from non-college families, while Msgr Michael V. Gannon
introduces his study of interactions between priests and the American
intellectual community by noting that in these decades there were
'precious few.'[11]

At the parish level, one seldom went to Mass to hear the sermon, and
seldom was a scriptural reading applied to contemporary problems.
Parishioners were still viewed as a passive flock, Msgr John Tracy Ellis
noting that before the Second World War 'one could not speak of a
middle class in terms of significant numbers and strength among Catholic
professional men, business executives, technicians, journalists, and educators,' but only 'an essentially mute laity that made little real contribution on their own, beyond their marvelously generous response in
material support to Catholic causes proposed to them by the clergy.'
While a few Catholics – Stella in painting, and John Ford (*né* Feeney)
and Frank Capra in film – were major visual artists, the indirect result of
the general trend among clergy and laity was a recurrent aesthetic
mediocrity, all the more disappointing because for almost two millennia the Church had fostered the West's highest achievements in art and
architecture. In 'The Catholic Theory of Art and Letters' (1923), Blanche
Mary Kelly wistfully characterized 'Catholic aesthetics' as elucidating
'the beauty of all the ways by which ... fallen, degraded nature has
sought to reproduce its lost, remembered heritage.' With 'the modern
theories of art and literature such as Futurism, Imagism, Dadaism, *Vers
libre*, etc.,' she added, Catholic aesthetics 'is concerned only to the extent
that it recognizes in them departures from the law of harmony which is
the ground of its philosophy,' considering such developments 'expres-

sions of revolt and anarchy.' Ralph Adams Cram noted in 1930 'not only amongst the clergy but in the public at large, a deplorable indifference to the claims of art, together with a wide inability to recognise its function as an integral part of the ecclesiastical organism.' Hilaire Belloc went further, alleging that the Church 'has not only abandoned, but deliberately turned enemy to, beauty.' In Harry Sylvester's novel *Moon Gaffney* (1947), a character introduced as 'our leading Catholic lay critic' describes American art, literature, and film as 'infected with a virus' of 'abominable paganism,' to be resisted by the 'strong, virile, realistic Catholic countermovement in the arts' as represented by such Catholic novelists as Frank Spearman and Lucille Papin Borden.[12]

Given such views, it was hardly surprising to hear John Pick tell a Catholic symposium in 1949: 'A Catholic culture in America is yet to be born.' In 1952 Fr. Walter J. Ong wrote that Catholics' 'immediate reaction' to the 'hostile environment' of America's unofficial anti-Catholic culture was not to understand it but to fight it with a 'strong minority mentality' which refused to judge intellectual achievement in an unbiased way, resulting in the paradox of the most conservative Catholic mentality in the world 'set in the midst of the nation whose genius seems to be adaptability and change.' In the same year, with the laity's donations for capital improvements at unprecedented levels, Sister Helene complained of a Catholic mindset in which every building had to be gothic and each lawn had to be 'dotted with assorted eye-catchers,' including grottoes and 'lattice arbors over statues of dubious merit.' The notable Catholic publisher Frank Sheed complained in 1954 that no first-class Catholic authors had emerged because there was no appropriate Catholic reading public to buy their books. A 'grown up Catholic mind,' Sheed went so far as to say, 'does not exist.' Father Ong complained of American Catholicism's perennial preoccupation with 'getting its bearings,' resulting in a subservience to European thinkers, as if knowledge were correlated with proximity to Rome. Msgr Ellis, professor at Catholic University, ventured an indictment even more general, claiming that with a few exceptions like the converts Hecker and Brownson, between 1790 and 1945 Catholics provided 'relatively little contribution ... to the nation's intellectual and cultural life.' Theodore Maynard wondered why a Catholic population approaching 30 million could not support one daily national Catholic newspaper.[13]

With both the high culture and the avant-garde culture dominated by non-Catholic artists, critics, and audiences, each writer was free to create the tastes by which he was enjoyed. And although prominent writers with Catholic backgrounds exceeded their statistical probability for achieving fame in the wider culture, they were all lapsed, *maudits*, at odds with or disapproved by Catholic officialdom. Theodore Dreiser, whose mother once saw the Virgin Mary in her garden, became the oft-censored scion of American naturalism, a mode of expression already disapproved of by the Church in its reaction to Dreiser's model, Zola. Given their respective subject matters, neither Eugene O'Neill nor F. Scott Fitzgerald could be embraced by the Church as 'Catholic writers.' O'Neill lived the life of a dockside derelict, delved into Nietzsche, and incorporated into his oeuvre the alcoholism and drug addiction that marked his family's life, Harold Bloom noting that O'Neill had transformed an Irish-Catholic Jansenism into 'anger at God.' Fitzgerald, having been introduced at Princeton to the beau ideal of Protestant lineage, employed his own Irish-Catholic background only as a scaffold from which to paint a social scene in which Catholic ideals played no role. John O'Hara, too, viewed Protestant society with the envy of a self-conscious aspirant, while James T. Farrell projected a rough urban milieu of sex and hard knocks quite contrary to the image of healthy and virtuous Catholic youth recommended in numerous prescriptive Church pamphlets. While abandoning and/or being abandoned by such writers, the Church (as John Cogley has noted) 'never lost the working class,' adding that some Catholic medievalist could always be called upon to say of the contemporary scene that there was a distinction between 'liberty' and 'license.'[14]

By the time Ellis in 1955 criticized Catholics for intellectual laziness, the problem was waning, albeit the perception lagged. In 1958, Fordham sociologist Thomas F. O'Dea wrote that non-Catholics often see Catholic enthusiasm for censorship as tied to a Catholic failure of intellectual achievement and even a Catholic anti-intellectualism. O'Dea bristled at the latter charge, arguing that it was not Catholicism but modern secularism that lacked appropriate intellectual rigour. Father Fulton J. Sheen, an accomplished Thomist with brilliant academic credentials, agreed. 'The spirit of modern thought,' he urged, 'whatever else it may be, is anti-intellectual.' Thomism was acutely intellectual, although confined in its interests and its logical method, causing George Bernard Shaw wittily to remark that he could never entirely agree with Catholicism because of its extreme rationalism. Catholicism retained one systematic theology and a set of doctrines, to be contrasted with multitudinous Protestantism's theologies and beliefs and the Enlightenment's secular philosophy of investigation and speculation. Chesterton defended the

Church as 'the one and only real champion of Reason,' implying that modern philosophies were not only more messy than the Church's but less rational. Archbishop McNicholas, a committed Thomist with a decided anti-Modernist perspective, excoriated the philosophical habit of 'separating all the connected parts of science ... issuing question-naires, cataloging facts, enumerating various mental processes,' so that, embracing no 'fixed law,' modern thought is 'a house built on sand.'[15] And while the Thomist and neo-Thomist methodologies urged by McNicholas and Sheen might have provided a base from which to address many modern problems, the Vatican's bunker mentality did not foster in anyone a desire to apply neo-scholasticism to those prob-lems in the popular, secular press, much less to challenge Protestant and secular thinkers regarding them.

An ongoing, many-sided Protestant prejudice, coupled with the Church's separate school system and the Vatican's regime of anti-Ameri-canism and anti-Modernism, bred continued insularity and – in some quarters – paranoia. Theodore Maynard, a convert, wrote in 1928 that America's 20 million Catholics refused to influence the wider society because 'they suffer – almost as much as do the Jews – from an inferior-ity complex. They are touchy; they start at the slightest sign of a threat; they are even afraid of the Ku Klux Klan.' For instance, although the prohibition of alcohol 'is demonstrably opposed to Catholic principles, they hesitate to oppose it lest they should be thought "un-American" by the Baptists of Kansas and the Methodists of Iowa.' While every semi-narian was invited to study Aquinas, no one was asked to replicate his method of finding Truth by arraying the best possible arguments against it. A Jesuit with legal training wrote: 'If a Protestant is asked why he believes a religious proposition to be true, he will rest his belief on the teaching of the Bible or perhaps on the inner testimony of conscience. But if a Catholic is asked the same question, he will reply that the proposition is true because the Church teaches that it is.' This foreclosed further debate. A Catholic was likely to say 'that since the dogma he holds by faith' is not 'an intellectual hypothesis ... but a divinely re-vealed truth,' he had no reason to discuss it with people outside the faith. Thus, the ordinary Protestant was left to consider Catholicism (a sociologist noted) 'an impenetrable jungle.'[16]

A New Catholic Activism

Despite several encyclicals on workers' rights, the Vatican steered clear of anything that challenged the rights of private property or otherwise smacked of socialism.[17] For American Catholics, the First World War proved to be a sort of watershed, with enlistment extracting thousands from urban ghettoes and credentialing them as patriotic and self-sacrificing citizens, while allowing rural Protestants to discover that Catholics were not horned beasts. The aging Cardinal Gibbons assured President Wilson that American priests and nuns 'will once again, as in every former trial of our country, win by their bravery, their heroism, and their service new admiration and approval. We are all true Americans'; that is, neither the Irish antipathy to the English, nor German-American sentiment, would bring Catholic patriotism into question. A chemistry teacher at Notre Dame, Knute Rockne, proved that Catholics could beat Protestants at their own game, then selflessly contributed seven members of his great football squad to the Students' Army Training Corps. And journalists who grew up reading about the Irish Brigade in the American Civil War were convinced that when they located the first American to fire a shot in France, he would be a red-haired 'Fighting Irishman,' war having suddenly afforded that term a positive connotation. Italian Americans, too, distinguished themselves, accounting for 10 per cent of U.S. casualties, although comprising only 4 per cent of the U.S. population.[18]

The National Catholic War Council won the right to contribute meaningful war work alongside the all-Protestant YMCA, then at war's end became the National Catholic Welfare Conference. In 1919, with Catholics comprising majorities or near majorities in major cities and one-sixth of the U.S. population overall, the American bishops issued a long Pastoral Letter addressing a variety of social and cultural issues, as if participation and sacrifices in the war had earned them the right to speak out. Thus, despite papal warnings against both Americanism and ecumenism, the earlier sense that the Church and America had a special, synergistic relationship now began slowly to re-emerge in a new form. Catholic University's Father John A. Ryan, a remarkable individual, had already established his intellectual credentials in the wider culture, and not as a Thomist but as an economist with a moral vision of a cooperative, non-socialist industrial plan. In 'The Bishops' Program of Social Reconstruction' (1919), Ryan urged not just the smashing of monopolies but the establishment of minimum-wage and child-labour laws. As senior executive of the National Catholic Welfare Conference, Ryan in 1922 – in the face of fierce opposition – received Pope Pius XI's approval of a plan to oversee various educational, social-action, and lay activities, with the Conference becoming the collective voice of the hierarchy and of the articulate laity on social and cultural issues. In

1921 John McNicholas, at the time bishop of Duluth, wrote of the NCWC: 'We have coordinated and united the Catholic power in this country. It now knows where and when it can act and is encouraged by the consciousness of its unity.'[19]

While Catholics were still a numerical minority, their relative position was constantly improving. From 1900 to 1920, the U.S. Catholic population grew from 12 million to 18 million, a growth rate averaging 4.5 per cent per year, versus 3.26 per cent among Protestants. The number of priests rose from 20,000 in 1917 to 32,700 in the early 1930s, with 18,400 parish churches as against 15,500. For some eugenicists, regionalists, and crackpots who thought Catholics (or Mediterraneans, or Slavs, etc.) genetically inferior, this unmistakable transformation of society was nothing to celebrate. In 1923, University of Iowa sociologist Edward Byron Reuter warned that the nation was letting in a predominantly Catholic peasant class, 'docile and stolid,' non-English-speaking, who did whatever priests told them and tended to drag down wages. A year later, the statutory closing of immigration from southern and eastern Europe, demanded by Protestant racists on the authority of eugenicist pseudo-science, forcibly ended a self-consciously 'immigrant' Catholic culture. Now three-fourths of American Catholics were U.S.-born, most others becoming 'naturalized' citizens. The number of foreign-born Italians in the United States topped off at the next census (1930) at 1.79 million, declining thereafter. Meanwhile, to the Church's gigantic educational system was added a health-care system of 640 hospitals, one-seventh of all non-government hospitals in the United States, one bed for every 231 communicants. Catholicism was for the first time 'going public,' via the National Catholic Welfare Conference, Father Ryan, and the brilliant new dean of the American hierarchy, Chicago's George William Mundelein. As exuberant as O'Connell in denouncing Modernism, Mundelein was as well favoured by Pius XI as O'Connell had been by Pius X. In 1926 he put American Catholicism on the world map by hosting the first Eucharistic Congress to be held in the United States, culminating in a Mass in Chicago's Soldier Field with one hundred thousand people, each holding a candle.[20]

Discomfort about thrashing out religious issues with Protestants entailed no lack of personal assurance. Michael Williams, principal founder of *Commonweal*, wrote in 1928 that the Church 'knows that the Modern Mind is simply the sum of the heresies against which the Church has struggled elsewhere, more or less successfully, since its beginning.' Thus it was time, Williams said, to 'put aside all lingering ... inhibitions of the "inferiority complex" that had for so long accompanied the American-Catholic identity.'[21] Francis X. Talbott, S.J., wrote: 'Personally, if I did not believe that God appointed a single way of religious life, that Jesus Christ was divine and originated a divinely guided church, and only one,' he added, 'I could not believe in a God of any sort.' 'We are so SURE,' an editor of *The Catholic Girl* wrote to a Jesuit friend in 1927. 'That characteristic would hurt me, if I didn't believe. I think I would hate people who are so certain and set apart.' Much energy and 'infallible certitude' could be derived from what Father Talbot in 1938 called the conviction that the Roman Communion comprised the only church 'instituted by Jesus Christ' and 'completely revealed.'[22]

On a tide of such assurance, a few lay Catholics now rose to national prominence. Joseph P. Kennedy splashily made serial fortunes in banking and securities, real estate, and movies. In 1928, Alfred Emanuele [Ferrara] Smith, descended from Italian, Irish, and other Catholic stock, raised in New York's Lower East Side, became the Democrats' candidate for the presidency. Despite his promises that 'no ecclesiastical tribunal ... would have the slightest claim' upon him in deciding any political issue, opposition to his Catholicism was steady, fierce, and ugly. Never – one student of the election reported – was there 'such a flood of literature let loose upon American Society to assault the religious beliefs and views of one portion of the population.' The editors of the Wesleyan *Christian Messenger* declared themselves 'strongly persuaded that Catholicism is a degenerate type of Christianity which ought everywhere to be displaced with a pure type,' while the editors of the prestigious *North American Review* granted space to Hiram Evans of the Ku Klux Klan to declare the Church 'fundamentally and irredeemably ... alien, un-American and usually anti-American,' rhetoric similar to that of the Know-Nothings seventy years before.[23] George Shuster commented that 'millions of people ... feel in their hearts that the accession of a Catholic to the presidency would be a deplorable national degradation,' while André Siegfried observed that not to see Protestantism as America's 'only national religion' was 'to view the country from a false angle.' Winfred Ernest Garrison, literary editor of the *Christian Century*, found in Catholicism the spectre of 'corporate control over the minds, consciences and moral conduct of its adherents ... by a very small self-perpetuating group,' ultimately by 'one man.' Garnering a mere 87 electoral votes against Herbert Hoover's 444, Smith noted that the time had not yet come when a man could say his rosary beads in the White House. This was an apt way to express his disappointment, since the image of a U.S. president reciting a rosary in the White House was exactly what many Protestant voters – when it came down to it – simply could not abide.[24]

The vituperative language issued during the campaign yielded among Catholics, including Father Ryan, the conviction that the Protestant majority remained hypocritical, ethnically prejudiced, and even fundamentally anti-democratic.[25] But the Catholic minority did receive ironic benefits, in that fair-minded Protestants now had a certain sympathy for Catholics, or at least an antipathy for anti-Catholics. Moreover, if Smith had won, many would have urged that the ensuing Depression was wrought by God to show His displeasure, much as some had called the Irish Famine divine punishment for the emancipation of Catholics in 1829, and others blamed the San Francisco earthquake on the influx of Japanese. Third, the Depression seemed to prove what Leo XIII and Pius X had said: that America's secular materialism was untrustworthy.[26] The Church, having colluded neither in the carnage of the Great War, nor in Wilson's failed peace plan, nor in the empty social froth and sexual immorality of the 1920s, nor in the flimsy financial pyramids that had all just collapsed, was still publicly committed to belief in God and revealed Truth, traditional family life, and the censorship of heterodox and salacious ideas, values which the devotees of Modernism had pushed aside as outmoded.

Hilaire Belloc, who ascribed his failure to get a fellowship at Balliol College, Oxford, to anti-Catholic prejudice, wrote in 1924 that Catholicism either controls a nation's moral life, or is persecuted by those who control it. In the United States, if with Al Smith's defeat a long era of explicit anti-Catholic prejudice had reached its climax and was in decline, a brief era of Catholic domination of American moral attitudes was about to begin. As Protestant evangelicals had already shown in leading a successful national movement to ban alcohol, a bold minority might deeply influence moral customs and habits by concentrating all of its collective effort on one issue. In 1928 Michael Williams argued that the Church, untouched by the 'paganism' of modern popular culture, was well positioned to assume the leadership 'of all those non-Catholic elements of the nation who share with Catholics a justified apprehension of the dissolving and destructive effects of movements such as Bolshevism, Communism, and materialistic science.'[27]

A severe economic collapse tends to attract new voices and new ideas. Propitiously, the Depression coincided with the end of a decades-long bunker mentality in Rome, since in 1929 Pope Pius XI and Italian premier Benito Mussolini in the Lateran Pacts agreed to recognize their respective nations, with the Vatican staying out of Italian politics in return for Catholicism's being declared Italy's state religion, adopted in the curriculum of its public schools. Although Mussolini just a few years earlier had written that he 'detested' Christianity, he soon recognized that Italy was worth a Mass, and now Pius hailed Mussolini as 'the man sent by Providence,' while the Vatican's quasi-official newspaper, *L'Osservatore Romano*, declared that 'Italy has been given back to God and God to Italy.' Replacing decades of Vatican insularism was a new expansiveness, with Pius proclaiming that the Church's teaching mission 'extends equally to those outside the Fold ... from the banks of the Ganges ... to frozen Alaska.'[28] Out of this came various Catholic organizations – appearing first in Italy – dedicated to projects deemed 'social' and 'moral' rather than 'political.' The primary post-Lateran organization in the United States, Catholic Action, exemplifying what Michael Williams in 1934 called 'that world-wide resurgence, or revival, of a progressive, positive spirit,' served the functions of forming an apostolate and educating the laity about getting involved in various issues, including immorality in film. Among its leaders was Bishop Bernard J. Sheil, auxiliary to Cardinal Mundelein and founder of the famous Catholic Youth Organization (CYO).[29] Another stimulant to lay Catholic thought (albeit without Vatican auspices) was the Catholic Worker movement, begun in the depths of the Depression by Peter Maurin, Dorothy Day, and Fr. Virgil Michel. Day, a socialist and ex-Wobbly, was converted to Catholicism by a trip to Guadalupe, Mexico, the site of the famous sixteenth-century Marian apparition, where she was impressed by the fact that at Guadalupe and again at Lourdes, it was poor peasants with whom Mary had chosen to have contact. By 1936 the Catholic Worker had sprouted thirty-three relief houses to provide food, clothing, and shelter to the down-and-out; by 1940 its periodical approached a circulation of 200,000.[30]

In the mid-1930s, 21.4 million Catholics comprised 20 per cent of the U.S. population, a third of its churchgoers. The Depression exchanged twelve years of Republican rule for a new era of liberal politics supported by new voting blocs, including organized labour and the Democrats' urban political machines. Two-thirds of union members were Catholic, and they were the backbone of various city organizations like New York's Tammany Hall, which had been Al Smith's base. James A. Farley, having successfully managed Franklin Roosevelt's nomination and election in 1932, was awarded the chairmanship of the Democratic

National Committee as well as that traditional sinecure, the job of postmaster general. The son of an Irish immigrant, Farley was one of Roosevelt's closest advisers as well as a de facto ambassador to the Catholic community. Traditionally an urban proletariat, Catholics benefited from FDR's various programs to jump-start the economy and to maintain social welfare, then watched as these programs were seriatim declared unconstitutional by an unsympathetic Supreme Court. With the 1936 election comprising a referendum on the New Deal, 75 per cent of American priests were in favour and – following their lead – so were 70 per cent of Catholics, emerging as an essential constituency. Despite the economic stagnation, some Catholics were moving into the middle class and into the suburbs, in what Andrew Greeley has described as 'a remarkable triumph over poverty and misery.'[31] And although Roosevelt failed in his effort to remake the Supreme Court, he did reshape the rest of the federal judiciary to reflect his political base. While the 214 federal judgeships awarded by Harding, Coolidge, and Hoover included only 8 Catholics, Roosevelt's 196 appointments included 51.

Another Catholic who rose to prominence in the 1930s was Father Charles Coughlin, the 'Radio Priest.' Initially he took his cue from Pope Pius XI, who in blessing the Catholic Action movement in 1931 showed the Church as favouring the average working man against abusive capitalists and moneylenders.[32] Coughlin became an early and vocal backer of FDR, daring even to call the New Deal 'Christ's Deal.' More substantive contributions to social amelioration came from Msgr Ryan, who analysed unemployment as stemming from insufficient buying power to keep the huge industrial process functioning, then proposed a stimulative, pro-labour program to jump-start the failed economy, at a time when Wall Street's plutocrats could think only of hoarding the cash they still had.[33] Ryan would serve on the Industrial Appeals Board of Roosevelt's National Recovery Administration and, along with Farley and Cardinal Mundelein, would broker relations between FDR and various Catholic groups. Father Coughlin, upon turning hostile to Roosevelt, dubbed Ryan 'the Right Reverend New Dealer,' while also accusing him of 'promoting the policies of the Communist Party in the Catholic Church.' Coughlin eventually had millions of followers, a major ecumenical force for divisiveness, proto-fascism, and anti-Semitism, until ultimately he was silenced by his bishop. A more winsome image of the Catholic priest as a domesticated and intelligent voice for meliorism was Father Fulton Sheen, whose own radio program, *The Catholic Hour*, grew from twenty-two stations in 1930 to ninety-five a decade later, a journalist calling him 'the finest Catholic orator since Peter the Hermit.' Despite the earlier papal criticism of 'Americanism,' Sheen, Coughlin, Day, and Ryan were all now driving a larger impulse whereby Catholics were positioned as the true followers of the American Dream, and of the even older myth of American 'innocence.'[34]

5 Protestantism Balkanized

Any institution said to be καθολικός has the attributes of universality, tradition, and cohesiveness, while Protestantism has been marked by variegation, schism, change. Under the 'covenant theology' of the seventeenth-century Cambridge Platform, adopted from the *Westminster Confession of Faith*, the individual may maintain a private, unmediated covenant of grace with God, an idea fundamentally contrary to Catholic doctrine. Although the Massachusetts Bay Colony started as a strict theocracy, it soon decentralized, the synod of the Massachusetts General Court in 1648 securing to each congregation's elders the right to hire and fire their minister, leaving to senior leaders such tasks as executing Quakers and exiling men and women who voiced heterodox ideas. Calvinism was intrinsically radical, insofar as one was not obliged to treat archbishops, bishops, or governors as God's deputed agents. Van Wyck Brooks wrote that Puritanism 'precluded in advance any central bond, any responsibility, any common feeling in American affairs,' making it an agent of anarchy which 'justified the unlimited centrifugal expediency which has always marked American life.'[1] In thus rejecting the hierarchical model found not just in Catholicism but in Presbyterianism and in Anglicanism, New England's Congregationalists have been commonly referred to as 'democratic,' 'American,' and 'modern.'

The Great Awakening of the 1730s and '40s, sweeping down the Connecticut River Valley, was the first of America's many religious 'revivals,' with thousands feeling 'converted,' 'born again,' in a 'state of grace,' irrespective of what their dour local cleric might tell them about humanity's propensity for sin. That first revival remained, Harold Laski noted, 'the supreme event in determining the character of American religious history' because it 'summarized and liberated' various forces which by the early nineteenth century would make Puritanism itself a 'backwater,' replaced by the belief in the perfectibility of humankind, America's own particular playing out of Enlightenment and Romantic ideals, with Emerson, Thoreau, and Whitman seeing an optimistic relationship between the individual and the universe that only Americans could conjure. God, it was now said, has entered into a new, personal covenant with and offers a fresh beginning for each person willing to make the requisite commitment, despite the lingering; murky presence of 'the old Adam' in us all.[2]

Having split from an international institution founded by Saint Peter, then from England's substitution for the Romish Church, then from the Massachusetts Bay theocracy, Protestantism kept splintering, the sharp contrast between the traditional belief in 'the old Adam' and the new belief in a personal Grace being only one of the many reasons for schism. The endless availability of land inevitably meant the persistent possibility of a new start, spiritually as well as economically. Religious speculation, already legitimate, became rampant. In 1836, Boston politician Harrison Gray Otis observed: 'All Christendom has been decomposed, broken in pieces, and resolved into new combinations and affinities.' With the rise of Tractarianism, Episcopalians could accuse other Episcopalians of becoming papists. In 1838 even Presbyterianism, consolidated by the hierarchical structure rejected by Congregationalists, split into factions. One, which adherent Lyman Abbott called the 'New Puritanism,' stressed that 'man is free, that religion is natural to him,' that he can choose between right and wrong, that 'all virtue is acceptable and all vice blamable in regenerate and unregenerate alike,' that God is an 'all-loving Father,' and that slavery is a sin and crime. The other, the 'Old Puritanism,' remained with the traditional Calvinist interpretation of Scripture, a 'fatalistic system, with God as sovereign Judge,' with a notion of the Elect, and with an apology for slavery on the ground that it was repeatedly mentioned in Scripture without being condemned.[3]

The nineteenth century saw additional Great Awakenings, sparking a general rise in formal church membership among the various Protestant sects, while yielding no greater doctrinal uniformity. Rather, the new brands of non-hierarchical Christianity, often led by charismatics who prided themselves on replicating the meagre educational credentials of the apostles, helped teach citizens of the new democracy to think for themselves, to make their own decisions.[4] The mother of Mormonism's founder, after considering the several denominations available in New Hampshire, determined 'that there was not then upon the earth the religion which I sought,' and thus proceeded 'to examine my Bible, and taking Jesus and the disciples as my guide, to endeavor to obtain from God that which man could neither give nor take away.'[5] Among the educated, as Ann Douglas has written, Protestantism between 1820 and 1875 evolved 'from a traditional institution which claimed with certain real justification to be a guide and leader to the American nation, to an influential *ad hoc* organization which obtained its power largely by taking cues from the non-ecclesiastical culture,' including the books, periodicals, and lyceum lectures which increasingly eclipsed the Sunday sermon as stimuli for middle-class moral reflection. While academic moralists borrowed from the Unitarian Charles Grandison Finney and other popular speakers the notion of transposing all issues to 'the moralistic octave,' old forms of collective piety were often replaced by resort to the individual conscience, to religion as philosophy and/or self-help. In 1841 Theodore Parker, a disciple of Emerson and deeply versed in Friedrich Schleiermacher and German biblical philology, dared say that although various religious practices were time-bound, Christianity itself was such an 'absolute, pure Morality' and such an 'absolute, pure Religion' that it would survive even if 'it could be proved that the gospels were the fabrication of designing and artful men' and that Jesus 'never lived.' Not surprisingly, Archbishop Cajetan Bedini, on a fact-finding tour for the Curia in 1853, could dismiss the majoritarian, non-Catholic population of the United States, as five million sharply divided Protestants and seventeen million 'indifferent people or *quasi*-pagans.' The Unitarianism of men like Parker came to wield such an immense influence among New England's educated and prosperous that by 1900, as Daniel Walker Howe has written, 'most respectable ... clergymen had little to say about the Trinity, atonement, or predestination.'[6]

Among the great disruptions in American Protestantism was slavery, splitting the northern and southern branches of the Methodists, Baptists, and Presbyterians. When the Civil War ended, few Protestant groups chose to recombine. Episcopalians, having avoided a schism over that issue, nevertheless fractured in the 1870s into High and Low. Contingents of Presbyterians, Methodists, and Baptists who wanted to harmonize their doctrinal differences by establishing the Disciples of Christ, ended up instead forming additional sects. Rural Protestants who had never met a Catholic or Jew spent substantial energy in sectarian animosities among themselves.[7] Mormonism attracted hard-working people and built an impressive church organization, but non-Mormon neighbours who could not abide its polygyny repeatedly drove its adherents into the wilderness, its founder being murdered by an Illinois mob.

Protestants who were seriously committed both to their faith and to their secular reading faced difficult choices. Many saw religion and science as mutually exclusive explanations for natural phenomena, with each new discovery another hostile incursion on religious credulity, as if playing out what Jefferson had confided to Adams: 'The day will come when the mystical generation of Jesus, by the supreme being as his father in the womb of a virgin, will be classed with the fable of the generation of Minerva in the brain of Jupiter.' Feuerbach described religion as a product of human yearnings, while Schleiermacher, who predicted that science would ultimately defeat all Christian tenets regarding the nature of the external world, dismissed the Virgin Birth as unnecessary either to faith or to salvation, favouring instead a religion of feeling, of a 'sense and taste for the infinite' which no scientific discovery can ever disprove. Certain Hegelians declared that the world was characterized by struggle and change, unmediated by Divine intervention but brought forward each day by an underlying force of dumb inevitability. Then in 1859 Darwin at a stroke transmogrified the story of Adam and Eve, undermining the account of humankind's beginning in an intimate if complicated relationship with God, by making the First Couple the offspring of simians. Many could accommodate religion and science by accepting that natural selection and other processes had been set in motion by a Divine Hand, and/or that there were now two stories of humanity's commencement, one objective, empirically discovered, and verifiable, the other metaphorical and moral, each acceptable and believable in its context. But many who, like Josiah Royce, still wanted a Pauline community of the faithful, nevertheless saw humanity as faced with 'an immeasurably vast cosmic process, at whose centre our planet does not stand.'[8]

The crisis was fueled by advances in German biblical scholarship, reported in English in hundreds of publications from *Essays and Reviews* (1860) to Andrew Dickson White's *History of the Warfare of Science with Theology in Christendom* (1896). By scrutinizing Scripture with the same methods scholars applied to ancient secular writings, invoking no a priori ground-rule either to harmonize everything or to ignore all disharmonies, much that had been embraced as divinely inspired revelation and/or as actual history required recharacterization as legend and myth, as merely human, or even as erroneous, thus making the Bible a 'lazy-Susan' of offerings one could accept or reject.[9] Could one still rely on the canonical gospels as divinely inspired, even after being told that Mark and Luke did not know Jesus? That Matthew and John did not write the gospels bearing their names? What is one to do with Matthew 13:31–2, where Jesus says mustard seeds grow into trees large enough for birds to roost in their branches, yet botany offers no such tree? For the Catholic scholar, how could one pursue one's researches after being warned that no discovery or exegesis could conflict with settled teaching? Once one reviewed two centuries of modern philology indicating that Moses could not be the author or supervising author of the entire Pentateuch, how could one continue to rely on it as the 'Mosaic Law'? What was one to do after 1906, when the Pontifical Biblical Commission, backed by Pius X as part of the Church's Magisterial authority, specifically rejected all that the philologists had accomplished?[10]

Miracles

The several New Testament words associated with Jesus' miracles indicate a power to demonstrate His divinity.[11] For such major figures as Origen, Justin Martyr, Athanasias, Gregory of Nyssa, Augustine, and Aquinas, as for the vast majority of Christians, miracles were proleptic proof, even if Jesus Himself in John 4:48 chides: 'Unless you see signs and wonders, you do not believe.' The Enlightenment would not accept 'signs and wonders,' Spinoza famously positing that every event accurately recorded in Scripture resulted from natural laws, not miracles, while Hume asserted that miracles should not be credited because they lie outside human experience. Sceptics, philosophical materialists, Hegelians, and socialists joined scholars and scientists in asserting that a belief in miracles was only a common attribute of ignorant credulity, Thomas Jefferson going so far as to carry with him a personal New Testament in which all of Jesus' miracles were razored out. Enlightenment scholars such as K.H. Venturini, K.F. Bahrdt, and H.E.G. Paulus made it their project to seek a 'rational' explanation for each recorded biblical miracle, including Jesus' birth, as a mere *Naturereignis*, a natural phenomenon, Paulus in 1802 suggesting what 'really' must have happened in a variety of incidents set forth in the gospels as miraculous. David Friedrich Strauss (*Leben Jesu*, 1835) explained each event as subject to neither a miraculous nor a naturalistic explanation, being instead a mythic exposition of philosophical Truth. In Mark 5:7–13, Jesus forces a legion of demons out of a crazy man and drives them into a herd of pigs, which then jump into the sea and drown. In 1837 August Neander argued that the passage might be an attempt to cover up an embarrassing accident, that of Jesus having caused such a commotion when he arrived among the Gadarenes that a herd of pigs panicked, stampeded, and drowned, to the great cost of their owner. Alluding to John 4:48, Neander wrote that in performing miracles, Jesus was just 'condescend[ing]' to 'human weakness.'[12]

Although in 1860 most American colleges and universities were still led by ordained ministers, by 1900 most presidents specialized in fields other than religion, many of them trained in the sciences and social sciences then centred in Germany and France. As versions of German historicism took hold in several top American divinity schools, the most brilliant scholars were no longer engaged in apologetics but in uncovering facts and making logical inferences from them, regardless of the consequences to faith. Personal piety was no requisite, and when a promising student at the Harvard Divinity School, upon inquiry, told biblical and patristic scholar Kirsopp Lake that he was a Methodist, Lake startled him by replying: 'Never mind. They're no worse than the others.' Among the subjects placed under scientific scrutiny was religious faith itself, treated as just another sublunary, psychological phenomenon to be exposed, tested, and analysed. G. Stanley Hall, the son of Puritan farmers from western Massachusetts, quit divinity school in favour of the cutting-edge science of experimental psychology in Germany, eventually becoming the president of the new, research-oriented Clark University, where his copious output included a two-volume study of Jesus 'in the light of psychology,' a natural extrapolation – in Hall's view – from all the German work on the biblical texts. Describing miracles as 'the baby talk of religious faith,' Hall proclaimed: 'I believe in the historical Jesus, but I have tried to show how ... the Church can get on ... without him, and that this might possibly ... make for greater spirituality.' In 1907 James Orr, in a book-length defence of the Virgin Birth, sadly noted that this crucial miracle had not been under such an unremitting attack since it was first promulgated in the second century.[13]

Among the achievements of Charles William Eliot was that of driving the stodgy faculty of the Harvard Medical School toward the acceptance of germ theory and microscopes. A Unitarian as well as a scientist, Eliot in 1909 argued for a religion that science could commend, one that 'will perform no magical rites, use no occult processes, count on no abnormal interventions ... and admit no possession of supernatural gifts.' Eliot thought 'miracles' akin to mesmerism and spirit rappings, popular gimmicks in the decades in which he had grown to maturity, but at bottom mere claptrap unworthy of a rational religious mind. A year later, George Angier Gordon, D.D., preacher at Boston's Congregationalist Old South Church, posited a Jesus worthy of belief without miracle-working. So long as one was preoccupied with such pyrotechnics as walking on water and making the blind see – Gordon urged – one was not close to the 'real' Jesus. As one 'moves from the circumference toward the heart of faith,' he wrote, miracles drop away as irrelevant, since one is instead 'dealing with the Eternal as it shines by its own light.' By this logic, no miracle – not even the Virgin Birth – is necessary. 'There are many,' Gordon wrote, 'to whom the tradition that Jesus had no human father is precious. As no one can prove that he had a human father, their sentiment on this subject is unassailable.' But neither in Mark nor in John 'is the subject mentioned ... [and] in all the New Testament writings outside ... Matthew and Luke, there is not a word in favor of it ... For the view that Jesus had no human father, the evidence in the New Testament is at best slight. If the belief was current in the apostolic church, it was considered of little moment.' Further, even the 'extremest champion of the miraculous' would not claim that if miracles are untrue, 'God is unreal.'[14]

To Catholics, all this debunking of miracles was gross heresy. Regarding several of the Church's traditional Enlightenment nemeses: Hume, deism, monism, and pantheism, J.J. Quinn wrote in 1892 that they are all categorically refuted by 'the simple exposition of a miracle,' that is, 'an effect which cannot be explained by the ordinary course of nature' but which demonstrates that God may 'suspend any of these laws, (if such is His holy will), for the benefit of man for whom they were principally intended.' In opposition to Gordon, Eliot, and a century of German researchers and philosophers, Quinn found the 'production of a supernatural effect' to be 'the only means by which God ... can communicate truth to us.'[15]

Forms of Protestantism

Charles M. Sheldon's *In His Steps* (1897) had readers pose the question in their business and personal decisions: 'What would Jesus do?' While Sheldon's book was very popular and many Protestants tried to apply

Jesus' ethical tenets to modern problems, only a small minority composed of intellectuals and the urbane had come to consider Christianity as essentially an ethical/philosophical enterprise. Many people strove for a preverbal, emotional relationship with the deity, of a kind suggested by Presbyterian minister Alfred Ackley's beautiful hymn, proclaiming: 'You ask me how I know [Christ] lives? He lives within my heart.' The Salvation Army succeeded brilliantly through its social commitment, its underlying evangelicalism becoming stripped of complicated sacrament and ritual, the better to trigger the simple, individual feeling of redemption of which each lost soul, in its way, was deemed capable. Billy Sunday, an ex–shoe salesman and ex–baseball player, projected the personal charisma by which Protestant multitudes recognized evangelical and Fundamentalist leaders as gifted and attractive interpreters of God and His love. The religious feelings such leaders generated rendered intellectualizing and philosophizing irrelevant to faith, as did other movements such as the holiness associations and Pentecostals, whose accent on the individual's personal relationship with God was exemplified in the solemn significance attributed to speaking in tongues. If one wanted to premise one's faith upon something beyond a warm feeling or glossolalia, one could read the Bible every day under the conviction that every syllable in it is not only divinely inspired but literally true, making its provisions – properly interpreted after study and contemplation – the final authority on all matters. 'We have the Bible for everything,' the Church of God's Ambrose J. Tomlinson declared, 'and we have no creeds, rituals, or articles of faith.'[16]

These developments brought Protestantism no closer to a collective theology. In most instances, any doctrinal and liturgical differences between a congregation in a rural southern hollow and one in Manhattan or Boston did not result in public wrangling, since they were unlikely to have any interaction. But to the degree Protestant groups were not totally isolated from one another, there would be clashes. In his inaugural speech at Union Theological Seminary in 1891, Professor Charles A. Briggs, an ordained Presbyterian minister trained in German historicism, called Mariolatry as wrong in its way as was the worship of the Bible as literally and inerrantly true. Although Union's faculty and various other academics sided with him, Presbyterian conservatives, most of them from the Midwest, initiated a widely publicized heresy trial, ultimately stripping Briggs of his Presbyterian ordination. In 1910, the General Assembly of the Presbyterian Church in the U.S.A. declared that no candidate would be ordained unless he affirmed what would be called five 'Fundamentals': the Virgin Birth, the inerrancy of Scripture, the atonement, the resurrection, and the authenticity of Christ's miracles. These requirements were affirmed in 1916, and in the early 1920s Presbyterian Church elder William Jennings Bryan demanded an affirmative stand against evolution. After Harry Emerson Fosdick, a Baptist minister, stood in the pulpit of a Presbyterian church in May 1922 and asked, 'Shall the Fundamentalists Win?' conservatives forced another reaffirmation of the five Fundamentals of 1910. The New York Presbytery rebelled by ordaining two young ministers who refused to affirm the Virgin Birth, and when Fosdick refused to affirm the Fundamentals, he was barred from preaching in Presbyterian churches. But the ouster of Briggs and Fosdick was not the only crisis in Presbyterianism, which by 1920 was divided into nine separate organizations. In the broad, liberal wings of Presbyterianism, as in several other denominations, the rejection of miracles, so radical when first proposed in the early years of the Enlightenment, was by the mid-1920s widely accepted by those demanding a religion vetted by science.[17] Bryan, meanwhile, made his anti-Darwinian argument the driving force of the prosecution of John Scopes in Dayton, Tennessee, in the summer of 1925, a trial which dramatized for the entire nation one of the great and abiding rifts in modern Protestantism.

The Protestant Episcopal Church, too, found itself organizationally adrift, pulled by conflicting impulses for ties to other Protestant denominations, to Episcopal/Anglican churches of other nations, even perhaps to a grand reunification with Rome, until it lost its focus, entertaining – William Adams Brown urged in 1922 – 'all shades of opinion from Catholicism without the Pope to the most radical Protestantism.' Episcopalians had long since lost traction in western states because their ministers were required to have college degrees, while the Congregational polity, continuing its two-hundred-year tradition of localism, failed to develop an appropriate strategy for programmatic westward expansion. The Disciples of Christ, with almost two million members, had gone through a succession of democratizing, anti-authoritarian disintegrations, all in keeping with its founding in 1832 over questions of 'restoring primitive Christianity.' Northern and Southern Methodists remained apart until 1939. Baptists, following generations of explosive growth, were split into four national factions, the possibilities of a central doctrine rendered impossible by their focus on the individual's right to his or her own beliefs, guided only by Scripture.

The Northern Baptist Convention comprised a spectrum of think-ing from Fundamentalism to such moderates as Fosdick, Walter Rauschenbusch, George Eastman, Charles Evans Hughes, and John D. Rockefeller, Jr. Lutherans fought among themselves whether to reach out to Reformed and/or other denominations, or to protect their culture by preserving German as the denomination's official language, a factor which had always limited growth. Many African-Americans, perma-nently lost to the large white organizations that had so grossly failed them several generations before, further developed their own church systems. As of 1925, the United States had over two hundred self-governing Protestant religious bodies, forty-eight of them with mem-berships above 50,000.[18]

Attempts to unify or at least to corral different Protestant groups uniformly failed. Delegates to the Federal Council of the Churches of Christ in America, established in 1908 to foster commitment to the 'Social Gospel,' included in their constitution a characterization of Jesus as 'their Divine Lord and Saviour,' high-sounding words chosen not for their euphony but rather to exclude Unitarians and Universalists. Epis-copalians and Lutherans refused to join, as did the Southern Baptist Convention and other conservatives, and those who did join failed to achieve consensus on the social issues that had supposedly brought them together. The Interchurch World Movement, intending to bring all Protestant charities and missionary work under one roof as a sort of business enterprise, went bust. Not until the 1950s and '60s did many Protestant churches begin to integrate racially. Looking at the whole picture, Robert T. Handy of Union Theological Seminary was devastat-ing: 'the racial, sectional, and class lines that were still drawn within Protestantism suggest rather disturbingly that the Protestant effort to permeate and Christianize society had not had too profound an effect even on her own social fabric.'[19]

Jesus as Chum

Protestant sects grew because of evangelicalism, exchanging transcend-ence for imminence, doctrine for feeling, driving out the Old Testament God of Judgment and replacing Him with an all-loving, all-forgiving Jesus. Then, to counter what seemed to many a feminized Jesus, came a 'manly' and even 'muscular' one, a Jesus whom Theodore Roosevelt might approve, exemplified by Fosdick's *The Manhood of the Master* (1913). If one thus had to 'sell' Jesus seriatim in mutually contradictory images, faith was obviously in trouble. Alexander Meiklejohn, resigning as president of Amherst in 1923, complained that educators were 'lost' because 'the old structure of interpretation of human life is wrecked,' leaving teachers without a 'gospel, a philosophy ... a religion' to convey to students. Not that the '20s lacked for cultural fashions claiming to be philosophies. Modern 'isms': not just socialism versus capitalism, but Freudianism, Coueism, Watsonianism, Adlerianism, and other psychologies summed up by conservatives as 'sensualism,' all rushed to fill the growing spiritual vacuum. A journalist claimed in 1923 that Protestantism's failure to maintain a viable supernatural element had led to 'an onrush of ardor, zeal and devotion almost as religion inspires, but which is in its nature contemptuously anti-religious.' As various intellectual factions began declaring their 'faith' in one or another of these new, atheistic explanations of humankind's place in the world, in the broader population the notion of a 'manly' Jesus took a new turn. The vaunted return to normalcy following the First World War soon included a capitulation by various Protestant ministers to the hegemony of business, with Jesus no longer ousting the money changers, but rather instructing them in finance. Jesus was now recaste as a regular guy, a pal, a chum, the 'ideal Rotarian.' The best-selling non-fiction book of 1925–6 was advertising executive Bruce Barton's *The Man Nobody Knows*, an entertaining attempt to purge the Sunday-school image of Jesus as the kindly, exhausted, pained visage on the wall, in favour of a bouncy repositioning of the Nazarene as the successful American-style organizer and entrepreneur, a Henry Ford–type who succeeds because he works the hardest and provides the best value, a man who picked out twelve nobodies as associates and conquered the world and – if that were not enough – was also 'the most popular dinner guest in Jerusalem' – the latter a grotesque absurdity in that Jesus was rejected by most people and went to Jerusalem intending to be martyred. 'You could take the "C" out of "YMCA,"' someone commented, 'and nobody would ever notice the difference.'[20] Well might historian Robert Moats Miller describe American Protestantism in the 1920s as 'The Church Corpulent and Contented.'

If Jesus was a chum, so also must be His local agent. Consistent with the old Congregational method, a layman in 1924 commented that to choose a minister, one should 'send him down on Main Street and around to the school buildings to chat with the business men and the children about politics, civic affairs, football, and geography, and then let the business men and the children vote for him.' That a minister should prescribe morality to those who placed their dollars on the collection plates, much less that he should pass judgment on their conduct and tweak their consciences in the name of the faith they purported to embrace, was to many white, middle-class Protestants only a faint memory of the distant past. Thus did the impulse away from institutionalism and proscription finally hit a sort of spiritual dead end, the local church becoming a social club. When the average American thinks of his church, wrote Harvard Divinity School dean Willard L. Sperry, 'he thinks not of the communion to which that church belongs, much less of any Holy Church Universal, but of the four walls of the building where he worships on Sunday and of the group of familiar friends and neighbours whom he meets there.' Although his minister might explain to him how his denomination is doctrinally and/or liturgically different from the others, he pays no attention.[21]

While some Protestants reacted to the Depression by flirting with socialism and even Communism, others refused to move as far left as Roosevelt. Although the economic collapse had demonstrated that the laissez-faire notion of 'rugged individualism' was an inadequate formula for understanding the complex business structures that had all just collapsed, J. Gresham Machen, an articulate spokesman for Fundamentalism, argued that the New Deal would yield enslavement to a government bureaucracy. Protestants who had made Prohibition their project could hardly be pleased to see FDR dispatch it to history as a misguided premise that had brought more evil than good. Still others reacted to the Depression by turning right, to the Klan and other supremacist groups that reiterated locally ideas growing popular in Europe.[22]

Amidst the business implosion, Reinhold Niebuhr reintroduced to Americans an idea from Genesis: that humankind encounters adversity because of its legacy of original sin. Opening his Rauschenbusch lectures at the Colgate-Rochester Divinity School in 1934 with a broadside against the 'superficialities' of modern, commercialized culture, he railed against its 'complacent optimism,' its failure to understand good and evil. Although the Niebuhrs' introduction of neo-orthodoxy augured to awaken the Protestant conscience among those who had forgotten the Fundamentals, their warnings did not tend to reach the local pulpit, much less the local pews. The same can be said of the Niebuhrs' source, Karl Barth, and of Paul Tillich, intellectuals of little relevance to the typical congregant.[23] Not that local ministers who had been hired under criteria thought relevant in the 1920s could retain their popularity in the 1930s. In 1936, Yale divinity professor Halford Luccock reported that

Protestant sermons demonstrated a gross naïveté regarding the hard times, as if religion had become so tied to the free-enterprise capitalism of the Roaring Twenties that it could no longer wage any effective protest against the evils in that system, afraid to bite the hand that had once fed it. Innumerable male churchgoers, chronically fretting about the possible unravelling of their very way of life, heard nothing valuable and stopped attending services. Many churches were kept from closing only through the efforts of the women, whose fund-raisers featured 'interminable bowls of cole slaw, tasteless meat loaf, embroidered flour sack dishtowels, and crazy quilts,' the latter perhaps symbolizing what American Protestantism had become.[24]

Oliver Wendell Holmes, a descendant of Anne Bradstreet, wrote of the Puritans: 'I love every brick and shingle of the old Massachusetts towns where once they worked and prayed, and I think it a noble and pious thing to do whatever we may by written word and molded bronze and sculptured stone to keep our memories, our reverence and our love alive and to hand them on to new generations all too ready to forget.' That was in 1902. By the time of Holmes's death in 1935, Old Testament lessons were long out of fashion and the Puritans had become a running joke, held up as the prime example in American history of prudes and censors being nothing more than Freudian neurotics, unconsciously driven by a 'reaction mechanism' at war with their own feared sexual impulses.[25] In *Puritanism and Democracy* (1944), Harvard philosophy professor Ralph Barton Perry advised: 'the way to be entertaining about a puritan is to caricature him. Secretly everyone would rather have an idealist *shown* up than *held* up – it relieves moral tension, and justifies that state of comparative failure which is the common lot.'[26] The white clapboard church on the typical New England town green, a symbol of 'traditional' American values reproduced on postcards and kitchen calendars, seemed to be a declining institution. In a typical New England community in 1945, the Congregationalists paid their minister a mere $23.50 a week, admonishing him to put wood in the stove only at mealtimes. The Unitarians, who a century earlier had pushed their way into authority on a tide of wealth and intellectual prestige, could no longer even support a full-time minister. The Methodist church had closed. None of the Protestant churches saw more than thirty persons on a Sunday, and the community's leading men no longer took an active role in religious affairs. With years of treating Jesus as a 'chum' and of seeing one's minister as a 'regular guy,' many Protestants had now blurred the traditional distinctions between God and creation, while others were so wedded to positivism, naturalism, or materialism that it was hard to find a place for God except as a synonym for 'values,' making Christ a sort of Gandhi. Richard Niebuhr in a Marxist moment declared that ethics deemed 'religious' or 'theological' were the social product of the class espousing them.[27]

With so many people no longer hungering to believe in the inerrancy of Scripture, or the truth of miracles, or even the authority of the local pastor, liberal Protestant moral authority had ebbed, with conservatives having gone their own way. In 1934 John Dewey in his Terry lectures at Yale made the extraordinary and sad declaration that 'many persons are so repelled from what exists as a religion by its intellectual and moral implications, that they are not even aware of attitudes in themselves' which, if they came to fruition, 'would be genuinely religious.' Edwin Aubrey found organized religion so moribund among the educated elite who now toyed with the idea of sending their children to Sunday school, that he began with utterly elementary advice: go to church yourself as a 'participant observer' and 'try to understand how the worshipers feel about the service,' much as one would try to understand a foreign sport by watching the fans react.[28]

Richard Niebuhr did not see in Catholicism a solution to the crisis, calling the Church 'petrified' (either a snide or an unconscious pun) with 'dogmatisms of another day,' its truths 'imbedded in an outmoded science,' its morality 'expressed in dogmatic and authoritarian moral codes.' But in fact it was liberal Protestantism, long since fractionalized, that was now dispirited and dysfunctional, while Catholicism had never been stronger, more cohesive, or more confident, capable – convert Theodore Maynard wrote – of cutting through Protestantism 'as through so much butter.'[29] Since the Church had fostered, not debate, schism, and individuality, but acceptance, uniformity, and submission, and since the parish priest did not treat his communicants as his 'chums,' much less as his employers, no crisis of belief would or could occur among the Catholic faithful in a time of material upheaval. *Commonweal's* Michael Williams began his book-length introduction to Catholicism (1934): 'few competent observers of the trends of the age would deny ... that since the close of the World War the Catholic Church has been positively active, in a higher degree and on a broader scale than at any time since just before the Counter Reformation,' being 'the one great institution to escape the confusion, or threatened confusion,' which has overtaken the world. Thomas Merton, apparently seeing no irony in James Joyce's depiction of the priest's sermon on Hell in *Portrait of the Artist as a Young Man* (1916), found in it 'something eminently satisfying in the thought that these Catholics knew what they believed, and knew what to teach, and all taught the same thing, and taught it with coordination and purpose and great effect.' Merton tossed off his nondescript and at times hypocritical personal Protestantism for a committed Catholic vocation, travelling up to the Cloisters in northern Manhattan's Van Cortlandt Park, newly replanted from Saint-Michel-de-Cuxa in the Pyrénées, in order to try on the monk's life for size, to uncover 'what kind of place a man might live in ... according to his rational nature, and not like a stray dog,' the latter apparently describing how Merton felt as a Columbia undergraduate in the mid-1930s.[30] And although back in 1907 Archbishop O'Connell had been speaking only of Boston, in retrospect his words also applied to the nation. 'The Puritan has passed,' he declared, 'the Catholic remains.'[31]

6 Reining In Hollywood

An Industry with an Image Problem

In 1919 the National Association of the Motion-Picture Industry (NAMPI) proposed a constitutional amendment to override *Mutual Film* (a silly fantasy, doomed at its inception) and developed a regime of self-censorship in which producers would withhold films from exhibitors who screened material of which NAMPI disapproved. In March 1921, NAMPI adopted 'Thirteen Points,' purporting to disapprove films which 'emphasize and exaggerate sex appeal,' or deal in 'an illicit love affair which tends to make virtue odious and vice attractive,' or 'unnecessarily prolong ... demonstrations of passionate love,' or 'instruct the morally feeble in methods of committing crimes,' or 'deprecate public officials,' or which show disrespect for any religion. These high-sounding principles impressed no one who noticed that few of the films NAMPI members were producing would pass muster under NAMPI's guidelines, and that the guidelines included no enforcement mechanism.[1]

The Reverend Dr Wilbur Fisk Crafts, known primarily for his involvement in banning alcohol, had in his time switched from Methodism to Congregationalism, then to Presbyterianism. Sufficiently sure of his righteous connections to dub himself 'lobbyist of the Lord,' as founder of the International Reform Federation he engaged in a variety of projects, including an initiative to pass a federal film censorship statute. Meeting with NAMPI president William A. Brady in 1921, Crafts promised to cease lobbying if NAMPI actually enforced its Thirteen Points, then reneged on that promise by incorporating the Thirteen Points into a federal censorship bill.[2] With Brady's efforts to fend off government censorship having thus backfired, the industry now formed a new organization, the Motion Picture Producers & Distributors of America, Inc. (MPPDA), hiring Will Hays to lead it.

Hays, a Presbyterian teetotaller from Indiana, was a brilliant and pragmatic Republican politician, one of those in the 'smoke-filled room' of the Blackstone Hotel who had engineered Warren Harding's victory. D.W. Griffith, when asked for comment about Hollywood's decision to hire Hays, said that the industry had been 'like a herd of wild elephants in the jungle' but was now positioned to protect itself. Hays had treated his short tenure as Harding's postmaster general, not as a sinecure, but as an opportunity to reform what he described in a businesslike way as 'the largest distribution system in the world,' his major achievements there including the reversal of his predecessor's vicious policy of using postal censorship to suppress free speech.[3] As the movie industry's new spokesman, Hays, in his first address to the National Publishers' Association, would have had a golden opportunity to describe film's newspaper-like functions in public affairs. But Hays harboured no foolish ambition to undo *Mutual Film*, that is, he would *not* argue that film deserved the same free-speech rights as the press. Instead, he openly embraced what Justice McKenna had said, describing movies as 'the principal amusement of millions,' their 'importance' to be measured 'only by the imperative necessity of entertainment,' their task being not to implant ideas but to *avoid* implanting them. If movies were ever to obtain the free-speech rights enjoyed by newspapers, he noted, they would have to earn them.[4]

He could hardly have argued otherwise, given the recent or pending murder, sex, and drug scandals involving major industry figures: William Desmond Taylor, Mary Miles Minter, Mabel Normand, Wallace Reid, Francis X. Bushman, Juanita Hansen, Olive Thomas, and Roscoe 'Fatty' Arbuckle. Hays's first task was to fix this image problem, just as federal judge Kenesaw Mountain Landis had recently been hired to fix the public image of professional baseball following the infamous 'Black Sox' scandal of 1919. Hays's second task would be to devise ways to stymie government attempts to regulate the industry's oligopolist trade practices, such as 'block-booking' and 'blind-buying,' whereby studios forced exhibitors to accept films in which they had no interest – even films they had never seen – as a condition for getting those they did want.[5]

Hays's third priority would be to minimize censorship. While he admitted being 'the cat's whiskers' for the industry, he also allowed the perception to develop that he was 'the Czar of all the Rushes,' empowered to command studios to delete salacious material. Knowledgeable observers knew otherwise, Pare Lorentz describing Hays as 'the super press-agent of the industry,' one who nobody should expect 'to present a factual picture of movie censorship or of the real purpose of his organization,' commonly referred to as 'the Hays Office.' To protect the industry while appearing to police it, Hays needed to be all things to all people, a skill at which he was nonpareil. In structuring Harding's campaign, Hays had managed to straddle 'the two broncos' of those who favoured the League of Nations and those who were opposed, 'riding them,' journalist Arthur Krock wrote, 'at the same instant in opposite directions without straining a ligament.' On the phone so often that people called him 'Telephone Bill,' Hays seldom recorded his ideas in memos, thus leaving no fingerprints and leaving himself free to change direction on a moment's notice. Indiana novelist Meredith Nicholson said of his friend that he 'presents as many different pictures as an old-fashioned kaleidoscope. He can be an 18th century gallant, a 20th century high-pressure executive, an exuberant playboy or a bashful country bumpkin. He can impersonate the impersonal.' Another friend said: 'I suppose Will Hays in many ways is a Babbitt. Yet in many other ways he is the greatest sophisticate I know. People may often think they are kidding him about this and that. But they never do.'[6]

The philosopher Mortimer Adler, Hays's choice to draft the MPPDA's annual reports, described Hays as 'a fascinating mixture of political astuteness and naiveté about the arts, the sciences, and philosophy.'[7] With no personal interest in film content, with no 'ideal' of what films 'could' theoretically be, and with no constituency demanding that film be treated as an art form, Hays would never have reason to assert that film-makers should be free to express themselves. Government censorship was to be minimized, not because this would foster a great flowering of creativity and insight, but because it would eliminate disruptions in the distribution process, increase the industry's margins by allowing more of the sex and violence audiences wanted to see, and, most important, impede governmental impulses for further regulation – such as outlawing block-booking – which would have a much graver impact on the bottom line.

To achieve these goals, Hays befriended and/or co-opted various so-called 'uplift' groups who would otherwise be lobbying for government regulation or giving anti-Hollywood speeches. Primary among their stated concerns was the allegedly pernicious effects of films upon children. Hays, a master of applied piety, gave a speech about Lockean epistemology that could have been cribbed from any Sunday sermon or parents' magazine. The industry, he said, 'must have toward that sacred thing, the mind of a child, toward that clean and virgin thing, that unmarked slate – we must have toward that the same sense of responsibility, the same care about the impressions made upon it, that ... the best clergyman, the most inspired teacher of youth would have.' So skilled was Hays at getting the politically naive to believe in his earnestness that Krock called him 'a professor of post-graduate Boobology.'[8] It is a measure of Hays's success in putting over the image of a hayseed, Puritanical disciplinarian that people still refer to the age of censored Hollywood as the era of 'the Hays Office.'

Hays put ministers, authors, and newspaper editors on retainer in order to argue for him. He never confronted would-be enemies but rather cajoled them with free trips to Hollywood, where 'consultations' about cleaning up the movies could be mingled with visits to sound stages and photo opportunities with the stars. Regarding the few for whom this was not enough, he slipped them remuneration so they would show up at conferences and hearings where government regulation of film was being considered, in order to voice their 'independent' opposition. And in his spare time he somehow avoided being sucked into the Teapot Dome scandal arising out of the early days of the Harding administration.

Hays staffed his office with people adept in the persuasive arts. His Committee on Public Relations a.k.a. the Studio Relations Committee was headed by Jason S. Joy, who carried the impeccable credential of having previously been national executive secretary of the American Red Cross. The leaders of women's groups, in particular, dilettantes with time on their hands and a need to be 'recognized' for having made a 'contribution' to the nation's moral improvement, were for Hays the easiest marks.[9] Joy soon gathered seventy-eight representatives of sixty-two national organizations, including the General Federation of Women's Clubs, the National Congress of Parent-Teacher Associations, the National Council of Catholic Women, the Jewish Welfare Board, the Child Welfare League of America, the Salvation Army, the Daughters of the American Revolution, the Camp Fire Girls, the Boy Scouts, and the American Academy of Political and Social Sciences. To Mrs Thomas G. (Alice) Winter, head of the largest collection of women's groups, he gave cash.[10] Under Hays's monitoring, film censorship never became a major project of such non-denominational Protestant groups as the

YMCA, the YWCA, or the Christian Endeavor movement. When in the mid-1920s a combination of Methodists, Presbyterians, and Baptists voiced their opposition to immoral films, Hays outflanked them by hiring as MPPDA secretary Carl Milliken, former governor of Maine, his influence being assured when he was appointed by the Northern Baptist Convention to the administrative committee of the Federal Council of Churches.[11] While thereafter the Council, a four-hundred-member umbrella group for twenty-seven denominations and over twenty million congregants, did periodically complain about film content, it was dubbed 'Hollywood's favourite Protestant stamp of approval' because it always stopped short of demanding censorship. At least one of the reasons for its cooperative spirit was that Hays had paid off one of its representatives.[12]

A career reformer equal in fame to the Reverend Dr Crafts was William Sheafe Chase, rector of Christ Church, Brooklyn. Canon Chase, joined by ex-film industry lawyer William Marston Seabury, demanded that Hollywood be subjected to the degree of detailed government oversight that had traditionally been used in regulating public utilities, an idea that would appear in the film censorship bill introduced in Congress in 1932 by Senator Smith W. Brookhart (R-IA). But Canon Chase, whom New York mayor George McClellan had once dismissed as not so much a 'canon' as a 'popgun,' was merely the current exponent of an American Protestantism that had complained about entertainment for more than two centuries.[13] While Chase and Crafts knew how to generate applause and make headlines, neither had the analytic ability to confront films as the actual cause of any psychological harm or social problems. Noisy but ineffective, the two talked about morality but really knew only about propriety. Although Seabury had the skills required for a more effective campaign against his former Hollywood bosses, Canon Chase somehow never gave him enough latitude to proceed.

More serious challenges were launched by Albert C. Dieffenbach, editor of the Boston-based Unitarian periodical the *Christian Register*, and by Guy Emery Shipler, editor of the *Churchman*, the periodical of the Protestant Episcopal Church, who in June 1929 gathered editors of the religious press in Washington to investigate how the Presbyterian Hays, the Baptist Milliken, and the Methodist Jason Joy went about the business of keeping religious groups from having any impact on Hollywood. Through the summer and fall of 1929, few editions of Shipler's *Churchman* lacked a vitriolic anti-Hays editorial. Soon that periodical's board of advisers received a letter from an Episcopalian mother of five from Staten Island, protesting these attacks on Hays. Then another defence of Hays was received from Rita C. McGoldrick of Brooklyn, head of the 80,000- to 100,000-member International Federation of Catholic Alumnae, who was also a member of Hays's committee of women, headed by Mrs Winter. Shipler reprinted both letters, noting that they were written with the same typewriter, on the same brand of paper, and were both mailed from the Grand Central post office, within walking distance of Hays's headquarters.[14]

While this was good evidence of underhandedness and Shipler's charges were reported by dozens of lay newspapers, the story went nowhere, demonstrating that Protestant film censorship was ultimately powerless. Nor was Protestantism's record any better with books. The New York Society for the Suppression of Vice and the New England Watch and Ward Society, both started in the 1870s by evangelical Protestants, by the early 1930s had suffered a series of humiliating court reversals when attempting to ban serious works of literature, and were ridiculed by intellectuals and serious readers as antiquated embarrassments.[15] Censorship, for all its supposed links with 'Puritanism,' did not accord with Luther's argument for the hegemony of the individual conscience, nor did it sit well with the gospel of entrepreneurship that had defined American economic genius. In Muncie, Indiana, where Protestants outnumbered Catholics fifteen to one, Robert and Helen Lynd noted a disapproval of censorship, whether governmental or clerical. People who make their living in a system of free enterprise believe that a customer should be free to make his/her own judgments about what to buy and what to avoid, with sellers enjoying a corresponding right to identify and exploit customer preferences. Justice Holmes was among those choosing the marketplace as the appropriate metaphor for the unfettered exchange of ideas, while the businessperson's retort to any attempt to ban anything has always been: But there's a market for it. Washington lawyer George McCabe observed in 1927: 'Enough people like smutty motion pictures to make it profitable for producers to manufacture them ... Some sincere but silly reformers account for the incidence of the indecent film by attributing to producers the sinister motive' of deliberately debauching America. 'There is nothing to that,' he urged; that is, what is shown on movie screens is just another example of supply and demand. In 1930, Maxwell S. Stewart in the *Christian Century* found the 'fundamental difficulty' with film censorship to be that 'the adult public which regularly patronizes the cinema actually prefers the kind of pictures which are now being offered. As long as this is the case, there is no use whatsoever in trying to legislate against them. After all, the influence of the movies upon these adults is probably negligible, and if they were denied the motion pictures they would doubtless find some other entertainment of much the same quality.'[16] While prominent women such as Mrs August Belmont, Mrs Calvin Coolidge, and President Franklin Roosevelt's mother, continued to inveigh against salacious movies, they neither had real power to force reform, nor did they actually seek such power.

Rationalizing Film Censorship

Film is a mass medium with numerous prints delivering 'the same message ... simultaneously through the length and breadth of the land.' However, inconsistent demands by various censoring agencies meant making different changes in different prints, leading Cecil B. DeMille to note in 1921 that although all thirty-five state and municipal censoring bureaus demanded alterations to his film *Carmen*, no two demanded the *same* alterations. Of the thirty exchange points that constituted the national film distribution network, twenty-four served more than one state, and thus a myriad of inconsistent censorship demands tended to disrupt the smooth functioning of the industry's integrated system of distribution, with the state or municipality having the most strict censorship dictating what all audiences throughout the relevant exchange saw. Pennsylvania trimmed a certain kiss down from its natural length to a mere snippet of five feet of film, and viewers in southern New Jersey, although under no censorship themselves, saw only the five-foot kiss approved across the river, just as many Missouri viewers saw what had been vetted by Kansas.[17] At the intrastate level, towns in northern Illinois with no censorship of their own would see only what Chicago's strict censorship board allowed.

It was to eliminate inconsistencies among its own cities that Ohio in 1913 had enacted the state censorship law approved in *Mutual Film*. Because Ohio was the distribution centre for Kentucky and West Virginia, its censorship dictated what those states saw. Among the subject matters proscribed by Ohio's statute were 'scenes which tend to give the idea that sexual vice accompanied by luxury makes vice excusable.' Since such scenes were exactly what people wanted to see, revenue-optimizing producers could not avoid censorship problems in Ohio. In fiscal 1916, following the victory of that state's censors in *Mutual Film*, they banned or made cuts in four of every ten films submitted.[18]

Of 17,836 movie theatres in the United States in 1925, 3,855 were in three states (Ohio, Pennsylvania, and New York) with state censorship bureaus. In 1926, George McCabe found that in one sixteen-week period, Pennsylvania forced 730 cuts in scenes and 560 changes in intertitle cards, while in twelve weeks Maryland required 116 cuts and 49 intertitle changes. For Herbert Brenon's *Dancing Mothers* (1926), Pennsylvania required 36 cuts and intertitle changes, while Kansas made 11, Maryland 6, and New York one. For the Dorothy Davenport Reid / Walter Lang film *The Red Kimona* (1925), Pennsylvania required 25 cuts and Ohio 7, while Virginia made none. Among the changes in intertitles required in Pennsylvania,

> Gabrielle, in the beginning a child – trusting, believing – had committed the sin of loving too well. Ground in the mire, numb with heartache, we find her in New Orleans – deserted.

became:

> Gabrielle had been a child – trusting, believing – taken from home by a blackhearted villain who married her under a false name. Ground down to desperation by working in a sweatshop, numb with heartache, we find her in New Orleans, living in the slums, and deserted.

'You just happened to be lucky – you got a wedding ring' became 'You just happened to be lucky, you got a rich husband,' the sexual element in both alterations being retained although immunized by a marital context. Similarly, with Wallace Worsley's *The Dancer of Paris* (1926), Pennsylvania replaced the intertitle 'You are obsessed by an insane desire to intrigue women – to make love to them – to hurt them' with 'You are obsessed by an insane desire to marry – when the state of your health positively forbids it.' Although a deletion was justified only if some statutory criterion was violated, these statutes were broadly drafted, their operative terms generally undefined. Of 2,960 cuts made by various states to the 579 features released by the nine top production companies in 1928, 155 were for nudity, 115 for over-passionate love-making, 509 for what was deemed 'suggestive' sex, and 249 for vulgarity. Journalist George Jean Nathan concluded that while the censors were 'idiotic' and their deletions 'unbelievably asinine,' they had done no damage to any reputable picture. That was not really so, in that censorship disrupted the distribution of the best as well as the worst of the industry's products; only 42 of the films produced in 1928 were left completely untouched by any government censor, that is, in the version originally issued by the studios.[19]

Faced with a nationwide mulligan stew of inconsistent demands, Hollywood decided to develop a self-policing code which might minimize disruption while also blunting demands for other forms of government oversight. Although since 1924 Hollywood's so-called 'Formula' code theoretically forbade turning certain racy novels and plays into movies, it had been largely ignored. In a conference convened by the Federal Trade Commission in 1927, MGM production chief Irving Thalberg, Paramount's E.H. Allen, and Fox's Sol Wurtzel promulgated Rule 21 of the Code of the Motion Picture Industry, a compilation of Hollywood's collective learning about what censors around the nation required. Included in its provisions were eleven absolute 'Don'ts' (among them, 'White slavery,' 'Miscegenation,' 'Sex hygiene and venereal diseases,' 'actual childbirth,' and 'sex perversion') and twenty-six 'Be Carefuls' (for instance, 'Sympathy for criminals,' 'a woman selling her virtue,' 'Man and woman in bed together,' 'dynamiting of trains' and 'hangings or electrocutions'). Some producers agreed to abide by some of these 'Don'ts' and 'Be Carefuls' some of the time. For instance, in turning Michael Arlen's novel *The Green Hat* (1924) into Clarence Brown's film *A Woman of Affairs* (1928), embezzlement replaces syphilis as the cause of a humiliation resulting in suicide. But compliance was again a problem; only half the producers cooperated, with only one feature in five being even submitted to Jason Joy's office for vetting. Nor could strict, good-faith compliance with the 'Don'ts' and 'Be Carefuls' assure government approval. In a farce called *Good Riddance*, a man wishing to get rid of his dog tells an aviator to throw it out of a plane. He does, but the dog lands in the back seat of the man's car and leans forward to lick his face. A New York censor demanded that the scene be deleted because it is cruel to throw a dog out of a plane.[20]

Changing intertitle cards was technically simple, and even if an entire scene had to be cut, the deletion could be smoothed over with redrafted intertitles. However, once the plotline moved forward by spoken dialogue, if the director failed to make so-called 'protection shots' which could later be substituted for material likely to excised by censors, the relevant actors, sets, costumes, and make-up people would need to be retrieved for additional takes, a logistical headache cleverly portrayed in Victor Fleming's fast-paced comedy *Bombshell* (1933), in which Jean Harlow's character must do retakes of scenes in Fleming's *Red Dust* (1932) (in which Harlow also starred).[21] Such work was even more onerous if prints had already been released. Since about two hundred prints were distributed, even one small change demanded by one state could become a Herculean enterprise, playing havoc with promotional schedules. While one could follow the lead of small producers not affiliated with national or regional film distribution centres by 'clearing' films on a state-by-state basis (so-called 'state-rights' distribution), that was itself expensive and time-consuming.

Catholicism and Film

The Church had always employed censorship to protect faith and morals and to guard against heresy. Acts 19:19 applauds new Christians for burning their own valuable books of magic, while the Epistle to Titus 1:10 excoriates the 'many disobedient, vain babblers and deceivers, especially those of the circumcision,' who 'must be rebuked, for they upset whole households, teaching things that they ought not, for the sake of base gain.' Heterodoxy, like knowledge itself in the Garden of Eden, was thought more dangerous by being more attractive; hence, the particular dangers of material stimulating sexual arousal. 'Concupiscence of the eye,' Aquinas wrote, generally arises 'from a visual stimulus, for as the book of Daniel so neatly phrases it, beauty has seduced you. Therefore, concupiscence of the eye should not be listed as distinct from concupiscence of the flesh.'[22] Nineteen years after Michelangelo completed his *Last Judgment*, Pope Paul IV ordered clothing to be painted on its nudes, presumably to avoid sexual arousal. But there were other evils to be avoided. As Cardinal Bellarmine proclaimed, 'freedom of belief' meant 'freedom to err.' Censorship criteria emerged from the particular rationales for banning particular works, and Pope Benedict XIV's *Sollicita ac Provida* (1753) became the Church's primary authority for banning books.[23] Thirteen years later, Clement XIII in *Christianae Reipublicae* condemned Enlightenment thinkers who 'lay open the mysteries of God,' with each inquirer's 'bold mind' examining everything and demeaning faith 'by seeking proof for it in human reason.' When several decades later a Philadelphia priest took the wrong side in a fight for control of a parish church, his writings became the first American works placed on the *Index Librorum Prohibitorum*, the ever-growing list of forbidden matter first compiled in the mid-sixteenth century.[24] In the encyclical *Mirari vos* (1832), Pope Gregory XVI described 'freedom to publish' as 'never sufficiently denounced' and 'liberty of conscience' as an 'absurd and erroneous proposition.'[25] In preparing a new edition of the *Index*, Leo XIII wrote: 'Nothing can be conceived more pernicious, more apt to defile souls,' than 'noxious literature,' so that 'remedies must be applied against this plague.' When in 1904 an organization called Daughters of the Faith pledged to fight various modern impulses in American life, Pius X applauded their desire to stop 'the shameless licence of spectacular representations and immoral books.'[26]

A significant advance in Church censorship was the *Codex Iuris Canonici* (1917), a commentary to which declared that the Church enjoys a *'natural right'* as an 'autonomous' and 'paternal' authority 'to ward off anything that may endanger the moral and physical welfare of [its] subjects, and to protect them against bad surroundings, company, literature, etc., in fact anything that is apt to cause insubordination, anarchy, or moral decay.' The clergy and laity were now required to report 'books which they consider pernicious,' and every bishop was obliged to forbid books which he judged harmful to faith or morality in his diocese, in particular, those 'which attack or ridicule any of the Catholic dogmas.'[27] No special immunity attached to works recognized for their brilliance, beauty, scholarship, or historical significance; thus the 1929 *Index* included Gibbon's *Decline and Fall*, Diderot and d'Alembert's *Encyclopédie*, J.S. Mill's *Principles of Political Economy*, and Flaubert's *Madame Bovary*, as well as works by Hobbes, Locke, Descartes, Pascal, Spinoza, Pierre Bayle, Berkeley, Hume, Condillac, Condorcet, Defoe, Addison and Steele, Richardson, Goldsmith, Sterne, Voltaire, Rousseau, Kant, Heinrich Heine, Bentham, Stendhal, Balzac, Dumas *père et fils*, Taine, Comte, Anatole France, Zola, D'Annunzio, and Bergson, as well as – not surprisingly – David Friedrich Strauss.

Prominent among categories of books barred by the *Codex* were those that 'inculcate lascivious and obscene things' or present these in a frivolous or alluring manner. Pius XI in *Studiorum Ducem* (29 June 1923), reiterating Leo XIII's proclamation that Aquinas was Catholicism's ultimate source of wisdom, declared that because 'the majority of young men' were 'caught in the quicksands of passion, rapidly jettisoning holy purity and abandoning themselves to sensual pleasures,' priests must urge on them that Thomas's highest virtue was chastity. In 1927 the Supreme Sacred Congregation of the Holy Office, successor to the Supreme Sacred Congregation of the Roman and Universal Inquisition, issued an Instruction under Canon 1399 to ban essentially all books portraying the Jazz Age zeitgeist, that is, showing 'a frivolous fascination with immorality' which would cause 'a very great loss of souls':

> For many of these writers depict immodesties in flaming imagery; relate the most obscene details, sometimes guardedly, sometimes openly and shamelessly, without the least regard for the requirements of modesty; they describe even the worst carnal vices with subtle analysis, and adorn them with all the brilliancy and allurements of style, to such a degree that nothing in the field of morals is left inviolate. It is easy to see how harmful all this is, especially to young people, in whom the fire of youth makes chastity more difficult. These books, often small in size, are sold at low prices in bookstores, on the streets and squares of cities, at railroad stations; they come very quickly into everybody's hands, and bring great and often fateful dangers to Catholic families. For it is well known that writing of that sort violently excites the imagination, wildly inflames the passions, and drags the heart into the mire of impurity ...
>
> Let no one make these excuses: that many of those books have a truly admirable brilliance and elegance of style; that they are remarkable for inculcating a psychology in accord with modern discoveries; that the lascivious bodily pleasures are reprobated in as much as they are represented in their true light as most foul, or are sometimes shown to be connected with qualms of conscience, or in as much as it is shown how often the basest pleasures give way at last to the sorrow of a sort of repentance. For neither elegance of style nor medical or philosophic lore – if indeed these things are to be found in that sort of writing – nor the intention of the authors, whatever it may be, can prevent the readers, who owing to the corruption of nature are usually very weak and much inclined to impurity, from being gradually enmeshed in the allurements of those unclean pages.[28]

Behind these warnings lay a cautious conception of human nature and its perpetual hunger for the fruit of the tree of knowledge. Rev. Joseph M. Pernicone in 'The Ecclesiastical Prohibition of Books' (1932), his dissertation in the faculty of the School of Canon Law at Catholic University, noted that the Church 'realizes full well that, because of the fall of Adam and Eve, human nature is so weak and prone to lust, that immoral writings generally pervert the minds of men and deprave their hearts, lead them to unbridle their passions, cause them to fall into all kinds of crimes and at times even to commit suicide.' Becoming 'enmeshed in the allurements' of 'unclean pages' was thus no mere offence to propriety. Nor were 'all kinds of sins,' even suicide, the worst that these authorities sought to minimize. Rather, at stake was nothing less than the failure to attain Heaven. Pernicone declared: 'The law of nature imposes upon all men the duty of shunning that type of literature which endangers their eternal salvation.' Thus, whatever the negative effects in this world of indulging in disapproved material, the ultimate penalty was going to Hell. The Preface to the 1930 edition of the *Index* proclaimed:

> Impious ... literature is written sometimes with great charm of style; frequently it deals with subjects that excite lascivious passions or flatter spiritual pride; always too, with specious arguments and quibbling of every kind, it aims at leaving a lasting impression in the heart and mind of the incautious reader. It is, therefore, only natural that the Church, like a provident mother, should with timely prohibitions warn the faithful lest they press their lips to deceitful cups of poison. Not, forsooth, from any fear of the light of truth does the Church forbid certain books to be read, but on account rather of the zeal of God animating Her, which does not tolerate the loss of a single soul.

If the ultimate result of dangerous knowledge is losing salvation, it is hardly surprising that the Church would do everything possible to save souls. As Pernicone noted, 'there is no more infringement upon liberty when the Church forbids a harmful book than there is when the State forbids swimming in polluted waters.'[29]

Justice Holmes's metaphor of a 'free trade in ideas,' a classic indicium of both Modernisn and Americanism, entailed a right to deal in a variety of potentially dangerous notions or (to change the metaphor) to swim in polluted waters – at one's own risk – if one chooses. Having committed itself, not to an open market for ideas, but to the saving of souls, the Church did not believe that communication should follow the law of supply and demand. Pius XI in *Mortalium Animos* (1928) and *Divini illius magistri* (1929) declared that cinema as well as radio and 'impious and immoral books, often diabolically circulated at low prices,' can cause 'moral and religious shipwreck' to 'inexperienced youth.'[30] While numerous Protestant groups argued that salacious films and books triggered sexual predation, only preachers of 'fire and brimstone' thought reading such material actually meant going to Hell. The vacuum of moral authority indicated by the silence of urbane Protestant liberals and the court defeats of the vice societies left room for clearer, more forthright arguments, and Catholics, by asserting that evil material ultimately ruined one's chance to enter Heaven, had such an argument. The bishops' deep commitment to the subject led in 1938 to the founding of the National Organization for Decent Literature (NODL), which would quickly become the nation's primary agency for pressuring local booksellers to keep disapproved books and magazines off their shelves. Organized by John F. Noll, bishop of Fort Wayne, Indiana, NODL sent subscribers lists of materials which its reviewers (predominantly graduates of Catholic women's colleges) had found objectionable, its evolving list eventually including works by Zola, Dos Passos, Hemingway, Farrell, and Aldous Huxley, as well as *God's Little Acre*, *Tobacco Road*, *The Naked and the Dead*, *Andersonville*, and *Catcher in the Rye*. In several American cities and towns, the NODL list – despite constitutional Church/State issues – was accorded quasi-official status.[31]

At its inception, film was a popular medium for promoting faith; Leo XIII was sufficiently pleased with film pioneer W.K.L. Dickson's recording of twelve scenes from papal daily life that he reportedly blessed the camera and all those who would see the film. Its exhibition at Carnegie Hall on 14 December 1898 was received enthusiastically, with few if any in the audience having previously seen Leo other than in the iconic photographs that hung from innumerable bedroom walls. Even earlier, a film of the Austrian *Horitz Passion Play* had opened in Philadelphia, accompanied by a lecture, slide show, and organ music, while *The Passion Play of Oberammergau* employed professional actors in a makeshift studio on the roof of Grand Central Station, imitating the Bavarian peasants who had been depicting the Passion since 1634. The film so impressed clergymen that its initial commercial run was followed by innumerable church screenings.[32]

Earnest depictions of the Passion would not be Hollywood's typical fare. Gerard B. Donnelly, S.J., stated in 1932 that because for Catholics 'the true principles of morality are Divine commands,' Hollywood's common themes – extramarital sex, murder, robbery, etc. – are 'violations of the Divine Will.' In his college text on family life, priest/sociologist Edgar Schmiedeler accused cinema as well as books and magazines of inculcating a false idea of marriage as a 'joy ride' arising out of 'love at first sight.' Even less offensive films, those that 'portray immorality as merely an offence against social mores,' are blameworthy because – Donnelly argued – they ignore the fact that sin is primarily 'an offence against the Creator.' The Vatican's *Osservatore Romano* was so disgusted with American films as to ask how such 'a triumph of paganism' could be permitted, while Michael Williams similarly thought movies part of a 'fatal flood of Paganism' which threatened the family, individual liberty, and private property. Cornelia McQueen Gibbs, active in various social and political causes in Maryland, provided the editor of a Baltimore-based Catholic periodical with a Bosch-like vision: 'The Octopus reaches out for box-office receipts from every age. The trade papers of the movie magnates give instructions how to lure back the children who grew bored when the talkies came in ... With the cunningness worthy of the evil one, the modern appeal of the Zeppelin, the airplane, the trip to Mars, become vehicles for wholesale nakedness and vulgarity. One of the few things left that was supposed to belong preeminently to the child were the animal cartoons ... Now "Krazy Kat" is having amorous adventures and dogs indulge in home-wrecking, with the usual triangle, and resulting murder and court trial.'[33]

Increasingly, Catholics made their views known to exhibitors, as when a Jesuit from Milwaukee in 1927 wrote that if a local theatre plays a film of which Catholics disapprove, the parish priest should write a letter of protest. 'The fact is,' he noted, 'that we, as Catholics, know a great deal more than the rest of the world' about moral questions and thus 'have a certain duty to manifest our conviction on such subjects ... [I]f a great number of the Catholic societies in our country would write frequently to express their convictions on the subject of the morality of the films, this would undoubtedly have a very good effect on raising the standard of this form of commercialized entertainment.' On *The Catholic Truth Hour* radio program in 1930, Mrs Francis E. Slattery, president of the Boston League of Catholic Women, said that the American housewife was – second only to the Church itself – 'the greatest single influence for the good of the people, for the protection of their morals and the preservation of their spiritual ideas ... Under the authority of her husband, she rules the Christian home, she influences the standards of the community, she leaves her impress upon the works of the State.' Well down Mrs Slattery's list of problems with which a Catholic housewife might choose to grapple were crime, bigotry, and prejudice. At the top were 'the conditions on the stage and screen,' along with such 'attacks on the family and home' as divorce, liberalized marriage arrangements, contraception, and feminism. She found it the 'particular province' of women 'to stress the moral virtues, to uphold the moral standards, to develop the underlying principles, spread a knowledge of them in the public mind, and insist upon their application to the great political and ethical issues of the present day.' But such comments had no impact on Hollywood. Soon there was a movement afoot to take Catholic protest beyond letters of outrage penned by housewives and parish priests.[34]

7 The Production Code

In 1915 George William Mundelein was transferred from Brooklyn to be installed in Chicago, at age forty-three, as the youngest archbishop in the United States. There he flourished, enhancing the power and influence of Catholics far beyond their 30 per cent share of the city's population, while fostering both assimilation and Catholic pride among the City's huge Polish, Italian, and German populations. That he had political clout was evidenced by the licence plate on his limousine, 'ILLINOIS 1,' an honour more typically reserved for governors. He would time his arrival at public gatherings – heralded by the blare of his motorcade's police sirens – to take place just after everyone else had settled in, leading some to call him 'the late Cardinal Mundelein.' In 1921 he constructed in a village near Chicago a seminary called St Mary's of the Lake and when, three years later, he became the youngest member of the College of Cardinals, the village was summarily renamed 'Mundelein.' When in 1930 the Sisters of Charity of the Blessed Virgin Mary established a local college, it too was named for him.[1]

As steward of the archdiocese's fiscal health, Mundelein had retained the investment banking firm of Halsey, Stuart & Co., which also underwrote debt and equity securities offered by the movie studios. Thus did Mundelein, under Harold Stuart's guidance, become a substantial investor in Hollywood.[2] In October 1929, with the industry's $500-million retooling for sound still in process, the U.S. economy collapsed. Investors, like underwriters, dislike uncertainty. Protests against the movies' alleged 'paganism' fuelled demands for federal regulation, which augured to be both disruptive and expensive. Stuart and Mundelein began discussing at their weekly lunches the benefits of a uniform, self-policing Hollywood code which might both clean up films and blunt the call for government censorship.[3] FitzGeorge Dinneen, S.J., pastor of St Ignatius Parish on Chicago's North Side and a member of Chicago's powerful film censorship board, had managed to purge several films from the local Granada Theater by inveighing against them from the pulpit. Martin Quigley, publisher of a prominent industry periodical later known as *Motion Picture Herald*, approached Dinneen about the notion of subjecting the movie industry to a code of practice which might somehow be enforceable by Catholic power, then asked public-relations man and journalist Joseph I. Breen, assistant to the head of Peabody Coal, to generate support among Catholic and secular newspapers. Breen proposed a successor to the 'Don't's' and 'Be Carefuls.'[4] To draft appropriate language, Quigley and Dinneen called upon a Chicago-born priest with the imposing name of Daniel Aloysius Lord, S.J.[5] Soon, consistent with Hays's strategy of making potential opponents feel like insiders, Jason Joy was copying Father Lord with dozens of letters written by the Hays Office to producers about various projects, as if Lord had somehow become Joy's consultant. In November 1929, Mundelein received Lord's draft of a code and directed Lord and Quigley to proceed to Los Angeles to present it to the industry.[6]

Father Lord was not without credentials for such an assignment. A prolific writer of pamphlets and hymns, he also taught drama at the Jesuit-run St Louis University.[7] As he later wrote, he had grown up on theatre, his mother having taken him to 'everything worth seeing' that came to late nineteenth-century Chicago. Nor would this be Lord's first junket to Hollywood; he had served as a technical adviser on DeMille's epic *The King of Kings* (1927), his success in immunizing that film from clerical attack having been attested by the Marxist film critic Harry Alan Potamkin, who declared it 'a pimple of sanctimony' and syco-phancy to the Church.[8]

Irving Thalberg, the only Hollywood executive about whom the word 'genius' was sincerely uttered, chose not to wait for guidance from Father Lord, instead drafting with Jason Joy a new version of the 'Don'ts' and 'Be Carefuls.' On 10 February 1930, Lord and Quigley met with them and with Hays, as well as Jack Warner, Sol Wurtzel of Fox, and Paramount's B.P. Schulberg and Jesse Lasky. Consistent with Hays's rhetoric about films being duty-bound not to implant ideas, Thalberg argued that a movie does not present its viewers 'with tastes and manners and views and morals' but only 'reflects those they already have,' so that if it does not comport with what people already think, feel, and believe, it will fail at the box office. Since many films were lascivious, or violent, or both, Thalberg's was the only position Holly-wood could take: to admit that films introduced the audience to lewd or violent ideas was tacitly to admit that censorship might be appropriate. But Lord saw through this, countering that the movies 'set standards,' 'inculcate ... customs,' and 'create fashions.'[9] Gloria Swanson's sumptu-ous bathtub in DeMille's *Male and Female* was not something each member of the audience already had at home. Indeed, few in the audi-ence could even imagine such a thing until they saw it on the screen. Once they did, they hungered for it as well as the life of decadent luxury it symbolized, thus justifying the characterization of Hollywood as a 'dream factory.' The producers were doing what all marketers of discretionary products do: not merely complying with what custom-ers say they desire, but creating desires in order to satisfy them. Human desires included – it would seem – impulses for sex and violence. While moral censorship is premised on stifling these im-pulses because of the dangers presumed to flow from their release, the movie industry was premised on extracting dollars by triggering that release as voyeurism.

While the pool of potential patrons might have a host of dissimilar interests, they might all be induced to buy a ticket because a particular film taps interests they have in common. Since the profit-maximizing way to exploit a mass audience is via its 'lowest common denominator,' Hollywood had no interest in raising audiences to a higher level of aesthetic appreciation. Rather, as scenarist Arthur Krows noted, the studios, 'for the sake of squeezing every possible dollar out of any film whatsoever,' made sure that it was 'reduced ... to a formula intelligible to fourteen-year-old minds.' In 1932, E.S. Bates, literary editor of the *Dictionary of American Biography*, wrote that what appears on the screen is not decided by Will Hays 'but by what Walt Whitman ... called the divine average,' the movies being 'the most shameless example of what comes from giving the public what it wants. What it actually wants is, quite obviously, "thrills" – chiefly sex-thrills, but in their absence any other kind of thrills will serve, particularly those derived from observ-ing the romantic habits of the rich. A smear of sentimentality over the whole completes the picture.' Since the essence of the studio system was to bring back the same patrons every few days, a film was likely to succeed if it threw together the same sex-thrills that had worked well enough the last time, the resulting pattern of patronage exemplifying Walter B. Pitkin's observation in 1930 that 'in a wide-open world mar-ket ... mean[,] crude, dull, stupid, false, childish' films 'always drive out

good ones.' The great historical and literary dramas, Edward M. Barrows wrote, yield no profit. This was the industry's position, reasserted
on numerous occasions. As Hays's general counsel, Charles C. Pettijohn,
told the Women's Republican Club of Boston: 'You are going to get
better pictures just as soon as you can develop a better public appreciation for the better type of photoplay and in no other way. That is the
cold, hard, answer.'[10]

The debate between Thalberg and Lord – between commerce and
morality – included nothing about art and its prerogatives, and while
many of Lord's complaints about sexual content could have been coun-
tered with trenchant references to Aristophanes, Plautus, or *Romeo and
Juliet*, Thalberg and the other executives were insufficiently conversant
with such works to enlist their aid. Before joining the industry, the
moguls had not engaged in the 'legitimate' theatre, but in more mun-
dane businesses where the gist had been to make a sale, punctuated by
the happy expression: 'Wrap it up.' Success in movies, too, was to be
judged at the point of purchase, yielding Adolph Zukor's brilliant
dictum: 'The public is never wrong.' They were tough and they were
cynical. Ex-jewellery merchant Lewis J. Selznick, upon hearing that
Czar Nicholas II had been deposed and imprisoned, reportedly sent
him a cable: 'WHEN I WAS A BOY IN RUSSIA YOUR POLICE TREATED MY
PEOPLE VERY BADLY. HOWEVER NO HARD FEELINGS. HEAR YOU ARE OUT OF
WORK. IF YOU WILL COME TO NEW YORK CAN GIVE YOU FINE POSITION
ACTING IN PICTURES. SALARY NO OBJECT. REPLY MY EXPENSE. REGARDS
YOU AND FAMILY, LEWIS J. SELZNICK.' (There was no reply.) Zukor, head
of Famous Players/Paramount, had been a fur merchant, having arrived from Hungary in 1889 at age sixteen. Another ex-fur merchant
was Marcus Loew. Joseph Schenck had managed a New Jersey amusement park, while Harry Cohn's several careers had included vaudeville
and song plugging. Louis B. Mayer had owned a junkyard and a bur-
lesque house, while the Warners had operated a nickelodeon in New-
castle, Pennsylvania, and Carl Laemmle, who had left Germany in 1884
at seventeen, had managed a clothing store. (The *wunderkind* Thalberg
had started as Laemmle's personal assistant.) William Fox arrived from
Hungary as an infant in 1880, sold stove-blacking door-to-door at age
seven, by thirteen headed a team cutting linings for suits, and at fifteen
prayed for rain so he could run to theatres and sell umbrellas to depart-
ing patrons.[11]

'Put that finger down,' John Barrymore once told a producer who
scolded him for an indiscretion, 'I remember when it had a thimble on

it.' Since they were catering to a mass audience, their failure to know the classics held them back not at all, but rather proved the quip Alva Johnston made in a 1933 *New Yorker* piece: 'You can roughly measure the importance of a man in the movie industry by the number of stories told about his ignorance.' When Zukor heard that the famous playwright Sir James M. Barrie had agreed to let his highly successful play *The Admirable Crichton* be filmed, Zukor cringed: a film about an admiral must have sea battles, and sea battles are expensive. Laemmle had Erich von Stroheim change the title of *The Pinnacle*, since no one wants to see a film about a card game; rather, 've vill call it *Blind Husbands* – den all de vimmen come.' Following the success of D.W. Griffith's *Pippa Passes* in 1914, a producer wrote to Mr Robert Browning, care of the studio, to ask if he had any other 'peppy, up-to-date stories' to sell. Samuel Goldwyn, né Schmuel Gelbfisz, had left Poland at age eleven to become a glove maker, glove salesman, then glove entrepreneur. To a director who found a script too caustic, Goldwyn replied: 'To hell with the cost. If it's a good picture, we'll make it.' Alva Johnston said the general drill was to ridicule Goldwyn for a while, then to denounce him for a while, and then finally to credit him with 'an instinctive love of beauty.'[12]

Cardinal Mundelein was ready to force the industry to reform itself via Father Lord's Code. On the other hand, undoubtedly to avoid the anti-Catholic backlash that might be expected in light of the treatment accorded Al Smith, Mundelein did not want the Code to be recognized as a Catholic document, and his public statement of support was circumspect.[13] While at one point Hays – still perceived by many as Hollywood's censor – tried to take personal credit for the Code, under scrutiny by Wilfrid Parsons, S.J., editor-in-chief of the Jesuit weekly *America*, Hays adroitly admitted that it was 'really the work of Lord, and the Lord.'[14] Pursuant to his traditional tactic of inclusiveness-*cum*-flattery, Hays sang Lord's praises to Mundelein while suggesting that Lord prolong his California sojourn.[15] Meanwhile, knowing that much of the language drafted by Lord and Quigley would never be approved by the MPPDA board in New York, and that simply rejecting their efforts might alienate Mundelein, Hays negotiated a compromise in which much material would be designated as explanatory annotation and – as such – would not require board approval.[16] Lord, for his part, decided to 'sell' the compromise to Mundelein.[17] On 17 February 1930, Thalberg, Schulberg, Wurtzel, Lasky, and Jack Warner voted to adopt the Code, and on 31 March the MPPDA board approved.

'Thou Shalt Not ...'

The Code revolved around three 'General Principles': to produce no film that 'will lower the moral standards of those who see it' by, for instance, eliciting audience sympathy for 'crime, wrong-doing, evil, or sin'; to produce no film which ridicules '[l]aw, natural or human' or which creates sympathy for the violation thereof; and to portray '[c]orrect standards of life.' Under these were twelve more specific prohibitions. Adultery had been outlawed in the Ten Commandments, and this as well as several other passages from the Old and New Testaments underlay much of the Code. The sanctity of married life was to be upheld, and 'low forms of sex relationship' were not to be portrayed either as common or accepted. 'Scenes of passion' were to be omitted if they 'arous[e] dangerous emotions on the part of the immature, the young or the criminal classes.' 'Impure love' was 'not [to] be presented as attractive and beautiful,' nor as 'right and permissible,' nor as 'the subject of comedy or farce,' nor 'in such a way as to arouse passion or morbid curiosity.' Also forbidden were obscenity, profanity, miscegenation, 'White slavery,' 'Sex hygiene and venereal diseases' (popular subjects in films of the Progressive era), and 'Sex perversion or any inference to it.' Clergymen could not be portrayed as either comic or villainous, dancing could not be too passionate, and nudity was forbidden outright, as were scenes of childbirth, consistent with a general prudery regarding this 'intimate' and – as many somewhat awkwardly described it – 'blessed' event.

Awash with ambiguous terms (e.g., 'correct standards of life,' 'impure love,' and 'law, natural or human'), the Code could also be oxymoronic, as when it allowed tasteful vulgarity and refined unpleasantness. Worse still is the discussion of film as 'art' in the annotations:

> Most arts appeal to the mature. This art appeals at once to every class, immature, developed, undeveloped, law abiding, criminal ... Art enters intimately into the lives of human beings. Art can be morally good, lifting men to higher levels. This has been done through good music, great painting, authentic fiction, poetry, drama. Art can be morally evil in its effects. This is the case clearly enough with unclean art, indecent books, suggestive drama. The effect on the lives of men and women is obvious.
>
> ... It has often been argued that art in itself is unmoral, neither good nor bad. This is perhaps true of the THING which is music, painting, poetry, etc. But the thing is the PRODUCT of some person's mind, and the intention

of that mind was either good or bad morally when it produced the thing. Besides, the thing has its EFFECT upon those who come into contact with it.[18]

Calling art 'morally evil in its effects' and using such expressions as 'unclean art' and 'authentic fiction' indicate that Lord – although a drama teacher – could not have been conversant with the work of major critics and aestheticians, much less could one imagine him having an appropriate reaction to *Tristan und Isolde*. Quigley's aesthetic is available at greater length in his book *Decency in Motion Pictures* (1937), witness such lines as: 'There is, it is to be feared,˙ much confusion between literalism and the proper realism of art ... Art was born of recording, but it grew great and powerful by selection of what it recorded. The argument for complete, literal recording, if that is what is meant by Mr. James Joyce and Mr. Ernest Hemingway, must presume a discriminatory approach by the audience that is not to be presumed of the commonality.'[19]

Although the Code and its annotations, riddled with such stuff, fairly cried out for denunciation by properly credentialed observers, few came forward. One who did (although not until 1938) was the Catholic-turned-Trotskyite novelist James T. Farrell:

The first paragraph of Part One ... reads: 'No picture shall be produced which will lower the moral standards of those who see it. Hence, the sympathy of the audience should never be thrown on the side of the crime, wrongdoing, evil or sin.' Herein is revealed an attitude pernicious to art, pernicious to the apprehension of art, pernicious even to the inculcation of the very moral standards Mr. Quigley has for years struggled to see upheld ... The notion implied ... is that the human response to art objects is similar to the response to advertising slogans. The wide variety of human responses to a work of art is neglected and ignored ... It is assumed that if allegedly false standards of morality are represented in a work of art, the audience will necessarily accept these false standards.

... It is assumed that if a work of art does not seem to weigh the balance in favour of virtue rather than sin, its audience will be inclined to be sinful rather than virtuous. This is psychologically unsound.

... If we accept ... the Production Code, we must adopt a view of the individual as a mere passive agent on whom stimuli work, but who does not himself select stimuli. The implication of such an acceptance is that the relationship between man and his world is a dead, mechanical, predetermined one.

In short, the Code 'contains just about every fallacy, every non sequitur, every irrelevancy, every false assumption, every mistaken psychological conception that has ever been used in this country to argue for censorship on moral grounds.'[20]

Under the doctrine of 'spectrum scarcity,' the federal government awarded radio bandwidth to station owners who promised to serve the public interest. Because this requirement introduced millions of people to great music (including *Tristan und Isolde*), these programs served to elevate tastes. The Code, on the other hand, denying the mass audience what the contemporary novel and the New York stage were providing to the 'swells,' virtually assured that, when adapting books and plays, film would delete what had given them punch. Beyond Farrell's bristling criticism, however, the Code was not appropriately denounced by intellectual and artistic leaders. Hays, meanwhile, expert in the art of seeming acquiescence, announced – with not a glimmer of irony – that the Code saved 'many valuable literary, dramatic and entertainment values' available in plays and novels by 'eliminating' from them 'the socially offensive and improper' during their transition to the screen.[21] With Hays in charge of enforcement, there was no reason for the industry to do other than take the Code in stride. In the 'Hail, Fredonia!' scene in *Duck Soup* (1933; dir. Leo McCarey), Groucho Marx, listing the several things which will require censorship in his perfect state, proclaims that wherever pleasure is 'exhibited,' it will be 'prohibited.'

Clerical Intimidation

As with earlier self-censorship efforts, the industry intentionally failed to provide in the Code any enforcement mechanism, leaving the studios free to ignore it whenever a cost/benefit analysis suggested moving forward with a project that was bound to incur problems with state and municipal censors, in the hope that the attendant publicity, coupled with whatever salaciousness remained following the various censorship efforts, might net out at the box office. An editorial in the *New York World* of 2 April 1930 advised: 'That the code will actually be applied in any sincere and thorough way we have not the slightest belief. It expresses neither what the best nor the worst directors and writers and actors in Hollywood think, but what Mr. Hays and the magnates think it would be good business for them to give the appearance of thinking.' Nevertheless, neither Quigley, nor Lord, nor Parsons intended to let this be just another of Hays's sanctimonious, hollow promises. As Jesuits,

Lord and Parsons were sworn not to take sides in any political controversy, and while censorship was plainly a political issue when enforced
by government, Hollywood self-censorship arguably was not. Parsons
publicly saluted the industry for having 'of its own accord' established
an 'ideal dreamed of by every educator and churchman,' that is, 'a state
of mind where the citizen ... obeys the public moral law.' Lord, too,
maintained the illusion that the Code 'did not originate in the Catholic
Church' and 'was not presented by me as a Catholic priest.'[22] But
something more was needed. 'If we pin [the producers] to it publicly,'
Parsons confided to Lord, 'we will have in Catholic public opinion a
weapon which we would otherwise lack.' Lord issued to the Church's
Episcopal Committee on Motion Pictures some suggestions for tricking
Hollywood into believing that the Church advocated federal censorship (in fact, it did not), so that the industry would consider compliance
with the Code a less onerous alternative.[23]

Pre-vetting film projects was now mandatory, and in 1932 Hays's
staff read 654 scripts and treatments, had 703 conferences, and issued
1,107 opinions. Box-office shortfalls from decreased sexuality and violence were offset by fewer disruptions from state and municipal censors.[24] Even before the Code, Jason Joy's staff had so mastered what
various governments demanded that by 1929 censors ordered only 1.9
cuts per film in which Joy had been consulted, as against a hefty 5.9 for
all others. Of 176 cuts in films Joy had reviewed, he had failed to predict
only seven.[25] When he successfully intervened to smooth the way with
state censors for *Madam Satan*, director Cecil B. DeMille wittily cabled
him: 'Let Joy be unconfined!' But Joy's predictive powers were not
perfect, and when he approved Jack Conway's *Red-Headed Woman* (1932),
involving a secretary's desire to land her married boss, Atlanta's censor,
Mrs Alonzo Richardson, called it a 'disgusting sex exploitation' film
that was bound to increase public support for Senator Brookhart's
pending federal censorship bill. Soon other producers pushed for similar
dispensations, in what became a virtual tide of 'fallen woman' films.[26]

As weekly admissions plunged to 40 million from a pre–Black Friday
high of 100 million, and average admission prices dropped from 35
cents to under a quarter, some producers believed that salaciousness
might ultimately constitute the margin between survival and insol-
vency. Joy, uncomfortable with being Hollywood's self-censor with so
much at stake, resigned to take a high-paying job with Fox. Nor could
the man replacing him, former New York State censor James Wingate,
be any more effective so long as the industry refused to invoke mean-

ingful sanctions against members who ignored the Code. A professor at the Harvard Business School noted that the Code 'has contributed suspiciously little' to ameliorate the expense and disruption arising out of government censorship, and that unless the industry 'takes rather drastic steps, those interested in obtaining.more rigid governmental regulation will succeed in forcing their views upon the public.' William Randolph Hearst told columnist Louella Parsons that Hollywood's failure to police itself would soon be followed by 'a revolt against indecency on the screen,' while Joe Breen, who had sufficiently impressed everyone to become Los Angeles–based assistant to the New York–based Hays, warned a producer that while the industry might continue to play games with women's groups, once the Catholic bishops lost patience, they would instruct parishioners to boycott the movies, with a devastating effect on revenues.[27]

As Breen settled in, he wrote to Quigley: 'Hays is not strong in qualities of leadership. He does, as you have frequently suggested, pull his punches. He raves and rants at us but seems to be in abject fear of certain of the executives of our member companies. Howard Hughes and Joe Schenck, for instance, have just given him the trimming of his life on the advertising and exploitation of "Scarface." Boy, but Hays backed down.' Personally disloyal to his immediate boss, Breen privately said of the Hollywood producers who paid his salary: 'They'd put fucking in Macy's window, if you gave them a chance, and they'd argue till they were blue in the face that it was "art."' Among the components of this seething resentment was a more than casual anti-Semitism. In a letter to Wilfrid Parsons, Breen referred to the 'lousy Jews out here' who 'think of nothing but money making and sexual indulgence,' adding that at Mass and Holy Communion he prayed that 'the Holy Ghost might let me in on the inside and sort of tip me off as to the proper thing to do in the situation.' 'I hate like hell to admit it,' he told Quigley, 'but really the Code, to which you and I have given so much, is of no consequence whatever. Much of the talk you hear about it from Hays, or Joy, is bunk ...' Breen proceeded to spew forth some vile anti-Semitic slurs, establishing that he considered himself, Parsons, and other Catholics in an adversarial relationship with L.B. Mayer, Thalberg, and other Hollywood executives who in his view ignored ethical issues and cared only about making profits. Breen concluded by noting that, given what he was up against in dealing with Hollywood's executives, 'All of this, and more, suggests, definitely, that I can't get very far out here with the work I had hoped to do.' Nor were anti-Semitic slurs limited to confidential correspondence. An article in the *American Ecclesiastical Review*, signed by Bishop John J. Cantwell of the Los Angeles / San Diego diocese but with detailed industry information undoubtedly supplied by Breen, declared that of the 'Big Eight' production companies, only Fox was 'definitely free from Jewish influence in its management and direction,' making Jews primarily responsible for 'all this vileness' on the screen.[28]

In January 1932, with each new film nominally vetted under the Code, Father Dinneen carped to Father Parsons that in fact nothing had changed and that the bishops seemed to be 'asleep.' Perhaps to stir them, Lord reported that Twentieth Century Pictures head Joseph Schenck had said of the bishops: 'they can go to Hell.' In his capacity as editor of a periodical reaching every Catholic high school and college in the United States, Lord began printing a blacklist of films his young readers should avoid – and tell their parents to avoid. The bishops apparently awoke from their slumber and at their 1932 conference issued a statement calling for an 'Organized Protest Against Corrupt Reading and Picture Matter,' while the National Council of Catholic Men resolved to address problems with the stage and screen. Lord told Breen and Hays that movies were getting 'worse and worse,' adding: 'we have been completely let down on the Code.'[29]

Quigley chose to direct his scorn not at the worst but rather at the best of the fallen-woman films: *Baby Face* (1933), produced by Darryl Zanuck and directed by Alfred E. Green. Barbara Stanwyck plays a mill-town girl whose father has her grant sexual favours to local authorities so that they will turn a blind eye to his cheap speakeasy and still. She heads for New York and sleeps her way to the top of a major bank, her progress there cinematically recorded, floor by floor, with everyone from George Brent to the young John Wayne desperately addicted to her cynical, tough-as-nails love-making. Wingate demanded substantial changes. With Stanwyck no longer available for retakes, Wingate got the end changed, with the bank's directors explaining that Stanwyck and her rich husband (the latter having defrauded the bank's shareholders) have sold her collected baubles to make everything right. Although the husband's manual labour had previously been confined to polo, the couple now dispatch themselves to the steel town she came from, to start an honest, working-class life. In this version of the film, the ambitious, sexually aggressive woman is to be forgiven because she relinquishes all the personal wealth she worked for and reverts to the squalor where she began, having brought down her husband with her, to live happily-ever-after with nothing.[30]

But even this was not enough. The narrator in Budd Schulberg's Hollywood novel *What Makes Sammy Run?* refers to film characters as mere sandwich-board men for various moral attitudes, and Stanwyck's home-town guru/mentor, one whose disapproval of Stanwyck's urban doings signals that he is our sandwich-board moral guide, warns her that she is following a 'Nietzsche philosophy.' While this intellectual touch delighted Wingate and the resulting mess of moral posturing satisfied many bluenoses, Quigley thought the film 'immoral' – even with the changes – because it shows 'that a girl is privileged to avail herself of any means to escape sordid and unhappy circumstances.' Quigley apparently believed that being forced by one's father to sleep with local pols is morally superior to sleeping one's way to the top for one's own benefit, since at least by staying home one never emerges from misery and squalor.[31]

With Hays's powerful Republican friends ousted in the 1932 election, rumours spread that the moguls would soon replace him with some similarly connected Democrat. Following Roosevelt's swearing in, Hays – as if to establish his continued utility – convened an all-night meeting of the MPPDA board to focus on the New Deal's likely intervention in Hollywood's oligopolistic, anti-competitive structure of production, distribution, and exhibition. Among the results of that meeting was a 'Reaffirmation of Objectives' whereby Hays could revamp and revivify Hollywood self-censorship, the better to portray the industry as good citizens requiring no government regulation. But if the industry had actually intended a housecleaning, it would have stayed clear of William Faulkner's *Sanctuary* (1930), in which an impotent man rapes a woman with an ear of corn. An utter mess was made of the novel in *The Story of Temple Drake* (1933), a film that was still sufficiently racy, even after substantial vetting by Hays's staff, to have Breen later call it 'above all others ... almost the *immediate cause* of the nation-wide outcry against offensive films.' In May 1933, the month it was released, Hays invited Lord to return to Hollywood, ostensibly to put some teeth in the Code, as if Hays himself had played no role in the industry's refusal to abide by the language already in force. While Hays had always succeeded in hoodwinking and co-opting Protestant leaders by inviting them to the land-of-milk-and-honey, Lord could resist such blandishments. If Wingate could not understand the Code and enforce it – Lord urged –

'he should be dismissed as thoroughly incompetent.' Lord now gave Hays a Mosaic warning: powerful forces were amassing, forces he had held back but would no longer contain, forces that would swamp the industry if Hays did not himself take a strong personal stand, there being not 'one man in twenty out there who has the slightest consideration for morality or decency.' On 21 August the National Council of Catholic Men reminded Hays of their 'repeated protests against the moral deterioration more and more evidencing itself' in Hollywood's products.[32]

   As Breen had said, the bishops had one weapon no Protestant leader could invoke: a boycott. In the summer of 1933, Dinneen suggested to Mundelein to make movies an issue at the bishops' conference at Catholic University in November. A.H. Giannini, who with his brother A.P. (the founder of the Bank of America) provided financing for several studios, had somewhat disingenuously described the film industry in 1926 as '[a] clean, wholesome business, managed by men with clear-eyed determination to render a great public service.' But now Giannini, joined by another prominent lay Catholic, Los Angeles attorney Joseph Scott, warned Hays and the producers that Bishop Cantwell was monitoring the situation and that if the studios continued to flaunt the Code, a Catholic boycott would follow.[33]

   On 1 October 1933 the Vatican's newly appointed apostolic delegate to the United States, Amleto Giovanni Cicognani, archbishop of Laodicea, addressed the National Conference of Catholic Charities at New York's Metropolitan Opera House. Cicognani, a former professor of canon law at the Pontifical Institute of Canon and Civil Law at S. Apollinare, had authored *Ius Canonicum* (1925), a commentary on the 1917 *Codex Iuris Canonici* which many in the audience of four thousand would have had reason to consult. Consistent with the Church's position that immoral material causes a loss of souls, he reasoned that films carried an 'incalculable influence for evil' with 'a massacre of the innocence of youth ... taking place hour by hour!' – adding that God and the pope called upon Catholics 'to a united and vigorous campaign for the purification of the cinema.' His listeners could have had no doubt that he spoke with the authority of Pius XI himself – even if the particular language may well have been handed to Cicognani at the last minute by John T. McNicholas.[34]

   McNicholas, a committed Thomist who had risen from his first assignment in an Italian parish to the bishopric of Duluth before becoming archbishop of Cincinnati, was now a vocal member of the episcopacy's growing opposition to Hollywood, forming at the bishops' November meeting a film committee to include Cantwell and Noll as well as Hugh C. Boyle of Pittsburgh. In a speech at that meeting entitled 'Priests and the Motion Picture Industry,' Cantwell proclaimed: '[S]ome action of heroic proportions must be taken if we are to save the youth of America from a pollution and debauchery the like of which America has never known ... In vain do we struggle to rear great educational institutions, if the invidious character of the cinema is permitted to prostitute the character of our adolescent youth. So great is the power of the motion picture to impress the youth of the land that 1 hour spent in the darkness of a cinema palace, intent on the unfolding of a wrong kind of story, can, and frequently does, nullify years of careful training on the part of the church, the school, and the home.' The speech probably had some input from Joe Breen and/or Quigley, given such metaphorical anarchy as: 'One whose moral antennae are attuned to the mouthings of the gutter, is not likely to react favourably to the wholesome atmosphere of the higher strata.' It was distributed through diocesan weeklies to some seven million subscribers, with versions also appearing in two national Catholic publications. The committee then took a substantial additional step, mailing questionnaires to all dioceses in order to develop a master-list of all owners and mortgage-holders of U.S. theatres. Newspapers began to note public demands by priests for movie boycotts. A Catholic periodical in St Louis noted: 'If the Catholic Church ever looses Her fulminations against the lust-purveying producers, there's going to be a hot time in Hollywood.'[35]

Breen attended the bishops' conference as the industry's representative, and apparently saw no ethical conflict in thereafter writing to Lord: 'I think you know about the proposal we made to Cantwell that his Committee request every bishop in the U.S. to address a personal letter to every exhibitor in his diocese protesting against dirty films ... What we hope to get out of this is 8,000 or 10,000 letters in reply, putting the blame on the Producers ... If this is what comes out of this particular endeavor, the accumulation will be a terrible indictment of Hollywood and will make a newspaper story that will rock the nation.'[36] In fact, few exhibitors disapproved of 'dirty films' if – as tended to happen – they attracted audiences. Despite a supposed moral 'uproar' about the clear-eyed salaciousness of Mae West's several films, an industry canvass found that not one U.S. theatre had ever asked to cancel *She Done Him Wrong* or *I'm No Angel*; rather, they were repeatedly held over. The exhibitors' actual complaint concerned block-booking, being forced to accept films with little box-office potential as a condition for getting the films (like West's) that people would pay to see. Speaking to the municipal censors of Worcester, Massachusetts, Hays's counsel asserted that although exhibitors would have the public believe that block-booking forced them to show prurient material, in fact it saddled them with unprofitable material, including such fare as William K. Howard's *The Power and the Glory* (1933), Mitchell Leisen's *Cradle Song* (1933), Frank Lloyd's *Cavalcade* (1933), Alfred E. Green's *Disraeli* (1929), and *With Byrd at the South Pole* (1930), that is, high-quality, praiseworthy films with only limited box-office appeal.[37] In any event, Breen, by secretly inviting exhibitors to 'put the blame on the Producers' for dirty movies, was unwittingly giving them an opportunity to undermine block-booking, a fundament of his employers' business plan.

8 The Legion of Decency

In January 1934, Breen told Lord that Bishop Cantwell was 'setting up a working committee to "do something" about the bad pictures.' Several prelates conferred but could not agree on a collective national strategy. On 11 March, following a speech by Father Lord to three thousand young members of the Catholic Action Convention in Buffalo, they passed a resolution to boycott objectionable films. On 10 April the bishops announced a 'Legion of Decency,' in which priests would invite Catholics 'to pledge themselves to refrain from patronizing motion pictures which offend decency and Christian morality,' so that eventually 'millions of Americans' would together 'rid the country of its greatest menace – the salacious motion picture.' In May an editorial in *Commonweal* concluded that the bishops had been more than patient and that Hays was only 'a dummy of respectability for the unscrupulous real masters of the Hollywood machine for the mass production of filth.' On 24 April, Lord threw down the gauntlet to Universal founder Carl Laemmle and Columbia co-founder Harry Cohn, stating that the producers had demonstrated 'a contempt for public opinion and a disregard for the high trust the nation placed in them in permitting them to supply it with entertainment. The Catholic bishops have determined that this shall not continue.' In short, it was time for the bishops to 'ask no quarter and give none.'[1]

Although a paucity of objective data about the psychological effects of movies had never stopped self-proclaimed moralists from engaging in jeremiads against Hollywood, the Payne Fund had recently commissioned nine state-of-the-art, psycho-sociological studies of the actual impact of film upon children. When a summary volume by H.J. Forman characterized that impact as both substantial and pernicious, a host of commentators seized upon Forman's book as 'proof' that movies harmed children, even though the studies themselves, by social scientists Herbert Blumer, W.W. Charters, Paul G. Cressey, Edgar Dale, Philip M. Hauser, L.L. Thurstone, and Frederic M. Thrasher, were substantially more circumspect.[2] Hays associate Carl Milliken was pleased to tell the Attorney General's Conference on Crime that no top social scientists actually knew what caused crime, but suggested (as tough-minded behaviourist J.B. Watson had famously said) that it was as likely to be caused by 'doting mothers.' Although the carefully conducted Payne Fund studies would dissuade any fair-minded person from throwing around loose accusations about the 'evil effects' of movies, the studies had no influence on the bishops, witness Cantwell's declaration that one hour with a bad film nullifies years of 'careful training,' a conclusion unsupported by state-of-the-art social science data, relying instead upon Catholic theological/moral tradition.[3]

Lord, too, believed that salacious films actually destroyed lives. He wrote to Hays: 'as one prominent Catholic laymen said to me ... "If the motion pictures continue at their present rate nothing can be done to save future generations."' Lord now drafted and the Legion of Decency began distributing a bristling pamphlet, *The Motion Pictures Betray America.* In 133 features released in the first five months of 1934, Lord claimed to have identified: twenty-six plots or episodes 'built on illicit love,' thirteen presenting 'seduction accomplished,' twelve with 'seduction as attempted or planned,' two 'based on rape,' one 'building on attempted incest,' and three with 'prostitutes as leading characters,' as well as eighteen characters 'liv[ing] in open adultery,' and twenty-five 'obscene or anti-moral' scenes, situations, dialogues, or dances. He characterized these elements collectively as 'treason' (presumably meaning that such material undermined the nation), then played the anti-Semitic card, calling the producers 'cheats' and 'pants-pressers' who portray glamorously on the screen 'the very things that did [Jesus Christ] to death' and who 'should not object to being reminded of their origins.'[4]

On 23 May, Cardinal O'Connell told a Boston audience: '[T]hese moving pictures with their unutterably filthy plots, are undermining the moral life of your children ... Do not imagine that ... little children, God's own little ones of the flock, can go into that atmosphere again and again and again and see the scenes which, to a poor little innocent child would in the beginning mean almost nothing at all, without being eventually influenced by them ... You are Catholics and you have the responsibility of Catholics, and you cannot be merely indifferent to these influences which are intended by plot and plan, not merely incidentally or by accident ... to ruin the faith of your children.'[5] Six days later, Lord told Breen that Archbishop McNicholas's committee had 'approved the plan of blacklisting' films and that letters were 'pouring in' from Catholic and non-Catholic groups asking for the lists. But another prelate was even more ambitious. Joe Breen's home town of Philadelphia was a citadel of Warner Brothers, with several first-run houses as well as seventy-five neighbourhood theatres. The city's archbishop, Dennis Cardinal Dougherty, departed for the Vatican in early June 1934. Several days later, in a sort of test case of Catholic power, the archdiocese released an announcement, approved by Dougherty before he left, barring Philadelphia's Catholics from going to the movies – any movies – because they constituted 'perhaps the greatest menace to faith and morals in America today.' Reportedly it was read aloud in all of Philadelphia's Catholic churches. Like Cantwell, Dougherty proclaimed that a 'vicious and insidious attack is being made on the very foundations of our Christian civilization, namely, the sacrament of marriage, the purity of womanhood, the sanctity of the home, and obedience to lawful authority,' a 'sinister influence ... especially devastating among our children.' He then cribbed Cantwell's most dramatic line: '[O]ne hour spent in the darkened recesses of a moving picture theatre will often undo years of careful training on the part of the school, the church and the home.'[6]

To formalize the boycott, the archdiocese distributed pledges to Philadelphia's ninety-two parishes for all adults and children to sign. On 11 June, local Methodist ministers urged their congregations to subscribe to the pledge, thereby becoming members of what had been theretofore an exclusively Catholic Legion of Decency. A week later the Central Conference of American Rabbis, meeting in nearby Wernersville, recommended forming a committee to work with 'other religious groups and civic bodies' to push Hollywood 'to elevate the moral standards of pictures.' On 22 June the Federal Council of Churches urged Protestants to abide by the Legion's pledge even if they chose not to sign it. The directors of the Philadelphia Federation of Churches, while approving Dougherty's goals and recommending that all church members avoid unwholesome films, also urged that 'as a church group' it would not 'approve the principle' of a boycott, any more than it would call for a boycott of German goods to protest against Hitler's disregard of human rights. But with most of the city's Catholics, along with some of these others, joining the boycott, film attendance in Philadelphia plummeted by 40 per cent.[7]

On 3 July, Warner Brothers' Philadelphia manager announced that he would be closing its local theatres. Independent owners, with an additional four hundred theatres, said they would do so as well. Some said the dramatic decrease in attendance simply made it unprofitable to stay open, while possibly the closings were intended to stimulate an entertainment-starved public and/or laid-off theatre workers to pressure Dougherty to relent. Warners' corporate headquarters, meanwhile, seemed to be surprised and/or confused by what its local manager had done. From Rome, Dougherty announced that he had Pope Pius XI's personal approval. The strength of Dougherty's negotiating position was its intransigence. To all appearances, he was not 'negotiating' at all, had given the industry no 'clean up or else' ultimatum, but had simply ordered all Catholics in Philadelphia to stop going to the movies. Even many months after the boycott began, he wrote in a pastoral letter: 'Motion picture theatres as they have hitherto been, and still are, must be shunned as occasions of sin; and the ban will remain upon them until they are transformed, even though the much-married, much-divorced actors and actresses and the Russian [read: Jewish] producers of lascivious filth, and theater owners who purvey crime and sex films, lose some of their fabulous incomes.'[8]

Dougherty had been ordained in 1890, Boyle and Noll in 1898, Cantwell in 1899, McNicholas in 1901. Those of their generation with a historical perspective must have felt that the warnings of Leo XIII and Pius X not to listen to the siren song of American materialism had been correct after all, that the nation's economic collapse and the popularity of 'filthy' movies had together revealed Americanist and Modernist ideas as hollow and untrustworthy. Among the laity, the Depression deepened parishioners' receptivity to Church teachings and invited (through, for example, the Legion of Decency and NODL) a new lay activism, even as the Catholic Worker movement invited personal commitment to social justice under a benevolent Catholic (rather than a Socialist or Communist) banner. And to those with a historical perspective predating even the era of Leo XIII and Pius X, it must have seemed that a 'true' Americanism was a Catholic version after all, that each American – regardless of faith – could participate in yet another Great Awakening by submitting to the adamantine moral leadership that Catholicism alone could now deliver. Thus could American Catholics – as in the days of Hecker – approach with pride the exhilarating possibility of an evangelical leadership, introducing non-Catholics to a clearly defined Catholic morality, even if it lacked the intellectual components Hecker had prized.

The Apostles' Creed and other vows, cast in beautiful liturgical rhythms, were part of the ritual of the average Catholic's life. The Legion's pledge had some of that same lyrical-*cum*-legal tone, the act of signing being intended – as McNicholas noted – 'to arouse millions of Americans to a consciousness of the dangers of salacious and immoral pictures and to take action against them.' Catholics were typically handed some version of the following, with instructions to read it on the Sunday within the octave of the Feast of the Immaculate Conception (8 December):

> In the name of the Father and of the Son and of the Holy Ghost. Amen. I CONDEMN indecent and immoral pictures, and those which glorify crime or criminals.
>
> I wish to join the Legion of Decency, which condemns vile and unwholesome moving pictures. I unite with all who protest against them as a grave menace to youth, to home life, to country and to religion. I condemn absolutely those salacious pictures which ... are corrupting public morals and promoting a sex mania in our land. I shall do all that I can to arouse public opinion against the portrayal of vice as a normal condition of affairs, and against depicting criminals of any class as heroes and heroines, presenting their filthy philosophy of life as something acceptable to decent men and women ... Considering these evils, I hereby promise to remain away from all motion pictures except those which do not offend decency and Christian morality.

Protestant, Jewish, and secular civic groups signed variant versions. The Legion also released a leaflet declaring the Legion's purpose to be that of insuring 'that motion pictures conform to the accepted and traditional morality upon which the home and civilization are founded.'[9]

As against the ideals and responsibilities of individual choice and judgment, here was a chance to suppress one's autonomy, to let others decide what one could and could not see, what one should and should not know. Tocqueville, at a time when republican democracy was still an isolated experiment, had apprehended in the United States a 'Tyranny of the Majority,' an empire of 'decent and ordinary' people who live 'in the perpetual practice of self-applause.' While even the Inquisition, Tocqueville wrote, could never stop the publication of a huge quantity of anti-religious books in Spain, in America the people can comprise a much more efficient censor since, once a population abandons freedom of mind, no one will purchase licentious books and thus no one will think to write them. That democratic phenomenon now presented itself as a formalized boycott of allegedly 'indecent' films by 'decent and ordinary' people. While many years had been required for Prohibitionists to persuade or outflank those (including prominent Catholics like Al Smith) who thought one should not – or could not – stamp out alcohol, opposition to the sudden crusade against films was minimal. Editorial comment was predominantly pro-Legion, although some papers analogized the movement to Prohibition (which had collapsed in 1933). Several journalists criticized the Legion's tendency to attack serious films like John Cromwell's *Of Human Bondage* (1934), and urged instead the more positive approach of helping audiences develop higher tastes. Nevertheless, millions who would otherwise have nothing to do with the Roman Communion now happily acquiesced in its leadership. Self-respecting citizens were as comfortable subscribing to the Legion's pledge as if they were being asked to support the principles of Home and Family – which in a sense they were. And the response was Capra-esque. At a time when the total U.S. population was 127 million and the Catholic population 20 million, between 7 million and 11 million people physically signed the pledge, making the Legion not only evangelical and ecumenical but the most famous and effective of the various movements loosely constituting 'Catholic Action.' The 600,000-member Knights of Columbus pledged its support. In Massachusetts alone, the pledge received 1.7 million Catholic signatures. In Mundelein's Chicago archdiocese, 800,000 signed.[10]

Methodist minister Worth M. Tippy of Indiana, secretary of the Federal Council of Churches, now led the national effort to get Protestants to sign or at least abide by the Legion pledge. The *Christian Century* repeated the common charge that Hays had successfully bamboozled Protestants for years, adding that the Catholic boycott had the attention of those who ultimately called the tune in Hollywood: the Wall Street underwriters. The *Los Angeles Times* of 10 June noted that the industry was 'in the midst of the most serious crisis in its history' and that the producers 'are in secret very deeply concerned about the outcome but have been sworn to silence.' The nation's powerful brewing industry had once mounted a substantial (if unsuccessful) fight against Prohibition. Although several papers carried rumours that Hollywood had raised a $2-million war chest to resist the boycott, Hays denied the allegation. The studios, with unprecedented power to influence public opinion, were now mute, left-leaning intellectual James Rorty calling the industry 'too cynical, too hypocritical, and too scared' to fight the Legion. New York critic Richard Watts credited the Legion with exposing 'the complete cowardice and utter lack of integrity and resourcefulness of the screen magnates,' leaving no reason for a 'comparative outsider' like Watts himself to 'join the brawl' on behalf of freedom of the screen if the producers had no interest in fighting for themselves. And Roy Howard, chairman of the Scripps-Howard newspaper chain, told Hays that 'a considerable part of the press' refused to challenge what was happening, because it, too, was 'frightened to death' of the Church.[11]

With millions of signatures already subscribed to the Legion's pledge, film attendances dropped by 15 million, although Quigley in June advised Lord: 'we can push the levels down a lot more.' In New York, Cardinal Patrick Hayes noted that the nation's 'moral forces ... have been too patient, tolerant, and long-suffering.' When the Legion arranged a boycott in St Louis, Archbishop John J. Glennon told local theatre owners that the 'good pictures' would have to 'suffer with the bad until the bad are eliminated.' Another boycott was planned by the Knights of Columbus for Massachusetts's 1.7 million Catholics. The plan, approved by Cardinal O'Connell, included a provision that, once a film was identified as inappropriate, the 'general public' would be 'reminded not to attend any theatre showing any picture, good, bad, or indifferent, of that particular producer for a period of one month or more.' Children in Catholic schools in Milwaukee boycotted theatres that played disapproved films. In forty-two dioceses, a total of 8 million Catholics had been asked by bishops to sign the Legion's pledge.[12] By mid-August, seventy-six dioceses were involved in Legion activities, and thirty-six bishops had issued public statements urging lay involvement.

The Legion emerged at what George Seldes described as 'a psychological moment.' Of 74 million Americans then over twenty-five, six out of ten had no schooling beyond the eighth grade. As demonstrated by the popularity of demagogues like Father Coughlin and Huey Long, people who were poor or at risk of being so, frightened by economic forces they could not begin to comprehend and over which they had no control, were prepared to forsake independence of mind in favour of the comforts of solidarity, of pride in their own collective purity, of what Tocqueville had called 'self-applause.' Mass movements, Seldes wrote in the ominous year of 1939, succeed through mass hysteria. Now everyone was resorting to 'armies' carrying banners and repeating shibboleths. The Legion brought to the streets of Chicago some 70,000 parochial school children carrying signs declaring that 'An Admission to an Indecent Movie is a Ticket to Hell,' a notion at which Cantwell, Dougherty, and Lord could nod approvingly. Cleveland bishop Joseph Schrembs, with apostolic delegate Amleto Cicognani attending, administered the Legion oath to a rally of 50,000 Catholics, then issued a pastoral read in every Catholic church in the diocese: 'Purify Hollywood or destroy Hollywood.'[13]

Although Eugene O'Neill, Robert Sherwood, Elmer Rice, Fanny Hurst, Sherwood Anderson, H.L. Mencken, George Jean Nathan, Louis Mumford, Harry Elmer Barnes, and Barrett H. Clark, all of them members of the ACLU's National Council on Freedom from Censorship, warned that the Legion of Decency was the first step toward censorship of other media, most intellectuals and artists were as silent as when the Production Code was promulgated four years before. While in the '20s intellectuals and artists positioned themselves as outsiders and derided mass movements, now many were themselves organizing, more interested in changing the world via collectivism than in urging people to retain rights of individual choice. Because free enterprise itself had failed, metaphors like Holmes's 'free trade in ideas' had lost their value. Meanwhile, the educated middle class, most of whom still had jobs, were scared. In an America that had clearly lost its way, the popularity of a new expression, 'The American Way,' was perhaps a bit defensive. When in 1937 Louis Adamic said Hollywood was churning out mediocre products, scenarist Ross Wills, as if having just read Tocqueville, replied that movies are what they are because the public is what it is, its limitations exercising a censorship that is 'more ruthless and dominating' than any a government might invoke. After all, Wills observed, producers never make the naïve mistake 'of assuming that they were also, or even incidentally, artists,' recognizing instead that they are in 'a business.'[14]

Alfred Kazin wrote in 1939 that while in the Roaring '20s people wanted 'to revenge themselves on their fathers,' in the 1930s they 'needed the comfort of their grandfathers.' Yale divinity professor Halford Luccock, quoting Kazin, noted in contemporary postage stamps a nostalgia for whiskered forebears: Lowell, Longfellow, Whitman. Instead of the previous 'era of debunking,' when biographers searched frantically for some respected figure who had not yet been exposed and trashed in the modern manner, now reverential biographies emerged of such near-mythic heroes as Abraham Lincoln and Robert E. Lee, alongside such exercises in nostalgia as Dr Arthur E. Hertzler's *Horse and Buggy Doctor* (1938) and Bellamy Partridge's *Country Lawyer* (1939). Some saw the pain and despair of the '30s as divine retribution not just for the economic but also the cultural and even the sensual excesses of the '20s. The Legion tapped this longing for a reaffirmation of 'old-time' values, when people had jobs and worked hard and when sexuality was publicly taboo – perhaps forgetting that back then the accepted way to deal with venereal disease and unwanted pregnancy was simply to let the wrongdoer suffer and perhaps die, the better to serve as an example to others. In *Decency in Motion Pictures* (1937), Quigley wrote that film, while not obliged to *reform* the audience, nevertheless may not '*deform* those ideas and ideals' which prior to its inception dominated the vast public which it undertook to serve.' Presumably he was alleging that Hollywood – unless monitored and regulated by people like himself – would nefariously undermine the 'ideas and ideals' in place *circa* April 1896, when Edison first projected films. That some of those 'ideas and ideals' should themselves be challenged – and that films produced prior to widespread censorship, such as *The Downward Path* (1900), *The Kleptomaniac* (1905), *Children Who Labor* (1912), *Traffic in Souls* (1913), *Damaged Goods* (1914), *The Governor's Boss* (1915), and *The Public Be Damned* (1917), had opened people's eyes to the social and political problems around them – were beyond Quigley's perceptual horizon.[15]

With Paramount Publix, RKO, and several other studios already insolvent, and with years of racy films and anti-Hollywood publicity having rendered the industry incapable of defending itself with high-toned arguments about free speech, it quickly became apparent that the bishops and the Legion could outlast Hollywood – and thus close it down. If the industry did die, with it would go the 290,000 jobs it supported, the $100 million it paid in taxes, the social/cultural anchor it had become for most downtowns, the cheer and diversion it gave a hard-pressed people, and the huge, amorphous role it played in America's evolving self-definition. Choosing capitulation rather than further losses or even bankruptcy, the studios were giving up not just the smut and violence which for several studios had been the difference between survival and dissolution, but also the freedom to deal with the full range of human subjects in an honest and straightforward way. If films like *The Story of Temple Drake* had to go, so did the cutting-edge wit of Mae West, that self-declared bulwark against 'depression, repression and suppression.' Artistic freedom was little enough to jettison, since the revenues lost by cleaning up the movies were minor when compared with the damage the boycotts were already exacting. 'The stalled ox,' Gilbert Seldes noted, 'rejoices in his 20 per cent higher ration of oats.'[16]

While a decade earlier Hays had been portrayed as the man who would step in and clean up the industry, he had by now spent all his credibility and would thus either have to resign or come up with someone upon whose promises Lord, Quigley, and the bishops' committee might rely. A career survivor, Hays was not about to quit. In one of the meeting rooms of New York's Harvard Club, across the street from the MPPDA, Hays and several studio heads in mid-June prepared Quigley and sent him off to Ohio to negotiate with the bishops. Joe Breen, elevated by Hays some months before to be Dr Wingate's successor as head of the Studio Relations Committee, was asked to go along, since he had already worked with Quigley and Dinneen. Unknown to Hays, the bishops already had absolute trust in Breen, their Trojan Horse inside the MPPDA.[17]

A meeting on the porch of McNicholas's residence in a Cincinnati suburb resulted in the bishops' decision to call off the boycott in exchange for vigorous Code enforcement by Breen. The Studio Relations Committee was to be revamped as a major unit of the MPPDA, to be renamed the Production Code Administration (PCA), with Breen as its head, no longer answerable to Hays but only to the MPPDA board. Films about to be released were now held up for additional vetting, and twelve projects were summarily dropped from production schedules. Columbia, Warners, Fox, MGM, Paramount, Universal, United Artists, and others gave independent exhibitors a partial dispensation from block-booking insofar as they could ascribe their rejection of any pre-PCA film to a protest by patrons regarding its morality. The MPPDA resolved to add to the Code a section called 'Compensating Moral Values,' requiring films to have 'good characters, the voice of morality, a lesson, regeneration of the transgressor, suffering, and punishment.' Thus did the new era begin with amended Code language mandating what had made the revised version of *Baby Face* such an odd mess.[18]

9 The Breen Office

The AP wire of 6 July carried a demand by Bishop James E. Cassidy of Fall River, Massachusetts, that any deal with the 'producers of past and present salaciousness' must include the firing of Hays. The bishops' committee, however, had no such vindictive goal, having afforded Hays a chance to save himself by investing Breen with the censorial power the public had always ascribed to Hays. If Hays was the 'czar of all the rushes' – some observer now joked – Breen was the 'czarewitch.' Hays had been hired at a kingly salary of $200,000; so that Breen might understand where his allegiances ultimately lay, he received a princely $18,000.[1]

Six feet tall and husky, experienced in dealing with labour strikes at Peabody Coal, Breen was adept in the arts of intimidation, confident in the knowledge that if any producer challenged one of his rulings and the MPPDA's board refused to back him, he could always complain to Cantwell. Thus the bishops, through their double agent inside the film industry and their proven boycott threat, established veto power over films, a power no less daunting for being unofficial and unspoken. As late as the fall of 1934, Cardinal Dougherty was still maintaining Philadelphia's boycott, awaiting unequivocal indications that Hollywood had learned its lesson. In other dioceses, priests were issuing 'white lists' of films people could see, while others formed committees to fight certain movies on the local level. When a theatre on Chicago's West Side refused to comply with a local priest's demand to stop playing Howard Hawks's *Barbary Coast* (1935), it lost substantial ticket sales. By July 1935 the Catholic periodical *America*, edited by Breen confidant Wilfrid Parsons, could declare Breen's emergence as a significant step forward, while the *New York Times* noted that Hollywood's Wall Street financiers were 'heeding the thunder.'[2]

Breen's seven-person staff reviewed all pre-production story treatments, then negotiated with the studios as successive draft scripts solved or failed to solve issues likely to be raised either by the bishops or by government censorship agencies. In its first year, Breen's office issued 27,000 opinions; few projects reached the soundstage until they had passed muster. Breen staffer Jack Vizzard, whose credentials had included studying for the priesthood, said Breen had 'a way of leaving you with egg on your face,' even if you could not articulate why. Although in confidential letters to Catholic friends Breen characterized himself as their much put-upon champion in a moral crusade against the Jewish, money-grubbing purveyors of evil, in fact his job was to ensure that his employers' films encountered only a minimum of objections from state and municipal censors, and he did that job efficiently and well. To spot problems before even the first dollar was invested in a project, Breen staffers attended New York plays to report on whether they would be objectionable when and if a studio negotiated for screen rights. As bargaining chips in the typically collegial negotiations with Breen's assistants, the studios would include in early shooting scripts risqué material they did not actually intend to use, eliminating it during negotiations in order to protect the slightly less objectionable material they actually wanted. Scenarist Philip Dunne later noted: 'often, especially when I was dealing with such inventive souls' as Vizzard or another Breen staffer, Geoff Shurlock, 'the sessions turned into lively story conferences in which we jointly explored ways of gliding around potential censorial boobytraps.'[3] Only self-declared adventurers like Howard Hughes proceeded unilaterally with projects that might be eviscerated or even barred by Breen.

Some of the works for which Cecil B. DeMille was justly famous – *Old Wives for New* (1918), *Don't Change Your Husband* (1919), *Male and Female* (1919), *Why Change Your Wife?* (1920), *Forbidden Fruit*, and *The Affairs of Anatol* (1921) – would never have been made under the standards enforced by Breen. Nor would audiences have ever been favoured with F.W. Murnau's brilliant *Sunrise* (1927), with its orgiastic sex-dance and murder/adultery theme, or G.W. Pabst's *Die Freudlose Gasse* (*Joyless Street*, 1925), with Garbo joining a brothel to keep her family from starving, or the great Garbo–John Gilbert vehicle, *Flesh and the Devil* (1926; dir. Clarence Brown), the story of a married woman's affair. Only after revetting would Breen re-release John Ford's *Arrowsmith* (1931) or the sound version of Lewis Milestone's *All Quiet on the Western Front* (1930). To get a retrospective seal, Frank Borzage's 1932 film of Hemingway's *A Farewell to Arms* suffered the insertion of a priest mur-

muring a marriage service behind Gary Cooper's hospital bed. Such classics as Alexander Korda's *The Private Life of Henry VIII* (1933) and Josef von Sternberg's *Der Blaue Engel* (*The Blue Angel*, 1930) were denied retrospective seals, as was the best talking film of the pre-Breen era, Ernst Lubitsch's *Trouble in Paradise* (1932). Some pre-Breen films have survived only as cut for reissue. Happily, some others, considered too sleazy to be revetted (e.g., *I'm No Angel*, *She Done Him Wrong*, and *Red Dust*), have therefore survived intact, Breen unintentionally guaranteeing their survival by condemning them – uncut – to studio film vaults, to await liberation decades later. But when Archie Mayo's raunchy *Convention City* (1933) could not be sufficiently re-edited to get a seal, someone in a fit of pique destroyed all known copies, thus depriving posterity of this particular cultural artifact.[4]

In 1928, Mary Pickford had starred in a filmed version of the George Abbott / Ann Preston Bridgers play *Coquette*, in which a southern flapper's father kills her boyfriend because he thinks they have spent the night together. In 1936, Breen rejected a proposal for a new version because he thought it 'calculated to lower the general moral standard and to arouse unpleasant and morbid curiosity,' adding that Pickford's early version of this 'highly dangerous' play itself violated the Code. The child born out of wedlock in Tolstoy's *Anna Karenina* was eliminated from the script of Clarence Brown's 1935 film. In 1939, during a conference regarding Sidney Howard's play *They Knew What They Wanted*, the play's theme of forgiving adultery came up against the Code rule that adultery is never to be forgiven. A frustrated Charles Laughton, contemplating Jesus' sympathetic treatment of the woman taken in adultery in John 8:3–11, finally asked: 'Do I understand, Mr. Breen, that the Code does not recognize the New Testament?' Breen, following an interminable pause, replied: 'That would be a rough way of saying it, Mr. Laughton.' Breen refused a seal to *That Hamilton Woman* (1941), and when Alexander Korda protested that it was an accurate portrayal of Lord Nelson and Emma Hamilton, Breen answered: 'I don't care who they are, they're adulterers.'[5]

In its first decade, Breen's office awarded seals to 10,000 films. In 1937, 98 per cent of the features shown in the United States, a total of 663 titles, carried seals. Of thirty-six finished films rejected by Breen that year, only nine were not re-edited and certified. Breen's written and unwritten rules became sufficiently well known that only seventy-five scripts were rejected, and of these only twenty-nine (dealing with venereal disease or containing 'grossly suggestive' dialogue) were dropped rather than revised. By 1939 the system had become so per-fected that only two completed features were rejected and only twelve needed to be reworked to achieve compliance, while no private censor-ship group seriously criticized any Hollywood feature. Breen was even more adept than Joy in identifying and eliminating what state and municipal censors might disapprove, a Pennsylvania censor comment-ing that only 2 per cent of the films presented in 1938 required any work, while Ohio censors could say in 1953 that of eighteen thousand films presented to them over the decades, they ultimately issued li-cences to all but forty-four. While such numbers show that Breen had rendered the censorship boards largely superfluous, in fact they were in no danger of closing down, since they comprised self-perpetuating political units, the 'cream of the jest' being (as William De Mille noted) that their operation was financed by the fees producers were obliged to pay to get their films examined and cleared.[6]

Breen, described as 'just dumb enough,' had a sensibility inferior even to Quigley's. During the vetting process for Dorothy Arzner's film of Emile Zola's *Nana* (1934), he described Zola as 'a filthy Frenchman who grew rich writing pornographic literature.' But such gothic igno-rance regarding art was of no consequence either to industry heads who gauged success solely in commercial terms, or to bishops who tended not to read great literature and who required of films, not that they be beautiful, creative, or profound, but only that they be 'clean.' Moreover, few of the story lines and scripts that came before Breen required any aesthetic sophistication, and in the punctilios of everyday propriety he was an expert. Among the many issues to be thrashed out regarding Michael Curtiz's *Angels with Dirty Faces* (1938) – including kidnapping for ransom, criminals using machine guns, and a sympathetic portrayal of a murderer, etc. – was the elimination of the word 'halitosis.' In Edmund Goulding's *The Great Lie* (1941), George Brent marries fast-living Mary Astor, only to be told days later that her divorce from an earlier husband had not been finalized, rendering his marriage void. He marries Bette Davis, then finds that Astor is pregnant. Breen told Jack Warner that the characters must not consider abortion as an option, and that when the baby arrives, there must be no changing of diapers. Al-though Breen had no problem either with the content or with the allusive title of Frank Capra's *It Happened One Night* (1934), he did de-mand the deletion of a scene in which a passenger whispers something to a Pullman porter, since it implied he was asking where the toilet was. Commenting on a version of Dalton Trumbo's Oscar-nominated script for Sam Wood's *Kitty Foyle* (1940), Breen wrote that the couple should not 'be dressed in sweaters and old pants,' since this would indicate 'that their stay at Lake Pocono has been an extended one.' Innumerable PCA files contain letters similar to one Breen sent to Harry Cohn regarding Henry Levin's *And Baby Makes Three* (1949): 'We assume that the hula dancer on the necktie will not be naked.'[7]

Addressing a version of Clifford Odets's script for *None but the Lonely Heart* (1944), Breen wrote: 'Ada's line "I'm not a ham sandwich, you know, to take a bite of and throw away" is unacceptably sex suggestive,' as was the expression '"the young ladies from the riding academy."' Sheilah Graham reported that a film her lover F. Scott Fitzgerald was working on, 'Infidelity,' had to be retitled 'Fidelity' – directly contrary to what the story was about. After the title of *Good Girls Go to Paris Too* was queried because it suggested that only bad girls went to Paris, the film was released as *Good Girls Go to Paris* (1939), thus unwittingly suggesting that it was somehow novel or headline-making for good girls to go to Paris. The French were not offended but amused, a correspondent for *Paris-soir* commenting in May 1938 that it was from the movies that America had the idea 'that love is always wholesome, genuine, uplifting, and fresh, like a glass of Grade A milk.' The term 'sex appeal' was off-limits; one had to use 'oomph' or Elinor Glyn's time-honoured 'It.' In Richard Boleslawski's 1937 remake of *The Last of Mrs Cheyney*, from the sophisticated 1925 play by Frederick Lonsdale, Breen must have been pleased to see Joan Crawford declare, 'I am not a modern woman,' and refuse to commit adultery – even with the man she loves – thus presenting a stark contrast both with Crawford's pre-Breen characters and with her own behaviour. In John Cromwell's *The Prisoner of Zenda* (1937), a commoner and a king look alike because they are both descendants of an elicit affair in the early seventeenth century. Although that three-hundred-year-old tryst is only alluded to, Breen nevertheless insisted that it be punished, and so the film includes a statement that the woman died in childbirth.[8]

Breen's requirements did not – as some producers had feared – ruin attendance. Although admissions had dropped from the pre-Crash figure of 100 million per week, even in 1935, with 9 million people out of work and 3,000 of the 16,400 sound-equipped movie theatres closed, movies could still draw 70 million per week. Although only one film in ten could be recommended for children, this comprised one film a week, a better yield than before Breen. While in 1927 only 40 per cent of pictures were approved by the International Federation of Catholic

Alumnae, under Breen this jumped to above 95 per cent. Breen's power was close to absolute, in that no producer of American features ever succeeded in getting the MPPDA to reverse him. So smoothly did the system function that cynics resurrected the old accusation that the Hays Office was only a front for the producers.[9]

Although he was neither a legislature nor a court formulating public policy, Breen – like legislatures and courts – believed in the 'If ... then ...' form of argument: if I make an exception here, then a flood of other people will demand the same or even more. Negotiating the script for *Gone with the Wind* (1939), however, he rose above principle and condoned 'Frankly, my dear, I don't give a damn,' where a refusal might have triggered deep antipathy toward the Code by the tens of thousands who would have been offended to see their favourite novel bowdlerized on the screen. But regarding *In Which We Serve* (1942), a heart-stirring piece of British propaganda directed by David Lean and Noel Coward, Breen resolutely protected Britain's staunch ally from the film's ten 'damns,' two 'bastards,' two 'hells,' two 'Gods,' and one 'lousy.'[10]

Richard Sheridan Ames wrote in 1935 that in the years before Breen, the studios ignored the 'real issues of potential importance to American democracy' because they were focused solely on profits, then again ducked these issues in order to comply with Breen. In 1937, Breen's former secretary, Olga J. Martin, wrote that until her boss arrived, the producers made up their minds as to what the public wanted, but because of Breen, the nation's movie fans could demand 'decent, wholesome entertainment.' Both Ames and Martin were wrong. Before Breen, the market mechanism dictated what the public saw, via the lowest common denominators: sex and crime. The same was true during Breen's tenure; he merely told the industry what it could and could not get away with. James Rorty noted that pre-Breen films provided neither 'honest sainthood' nor 'honest sin,' but only 'fake sin, fake sex, fake social and moral values,' a diet of which cannot yield a culture of 'healthy maturity.' To the degree that producers had been injecting sex solely as the gimmick likeliest to attract audiences, Breen's office may have been a 'refining' influence, since suggestion, subtlety, indirection, and renunciation are often dramatically superior to explicitness and indulgence.[11] But art and sensuality are not at antipodal ends of the aesthetic spectrum. Insofar as creative people had to pull their punches to satisfy Breen, his influence was negative. The tangible net results are the 25,000 films made and released under the watchful eye of the PCA.

Vigilanti Cura

On 29 June 1936, Pope Pius XI issued the encyclical *Vigilanti Cura*, directing the world's priests to replicate the Legion's program of black-listing films which through 'vivid and concrete imagery' can influence even 'the crudest and most primitive minds,' clouding ideals and seducing young people 'along the ways of sin by glorifying the passions.' The genesis of the encyclical is unsettled. On 8 July 1936, John Killeen, S.J., wrote to Father Lord from Rome:

> As far as I can make out, the author of the Encyclical remains a deep secret ... As you know, [Amleto Giovanni Cicognani, apostolic delegate to the United States] arrived in Rome a couple of weeks ago and I am thinking that everyone suspects he brought the text over with him. Mons. Cicognani is staying at the Maryknoll House. The night the Encyclical appeared in the *Osservatore Romano*, the superior of the house took a copy of it to Cicognani immediately, only to be met with the reply: 'I have already read it' ... The Maryknoll superior told us of the incident and then laughed and said: 'He had already read it and I wonder if he didn't write it, too.' Some of your friends in the States, though, may have a different opinion.

Martin Quigley's son later recounted that credit for the encyclical (if not for its particular words) should go to Quigley, in that when Vatican secretary of state Eugenio Cardinal Pacelli was touring America under the guidance of Bishop Francis Spellman in the fall of 1936, it was Quigley who complained to Pacelli that Rome had failed to salute the American bishops' success at tackling a major moral issue. Others said to have been the actual authors of the encyclical included Cardinal Dougherty and Father Lord.[12]

The boycott, Breen's ultimate threat, now carried Rome's implicit endorsement, along with the express approval previously noted by Dougherty. In 1938, Elizabeth Yeaman noted that for four years Breen had enforced a morals code against the '99-per cent Jewish' film executives by having at his back 'a mighty army, the 18,600,000 Catholic communicants of the United States. Their captains are the parish priests, their generals are the archbishops, and their war college is the Vatican. Their bullets are mass boycott and they are well supplied with bombs of public protest.' The Legion's original mandate did not include rating individual films, a task carried out since 1922 by the International Federation of Catholic Alumnae. But in February 1936, New York cardinal Patrick J. Hayes announced that the Federation's staff (seventy women in New York, thirty-five in Los Angeles) would now work under Legion auspices. Following special pre-screenings arranged by the studios, the women would file reports with the Legion, read by the Very Reverend Msgr John J. McClafferty, the Reverend Patrick J. Masterson, and Mary Harden Looram (Mrs James F. Looram), chairwoman of the Federation's Motion Picture Council. Among their sources of moral authority were Quigley's book *Decency in Motion Pictures*. Classifications included 'A-I' ('Morally Unobjectionable for General Patronage'), 'A-II' ('Morally Unobjectionable for Adults'), 'B' ('Morally Objectionable in Part for All'), and 'C' ('Condemned'). But Breen's office functioned so effectively that the Legion became as redundant as the various government censors. Of 1,271 films reviewed by the Legion from February 1936 to November 1937, 1,160 received the approved (A-I and A-II) categories, a mere 13 getting a 'C,' most of these being foreign films shown in small 'art' houses outside Breen's jurisdiction. Of 535 features released in 1938, the Legion approved 496 as morally unobjectionable. Of 439 films classified in 1943, only 55 received a 'B' and only 4 a 'C.'[13] Pius rewarded Breen's efforts by making him a Knight Commander of the Order of Saint Gregory.

Like the Production Code and the Legion's pledge, the Legion's rating system was negative, disapproving films thought to be evil while fostering nothing constructive. Although evil was most commonly associated with sexuality, on more significant moral issues the Legion was obtuse. Of the 120 Nazi-made pictures it reviewed between February 1936 and November 1937, not one – not even the viciously anti-Semitic *Friesennot* – received a 'C' rating. Regarding the Spanish Civil War, the Legion was stridently pro-Franco, and although William Dieterle's *Block-ade* (1938) had been so puttered with to avoid signs of bias that in the end the staunchly pro-Loyalist Lillian Hellman could not determine which side the film favoured, the Legion issued its rare 'Separately Classified' rating, believing that Dieterle had strayed beyond the boundary of 'entertainment' into 'propaganda.' The Knights of Columbus, similarly pro-Franco, called *Blockade* 'historically false and intellectually dishonest' in its 'suppression of the facts of the Communist-inspired reign of terror' necessitating Franco's resistance.[14]

Hollywood avoided projects dealing with Fascism, both to protect its substantial markets in Germany, Italy, and Spain, and to avoid criticism by the Legion, the Knights of Columbus, and the several vocal congressmen who periodically charged Hollywood with exceeding its entertainment function by trying to influence public opinion. Msgr McClafferty, when called upon to opine regarding the widely hailed public-health documentary *Birth of a Baby*, reportedly remarked: 'The fundamental concept of the Church on the place of the cinema in American life is diametrically opposed to that of the producers of the Birth of a Baby. You ... believe with all sincerity the cinema can and should produce educational films, and you state that this picture is such a film. But the official position of the Catholic Church (... this is not my ruling, but that of the Church) on the place of cinema in American life is that the cinema should be for entertainment, escape, and not for education.'[15] Like Justice McKenna in *Mutual Film* (although without the force of law), the Church was telling film-makers that their role in American life was restricted to that of helping audiences pass the time. But *The Birth of a Baby* was not produced in Hollywood, where most executives had no interest in provoking the public with either educational or political fare, much less in violating the Code by showing films of the birthing process. *New York Herald Tribune* critic Howard Barnes called movies 'the ostrich of the arts.'

Father Paul (Frank Sinatra) and Bill Dunnigan (Fred MacMurray) in *The Miracle of the Bells*. © 1948 RKO Radio Pictures. Production still courtesy of RKO and the Academy of Motion Picture Arts and Sciences.

Joe Smith (James Whitmore) in *The Next Voice You Hear*. © 1950 Turner Entertainment Co. A Warner Bros. Entertainment Company. All Rights Reserved.

Cartoon concerning papal declaration of infallibility, *Harper's Weekly*, vol. 14 (30 July 1870).

'The Descent of the Modernists,' illustration from William Jennings Bryan, *Seven Questions in Dispute* (New York: Fleming H. Revell Co., 1924).

Caricature of Will Hays by Hans Stengel, originally published in the *New Yorker* (9 May 1926).

Bernadette Soubirous (Jennifer Jones) in *The Song of Bernadette*. © 1943 Twenti-eth Century-Fox. All rights reserved. Production still courtesy of Twentieth Century-Fox and the Academy of Motion Picture Arts and Sciences.

Newspaper advertisement for the *Bicycle Thief*, featuring illustration by Al Hirschfeld, November 1950. © Al Hirschfeld. Reproduced by arrangement with Hirschfeld's exclusive representative, The Margo Feiden Galleries, Ltd, New York.

The bishop (Basil Ruysdael), Msgr. Talbot (Regis Toomy), Sister Margaret (Loretta Young), and Sister Scholastica (Celeste Holm) in *Come to the Stable*. © 1949 Twentieth Century-Fox. All rights reserved. Production still courtesy of Twentieth Century-Fox and the Academy of Motion Picture Arts and Sciences.

The Stranger (Federico Fellini) and Nanni (Anna Magnani) in *The Miracle*. Image courtesy of Archivio Fotografico del Fondazione Centro Sperimentale di Cinematografia, Rome. All rights reserved.

Nanni (Anna Magnani) in church. Image courtesy of Archivio Fotografico del Fondazione Centro Sperimentale di Cinematografia, Rome. All rights reserved.

Nanni (Anna Magnani) playing with a child from the village. Image courtesy of Archivio Fotografico del Fondazione Centro Sperimentale di Cinematografia, Rome.

Rossellini on the set of *The Miracle*. Image courtesy of Archivio Fotografico del Fondazione Centro Sperimentale di Cinematografia, Rome.

Joan (Ingrid Bergman) in *Joan of Arc* (1948). © RKO Radio Pictures. Production still courtesy of RKO and the Academy of Motion Picture Arts and Sciences.

10 The *Paramount* Case

Vertical Integration

In 1908 and 1909 ten major film producers formed the Motion Picture Patents Company, thus achieving three goals: the termination of lawsuits among themselves over their respective patents for various components of motion-picture cameras and projectors; the rationalization of methods to meet exhibitors' bottomless hunger for films; and, most important, the formation of a huge cartel to hobble outside competitors. Over the next five years, this so-called 'Edison Combine' would file over forty patent lawsuits against outsiders, also employing strong-arm men to grab or destroy the independents' equipment. They contracted to purchase *all* of George Eastman's perforated movie film stock, not because they needed it but to keep others from getting it. They had a virtual lock on domestic distribution, acquiring fifty-seven of the fifty-eight major film exchanges, while establishing exclusive distribution licences with dozens of other, smaller exchanges, thus driving competitors out of business. With a monopoly on production and (with the exception of William Fox's fifty-eighth exchange) distribution, some members of the Combine also had substantial holdings in the third element of the film industry: theatres. With ten to twelve thousand independent exhibitors, they entered into contracts for a flat fee-per-foot of film – any film – thus disincentivizing any instinct to improve content, production values, or overall quality.[1] As far as the Combine was concerned, movies were fungible, like scrap iron or soybeans.

When people restrain trade, they can become very rich. Edison's influence in the film industry, like Henry Ford's in the car business, was to foster a top-down regime in which producers became wealthy by dictating what consumers could buy. But such oligopolies work only so long as they maintain market control. Independents – William Fox, Carl Laemmle, Adolph Zukor, William Swanson, and others – having learned in various businesses (gloves, furs, vaudeville, nickelodeons, amusement parks, etc.) the basics of customer service, now learned how to fight the succession of obstacles the Combine threw in their path, and gradually gained market-share. Disregarding their own rivalries, they formed the Motion Picture Distributing and Sales Company, then proceeded to sue the Edison Combine under the antitrust statutes. By the time (in October 1915) a court finally found the Combine to have violated the federal Sherman Anti-trust Act, Laemmle had opened Universal City and was making dozens of films, joined by Fox and other independent Davids in capturing the business from the tottering Goliath. By 1921 the Combine had disintegrated, and most of its constituent members had folded.[2]

That year the industry produced 700 films, attracting 50 million weekly admissions. Some urged that Hollywood was producing 25 per cent more product than the nation's 14,000 theatres could profitably handle, since audiences would no longer watch just anything, but rather demanded to see their favourite stars in suitable fare. Mary Pickford, joining Douglas Fairbanks, D.W. Griffith, and Charles Chaplin in a brilliant marketing concept called United Artists, correctly grasped that if a star was sufficiently in demand, she could distribute her own films outside the block-booking, blind-selling regime and thus take all profits to be made by distributing to exhibitors only the star-vehicle films their customers preferred. But UA's idea worked only for the most sought-after screen talents, and it remained an exception to the studios' standard business model: churning out a large number of films, then promoting and playing the best of them in the downtown, first-run theatres the studios owned, while using block-booking contracts with theatre chains ('circuits') and independents, both to exploit the best stuff further and to slough off everything else.

The Federal Trade Commission tried but failed to convince federal judges that one studio's block-booking practices were monopolistic, while various congressmen attempted to stop the practice legislatively. After Hays's skilful lobbying in 1927 handily defeated Senator Smith W. Brookhart (R-IA)'s bill, Senator Matthew M. Neely (D-WV) introduced a bill to bar producers and distributors from owning theatres. This, too, Hays quashed.[3] As of 1930, the industry was dominated by the so-called 'Big Five' a.k.a. the 'Majors': Paramount, Twentieth Century-Fox,

Loew's (Metro-Goldwyn-Mayer), Warner Brothers, and Radio-Keith-Orpheum Corp. These, along with the 'Little Three' – Columbia, Universal, and United Artists – constituted a $2-billion industry. The Big Five divided among themselves ownership interests in lucrative first-run theatres, the profits from which were often larger than from production itself. They also set up cozy arrangements among themselves and with several large chains of independently owned theatres, thereby affording themselves access to 75 per cent of the gross revenues of exhibition.[4] When Joe Breen's strict enforcement of the Production Code deprived smaller exhibitors of the emotionally rousing argument that block-booking was the nefarious scheme by which Hollywood forced them to show dirty films, they reverted to the less compelling premise that they had to accept Hollywood's failures as a condition for getting what people would pay to see.[5]

Among the tasks assigned to Franklin Roosevelt's famous Brain Trust was that of ending the laissez-faire system which many people blamed for the Crash. Although the New Deal's resulting legislative solutions were widely viewed as 'creeping socialism' and were eventually declared unconstitutional by a Supreme Court dominated by conservatives, FDR remained undeterred. While the House Commerce Committee itself held extensive hearings on block-booking and blind-buying, Roosevelt's National Recovery Administration invoked oversight via rules of fair competition for the industry, albeit Hays managed to have the rules, and the group organized to enforce them, weighted in the studios' favour.[6] Of 18,370 theatres in the United States as of April 1934, the so-called Big Eight owned 1,950, leaving 2,850 to other circuits and 13,570 to independents. While the Big Eight controlled only 25 per cent of total seats, their holdings included four of every five first-run venues in the ninety-two largest markets, where 40 per cent of a typical film's total revenues were generated. Exhibitors outside this alignment, requiring each year from eight national distributors a total of 250 features, 500 shorts, and 250 newsreels, continued attacking the distribution regime by which Hollywood kept them in a second-class status.[7]

In 1938, Thurman Arnold, a Yale law professor and author of the trenchant *Folklore of Capitalism*, became head of the U.S. Justice Department's Antitrust Division.[8] That summer, Arnold filed the first of four cases against the movie industry, asserting, among other things, that the big studios' lock on production, distribution, and exhibition strangled small exhibitors as well as small producers. Since no theatre or distributor could get Production Code films without undertaking never to handle non-Code films, no independent film could get wide distribution unless it was vetted by Breen, who was thus dictating what kinds of films independent producers could make. Breen discriminated against the independents, denying Code seals to their films while awarding seals to studio films with similar content.[9] Thus, the Code evidenced an antitrust conspiracy against independent voices, much as a case against the automobile industry would be evidenced by an agreement to exclude manufacturers who offered extra options, styles, or colours.

Arnold chose not to include such allegations in his petition, however. While it would be easy to convince a juror or judge that an agreement among automakers to limit options was baneful because it limited consumer choices, an agreement among producers to limit what audiences could see was widely thought to be salutary, not criminal, witness the swelling membership of the Legion of Decency. The small exhibitors had been demanding an antitrust case for a decade, and they were its immediate beneficiaries. Having claimed that salacious films had been thrust upon them as part of the antitrust conspiracy, they could not now credibly testify that the Code, having stopped such films, was itself illegal. Thus, while the Code narrowed the range of available product and thus consumer choice, there was no constituency for freedom of the screen, namely, for a market-driven regime that allowed producers to make whatever they wanted to make and allowed people to see whatever they wanted to see.

The First Amendment and Antitrust Law

In October 1940 the Big Five of the studios signed a consent decree mandating, among other things, that exhibitors could view films before buying them, and that a studio could sell no more than five films in a block. Although the Government, for its part, agreed to refrain from prosecuting its demand that the studios divest their theatres, when the decree finally ran out, the Government did revivify the suit and eventually brought it to trial.[10] In an unrelated prosecution against the Associated Press news combine, Arnold's lawyers formulated an extraordinary legal theory, structuring a novel antitrust argument around a novel free-speech question. The Associated Press was a colossus bestriding the world of news, with 7,200 full- and part-time employees in ninety-four bureaus in the United States, a Washington headquarters housing 150 professionals, and another 250 offices abroad. Eighty-one per cent of U.S. morning newspapers were AP members, comprising 96 per cent of total morning circulation, as were 69 per cent of evening papers, totalling 77 per cent of evening circulation. Of sixty-four morning newspapers with circulations over 50,000, all but one, the *Chicago Sun*, were AP members.

Despite these impressive figures, AP did not control the national news market. The *New York Daily News*, begun in 1919, had by 1924 achieved America's highest circulation, and without AP membership. Two other large news organizations, Scripps's United Press (UP) and International News Service (INS), a branch of King Features Syndicate, survived and flourished. In 1929 two AP stalwarts, the *New York Herald Tribune* and the *Chicago Daily News*, switched to UP affiliations, while the *New York Times* opted to initiate its own syndicate. Twenty to thirty other news-gathering associations flourished.

The Justice Department's suit was prompted by AP's refusal to admit the *Chicago Sun*. The *Chicago Tribune*, a morning daily and long-time AP member run by the formidable Robert R. McCormick, engaged in such classic predatory conduct as threatening to withdraw from news dealers who also wanted to carry the *Sun*. Not that McCormick could deliver a deathblow. The *Sun*, backed by the fortune of department-store magnate Marshall Field and benefiting from the plain good luck of premiering just three days before Pearl Harbor, attained in less than a year the eighth largest circulation of all non-tabloid morning dailies in the United States, supported by eleven million lines of advertising. It did all this by utilizing the wire services of five agencies other than AP, thus demonstrating that AP membership was unnecessary for success and that AP did not have the power to drive non-members out of the market.[11]

Because Marshall Field was pro–New Deal and McCormick was rabidly anti-Roosevelt, many saw the Justice Department's suit against McCormick's paper as tainted by politics. Thurman Arnold said that the original impetus to file the case was his, albeit Field convinced the Administration to approve.[12] The case, carrying this political flavour, was assigned to a panel of three federal judges: Learned Hand, his cousin Augustus Hand, and Thomas Swan. Following an exchange of documents and the taking of depositions, the Justice Department moved for summary judgment, asserting that AP had presented no factual issues requiring a trial. Learned Hand, joined by his cousin 'Gus,' agreed, holding that AP's exclusionary by-laws violated the Sherman Act. Judge Swan filed a parlous dissent.[13]

In the three decades since *Mutual Film*, several courts had so broadened free speech that the First Amendment bore little resemblance to the provision as it had been construed throughout its first 124 years. In 1913, two years before *Mutual Film*, Learned Hand, then a forty-two-year-old judge in Manhattan's federal district court, had been called upon to deal with whether a new novel, *Hagar Revelly*, was 'obscene' under New York law. The book's author, Daniel Carson Goodman, M.D. (1883–1957), counted himself a staunch advocate of 'social hygiene,' the fostering of sexual knowledge to avoid what Progressives had proven to be the two dread consequences of sexual ignorance: venereal disease and unwanted pregnancy. Among the social hygienists' projects was a crusade against the low wages paid by department stores and factories, which tended to push young, unmarried women into prostitution in order to earn enough to live on. The novel concerns such a woman.

Since the word 'obscene' was not defined in the various state and federal statutes prohibiting it, courts turned for guidance to common-law sources, especially to *Regina v. Hicklin*, a British case decided in 1868. There Sir Alexander Cockburn, Lord Chief Justice of the Court of Queen's Bench, proposed a test for obscenity: 'Whether the tendency of the matter ... is to deprave and corrupt those whose minds are open to such immoral influences, and into whose hands a publication of this sort may fall.'[14] In numerous cases employing Cockburn's test, the two-pronged issue reduced to: (a) whether a judge or jury thought the item under scrutiny was the kind of thing likely to deprave those who could be depraved by it; and (b) whether it was likely to find its way into their hands. Thus, a cheap reprint of *Fanny Hill* sold in the Strand might trigger liability, while a leather-bound folio edition of Rabelais in the library of a Pall Mall men's club would not. The particular item at issue in *Hicklin* was a pamphlet widely distributed in the Midlands in connection with a series of virulently anti-Catholic speeches by an itinerant lecturer. In 1850 Pius IX in *Universalis Ecclesiae* restored in England a Catholic hierarchy that had been outlawed since the reign of Elizabeth I. Even before this resurgence of organized Catholicism, anti-Catholic elements in Britain, as well as in Europe and in the United States, had stirred great notoriety by publishing titillating pseudo-exposés of sexual misconduct within the walls of convents and seminaries, accounts whose sexual content might be excused by sympathetic judges because it was in the service of anti-Catholic editorial themes. That is, the ultimate goal of such pamphlets was not sexual arousal but sectarian hate-mongering. The pamphlet in *Hicklin* fell within a related genre of writings that mocked Catholicism by quoting – verbatim – works on sexuality used to train priests in preparation for hearing confessions. By quoting these explicit discussions, pamphleteers provided the double impact of suggesting both that Catholic wives confessed their sex lives to parish priests, and that Catholicism's public reticence about sex was hypocritical, while also triggering in the intended Protestant readership a certain negative synergy between sexual stimulation and puritanical hatred.[15] The case brought wide attention in Britain, neither because of the pamphlet's sexual content, nor because of Cockburn's definition of obscenity, but because the itinerant lecturer's several anti-Catholic speeches had triggered violent riots in several Midlands cities.

Cockburn's formulation, a cascade of undefined words, was no model of jurisprudential clarity. The two classes thought to be open to corrupting influences were children and riff-raff, both groups having participated in the Midlands rioting. Any book deemed in court to have such a 'tendency' would be suppressed outright, even if this also meant blocking access by 'mature' readers. In a legal environment untouched by any appropriate psychological or sociological analysis regarding what causes depravity and who is most likely to become depraved, there emerged from the dozens of British and American cases relying upon *Hicklin* no seamless web of legal authority, but only a high conviction rate and a sense that neither judges nor juries were obliged to articulate why a given work would injure children and/or low-lifes. On rare occasions, however, the *Hicklin* test was applied intelligently. In 1906 the U.S. postmaster general decided that Upton Sinclair's novel *The Jungle*, while containing several passages that were admittedly of a 'coarse and of a vulgar tendency,' nevertheless was not 'obscene' within the meaning of *Hicklin* since, among other things, Sinclair's description of a police raid on a house of prostitution did not tend to corrupt the morals of those into whose hands the novel might fall, but rather suggested compassion for the women being arrested.[16]

In dealing with *Hagar Revelly*, Learned Hand well understood that as a trial-level judge he was not allowed to ignore *Hicklin* and make up his own test for what was and was not obscene. Nevertheless, he saw fit to note 'that the rule as laid down, however consonant it may be with mid-Victorian morals, does not seem to me to answer to the understanding and morality of the present time ... I question whether in the end men will regard that as obscene which is honestly relevant to the adequate expression of innocent ideas, and whether they will not believe that truth and beauty are too precious to society at large to be mutilated in the interests of those most likely to pervert them to base uses.' Hand thus suggested an alternative, albeit one he as a district judge was not himself free to use: that 'obscene' should indicate 'the present critical point in the compromise between candor and shame at which the community may have arrived here and now.' That is, if literature 'must, like other kinds of conduct, be subject to the social sense of what is right, it would seem that a jury should in each case establish the standard much as they do in cases of negligence,' in which jurors must decide whether – given the facts presented – the defendant acted *reasonably*.

As a 'Progressive,' Judge Hand thus questioned the wisdom of suppressing the literary offerings of 1913 by invoking a test formulated in 1868, and of blocking all readers from access to a book because of its presumed impact on those deemed least able to respond to it appropriately. 'To put thought in leash to the average conscience of the time,' that is, to the average juryman's ideas of right and wrong, was in Hand's view 'perhaps tolerable, but to fetter it by the necessities of the lowest and least capable,' that is, to those 'whose minds are open to ... immoral influences,' seemed to him a 'fatal policy,' albeit one he was obliged to apply. Hand's perspective was radically new. Felix Frankfurter described him as 'this new planet in the judicial sky,' one with whom 'the convention-minded in the law' were not immediately comfortable. Free-speech lawyer Morris L. Ernst later called Hand's opinion the turning point, after which the quasi-official 'vice societies' started by bluenoses like Anthony Comstock in the heyday of the *Hicklin* standard began losing their attempts to ban serious literature issued by reputable publishers.[17]

Six years later, in 1919, Justice Holmes in *Schenck v. United States* haltingly and ambiguously introduced a new era in First Amendment jurisprudence by stating that the provision not only barred most prior restraints by the federal government, but also immunized speech against federal censorship unless the Government could show that the words used, given the situation in which they were used, created a 'clear and present danger' that they would cause 'substantive evils that Congress has a right to prevent.'[18] In 1925 the Court in *Gitlow v. New York* stated that 'freedom of speech and of the press – which are protected by the First Amendment from abridgement by Congress – are among the fundamental personal rights and "liberties" protected by the due-process clause of the Fourteenth Amendment,' so that these freedoms were now for the first time protected from impairment by the states as well as the federal government. In *Stromberg v. California* (1931), a state statute criminalized displaying 'a red flag ... as a symbol ... of opposition to organized government or as an invitation or stimulus to anarchistic action or as an aid to propaganda that is of a seditious character.' A young woman was convicted because at an indoctrination camp she had children salute a Soviet flag and recite: 'To the workers' red flag, and to the cause for which it stands, one aim throughout our lives, freedom for the working class.' While many people bristled at this grotesque twisting of the flag salute engaged in by all American school children every day, the Court found the California statute 'so vague and indefinite' in its blanket criminalization of nonviolent activity as to be 'repugnant to the guaranty of liberty contained in the Fourteenth Amendment.'[19]

Learned Hand and Augustus Hand, meanwhile, had earned reputations for brilliance and diligence, and by 1933 both had been elevated to the U.S. Court of Appeals. That year a district-court judge in Manhattan, John Monroe Woolsey, was faced with applying *Hicklin* to James Joyce's *Ulysses*, a copy of which lawyer Morris Ernst had ingeniously caused to be mailed from France and seized by Customs officers so that he could force a test case under the statute banning the importation of 'obscene' materials. The case was against neither the European publisher, nor Joyce, nor the person to whom the book was addressed (Ernst's client, Random House, which hoped to publish an American edition). Rather, the litigation, styled *United States v. One Book Called 'Ulysses,'* was against the novel itself, the judicial remedy in such so-called *in rem* actions being not a fine or prison term for anyone, but the physical destruction of the copy seized. Woolsey, a trial-level judge, was no more privileged than Learned Hand had been two decades earlier either to ignore *Hicklin* or to make up his own test for what was and was not obscene. After making the unusual judicial commitment of spending several months studying Joyce's novel, Woolsey in a lucid and probing decision declared it to be not obscene in that it did not tend to deprave and corrupt. Martin Conboy had been counsel to the New York Society for the Suppression of Vice as well as a director of the National Council of Catholic Men, before being made U.S. Attorney by his long-time political mentor, President Franklin Roosevelt. Although Conboy had not been involved in the case presented at trial, he now decided to take the case to the U.S. Court of Appeals. The *Evening Post* mocked him for 'riding his little purity hobby' at taxpayers' expense.[20]

While Judge Woolsey's thoughtful opinion would be impossible to outdo as a groundbreaking exposition of the relationship between modernist art and traditional censorship, Augustus Hand, in an opinion joined by Learned Hand, saw fit as a member of an appellate court to add some perspectives which might have been deemed presumptuous if uttered by a trial judge. He found 'numerous long passages' in the book which could be called 'obscene' either under *Hicklin* or 'under any [other] fair definition of the word,' while finding other passages 'blasphemous,' still others 'coarse.' Voiced by most judges, such conclusions would compel a reversal of Woolsey's decision. But the U.S. Supreme Court had never itself declared *Hicklin* to be the law of the land, nor had it otherwise defined obscenity, leaving this federal circuit court free to make its own way. A well-settled common-law rule required that judges and juries in obscenity cases consider *solely* the allegedly obscene passages, so that an entire novel could be banned because of what is written in one sentence. If the court applied that rule, Joyce's novel was sure to be found obscene and ordered shredded. But Augustus Hand, embracing a differentiation proposed by Woolsey between art and 'dirt for dirt's sake,' said that the 'obscene' as well as the 'blasphemous' and 'coarse' passages in *Ulysses* are not to be scrutinized in isolation since they support 'the purpose of depicting the thoughts of the characters and are introduced to give meaning to the whole, rather than to promote lust or portray filth for its own sake,' the 'net effect' of the combination being not 'lustful' but 'pitiful and tragic.' Thus, material in the novel which would qualify as obscene if considered in isolation, was held not to be so if Joyce had enlisted it in support of what Learned Hand back in the *Hagar Revelly* case had called 'innocent ideas.' The majority of a federal appellate tribunal had announced for the first time that modernist works had their own prerogatives.

Judge Martin T. Manton, a Catholic, dissented. Having studied the twenty-eight passages in *Ulysses* alleged by Conboy to be obscene (the locations of which Conboy helpfully listed for those who did not wish to get bogged down in the novel's non-obscene connective tissue), Judge Manton forthrightly declared: 'Who can doubt the obscenity of this book after a reading of the pages referred to, which are too indecent to add as a footnote to this opinion? Its characterization as obscene should be quite unanimous by all who read it.' Judge Manton saw no reason to abandon the common-law rule of declaring a book obscene because of individual passages, nor did he have anything to say about the meaning of the book as a whole. After all, he opined, *Ulysses* is only 'a work of fiction,' written solely for the reader's 'alleged amusement.' His perspective on novels was thus the same as Justice McKenna's on films: they are for entertainment only and have nothing to teach.

Although Conboy had convinced U.S. Attorney General Homer Cummings to let him appeal Judge Woolsey's decision to the Second Circuit, Cummings now refused pleas by Conboy and by the New York Society for the Suppression of Vice to petition the U.S. Supreme Court. And so the case ended. Thereafter, all federal trial judges in the Second Circuit (New York, Connecticut, and Vermont) were on notice that in trying obscenity cases they would need to differentiate art from 'dirt for dirt's sake.' As far as the Supreme Court was concerned, however, Chief Justice Charles Evans Hughes had noted in 1931 that obscenity was outside the protections of the First Amendment, and the decision in the *Ulysses* case, with its unusual distinction between a work's *containing* obscenity and *being* obscene, was binding only in the Second Circuit. Conboy, like Joe Breen, would be made a Knight Commander of St Gregory the Great by Pope Pius XI, thereafter becoming a distinguished federal judge. Judge Woolsey, for his part, achieved a unique kind of judicial fame, in that his opinion was appended to both the American and the British editions of the book he had allowed people to read, thus insuring his worldwide eminence in the history of free speech, while also rendering his analysis the most widely disseminated commentary on Joyce in the world.[21]

Although the Supreme Court was not asked to decide whether *Ulysses* was obscene, or to elucidate further its rule that obscenity is not protected by the First Amendment, in 1936 it did hold in *Grosjean v. American Press Co.* that the First Amendment would no longer be limited to Blackstone's immunity from prior restraints, but instead would protect against 'any action' by government which 'might prevent such free and general discussion of public matters as seems absolutely essential to prepare the people for an intelligent exercise of their rights as citizens.'[22] In *Lovell v. City of Griffin* (1938), the Court held that a Georgia town violated the First Amendment by requiring anyone who wished to hand out handbills or pamphlets to obtain a licence. To the town's argument that its ordinance did not impair a free press because newspapers were exempt from the licence requirement, the Court responded that Thomas Paine communicated via pamphlets and that the press 'comprehends every sort of publication which affords *a vehicle of information and opinion.*' And in *Thornhill v. Alabama* (1940), the Court declared that freedom of speech and of the press 'embraces at the least the liberty to discuss publicly and truthfully *all matters of public concern* without previous restraint or fear of subsequent punishment.'[23]

The italicized words quoted from *Lovell* and *Thornhill* suggest that the Court sought to expand First Amendment protections far beyond the particular circumstances presented in these two cases. This was again evident in *West Virginia State Board of Education v. Barnette* (1943), in which children of Jehovah's Witnesses had been expelled from a public school and threatened with prosecution as delinquents because their parents construed the American flag as an 'image' and refused to let their children salute it, since Exodus 20:4–5 forbids bowing to any 'graven image.' Since the flag pledge did not include the words 'under God' (these were not added until 1954), the pledge and the accompanying gestures used in saluting the flag had religious ramifications only if one accepted the parents' view that an American flag is an 'image' within the meaning of Exodus. Justice Robert H. Jackson might have drawn the issue narrowly as whether the flag salute comprised government intrusion on the First Amendment right to the free exercise of one's religion. But he instead chose a much broader perspective, seeing this governmental coercion of speech and gesture as the power to compel a citizen 'to utter what is not in his mind,' that is, to say something he does not actually believe. Jackson concluded that government may not 'prescribe what shall be orthodox,' not just in religion, but 'in politics ... or other matters of opinion,' nor may it 'invade the sphere of intellect and spirit which it is the purpose of the First Amendment ... to reserve from all official control.' He thus declared the coerced pledge to violate the First Amendment, not because it interfered with the children's religious beliefs, but because government had no business intruding upon *any* 'matters of opinion and political attitude.'[24]

Since the 1880s, legal scholars had been discussing an unspecified but nevertheless significant right under Anglo-American legal principles: the right 'to be let alone.' *Barnette* became a dramatic example of this amorphous concept, of particular interest because the decision was premised, not on the Fourth Amendment's traditional prohibitions on illegal searches of one's home and private papers, but on this new First Amendment right not to be forced into false, regimented statements about one's beliefs and opinions. The idea, with roots in Locke, Jefferson, and Madison, was that in matters of individual conscience, government has no coercive authority. As Thoreau had written in *Civil Disobedience* (1849), no citizen should be obliged to 'resign his conscience to the legislator.'[25]

The result in *Barnette* was of interest for two additional reasons. It was that Supreme Court rarity, a 180-degree reversal from a decision rendered by the Court not long before. And it was issued in June 1943, when tens of thousands had already given their last full measure of devotion to the flag which these children were now permitted to ignore. While many thus found the decision to be shocking, viewed from another perspective, the holding was consistent with the popular view that this was a war between totalitarianism and freedom, regimentation and individuality, coercion and the right 'to be let alone.'[26] Norman Rockwell's appealing series of paintings entitled 'Four Freedoms,' including a working man speaking his mind in a Vermont town meeting, parents tucking their children in bed, a family celebrating Thanksgiving, and people of different ethnicities praying in different ways under the caption 'EACH ACCORDING TO THE DICTATES OF HIS OWN CONSCIENCE,' had appeared in the *Saturday Evening Post* in February and March of that year, the four images so galvanizing public sentiment that Rockwell's original paintings went on a sixteen-city war-bond tour. The first stop, at a Washington department store in late April and early May, yielded 50,000 visitors and over $1 million in bond sales.

As the *Associated Press* antitrust case went forward, *Barnette* and its broad language opposing government coercion was still fresh. Part of the legal bedrock of the Anglo-American free-enterprise system had been the businessperson's right to refuse to deal with anyone, for a good reason, a bad reason, or no reason. Yet several old common-law antitrust cases, cited as authoritative in early litigations under the Sherman Act, had made inroads on that doctrine by suggesting circumstances in which a monopolist, like a person who owns the only ferry service across a river, might be legally obligated to deal with anyone who demands service and is willing to pay a reasonable fare. AP's lawyers, denying that AP had such utility-like attributes, argued that if the First Amendment meant anything, it meant the right not to be forced by government to share information (more particularly, news stories) with people not of one's choosing.

While *Barnette* had struck broadly and forcefully at anything smacking of totalitarian meddling with private rights, Learned Hand was not about to find that the mammoth Associated Press had the same right as *Barnette*'s schoolchildren to be 'let alone' by government. Rather, he held that AP, despite its less than absolute dominance, was nevertheless a monopolist of news and thus had a utility-like obligation to share news with non-member newspapers. The newspaper industry, he wrote, 'serves one of the most vital of all general interests: the dissemination of news from as many different sources, and with as many different facets and colors as is possible. That interest is closely akin to, if indeed it is not the same as, the interest protected by the First Amendment; it presupposes that right conclusions are more likely to be gathered out of a multitude of tongues, than through any kind of authoritative selection. To many this is, and always will be, folly; but we have staked upon it our all.'[27]

The primary rationale for maintaining a free press had always been to expose the population to the variety of perspectives that would best serve them in exercising their right to choose, as citizen-sovereigns, how and by whom they should be governed. This seemed clear enough, but was rather less than saying – as Learned Hand was now saying – that to optimize a diversity of views, antitrust law was to be invoked in service of the First Amendment against private news sources. This was novel, even radical, the kind of major synthesis one might have expected, not from a mere appellate judge, regardless of his tenure and reputation for brilliance and wisdom, but from an 'activist' or 'liberal' Supreme Court justice interested not only in construing statutes but in forging public policy.

The AP appealed to the Supreme Court. On 18 June 1945 the Court majority, in an opinion written by Justice Hugo Black, affirmed Judge Hand. 'It would be strange indeed,' Black wrote,

if the grave concern for freedom of the press which prompted adoption of the First Amendment should be read as a command that the government was without power to protect that freedom. The First Amendment, far from providing an argument against application of the Sherman Act, here provides powerful reasons to the contrary. That Amendment rests on the assumption that the widest possible dissemination of information from diverse and antagonistic sources is essential to the welfare of the public ... Surely a command that the government itself shall not impede the free flow of ideas does not afford non-governmental combinations a refuge if they impose restraints upon that constitutionally guaranteed freedom. Freedom to publish means freedom for all and not for some. Freedom to publish is guaranteed by the Constitution, but freedom to combine to keep others from publishing is not ... The First Amendment affords not the slightest support for the contention that a combination to restrain trade in news and views has any constitutional immunity.

Justice Frankfurter concurred: 'the freedom of enterprise' protected by the Sherman Act, he wrote, 'necessarily has different aspects in relation to the press than in the case of ordinary commercial pursuits. The interest of the public is to have the flow of news not trammeled by the combined self-interest of those who enjoy a unique constitutional position precisely because of the public dependence on a free press.'

Thus, the Associated Press, with less than absolute dominance of the market for news, was forced to sell its news stories to any newspaper wanting them and ready to pay for them. The decision was issued in June 1945. Several months earlier, AP executive director Kent Cooper had come up with a crisp new expression: 'the right to know,' a phrase that continued to resonate even after Justices Black and Frankfurter determined that AP's own exclusionary practices trampled on that right.[28]

Free Speech and the Demise of the Studio System

The *Paramount* antitrust case initiated by Thurman Arnold against the movie industry in 1938 was placed in the hands of U.S. Attorney General Tom C. Clark, who in October 1945 brought it to trial before a three-judge federal panel in New York. In 1946 that court, in an opinion by Judge Augustus Hand, found that the Big Five had engaged in practices violative of the Sherman Act, and ordered them, among other things, to develop a system in which all theatres, including small, independent exhibitors, could bid competitively for films. The case was appealed to the Supreme Court, which in May 1948 affirmed many of the panel's conclusions but directed it to craft the drastic remedy the Big Five had always feared: total divestment of their theatre interests, thereby at a stroke dismantling the industry's vertically integrated structure. In the following months, all but Warner Brothers began the process of selling off their theatre interests. In July 1949, Augustus Hand issued an order of divestment.[29]

Associated Press had established that by monopolizing a medium of information, an oligopoly deprives the public of not only particular pieces of knowledge but also varieties of emphasis, tone, even sensibility, that would be present in any free and vigorous marketplace for information and ideas. In 1942 the studio defendants in *Paramount* had tried to blunt the Justice Department's antitrust case by releasing the theatres (but not the distributors) from the Hays Office's $25,000 fine for showing films that did not carry a seal from Joe Breen. This gesture, a tacit acknowledgment that the seal had been an enforcement tool of the studios' monopoly, had been too late and was not nearly enough to dissuade the Government from continuing its prosecution.[30] In the Supreme Court, with Thurman Arnold now in private practice and representing the American Theatres Association, the Government's next generation of antitrust lawyers put forward a version of the argument Arnold had omitted from his initial petition against the studios, then used against Associated Press: that an oligopoly's stranglehold on the distribution of information raises substantial issues of free speech.

Since Arnold had not used the argument, the studios had not been called upon to refute it, nor had the Court been called upon to adjudicate it. Yet the Government had mentioned the issue in its appeals papers, and the American Civil Liberties Union had submitted an *amicus* brief, extrapolating from *Associated Press*, proposing that 'maximum diversification in the production and the exhibition of motion pictures is guaranteed by the First Amendment' because it is via movies that 'millions of people are given social, economic, and political notions.' Thus – the ACLU suggested – the Big Eight, by providing only films Breen approved, were 'stifl[ing] the freedom of expression of diverse minds which wish to produce and exhibit motion pictures designed to be most responsive to the real needs and tastes of the general public.'[31]

The Court's opinion in *Paramount* was written by one of Roosevelt's appointees, Justice William O. Douglas. Seemingly *en passant*, Douglas observed: 'We have no doubt that moving pictures, like newspapers and radio, are included in the press whose freedom is guaranteed by the First Amendment.' This was new. After all, the Court in *Mutual Film* had left 'no doubt' that moving pictures were *not* protected by any free-speech principle. But the studios, riveted as they were on the court-ordered dismantling of their industry, paid scant attention to Douglas's off-hand comment. A discussion of the case in the *Yale Law Journal*, although promising much by being entitled 'Motion Pictures and the First Amendment,' buried Douglas's statement in a footnote. If, however, anyone had cared to review the *Associated Press* decision and the line of earlier First Amendment cases leading up to it, Douglas's remark would have sounded very much like a bellwether. This would have been even clearer after a Roosevelt appointee with a judicial philosophy very unlike Douglas's, Felix Frankfurter, noted in 1949 that movies and other forms of mass communications presented free-speech problems that Jefferson and Madison never contemplated. This was something he too was thinking about, and in the context of *Associated Press* and *Mutual Film*, both of which he cited.[32]

Although most producers took no interest in free speech, in 1939, amidst the controversy surrounding *Blockade*, an article ghostwritten for Walter Wanger in the prestigious periodical *Foreign Affairs* urged Hollywood to take the issue of free expression to the Supreme Court, and in 1947 the Commission on Freedom of the Press, including such luminaries as Reinhold Niebuhr, Archibald MacLeish, Harold D. Lasswell, Arthur M. Schlesinger, and Zechariah Chafee, Jr, recommended that the Supreme Court overrule *Mutual Film*. What that might mean in any given dispute was anyone's guess. Although the line of cases leading up to *Associated Press* comprised a dramatic expansion of free speech, the Court had only begun to articulate what media and content might be included. If it decided that the First Amendment applied to film, a burden would fall upon state and municipal censors, whenever challenged by a studio in court, to show that any particular cut or alteration they demanded was *not* protected, until, from a slow and piecemeal succession of such challenges, a body of law would evolve revealing just where the parameters of the studios' freedom lay. While this would comprise a profound change in the legal milieu, the industry – with isolated exceptions like Walter Wanger and Charlie Chaplin – did not care, having learned to fine-tune the content and promotional formulas thought necessary to attract customers, while at the same time presenting nothing that might require re-editing or provoke another boycott. At a *Life* magazine roundtable on film in 1949, an industry leader who refused to be quoted for attribution said that the studios would never fight the Legion of Decency because they would not risk even one week's cash-flow disruption, so that whatever free-speech 'rights' Hollywood might have had were now 'lost, presumably for good.' Another participant, similarly demanding anonymity, concurred that the Legion now 'holds the whip hand over Hollywood, and nothing can be done about it.'[33]

Like the AP's control over news, Hollywood's censorship was no less effective for being part of a private, self-imposed industry oligopoly rather than a government edict. If there had been a moment for the Justice Department to go after this private self-censorship mechanism as an instrument of unlawful monopoly, it was in the *Paramount* prosecution, and Arnold had not pursued it. In fact, his lawyers had abandoned the notion that the Big Five monopolized the *production* of films, proving instead that, through theatre ownership and licensing, they controlled the lucrative, first-run *exhibition* of the films they produced. Since – Justice Douglas wrote – all audiences would eventually see all films produced by the major studios, even if these films would not appear in local theatres at reduced prices until their initial run in one of the downtown palaces was over, audiences were not being deprived of the right to see any studio film. The argument that Breen, through his enforcement of the Production Code, was in effect censoring what independent filmmakers produced, thus depriving audiences of a variety of perspectives and styles, Douglas simply ignored.

Whatever 'free speech for the screen' might augur for Hollywood's dealings with state and municipal censors, the Production Code and its enforcement by Breen were primarily the producers' device for keeping the bishops and the Legion at bay, and no liberalization of the First Amendment by the Supreme Court, even one that struck down all state and municipal censorship agencies, would embolden Hollywood to risk another Catholic boycott. Nor did independent exhibitors wish to challenge the status quo. In June 1949, just prior to the *Paramount* divestiture decision, an ACLU affiliate offered to test the ongoing viability of *Mutual Film* by offering legal services *gratis* to any exhibitor who would show a film prior to submitting it to any state or city censor. None came forward.[34]

11 Cocktails and Communism

The Money Helps

A successful film typically combined several elements that had already worked, varied sufficiently that the audience would somehow be satisfactorily diverted yet again. Warner Brothers was so habituated to imitating its own prior successes that its script department was dubbed 'the Echo Chamber.' While attractive people could be hired to recite the dialogue and others could show them where to stand and when to light a cigarette, the industry's real 'stars' were the senior executives. Monroe Stahr, the fictionalized Thalberg in Scott Fitzgerald's *The Last Tycoon* (1940/41), understood that screen credit was something one doled out to others; if one needed it, one did not have real power. Proof that Stahr had reached the top 'was the spying that went on around him – not just for inside information or patent process secrets – but spying on his scent for a trend in taste, his guess as to how things were going to be.'

In the 1930s most of the actors, writers, and those in their social stratum were pro–New Deal, although lightly so, social consciousness being for them less a commitment than a fashion. But some toyed with leftism. For them, as Murray Kempton later wrote, 'life was a scenario,' with 'the Comintern ... a musical and Spain the Rose Bowl.' In 1938, Matthew Josephson, visiting Scott Fitzgerald, asked if it was true that many Hollywood writers had 'gone left.' Fitzgerald 'nodded, looking thoughtful, then ventured: "I have been reading Marx too – very impressive."' At a cocktail party, the Exeter- and Yale-educated screenwriter Donald Ogden Stewart, chairman of the Hollywood Anti-Nazi League, waved a champagne glass in one hand and a caviar-on-toast in the other, proclaiming: 'Comes the Revolution, none of you will have any of this; none of you will have anything. Join us while you can, because we are going to take this away from you.' Stewart's commitment to social upheaval had come on precipitously: he had asked the doorman at Claridges for a book on the subject, and by the time Stewart's ship docked in New York, he had finished it, John Strachey's *The Coming Struggle for Power*, and had been transformed into a true believer – vociferously and unpleasantly so.[1] Numerous craft workers below Stewart's social level entertained various leftist projects with no fanfare, even if the industry's largest union was vehemently anti-Communist. For most of those whom sophisticates like Dorothy Parker would have known, however, her conclusion was accurate: the only 'ism' Hollywood really believed in was plagiarism.

While occasionally Breen's censorship held writers back from fulfilling their artistic ambitions, more commonly the deletion of creative or heterodox ideas came not from Breen but from executives who had become rich by delivering a biweekly succession of unexceptional, predictable products to a drowsy and undemanding public. When Ivor Montagu was interviewing for a writing job at Paramount, he listened as producer B.P. Schulberg and an associate asked a staff writer to summarize his progress on a certain project:

> 'Moscow, August 1914, the eve of the Great War. It is night, the lights are glittering on the snow ...' I interrupted. 'One moment. There's no snow in Moscow in summer ...' The three men looked at each other. Schulberg gave another twist on his cigar. 'That's a new angle ... Moscow without snow. The public will like that.' I was in.

The head of MGM's script department, Ross Wills, commented that for every Dorothy Parker, Donald Ogden Stewart, Claudine West, Robert Riskin, or other writer of talent, there were five hundred hacks, so 'helpless' that 'they can write only in gangs of four to eight on a picture,' even then being wet-nursed by the producer and director. H.L. Mencken groused in 1927 that the magnates 'continue to buy bad novels and worse plays, and then put over-worked hacks to the sorry job of translating them into movies. It is like hiring men to translate college yells into riddles. Aeschylus himself would have been stumped.' Few ever read a book of their own volition, and those who did would avoid books on vital social, political, or economic questions, for fear that they would 'somehow injure their effectiveness as movie writers,' since success lay in nothing more complicated than a story ripped from a tabloid newspaper.[2]

The writers were psychically scorned by Hollywood's powers-that-be, witness Jack Warner's classic assonance: 'Schmucks with Underwoods.' It was said that when the famous Belgian playwright Maurice Maeterlinck arrived for his first day of work, Samuel Goldwyn handed him a pencil and said: 'Now I want to see this worn down to here by five o'clock.' In the middle of an argument with Clara Bow, a director raised his voice. 'For heaven's sake, don't speak so loud!' she urged. 'You'll wake all the authors.' In Michael Curtiz's *The Strange Love of Molly Louvain* (1932), the wise-cracking Chicago reporter wants to go to Paris to write a novel, then contemplates writing movies, then reflects that Hollywood is the place where reporters go to die. S.J. Perelman said never to tell people back home that one was a scriptwriter – better to say one played the piano in a whorehouse. A successful scenarist observed that Hollywood was the worst town in the world to be broke, since 'it denotes lack of virtue not to be in a position to command a price for one's virtue.'[3]

Monetarily, Hollywood's writers were no oppressed underclass. In 1933 the 307 who worked steadily averaged a princely $13,500 per year, while 707 who were more casually employed ranged around a still quite handsome $2,750. In 1939 their median weekly income was $120, excellent for the time, even if only a few got rich. Of Albert Ellsworth Thomas, formerly a successful playwright specializing in light comedy, it was said:

> They gave him an office. They paid him every Saturday morning: such a nice, round check. But they neglected to explain the mystery ... what is a screen play and why. 'Here is a story,' they said. 'A fine, successful story by a famous novelist. We own it. We paid fifty thousand dollars for it. It won't do for the screen. Re-write it.' So he did. They said, 'Thank you very much,' and gave him another ... No one spoke to him. No one read what he wrote.

Scenarist and Hollywood fixture Elinor Glyn commented:

> All authors, living or dead, famous or obscure, shared the same fate. Their stories were re-written and completely altered either by the stenographers and continuity girls of the scenario department, or by the Assistant Direc-

tor and his lady-love, or by the leading lady, or by anyone else who happened to pass through the studio; and even when at last after infinite struggle a scene was shot which bore some resemblance to the original story it was certain to be left out in the cutting-room, or pared away to such an extent that all meaning which it might once have had was lost.

Ben Hecht and Charles MacArthur found a gas station attendant who happened to be English. Apparently out of pure bloody-mindedness, they renamed him 'Percy Wintoon' and got Metro-Goldwyn-Mayer to hire him at $1,500 a week, telling him to write nothing (easy enough, since he was functionally illiterate) and to say nothing at story conferences other than to ask for a cigarette. 'Wintoon' stayed on for a year, then resigned with his nest egg and returned home.[4]

The New York writers of talent were disdainful. We could always go out there, Ivor Montagu later wrote, 'adventurous flies ready to grow fat on the rich carrion we anticipated, and then, if something went wrong, we could always come back and raise a laugh about the foibles of our hosts.' 'In that lavish heyday of the parvenu,' the F. Scott Fitzgerald character in Budd Schulberg's *The Disenchanted* mused, 'when everything was built to look like something it wasn't, a bungalow court with accommodations indistinguishable from a hundred other bungalow courts came to be called the Garden of Allah,' a name taken from a 1935 David O. Selznick film. In the moonlight its apartments 'looked like mausoleums. It was uncanny how many talented men ... had chosen these stucco tombs.' One of its denizens, Dorothy Parker, repeatedly groused that she was 'working for cretins.' Schulberg contemplated Parker, her fellow tenant Robert Benchley, and others who vied with each other 'in witty denunciations of this Capital of the Philistines.' Yet most who ended up returning to New York did so simply because they failed, while the successful ones, those who clawed out a screen credit and got more significant work, remained in Hollywood and, 'like the prince and princess, liv[ed] happily ever after.' When Clifford Odets, writer of the hard-hitting play *Waiting for Lefty* (1935), went to Hollywood and turned Charles C. Booth's story *The General Died at Dawn* into a script, it was so lacking in the power his sophisticated New York friends had known that one quipped: 'Odets, where is thy sting?' Another who could not make the transition was the burned-out Scott Fitzgerald, returning to Hollywood in the wake of his unsuccessful novel *Tender Is the Night* (1934), and still unable to fit his talent to Hollywood's requirements. Nor would the town take much notice of this ex-literary/cultural icon in its midst. When Sheilah Graham told Fitzgerald she wanted to read all of his books, she found that local stores no longer carried them.[5]

Given all this, the writers were – as a group – a sort of lumpen bourgeoisie. After Louis B. Mayer in March 1933 forced all employees to take pay cuts as an alleged necessity to save MGM from bankruptcy, a disgruntled screenwriter commented: 'Oh that L.B. Mayer. He created more Communists than Karl Marx.' When in short order hundreds of writers joined the Screen Writers Guild and there was talk of merging it with the New York–based Authors League of America, not only Mayer and Jack Warner but even Thalberg claimed an infestation of left-wing agitators, while other executives scoffed at the notion of someone making $750 a week purporting to need union help. From the mid-1930s to mid-1950s, with the film industry employing 30,000, the Communist Party USA counted among its members 300 writers, directors, actors, and designers, with others joining such pro-Soviet groups as the Hollywood Anti-Nazi League and the Hollywood Writers' Mobilization. A collective feeling that writers did not get 'respect,' often coupled with a real sympathy for the world's have-nots, attracted them to 'progressive' causes. Some were appalled by American racism, at a time when Communist and other progressive groups seemed to offer the only aggressive leadership in righting this great wrong. In Josephson's view, many writers considered themselves prostitutes by day and social idealists at night, finding in the great works of Eisenstein and Pudovkin 'a great hope – perhaps a grand illusion – of what true works of art might yet be achieved under some form of socialism, even the authoritarian regime of the Soviets.' Yet Murray Kempton observed: 'We are told now that this was a time when the Communists influenced Hollywood's most passionate creative minds; if that is true, we may wonder why so few of them felt any impulse to take time off and form independent companies to produce films of deeper social content and involvement than the stuff they were fabricating for the big studios. The answer must be that they did not really care and were not fundamentally ashamed of what they were doing.'[6]

Martin Quigley, warning of a growing left-wing consciousness in Hollywood, believed movies should be only 'a door into a world of charm, beauty, fantasy, romance and vicarious adventure' by which we 'escape from the hates, hurts and fears of the world-as-it-is.' In January 1939, having been appointed to the New York Archdiocesan Council of the Legion of Decency, Quigley told Breen that although the battle for decency had been won, soon 'Red propaganda on the screen is going to represent ... a greater problem,' in part because Hays, 'as might be expected, is ducking the issue,' while 'in many places in the industry, especially amongst our Semetic [*sic*] brethren, there seems to be growing an acceptance of the idea of radical propaganda on the screen.' Quigley then became more specific, warning his old friend that a 'bitterly anti-Catholic and ardently pro-Red' member of Hays's own staff (unnamed) was heading a cabal to oust Breen, presumably so that the remaining censors would then let Communist ideas drift into Hollywood films.[7]

Since no screenwriter's 'vision' of the world, whether conjured by himself or suggested to him by Communist operatives during cell meetings, was of any interest to the moguls or of any relevance to the kind of movies they were making, and since numerous hands were involved in reworking scripts in order to give them the 'vanilla' quality thought necessary to attract a mass audience, the chances of having leftist ideology sneak into a film were statistically negligible. Controversial subjects were to be avoided because they might lead to protests, boycotts, government investigations, and/or more censorship, and any overtly political dialogue that somehow got by the various people developing a script would be red-pencilled by Breen. In 1936, Hollywood refused to proceed with a film of Sinclair Lewis's novel *It Can't Happen Here*, recounting the rise of a Fascist government in the United States, at least in part because the film might displease Hitler and Mussolini. When a young scriptwriter in Budd Schulberg's *What Makes Sammy Run?* (1940) says he is reading a novel by Ignazio Silone about a peasant uprising against Mussolini, Sammy replies: 'Well, for Chri'sake, who do you think's gonna make a picture about a lot of starving wops? In the first place, you'd lose your whole foreign market.' When Fitzgerald's character Pat Hobby, a down-and-out screenwriter not unlike Fitzgerald himself, is assigned to edit a certain script, he is advised: 'Clean up the stuff about Spain ... The guy that wrote it was a red.' In 1940, Frederick Lewis Allen said that if in the future one showed two dozen Depression-era features to an audience, they would derive from them 'not the faintest idea' that the United States had gone through an agonizing time. The executives' nervousness about Darryl Zanuck's decision to make a film of *The Grapes of Wrath*, and about Sam Goldwyn's decision to produce *Dead End*, demonstrated a collective fear of anything critical of U.S. society.[8]

'Asleep All Over America'

Although several studios had tried to preserve their German market by complying with a Nazi law requiring them to fire all Jews working in their German subsidiaries, Warner Brothers refused, choosing instead to withdraw from that market while leading the industry in producing films critical of Europe's dictators. Warner Brothers' *Confessions of a Nazi Spy* (1939) presented a fictional American Bund, its melodramatic fearsomeness driven home by director Anatole Litvak's use of the familiar 'March of Time' newsreel format. While some intellectuals thought the film's anti-Nazi position so blatant that it would make audiences uncomfortable, in fact the public was so unaccustomed to 'message' pictures that it could not recognize one as such, treating the film as a mere espionage story with no real-life implications. The newspaper of the German-American Bund printed a list of each of the film's credits, preceded by the word 'Jew,' while Groucho Marx saluted Warner Brothers as 'the only studio with any guts.' Jack Warner later suggested that during production he had received a veiled death threat from the Nazi consul in Los Angeles, Georg Gyssling. Mussolini, meanwhile, had banned the Marx Brothers' films as 'exemplars of the full flower of anti-fascist culture,' an intended vilification they could happily accept.[9]

As Gyssling applied pressure to suppress films that might put Nazism in a bad light, politicians in Washington saw a new angle from which to attack Hollywood. In May 1938, Rep. Martin Dies (D-TX), described by a seasoned Washington journalist as the most cynical man he had ever met, formed a Special Committee to Investigate Un-American Activities, its stated purpose being to probe: '(1) the extent, character, and objects of un-American propaganda activities in the United States, (2) the diffusion within the United States of subversive and un-American propaganda ... [which] attacks the principle of the form of government as guaranteed by our Constitution, and (3) all other questions in relation thereto that would aid Congress in any necessary remedial legislation.' Among those ordered to appear before Dies's committee in Los Angeles was Shirley Temple, because she had allegedly once sung and danced for a 'subversive' group.[10] As it became clearer that Germany and Italy considered America their enemy, Hollywood, led by Warner Brothers, increasingly turned out action adventures about Nazis and Fascists operating in secret cells within the United States. Dies urged that similar films should be made about infiltration by Communists. But Hollywood did not see fit to follow that advice. Leftist screenwriter Donald Ogden Stewart, thumbing his nose at Dies's committee, wrote a skit that closes with a speech delivered by Dorothy Parker: 'The people want democracy – real democracy, Mr. Dies, and they look toward Hollywood to give it to them because they don't get it any more in their newspapers. And that's why you're out here, Mr. Dies – that's why you want to destroy the Hollywood progressive organizations – because you've got to control this medium if you want to bring fascism to this country.' At the conclusion of Dies's hearings, the public could read (with either relief or amusement) that Shirley Temple, Humphrey Bogart, Fredric March, James Cagney, Franchot Tone, and Melvyn Douglas were not out to subvert the nation. Dies – Murray Kempton later wrote – was 'almost hooted out of town.'[11]

Dies was not the only politician beating up on Hollywood. Senator Gerald P. Nye (R-ND), a strident isolationist, charged the industry with producing pro-interventionist newsreels. In a radio address on 1 August 1941, Nye restated the position that had already made him famous in prior hearings: that the U.S. public had been duped into the First World War by Wall Streeters who had loaned so much money to Britain that they could not afford to let their debtor lose. Now arguing that the movie business wanted to push the United States into a second world war, Nye alluded to an investment banking study indicating that if Britain lost to Hitler, the elimination of the British market for American films would bankrupt most major studios. 'Before we plow a million American boys under the dust ... to make the world safe for Empire and Communism,' he urged, it was time to ask who wanted to get the United States into war: Harry and Jack Cohn, Louis B. Mayer, George J. Schaefer, Barney Balaban, Sam Katz, Adolph Zukor, Joseph Schenck, Darryl Zanuck, Murray Silverstone, Samuel Goldwyn, the Warners, Arthur Loew, and David Bernstein, and with them their employee directors, 'many of whom have come from Russia, Hungary, Germany, and the Balkan countries.' Those named, who 'only a few years ago filled their pictures with so much immorality and filth that the great Christian churches had to rise up in protest,' were the kind of people who are 'interested in foreign causes' and 'naturally susceptible' to 'national and racial' emotions, whereas the American public did not want to see war films but only to 'escape the realities of life.'[12] Thus, to Justice McKenna's conclusion in *Mutual Film* that film should have no free-speech rights because it was only a form of entertainment, and to Quigley's view that Hollywood should never cross the line from entertainment to propaganda, was now added a new slant: the moguls are Jews, unfairly forcing the American public to face European events in which it has no interest.

Feeding the long-standing perception that Jews tended to be leftists and even radicals, on 7 May 1938 the Jesuit periodical *America* editorialized: 'If more Jewish spokesmen reiterated opposition to Communism and fewer Jewish people joined the Communist ranks, the American people would, on this point, have a kindlier feeling toward the Jew.' A handbill distributed in California by a group called the Anti-Communist Federation, reproduced in the 6 March 1939 issue of *Life*, featured a male Jewish caricature against a Jewish star and a nude woman with a serpent. The text ran: 'Christian Vigilantes Arise! Buy Gentile Employ gentile Vote gentile. Boycott the Movies! Hollywood is the Sodom and Gomorrah where International Jewry controls Vice – Dope – Gambling.' Most Jewish studio heads were, in fact, politically conservative, witness L.B. Mayer's earlier endorsement of Herbert Hoover, or the forced commitment of the industry's salaries and media talent to engineer the derailing of Upton Sinclair's California gubernatorial campaign, going so far as to paint Sinclair as wanting a Soviet system in the United States. To the degree Hollywood's Jews sensed more acutely than their gentile countrymen just where European anti-Semitism was headed, any pro-interventionist propaganda generated in Hollywood would have to climb a national wall of ignorance and hostility, in that domestic anti-Semitism was – as exemplified by Nye's vile rhetoric – a significant component of American isolationism. Jews comprised under 4 per cent of the U.S. population. With seven out of ten living in the nation's eleven largest metropolitan areas, in most other places they were known only by hearsay and by the slurs which periodically found their way into the public media. The January 1936 *Fortune* carried the result of a survey of 3,000 Americans to the question: 'Do you believe that in the long run Germany will be better or worse off if it drives out the Jews?' Even in the heavily urban Northeast, 15.1 per cent of those surveyed answered 'Better off,' with another 32.2 per cent voting 'Don't know.'[13]

Nye's charge of interventionism was not flimsy. William Keighley's *The Fighting 69th*, released in January 1940, seemed to be saying that the only place for any red-blooded Irish American to be was fighting in a war, backed by the iron courage of an Irish-American priest. Upon the release of Charlie Chaplin's *The Great Dictator* (1940), Frank Borzage's *The Mortal Storm* (1940), Alfred Hitchcock's *Foreign Correspondent* (1940), and Henry King's *A Yank in the RAF* (1941), Nye and Senator Bennett Champ Clark (D-MO) initiated hearings on the issue of pro-war Hollywood propaganda. In September 1941, Nye urged that he was being unfairly attacked by 'many Jewish and other writers' who 'were, no doubt, getting their cue from the moving-picture heads against whom my effort was extended':

> There would have been no differing approach by me to the subject had those primarily responsible for propaganda in the movies been in the main Methodists, Episcopalians, Catholics, or Mohammedans. The fact is that of those I named, not all were Jews as has been so often insinuated. However, if I had it to do over and were I determined to name those primarily responsible for the propaganda in the moving-picture field, I would, in light of what I have since learned, confine myself to four names, each ... of the Jewish faith, each except only one foreign-born. But I would do that without any spirit of prejudice and without prompting by any cause as foreign to my thinking as is Anti-Semitism.

Wendell Willkie, representing the motion picture industry, thought it appropriate to remind Nye's committee that 'neither race, creed, nor geographical origin is an essential qualification to participate in American business.' Although gentiles like Cecil B. DeMille and Darryl F. Zanuck could be subjected to anti-Semitic remarks because of their exotic names, Zanuck testified at the hearing regarding his Methodist upbringing in Wahoo, Nebraska, also pointing out that it had been he who had drafted Ma Joad's 'we're the people that live' speech in *The Grapes of Wrath*. (Here the official transcript noted applause.) A growing sense in that autumn of 1941 that Nye's investigation was indeed anti-Semitic helped get the hearings adjourned.[14]

Winston Churchill, well aware that Nye and others had long since exposed the subtle British propaganda efforts that had helped lure the United States into the First World War, grasped that if the British were again to enlist America's help, they would have to be even more subtle. When British director Alfred Hitchcock arrived in Hollywood in 1939, his *sub rosa* assignment was to craft secondary British characters whom the American public might find endearing. Such were already in place in Hitchcock's *The Lady Vanishes* (1938), in which the two cricket fans seem at first to be perfect dolts, included only to provide comic relief. But when the Nazis show up and start pushing people around, it is the two Brits who turn out to be paragons of *sang froid*. In one scene in

Alexander Korda's *That Hamilton Woman*, Lord Nelson tells the Admiralty: 'Napoleon can never be master of the world until he has smashed us up – and believe me, gentlemen, he means to be master of the world. You cannot make peace with dictators, you have to destroy them.' It was rumoured that Churchill himself had penned this line and handed it to Korda for insertion. Nye subpoenaed Korda to testify when his hearings reconvened. Meanwhile, both Georg Gyssling in Los Angeles and the Nazi ambassador in Washington were circulating rumours about British agents engaging in subversive activity in the United States. Korda believed the Germans were aware of his efforts to gather useful intelligence and were feeding Nye information about it.[15]

Joseph P. Kennedy, a veteran of the movie business but then ambassador to Great Britain, warned studio heads that they should 'stop making anti-Nazi pictures' or using the film medium to promote or show sympathy to the cause of the 'democracies' versus the 'dictators,' because 'the Jews' – including the studio heads – were 'on the spot.' Will Hays, himself subpoenaed by Nye, was sufficiently concerned that he retained philosopher Mortimer Adler to draft his presentation, called 'Freedom of the Films.' But in the end neither Hays nor Korda had to testify, since Japan's attack on Pearl Harbor mooted Nye's theory that Hollywood wanted to trick the United States into a war that was none of its concern. All isolationist sentiment spontaneously evaporated. Churchill had Korda knighted. William Wyler's *Mrs Miniver* (1942), bringing the American public into the home of an earnest, brave, and attractive fictional English family in wartime, garnered seven Academy Awards.[16]

Monday, 8 December 1941, the day Nye had to call off further hearings into Hollywood's alleged pro-interventionist bias, happened also to be the day a script arrived at Warner Brothers called *Everybody Comes to Rick's*. Julius and Philip Epstein worked it over, as did Howard Koch and Casey Robinson, although it was still undergoing substantial rewrites as shooting went forward. In the final product, released in New York as *Casablanca* in November 1942, Humphrey Bogart asks Dooley Wilson: 'Sam, if it's December 1941 in Casablanca, what time is it in New York? ... I bet they're asleep in New York. I bet they're asleep all over America.' And the public had been asleep, to the extent that powerful forces had again intimidated Hollywood into sticking with 'entertainment' and avoiding significant, controversial subjects. Well might Warner Brothers indulge in this politically pointed comment about America having been caught napping. In a film pitting selfless patriotism and courage against Nazi evil and lawlessness, the Warners were justified in noting that they had been right and that Nye, Dies, Champ Clark, Joe Kennedy, Charles Lindbergh, and dozens of other isolationists and anti-Semites had been wrong.

'The Gallant Russian Bear'

Stalin's non-aggression pact with Hitler in August 1939 caused many previously sympathetic Americans to feel that their commitment to Communism had been betrayed, while others, having surrendered the ability to think for themselves, scrambled not for answers but for ideological justifications for Stalin's decision. When in June 1941 Hitler broke the pact and invaded Russia, the Soviet Union was suddenly not just a 'victim' of Hitler's betrayal but the indirect saviour of Britain, since the opening of the Eastern Front signalled Hitler's abandonment of a cross-Channel invasion. The Russians' new role in what promised to be a world war was not lost on Franklin Roosevelt, who in November 1941 made them beneficiaries of Lend-Lease. After Japan attacked Pearl Harbor and Hitler within days declared war, the United States and the Soviet Union, like two oblique planets, were now for a time aligned.[17]

Since Russia had not been a serious market for American films, Hollywood had used Soviet characters as buffoons in comedies and villains in melodramas, when an unattractive Nazi or Fascist character would cause problems in markets not yet closed.[18] Now, to jump-start popular support for America's new friend, Roosevelt reportedly prompted Hollywood to make unequivocally pro-Soviet films.[19] Bob Hope wrote into his signature tune, 'Thanks for the Memory,' a salute to 'the gallant Russian bear.' Frank Capra in *The Battle of Russia*, produced by the Army Signal Corps as part of the 'Why We Fight' series, refused to portray Soviet life as rosy, making do with the plain fact that the United States and Russia were allies because they were fighting the same enemy. Beyond that utilitarian logic, the most credible way to soften twenty-five years of anti-Soviet feeling was to ignore everything but the common Russian soldier. Zoltan Korda's *Counter-Attack* (1945), written by John Howard Lawson and co-starring Larry Parks and Paul Muni, involved the heroic exploits of Soviet paratroopers behind German lines. Jacques Tourneur's *Days of Glory* started out well enough as a heroic story of Russian guerrillas fighting the German invaders, before crumbling into a weak love story which somehow did not end the career of its young male lead, Gregory Peck. Some films, however, dared project pro-Soviet propaganda so outlandish, vile, and ill-suited for domestic audiences that they seemed to have been produced solely to please America's new 'comrades.' One such was MGM's execrable *Song of Russia* (dir. Gregory Ratoff, 1944), co-scripted by Richard J. Collins, a member of the Communist Party USA. Lewis Milestone's *The North Star* a.k.a. *Armored Attack* might have been as bad, but for the deletion of twenty-three minutes of pro-Soviet material from Lillian Hellman's script prior to the film's release in November 1943. And Warner Brothers' *Mission to Moscow* (dir. Michael Curtiz, 1943), picturizing the thoughts of U.S. ambassador Joseph Davies as recorded in his best-selling book, provides a disgustingly positive account of the Moscow Show Trials of 1936–8, despite the fact that a U.S. investigation had already exposed them as totalitarian frauds. The film was scripted by Howard Koch, whose contributions to the patriotic *Sergeant York* (1941) and *Casablanca* (1942) would not later immunize him from Government scrutiny.[20]

The HUAC Hearings

By 1944, the Communist Party USA, on the strength of its progressive labour and race policies and the officially collaborative relations between the United States and Russia, had 100,000 members. Once V-E Day ended the two nations' brief *entente cordiale*, the CPUSA suddenly – on cue from Stalin – took a hard left turn. The House Committee on Un-American Activities (HUAC), vigorously at work before the war, was now rejuvenated by John E. Rankin (D-MS), joined by J. Parnell Thomas (R-NJ), who had been a founding member. Rankin, later described as 'a symbol of all that is dark and evil' in HUAC, would fly into rages and interrupt testimony with irrelevancies or erroneous assertions, calling an article by Eleanor Roosevelt 'the most insulting, Communistic piece of propaganda that was ever thrown in the faces of the women of America.' Believing that Communism was led by Jews, he said that it 'hounded and persecuted the Savior during his earthly ministry, inspired his crucifixion, derided him in his dying agony, and then gambled for his garments at the foot of the cross ... These alien-minded Communistic enemies of Christianity, and their stooges, are trying to get control of the press of this country. Many of our great daily newspapers have now changed hands and gone over to them ... They are trying to take over the radio. Listen to their lying broadcasts in broken English and you can almost smell them.' No better was Parnell Thomas. '[I]t

would be hard to imagine,' a scholar later wrote, 'a person less qualified' to chair such a committee, given his 'complete lack of dignity' in
presiding over the hearings and his 'utter irresponsibility in making
charges in the absence of supporting evidence.'[21]

Although leftism had a foothold in some unions, in some universities,
with a few New Yorkers, with isolated ideologues and crackpots, and
among Hollywood intellectuals, it had failed to attract the vast group of
American workers who were supposed to be its beneficiaries, a conclusion admitted by William Z. Foster, general secretary of the CPUSA.
While Foster, Eugene Dennis, and other Party leaders would be indicted under federal statutes and undergo very public trials, these were
not people whose views or personalities could possibly mean anything
to the middle-class public, except as objects of scorn. That public did
care very much, however, about movies and those who made them, and
thus the ferreting out of Hollywood leftists promised politicians bank-
able publicity. While the industry had once been accused of destroying
the nation's moral fabric by spreading lasciviousness, then of trying to
get the United States into a war, now Hollywood was said to be –
Rankin charged in July 1945 – the 'headquarters' of 'one of the most
dangerous plots ever instigated for the overthrow of this Government,'
a plot aimed at 'trying to spread subversive propaganda, poison the
minds of your children, distort the history of our country, and discredit
Christianity.'[22] Here was a chance for conservatives to 'get even' retrospectively with an industry inhabited not only by leftists but by supporters of Roosevelt and of the defeated cause in Spain. Many anti–New
Dealers were disappointed when another widely publicized post-war
congressional investigation failed to prove that FDR was the evil genius
behind Japan's attack on Pearl Harbor. And while no mere congress-
man or government *apparatchik* could hope to stimulate for his own
benefit the complex of positive emotions conjured by movie stars, hearings that featured the actors afforded government men the chance to
catch some reflected glory; thus did Richard Nixon, among others,
launch his national career.

Although the public and major newspapers were initially indifferent
to or vaguely distrustful of HUAC, appearances by Jack Warner and
other 'friendly' witnesses at the Los Angeles Biltmore in May 1947
helped foster some positive national coverage, as did Parnell Thomas's
statement that he had a 'complete list of all the pictures which have
been produced in Hollywood in the past eight years which contain
Communist propaganda.' When subpoenas were issued for further

hearings to be conducted in October in Washington, directors John Huston and William Wyler, screenwriter Philip Dunne, and actor Alexander Knox met for lunch at Lucey's restaurant on Melrose Avenue in Hollywood, there forming what would be called the Committee for the First Amendment, the group apparently believing that this provision of the Constitution somehow barred the Government from asking people questions about their political affiliations. A subsequent organizational meeting at Ira Gershwin's house yielded a capacity crowd, and in short order the group numbered 500, including Rita Hayworth, Humphrey Bogart, Lauren Bacall, Gene Kelly, Judy Garland, Frank Sinatra, Katharine Hepburn, and Orson Welles.[23]

Since HUAC's mandate was to probe leftist influence in the medium, it was not surprising that it did not target costumers, carpenters, or electricians. Of the original nineteen 'unfriendly' witnesses subpoenaed for the October hearings, sixteen were or had been writers. Although most were relatively unknown and thus easily expendable, the moguls were not pleased about the public knowing that they had been employing recognized talents like Dalton Trumbo who had been affiliated with organizations that prophesized the collapse of an economic system that had made them all rich. Thus John Houseman may have been right in later observing that Hollywood was 'not altogether averse to a little blood-letting among those of its employees whom it found disturbing.'[24]

In the post-war years, any witness in any forum could immunize himself by reference to his war record. Significantly, of the nineteen unfriendly witnesses targeted by the Government, only Richard Collins and Adrian Scott had served in the war. Most were Jewish. Although Senator Nye had been criticized for the anti-Semitic atmosphere of his pre-war hearings, and now revelations regarding the Holocaust might have suggested reticence, Rankin was undeterred: 'I want to read you some of these names. One ... is June Havoc. We found ... that her real name is June Hovick. Another one was Danny Kaye, and we found out his real name is David Daniel Kamirsky ... Another one is Eddie Cantor, whose real name is Edward Iskowitz. There is one who calls himself Edward [G.] Robinson. His real name is Emmanuel Goldenberg. There is another here who calls himself Melvyn Douglas, whose real name is Melvyn Hesselberg.' As before the war, Hollywood's Jewish executives saw no benefit in challenging anti-Semites. Some were worried about how the public would react to the Darryl Zanuck / Elia Kazan film *Gentleman's Agreement* (1947), exposing the 'polite' anti-Semitism found in major hotels and the 'better' country clubs. A less confrontational method of self-defence is drafted into *The Miracle of the Bells* (1948), where Marcus Harris, projected as Jewish by Lee J. Cobb's acting style, demonstrates that the archetypal Hollywood producer, although admittedly rough around the edges, operates ethically.[25] The reason Harris has given a young unknown the chance to play Joan of Arc is that he has fired the petulant European star originally cast in the role because she had made an unacceptable crack about America.

On 16 October, four days before HUAC's Washington hearings opened, the nineteen unfriendly witnesses ran in *Variety* and elsewhere a notice inviting studio heads to step forward and show that they – and not the Government – were still in charge of their business. Under the heading 'AN OPEN LETTER TO THE MOTION PICTURE INDUSTRY ON THE ISSUE OF FREEDOM ON THE SCREEN FROM POLITICAL INTIMIDATION AND CENSOR-SHIP,' it read, in part:

> Let us be clear. The issue is not the historically phony one of the subver-sion of the screen by Communists – but whether the screen will remain free. The issue is not the 'radicalism' of nineteen writers, directors, actors who are to be singled out, if possible, as fall guys. They don't count. No one of them has ever been in control of the films produced in Hollywood. The goal is control of the industry through intimidation of the executive heads of the industry ... and through further legislation. The goal is a lifeless and reactionary screen that will be artistically, culturally, and financially bankrupt.[26]

No studio executive would have disagreed. As *Mutual Film*, and the Catholic bishops, and the Legion of Decency, and the controversy fol-lowing the release of *Blockade*, and Nye, Dies, and Ambassador Kennedy had all demonstrated, the powers-that-be had never wanted Holly-wood to be a Fifth Estate of meaningful social, cultural, or political commentary. If on occasion a Howard Hughes, Chaplin, or the Warners chose to say something or stand for something, they did so at their peril. So, for any mogul who had seen it all, the Hollywood Nineteen's appeal was clear enough: What HUAC really wants is to cow you into submission; by standing up for our political rights, you ultimately protect your own right to control the film industry.

Parnell Thomas and Jack Warner opened the Washington hearings by inculcating the ominous sense that the nation was being manipulated from within by sinister forces. 'Subversive germs breed in dark corners,' Warner declared. 'Let's get light into those corners. That, I believe, is the purpose of this hearing.' Ronald Reagan, an articulate anti-Communist unionist who had risen to the presidency of the Screen Actors Guild, testified forthrightly that a small group within the Guild 'has been suspected of more or less following the tactics that we associate with the Communist Party,' while director Sam Wood said that directors Irving Pichel (*The Miracle of the Bells*) and Edward Dmytryk (*Murder, My Sweet; Crossfire*) had tried to steer the Screen Directors Guild 'into the Red river.' The questions put to another friendly witness, Adolph Menjou, as well as his detailed and modulated responses, suggest not only the brilliant showmanship for which he was known in a succession of films, but also a more thorough rehearsal than could be accommodated in the production of a typical studio feature. Playwright Bertolt Brecht, one of eleven unfriendly witnesses called to the stand, testified that he was not and had never been a Communist, then immediately fled and found his way to Communist East Germany, where for a generation he enjoyed the status of being that totalitarian state's most famous dramatist. The others, the so-called Hollywood Ten, were not the mere hacks no one cared about, but very successful movie people: writers Dalton Trumbo, John Howard Lawson, Albert Maltz, Alvah Bessie, Lester Cole, Samuel Ornitz, and Ring Lardner, Jr, writer/producer Adrian Scott, and directors Herbert Biberman and Edward Dmytryk.[27]

When the original Hollywood Nineteen had first met with their lawyers, Howard Koch was among those urging a strategy of simply telling everything: organizations joined, names of other members, subjects discussed at meetings, etc. Richard Schickel later commented that if that plan had been adopted, 'no moral opprobrium could have been attached to anyone' and the whole matter might have been quickly over. While this might have worked for those who regretted their involvement and had made a clean break, most were still committed leftists, and the studios would have been subjected to overwhelming pressure to fire and blacklist them. Dmytryk later alleged that he and Scott talked over the virtues of this tell-all strategy with their own chosen lawyer, Bartley Crum, but that four lawyers sent by the CPUSA, after holding private meetings with those of the Nineteen thought to be the most committed, manipulated the entire group into a unanimous strategy of refusing to testify at all. This strategy, which Dmytryk later claimed had issued from Moscow, was designed to protect the many CPUSA members not subpoenaed to testify, since any tell-all approach would inevitably mean that dozens of Party members would be exposed. If, then, all the witnesses had testified fully and truthfully, HUAC would have proven its premise that Hollywood was infiltrated by Communists. In the end, Crum and ex-California attorney general Robert W. Kenny, the other lawyer for the Ten who had known nothing about the extra meetings, acquiesced in a 'unanimous' strategy of non-cooperation, to the great injury of those who would have been well served by testifying freely and fully.[28]

This strategy of non-cooperation was fraught with legal difficulties. The Fifth Amendment provides that no one 'shall be compelled ... to be a witness against himself.' A witness at a trial or hearing who has committed a crime is well advised to 'take the Fifth,' that is, to refuse to say anything that might help the prosecution prove a subsequent criminal case against him. But invoking this time-honoured right against self-inculpation has – ironically – a self-inculpating effect, in that it tends to make the public, as well as the witness's employer, believe that he has in fact engaged in criminal activity. Although the federal Smith Act criminalized advocating the violent overthrow of the U.S. Government, none of the Ten had done so.[29] Although they were or had been affiliated with leftist organizations, that was not in itself unlawful.

Nor, once a witness invokes the Fifth Amendment, does he necessarily avoid further inquiry, since Congress may force upon him a partial immunity by declaring that the evidence he presents, as well as any other evidence derived from it, may not be used in any subsequent criminal prosecution against him. Once Congress issues such an immunity, the witness must either testify fully or invite the consequence of refusing to do so: a prosecution under the federal contempt statute, 2 U.S.C. § 192. Thus, the negative publicity of 'taking the Fifth' when there is no crime to hide, coupled with a possible jail term for refusing to testify once an immunity is imposed, made the Fifth Amendment an unattractive basis for refusing to cooperate with HUAC.[30]

John Huston and Philip Dunne suggested that the witnesses should refuse to cooperate, then find a Supreme Court justice such as Felix Frankfurter to put them under oath at a press conference, where they would tell all, thus demonstrating that their refusal to answer these questions when posed by HUAC was a principled position rather than an attempt to hide anything. This strategy was inconsistent with CPUSA's agenda, and was rejected. Instead, the Ten chose (or were manipulated by CPUSA's lawyers into accepting) a highly tenuous basis for avoiding HUAC's questions, by invoking the First Amendment's guarantees of freedom of expression and of assembly. According to this theory, the First Amendment, coupled in one variant with the Fourth Amendment's 'right of the people to be secure ... against unreasonable searches and seizures,' comprised a Constitutional right to remain silent about one's beliefs and associations. Derived in part from the Supreme Court's investing the children in *Barnette* with a First Amendment right to refuse to salute the flag, the theory posited a right not to be coerced into cooperating with the Government, a right to be 'let alone.' 'If there is any fixed star in our constitutional constellation,' Justice Jackson had written in *Barnette*, 'it is that no official, high or petty, can prescribe what shall be orthodox in politics, nationalism, religion, or other matters of opinion or force citizens to confess by word or act their faith therein.' This 'seemingly unequivocal' language in *Barnette*, Ring Lardner, Jr, later wrote, constituted the Ten's basis for relying on the First Amendment in refusing to answer HUAC's questions.[31]

This putative extension of *Barnette* was already being tested by others, among them Edward K. Barsky, who during the Spanish Civil War had formed a medical corps to aid anti-Franco forces. In 1942, Dr Barsky organized the Joint Anti-Fascist Refugee Committee to help pro-Loyalists then living in refugee camps in France and to keep their cause alive in the United States. When in February 1946 HUAC demanded to see that organization's records, Dr Barsky refused, urging that the exposure of refugees' names would endanger the lives of their relatives still living in Franco's Spain. Congress held him in contempt, and he was convicted in a subsequent trial. As the Washington hearings against the Hollywood Ten went forward, Dr Barsky's lawyers were preparing their submission to the Court of Appeals.[32]

Another theoretical basis for refusing to cooperate with Congress derived from the Constitution's basic premise of limited and specified federal powers, the same premise that had caused Alexander Hamilton to urge that the best way to insure free speech in the federal Constitution was to say nothing about it. The contempt statute provides for up to a year in prison for refusing to answer 'any question' by a congressional committee which is 'pertinent' to the issue under inquiry. HUAC's mandate was extremely broad, including inquiry into anything likely to help Congress draft legislation to protect against 'the diffusion within the United States of subversive and un-American propaganda ... [that] attacks the principle of the form of government as guaranteed by our Constitution.' All governments retain inherent authority to protect themselves from attack, and Article I, section 8 of the Constitution authorizes

Congress to provide for the nation's 'common Defence and general Welfare.' Although a wide range of activities could thus be 'pertinent' to HUAC's inquiry, some scholars believed that the Constitution did not grant Congress authority to investigate propaganda which, although criticizing 'the principle of the form' of the U.S. Government, did not advocate its violent overthrow or otherwise constitute a crime. They reasoned that if HUAC could not show that a witness possessed information about actual criminal activity, it would be asking him questions about his affiliations and beliefs, subjects concerning which Congress could not legislate, and which thus were also beyond its investigative authority.[33] Thus, some hoped to challenge Congress's authority to hold witnesses in contempt for refusing to answer its questions, by arguing that it had no authority to ask them.

Unfortunately, the only way to test such theories was to do what Dr Barsky and others had done: refuse to cooperate, be held in contempt by Congress, and attack that contempt holding in a subsequent federal trial and appeal. Nor were the chances for ultimate vindication very good, in that Chief Justice Fred Vinson's Supreme Court comprised 'a compliant instrument of administrative persecution and Congressional inquisition' which (as a former law clerk there admitted) 'dutifully reflected the prejudices of the period.' If the Court found that questions about leftist affiliations had the required connection with 'subversive and un-American propaganda,' and that Congress was authorized to legislate regarding such propaganda even in the absence of a criminal conspiracy to overthrow the Government by violence, the First Amendment would avail a witness nothing.[34]

As a final bit of advice prior to HUAC's hearings, Kenny told the Ten that instead of flatly refusing to answer the Committee's questions, they should say at least *something*, so that they might be able to argue in their subsequent contempt trial that they had at least 'tried' to answer.[35] Thus, when a principled refusal to answer might have allowed the witnesses to at least retain some personal dignity, Kenny recommended something like double-talk, verbal evasion. With this final piece thrown into a mixed bag of advice – none of it very helpful or likely to succeed – the Ten went to face Rankin and Parnell Thomas.

As with the earlier hearing held by several members of the Committee in Los Angeles, HUAC orchestrated its cavalcade of 'friendly' witnesses in an attempt to establish its own virtue with the public. The typical friendly witness praised HUAC's work, testified that he personally hated Communists and would sock one in the nose if he met one, spewed out some names of people he thought might be Communists because of something they might have said or something someone else might have said about them, and then, when asked whether Hollywood should make anti-Communist films, heartily agreed that it should. Some months earlier, in response to an invitation by Hollywood's free-speech advocates, Thomas Mann in a nationwide radio broadcast assured listeners that in the nine years he had been in the United States, he had seen many films and that 'if Communist propaganda had been smuggled into any of them, it must have been most thoroughly hidden,' since he, for one, had 'never noticed anything of the sort.' That was absolutely true in the pre-war period, and a substantial amount of pro-Soviet material had been cut out of the pro-Russian films of the mid-war period, as when Joe Breen had ordered deleted from the script of Gregory Ratoff's *Song of Russia* such un-American lines as 'I hear that in America there's no real family life at all. You want a divorce – You're divorced. They don't even take care of the children.' Robert Taylor, the most sycophantic of the 'friendly' witnesses, had starred in that film, telling the Committee he had objected to being in it and had succeeded in having much pro-Soviet stuff deleted during production. Richard J. Collins, the film's co-writer, would later corroborate Taylor's testimony.[36]

Since John Howard Lawson was known to be a doctrinaire leftist hothead, HUAC smartly called him as its first unfriendly witness. When asked whether he was or had ever been a member of the Communist Party USA, he replied that 'the question of Communism is in no way related to this inquiry.'[37] The legal question of what was or was not an appropriate area for congressional inquiry was a complicated one, properly to be raised by lawyers in later court proceedings, not in a harangue by a witness, and Lawson ended up looking surly, evasive, and foolish. Although his testimony and demeanour were the worst, none of the Ten – all industry veterans – ever managed the kind of winning, Hollywood-style speech by which the overflow audience in the Caucus Room might by its applause have made HUAC look like political villains in a Capra film.[38] Thus, the particular kind of non-cooperation previously agreed upon, when coupled with the initial impression left by Lawson, ended up destroying the public sympathy the Ten would otherwise have elicited. In a succession of compellingly dramatic scenes, each unfriendly witness fell into a verbal shouting match with the Committee and was ordered to move away from the microphone, whereupon HUAC investigator Louis Russell would produce a portfolio of evidence of leftist organizations the witness had joined, meetings he had attended, etc.

The hearings were rife with missed cues and lost opportunities – on both sides. Howard Koch, if the Committee had called him to the stand and if he had agreed to testify, would have said that he wrote the script for *Mission to Moscow* only because Jack Warner ordered him to do it, after Franklin Roosevelt had personally asked Warner to make the film so that the American public would have 'a more sympathetic understanding' of the Russians.[39] Such testimony would have undercut Warner's value as a friendly witness and would have comprised a complete and patriotic rationale for pro-Soviet material in all the other mid-war films. Not surprisingly, Koch was not asked to testify. Albert Maltz, a graduate of Columbia and Yale Drama School, had written for leftist theatre productions in New York and co-wrote Edward G. Robinson's narration for *Moscow Strikes Back* (1942), the Oscar-winning American adaptation of a Soviet propaganda film, before contributing to the staunchly patriotic *Destination Tokyo* (1943) and *Pride of the Marines* (1945). When Maltz wrote in the leftist *New Masses* that 'the artist is most successful' who avoids abjectly serving a leftist agenda but instead 'most profoundly and *accurately* reveals his characters, with all their motivations clearly delineated,' the CPUSA forced him to recant and to 'admit' that art was not to be judged by its own rules but by its compliance or non-compliance with approved Communist doctrine.[40] Thus, a skilfully conducted cross-examination of Maltz could have destroyed the argument that Hollywood's leftists should be allowed their intellectual freedom, by showing that they had none, being willing tools for the Party line. But because Maltz refused to cooperate, no such examination took place; nor was anyone else called to the stand to recount the facts.

The actual evidence adduced of Communist influence in films was minimal and equivocal. While Jack Warner lambasted writers by name and writers generally, and said he had often had to purge scripts of leftist material, his actual proof was hardly impressive. Another friendly witness, Gary Cooper, proved to be an unsophisticated toady, swearing that he had 'turned down quite a few scripts because I thought they were tinged with Communistic ideas,' yet finding himself unable to name even one. Ginger Rogers's mother testified that her daughter turned down a script of *Sister Carrie* because it was 'open propaganda,' then spoke of her failed effort to stop the production of *None but the Lonely Heart* (1944), directed and scripted by Clifford Odets, because she had heard that Odets was a Communist and she found the story 'filled with despair and hopelessness.' Yet what really bothered her was the apolitical fact that she did not consider such a gritty film to be an appropriate vehicle for a star like Cary Grant.

Another film mentioned was *Tender Comrade* (1943), scripted by unfriendly witness Dalton Trumbo and directed by unfriendly witness Edward Dmytryk, which portrays five wives whose husbands are off at war, the purportedly 'subversive' element being that five mature women can live together in an informal 'women's collective.' 'Share and share alike,' Ginger Rogers's character says, 'that's democracy.' In Sam Wood's *Kitty Foyle* (1940), with an Oscar-nominated script by Trumbo, the heroine's poor and idealistic doctor/boyfriend, delivering babies in tenements redolent of Margaret Sanger's early days on New York's Lower East Side, points to a ragamuffin boy on the subway and offers the 'unAmerican' prediction that the boy's whole life will be a failure merely by virtue of the grinding poverty into which he was born. The heroine's other boyfriend, meanwhile, from one of Philadelphia's oldest families, invites her into a sexual relationship (which she declines). Although Trumbo could have outwitted the Committee in any substantive discussion of the film and thus demonstrate the weakness of its case, by refusing to testify he denied himself the opportunity.

None of the Hollywood Ten had worked on King Vidor's *Our Daily Bread* (1934), a prize-winner at the first Moscow Film Festival, in which unemployed Americans collectivize an abandoned farm. None had worked on *Song of Russia*. Nor could HUAC do anything with *Dead End* and *The Grapes of Wrath*, both of which had made conservative industry executives so nervous. As neither of the scenarists on those films (Lillian Hellman and Nunnally Johnson) was now among the Ten, no crossexaminer could ask questions about the ideological underpinnings of Tom Joad's 'Wherever there's a fight so hungry people can eat, I'll be there. Wherever there's a cop beatin' up a guy, I'll be there.' Because director John Ford was not among the Ten, no one could cross-examine him about his observation that *The Grapes of Wrath* depicted the replication in the American 1930s of what had happened in Ireland in the 1840s: throwing people off the land to let them starve on the roads. In the end, neither the films mentioned nor the testimony adduced constituted solid evidence upon which HUAC could premise a report that the Hollywood Ten had filled movies with 'subversive' and 'un-American' propaganda. If the Ten had decided upon a tell-all approach concerning the films they had worked on, the Committee would undoubtedly have had to issue a report indicating that while there were Communists and leftists working in the industry, the complicated process by which ideas are turned into scripts and then into films made Communist propagandizing nearly impossible unless (as with the pro-Soviet mid-war films) the moguls approved, a fact later shown in a study of the 159 films in which the Hollywood Ten had credits. Meanwhile, most of those who followed the hearings in newsreels, on the radio, and in the new medium of television, whatever they thought of the unfriendly witnesses, found HUAC's handling of the hearings incompetent and distasteful. After publicly questioning only eleven of the sixty-eight unfriendly witnesses it had promised to subpoena, HUAC abruptly ended the hearings, issued no report or findings, and would not start new Hollywood hearings for another three and a half years.[41]

In the end, all HUAC had on these witnesses was that they had not cooperated. This was, however, enough to ruin them. Representative Nixon led the effort to have the Ten held in contempt, and, following overwhelming congressional votes, they were indicted and faced federal trials. Although most studio heads had stayed well clear of the hearings, once the indictments were issued, they emerged. On 20 November 1947, despite ample industry talk over the previous months about civil rights and freedom of expression, the board of Twentieth Century-Fox – theretofore known as 'the writers' studio' – voted to bar from employment anyone held in contempt for refusing to cooperate with HUAC, and proceeded to instruct Darryl Zanuck to fire Ring Lardner, Jr, then under contract. RKO, over the objection of Dore Schary, fired Dmytryk and Adrian Scott. On 22 November, Schary of RKO, Louis B. Mayer of MGM, Barney Balaban of Paramount, Nicholas Schenck of Loew's, Spyros Skouras of Fox, Harry Cohn of Columbia, and Samuel Goldwyn, plus various advisers, held what journalist Westbrook Pegler called 'a solemn frightened huddle' at New York's Waldorf-Astoria, chaired by Will Hays's successor, Eric Johnston. The group emerged on 24 November, revealing nothing, then two weeks later released the so-called 'Waldorf Manifesto,' summarily firing and blacklisting the remaining members of the Hollywood Ten. Only a few weeks had passed since the subpoenaed witnesses in the trade papers had asked the moguls to consider that if the Government could attack mere writers, the moguls would be next. Once the Ten were indicted, however, pressure from the industry's Wall Street underwriters, derived in part from uncertainty regarding what the Supreme Court would do to Hollywood's business structure in the pending *Paramount* case, and in part from seeing febrile demands by the Hearst newspapers for federal regulation of the studios and their wayward personnel, resulted in the purging of the Hollywood Ten. Earlier idealism was all now ancient history, except insofar as the Waldorf Manifesto proclaimed that Hollywood would not 'be swayed by hysteria or intimidation' and was pledged 'to protect the innocent, and to safeguard free speech and a free screen.'[42] But this was Orwellian double-talk, directly contradicting what was happening.

A number of Hollywood stars had gone to Washington in support of free speech. Stopping in New York before returning to California, Humphrey Bogart, Lauren Bacall, John Huston, and Philip Dunne were told by a cabbie: 'You guys are right. No senator's going to tell *me* what to think!' But they had felt betrayed by the Ten's failure to present the case for freedom in a dignified way, and once the Waldorf Manifesto appeared, these megastars ran for cover, witness Bogart's soft-boiled *mea culpa*, 'I'm No Communist,' published in the March 1948 *Photoplay*.[43] In the months that followed, Lawson and Trumbo challenged their congressional contempt citations in federal court, the other eight defendants having agreed with the Government to be bound by the result. When Lawson and Trumbo lost, all were fined and sentenced to prison. Two federal appeals courts rejected the similar legal arguments of two other witnesses who had refused to cooperate with HUAC, Dr Barsky and Leon Josephson, although each decision was accompanied by a substantial dissent, thus raising hopes for Supreme Court review. In the end, however, the Court accepted neither case, nor several others premised on the same First Amendment theory upon which the Hollywood Ten had staked everything. This sealed their fate, and in April 1950 the Court denied their petitions.[44]

Nine of the Hollywood Ten now brought claims against the industry for an unlawful conspiracy to blacklist them, citing the joint Waldorf Manifesto as direct evidence. Since five of the Ten also had employment contracts which their respective studios refused to honour, they sued for their contractual salaries. Four of these contracts contained a so-called 'morals clause,' found in most Hollywood personnel contracts following the Arbuckle and other scandals of the early 1920s. In court, the studios argued that an employee's refusal to cooperate with a congressional committee constituted a violation of the 'morals clause' because it tended to bring his employer into public disgrace. Dore Schary later revealed that during the 'frightened huddle' at the Waldorf, Eric Johnston had set forth four reasons for the blacklisting, reminiscent of the economic considerations for which the producers had caved in to censorship thirteen years before: the Legion of Decency was again threatening a massive boycott; there were already isolated boycotts of films in which the Ten were involved; an audience in Chapel Hill, North Carolina, had stoned the screen of a theatre playing a film starring Katharine Hepburn, who had criticized HUAC and visibly supported the Committee for the First Amendment; and the right-wing governments of Spain, Chile, and Argentina were going to boycott the films of any studio that employed any of the Ten. But in these employment-contract suits, the studios could adduce little evidence that they were actually injured by their employees' refusal to testify, and juries in three of the cases awarded the ex-employees damages. The cases brought by Ring Lardner and Adrian Scott against their respective studios were tried to a Pasadena jury, which awarded them damages despite such reported comments from the trial judge as: 'I don't respect people like you jailbirds.' Lardner's $25,000 award of accrued salary was reversed on appeal, the Ninth federal Circuit holding that Twentieth Century-Fox should not be bound by Darryl Zanuck's statement that he did not care about a man's politics but only his ability to do the job. Although Zanuck was co-founder and chief of production at Fox, the Ninth Circuit concluded that it was factually unclear whether Zanuck's position at Fox was of sufficient authority to render the company liable for things he said. Adrian Scott's jury award was overturned by the trial judge as against the weight of the evidence, and he then lost a subsequent non-jury trial before the same judge. Affirming, the Ninth Circuit noted that it would not wish to reach a result in Scott's case different from what it had decided in Lardner's.[45]

Lester Cole's employment suit against MGM and its then parent, Loew's, was assigned to federal judge Leon Yankwich, who had earlier told a state investigative committee that he reserved the right to give a speech to any organization, even one identified as a Communist front. That committee declared Yankwich unfit to sit as a federal judge, even though as a state committee it had no jurisdiction to do so. When Loew's filed a motion to disqualify Yankwich from presiding over Cole's case because his prior statement about speech-making showed an alleged pro-Communist bias, Yankwich denied the motion, then approved the jury's verdict in Cole's favour, noting that Cole's victory was to be ascribed to the testimony given on Cole's behalf by L.B. Mayer. Although the jury found that Cole's conduct did not violate the 'morals clause' of his contract with Loew's, the Ninth Circuit reversed and remanded for a new trial. The Supreme Court refused to accept Cole's case, or Lardner's, or Scott's. Cole and fellow MGM employee Dalton Trumbo were owed over $300,000 in back salary; rather than try the case again, they settled for $62,500 each. After paying their lawyers and giving some of the money to other members of the Hollywood Ten, they were left with almost nothing.[46]

When testifying as plaintiffs in support of their contract claims, some of the Ten noted that the producers had originally been very support-ive, telling them not to be intimidated by HUAC, as when Eric Johnston had said – just prior to the hearings – that the industry would never invoke a blacklist. Whatever the sincerity of those words when uttered, the Waldorf Manifesto demonstrated that the Ten were without friends. Some inferred that they had all been 'set up,' that the one thing the studios had not wanted the Ten to do was openly to declare their leftist affiliations, since this would have indicated that the studios had hired them and/or had continued to employ them while knowing of those affiliations. Paul Jarrico, co-scenarist of *Song of Russia*, later said that L.B. Mayer told him that 'he knew I was a Communist and that he wouldn't have me on the lot for a minute except that I was such a good writer.'[47] Better to inculcate among the Ten a belief (however dubious legally) that HUAC had no right to ask about their politics, and that the industry would welcome them back when it was all over. Once the Ten had committed themselves to saying nothing and implicating no one, it was easy enough to sacrifice them, much as the hapless Arbuckle had once been sacrificed so that the industry might demonstrate collectively its *bona fide* intention to clean house.

And the studio heads had set them up, insofar as it let Johnston make on their behalf promises that ultimately they decided not to keep. More at fault, however, were the lawyers, the CPUSA's lawyers (if we are to believe Dmytryk) and Crum and Kenny, causing the Ten jointly to take a 'principled' position against Government intrusion, using a legal theory known to be avant-garde and likely to fail. When Parnell Tho-mas asked Lardner whether he was or had ever been a member of the Communist Party, Lardner gave the Ten's only brilliant line: 'I could answer ... but if I did, I would hate myself in the morning.' Having all made that decision, the Ten jointly bound themselves to the only long-shot legal principle by which they might ultimately be vindicated. Failing in that effort, they suffered the consequences, including not just personal ruin but the suggestion that they had no one to blame but themselves and their lawyers. The Ninth Circuit, for instance, not only

overturned the jury verdict Lester Cole had obtained on his employment contract, but told him that 'a more reasonable course of conduct
would have enabled him to trumpet his protest without danger to
himself.' Adding insult to injury, the court actually quoted L.B. Mayer's
recollection of what he had said to Cole after the HUAC hearing had
gone sour:

> We talked about the hearing and I said it is very unfortunate; that I
> thought he acted very unwisely and had bad advice, because, if he be-
> longs to the Communist Party, the FBI no doubt has got a record of it, and
> it was no crime, as I saw it, to belong to the Communist Party ... and he
> should have answered. Well, he thought some personal rights were in-
> volved. And I said, 'You could have told the chairman that "I am advised
> you have no right to ask me these questions but I can't afford not to
> answer them. No; I am not a Communist" or "I am a Communist or
> belong to the Communist Party but I never heard anything subversive or
> [advocating] any violence or I would have walked out on them," which-
> ever the case may be, and then you are clear. You wouldn't have any
> problem on your hands.' 'Well,' he said, 'I had to stick with the gang. They
> agreed to do it that way and I had to be with them.'[48]

Held in abeyance for three and a half years, HUAC's movie hearings
reopened in March 1951, with the fate of the Ten demonstrating to those
now being subpoenaed what awaited anyone opting for a 'principled'
refusal to cooperate. Larry Parks, co-star of *Counter-Attack*, chose to
name names, including that of Lee J. Cobb. For two years, Cobb refused
to cooperate, but finally caved in, named names himself, and confessed
to having been a member of the Communist Party USA during 1945–6,
shortly before he began rehearsals for *The Miracle of the Bells*. Dmytryk
admitted a Communist affiliation for several months of 1945, his primary stated reason for his recent decision to cooperate being that the
attack on South Korea suggested aggressive tendencies by the Soviet
Union and Communist China, to which he purportedly took exception.
One of his questioners, endeavouring to make *High Noon* scenarist Carl
Foreman similarly fess up, called Dmytryk's testimony 'among the
finest and most complete ever received by this committee' – as if HUAC
could itself award Oscars. Roy M. Brewer, head of the Hollywood unit
of the International Alliance of Theatrical Stage Employees (IATSE),
played a central role in the 'clearance' process by which personnel
whose background had been questioned could purge themselves of

leftist taint via formal disavowals or – where something more was deemed necessary – by naming names. Warner Brothers hired so many writers who had undergone this cleansing process that someone put up a sign in the commissary: 'IT IS NOT ENOUGH TO HAVE INFORMED – YOU MUST ALSO HAVE TALENT.' A group of twenty-three blacklisted actors, writers, and editors filed a collective complaint against the studios which was dismissed by the court on a technical point, since it lacked an allegation to the effect that 'but for' the blacklisting, the plaintiffs would have been able to find work in Hollywood. While some industry spokesmen continued to claim that there was no blacklist, no honest observer could agree.[49]

Hollywood was now careful. In Sam Fuller's *Pickup on South Street* (1953), a film so filled with corruption (a Britisher observed) that the only clean thing in it was the subway, not even a pickpocket and his tramp girlfriend would stoop so low as to sell secrets to the Reds.[50] HUAC had caught the studios in the awkward position of having to admit that they had no anti-Communist films in production, and they hastily corrected that omission with such low-budget fare as *Guilty of Treason* (1949), *The Red Menace* (1949), *Sky High* (1951), *Invasion U.S.A.* (1952), and *My Son John* (1952), the latter directed by Leo McCarey after he named names.[51] In Harry Horner's *Red Planet Mars* (1952), the Americans perfect a technology for interplanetary communication and find that God is speaking to them from Mars. They rebroadcast His communication on Radio Free Europe, and some Russian peasants, hearing it on contraband radios, dig up a box containing a picture of the Madonna and Child and perform an outdoor Mass, before Russian soldiers arrive and machine-gun them all. Soon Russia's religious revival becomes a coup d'état, and a Christian patriarch, newly installed in the Kremlin, ushers in a world of Christian peace.

12 New Realities

In December 1947, as the Hollywood Ten prepared the appeals of their convictions for contempt, journalist Dorothy Thompson derided HUAC's whole premise, finding Hollywood's problem to be 'not that it is revolutionary, but that it is asinine.' On 6 December, *The New Yorker* proclaimed: 'If it is American to aim high and to respect one's own intelligence, then ninety per cent of Hollywood films are un-American.' Communist writer Isidor Schneider had said as much, asserting that Hollywood's 'reactionaries ... defend the world of "escapism" as a world of beauty and virtue opposed to evil and ugly reality,' thereby diverting attention from the 'shallowness' and 'hypocrisy' of the films they produce. John Houseman, in the middle of co-producing *Joy to the World*, a Broadway play about Hollywood's firing an executive for defending the idea of a free screen, complained that while Hollywood might set trends in clothing, it otherwise 'trots along ... somewhere quite near the rear end of the cultural parade.' At a *Life* roundtable on movies held in 1949, Dore Schary described the studios as so busy complying with censorship demands that they had adopted 'the barren and self-defeating aim of not displeasing anyone.' Samuel Goldwyn agreed, noting that fear of the censors had turned Hollywood movies into 'empty little fairy tales,' while Broadway producer Mark Hellinger said one could not make an 'honest, forceful' picture in Hollywood because the industry was 'gutless ... the whipping boy ... for all kinds of pressure groups,' with only itself to blame 'for everything that has happened to it.' Budd Schulberg stated that although Hollywood had 'gathered more geniuses, assistant geniuses, and apprentice geniuses than were assembled in Athens,' more creative ideas are thrown away during shop-talk banter at Hollywood parties than are seen in a year of movies. Thus, despite demands by Bosley Crowther and other critics 'for more films dealing honestly with contemporary American life,' for most Hollywood executives, 'the safest stories still seem to be those which do the people's dreaming for them.'[1]

Although similar allegations had been levelled against the industry ever since Breen took over, in Schary's view the problem was post-war America, where the 'way of life' had become a yearning 'for peace of mind' and 'security,' a yearning Schary had not only identified but meant to exploit in the film he was then producing, *The Next Voice You Hear*. Yale psychologist Leonard Doob, in response to the common charge that the studios inculcated inaccurate perceptions of America abroad, replied that Hollywood merely 'swims with the tide of public opinion,' and if its films mislead, it is only because everyone everywhere expects American life to be 'portrayed in one way and not in another.' Certainly the depiction of what was appropriate or inappropriate by way of behaviour or language, what was acceptable and what was questionable, what was deemed common or uncommon, was the same in movies as it was in the popular magazines and on the radio. But something was changing; some new movies really did have 'bite.' In April 1946 the Legion of Decency announced that the number of films rated 'B,' 'Objectionable in Part,' had doubled in only a year, a sort of seismic signal of disruptive forces at work beneath the surface.[2]

Nineteen forty-six, the year of William Wyler's *The Best Years of Our Lives*, was also the best year of Hollywood's financial life: of every dollar spent on entertainment, 90 cents went to movies, with 75 million to 90 million seatings a week and gross revenues totalling $1.7 billion.[3] Yet, even before *Paramount* shattered the industry's business model, the entertainment market had a new competitor. The Golden Age of movies had been saved from competition because of the radio manufacturers, who in the 1930s slowed the introduction of television for fear that this new home-entertainment device, superior to radio because it added moving visual images, would upset the retail market for radio sets, which had become a perpetual cash cow. War further delayed television, and with a paltry 8,000 sets operating in 1946, the new medium seemed no threat to the more than 17,000 theatres. As television prices began to plunge from the $400-$500 level, however, a booming economy afforded many people enough disposable income to buy a set, while easy credit let others pay over time. By 1948 televisions were selling briskly at 200,000 per month, and within a year they were in four million homes, leapfrogging in 1950 to 10 per cent of all households, yielding such 'status' that those with neither cash nor credit were installing aerials on their chimneys before they could afford the television itself. In 1952, with 108 television stations in 68 cities broadcasting to 15 million homes, the Federal Communications Commission stimulated growth by issuing many new station licences. By 1956 television was a mature industry with 500 stations reaching 35 million households.[4]

Gathering Darkness

Not until 1946, two years after it was liberated, did Paris experience that singular artifact of French/American friendship, *Casablanca*, with its patriotic prostitute joining the crowd in 'La Marseillaise,' drowning out the German officers' marching song. French critics were undoubtedly flattered by the film's *hommage* to a similar scene in Jean Renoir's *Grand Illusion* (1937), while also feeling a special resonance in other Hollywood fare. Jean-Pierre Chartier and Nino Frank coined the term 'film noir' to describe John Huston's *The Maltese Falcon* (1941), Billy Wilder's *Double Indemnity* (1944), Fritz Lang's *The Woman in the Window* (1944), and Edward Dmytryk's *Murder, My Sweet* (1944), all of which translated into film the 'tough' American detective stories the French loved. Among the translations of Raymond Chandler, Dashiell Hammett, James Hadley Chase, and James M. Cain were several in Gallimard's popular 'Série noire.'[5]

While France had looked to U.S. films to satisfy its own dark, post-Vichy, post-Occupation mood, it saw in them not just an occasional *hommage* but substantial borrowing from pre-war France, including Marcel Carné's *Quai des Brumes* (1938) and Julien Duvivier's *Pépé le Moko* (1936), the latter reprised by John Cromwell as *Algiers* (1938).[6] It was *Algiers* that Hal Wallis had wanted to churn through Warner Brothers' 'echo chamber' when he bought the rights to what would become *Casablanca*.[7] In Carné's *Le Jour se lève* (1939), written by Jacques Prévert, Jean Gabin lives in a one-room bedsitter in a nasty neighbourhood, where his unusually nasty job is sandblasting huge machine tools. While one of his two girlfriends says he should cut down on his smoking, he replies that his cough is only the sand in his lungs. After he shoots the man who had been the other boyfriend for both women, he observes of the police outside his door: 'What could they understand? You suddenly do it and that's that.' *The Long Night* (1947), Anatole Litvak's American remake, is that oddity, a studio film in which one could invest as much attention as in reading a Camus novel.

Among the characteristic elements of noir is the cold-hearted, murderous, double-dealing woman, such as Mary Astor in *The Maltese Falcon* and Jane Greer in Jacques Tourneur's *Out of the Past* (1947). The experienced male protagonist quickly realizes he is dealing with a *femme fatale* but must struggle mightily to keep from capitulating, as in Robert Montgomery's *Lady in the Lake* (1946), where the cynical gumshoe figures the vampish Audrey Totter is playing him for a sucker. When Totter goes to the kitchen to get some ice for the drinks, he comments: 'Imagine you needing ice cubes.' Barbara Stanwyck in *Double Indemnity* is bored enough with her comfortable California existence to take a lover and conspire with him to kill her husband for the insurance.[8]

Another signature noir element is the corrupt cop, a categorical Production Code violation. In H. Bruce Humberstone's *I Wake Up Screaming* (1941), the policeman who keeps hounding the protagonist to confess to the starlet's murder, turns out not only to have killed her himself, but to be insane, having turned his apartment into a quasi-religious shrine to her sainted memory. In Otto Preminger's *Fallen Angel* (1945), any number of people could have killed the sexy girl who works at the diner, but it turns out to have been the detective investigating the case, because he could not tolerate his own secret lust for her. In Stuart Heisler's 1942 version of Dashiell Hammett's *The Glass Key*, the whole municipal government is crooked, and we are invited to admire the two men who run the city that way, while Nicholas Ray's *On Dangerous Ground* (1951) features Robert Ryan as a brutalized inner-city cop. Abraham Polonsky's *Force of Evil* (1948) shows a corrupt political system from which a skilled lawyer wrongly thinks he can make a quick profit without bending his ethics too far, while Jules Dassin's *Brute Force* (1947) offers compelling portraits of prisoners as individual human beings, all brutalized and doomed under a sadistic head guard, the personification of a corrupt system.

In these films, not only politics, government, and 'dames' are nasty, but existence itself. In *The Glass Key*, William Bendix plays a sadistic thug with a glint in his eye for Alan Ladd. A newspaper magnate's gorgeous wife finds out that her husband is bankrupt, asks Ladd to sit down next to her on the couch, starts necking with him and tells her husband to go upstairs. Later the husband comes back down begging her to please come up to bed, but she refuses. A shot is heard; the husband has committed suicide. Neither the wife nor Ladd seems to care. Robert Siodmak's *Criss Cross* (1949) ends with the two lovers getting shot dead by the villain, for no reason other than because existence is arbitrary – a theme bound to strike a responsive chord with the existentialist French. In Andre de Toth's *Pitfall* (1948), Dick Powell has a good job in an insurance company, a beautiful wife, and a nice little boy, but chooses to have an affair. While it would have been easy to explain away his conduct via some horrific war experience disabling him from settling in comfortably in the post-war American Dream, Powell's character has no such excuse, since his war service had been in Denver. In Mark Robson's *Champion* (1949), up-from-nothing boxer Kirk Douglas leaves his wife, has affairs, treats his manager and his brother like dirt, and then – minutes after successfully defending his title – dies of a cerebral haemorrhage. In Robert Wise's *The Set-Up* (1949), Robert Ryan is a worn-out fighter still looking for a big break. His handlers think so little of his ability that they see no reason to tell him that the syndicate requires that he lose. When he wins, gangsters beat him to within an inch of his life. As Manny Farber noted, the film is packed with unrelenting malice, as when a blind boxing fan yells: 'Go for his eyes!'[9]

Earlier American films with a similar feeling were the crime movies of the late '20s and early '30s. Joe Breen had refused retrospective seals to Mervyn LeRoy's *Little Caesar* (1930), Howard Hawks's *Scarface* (1932), and William Wellman's *Public Enemy* (1931), leading Gilbert Seldes, one of the few who claimed that Breen was having a negative impact on art, to praise these pre-Breen gangster films for always having 'a character who drastically or sourly says what human beings really think, or mocks at heroics, or deflates pretensions.' LeRoy's courageous *I Am a Fugitive from a Chain Gang* (1932) could not have been produced two years later, as it tells of an innocent man driven to become a criminal by a corrupt and sadistic state prison system. (That the story was true, Breen would have found irrelevant.) However that genre might have developed if left to evolve on its own, Breen had robbed it of the moral anarchy and municipal corruption that had given it punch. And now, given Breen's limited conception of what comprised appropriate 'entertainment,' the new noir material seemed too much for him. He approved Fritz Lang's *Scarlet Street* (1945), even though in it the wrong man is executed for murder. Then, to Breen's great embarrassment, New York censors took the extraordinary step of banning the film outright, as if no amount of recutting – despite its PCA seal – could rectify its immorality. Regarding *Crossfire* (1947), he allowed a married man to come on to a 'B- [=Bar] girl.' The Legion of Decency thought Breen's vetting of King Vidor's *Beyond the Forest* (1949) totally inadequate (one theme is abortion) and issued an unprecedented 'C' ('Condemned') rating. In the vetting process for Jacques Tourneur's remake of *Easy Living* (1949), Breen's staff allowed Lucille Ball, playing a decent woman, to kiss Victor Mature and hint that she was in love with him, although she knew he was married. With Breen's formerly iron-fisted control of film content somehow slipping, in soliciting commiseration from Quigley he seemed uncharacteristically passive: 'There is, quite frankly, a disposition ... to fight the Code, and to kick over the traces. We are really having a desperate time of it. During the past month, at least, more than half of the material submitted here has had to be rejected. We have had nothing like this situation since the early days of '34 and '35.'[10] Thus, from an industry beset by television, by the *Paramount* litigation, and by HUAC, came a number of films – and a film genre – characterized by bitterness and achieving high artistic integrity by ignoring and rising above rules which Breen had thought essential for the nation's moral welfare, but which he now seemed unable to enforce.

If the Depression could escape its own pain via Busby Berkeley, Shirley Temple, and Andy Hardy, it could also summon up *Dead End* and *The Grapes of Wrath*, despite protests by studio executives who thought both projects anti-American. If the noir films happened to be in sync with the cynicism of a film industry beginning to unravel, did they also reflect a general public ennui, some new, dark underside of American life, in the midst of a post-war economic boom? In August 1946, Siegfried Kracauer wrote that movies not only intentionally cater to popular demands but also unwittingly 'reflect popular tendencies and inclinations.' While any run-of-the-mill anti-Nazi film, he noted, would include a character preaching about the superiority of democracy, in fact, the 'scenes of life under democracy' depicted in such films are 'strangely evasive,' indicating 'indecision rather than confidence, lip-service instead of action,' with 'pure cloak-and-dagger' dramatics taking the place of any solid repudiation of the Nazi ideology from which Kracauer was himself a refugee. And while run-of-the-mill Hollywood films could be dismissed as merely culturally incompetent, Kracauer also found deep cultural ambivalence in films of high competence, Alfred Hitchcock's *Shadow of a Doubt* (1943) and Orson Welles's *The Stranger* (1946), both of which borrow the chronic insecurity of living in a Nazi state, then transplant it into everyday America, where 'everybody is afraid of everybody else, and no one knows when or where the ultimate and inevitable horror will arrive' because we cannot know which of our smiling neighbours is in fact the psychopathic murderer. Kracauer found such themes to be not (as they were intended) suspenseful, but instead discomforting, revealing an 'inner disintegration' of society, arising from an 'uncontrolled sadism and apprehensiveness' to which the films offer no 'counter-measures that would work to restore mental stability,' because American life itself offers none.[11]

One could not imagine a more devastating critique of a society unintentionally exposed in its films: a society unstrung and lacking integrity. A few months later, John Houseman similarly observed that the contemporary 'tough' subjects did not express Hollywood's free will to make the films it wanted, but only reflected America's 'neurotic personality.' Irving Howe wrote:

> If only because it must conform to the psychological patterns of industrial society, mass culture is inseparably related to common experience. The notion that it concocts a never-never world of irrelevant fantasy is nonsense spread by the kind of people whose only complaint about Hollywood is that it isn't 'realistic' enough. In actuality, the audience accepts both mass culture and daily experience precisely to the degree that the two blend. By now neither can be maintained without the other, which is one reason why there prevails in this country such a blurred notion of what human experience is and such an inadequate notion of what it should be.

Howe related that a group of soldiers watching *The Ox-Bow Incident* (1943) sided with the lynch mob, a reaction directly contrary to what was intended by or reasonably to be expected from the film, but which did evidence the cultural ambivalence Howe sensed. Kracauer wrote: 'American audiences receive what Hollywood wants them to want; but in the long run audience desires, acute or dormant, determine the character of Hollywood films.' Every popular film 'conforms to certain popular wants; yet in conforming to them it inevitably does away with their inherent ambiguity. Any such film evolves these wants in a specific direction, [then] confronts them with one among several possible meanings. Through their very definiteness films thus determine the nature of the inarticulate from which they emerge.'[12] Hollywood, that is, simplifies, objectifies, and concretizes inchoate feelings. With the war over, the economy booming, and everything supposedly looking up, intelligent commentators sensed a culture of ambivalence and neurosis, and the signature theme of one significant home-grown genre, American noir, was a cynical malaise.

The first filmed version of James M. Cain's noir novel *The Postman Always Rings Twice* (1934) was French, Pierre Chenal's *Le Dernier Tournant* (1939). In 1942, Luchino Visconti directed an unauthorized adaptation, *Ossessione* (1942), having learned the new style under Jean Renoir. Not until 1946 would a U.S. version appear, directed by Tay Garnett, revealing adultery, murder, and sin, with an explicitness and cynicism that Joe Breen in his heyday would never have allowed to reach the screen. Albert Lewin's *The Private Affairs of Bel Ami* (1947) demonstrated that a Hollywood film could have a sufficiently authentic European flavour to merit praise by Jean Renoir. And by the time of Fritz Lang's extraordinary *Human Desire* (1954), derived from Renoir's *La Bête Humaine* (1938) and Zola's brilliant novel, the French influence seems fully realized and at home in a U.S. culture that had matured on a decade of domestic noir themes and nearly a decade of political paranoia. Gloria Grahame has been providing sexual favours to a rich man since she was sixteen. Her hothead husband, a railroad foreman (Broderick Crawford), gets fired and asks her to help him get reinstated. She does, by again bedding the rich man. Crawford finds out and makes her watch as he kills the man, thereafter forcing her to stay with him by keeping a compromising letter he forces her to write. She is now physically repulsed by Crawford and falls in love with railroad engineer Glenn Ford, whom she invites to kill her husband. Ford follows Crawford one night through the deserted railroad yard, but then decides not to carry out the crime and instead ends the affair with Grahame. Crawford sees Grahame boarding a train, and, believing that she is skipping out on him to join Ford, he finds her compartment and strangles her. Up in front – oblivious to all this – Ford is driving the train.

Neo-realism

Of the handful of films produced in Italy at war's end, Roberto Rossellini's *Roma città aperta* (*Open City*), premiering in Rome in September 1945, was the masterwork. Despite mixed critical notices, bans in some places by Church officials embarrassed about Catholic collaboration with the Nazis, and a determination by the Catholic Film Office that it was unsuitable for children, the film did fairly well in Italy, then won no prizes at Cannes.[13] While *Ossessione* was 'tough' in the stylish French manner then being imitated in the United States, Rossellini's film was 'realistic,' its pain arising not from a pastiche of existential cynicism superimposed on the story, but from what seemed a straightforward presentation of documentary-like facts.

Early in the war, the British had asserted that unless the Vatican illuminated itself at night, British planes would have no way to avoid bombing it when they appeared over Rome. When the Vatican replied that Mussolini would construe any illumination as an intended beacon for Allied bombers, the British said the Vatican had to choose which side it was on. In August 1943 the new Italian government of Pietro Badoglio, about to sign with the Allies the technical surrender of all Italian forces, declared Rome a demilitarized 'open city.' This was meaningless, because Germany reacted by invading Rome, itself declared Rome an open city, then militarized it, while setting up Mussolini in a puppet government in the north. Italian soldiers surrendered to the Allies or the Germans, or joined Mussolini, or became partisans against the Germans, or simply quit. Chaos reigned. A thousand Roman Jews were rounded up and sent to the death camps and, pursuant to Field Marshall Albert Kesselring's order, ten Italians were shot for each German killed by *partigiani*. As Francis Spellman, Giovanni Cicognani, and other high Church officials negotiated with President Roosevelt for a third – American – declaration that Rome was an open city so as to spare it from Allied bombing, Pius XII argued that if it were bombed, Italians would not just lose faith in the Allies but turn toward Communism. On the other hand, Roosevelt aide Harry Hopkins stated that there would be 'one hell of a row in the U.S.A. if Rome were not bombed owing to Catholic pressure.' The Curia thought FDR would take Rome in order to swell support in the November 1944 elections. Then, in June 1944, the first U.S. troops entered Rome through the Cinecittà complex on the Via Tuscolana, just as the last of Kesselring's units pulled out on the Via Flamina.[14]

In the end, a mix of strategic, tactical, and diplomatic considerations had combined to spare Rome, albeit leaving the exhausted and starving citizens to find in the term '*città aperta*' a bitter joke. Edmund Wilson, in Rome in the summer of 1945, observed that the Surrealist works of Leonor Fini, a painter he was visiting in the Piazza del Gesù, had lost the power to shock they had had when first shown to him in New York and Paris, since Rome itself had become Surrealist. Rossellini's film included real German soldiers who had been captured and interned by the new pro-Allied government during the German withdrawal. When a crowd watching the filming of a street scene saw these men, then saw Italian extras wearing German uniforms to earn a few lira, it turned hostile. The actress playing the female lead, Anna Magnani, later recalled the sequence in which her character is shot dead:

I hadn't rehearsed ... With Rossellini, great director that he was, we didn't rehearse: we filmed. He knew that once he had prepared the surroundings I would function ... [W]hen I came out the door onto the street ... I went back to the time when all over Rome the young people were being taken away ... The people against the wall were real people, ordinary people. The Germans were real Germans ... All of a sudden I wasn't me anymore, understand? I was the character. And, yes, Rossellini had prepared the street in a way that was really hallucinatory. The women had actually turned white telling each other how much they resented the Nazis! This made me feel the anxiety I showed on the screen. It was terrible! That was the way Rossellini worked. And at least with me, it worked ... He materialized what I felt. All it took was a gesture, a movement of an eye, and I was on my way.

Rossellini, who had accommodated himself to Mussolini's regime insofar as necessary to make films, described *Open City* as 'a sort of balance sheet of ... those twenty years of Fascism that ended with the great drama of the war, fruit of something that had been much stronger than us and had overwhelmed, crushed, and implicated us. Once the balance sheet had been drawn up, perhaps we could start with a fresh page.'[15]

Two months after Cannes, *Open City* was rediscovered in Paris, where it predated the influx of American noir. It crossed the Atlantic unceremoniously in a GI's duffle, and on 25 February 1946 opened at the tiny World Theater on West 49th Street. So-called 'art houses' were proliferating, from fifty at war's end to three hundred within several years, the reincarnation as well as the salvation of marginal second-run houses whose former patrons had been lost to television. Released from the $25,000 penalty for exhibiting non-seal films, these theatres were free to show foreign products as well as the handful of what would later be called 'independent' American films.[16] For a time, the *New Yorker*'s 'Current Cinema' listings included a category called 'Foreign, Special, etc.,' the issue of 17 December 1949 indicating thirteen such venues.

Open City's release – critic Bosley Crowther later wrote – had the effect of a lightning bolt. John McCarten in the *New Yorker* issue of 2 March 1946 called it the best film ever to come out of Italy, a meaningless comment for the vast majority of Americans who had never seen one. The lore surrounding *Open City* included rumours that it had been shot on whatever film could be had, such as the oddments Rossellini scrounged from Rod Geiger of the U.S. Signal Corps because they were scratched or fogged. Thus *Open City* seemed like scraps of newsreel, consistent with its original title: *Storie d'ieri* (*Yesterday's Stories*). For a small audience of New York's sophisticates and intellectuals, years of watching grainy war footage, coupled with the chronic disappointment of experiencing thematically weak Hollywood fare notable only for its lavish production values, had primed them both for such 'realism' as Magnani's death in the street, and for technical shortcomings no domestic studio would ever tolerate. During the filming of *Sunset Boulevard*, Billy Wilder reportedly quipped to cameraman John F. Seitz: 'Johnny, keep it out of focus. I want to win the foreign-picture award.'[17]

Anna Magnani, 'La Lupa,' the perennial toast of Rome as well as its living she-wolf symbol, was said to have been born in Alexandria of an Egyptian father and an Italian/Jewish mother, earning her way through Rome's Academy of Dramatic Art by singing off-colour songs in questionable venues. *Time* described her as 'fiery,' a less reticent Harold Clurman choosing 'volcanic,' while Rossellini called her the greatest acting genius since Eleonora Duse. But *Open City*'s most important character is an anti-Gestapo priest, amalgamated from two actual priests who had been shot by the Germans for coming to the aid of the partisans and Allied prisoners. For him, Rossellini cast Aldo Fabrizi, Italy's best-known vaudeville performer. The priest's middle-aged, slightly overweight persona seems at first sentimentally conventional, as when in a store he turns a statue of Saint Francis around so it will not be 'looking' at a statue of a nude woman. But this is no insipid, bicycle-riding, kite-flying Hollywood padre. Focused on large moral issues, he chooses not to lecture the haggard heroine for getting pregnant before marriage. In his anti-German commitment, he is not reluctant to work hand-in-glove with Communists, the Church's sworn enemies. He hides a partisan's rifle in the bed linens of an old man, and when the latter tries to betray him by yelling to the Germans downstairs, the priest hits him over the head with a frying pan and tells the Germans he is administering last rites.[18] In the end, in a vacant lot, when the Italian firing squad refuses to execute him, a German officer shoots him with a pistol.

James Agee's review in the April 1946 issue of the *Nation* included a comment Rossellini would have endorsed: 'I have no doubt that plenty of priests, in Italy and elsewhere, behaved as bravely as this one. Nor do I doubt that they and plenty of non-religious leftists, working with them in grave danger, respected each other as thoroughly as shown here. I see little that is incompatible between the best that is in leftism and in religion – far too little to measure against the profound incompatibility between them and the rest of the world.' While one could hardly expect Agee's perspective to be endorsed by the virulently anti-Communist bishops of the American Catholic Church, the liberal lay Catholic publication *Commonweal* did praise the film, while Martin Quigley's son in the *Motion Picture Daily* of 6 March 1946 said of it: 'the courage of ... the priest is heroic and gives a high over-all character to the picture,' with Fabrizi 'superb in a moving role.' The Legion of Decency rated it 'B,' objectionable in part but not forbidden, the same rating given *Best Years of Our Lives*, a film similarly combining strong patriotic themes with certain disapproved elements (there, a young woman's decision to break up the failing marriage of the man she loves). While *Open City* has often been acclaimed as the greatest work of Italian neo-realism, Peter Bondanella has characterized it as exemplifying 'Rossellini's message of Christian humanism.'[19]

In 1945 a blue-ribbon Harvard panel, including historian Arthur Schlesinger, language specialist I.A. Richards, classicist John Finley, and biologist George Wald, had concluded that one did not need to be a 'soft paternalist' to believe that never in history 'have vulgarity and debilitation beat so insistently on the mind as they now do from screen, radio, and newsstand. Against these the book or movie which speaks with authentic largeness to the whole people has no easy victory.' *Open City* spoke with authenticity, even if not to 'the whole people,' there being in America no cultural infrastructure by which to embrace such a work. John Houseman called it a 'deeply moral picture' of people heroically sacrificing their lives against oppression, to be contrasted with Garnett's version of *The Postman Always Rings Twice*, one of Hollywood's contemporary 'tough' films, portraying the United States as 'a hung-over people with confused objectives groping their way through a twilight of insecurity and corruption.' But Kracauer's was the highest compliment, noting that American culture would not be redeemed until its films portrayed, like *Open City*, 'the principles of human integrity at grips with a deranged world – and shows them as positive forces, with a reality at least equal, if not superior to, the forces of cruelty and violence and to the fear upon which these feed.'[20] While the subject matter of Rossellini's film is a world come apart, the 'human integrity' of his characters promises the possibility of restoring moral sanity, while America, neither bombed in the war nor invaded and occupied, nevertheless could offer in its films nothing more than the passive reflection of a domestic culture that had lost its moral compass, as if neither U.S.

film-makers nor U.S. audiences were capable of recognizing and saluting real courage.

Open City ran at the World Theater for an extraordinary twenty months. Contemplating a broader audience, distributor Joseph Burstyn and his partner Arthur Mayer applied to Breen for a PCA seal. In May 1946, Breen conditioned a seal on, among other things, the following: 'Eliminate ... "Yes – and in my condition – a rather late wedding." Also eliminate shots of [Magnani] rubbing her swollen stomach. This rubbing of the stomach to call attention to pregnancy not only will be "repellent" to mixed audiences in American theatres, but it violates the provision of the Production Code prohibiting explicit treatment of illicit sex relationship[s].' Burstyn and Mayer chose for over a year to ignore Breen's demands, seeing no need to cut a film that continued to do well in art theatres in unexpurgated form. It received helpful publicity when the 4 March 1946 issue of *Life* noted that its 'violence and plain sexiness steadily project a feeling of desperate and dangerous struggle which Hollywood seldom approaches.' Once the film had saturated the art-house market and attained sufficient notoriety to warrant a wider distribution, Burstyn and Mayer made the deletions Breen demanded and obtained a PCA seal.[21]

Open City's success led to U.S. financing for *Paisà* (1946), called by Kracauer 'one of the greatest films ever made.' Again Rossellini chose a title with an ironic barb, *Paisà* (*Paisan* in the United States), the colloquial blend of fondness and disdain by which American soldiers referred to the locals, their friends/enemies/captives. Among the film's surprises, the GI who befriends a homeless orphan in wartime Naples is an African-American. But the importation of Dots Johnson and several other professional American actors had been a condition of the U.S. financing. Rossellini's own preference was either for actors of Magnani's and Fabrizi's stature or for 'nobodies who can be properly directed. No one in between.'[22] Commonly, Rossellini would employ people who happened to be standing around watching the production, much as the artist Kurt Schwitters fabricated his work from 'found objects' like buttons and ticket stubs. Two of the other Americans in the film, Gar Moore and Robert Van Loon, were actual U.S. soldiers, while the German POWs are played by real German POWs, and the monks by real monks, their on-screen conversation regarding religious issues resembling their discussions with Rossellini between takes.

Paisan looks unsparingly at human cruelty, unmediated even by the slick cynicism of American noir. Although *Paisan* violated the Code in several significant respects, Rossellini's reputation was already so high that Burstyn and Mayer obtained for it a PCA seal, Breen later chastising the employee who issued it. While the film warranted a 'C' (Condemned) rating under the Legion's published criteria, it obtained a 'B,' as had *Open City*. It played at the World Theater at an admission price of $1.80, the highest in New York. Martin Scorsese has related that when his grandparents saw *Open City* and *Paisan*, they cried, Rossellini having delivered 'both the tragedy of the war and the spiritual fortitude of the Italian people,' yielding 'an indelible achievement.' Among other Rossellini films suddenly finding U.S. distribution was *Deutschland im Jahre Null* (*Germany, Year Zero*, 1947), portraying a boy in bombed-out Berlin who lives by stealing and who, at the suggestion of his predatory, child-stalking, pro-Nazi teacher/pimp, poisons his own father. In January 1949, New York's censors, perhaps willing tacitly to acknowledge Rossellini as a genius outside the usual rules, or recognizing that the film would never get a distribution wide enough to offend middle-class tastes, approved it without changes. Ohio, Maryland, and Pennsylvania required some deletions. Its distributor was misguided even to apply for a seal, and Breen in October 1949 described the film as 'thoroughly and completely unacceptable' under the Code, in part because 'the prospect of a child of twelve murdering his ailing father ... and of destroying himself by hurtling himself from a wrecked building, are hardly fit subjects, to say the least, for general family patronage.' Jack Vizzard, a former seminarian on Breen's staff, thought the film unfairly concentrated on people who had been 'damaged spiritually and morally' by the war, when perhaps '70% or 80%' of Berlin's population had undoubtedly 'retained some semblance of moral health.' Martin Quigley, still commending films that offered 'charm' and 'escape,' condemned works 'from the unhappy foreign left, dripping with the bitter juices of the complaining art of a defeated world.' More recently, however, Mira Liehm has written that the boy's story, inspired by the death of Rossellini's own son, is the 'foremost example' of the director's 'absorption with the fundamental sentiments of Christianity.'[23]

The drug-taking, corruption, prostitution, criminality, patricide, and similar themes in these films show the degradation of war and a civilization threatened with collapse. They were far 'tougher' (borrowing John Houseman's word) than noir in that they depicted – relentlessly, up close, and on location – a civilization unstrung. As Rossellini commented in 1952, neo-realism expresses 'a need that is proper to modern man, to tell things as they are, to understand reality ... in a pitilessly concrete way, conforming to that typically contemporary interest' in 'statistical and scientific results.' Fred Zinnemann borrowed heavily from Rossellini in *The Search* (1948), portraying orphans in the American sector of Berlin, keying off the relationship between one of them and a friendly GI, played by Montgomery Clift.[24] Particularly disturbing is the scene of a boy who, under the terrifying delusion that American Red Cross workers want to gas him, tries to escape and drowns in a river. To portray such a thing in an American film would have been unimaginable without Rossellini's influence.

The Bicycle Thief

Another landmark in neo-realism, Vittorio De Sica's *Sciuscià* (*Shoe-Shine*, 1946), portrays a prison for juvenile delinquents. Hollywood was sufficiently impressed to award it a 'Special' Oscar in 1947, nine years before the Motion Picture Academy established a 'Best Foreign Language Film' category. Burstyn, U.S. distributor of *Open City* and *Paisan*, now imported De Sica's *Ladri di biciclette* (1948), a heart-rending portrayal of moral breakdown caused by desperation and poverty. De Sica had reportedly rejected the substantial Hollywood budget that would have come with casting Cary Grant in the lead role, choosing instead the metal worker whose haggard visage and shabby jacket would thereafter become – alongside Magnani's death scene in *Open City* – a poster-like image that could summon the feelings evoked by the films themselves. Uncut, *The Bicycle Thief* (the Americans imitating the French by translating the title into the singular) won the New York Film Critics Circle award for Best Foreign Film in 1949. Although it was nominated for the same 'Special' Oscar *Shoe-Shine* had garnered earlier, Breen nevertheless refused to award it a seal, thus placing Hollywood in the awkward position of saluting a film's excellence while disapproving its distribution. Breen had successfully demanded the deletion of a few frames revealing a little boy's genitals in *Open City*, and the brief full-frontal shot of boys taking showers in *Shoe-Shine*. He now wanted cut from *The Bicycle Thief* one short scene in which the boy, his back to us, is about to urinate against a wall, and another where the hero runs through a bordello whose employees, fully clothed, are eating breakfast. De Sica responded to these demands by cable: 'Let's be frank. Is there more sex in this picture or in the average American [film] ... ? May I recall that noble religious town of Brussels, Belgium whose emblem is a boy in said circumstances whose statue stands in one of its squares.' While

Breen was only enforcing his adamantine rule against toilet gags, Bosley Crowther pointed out that in *Cheaper by the Dozen*, Clifton Webb gets away with telling his children: 'Anyone who wants to see Mrs Murphy had better do it now.'[25] De Sica's film, its general distribution still blocked by Breen, won the 'Special' Oscar in 1949, as well as the Best Foreign Film award at the Golden Globes.

Burstyn could repeat the manoeuvre played out earlier with *Open City* by showing *Bicycle Thief* in a scattering of art houses as word-of-mouth generated interest, before making the cuts necessary for a seal and a wider distribution. But the several works Burstyn had previously imported had by now established a viable U.S. market for Italian cinema. This fact, coupled with the easily accessible sentimentality which differentiated *Bicycle Thief* from Rossellini's more astringent aesthetic, suggested moving forward immediately with a wide release. Burstyn thus told Breen that since *Bicycle Thief* had been deemed acceptable to the Legion of Decency (albeit with a 'B') and to the censors of Ohio, Pennsylvania, and New York, he would appeal Breen's decision to the full board of what was now called the Motion Picture Association of America (MPAA).[26] While his chances of success were mathematically hopeless and he lost, he could at least exploit the appeal by clever newspaper advertisements featuring a little boy pleading with the public not to let him be cut out of the film.

Given Burstyn's newspaper advertisement inviting the public to side with the winsome little boy against the censors, as well as his prior gambit of simply disregarding Breen's demands until the art-house market had been tapped out, Breen was angry, confiding to another MPAA employee: 'I share, thoroughly, your worry concerning people like Burstyn, who give us an immense amount of trouble ... refuse to accept the judgment of our Board, capitalize on the whole matter in their advertising, and then – after they have sucked their limited market dry – come around looking for our seal.' Burstyn pointedly told Breen: 'I reluctantly have come to the conclusion that there may be motives involved in your refusal to issue a seal of approval for this artistic masterpiece other than those mentioned in your letter.' His meaning was clear: Burstyn had injected competition into what was otherwise a closed, monopoly business, the extraordinary films he distributed having repeatedly prompted respected U.S. critics to deride Hollywood's domestic product as insipid and inferior. Therefore, just as the Government was dismantling Hollywood's monopoly and audiences were staying home to watch television, Burstyn was accusing the industry of essentially what the Justice Department had identified years earlier: the use of Breen's office to block outside competitors from offering the public alternative artistic perspectives. Breen and Burstyn were now confirmed enemies. With Burstyn intransigent, De Sica went around him by having a lawyer approach Breen about a compromise: deleting the brothel scene, while keeping the scene of the little boy. Meanwhile, in October 1950, Burstyn announced that the powerful Skouras Theatres chain would flout the Code and book the uncensored version of *Bicycle Thief* into all of their New York–area theatres. The owners of two other large chains did the same.[27]

Not that *Bicycle Thief* and Burstyn's other offerings posed any serious economic challenge. But Hollywood was becoming desperate, in a tailspin without knowing how to right itself. Since the industry had been premised on the fact that everyone went to the movies, and since the market had always been saturated with whatever the studios produced, Hollywood had failed to monitor customer preferences, moods, and attitudes in any scientific way. Harry Cohn announced that he judged whether a film would be profitable by whether he squirmed in his seat, leading Herman Mankiewicz to the unpleasant observation that the whole world was wired to Harry Cohn's ass. Jack Warner was similarly visceral; if he got up to pee, the picture stinks. But the moguls were now old men. Visual entertainment was a zero-sum game, a poll indicating that its availability at home would decrease people's desire to go out. Television had no admission price, allowed one to stay put, and constituted a free babysitter. Goldwyn now faced facts with a characteristic locution: why should anybody go to the movies, when he can see 'no worse' at home? Since Breen's arrival, Hollywood had dictated a standard 'taste' in visual family entertainment, only to find that in fact Americans had no loyalty to Hollywood films once they could get 'no worse' from a competitor at home. Between 1946 and 1949, weekly movie attendances fell to 50 million and the profits of the eight top studios plummeted from $120 million to $33.6 million. By 1950 only 10 per cent of films broke even on U.S. bookings, down from 80 per cent pre-war. A survey showed that among children who lived in homes with televisions, movie-going was down 49 per cent.[28] In and around Philadelphia, television succeeded in doing what even the combined forces of Cardinal Dougherty and the Depression could not do: the closure of over 100 theatres in two years. In Southern California, 134 venues closed. By 1953 the total number of functioning cinemas nationally sank to 3,000. Fewer than a third were profitable from ticket sales, with another 38 per cent managing to stay afloat via the high margins at the refreshment counter.[29]

Although foreign films (unlike television) represented only a minor financial irritant, several films were irksome for the additional reason that they demonstrated a success formula utterly unlike Hollywood's. Laurence Olivier's *Henry V* (1944), a film Hollywood neither would nor could have made, grossed $1 million following its release in the United States in 1946, impressing Hollywood both by its special beauty (which yielded Olivier a special Oscar) and by the advanced marketing techniques used to attract American audiences to such highbrow stuff. Then the industry awarded Olivier's *Hamlet* the Academy Award for Best Picture in 1948, over *Johnny Belinda*, *The Treasure of the Sierra Madre*, and *The Snake Pit*. Although another nominee, *The Red Shoes* (1948; dir. Michael Powell and Emeric Pressburger), had shown no particular promise in Britain, it ran for over a year in New York and eventually grossed over $2 million.

Since producers no longer knew what audiences wanted, no one was more shocked than they when Billy Wilder's *The Lost Weekend* (1945), dealing with the ugly subject of delirium tremens, became a blockbuster success, then beat *The Bells of St Mary's* for the Best Picture Oscar. That two unlikely British films were nominated for Best Picture in 1948, that a black-and-white rendition of *Hamlet* won, and that both films were highly profitable in the U.S. market, were indicia that Hollywood's long-standing relationship with its foreign markets was no longer a one-way street. Great Britain, France, and other nations imposed regulations geared to stimulate local production by limiting the proportion of total screen time allowed to Hollywood products, and although several studios hoped to get such restrictions lifted by importing several foreign films, and producing several abroad using local professionals, the net result of these foreign regulations gave Hollywood the sense that with the world's theatres finally open again, it was being deprived of what had been 'gravy' in good times, a safety margin in bad times.

And these were the bad times. Industry bankers asserted that if an 'A' picture costing $2 million grosses only $2 million, it makes more sense to produce a '$150,000 stinker that grosses $160,000.' While $150,000 stinkers proliferated, they too failed to get back their costs. And as Paramount, RKO, Warners, Twentieth Century-Fox, and Loew's/MGM began selling off their downtown, first-run theatres under *Paramount*'s divestment order, they found that television's impact on ticket sales had depressed the market, so that the smaller, independent exhibitors who for a generation had been frozen out of the handsome cash flow these first-run theatres had generated, no longer wished to purchase them. Now vast caverns of empty seats, their sheer size and opulence rendering them too expensive to maintain, they soon became musty hulks, the real estate on which they stood becoming their only selling point, although the post-war flight to the suburbs had left many downtowns as moribund as the shuttered picture palaces that had once been their pride. In perhaps the most ironic twist, Chicago's sumptuous Sheridan Theater, built in the late 1920s by the brilliant architect J.E.O. Pridmore in a flamboyant mix of baroque and Corinthian, was converted into a synagogue.[30] By 1956, despite a post-war baby boom that netted 26 million more potential customers, the movie business was dying.

13 Visions of Mary

The Virgin Birth and the Immaculate Conception

For some, it is Mary's Davidic lineage that makes Jesus the Messiah prophesied in the Old Testament, since for them, Joseph's own ancestry in the House of David is genetically irrelevant. While the question of Mary's biological heritage will never be resolved, it is clear that she had neither wealth nor social station. As Mary Hines has written: 'God chose a marginalized person, someone whom society would have regarded as unworthy, for a central role in human salvation.'[1] Paul (Rom. 1:3–4) calls Jesus the 'foreordained Son of God,' 'born of him according to the flesh of the offspring of David,' without seeing fit even to mention the name of Jesus' mother, as if she were only a vehicle for her child's Davidic genes. Most of the Bible's scattered references to Mary deal with her only tangentially and always in reference to Jesus or the Holy Ghost. In several passages Jesus curtly distances himself from her and from the trappings of a nuclear family, preferring the spiritual family of the faithful.[2] And in the crucial passage of Jesus rising from the dead, it is not his mother, but Mary Magdalene, who is prominent.

Elsewhere, however, Mary is the focus of attention. In Luke 1:26–38, God sends the angel Gabriel to tell her that as a virgin she will be visited by the Holy Ghost and that she will give birth to a 'Holy One ... called the Son of God.' Gabriel tells Mary she is 'highly favoured' ($\chi\alpha\rho\iota\tau\delta\omega$) with God, and Elizabeth in Luke 1:42 calls her 'blessed' ($\varepsilon\dot{\upsilon}\lambda o\gamma\dot{\varepsilon}\omega$). Textual evidence is strong both for God's choosing Mary, and for the miracle of the virginal conception and birth. Luke, said to be a physician, had no doubts, and Matthew (1:18) could not be plainer: 'Now the origin of Christ was in this wise. When Mary his mother had been betrothed to Joseph, before they came together, she was found to be with child by the Holy Spirit.' An angel of the Lord visits Joseph in a dream to explain: 'that which is begotten in her is of the Holy Spirit,' in fulfilment of Isaias 7:14: 'Behold a virgin shall conceive, and bear a son, and his name shall be called Emmanuel.' And in John 19:26–7, Jesus addresses his mother from the cross ('Woman, behold, thy son') and tells a disciple, 'Behold, thy mother,' which the disciple takes as an instruction to take Mary into his home, but which readers may take to indicate that Mary (rather than Eve) is the mother of all.[3]

Out of Luke, Matthew, and John emerges Mary both as Virgin Mother and as Θεοτόκος, 'Mother-of-God.' In Luke 1:22–56 and 2:8–20 she is an extraordinary figure, the Annunciation unfolding the story of a rural, adolescent girl chosen as God-bearer and receiving divine knowledge, exclusively and in confidence. Luke's account of the Visitation with the post-menopausal Elizabeth, similarly, is a touching story of confidential knowledge. Mary and Elizabeth are both pregnant, not by their husbands but through miraculous interventions. When Mary speaks, the fetus within Elizabeth 'leap[s]' in her womb and Elizabeth is filled with the Holy Spirit, causing her to exclaim: 'Blessed art thou among women and blessed is the fruit of thy womb!' – words later incorporated into the *Ave Maria* and then into the rosary. It is a powerful moment. Thus did Luke grasp and elucidate the special, confidential relationship among the young, rural girl, the older Elizabeth, and God, concerning the miraculous births with which both women are blessed.[4]

This extraordinary account appealed to women, including those who looked forward to having a baby and those who prayed to have one when it seemed impossible. For those who instead chose a life of abstinence, the *Protoevangelium* or *Infancy Narrative* of James, circa 150 C.E., provides an account of Mary's parents, Joachim and Anna, a sterile couple who asked God for a child and, when their request was answered, raised their daughter as a holy person, providing to all women an exemplum of chastity.[5] In patristic times, with martyrdom no longer a common conclusion to an ideally Christian life, the consummation devoutly to be wished was the self-willed asceticism Mary shared with the Pauline Christ.[6] Pursuant to that tradition, Mary remained *semper virgo*, a virgin throughout her life.[7] Another tradition posited that Mary maintained her virginity during Jesus' birth.[8] Summing up, Pope Paul IV in the mid-sixteenth century declared Mary's virginity *ante partum*, *in partu*, and *post partum*.[9]

Mark and John do not mention the Virgin Birth, while Paul, rather than simply declare Jesus' divine paternity, instead describes him (Rom. 1:3–4) as descended from the seed of David and then marked out, designated, or fore-ordained ($'ορίζω$) to be the son of God, as if in fulfilment (Acts 13:3 ($'εκπληρόω$)) of a prophecy. Nevertheless, that a divine miracle was responsible for Jesus' conception became the plain and complete answer to pagans, Jews, sceptics, and heretics who asserted that Jesus was an ordinary man, conceived and born in the ordinary way. The Council of Ephesus (431 C.E.) determined that Jesus' divine birth would be a fundamental tenet of Christianity, denouncing as heresy the Nestorian theory that Mary was the mother of Jesus the man but not the God.[10]

Regarding Mary's own birth, most accepted that human generative activity was at work when Joachim and Anna conceived Mary, but debated whether Mary was initially conceived in the state of sin common to all humanity after the Fall, then sanctified in the womb, or whether she was free from original sin from the first instant of insemination. To choose the latter (Bernard of Clairvaux and Thomas Aquinas argued) was to take Mary outside the Fall and thus to undermine the fundamental doctrine (Matt. 1:21; Rom. 3:9–25, 5:12–21) that all humans are in a state of sin and require redemption by Christ.[11] Some urged that only a human soul can be redeemed by Christ, and that at fertilization a fetus has no soul, so that Mary's redemption occurred, not at the original fertilization (so-called 'active conception'), but at a later moment of 'ensoulment' when the fetus is invested with what makes it human (referred to as 'passive conception').[12] When ensoulment occurred remained unsettled, although many adopted the Aristotelian theory (forty days from fertilization for males, eighty or ninety days for females), and many, equating ensoulment with 'animation,' believed it to be marked by the mother's first sense of movement. Then around 1300 the Franciscan Duns Scotus took Mary outside the Fall by declaring that Christ spared her from original sin, making her the only human to merit that status.[13] The fifteenth-century Council of Basel, better known for its condemnation of Joan of Arc as a witch, affirmed this view. In 1482, Pope Sixtus IV held that it was not heretical, while in 1546 the Council of Trent affirmatively held it to be true. In 1617 the Church prohibited works contending that Mary had partaken of any earthly sin, most Catholic thinkers thereafter accepting this as the doctrine of the Immaculate Conception.[14]

Mary was thus viewed as a unique human: virgin, mother-of-God, and sinless because she was not implicated in the Fall. 'Spell Eva back,' the sixteenth-century poet Robert Southwell wrote, 'and Ave shall you finde.' Eve, it was said, was the woman of disobedience, sin, intercourse, the agonies of childbirth, the parent of fallen humanity and death, while Mary was the woman of purity, virginity, the bearer of God and of everlasting life, an Eve restored into an unashamed and presexual Eden, thus replicating Paul's contrast between Adam and Christ in Rom. 5:12–21. Ephrem the Syrian (d. 373 C.E.) chose a succinct legal metaphor: Mary paid Eve's debt and tore up the note.[15]

Ineffabilis Deus

While many mid-nineteenth-century American Protestants saw the papacy as a foreign monarchy whose edicts contravened republican and democratic values, in Italy these same republican and democratic values were threatening the papacy's very existence. Early in his pontificate, Pius IX impressed many as a liberal reformer. 'He was the idol of Italy,' E.E.Y. Hales has written, 'fantastically popular ... Any crowd, in any town or village, shouted viva Pio Nono, whatever the object it had in view.' The laser-eyed Metternich, however, could see that in fact Pius was too naïve and too ill-advised to be the universal solution everyone wanted or needed him to be. G.M. Trevelyan described him as 'kindly, narrow, pleasingly childish, shrewd in small matters and stupid about great affairs,' while F. Marion Crawford called him 'politically too credulous for any age, and too diffident, if not too timid, for the age in which he lived. His private virtues made him a model to the Christian world, while his political weakness made him the sport of his enemies. The only stable thing in him was his goodness; everything else was in perpetual vacillation. In every true account of every political action of Pius the Ninth, the first words are, "the Pope hesitated."'[16]

The Risorgimento, the ongoing drive for the unification of Italy, reached its first crescendo in 1848, intimidating Pius IX into promising democratic reform in the Papal States, the wide expanse of north-central Italy stretching as far as Rimini and Ancona on the Adriatic, and halfway to Naples on the Tyrrhenian. In November of that year, Pius narrowly avoided arrest and perhaps assassination by escaping in the garb of a common priest, while the man he had appointed to administer the Papal States, hated by the vast majority of Pius's three million subjects, was murdered.[17] In February 1849, a newly convened legislative body voted overwhelmingly to end Pius's temporal rule and to establish a democracy called the Republic of Rome. Pius found refuge at Gaeta under the protection of the Bourbon despot, Ferdinand II of Naples, and then obtained the military support of France, Austria, and Spain. He did not return to Rome until 1850, after the arrival of a French garrison staved off Italian forces.

Allied with three foreign, Catholic states against Italy's republican, democratic, and nationalistic movements, Pius would evolve into 'the most resolute of the public enemies of liberalism,' even while his personal honesty, simplicity, cheerfulness, and piety caused his name still to be bandied about as the natural choice to rule any federated Italian nation. While negotiations in the late 1850s between Napoleon III and Italian nationalist Camillo Cavour might have yielded this result, they ultimately collapsed. While Napoleon III's troops continued to provide Pius with personal protection, the pope's own armies lost successive battles with troops under Victor Emmanuel II of Savoy, and by the autumn of 1860 the papal territories had shrunk to the immediate environs of Rome. Among Pius's reactions was a lashing out against all 'modernist' ideas, as a traveller found when, arriving at the Civitavecchia, a guard confiscated not only his Machiavelli but also his Molière. Pius wrote to Napoleon III: 'I remain almost without Temporal Power ... but without spiritual dominion will I never be, for all men are powerless to take that from the hands of the Vicar of Jesus Christ ... who enjoys a promise which is infallible and omnipotent, whatever certain wretched books may say.' A letter Metternich had written back in December 1847 now seemed prescient: 'What the Pope has already destroyed by his liberalism is his own temporal power; what he is unable to destroy is his spiritual power; it is that power which will cancel the harm done by his worthless counselors. But to what dangerous conflicts have not these men exposed the man and the cause they wanted to serve!' Among Pius's strategies to replace temporal with spiritual power was to foster the arts of popular piety, such as granting indulgences in exchange for engaging in specific Marian devotions.[18]

By 1848 the doctrine of Mary's Immaculate Conception enjoyed wide acceptance and had been embraced by most Catholic orders, with Giovanni Perrone's De Immaculato B.V. Mariae Conceptu (1847) meriting ten reprintings in five years. Pius IX appointed several commissions to poll the world's bishops regarding the feasibility of elevating the doctrine of the Immaculate Conception to the level of Church dogma, that is, a truth deemed to have been revealed directly by God or through the apostles and – as such – irrevocably binding on all Catholics. Toward that end, on 2 February 1849, having fled to Gaeta not to save his own life but rather (as one scholar has said) to enlist the Holy Mother's favour in his time of troubles, he issued the encyclical *Ubi Primum*, which stimulated further discussion. Although the United States was a democratic republic and the Papal States were said to be the most arbitrarily administered monarchy in Europe, the American bishops, meeting in Baltimore, not only responded affirmatively to Pius's Marian initiative but provided the embattled pope with their collective moral support.[19]

Although sixteenth-century Jesuits claimed to have discovered a parchment yielding apostolic proof for the Immaculate Conception, Dominicans proved it to be a forgery. The first challenge Pius IX thus faced was that of overcoming the fundamental tenet that the *depositum fidei*, the evidence comprising the deposit of faith, was complete upon the death of the last apostle, by declaring a dogma in the absence of apostolic authority. While such a declaration would have been an extraordinary act even if ratified by the College of Cardinals and/or by the world's bishops, Pius IX set himself an even more ambitious goal. With the temporal rule of the papal monarchy disintegrating, he chose to declare the dogma by himself, thus establishing that a pope, acting unilaterally and irrespective of his temporal status, could – in effect – speak 'infallibly.'[20]

Orestes Brownson, sensing in 1853 a widespread desire to have the Immaculate Conception declared a Church dogma, wrote: 'Even if it were true that the devotion to Mary holds a more prominent place in modern than in ancient devotion, it would not be any argument against it, for the times specially demand it, and it is only by the general prevalence of this devotion that the age can be saved from heresy, idolatry, superstition, and irreligion.' Pius asked the writers of one of the draft declarations to combine with the dogma of the Immaculate Conception a denunciation of modernism. That Mary could be the Church's champion against democracy and republicanism was the view of the French abbot Jules Morel, who wrote in 1857: 'If Mary alone has been conceived without sin, then the whole of humanity is conceived in sin and bears the consequences of it ... [I]t follows that the government of men will always have need of a preventive and repressive system, and that self-government is nothing but a utopia. The United States, whose success has for a moment disturbed the faith of the weak, will not delay long in proving this by its history, young as it is.' Although Pius himself issued similar attacks against values Americans held dear, he opted not to do so in this instance, and in fact included five Americans among the bishops he chose to peruse a late draft. Archbishop Francis Patrick Kenrick of Baltimore and Bishop Michael O'Connor of Pittsburgh both offered substantive comments, recommending that historical objections to the doctrine of the Immaculate Conception be acknowledged, and that questionable historical authorities be deleted. While O'Connor wanted the declaration to include a statement to the effect that it had the bishops' consent, this was rejected, an archbishop noting that since the document purported to be an infallible papal decree, to suggest that it required conciliar approval was not just counterproductive but even smacked of Protestantism. Pius received word of what Mary had told two children at La Salette, near Grenoble in 1846, and although he did not reveal the message, he reportedly did relate that one of the children in the course of writing out the message had asked how to spell 'infallibility.' Then in *Ineffabilis Deus* (8 Dec. 1854), Pius unilaterally declared:

> The doctrine which teaches that the Most Blessed Virgin Mary, in the first moment of her conception, by a special gift of grace from Almighty God, in consideration of the merits of Jesus Christ, the Saviour of mankind, was preserved pure from all taint of original sin, is revealed by God, wherefore it shall also be the object of sure and certain faith on the part of all believers. If therefore, any – which God forbid! – should dare to think otherwise in their heart, than as we have determined, they shall learn and know, that they are condemned by their own judgment, that they have made shipwreck of the faith, and are separated from the unity of the Church, and that further they are liable by their own act to the punishments fixed by law, if they presume orally or in writing, or in any other outward way, to make known what they think in their hearts.[21]

Mary and Bernadette

In 1849, Pius founded the Feast of Our Lady, *Mater admirabilis*, establishing the adolescent Mary as a subject of devotion, after seeing a fresco of her by a young French postulant in the Convent of the Sacred Heart at the top of the Spanish Steps. By one account, the fresco was so amateurishly garish when painted in 1844 that the mother superior kept it behind a curtain, although when Pius visited in 1846 and asked what was behind the curtain, the fresco was revealed and was found to be beautiful. Soon it was held responsible for several miracles, and reproductions were sent to all Sacred Heart schools.

Pius was much taken by the idea of an adolescent Mary, and in *Ineffabilis Deus* he declared her 'free of all stain and sin, all fair and perfect ... possess[ing] that fulness of holy innocence and sanctity than which, under God, one cannot even imagine anything greater.' Then, in 1858, a vision of such an adolescent appeared in the French town of Lourdes to the fourteen-year-old Bernadette Soubirous. The apparition was that of a slight youth not unlike Bernadette herself, yet also maternal:

> Gathering firewood at the grotto of Massabielle, I lost all power of speech and thought when, turning my head toward the grotto, I saw ... a rosebush ... moving as if it were very windy. Almost at the same time there came out of the interior of the grotto a golden-colored cloud, and soon after a Lady, young and beautiful ... She looked at me immediately, smiled at me and signed to me to advance, as if she had been my mother. All fear had left me but I seemed to know no longer where I was. I rubbed my eyes, I shut them, I opened them; but the Lady was still there continuing to smile at me and making me understand that I was not mistaken. Without thinking of what I was doing, I took my rosary in my hands and went on my knees. The Lady made a sign of approval ... and took into her hands a rosary which hung on her right arm. When I attempted to begin the rosary and tried to lift my hand to my forehead, my arm remained paralyzed, and it was only after the Lady had signed herself that I could do the same.

Over a period of five months, the vision came to Bernadette a total of eighteen times. While her description naturally caused people to suggest that the apparition was the Virgin Mary, Bernadette simply called it (in the local dialect) 'Aquerò,' meaning 'Cela,' 'That Thing.' Finally, in late March, Aquerò announced her identity: 'Que soy era Immaculada Councepciou,' 'I am the Immaculate Conception.' When asked by a local priest to explain what the Immaculate Conception was, Bernadette, having failed her catechism, could not do so, although she would have heard the expression many times locally in the four years since Pius IX had declared the dogma.[22]

In the *Magnificat* (Luke 1:46–56), the young Mary, exhibiting the same radical independence by which her Son would seek and find martyrdom, rejoices in God her saviour 'because he has regarded the lowliness of his handmaiden,' 'exalted the lowly,' and 'scattered the proud in the conceit of their heart.' After Jesus' birth, shepherds arrive in Bethlehem saying an angel had called Him Christ the Lord. Here would be an opportunity for Mary, the proud new mother, to reveal something of what she has been told by Gabriel and Elizabeth. Instead, she maintains the intense dramatic irony, pondering in her heart (Luke 2:19) the private knowledge that what the shepherds had said about heavenly intervention was true. By the fifteenth century, Mary's status had risen sufficiently that in Botticelli's *Annunciation*, the angel Gabriel is bowing to her rather than the other way around, although she would never lose her unique role as the meek, all-loving, all-sacrificing mother. Botticelli's Madonnas, Walter Pater observed, 'shrink from the pressure of the divine child,' since Jesus, even in infancy, was too saintly, too iconic, while these Marys 'plead in unmistakable undertones for a warmer, lower humanity.' In Pater's interpretation of the Florentine, 'the high cold words' of the *Magnificat* 'have no meaning' for Mary. Dejected under the 'intolerable honour' of being the God-bearer, she more comfortably connects with her 'true children,' those she had known 'in her rude home,' resembling the gypsy children Pater saw in Apennine villages, 'hold[ing] out their long brown arms to beg of you.'[23]

It would have been difficult for Mary, herself born into poverty, to find anywhere in France a child of lower social status than Bernadette Soubirous, living with her slovenly, no-account parents and five younger siblings. A local prosecutor called the family 'miserable people' whose 'language,' 'habits,' and 'reputation' were so low that for him any 'charm' the story might have had was replaced not just by 'doubt' but 'disgust.' The family's hovel, once a jail, was a room so nasty it was no longer deemed habitable even for its former purpose. Bernadette's asthma and general sickliness worsened there, making her look, not fourteen, but eleven or twelve. When, shortly after her visions, the town authorities saw fit to post a notice barring the curious from entering the Massabielle grotto, they used a board that had been retained as evidence in a law case, Bernadette's father having previously been accused of stealing it.[24]

While dozens of villagers had watched Bernadette in alleged communication with the apparition, none saw the apparition itself, and local priests were barred from attending, so as to avoid the implication that the Church approved. Nor had Bernadette herself wished to tell adults about her initial vision; it was her sister who first revealed the secret. In one version of events, her mother chided her: 'So you want to make us the laughing stock ... I'll give it to you with your hypocritical airs and your stories of the lady.' In another version, the mother figured the vision was nothing more than the soul of a relative in purgatory. Bernadette's father contemplated only more scandal and misery.

In seventeenth-century Spain, Mary could reveal to an abbess a variety of messages about articles of faith and appropriate conduct, and the abbess could record them at length, without being charged with either delusion or fraud. In France in the 1850s, however, things stood rather differently. Municipal elders feared that Lourdes would get a bad reputation and that the Compagnie des chemins-de-fer du Midi would decide not to extend a railway line south from Tarbes, thus depriving local businessmen of this substantial commercial opportunity. Bernadette was cross-examined by the eminent physician Pierre-Romain Dozous, by M. Dufo the advocate, by M. Pougat, president of the Tribunal, M. Vital Dutour, procureur imperial, M. Duprat, juge de paix, and by M. Dominique Jacomet, commissaire de police – among them self-professed Voltaireans and free-thinkers who represented collectively everything Pius IX despised. 'Be sure of one thing,' Henri Lasserre in his reconstruction had these savants say, the supernatural does not exist. 'Science has abolished it. Science explains everything, and in science alone can you find anything certain ... In the present instance, we have an example of the stupidity of the common people. Because a little girl ... has all kinds of crotchets in her head, these blockheads loudly proclaim a miracle.' Lasserre compares Bernadette's cross-examiners with Herod, Caiaphas, and Pilate.[25]

Jesus had praised God for hiding truths 'from the wise and prudent' while 'reveal[ing] them to little ones,' and Bernadette's story is rich with dramatic themes: the most abject family, the nay-saying clerical elders, the secular, miracle-deriding intellectuals, and the commerce-loving municipal officials, all conspiring to intimidate the small, sickly girl into disavowing her private relationship with the compassionate, brilliant deity. This is a sort of Cinderella story, albeit without a Prince Charming – that is, without a handsome man to fall in love with and thus lose one's own girlish identity. Bernadette had pluck. Taken to a dress shop to identify what Aquerò was wearing, she was shown a piece of Lyonnaise silk and said: 'Nothing like it.' The dressmaker replied, 'But, Mam'selle, this is the whitest and silkiest fabric in the city.' She responded, 'That only shows that the Blessed Virgin did not have her dress made by you.' As with the scriptural account of Mary's private knowledge that she is carrying the Christ Child, or Joan of Arc's conversations with saints, Bernadette shows that a girl may attain fulfilment by maintaining her secret spiritual commitment, rather than submitting to the intimidations of the sublunary men around her.[26]

With the deposit-of-faith complete in the apostolic era, the Church disapproved almost all reports of communications with saints, even while criticizing anyone who proposed earthly explanations for those rare phenomena the Church itself recognized as miraculous.[27] Only after Bernadette passed a battery of cross-examinations would the Church countenance any connection between its dignity and the poor girl's story. Nevertheless, for an institution experiencing geopolitical catastrophe, solace and glory could both be found in this visitation by Mary Immaculate, coming – as it did – just after Pius IX's declaration. Bernadette, entering the Saint Gildard convent at Nevers and there assuming the name Marie-Bernard in 1866, wrote a flattering letter to Pius suggesting that Mary had appeared to her in order to 'confirm' the correctness of Pius's action in declaring the Immaculate Conception as dogma, adding that Mary probably often looked down on Pius 'in her maternal way.'

Bernadette's vision came just six years before another papal announcement of signal importance. In 1863, J. Ernest Renan published a life of Jesus that characterized miracles as the psychological products of the credulous and ignorant. The following year, Pius IX in *Quanta Cura* and its accompanying 'Syllabus errorum' excoriated virtually all aspects of the modern political, social, and scientific ethos that not only had been the driving forces depriving him of temporal rule, but that also had propounded naturalistic, positivist explanations for scriptural miracles. In 1869, with the Papal States gone, Pius wrote that in Bernadette's story people would see 'how, even in the absence of all material force, this Religion is all-powerful for the maintenance of order.' On 8 December of that year, the Feast of the Immaculate Conception, Pius opened the Vatican Council, which seven months later declared 'infallible' all papal pronouncements regarding faith and morals. As Thomas Kselman has said, the assertion of miracles was potentially subversive, while maintaining control over them by investigating them, scrutinizing the evidence, cross-examining the witnesses, and then declaring some miracles valid, others false or unproven, demonstrated the 'unique ability' of miracles 'to verify the Church's claim to be God's sole representative on earth.' Pius IX's successor, Leo XIII, forbade all books recounting new miracles and apparitions that were not Church-approved.[28]

Although the centuries have witnessed many recorded appearances of Jesus, more notable and influential have been the visions of Mary, seen first by the Apostle James at the Rio de Ebro in Spain in 40 C.E., with countless sightings thereafter. Of ten Marian visions declared by the Church to be worthy of pious belief, only one (at Guadalupe, Mexico,

in 1531) fell outside the period from the 1830s to the 1930s, what
Jaroslav Pelikan has called 'the great century of Marian apparitions.'[29]
Among these, Sister Catherine Labouré, an uneducated French nun,
saw Mary periodically between July 1830 and September 1831, receiving from her instructions to 'have a medal struck' derived from what
she saw, and to have people wear it around their necks in order to
receive 'great graces.' Copies of the resulting 'Miraculous Medal' were
cast starting in 1832, with a papal approval issuing in 1842. On one side
of the medal is Mary joyful and triumphant, standing on a globe and
crushing a serpent as beams of light emanate from her hands. Included
there is the famous prayer: 'O Marie, conçue sans péché, priez pour
nous qui avons recours à vous.' The other side is sorrowful: the heart of
Mary pierced with a sword and the heart of Jesus crowned with thorns.
Bernadette Soubirous recounted that the Lady she saw 'was just like she
is on the Miraculous Medal.' She may also have heard of the vision at
La Salette in the French Alps in 1846. There the weeping Virgin, speaking in French and in *patois* to two shepherd children in a ravine, warned
that if religious observance remained lax she would not be able to keep
her Son from striking. 'If the potatoes rot, it is your fault,' Mary reportedly said. 'I made you see it would happen a year ago, and you did
nothing about it.' Thus, although the potato blight, proximately caused
by the fungus *Phytophthera infestans*, had the worst effects in Ireland
because there peasants depended upon potatoes almost exclusively for
subsistence, it also caused hardship in other European countries, where
– as in Ireland – some ascribed the blight to inadequate piety.[30]

In the two decades following the brutal French Commune of 1871,
France recorded fourteen notable Marian apparitions. Pius X, declaring
officially in 1904 that the vision appearing to Bernadette was indeed the
Virgin Mother, voiced again what had been a conviction in Pius IX: that
'the prodigies which still continue to take place through [Mary's] inter-
cession furnish splendid arguments against the incredulity of our days.'
In 1910 republican forces headed by Freemasons toppled the Portu-
guese monarchy, announced the separation of church and state, and
made the purging of Catholic faith there a major project. As the process
of secularization went forward, in 1916, a group habit of prayer began
called 'the Crusade of the Rosary,' wherein the faithful asked Mary to
intercede. From May to October 1917, near the village of Fátima, eighty
miles north of Lisbon, a nine-year-old girl named Lúcia dos Santos, and
her two cousins, aged eight and six, were reportedly visited by Mary,
who told them to 'pray the Rosary every day to obtain peace for the

world and the end of the war.' Although Lúcia told her cousins to say nothing about Mary's visit, one could not keep the secret. In one account, Lúcia's straight-laced mother called her a liar. In another, officialdom threatened the children with horrific punishments if they were found to be lying. In a subsequent visit, Mary reportedly told Lúcia: 'Jesus wants you to make me known and loved, and wants to establish in the world devotion to my Immaculate Heart.' Locals, spontaneously declaring their village a sort of spiritual outpost against the government crackdown on faith, were proud that Mary had chosen to appear at Fátima when she could easily have opted again for Lourdes.[31] In Beauraing, Belgium, in November 1932, a youthful Mary was reportedly seen by five children, and then appeared to Mariette Beco, age eleven, in Banneux, fifty-six miles away, directing Mariette to a nearby spring which soon was said to produce cures. In both instances, local authorities disbelieved the children.

Although Lourdes' municipal leaders thought Bernadette's visions might prejudice the town's bid for the rail line, in fact she put the town on the map, the new railroad bringing millions of pilgrims. Bernadette's vision had directed her to dig in the ground and to drink from the muddy trickle she found there. When, in Bernadette's presence, that water was applied to a quarryman's injured eye, his sight was reportedly restored, thus destroying every modern physician's 'façade of philosophic scientific skepticism.' The spring was soon issuing several dozen gallons a minute, and some of the water was eventually channelled off to a special bathhouse where immersion might effect cures. Its popularity grew, decade by decade, and in 1971, 261,000 women and 107,000 men used Lourdes' communal bath. Imitation Lourdes grottoes went up in Oregon, Maryland, Missouri, and on the campus of Notre Dame. Lourdes water became central to the spa's popularity; bottled and sent throughout the world, it could in a sense put the faithful in touch with the miracle of the Blessed Mother's intervention.[32] At the Rhineland, Missouri, shrine, a well was dug to imitate Bernadette's spring, its initiation primed by pouring in some water from Lourdes.

14 Mary or Communism

In *Devotion to the Blessed Virgin Mary in North America* (1866), the Reverend Xavier Donald Macleod observed that from the moment Columbus's ships weighed anchor in Andalusia, 'the love and protection of our dear Lady and Mother floated over the Atlantic.' When the largest of Columbus's ships, the *Santa María*, ran aground on Hispañola on Christmas Eve 1492, the sailors fabricated from its timbers a fortified settlement on the island which they named Navidad. Columbus called one of the other islands Santa María de la Concepcion, although later visitors substituted the less euphonious Rum Cay. Jesuit missionary Jacques Marquette called the Mississippi the River of the Immaculate Conception and in 1675 established a mission for the Kaskaskia Indians under that name. Since then, Macleod wrote, 'Mary has gained vast possessions in this country. One day, let us hope, she will conquer it all, and annex it all.'[1]

Other early salutes include the naming of Maryland's first capital, St Mary's City, on St Mary's River, with Maryland itself publicly recognized as a tribute to Queen Henrietta Maria, privately to the Queen of Heaven. The colony became a prophetic working model of religious tolerance under Catholic proprietorship, at a time when the ministers of Massachusetts Bay executed Quakers, burned witches, and exiled dissenters. Alphonso Maria de' Liguori's *Le Glorie di Maria* (1750), frequently reprinted and distributed in America, provided extensive commentaries for hundreds of Marian devotions, while 1844 saw an extended account of various Marian practices in Italy, along with excerpts from European prayers, devotions, and votive offerings. On 8 December 1846, the Feast of the Immaculate Conception, America's Catholic bishops declared 'the Mother of God, whose Immaculate Conception is venerated by the piety of the faithful throughout the Catholic Church,' to be Patroness of the United States, a declaration ratified by Pope Pius IX. Prominent in the American bishops' famous pastoral letter of September 1919 was a commentary about the nation's 'heavenly Patroness,' and construction of a 'National Shrine of the Immaculate Conception' began in Washington in 1920.[2]

As American Protestantism continued its perpetual process of schism, and as science pursued its positivist goal of crushing credulity with empirical fact, the Church Universal continued to satisfy the human thirsts for beauty, sympathy, and mystery. After observing a Catholic service in Philadelphia, John Adams wrote to Abigail (9 Oct. 1774): 'Here is everything which can lay hold of the eye, ear and imagination – everything which can charm and bewitch the simple and ignorant. I wonder how Luther ever broke the spell.' In 1840, Elizabeth Cady Stanton, having just arrived in Europe, found herself in Exeter Cathedral:

It was just at the twilight hour, when the last rays of the setting sun, streaming through the stained glass windows, deepened the shadows and threw a mysterious amber light over all. As the choir was practicing, the whole effect was heightened by the deep tones of the organ reverberating through the arched roof, and the sound of human voices as if vainly trying to fill the vast space above. The novelty and solemnity of the surroundings roused all our religious emotions, and thrilled every nerve in our being. As if moved by the same impulse to linger there a while, we all sat down, silently waiting for something to break the spell that bound us. Can one wonder at the power of the Catholic religion for centuries, with such accessories to stimulate the imagination to a blind worship of the unknown?

Similar admiration came from Hawthorne, Ruskin, and Henry Adams. George Santayana, Catholic in background and atheist by philosophical commitment, was philosophically attracted to the religion's deep romanticism. 'There is no God,' he reportedly quipped, 'and Mary is his mother.' To read the greatest poets (Dante, Chaucer, Petrarch, Boccaccio, Donne, Jonson, Milton, Crashaw, Coleridge, Wordsworth, Shelley, Byron) is to see Mary repeatedly and earnestly saluted. Americans read in the works of thoughtful celebrants like John Henry Newman the idea of Mary the all-forgiving mother, sheltering all humanity in the folds of her blue cloak, the intermediary to approach when going directly to the iconic Christ would be too humiliating. Whatever 'Catholicism' meant to rabid Know-Nothings, Americans sufficiently curious about the major achievements of Western culture to take the Grand Tour (some 25,000 per year in the 1870s) could experience the Mary of the *bellezza corporale*, of a mother's love in Michelangelo's *Pietà* in St Peter's Basilica, then as 'the receptacle of light' in Caravaggio's breathtaking *Death of the Virgin* (ca. 1601–2) in the Louvre. Mary's complicated relation with God held fascination for the poets, 'a Woman-Trinity,' Rossetti wrote, 'daughter born to God, / Mother of Christ from stall to rood, / And wife unto the Holy Ghost.' Protestantism offered nothing as rich, except insofar as the Oxford Movement sought to recapture Catholic ritual, and Protestant poets and artists indulged their hunger by borrowing Mary from Catholicism.[3] In 'Maternal Lady with the Virgin Grace' (1805), Mary Lamb wrote: 'when thy sinless face / Men look upon, they wish to be / A Catholic, Madonna fair, to worship thee.'

But not all Protestants yearned for what Catholics had. In 1946, J.A. Mackay, president of Princeton Theological Seminary, wrote that because Protestants embrace the 'overwhelming thought' that Christ is 'the ever present and living Lord,' they sense no need for Mary or the saints. This averred positively what for centuries had been an accusation: that Catholic devotion to Mary was idolatrous, even anti-Christian. Thus, for many, on Mary was focused the question of which faith was the true faith. As John Lancaster Spalding wrote: 'To defend the true doctrine of the Incarnation against ... heresies[,] the Church could discover no more certain and effectual means than to declare the Blessed Virgin Mary to be the Mother of God ... To think of Mary as only a good woman implies a doubt of the divinity of Christ ... Protestants shrank from calling Mary the Mother of God, and the force of logic has driven them in large numbers to deny that Christ is God.' Orestes Brownson, a former Protestant, had said much the same thing. A third Catholic bitterly called the Gospels 'the very stronghold of Protestant argument against our devotion to the Blessed Virgin' – as if this were somehow unfair.[4] The impulse among many Protestants to rely solely on Scripture, whether as the absolute and complete Truth, or as adjusted by the findings of archaeologists and linguistic scholars, and the impulse for a 'modern,' 'scientific' religion in which miracles had no place, could all be construed as an insult to Catholic faith, experienced viscerally as an insult to the Blessed Mother.

Bernadette Soubirous died in 1879 and was beatified in 1925. That year, Sister Lúcia of Fátima, like Bernadette six decades before, entered a convent. In the wake of the Russian Revolution, the Vatican's concern for Russian Christians of the Latin Rite was sufficiently strong that in 1930 Pius XI ordered a Pontifical Commission for Russia. In 1941, Lúcia obliged her superiors by writing down several secrets the Virgin had told her back in July 1917. One was that the First World War would end, but that if people continued to offend God, a worse conflict would break out during the pontificate of a pope who would be named Pius XI. (The Second World War had commenced in September 1939, the last year of Pius XI's reign.) Lúcia also described a visit by Mary back in 1929, when she said: 'The moment has come in which God asks the Holy Father in union with all the bishops of the world to make the consecration of Russia to my Immaculate Heart, promising to save it by this means.'[5] Thus was Mary, the epitome of virginal chastity and loving motherhood, becoming Catholics' champion against not just Protestantism and Modernism but Communism as well.

On 8 December 1933, the Feast of the Immaculate Conception, Bernadette was canonized by Pope Pius XI, thus officially declaring her sainthood. In 1937 he proclaimed, 'anyone who studies with diligence the records of the Catholic Church will easily recognize that the true patronage of the Virgin Mother of God is linked with all the annals of the Christian name. When ... errors everywhere diffused were bent upon rending the seamless robe of the Church ... our fathers turned with confident soul to her'; thus he urged the rosary (Bernadette had seen Mary reciting it at the grotto) to 'overcome the enemies of God and Religion.' A few years later, Franz Werfel, a Jewish refugee reportedly killed by the Nazis but actually hiding out at Lourdes, swore that if he managed to escape he would honour Bernadette by writing her biography. Reaching Los Angeles, he wrote *The Song of Bernadette*, in which he turns the 'Heralds of Science' and 'disciples of Voltaire' who cross-examine Bernadette into two-dimensional stock characters, less subtle even than the nay-saying public men found in Hollywood films like *Miracle on 34th Street*.[6] Werfel's book became America's best-selling novel of 1942.

Bernadette had been, among other things, the first photographed saint, making her melancholy visage a timeless if not wholly heart-warming memento of Mary's most famous interaction with the post-Resurrection world. Although Werfel's novel, with its municipal villains scheming to silence the girl in order to get the railroad, fairly cried out for Hollywood treatment, in March 1943 Joe Breen told Father Lord he doubted such a project would appeal to 'audiences in a pagan country such as this – but we shall see what we shall see.' Cantwell reportedly provided a detailed list of requirements for any actress playing the part. Director Henry King gave screen tests to Teresa Wright, Anne Baxter, and Phyllis Isley Walker, concluding that while the first two 'looked at' the make-believe vision they were told to imagine, only Walker, a devout Catholic educated by the Benedictines at Tulsa's Monte Cassino Junior College, 'saw' the vision. Although Phyllis was married and a mother of two, producer David O. Selznick, married to L.B. Mayer's daughter Irene, apparently did not deny himself the rites of the casting couch, a tradition with which Phyllis happily complied. He gave her the screen name 'Jennifer Jones,' combining everyday Americanism with a certain alliterative spunk appropriate for the role she was about to play. The film, shot in black-and-white to replicate the stygian bleakness of Bernadette's life, further avoids DeMillean grandeur by reducing the resplendent Aquerò (played by Linda Darnell) to a bit part. For her portrayal of Bernadette, Jones won an Oscar, beating out Ingrid Bergman in *For Whom the Bell Tolls*. With statuette and stardom safely in hand, Jones on the day after the awards ceremony filed for divorce from actor Robert Walker, the better to carry out with Selznick what the April 1949 *Screen and Television Guide* would call 'one of the most genuine, tempestuous love affairs in the long hectic history of Hollywood.'[7]

Mary versus Communism

In 1937, Pope Pius XI declared of Nazism: 'Whoever exalts race, or the people, or the State ... and divinizes them ... distorts and perverts an order of the world planned and created by God.' Five days later, he condemned 'atheistic Communism' and what he deftly called its 'false messianic idea.' His successor, Pius XII, was not similarly even-handed. In June 1941, just days after Hitler invaded the Soviet Union, Pius XII in a radio address noted that 'in the midst of ... darkness and storm, signs of light appear which lift up our hearts with great and holy expectations – these are those magnanimous acts of valour which now defend the foundations of Christian culture, as well as the confident hope in victory.' In September, with Hitler's divisions seemingly primed to overwhelm the Soviets, Pius received a letter from Franklin Roosevelt stating that 'the survival of Russia is less dangerous to religion, to the church as such, and to humanity in general than would be the survival of the German form of dictatorship.' Pius, however, disagreed, seeing Nazism as the lesser of the two evils.[8] On 31 October 1942, with the fate of Stalingrad in doubt, Pius in a radio address discussed what Mary had reportedly said to the children at Fátima, then consecrated the world and – by clear implication – Russia, to the Virgin's Immaculate Heart, in effect putting Russia in Mary's hands, not so it would win against Hitler, but so that it would return to Christianity.[9] He must have felt a prophetic bond with Mary for such purposes, since he had become a bishop on 13 May 1917, the day she first appeared to the three children at Fátima. Nor would it have been lost on Pius XII that the Fátima visions continued throughout the summer of 1917, as Russia moved toward the October Revolution.

In a passage in Cardinal Spellman's novel *The Foundling* (1951), taking place on the day after Pearl Harbor, a character notes that 'America has been dedicated to Our Blessed Mother, and ... if our country was being forced to declare war on her feast day [8 December], Mary would see us through.' Throughout the war, Pius XII, Spellman, and countless other prelates repeatedly instructed Catholics to seek Mary's guidance through prayer, and at war's end many believed that Mary had played a crucial role in the Allied victory. The circumstantial evidence was worth considering. In *Communism and the Conscience of the West* (1948), Msgr Fulton J. Sheen noted not only that the United States declared war against Japan on the Feast of the Immaculate Conception, but that it was on 13 May 1945, Mother's Day as well as the Sodality Day of Our Lady, that V-E Day was declared, that on 15 August 1945, the Feast of the Assumption of Our Blessed Mother, Japan surrendered, and that V-J Day was an anniversary for one of Mary's appearances at Fátima. Spellman, who visited thousands of soldiers during the war, dedicated his 1946 collection of poems on themes of war and victory 'To Mary / whose only Son died that other mothers' sons might live in love and peace.'[10]

A poll revealed that U.S. soldiers believed military service had enhanced their religious convictions, and an estimated 10,000 GIs visited Lourdes during 1945–6. On 9 September 1945, a few months after V-E Day and a month after two atomic bombs rendered an American invasion of Japan unnecessary, the military newspaper *Stars and Stripes* reported: 'A group of soldiers and WACs walked slowly toward the grotto ... They approached Bernadette's shrine ... Three WACs kneeled before the iron railing ... [making] the sign of the cross and [counting] the beads, offering prayers to the Mother Mary for their families, friends and themselves ... A WAC stepped down to a spigot and washed her hands and face with the water as Bernadette had done when she discovered the spring.'[11]

Eugenio Pacelli, Pius XII, has been called 'the first cold warrior.' Although the Vatican had intervened to save thousands of Soviet citizens from dying of starvation in the early 1920s, Pacelli failed over the next few years to negotiate some form of permanent diplomatic relationship between the Vatican and Moscow, and when the United States recognized the Soviet Union in 1933, Stalin saw no further strategic value in befriending the Holy See. Although the Lateran Pacts with Mussolini (negotiated by Pacelli's brother, Francesco) had foreclosed Vatican involvement in Italian politics, in the spring of 1948 Pius worked with the Americans to keep the Communists from winning Italy's national elections. Alcide De Gasperi's Christian Democrats, an offshoot of Catholic Action, reportedly received over $500,000 in American campaign funds, and Frank Sinatra, Bing Crosby, and Gary Cooper all gave radio broadcasts to the Italian people, urging that the election would answer whether Italy would live in freedom or slavery. Arthur Miller, in Rome at the time, wrote that although the Italian Communist Party was already the largest in Europe, it was discreetly but pragmatically instructing citizens to vote for the Christian Democrats, since a Communist victory would mean an end to American largesse, with no offsetting benefits from Stalin, who earlier had demanded war reparations from Italy. And De Gasperi's coalition prevailed, albeit with less than half the votes cast.

As Pius XII had predicted, Russia's victory was a defeat for Christianity, as Soviet-backed regimes grabbed the nations of Eastern Europe, closing and/or desecrating all churches. Priests and nuns presented innumerable cases of personal bravery, facing the punishments and tortures by which the new dictators forced them to abandon their parishioners and disavow their faith. Alojzije Stepinac, wartime archbishop of Zagreb in Croatia, was jailed by Yugoslavian boss Josef Tito's Communist government for alleged collabouration with the Nazis. The plight of Stepinac, a personal favourite of Pius XII, was monitored closely in America, and when in 1946 Cardinal Spellman asked for contributions to build a high school in Stepinac's honour, he received funds sufficient to build not one school but two. Joÿsef Cardinal Mindszenty of Hungary was first jailed by the Nazis, then by the Communists. In February 1949, drugged and sleep-deprived, he publicly 'confessed' to conspiring with the United States to overthrow the Communist regime, for which he was sentenced to life imprisonment. Spellman mounted the pulpit of St Patrick's Cathedral to decry Mindszenty's mistreatment and to warn Americans against the 'demoniac people now using every foul means to overthrow our republic' with their 'Satan-inspired Communist crimes.'[12] In July 1949, Pius XII decreed that Catholics who advocated Communist doctrines would be excommunicated. In September 1951 he urged priests to ask the Virgin Mother of God to revive the hearts of the priests and laymen 'who languish miserably in ... concentration camps,' and in December 1952 issued an encyclical concerning the 'Persecuted Eastern Church.'[13]

Cynics considered the descent of an Iron Curtain in Eastern Europe to be merely the Soviets' inevitable spoils of victory, after bearing the brunt of the fighting and dying, inflicting seven of every ten German casualties. Some thought a declining FDR had been too trusting of 'Uncle Joe' Stalin, while Republicans rushing to obliterate Roosevelt's entire legacy included some – Alistair Cooke wrote – who conjured a long-standing plot between fellow travellers and New Dealers. Polish Americans characterized the Truman Administration's recognition of Poland's Soviet-backed puppet government as appeasement. By March 1947, with Eastern Europe in captivity and signs that additional nations might fall like dominoes, Truman proclaimed that U.S. policy would be to contain Communism – categorically and universally. In June, Secretary of State George Marshall announced what became a plan of massive financial and logistical commitments to the crippled European states, in part an act of simple humanitarianism, but also intended to keep them from being sucked into the Soviet sphere.[14]

May was Mary's month, and in May 1946 at least 700,000 pilgrims came to Fátima to thank Mary for the end of the war. Bishop Sheen was among the many recognizing that Mary's appearance at Fátima, when contrasted with the Godless materialism of the Soviet state, held the key to world peace. Pius's consecration of Russia to Mary's Immaculate Heart had been a dramatic way to reiterate what the Fátima message had already shown: that the mere existence of the atheistic, materialist Soviet regime might be such an offence to an angry God that He might destroy the entire world Himself rather than wait for that result in a nuclear exchange. Thus in 'Will Fátima Save America?' did the Rt Rev. W.C. McGrath suggest the 'terrifying possibility ... that the Hand of God may strike before a Russian bomber ever takes off from Moscow.' In the yearly collection of Marian appearances reported between 1928 and 1975 by the Société Française d'Études Mariales, 1948 led, with forty-eight. In 1949, Mary appeared to some children in Heroldsbach-Thurn, West Germany, promising that she would be their protectress if the Russians came sweeping through town. On 15 August 1950, the Feast of the Assumption of the Blessed Virgin Mary, a crowd alleged to number 100,000 assembled in Necedah, Wisconsin, as Mary reportedly told a farmer's wife: 'Your country is in grave danger from the enemy of God. Much of your trouble will rise from within; then through this the enemy from without will strike causing much suffering.' Pilgrims to the Necedah shrine reported that their rosaries turned colour, some changing to gold. The Church refused to recognize the alleged visitation.[15]

For Catholics, Cardinal Spellman noted, the blue in the American flag represented Mary, the Patroness of the United States, 'the last unfailing hope of embattled humanity struggling for survival against the menace of atheistic Communism that would desecrate and destroy both the flesh of man and man's spirit!' In 1947, a year in which a record 115,214 Americans converted to Catholicism, Mary's earlier message at Fátima about the conversion of Russia became a focal point for anti-Communist fervour. Msgr Harold Colgan of St Mary's Catholic Church in Plainfield, New Jersey, suffering from heart disease and given three months to live, promised Mary that he would preach the message of Fátima regarding Russia's conversion, and suddenly was cured. In spiritual opposition to Russia's Red Army, he named his grass-roots sodality the 'Blue Army of Our Lady of Fátima.' Chapters proliferated rapidly into almost every U.S. diocese, with members' obligations including the recitation of five decades of the Rosary each day and the wearing of a blue Miraculous Medal or other blue object. A statue of 'Our Lady of Fátima' toured the United States, attracting over three million onlookers by December 1948. A month later, Jesuit priest Leonard Feeney founded the Slaves of the Immaculate Heart of Mary.[16] A Franciscan who worked in the reference department at the Library of Congress wrote a life of Mary compiled from the visions of Anna Katharine Emmerich, Maria of Agreda, and two other mystic women. Boston's archdiocesan newspaper serialized João de Marchi's book *The Immaculate Heart: The True Story of Our Lady of Fátima*. Thousands of sick pilgrims came to Lourdes in search of Mary's help. While many claimed to have been helped, each report of a miracle cure was analysed by a qualified medical committee, which between 1948 and 1993 ratified only eighteen cases. Ironically, the most reliable proof for miracles came from science, as when before-and-after X-rays recorded and memorialized the presence of dangerous lesions on lungs, then their utter absence.[17]

In the common form of the rosary, vignettes of Mary's life interlace with those of Jesus, and each 'Our Father' and 'Glory be to the Father' is answered by a battery of ten 'Hail Mary's.' By 1947 the Sorrowful Mother novena, popularized a decade earlier by a priest of the Order of Servants of Mary at Chicago's Our Lady of Sorrows Basilica, had become widely adopted. In June, Pius in a radio address to a Marian congress in Ottawa told young listeners that 'a loving Mother's eyes are upon them' and that they should 'vindicate the glory of your Immaculate Mother in the face of a vicious world' by proving that 'young hearts can still be chaste.' July saw the canonization of Sister Catherine Labouré, whose visions of Mary in 1830 had yielded the Miraculous Medal. A nun published *I Sing of a Maiden*, a book-length compendium of poetic salutes to Mary. In May 1948, Pius invited the faithful to implore Mary to intervene regarding the unsure post-war environment, and in 1949 the Vatican ratified Mary's earlier appearance to the eleven-year-old Mariette Beco in Banneux, Belgium. While in all of Pius XI's pontificate there had been only four Marian congresses, there were four in 1947, seven in 1949, and fifteen in 1950. In *Bis Saeculari* (27 November 1948), Pius XII gave a flavour of social activism to the growing number of Marian sodalities by declaring them to be part of the Catholic Action movement.[18]

When film star Loretta Young first met Msgr Sheen in 1940, she took his advice by committing herself to say the rosary every day. On 8 May 1949, Mother's Day, she joined Charles Boyer in a network radio broadcast discussing Mary's instruction to the three peasant children at Fátima to 'Pray the Rosary always.' Evelyn Waugh, a British Catholic visiting the United States, although surprised to find movie stars broadcasting rosary instructions, concluded (despite the earlier pronouncements of Pius IX, Leo XIII, and Pius X) that Catholicism was 'not something ... opposed to the American spirit but an essential part of it.' In 1951, as if to seal the new Marian regime against Communism, Pius recommended that families at close of day recite the rosary together, recognizing its 'powerful efficacy to obtain the maternal aid of the Virgin' whereby, 'like a loving mother, in the circle of her children,' she bestows on them 'an abundance of the gifts of concord and family peace.' Addressing thousands of pilgrims at Fátima by radio, Pius similarly urged 'the Virgin Mother's insistence on the recitation of the family Rosary.' The Central Association of the Miraculous Medal, founded in Philadelphia in 1915, was now so busy manufacturing and distributing these amulets that it expanded into a block-long building, 'Our Lady's Workshop,' across the street from Mary's Central Shrine.[19]

Catholic universities began naming professorships and even whole institutes dedicated to Marian study. At the University of Dayton, Fr. Lawrence Monheim in 1943 founded the first American library solely for works about Mary. Among major studies, in 1947 appeared the first volumes of *Katholische Marienkunde*, edited by Paul Sträter, S.J., and of Fr. Gabriele Maria Roschini's *Mariologia*, followed in 1949 by the first volume of *Maria: études sur la sainte vierge*, edited by Hubert du Manoir, S.J. In 1949, Fr. Juniper P. Carol and thirty-nine theologians formed the Mariological Society of America. Two new periodicals, *The Marianist* and *Marian Studies*, were inaugurated to deal exclusively with Mary, while articles about her so proliferated as to require a bibliography, *Our Lady's Digest*. Books about Mary, totalling a substantial 982 during 1948–9, jumped to 2,209 during 1950–1.[20] In 1951, Philadelphians Edward McTague and John Stokes, playing out an idea started at St Joseph's Church on Cape Cod twenty years earlier, began planting gardens of marigolds and other flowers whose pre-Reformation names honoured Mary. Soon various churches, organizations, and families were purchasing seeds for up to twenty-five Marian varieties.

Amidst this intense focus on Mary, a papal message of deepest significance was in process. The doctrine of the Assumption provided that, following Mary's natural life on earth, not only her soul but her physical body was assumed into Heaven. Mary is last mentioned in Acts 1:12–14, in an 'upper room' in Jerusalem shortly after Christ's ascension, thus revealing nothing about the time, place, and circumstances of Mary's death. While the Assumption was thus uncorroborated by apostolic authority, it was supported by two inferences: that God, having lived in Mary's body, would not have allowed it to decompose; and that since early worshippers revered the bones and other remnants of the first Christians yet no mention was made of Mary's body, it did not remain on earth. In 1863, nine years after Pius IX had defined Mary's Immaculate Conception as a dogma of the Church, Queen Isabella II of Spain asked him to do the same for the Assumption. He declined, stating he did not consider himself worthy to declare as dogma this 'second mystery of the Madonna.'[21] Pius XII's reopening of the matter thus comprised an opportunity to complete Marian developments started by his namesake a century before.

In 1939, at the start of his pontificate, Pius XII had directed two different groups to study the feasibility of defining the Assumption as a dogma. In *Deiparae Virginis Mariae* (1 May 1946), he alluded to two volumes of petitions, all 'begging' for such a declaration, adding that this had been the fervent request of almost two hundred bishops at the

Vatican Council in 1870. Following the procedure used by Pius IX as a prelude for declaring the dogma of the Immaculate Conception, Pius XII asked the opinions of bishops, lower-level clergy, and parishioners. The response was over 98 per cent in favour, and on 1 November 1950, addressing a crowd of two hundred thousand in St Peter's Square, Pius read out *Munificentissimus Deus*: 'The Immaculate Mother of God, the ever-Virgin Mary ... was assumed body and soul into heavenly glory.'[22] Members of the crowd below clapped, cried, prayed. In 1854, Pius IX had conclusively established that the fetal Mary was outside the curse of the Fall, and now Pius XII, who as a child had poured out his heart to the iconic *Madonna della Strada* in Rome's Church of the Gesù, now officially declared Mary outside physical death.[23] Professor Pelikan linked Pius XII's action with that of Pius IX ('reinforced' by the Lourdes appearance) and with the related dogma of papal infallibility in 1870, as the 'most important "new" doctrines to have been defined by the Roman Catholic Church in the entire modern era.'[24]

A papal legate told a substantial throng at Fátima that on three successive days just before the announcement regarding the Assumption, Pius XII, while walking in the Vatican gardens, saw unusual activity around the sun, something like what the three peasant children had seen at Fátima, taken by him as a sign that the Soviet Union would indeed be converted to Mary's immaculate heart. Several months earlier, Pius XII had issued the encyclical *Humani Generis*, 'False Trends in Modern Teaching.' In the tradition of Pius IX's 1864 encyclical *Quanta Cura* and Pius X's *Pascendi* and *Ad Diem Illum Laetissimum*, it declared 'the principles of Christian culture' to be 'attacked on all sides,' as by the Communists' insistence that evolution, with its 'fictitious tenets,' 'explains the origin of all things,' although the soul – Pius XII urged – does not emerge from material sources. He proceeded to choose Pius X, the staunch anti-Modernist, as the first pope since the Counter-Reformation to be canonized. A group of militant young Catholic intellectuals at the University of Chicago, having sought to harmonize belief and science, now lost heart.[25]

Bishop Sheen had ascribed the *nausée* of modern life not just to Communism but to Freud's popular theory that civilization was based upon underlying instincts for sex and for death. The day after *Munificentissimus Deus*, Pius XII voiced his hope that the dogma of the Assumption would cause 'a spirit of penance to replace the prevalent love of pleasure, and a renewal of family life,' despite the growing use of contraceptives and the prevalence of divorce. A few days later,

Bertrand Russell told an audience at Columbia University that Catholicism was not capable of fighting Communism. Although it would take some years, Russell would be proven dead wrong. For now, Mary, through several reported visitations and through her compassionate personality, had become Catholicism's powerful antidote to Godless totalitarianism, when all the philosopher Russell could offer – even after decades of reflection and political involvement – was the defeatist notion that he would rather be 'Red' than 'dead.' Fulton Sheen, in contrast, summed up the contest brilliantly, describing Mary's Assumption as the absolute answer to 'the mystical body of the anti-Christ' which gathers around 'the tabernacle doors of the cadaver of Lenin, periodically filled with wax to give the illusion of immortality.' 'De Maria numquam satis,' it was now said: there can never be enough Mary. The period from 1854 through 1950 would become known as 'the Marian Age.'[26]

Hollywood Priests

Come to the Stable (1949) begins in the snow-covered fields of New England, through which two French nuns, Sister Margaret (Loretta Young) and Sister Scholastica (Celeste Holm), are trudging on foot in a starlit night, eventually reaching a stable in Bethlehem, Connecticut. Sister Margaret explains that when the Nazis occupied her pediatric hospital in France, she asked the advancing American Army not to bomb it, then promised God that if the building was spared, she would come to America and build a children's hospital. She had seen a post-card of a painting entitled 'Come to the Stable,' by the artist now using the building as her studio, and thus made this place her destination, having already spotted a nearby hill as the probable construction site.

When the nuns tell the local bishop that they have no money for the project, he is dubious about their prospects, particularly because the hill they have chosen is owned by Luigi Rossi, a racketeer. Undaunted, they borrow a jeep and head for Rossi's office, merrily travelling well above the speed limit while they invoke Mary's help. Rossi's gang, discussing the merits of a certain horse at Santa Anita, at first refuse to admit the two nuns, but then they slip through in the general confusion provoked by Sister Scholastica's observation that the racetrack was named for Mary's mother. When it turns out that the nuns are from the town where Rossi's son was killed in the war, he agrees to donate the land. The nuns start raising the construction money, and when this proves difficult, they ascribe it to their having failed to build an appropriate shrine on the designated hill. A successful songwriter who has a country house nearby wants the whole project stopped, but gives in when he finds that the beautiful melody he has just written was in fact subconsciously plagiarized from a Gregorian chant he had heard as a soldier in France. Overcoming a series of such obstacles, the nuns are still $500 short of their goal when Sister Scholastica reveals that she is a veteran of the French Open and decides to play a match – in her nun's habit – to make up the shortfall. Each unlikely step in their project works out because, as the wise bishop observes, 'simple, blind faith' can be 'sublime,' comprising an 'irresistible force against which there has been no defence for 2,000 years.' The nuns approach each challenge with a Franciscan naïveté which director Henry Koster intended to be winsome, although it instead comes out saccharine.

The story was Clare Boothe Luce's fictionalized account of the founding of Connecticut's Regina Laudis Abbey, although it is also reminiscent of Mother Cabrini's early collaboration with Archbishop Corrigan in 1889. Luce was one of several prominent people converted to Catholicism by Loretta Young's friend and adviser, Fulton Sheen. Among Sheen's extraordinary achievements was the funding in 1938 of a maternity hospital for African-American women in Birmingham, Alabama, the unusual idea coming to him because he had preached there, and because he was fond of his African-American housekeeper. Perhaps Sheen's unusual achievement played some role in the genesis of Mrs Luce's story. Like Sheen, the bishop in *Come to the Stable* is a perfect mix of charity, irenic faith, probity, and sagacity. And while perhaps the smart thing would have been to send these two naïve, penniless nuns back to France, he is prepared to give them a chance at wonder-working. Not that the bishop in Luce's story is a mere copy of her friend: Sheen would have raised the money and built the hospital himself. His fund-raising talents were extraordinary. In one year, 1955, he sent to Rome $24.6 million. Over the course of his life, he would raise something approaching $200 million. But he was best known for his immensely popular prime-time show, *Life Is Worth Living*, first airing in 1952. Among the props in its tiny set was a statue of Mary, later dubbed 'Our Lady of Television,' which became so popular that Sheen sold copies to raise money for the Vatican's World Mission Society for the Propagation of the Faith, of which Cardinal Spellman had made Sheen the U.S. director.[1]

Los Angeles bishop John Cantwell had assigned his former secretary, the Irish-born John J. Devlin, to be 'padre of the films,' that is, the Legion of Decency's formal adviser to Hollywood on Catholic matters, including the question of how to portray priests. Father Devlin's presence at story conferences and on the set, when coupled with Joe Breen's vigilance and with the Code provision barring clerical caricatures, meant that priests could never be portrayed as confused, mistaken, unsure, depressed, or overbearing, much less dishonest, uncharitable, or tipsy. Graham Greene's novel *The Labyrinthine Ways* a.k.a. *The Power and the Glory* (1940) concerns an outlawed priest in the vicious battles between the Mexican government and the Catholic Cristeros during 1927–8. Produced as *The Fugitive* (1947, dir. John Ford), the film eliminated all references to the priest's alcoholism, leaving the character (played by Henry Fonda) oddly flat and the film oddly uncompelling.[2] One could, of course, invest the character of a priest with all the requisite lyricism without alcohol, the highest achievement along these lines being Leo McCarey's *Going My Way* (1944), a multiple Oscar-winner pairing Bing Crosby and Barry Fitzgerald as two priests, each with his own beautiful intonation, each in his way morally flawless. Its success yielded a sequel, *The Bells of St Mary's* (1945), in which Fitzgerald's ailing priest is replaced by Ingrid Bergman as an ailing nun.

The American Catholic hierarchy succeeded brilliantly with 'bricks-and-mortar,' Archbishop Hughes having set a high standard with St Patrick's Cathedral. The common joke was that when an American bishop died and Saint Peter asked him his profession, he replied: 'real estate agent.' Since the nation's founding, the hierarchy found itself in a variety of real estate disputes with the lay trustees of church properties, many of whom claimed the right to hire and fire parish priests. John Carroll, the nation's first Catholic bishop, soon realized that the trustee system so localized authority and power as to turn American Catholicism into a sort of New England congregationalism. As bishops tried to wrest back diocesan control from local trustees, the latter enlisted various state legislators who were eager to impede any and all forms of centralized power in a unified episcopy answerable only to Rome. In the 1850s, for instance, New York's legislature saw fit to void any bequest that purported to pass property to 'any person and his successors in any ecclesiastical office,' a blatant (although ultimately unavailing) attempt to keep the ownership of Catholic churches in lay hands.[3]

A hallmark of the local pastor was his fundamental selflessness. Finley Peter Dunne's famous character, the Chicago bartender 'Mr. Dooley,' noted that the parish priest, Father Kelly, 'spint all th' money that he ought to be usin' to buy a warm coat f'r his back, spint it on th' poor, an he dipt into th' Easter colliction that ought to've gone to pay interest in th' church morgedge. It'll be a smooth talk he'll have to give his grace th' archbishop this year.'[4] Not surprisingly, the Depression of the 1930s entailed severe economic pressures on the mortgaged churches, schools, and hospitals under the care of innumerable Father Kellys. In Norman Taurog's *Boys Town* (1938), Spencer Tracy as Father Flanagan constructs a multi-building complex for juvenile delinquents, then resists the pressures invoked by three different mortgage holders by maintaining the simple faith that everything will somehow work out. (It does.) In Ted Tetzlaff's *Fighting Father Dunne* (1948), Pat O'Brien happily commits to a two-year lease on his home for boys with a down payment of everything he has: $2. In *Going My Way* and *Bells of St Mary's*, Bing Crosby's character is assigned by the bishop to resolve serious real estate problems. In each film he is the consummate professional, in the first dealing with a worn-out parochial school, in the second with a worn-out church. In each he faces a secular and worldly opponent, a builder in one, a mortgage holder in the other, each wishing to tear down the religious edifice to make room for that ultimate handmaiden of American materialism: a parking lot. In each film, one of the plot elements is the process of bringing the secular businessman 'round to the Church's own charitable perspective.

In *Going My Way*, Crosby's character is a classic *eiron*, allowing everyone to consider him plainly inadequate for his assigned task. No one, particularly the aging parish priest played by Fitzgerald, may know that Crosby's real assignment is to ease the old man into retirement, with all the respect due to one who has dedicated his life to his downtrodden parishioners. In *The Bells of St Mary's*, no one, particularly the nun played by Ingrid Bergman, may know that Crosby's real purpose in transferring her out of the school is to protect her deteriorating health. With Celtic alacrity but no hint of ethnic foreignness, Crosby establishes in both films that the priest's job is to be smart, kind, supportive, non-egotistical, and, above, all subtle, working *sub rosa* to make good things happen. In *Going My Way*, Crosby is faced with an attractive eighteen-year-old who has left home to be a nightclub singer. Smarter than all the dour head-shakers, Crosby decides neither to scold her nor to send her back to her parents, but rather to give her a singing lesson. In *Bells of St Mary's*, an attractive woman, abandoned by a musician, engages in an unspecified but lucrative profession, and is worried about the influence that profession is having on her sexually precocious and troubled daughter. After examining an early script, Joe Breen thought the character 'ugly,' 'hardly more than a prostitute,' her child 'illegitimate.' Nor did Breen like the fact that Crosby's character exuded 'the flavour of a kind of mild condonation ... for the acts of the erring woman. It all seems to be taken by the priest as a matter of course and this, we think, is not good.' By the time of the shooting script, however, it is clearly established that the woman and musician are married, and everything has been cleaned up just enough to make the situation allusively interesting, with McCarey leaving to Crosby's considerable acting talents the responsibility to make everything come out right. When the woman asks Crosby to look after the girl, he blithely replies: 'I'll take care of your daughter if you take care of yourself,' delivered mellifluously as a Der Bingle throw-away line, but one no reasonable person could ignore. And he does quietly save the day, dragging back the wayward husband and re-establishing a functioning family. One simply could not have a more selfless, more charitable, more perfect person than Crosby's priest, as saintly in his way as the aging priest he has been assigned to help. No less perfect is the nun portrayed by Bergman, as she selflessly coughs her tubercular way through a gaggle of adoring children.[5]

Both films were vetted by Father Devlin. Howard Barnes commenced his review of *Bells of St Mary's* in the *Herald Tribune* of 7 December 1945 by noting that McCarey 'has pursued a hazardous path with surefooted daring and serenity.' *Going My Way*, too, as an implement of emotional manipulation, is as perfect a work as the studio system produced, as perfect in its way as *Casablanca*. While some found Crosby's 'piano-pounding, golf-playing clergyman,' Andrew Greeley later wrote, 'a dangerous distortion of the sacramental role of the priesthood,' others saw 'a major propaganda victory for the Church,' and Pope Pius XII reportedly thanked Crosby for projecting the priesthood as 'humanised.'[6] This was the overwhelmingly dominant view, McCarey doing perhaps more than any person alive in the 1940s to burnish the image of Catholicism, not just with the Catholic laity, nor just with the American Protestant majority, but with the entire world. Testifying before HUAC as a friendly witness in October 1947, McCarey noted that neither *Going My Way* nor *Bells of St Mary's* made any money in Russia. The chief investigator asked why:

A. Well, I think I have a character in there that they do not like.
Q. Bing Crosby?
A. No; God.

Cardinal Spellman

Boston archbishop William Henry O'Connell had a certain flair that made him a celebrity priest, moving as something like an equal in the higher echelons of Boston's staunchly Protestant social circles, the award of a cardinal's hat in 1911 signalling to all Boston Catholics that they had 'arrived.' With a huge endowment from theatre owner B.F. Keith, O'Connell built a princely home in Brighton and purchased a summer house in fashionable Gloucester. So often did O'Connell appear in newspapers on his way to Europe or to his winter home in Nassau that he was called 'Gangplank Bill.' Cardinal Mundelein, while rationalizing the finances of Chicago's archdiocese, established a similar regime of personal splendour.[7] But by the late 1940s the American Church's acknowledged leader was New York's less grandiose archbishop, Francis Spellman.

Although O'Connell had owed his position to the fact that a good friend from his days in Rome, Rafael Merry del Val, had become Pius X's secretary of state in 1903, O'Connell's relations with Rome suddenly and permanently chilled shortly after Pius X's death in 1914, when, queried by the new pope, Benedict XV, about the decision of O'Connell's nephew to leave the priesthood and marry, O'Connell reportedly denied it, upon which Benedict produced from his desk a copy of the Indiana marriage licence. O'Connell was thereafter so stripped of prerogatives that he could not even name his own auxiliary bishops, and in 1932, Francis Spellman's friend from his days in Rome, Eugenio Pacelli, who had become Pius XI's secretary of state, imposed Spellman on O'Connell. O'Connell did not try to hide his disgust, perhaps failing to see that this was only replicating the process by which – thirty years before – O'Connell had landed the same job because of his friendship with Pacelli's predecessor, Merry del Val. With Spellman's appointment came a new coat of arms, Columbus's *Santa María* on an azure field, designed personally by another of Spellman's Roman patrons. Although O'Connell did his best to make the next seven years extremely unpleasant for his unwanted auxiliary, in 1936 Cardinal Pacelli let it be known that Spellman was destined for higher office, by choosing him as a guide during Pacelli's widely publicized American tour.[8]

In 1938, upon the death of Cardinal Hayes, Mundelein wanted a fellow German American, New Orleans archbishop Joseph Rummel, to be New York's new archbishop, although Cardinal Dougherty – given German belligerence in Europe – thought that suggestion misguided.

Pius XI had been considering John T. McNicholas, a man with a long record of extraordinary achievement, from pastoral work among Italian immigrants to a key role in forcing Hollywood to clean up its films. McNicholas had already cleared his desk in Cincinnati and would have been confirmed, but for Pius XI's death. Upon Pacelli's election as Pius XII, however, the New York archbishopric went instead to Spellman. Msgr Sheen, who had apparently taken at face value some press reports that he was himself being considered, leaned over to John Tracy Ellis during a lunch and said of Spellman: 'It is incredible. It is incredible. He has nothing.' Since all four of Spellman's grandparents had come from Ireland and his training included a long stint in Boston under the autocratic O'Connell, his appointment constituted Rome's 'seal of approval' on the 'conservative, Irish, pragmatic, centralized style' that had long been the hallmark of the American hierarchy.[9] When Mundelein died in 1939, Spellman became the Vatican's most significant agent in its relations with FDR. In a glowing cover story, *Life* on 21 January 1946 called Spellman Pius XII's 'intimate friend and probably his most influential adviser,' making him the 'the No. 2 man among the 350,000,000 Roman Catholics of the world.' Although no non-Italian had been elected pope in several centuries, there was even talk of Spellman's having the inside track to the papal succession.

In 1928, the year of Al Smith's presidential bid, Msgr John A. Ryan wrote that the American episcopacy was 'well satisfied' with the separation of church and state, admitting that in matters 'purely political' the Church 'has no right whatever to issue commands or to give official advice,' and that on issues with a moral component, issues 'of right and wrong,' the Church's authority was limited to 'direct[ing] the Catholic citizen.' This soon changed. While some Catholics were surprised by the bishops' public assertions of national power in the 1930s in their quest to purify movies and books, some thought they could and should go even further. In 1941, Theodore Maynard bugled a call-to-arms: 'Unfortunately American Catholics, upon the whole, have not begun to wake up to their responsibilities and opportunities. Protestantism ... is now so doctrinally decayed as to be incapable of offering any serious opposition to the sharp Sword of the Spirit, as soon as we can make up our minds to use it. Except for isolated "fundamentalists" – and these are pretty thoroughly discredited and without intellectual leadership – Catholicism could outmuscle Protestantism at will.' Spellman's answers to such calls-to-arms included a substantial dispensing of the *odium theologicum*, as when in 1941 he had a message read from New York pulpits denouncing George Cukor's film *Two-Faced Woman* (1941), a screwball comedy in which Greta Garbo tests her husband's fidelity by pretending to be her own twin sister, a courtesan. 'When I went to school,' Spellman wrote in 1942, 'freedom of the press meant the presentation of facts with decency and sincerity. Now, there are those to whom freedom of the press means license to publish pornographic literature and to distribute it freely with the resulting corruption of minds and morals.' Further, 'the "fifth column" of the saboteurs of our factories and public utilities has its counterpart in the "filth column" of those who piously shout "censorship" if they are not permitted freely to exercise their venal, venomous, diabolical debauching of the minds and bodies of our boys and girls. I am against "censorship," but that does not mean that I must condone those who wish to include among America's freedoms the freedom to kill the bodies and souls of their fellow-Americans.'[10]

If one knew about the Second World War only by reading Spellman's *The Road to Victory* (1942), one would not know whether the primary enemy was Nazism or Communism. Once the war ended, Spellman became American Catholicism's primary voice against Communism, both as practised in the Soviet Union and as the source of domestic subversion. In 1946 he told graduating FBI agents: 'To help save America you must constantly and loyally labour to unmask traitors who give lip service to democracy while anarchy and tyranny nestle in their hearts.' He 'earned the admiration of Catholics and the enmity of non-Catholics,' David O'Brien has written, 'by regularly insisting that Catholicism more than any other religion affirmed the basic principles of American democracy and offered the firmest support to the nation in its resistance against Communism.'[11]

In addition to its language about freedom of speech, of the press, and of assembly, the First Amendment provides: 'Congress shall make no law respecting an establishment of religion, or prohibiting the free exercise thereof.' In March 1948 the Supreme Court in *McCollum* held that this provision, applicable to the states via the Fourteenth Amendment, was violated when a public school invited Protestant, Catholic, and Jewish instructors into schoolrooms during regular school hours to teach children who wished to learn their respective traditions. In an earlier free-speech case, Justice Frank Murphy, the only Catholic on the Court, confided to his colleague Felix Frankfurter 'that he wanted always to err on the side of religion.' Frankfurter responded that as judges 'it is our business not to err on either side,' a perspective which seemed to strike Murphy as novel. On the day *McCollum* was announced, Murphy told Frankfurter that he feared Catholics would fault him for having joined in the Court majority's holding that public schoolrooms could not be used for Catholic education. Frankfurter responded that although that might be the reaction of some, the decision was likely to increase Catholic solidarity and militancy, in that it would lead more Catholics to transfer their children into parochial schools and might even buttress the long-standing Catholic belief that public schools are 'inherently irreligious.' Frankfurter's haughty attitude toward Murphy was evidenced some years later when, in a letter to Judge Learned Hand, he snidely referred to his colleague as 'Saint Frank.'[12]

Just as Murphy feared, Catholic reaction to *McCollum* was vociferous. Boston archbishop Richard Cushing openly asked how Murphy 'could do such a thing.' Bishops urged that the decision was premised upon a presumed 'separation' between church and state, itself a 'shibboleth of doctrinaire secularism' which is not found in the First Amendment itself but in a letter Thomas Jefferson wrote decades later.[13] Retired Fordham president Robert Gannon, S.J., spoke of the 'current fraud of separation of church and state,' while the *National Catholic Almanac* accused the Court of 'pay[ing] scant attention to logic, history or accepted norms of legal interpretation.' Wilfrid Parsons, S.J., noted that the First Amendment's language reflected a mere compromise among the states to the effect that none of their respective established churches could be a national established church. Robert Drinan, S.J., said the Court had adopted a 'philosophy of secularism' which gave atheists and agnostics the right to stop government from even recognizing religion, thus putting 'the believer at a disadvantage since a comparable right to enjoin all atheism or agnosticism is not given to religionists.' Drinan, a graduate of Georgetown Law School, was trained to choose his words carefully and to understand that an argument can be persuasive and dramatic without becoming sibilant. This differentiated him from James M. O'Neill of Brooklyn College, who dared call the Supreme Court a 'Politburo.'[14]

Paul Blanshard had been, among other things, a Congregationalist minister, a lawyer in the office of free-speech specialist Arthur Garfield Hays, an investigator of Tammany corruption for Fiorello LaGuardia, a leader of the textile workers' strike in Utica, New York, an anti-Communist influence in the American Labor Party, a journalist investigating conditions in Southern textile mills. In 1947–8, *The Nation*, a left-leaning periodical founded in 1865, syndicated segments of a book by Blanshard attacking the Catholic Church on a range of issues, including its censorship policies and its relationship with Fascism. Although American history had been rife with merely vicious rhetorical attacks on Catholicism, here was a serious investigative work that subjected the Church – someone observed – to the careful, detailed scrutiny that Ida Tarbell had used in her classic exposé of Standard Oil. Shortly after the last installment, the Board of Superintendents, the highest administrative agency of New York City's public school system, deleted *The Nation* from its subscription list, thereby withdrawing it from the schools' libraries. *The Nation* objected, arguing that Blanchard had not attacked Catholic faith but only the Church's stands on a variety of public issues. In reply, the Board's chairman cited to the 15 and 22 May issues, wherein Blanshard had criticized Catholic beliefs in miracles, relics, and apparitions, adding that public schools were places neither to teach religious beliefs, nor to foster attacks on them, but rather to encourage good will. The chairman, a Lutheran, repeatedly denied that the Superintendents had been subjected to outside pressure. Blanshard's opus now came out in book form under the title *American Freedom and Catholic Power* (1949). The press, perhaps fearing reprisals, was generally reluctant to acknowledge its existence, even by accepting paid advertising for it. *The New York Times* reviewed it, but negatively. The book nevertheless sold an extraordinary 240,000 copies, the efforts at suppression having supplied – *gratis* – the equivalent of a major promotional campaign. A priest from Catholic University claimed that Blanshard, consistent with Soviet strategy, was part of a group trying to make the Catholic laity distrustful of the hierarchy.[15]

Among those speaking out against the Superintendent's ban of *The Nation* was Archibald MacLeish, a major poet and former Librarian of Congress, who had been FDR's consultant on cultural matters. Not just in this instance, but generally, there was evidence of a growing impatience – even discomfort – with what many had gradually come to see as Catholic high-handedness, as when Edmund Wilson in 1945 called the Church a 'pressure group' that was playing a 'new and rather sinister role.' Denis Brogan wrote that although Protestants had acquiesced in Catholic censorship efforts, 'the imposition on a cosmopolitan population of the sexual standards of Irish Catholic Puritanism has its dangers, if only because it attracts attention to the real or alleged political power' of a hierarchy which most Americans 'are prepared to tolerate but not to love or admire.' William Warren Sweet, a Methodist and the pre-eminent authority on American religious history, revived the traditional allegation that wherever Catholics have a numerical dominance, Protestant opinions risk being censored, while wherever Catholics are a minority, 'there and there only do they give even lip service to complete religious liberty.' Writing of 'The Catholic Issue,' George West asked readers of the *New Republic* whether it might not be time for Americans, after 'dodging and postponing a distasteful chore,' to revise downward their appraisal of the Church and its right to dictate American morals. After all – West urged – Catholic militancy had reached a point where some 'alarmed Americans' feel 'that the first concern of our local and national governments is the appeasement of Catholic opinion.' That 'opinion' seemed no longer to be the tempered views of Cardinal Gibbons, Al Smith, or Monsignor Ryan, but rather the pronouncements of 'the most arrogant and bigoted,' those who had engaged in censorship and fought contraception while 'perverting our foreign policy' by keeping munitions from the Loyalists in Spain and threatening boycotts against any American newspaper that dared criticize the dictator Franco. Peter D'Agostino thought this new, post-war feeling derived not just from reviewing the Church's relationship with Fascism, but from 'the near absence ... of any self-critical ... evaluation' by Catholics themselves.[16] Thus, with Protestant leaders having for years induced no general public interest in any alternative or countervailing ideas regarding major public issues, it seemed that the Catholic bishops had simply not known when to stop.

When producer Pandro Berman in 1947 submitted to the Legion of Decency a scenario for *The Three Musketeers*, he reportedly received back a suggestion that the character of Cardinal Richelieu (who was not going to be shown in clerical garb or performing priestly functions) should be cut out completely, because the underlying book by Alexandre Dumas, published in 1844, had portrayed Richelieu as worldly and unscrupulous. Someone saw an opportunity too rich to forgo, and proceeded to leak the story to the *New York Times*. While this should have served as notice to the Legion that it was wearing out its welcome, in November 1949 it objected to Henry Levin's comedy *And Baby Makes Three* because it contained the line 'There hasn't been a miracle since the thirteenth century,' which the Legion construed as failing to give miracles appropriate currency or respect. Producer Robert Lord leaked to the press what he considered the Legion's 'preposterous' objection. Some Catholics, too, thought things were getting out of hand, Mason Wade in *Commonweal* characterizing Catholicism's censorship efforts as 'a pathetic attempt at gentility on the part of those of no great culture.'[17] During the Depression, it had seemed sensible to allow those who promised moral leadership to make decisions for everyone, as a way of maintaining some sort of order in a society that had partially unravelled by pursuing the Enlightenment philosophy of laissez-faire. Now, millions had been involved in a world war against totalitarianism and for freedom of thought, while tens of thousands were using the 'GI Bill' to enroll in colleges where they were being invited – many for the first time – to embrace freedom of thought as a working principle in their own lives. In this changed atmosphere, institutional censorship – whether Catholic or governmental – would no longer go unchallenged.

While the *Nation* ban amply demonstrated Catholic power over public education in New York, Cardinal Spellman was best known for his 'bricks-and-mortar' skills in building Catholic schools, from 130 elementary and secondary schools when he arrived in 1939, to 429 schools by 1964, giving the archdiocese the largest school system in New York State other than New York City's own public system. With so many Catholic children not using the public schools, non-Catholic taxpayers received a huge de facto tax break, while many Catholics were in effect paying twice, in taxes to the government system, in tuition or donations to the private system. Among the arguments raised against this economic inequity, Spellman urged that Catholic schools, which enrolled close to three million students, should receive federal education money. In June and July 1949, Eleanor Roosevelt in her syndicated column took issue with him.

Although many would have considered President Roosevelt's internationally admired widow to be off-limits for purposes of personal attack, on 21 July Spellman accused her of participating in a 'continued anti-Catholic campaign.' Donald Crosby, S.J., has written that Spellman, a 'stubborn if inarticulate polemicist,' carried forward 'New York City Catholicism's grand tradition of warfare with local Protestants,' thus epitomizing everything 'that American Protestants feared and disliked in American Catholics.'[18] Spellman alleged that by opposing the commitment of tax dollars to Catholic schools, she was denying equality to Catholic youths whose 'broken bodies' lay 'on blood-soaked foreign fields' in 'a long and bitter fight to save all Americans from oppression and persecution.' If that were not enough, he dared tell Mrs Roosevelt (of all people): 'your record of anti-Catholicism stands for all to see – a record which ... cannot be recalled – documents of discrimination unworthy of an American mother!' Thus ignoring or implicitly denigrating the contribution not only of her husband but her children to the war effort, he seemed also not to know or not to care that Mrs Roosevelt herself had not only visited with hundreds of injured GIs in stateside hospitals, but had overcome substantial opposition from her husband, from General Douglas MacArthur, and from Admiral William Halsey, in order to visit the 'blood-soaked foreign fields' of Guadalcanal so that she could honour the dead and comfort the men still hospitalized there.[19]

The *New York Times* characterized Spellman's letter as 'caustic,' noting that his calling Mrs Roosevelt anti-Catholic was belied by her having campaigned for Al Smith. Herbert H. Lehman stepped in on Mrs Roosevelt's behalf, urging that 'her whole life has been dedicated to a constant fight for tolerance and brotherhood of men as children of one God.' Lehman, the only Jew in the U.S. Senate, added that the issue presented by Spellman's attack was one of free speech, that is, 'whether Americans are entitled freely to express their views on public questions without being vilified or accused of religious bias.' In the end, Mrs Roosevelt had the best of it rhetorically, seeing fit to tell her adversary: 'I assure you that I have no sense of being "an unworthy American mother." The final judgment, my dear Cardinal Spellman, of the worthiness of all human beings is in the hands of God.' News of the controversy reached Rome, and it was reportedly on orders from Pius XII that Spellman travelled to Hyde Park to make peace. It was noted that Spellman's attack on the president's widow had been a major stimulus to sales of Paul Blanshard's book.[20]

Several years before, Rep. Parnell Thomas's verbal references to a 'list' of all Communist-tainted Hollywood films had seemed to tweak public curiosity. Another man with an unrevealed list was Senator Joseph McCarthy. Although both the Jesuit weekly *America* and the Catholic lay weekly *Commonweal* refused to endorse him, Cardinal Spellman became a vocal supporter. Donald Crosby has commented: 'In his haste to exorcise American life of Marxism, Spellman seemed all too ready to reject social reform ... and even liberalism itself.' On 10 February 1950, the day after McCarthy first alluded to his list of Communists in the State Department, the head of the Harvard Law School Forum, oblivious to the story (only a handful of AP newspapers thought it worth carrying), introduced a debate between Paul Blanshard and Father George H. Dunne, S.J., with the remark that the topic to be addressed, 'The Catholic Church and Politics,' had become a 'red hot' issue.[21]

16 'Woman Further Defamed'

The Miracle Comes to New York

At forty-one minutes, *Il miracolo* was too short to be released as a feature. In Italy it was paired with Rossellini's *Una voce umana* (*A Human Voice*), based on a Jean Cocteau play, a Magnani tour-de-force in which her character agonizes over the telephone with a lover who is about to marry someone else. The two films, coupled under the title *L'Amore: Due storie d'amore*, were said to portray in different contexts the suffering intrinsic in the way women love. In 1949 a print of *L'Amore* passed through U.S. Customs without incident. Although Joe Breen's Code enforcement had rendered state censorship offices largely super-fluous, New York's Motion Picture Division was among those still actively engaged. It had banned *Scarlet Street* outright after Breen passed it, and refused to license Marcel Pagnol's *Harvest*, a pastoral story of Provence, because the couple portrayed therein had not been married by a cleric.[1] Not that New York was particularly restrictive: of 9,463 films screened by its censors during 1935–40, only 99 were rejected, and of these 20 were revised and subsequently licensed. Nevertheless, 703 of the 9,463 films required a total of 5,775 eliminations, making government censorship a not inconsiderable factor in what New York audiences saw and did not see.[2] On 2 March 1949 the Division, under the directorship of Ward C. Bowen, saw *L'Amore*, found nothing violative of the statute, and issued a licence to its distributor, Lopert Films, Inc. Distributor Joseph Burstyn then bought the rights and uncoupled *Il miracolo* from *Una voce umana*, combining it with two French films, Marcel Pagnol's *Jofroi* (1933) and Jean Renoir's rendition (1936) of de Maupassant's *Une partie de campagne* (1881), entitling the resultant trilogy *Ways of Love*.[3]

Mary Looram of Queens, New York, chairwoman of the Motion Picture Council of the International Federation of Catholic Alumnae, had been interested in film censorship since the early 1920s when she started a syndicated program about movies in the then-new medium of commercial radio. Now a major voice in the Legion of Decency, she had seen *Il miracolo* at the Venice Film Festival in 1948 and thought it 'sacrilegious,' a characterization she conveyed to Burstyn when she spotted him there negotiating U.S. distribution rights with Rossellini's lawyer.[4] Although New York's Motion Picture Division had already approved *Il miracolo* as a component of *L'Amore*, Burstyn resubmitted it because it was now repackaged with two other films. On 30 November 1950 the Division issued *Il miracolo* a second licence.

At a Mass held on Friday, 8 December 1950, the Feast of the Immaculate Conception and the ninety-sixth anniversary of Pius IX's declaring that doctrine as dogma, Catholics were handed and recited a short version of the pledge of the Legion of Decency, thereby renewing their commitment as they did on that special day each year.[5] On Monday, 11 December, the *Ways of Love* trilogy opened at Manhattan's Paris Theatre. The next day, the Reverend Patrick J. Masterson, senior executive of the Legion of Decency and vice-president of the Vatican's Pontifical Film Commission, purchased a ticket, undoubtedly having already been told about the film by Mrs Looram.

In *The Miracle*, Nanni (played by Anna Magnani) is a homeless woman living in and around a village on the Amalfi coast, doing odd jobs and scraping together an existence on the food, clothing, and shelter provided to her by charity. While tending goats one day in the hills, she sees a stranger walk by (played by Federico Fellini) and tries to engage him in conversation. Having heard and seen saints many times, she believes he is Saint Joseph and says she has been waiting for him. Babbling with excitement, she recounts that one of the voices she hears told her to jump off the cliff into the sea, but she refused because she recognized it as the devil's voice. She adds, however, that she would happily jump off the cliff with Saint Joseph, so that they could together fly to heaven with the archangel Michael, whose church stands atop a nearby mountain. The stranger says nothing but plies her with wine. She lies on the ground next to him and appears to undergo a sort of feverish ecstasy, as she mumbles words from Matthew's Gospel about Christ's birth.

Nanni awakes from her reverie to find the goats licking her face. The stranger is gone. She proceeds down to the village and, upon inquiry, is reassured by a local monk that visions of saints are real, since he sees the Virgin Mary every day. She goes to a church service, where she steals an apple and eats it. Several months later, Nanni is merrily playing with the young children of the village when she gets dizzy and faints. One of those who come to help inadvertently touches Nanni's stomach and declares that she is pregnant. At first distraught and confused, Nanni tells them, 'Don't touch me,' and announces, 'It is the grace of God.' She runs into a church and prostrates herself before the host, by this time beaming with joy. Soon the whole village knows that she is pregnant. When dozens of people crowd around her in the street, she believes they are duly recognizing her as carrying the Christ Child and announces: 'It is the will of God that I be among you.' But in fact they are deriding her and place a wash-basin on her head as a mock halo, while they sing the traditional 'Evviva Maria.' Finally grasping that they are mocking her, in a panic she escapes back into the hills, where she puts her hand on her stomach and says: 'My blessed son, don't fear, I will protect you.' Several more months pass. Her labour begins and she starts down toward the village to have the child, but then, upon seeing a real Evviva Maria procession, she turns back and again ascends the hills. Led by a goat, she stops at a grotto and drinks from a spring, and then ascends further, arriving at the church of Saint Michael. It is locked, but she finds a storeroom where she gives birth and whispers: 'God, my God, my creature, my blood, my baby!'

How the story came to be has been variously reported. In the June 1948 number of Jean-George Auriol's *Revue du Cinéma*, Fellini recounted that with no scenario in hand and only five days before shooting was scheduled to begin, he himself blurted out the notion of a crazy woman seeing a vagabond and mistaking him for Saint Joseph. Pressed to tell where he had read this so that any appropriate permissions could be sought, he claimed it to be his own idea.[6] Not that the premise was new; it had about it the sense of a folktale and of early miracle plays and similar vernacular literature. When Rossellini first outlined the plot to Magnani, he reportedly referred to it as a Russian folktale, a credible possibility no film reviewer, commentator, or copyright lawyer was likely to pursue further.[7] *Osservatore Romano* and *Corriere della Sera* both found the story to be reminiscent of Gabriele D'Annunzio's collection, *Le novella della Pescara*, the latter reviewer going so far as to accuse the film of exuding 'troppo di letteratura.'[8] When in September 1948 *Il miracolo* opened in Buenos Aires, writer and film critic Francisco Madrid, author of a book-length study of the Spanish writer Ramón del Valle-Inclán (1869–1936), accused Fellini of plagiarizing Valle-Inclán's novella *Flor de Santidad* (1901/1904), which does present a few parallels.[9]

The film's genesis never became any clearer. In 1954, Rossellini claimed as his 'inspiration' for *Il miracolo* a sermon by the fifteenth-century Franciscan friar San Bernardino of Siena, in which a man finds his young son dead with two teeth marks in his neck as the family dog, Bonino, waits nearby. In anger the man kills the dog, but then sees nearby a dead snake, which the dog apparently had killed in trying to save the boy's life. In penance, the man buries Bonino and puts up a headstone, to which successive generations of pilgrims pray. When through their prayers a number of miracles have been effected, they decide to build a church in honour of this 'saint' and – exhuming the object of their veneration – discover the bones of a dog. Since their prayers had resulted in miracles, Bernardino concluded, the fact that they had mistakenly prayed to a dog was unimportant. In another interview a few years later, Rossellini again mentioned Bonino, this time characterizing the story not as his 'inspiration' for the film but only as a reputable Catholic authority for the proposition that legitimate faith accrues in a variety of circumstances which some might deem inappropriate or even blasphemous.[10]

In 1970, having either forgotten or simply grown tired of these other accounts, Rossellini explained that while filming *Paisan* (1946), he needed some props from a U.S. Army unit, which ended up handing over to him, among other things, three German prisoners. With no one to guard them, they wandered off to a monastery to take a nap, and, going to retrieve them, Rossellini came upon the monks he would enlist to play in *Paisan*. Among these was Frà Raffaelle, who told him about the wild beggars living in the poor areas of the Amalfi coast. He then asked Frà Raffaelle if he had ever had visions. 'Yes, always,' he replied. 'What do you see?' asked Rossellini. 'The saints.' 'Which saints?' 'All of them.' 'And the Virgin Mary?' 'Yes, signore, from head to foot.' That – Rossellini recounted – was 'how I thought up Anna Magnani's part.'[11] This anecdote, whatever its actual place in the genesis of *Il miracolo*, is evidenced in the scene where the monk assures Magnani's character that her visions are legitimate by saying that he sees the Madonna every day. (When a second monk says he has never seen a miracle, the first dismisses him as a 'materialist,' the only comic moment in the entire film.)

Whatever the collective value of this mixed bag of comments in showing how a director can lead drowsy journalists and critics on a merry chase, it did not induce them to re-examine the film itself, which quietly settled into a supporting role as a minor artifact in the Rossellini canon, known primarily because it had stirred some controversy in

New York when it opened. In February 1973 the *New Yorker*'s squib for a two-day revival at the Art Theatre on East 8th Street called it 'perhaps the most fully achieved' of all Rossellini's works, an odd sort of compliment for a film only forty-one minutes long, grossly misunderstood when it was first released, and never analysed at length.

The common reaction to Nanni – both among the film's other characters and critics – is that she is 'delusional,' 'schizophrenic,' 'crazy.' Rossellini said as much. But if we are to understand the character in anything like the terms in which Rossellini, Fellini, and Magnani created it, this is – as when approaching Giulietta Masina's Franciscan heroine in Fellini's *La strada* (1954) – the wrong way to begin. If to see saints is 'crazy,' then so is the monk who told Rossellini that he sees the Virgin Mary every day, a statement which deeply impressed the director as both sincere and sane. Whatever Rossellini personally believed regarding miracles (and he consistently rejected journalists' suggestions that his films might reveal anything about him), it is clear enough that his presentation of characters who believe in miracles is sympathetic.

While we accept that Nanni's pregnancy is the result of intercourse with a stranger, she does not accept that, nor could she, since she understands from the Matthew Gospel that Joseph was Mary's protector but not the father of Christ. She knows nothing of what has happened, and when a nun tells her that she must confess the sin of getting pregnant, she indignantly replies that her conscience is clear and that she is loved by the Lord. If the biblical Joseph had similarly abandoned the Virgin Mary to the vindictive eye of *her* village, she would have been in much the same situation, and would have said much the same thing. Although Nanni is pregnant in the sublunary way, psychically she is no less innocent – her 'craziness' notwithstanding. And because the stranger was not in fact Joseph but merely a drifter who exploited her and absconded, Nanni is alone and unprotected, living on the psychic as well as the physical margin of a community which had theretofore ignored her or indulged her as a sort of village fixture. She is deemed worthy of notice only when to her bizarre accounts of conversations with saints is added a diverting bit of salacious scandal, her pregnancy being all the more entertaining because she preposterously ascribes it to one of these divine visitations. While one of the village's other homeless people had once proposed marriage, she had rejected that as ridiculous, and as we glimpse how truly 'crazy' her ex-suitor is, we can see why. Not that it is fair that Nanni is deprived of a family life. She adores the village children, and thus there is an abject irony in her statement to the stranger that she is glad she has none of her own because that leaves her free to die and fly to heaven with him. In fact, the world, which she describes as full of demons, offers her no reason to stay. As she repeatedly tells the stranger, if Jesus is not going to return, either to kill all the demons or to end the world, then all she wants is to leave, in a sort of farewell defiance of villagers who told her that 'crazy people can't go to heaven.'

Some directors would have manipulated the audience's sympathy by making the villagers ignorant peasants from whose cruelty we could easily distance ourselves. Rossellini does not permit that. The Amalfi coast was dotted with fashionable resorts, and among those who taunt Nanni are a number of people wearing stylish clothes, that is, people like us. They are well versed in the mechanics of religious observance, but they so lack any spiritual connection with Mary and Mary's radical messages of forgiveness and unconditional love that they thoughtlessly use the mechanics of Marian adoration to mock this outcast, as much an insult to Mary as it is to their intended victim. Thus refusing, on the one hand, the trite ploy of befriending his audience, Rossellini also avoids the sentimental option of making Nanni a misunderstood saint or a modern-day, unrevealed Mary, Mother-of-God. Nanni is 'devout' insofar as she goes to church and communes with saints, but the devil also talks to her, and at Mass she cannot refrain from stealing an apple and devouring it guiltily. An objective viewing of her scene with the stranger reveals that it is she who unwittingly seduces him, constantly begging him to stay when he is about to leave, lying down on the ground, opening her blouse in a swoon, etc.

The apple is not Rossellini's only biblical allusion. Goats are historically associated with lechery, and when Nanni awakes from her encounter with the stranger, goats are licking her face. In Leviticus 16:7–26, Aaron transfers to a goat all the people's sins, then sends it off to be released in an unforgiving, mountainous wilderness (Heb.: *'ăzâ'zêl*) ruled by the horned chief of the goat demons, from where neither it nor the sins it carries can return. Although this goat carries the people's sins and is banished to a world of demons, it is itself innocent, a 'goat that departs,' a scapegoat. Another goat, similarly innocent, Aaron merely slaughters as a sacrifice for the people's sins. This slaughter became a yearly Jewish ritual, and when John the Baptist in John 1:29, 35 calls Jesus 'the lamb of God, who takes away the sin of the world,' he is alluding to Leviticus, although the negative associations are eliminated by substituting for the goat a lamb, a symbol of innocence. In John's account, Jesus is crucified on the day of the Preparation of the Passover, that is, the same day the paschal lambs are slain. Matthew's account of Christ's birth includes the advice from the angel to Joseph that Jesus 'will save his people from their sins,' and among the reasons given by the author of Hebrews (9:23–10:18) for the superiority of Christianity over Judaism is that Christ, by sacrificing himself, can bear the sins of many, while the Jews' yearly sacrifice of a goat cannot.[12]

One of Nanni's goats, her guide through the wilderness, leads her to San Michele, the hilltop church she has identified as the place where the archangel Michael will join Nanni and Saint Joseph on their way to heaven. Before reaching the church, she drinks water from a grotto. Saint Michael, whose own grotto near the Monte San Angelo was sufficiently revered to have been visited by Saint Francis, is associated with, among other things, healing the sick through the powers of water. In Revelation 12, a woman 'clothed with the sun,' construed as the people of Israel, the Church, the Blessed Virgin, or a descendant of Eve, cries out 'in the anguish of delivery' of the 'male child who is to rule all nations.' Satan, a serpent in Genesis, is in Revelation a dragon intent upon devouring the woman's newborn son. It fails, and the infant is 'caught up to God and his throne.' Saint Michael leads an army of angels to defeat Satan and his demons by throwing them out of heaven, Christ's followers thus having conquered Satan 'through the blood of the Lamb.' 'And when the dragon saw that he was cast down to the earth, he pursued the woman who had brought forth the male child. And there were given to the woman the two wings of the great eagle, that she might fly into the wilderness unto her place, where she is nourished ... away from the serpent.' Nanni wants to fly off with the saints Michael and Joseph because the world is filled with demons and although Christ can kill demons, He is not coming back. Perhaps Nanni, led by the goat, has taken on the sins of the world as its martyr and/or exile in the wilderness. Perhaps, having been led by the goat to the church of Saint Michael, the archangel, 'through the blood of the Lamb,' has driven out Nanni's demons. As Rossellini himself later said, Nanni's giving birth yields her the 'sanity' of maternal love.

These suggestions about the film are speculative, and no one will 'solve' the story and/or the character of Nanni via the manipulation of biblical symbols. It was not Rossellini's method to choose symbolic elements in order to construct from them a grid of meanings to be uncovered and neatly deciphered. Il miracolo is a work of art – taut, complex, and ambiguous – not an academic puzzle to be 'solved' by some 'key.' The film is highly compressed, its forty-one minutes fairly reverberating with the intense sacramentality one finds in the ambient atmosphere of Italian-Catholic culture. This is so, even if the up-to-date community portrayed in the film has lost touch with the spiritual and moral meanings of that sacramentality.

In August 1948, Italy's Council of Ministers gave Rossellini's film a 'nulla osta' (no opposition) for public viewing, under a regulation dating from 1923 empowering the Council to bar any film containing 'scenes, actions or subjects offensive to ... chastity, morals, good customs and public decency.' The Vatican, characterizing *Il miracolo* as a 'modern version' of the 'miracle of the virgin' (which in some limited sense it is), could have banned the film in Italy, pursuant to its authority under the Lateran Pacts signed with Mussolini in 1929. It chose not to, nor did it exercise another of its prerogatives, that of blocking *Il miracolo* from the Venice Film Festival. In his review, the Vatican's film critic, Piero Regnoli, wrote that while opinions might vary about the film and it raised religious questions – even grave ones – these were of no more apparent concern to Regnoli than the film's overly cerebral tone. Moreover, he was quick to add that the film had scenes of indubitable cinematic distinction, and that he still believed in Rossellini's art. The film opened in Rome in September 1948, and in October the Centro Cattolico Cinematografico, organized by Azione Cattolica Italiana in imitation of America's Legion of Decency, was substantially more negative, calling it 'an abominable profanation from religious and moral viewpoints' and 'a parody of that sublime evangelical narrative which forms the basis of every Christian belief. We advise everybody, nobody excepted, not to see this film.' One could not call that a favourable notice, just one step short of demanding an official ban. Then, on 3 November 1948, *Il Popolo*, the official organ of the Christian Democratic Party, took a contrary view, calling the film a 'beautiful thing, humanly felt, alive, true and without religious profanation ... because ... the meaning of the characters is clear and there is no possibility of misunderstanding.'[13]

As the lights went up following the 12 December showing at New York's Paris Theatre, Father Masterson told the management to cease showing the film. It refused. The next day, Bosley Crowther in the *New York Times* invited contention by writing that Nanni 'may be logically accepted as a symbol of deep and simple faith, horribly abused and tormented by a cold and insensitive world; or she may be entirely regarded as an open mockery of faith and religious fervor – depending on your point of view,' a rather flip suggestion that the film supported both interpretations. *Newsweek* called *The Miracle* 'strong medicine for most American audiences,' in which Magnani 'appears as a half-wit Italian peasant girl whose religious passion bursts violently into expression.' Wanda Hale in the tabloid *Daily News* declared that Nanni's faith placed her 'above ridicule and insult by those whom she thinks are ignorant,' while Hearst's *New York Daily Mirror* called the film 'stirring.' *Cue*, a weekly guide to the arts in New York, found it 'strange and wondrous ... a brilliant climax' to the evening, while the National Board of Review thought it 'especially worth seeing.' In Hearst's flagship paper, the *Journal-American*, Rose Pelswick said *The Miracle* might be 'in questionable taste,' while *Time* called it a 'curiously spotty' and 'second-rate' film that had been a 'flop' in Italy, failing to recover more than half of its $60,000 cost. Crowther, perhaps realizing that his earlier comment might be exploited in some censorship effort, now wrote a second review: 'Obviously, this story, with its symbolic parallels, might by some be considered a blasphemy of the doctrine of the Virgin Birth. And with its poor, crazy woman crying desperately to God while goats bleat at her, it might also be considered a mockery of religious faith. But because of the humble framing that Rossellini has given this simple tale and because of Magnani's great performance, it seems to this reviewer to be just a vastly compassionate comprehension of the suffering and the triumph of birth. Here is an understanding of the feebleness and loneliness of men.'[14] Although the film had passed without objection through federal Customs and through not one but two screenings by New York censors, Masterson of the Legion of Decency asked Hugh M. Flick, the new director of the Motion Picture Division, to view *The Miracle* once again, to decide whether it was 'sacrilegious' and thus censorable under New York's film censorship statute.

Among movies identified by the National Board of Review in 1915 as requiring strict scrutiny by its examiners were those found to be 'sacrilegious or offensive to well established religious convictions,' while Kansas in its 1915 film censorship statute barred films that were 'sacrilegious, obscene, indecent or immoral.' Pennsylvania's law had identical language.[15] Six years later, New York legislators borrowed language from these and other state statutes, enacting a law barring any film that was 'obscene, indecent, immoral, inhuman, sacrilegious, or ... of such character that its exhibition would tend to corrupt morals or incite to crime,' although the draftsmen did not favour the public or the courts with definitions of the statute's several operative terms, including the word 'sacrilegious.'[16] In 1922, the year after the law passed, New York censors reportedly cut a total of twenty-six scenes and intertitles on grounds of sacrilege. Once Breen took over in Hollywood a decade later, the number of films found by New York censors to be sacrilegious dwindled.[17]

The head of the Motion Picture Division, Hugh Flick, was no mere patronage appointment, holding a PhD and having previously served as state archivist. Nor did his staff include any time-servers or hacks, since qualifications included a bachelor's degree and a minimum of four years' additional academic, educational, or social-work experience or foreign travel. One staff opening had yielded two hundred applicants, many with PhD's and MA's. The job paid between $4,500 and $5,200, making the Division's personnel the highest paid government censors in the nation. Dr Flick described them:

> One is beginning his doctorate work in psychology and has had a wide experience with foreign attitudes and customs through foreign residence. He is also, incidentally, one of the ranking chess players of the country. The next member ... in order of seniority has spent the major portion of his experience in attending the courts of New York City on problems of juvenile delinquency. He brings to our discussions a very useful fund of information. The next member ... has worked also with the City of New York but mostly in social welfare and truancy. His professional experience is also of extreme use. The last member ... has worked with various radio programs and other forms of mass communication, more especially with the Voice of America in the preparation of foreign language broadcasts ... This ... is of immense benefit in understanding the real meaning of slang used in various fields.
>
> Four members ... are male and three female ... there is a fairly good representation in regard to religious backgrounds including Catholic, Jewish and Protestant.

Flick saw the film on 21 December and confirmed the decision already made twice by his agency: that *The Miracle* did not violate New York's film censorship statute, including the clause barring 'sacrilegious' films.[18]

Edward T. McCaffrey, a former state commander of the Catholic War Veterans, was the New York City commissioner of licences, a post having no connection with Dr Flick's State Motion Picture Division. A Bronx Democrat held over from the administration of ex-mayor William O'Dwyer, McCaffrey had been Masterson's invitee at the 21 December screening attended by Dr Flick, and had apparently become sufficiently upset by viewing *The Miracle* that the Paris Theatre's staff noticed him. On Christmas Eve the news broke that he had suspended the theatre's licence. Although he had received no complaints, he said he felt compelled to act because he considered *The Miracle* 'both officially and personally, a blasphemous affront to a great many of the citizens of our city.'[19] To avoid a permanent revocation of its licence, the Paris immediately replaced *The Miracle* with a 1935 film of Synge's *Riders to the Sea*. On Christmas Day, *The Miracle* received a 'C' (Condemned) rating from the Legion of Decency. Two days later, the New York Film Critics (whose members included Crowther and Pelswick) reacted to McCaffrey's ban by sending protest letters to him and to New York's new mayor, Vincent R. Impellitteri, then voted the *Ways of Love* trilogy the best foreign film of the year. Spellman noted to his friend, Hollywood gossip columnist Louella Parsons: 'it is certainly an interesting comment on ... the American scene when the film critics of New York give an award for the best foreign film to one which so many millions consider to be the worst.' In fact, only a few thousand people had seen the film, and there was no evidence that any substantial number had reacted negatively. As the ACLU and others asked Impellitteri to stop McCaffrey, poet Muriel Rukeyser arranged for persons interested in the arts to attend a private screening, presumably to enlist their support to fight the ban. Although the story had been covered by the New York newspapers and the Hollywood press, it became 'national' when *Life* magazine called McCaffrey's action 'a striking example of how minor bureaucrats can find ways to establish their personal prejudices as law.' The New York periodical *France Amérique*, allying itself with the French-owned Paris Theatre, suggested that for consistency's sake, perhaps Radio City Music Hall's annual Christmas production should remove the scene of the Infant Jesus from its place between Mickey Mouse and the trained-seal act.[20] Burstyn's lawyers sued to enjoin McCaffrey, appearing before Justice Henry Clay Greenberg on 29 December.

The *Outlaw* Precedent

A state statute generally overrides an inconsistent municipal ordinance on the same subject, and a federal law generally overrides both. In December 1915 the Supreme Court, having concluded some months before in *Mutual Film* that movies had no free-speech rights, affirmed Customs' authority to confiscate and destroy obscene films at the port of entry, pursuant to the statute later involved in the *Ulysses* litigation.

In 1934 a version of the Czech film *Extase* ('Ecstasy,' 1933) was seized at Customs because the face (only) of Hedwig Kiesler Mandl (a.k.a. Hedy Lamarr) is shown during a portrayal of intercourse. Representing the Government in the case was U.S. Attorney Martin Conboy, who had failed several years earlier to have Joyce's novel destroyed. Here he convinced a federal jury that *Ecstasy* was obscene. On the appeal to Learned Hand, Thomas W. Swan, and Martin T. Manton, Judge Hand noted: 'I may be wrong [he seldom was], but I saw nothing in any sense immoral' in *Ecstasy*. Because, however, a U.S. marshal had already destroyed the offending print, the controversy was now declared moot, depriving Hand and Manton of the opportunity to reprise with *Ecstasy* the give-and-take they had exchanged regarding *Ulysses*.[21]

In a related case brought before Judge Manton, a lawyer argued that since federal Customs officials had declared another version of *Ecstasy* admissible to the United States, no state official could bar it from exhibition. Judge Manton disagreed. Although states could not generally stop goods from entering the United States or from moving in interstate commerce, Chief Justice Taney concluded in 1847 that a state may block at its own borders anything likely to introduce 'immorality' and 'vice,' while Justice McKenna in *Mutual Film* noted that although only Congress may regulate interstate commerce in films, any state could ban the public *exhibition* of films within its borders. Judge Manton found this principle to be controlling.[22] But if a state instead issued a film a permit, could a city within that state nevertheless ban it? In 1935, Louisiana resolved this question by providing in its state censorship statute that no parish or municipality could censor films. And in 1940, Virginia's highest court held that since the Commonwealth had issued a film permit for the famous health documentary *The Birth of a Baby*, the city of Lynchburg could not ban the film as 'obscene' under a local ordinance.[23] In the litigation Joseph Burstyn brought in New York against Commissioner McCaffrey, apparently none of the lawyers on either side had found the Louisiana and Virginia precedents. Nor were they aware of another legal precedent closer to home, involving Howard Hughes's film *The Outlaw* (1941).

Upon reading *The Outlaw*'s script in December 1940, Joe Breen warned Hughes to 'avoid sexual suggestiveness,' an odd admonition since Hughes could have had no other reason for making the film. Hughes, who had made no movies since co-producing the highly praised and highly censored *Scarface* during 1930–2, now fired *The Outlaw*'s director and took over, often working late at night when he could spare time from designing and building planes at the Hughes Aircraft Company. His eccentric methods and freedom from budgetary constraints yielded a reported eighty-five miles of film, while his flair for engineering resulted in a special brassiere designed to optimize Jane Russell's not inconsiderable endowments. Breen told Hays in February 1941 that in ten years of examining films he had 'never seen anything quite so unacceptable as the shots of [Russell's] breasts,' a determination Hughes might have found complimentary. Following script changes and cuts, the film received a PCA seal, conditioned on approval of its advertising. Hughes retained the brilliant publicist Russell Birdwell, already famous for stimulating frenetic public interest in the search for an actress to play Scarlett in *Gone with the Wind*.[24]

As the Second World War progressed, Hughes struggled with the construction of his huge wooden plane, the 'Spruce Goose,' a bigger project than the Russell bra, albeit one doomed to enjoy no greater public utility. Birdwell, meanwhile, created and exploited the general atmosphere of salaciousness that had accreted around *The Outlaw*, using such gimmicks as a billboard featuring Russell in a low-cut blouse with the words 'How would you like to tussle with Russle?' and another captioned: 'What are the two great reasons for Jane Russell's rise to stardom?' The war occasioned a huge new market for 'pin up' pictures one could tack above one's bunk or stick in one's helmet liner. While the most famous of these featured Betty Grable's legs and backside, Jane Russell was in the forefront of establishing a breast culture. Twenty-five-cent pulp paperbacks featured 'chest art' on their covers, and a cheap magazine appealed to a troglodyte mentality by being entitled 'Titter.'[25] The real facts surrounding Jane Russell: that she had devoted herself to Jesus at age six, that she helped out her widowed mother, that she married her high-school sweetheart, that she would adopt three children, found an adoption organization, build a chapel, etc. – stuff that twenty years earlier would have been a perfect response to charges that a film was not 'refined' – would have no place in any promotional strategy for Russell.

In 1942, New York's Motion Picture Division rejected a recut version of Hughes's film. A third version received a seal from Breen, was accepted by state censors, and opened in February 1943, albeit with a 'C' (Condemned) rating from the Legion of Decency, the first film since 1936 to get a 'C' after being passed by Breen. The press hated the film and Hughes withdrew it from distribution, perhaps hoping that the tawdry advertising and whiff of scandal would outlive the bad notices and prime some later re-release. And in 1946, in preparation for that re-release, Birdwell hired a skywriter to fly over Pasadena and scribe the words 'The Outlaw' above two circles with a dot in each.[26] One of the new newspaper ads – 'Exactly as it was Filmed – Not a Scene Cut' – was a palpable falsehood, given the heavy editing that Breen had required in 1941 before giving it a seal. The film's achievement was that of giving new meaning to Will Rogers's adage: 'You can't make a picture as bad as the ads lead you to believe it is.'

Breen, having initially been more liberal than the Legion, now insisted that Hughes raise Russell's blouse line, necessitating retakes for a film already five years old. When Hughes rejected that demand, Breen took the highly unusual step of withdrawing the original seal. Hughes appealed Breen's decision and lost, thus temporarily consigning the film to a scattering of non-seal venues.[27] He then gave in, made the required changes, was reissued a seal and received a 'B' ('morally objectionable in part for all') rating from the Legion. With millions of dollars in free publicity for an intrinsically worthless film, Hughes now cashed in with a wide distribution. Although ten years earlier Breen had had the power to enforce a regime of 'family entertainment,' it was now universally acknowledged that the sole reason to see *The Outlaw* was to stare at Jane Russell's breasts.

Duel in the Sun (1946), produced to exploit the market for sexiness just stimulated and tapped by Hughes, starred Jennifer Jones, who exchanged the role of Bernadette for that of a 'half-breed' whose life ends in a slow, stylized, bloody, and colourful shoot-out with her lover, played by Gregory Peck. Jones was in fact third choice for the part, the pregnancies of Hedy Lamarr and Teresa Wright having rendered them both unavailable. During production, David O. Selznick finally told his wife, Irene, about his ongoing affair with Jones, and it has been said that his frenetic presence on the set, while struggling to decide which woman to keep and which to dump, translates into the crazed emotional intensity of Jones's performance. Post-production disputes with Breen and the Legion were intense, and while at the end of the film both characters die, Breen's office complained that their deaths did not comply with the Code's requirement of just deserts, since 'Peck kisses Jones and dies, and she kisses him and dies. In this way they both get, not only what they deserve, but what they want [so it] actually amounts to a scene of sublimation and exaltation.' When Breen's office nevertheless issued a seal for the film and Father Lord asked how it could have happened, Breen said he had been out sick. Masterson of the Legion berated Breen, angry that the lovers treated their own deaths as a 'triumph,' with 'no regret, no sorrow ... Audiences cannot help but be influenced by it. The influence cannot be anything but evil.' Presumably he meant that a film will persuade viewers to engage in illicit sex insofar as it also persuades them that death by violence is not too high a price to pay for doing so. A few weeks later, Memphis municipal censor Lloyd Binford described *Duel in the Sun* as 'the fleshpots of Pharaoh, modernized and filled to overflowing ... a barbaric symphony of passion and hatred ... mental and physical putrefaction ... God help America!!' Binford sent a copy of the letter to Rep. John Rankin, one of the driving forces behind the 1947 HUAC hearings, who read it into the *Congressional Record* and introduced H. Res. 250, asking his congressional colleagues to exercise their jurisdiction over the District of Columbia by forcing the closure of the local theatre where *Duel in the Sun* was then playing.[28]

In October 1947, Spellman issued a letter to all priests in the New York archdiocese regarding the Otto Preminger / John M. Stahl film of Kathleen Winsor's tawdry best-seller *Forever Amber*, stating that 'Catholics may not see this production with a safe conscience.' The Legion issued a 'C' rating. On 11 November, after Cardinal Dougherty threatened a boycott against any Philadelphia theatre that showed either *Forever Amber* or *The Outlaw*, the downtown Erlanger Theatre withdrew *The Outlaw*. When the Central-City Fox Theatre refused to pull *Forever Amber*, Dougherty directed the city's one million Catholics to boycott that theatre for a year. On 4 December, Twentieth Century-Fox president Spyros P. Skouras, fresh from the Waldorf meeting, promised that *Forever Amber* would be edited and toned down. First came a new prologue: 'This is the tragic story of Amber St Clare ... Slave to ambition, stranger to virtue ... fated to find the wealth and power she ruthlessly gained wither to ashes in the fires lit by passion and fed by defiance of the eternal command ... The wages of sin is death.' Then a new voice-over epilogue was added, repeating something said earlier in the film by one of her lovers: 'Amber, haven't we caused enough unhappiness? May God have mercy on us both for our sins.' Although these immunizing insertions placated the Legion of Decency, this was not enough for Spellman, who apparently found intolerable Amber's successive, ladder-climbing relationships (although their sexual aspect is left entirely to inference), the birth of a love child, and the fact that in the end Amber is alive and rich, an archetypal survivor. Perhaps he felt as an executive of the Legion had felt: 'We banned the book. Why make the picture at all?'[29]

Regarding *The Outlaw*, the New York State Motion Picture Division issued a licence under the state film censorship statute, while the city licence commissioner banned it as obscene. Justice Carroll G. Walter affirmed the city's ban, under another state law which permitted local authorities to prosecute obscenity in any medium, adding that if a court ultimately found *The Outlaw* to be obscene, then the Motion Picture Division's contrary decision would be void. That position was affirmed by the Appellate Division on 29 November 1946, thus setting up a crisis in state/municipal jurisdictions. In order to resolve that crisis, the state legislature on 14 April 1950 imitated what Louisiana had done, providing that once a film is licensed by the state, it may not be prosecuted locally as 'obscene, lewd, lascivious, filthy, indecent or disgusting.'[30] The new law, whether by a draftsman's oversight or otherwise, did not include the word 'sacrilegious,' thus arguably leaving a local licence commissioner free – in an exercise of broad discretion – to ban a film because it was offensive to local religious groups, even after the Motion Picture Division had declined to do so.

In the rush to prepare for the hearing in the *Miracle* case, apparently neither Burstyn's lawyers nor McCaffrey's nor Justice Greenberg seemed aware of this new legislative enactment and the theoretical opening it left for a city licence commissioner to ban a religiously offensive film. Greenberg decided the case on other grounds: 'Now, here is a case where a license commissioner has seen a film; he finds that it is personally and officially obnoxious to him, and he closes the picture houses down and after he closes them down, in effect, offers them a hearing to determine whether or not what he has done was right or wrong ... That is not the way we do things in this country. Certainly not in this community.' Just as Greenberg was about to sign an order lifting the ban, the city's lawyer asked for a ten-minute delay and telephoned McCaffrey, returning to court with a message that McCaffrey 'did not want to be tyrannical' and was willing to withdraw his own ban 'voluntarily' until the matter could be resolved at a fuller hearing. The next day, Cardinal Spellman's secretary, Walter P. Kellenberg, released a statement that *The Miracle* was an 'open insult to the faith of millions of people in this city and hundreds of millions throughout the world.' In Britain, meanwhile, the county councils of Middlesex, Essex, and Sussex banned *The Miracle*, although it was licensed by London's county council and opened at the prestigious Academy Cinema on Oxford Street.[31]

New York's rescheduled hearing took place on 3 January 1951, this time before Justice Aron Steuer. McCaffrey's lawyer, still unaware of the

Outlaw statute and its theoretical loophole by which he might ban religiously offensive material, argued that the state's film censorship statute itself contained an unfortunate and unintentional loophole in that it included no mechanism for withdrawing a licence that had been improvidently granted. Because of this alleged deficiency in the state statute, he asserted, a city commissioner should be able to ban a film on his own authority. The argument, sensible enough in theory, bore no relation to the facts at hand, since Dr Flick would not have withdrawn the licence even if the state statute authorized him to do so. His office had licensed *The Miracle* not once but twice, and when he was specifically asked to see it again, he himself reaffirmed that *The Miracle* was not sacrilegious. McCaffrey's position thus reduced to the plain fact that he wanted the film banned and Dr Flick and his staff did not.

When asked whether he wished to see the film before deciding the case, Justice Steuer declined, indicating that he was not himself a censor but a judge deciding which censor had jurisdiction. On 5 January he ruled against McCaffrey. 'It may not be amiss' to observe, Steuer noted, that the city licence commissioner 'is not the protector from affronts of a large portion of our citizens,' who can protect themselves either by not seeing the film or by asking the Board of Regents, the Motion Picture Division's parent agency, to reverse its subsidiary by revoking the licence. Finally, Steuer noted that if anyone presented him with evidence that the state licence had been issued through an abuse of power, he would be just as ready to restrain the state as he was to restrain McCaffrey. McCaffrey appealed, stating that because *The Miracle* ridiculed, affronted, and attacked a segment of the population (i.e., Catholics), he would consider himself remiss in his official duty if he did not pursue the matter.[32]

After Justice Steuer's decision was reported in the newspapers on Saturday, 6 January 1951, Masterson asked Spellman to have a message read from the pulpit at St Patrick's Cathedral the next day. In that message, Spellman advised that it had been just a month since he and countless others had renewed their Legion pledge to 'remain away from indecent and immoral films,' and he was now calling upon not just the 1.25 million Catholics in the New York archdiocese, but all 26 million Catholics in the United States, to boycott *The Miracle*, a film whose very existence would have been unknown to them but for the publicity McCaffrey and Spellman were generating. He called for stricter federal and state censorship 'to make it impossible for anyone to profit financially by blasphemy, immorality and sacrilege,' and urged that Dr

Flick be 'censured' for licensing *The Miracle*, deeming it 'a blot upon the escutcheon of the Empire State' that the film statute did not include a provision whereby citizens could appeal to the Board of Regents to correct Dr Flick's error. Although it does not appear that Spellman actually saw *The Miracle*, he had no cavil about declaring that 'Satan alone' would make such a film. Characterizing its theme as 'the seduction of an idiotic Italian woman,' he noted: 'The seduction of any idiot woman, regardless of race, is revolting. It is art at its lowest. To give to this story of the seduction of an idiot-woman the title, "*The Miracle*," is diabolical deception at its depths. The picture should very properly be entitled, "Woman Further Defamed," by Roberto Rossellini.'

To Catholics who had not seen the film (and Spellman had just commanded all Catholics to avoid it), the gist of his message, presumably derived from information provided to Spellman by Masterson, Mrs Looram, and/or others, was that the 'miracle' referred to in the title was Nanni's seduction by the stranger. What Spellman meant by 'Further' in 'Woman Further Defamed' was not hard to grasp, since the media had already had a feeding frenzy with the story of Rossellini's having recently 'defamed' Ingrid Bergman. Thus there was some truth to what a Tennessee newspaper had said: that the *Miracle* controversy was really about Rossellini's 'actual sacrilege': 'dragg[ing] Ingrid Bergman, the Hollywood Diana, from her plaster-of-Paris pedestal.' Within hours of Spellman's speech, Catholics were picketing the Paris Theatre. One of the placards read: 'This Picture is an Insult to Every Decent Woman and Her Mother.'[33]

Ingrid Bergman

From the moment she had arrived in Hollywood, Ingrid Bergman seemed more 'moral' than earlier European imports (she was married to a Swedish dentist and was raising their daughter) and more 'natural' than Hollywood's home-grown types. 'Hollywood,' she had said, 'has a queer way of taking an individual and fitting her into the American mold. I have worked hard to develop my style and I don't want anything to do with bathing suits and plucked eyebrows.' She did not exemplify what the studios (and, thus, America) defined as classic elegance and glamour, much less did she exude vampish sexuality. When Bergman was first introduced at a dinner party held at Don the Beachcomber just off Hollywood Boulevard, Joan Bennett was heard to say: 'We have enough trouble getting jobs as it is. Do they have to import kitchen maids?' She did well in Gregory Ratoff's remake of *Intermezzo* (1939), then in *Casablanca* (1942) she became, 'overnight,' Garson Kanin later wrote, 'the biggest star in pictures.' The film showcases the breadth of her skills as she plays one character in three sequential dimensions: the *femme fatale* betrayer, the devoted wife sacrificing her personal happiness, and finally the 'you'll-have-to-think-for-both-of-us' victim of love, out-moralized by her hard-bitten lover into staying with her heroic husband. It is an impressive, multi-faceted portrayal, facilitated somewhat by the fact that from day to day Bergman did not know how her character would turn out, since none of those who were tinkering with the script had provided her with an ending.[34]

Following Bergman's performance in *For Whom the Bell Tolls* (1943), *Time* magazine put her on the cover, over the caption: 'Whatever Hollywood's bell tolled for, she rang it.' Repeating *Casablanca*'s soft-focus vulnerability in an Oscar-winning performance in George Cukor's *Gaslight*, Bergman then took the role of Sister Mary Benedict in *The Bells of St Mary's* (1945), the sequel to *Going My Way*. Although neither the Church nor the cultural norms of the 1940s would tolerate any hint of heterosexual love between a nun and a priest, even one hermetically sealed against physical desire, a decade of film-vetting by Breen had apparently prepared the audience to accept such an intense relationship, in which the erotic component between the crooner/priest and the gorgeous nun, filmed under the watchful eye of Father Devlin, is somehow held within appropriate bounds.[35] Thus, while Bergman achieved with Humphrey Bogart in *Casablanca* the ultimate Production Code version of renunciation as more interesting than consummation, the Bergman/Crosby matching does something similar.

Although the public could admire Bette Davis or Ethel Barrymore for bravura acting talent, its feeling for Bergman was different, since she 'represented' or 'personified' the idea that 'clean' could be alluring. In 1945 screenwriter/reporter Frank Nugent drafted some hagiography for the *New York Times* that would have been suitable for Mary Pickford a generation before: 'Miss Bergman just can't help being a good girl on the screen because that's the way she is.' She 'does not drink, does not smoke, does not stay out late nights, does not use make-up for street wear, never so much as carries a compact.' David Selznick called her 'the Palmolive Garbo,' while Andrew Sarris later gave a Freudian twist to the phenomenon, commenting that with 'the censors and the puritans ... in complete control of Hollywood ... a great deal of eroticism had to be sublimated in the increasingly neurotic nice girl.'[36]

Bergman moved seamlessly into the role of a psychoanalyst in Hitchcock's *Spellbound* (1945), then in *Notorious* (1946) played a sexually loose drunk who reforms herself and marries a man she does not love in order to uncover a Nazi plot for the FBI. From there she assumed the role of a sexual schemer in Sam Wood's *Saratoga Trunk* (1946), and in Lewis Milestone's *Arch of Triumph* (1948) played a sexually loose and suicidal refugee who almost dies of a botched abortion. Despite these films, her Palmolive reputation survived intact, to be further underscored as she took on the world-historical icon of Catholic martyrdom in Victor Fleming's *Joan of Arc* (1948).

Joan of Arc (1412–31), an illiterate, visionary peasant girl, heard the voice of the archangel Michael and saints Margaret and Catherine. Keeping these communications from her father for fear of his reaction, she nevertheless embraced the prophecy divinely relayed to her from God that she would lead France in war. She repeatedly demanded an audience with the Dauphin, and when he finally complied, he was sufficiently impressed to entrust her with an army numbering several thousand. Because of Joan's inspired leadership in battle under the banner 'Jesus Maria,' the Dauphin was crowned as King Charles VII of France. She was subsequently captured by the Burgundians, who handed her over to the English. Despite her extraordinary service, Charles did not lift a finger to save her life. She was tried by the Inquisition, headed by Pierre Cauchon, bishop of Beauvais, who hoped that as a reward for executing her he might get the archbishopric of Rouen. Also involved in her trial were five other bishops, sixteen bachelors of theology, and one cardinal, all of whom ignored her repeated demands to communicate with the pope. Following ten weeks of cross-examination by Bishop Cauchon's panel of local clerics and lawyers, she was declared a heretic, blasphemer, and sorcerer. Faced with death, she recanted. But then, on dubious allegations that she relapsed and refused to give up the men's clothing she preferred to wear, she was burned at the stake.[37]

Several decades after her death, Joan was juridically 'rehabilitated' by a new trial. She remained a popular although rather blurred French heroine, until in the 1840s historian Jules-Étienne Quicherat republished the documents pertinent to the trial condemning her and the posthumous vindication. With mid-nineteenth-century France in perpetual turmoil, every segment of opinion wishing to claim the true spirit of France now arrogated Joan as its prophet. In 1869, thirteen French bishops asked Pius IX to initiate the process of declaring her a saint, a simple way to make French Catholicism the *sine qua non* of

French nationalism. But then the anticlerical Third Republic, the bloody Commune, France's defeat in the Franco-Prussian War, and the tumult of the next two decades left the canonization process in limbo. In 1892, Leo XIII, although noting a 'vast conspiracy ... for the annihilation of Christianity in France' via a proposed separation of church and state, nevertheless instructed reluctant French Catholics to accept the Third Republic, which he saw as a potential ally in his ongoing dispute with secular Italy. Two years later, Leo attempted further accommodation with France by commencing the process of Joan's beatification, an intermediate step toward canonization. While beatification has fewer requirements when the subject has been martyred, this easier procedure was not chosen, for the rather awkward reason that Joan's death had been engineered by Catholic bishops.[38] This meant that four proven miracles were required, although one was said to be satisfied by Joan's having saved France.

Although France in 1904 broke diplomatic relations with the Vatican and in 1905 declared a statutory separation of church and state, Pope Pius X went forward with Joan's beatification, amidst suggestions in some quarters that the French government, by dismantling the French Church, had unwittingly strengthened the pope's direct power over French Catholics. While documents generated during Joan's posthumous rehabilitation trial contained testimony of several miracles, Pius chose to rely instead on miraculous cures recorded by competent medical eyewitnesses in his own time, in their respective attendances upon three different ailing nuns, each of whom invoked Joan's name and was cured. In 1921, C.A. Bachofen wrote that canonization was 'an act by which the Sovereign Pontiff definitively and, we may add, infallibly declares an individual ... to be a Saint.' The canonization of Joan of Arc thus demonstrated in papal hands a power to exalt a French heroine which no French government could hope to replicate. For canonization, two miracles were required which occurred *after* the official beatification. These were soon found, one of them taking place at Lourdes in 1909, where the invocation of Joan by a pilgrim suffering from tuberculosis was held responsible for a cure. In canonizing Joan in May 1920, Pope Benedict XV noted the felicity of using the miraculous cure recently effected at Lourdes, 'thus linking, in French hearts, the Immaculate Mother with the Virgin Warrior.' In July 1920, France established a national holiday in Joan's honour, then announced in November that diplomatic relations with the Vatican would be restored. Joan now joined Bernadette Soubirous as a patron saint of those who are ridiculed for their piety. The fact that Joan had been condemned by bishops, Marina Warner has written, was overcome by Benedict's claim that the judicial proceeding orchestrated by Cauchon was not under the auspices of Rome but of the schismatic Council of Basel.[39]

Joan's story, with its divine visitations, its peasant-girl-makes-good, its knights-in-armour, and its culminating trial and immolation, was in a sense a 'natural' for Hollywood, and the production of a film about Joan is the off-screen subplot of *The Miracle of the Bells*. Yet any cinematic portrayal raised both clerical and political issues, since what happened to this great French Catholic was far from flattering either to the Church officials who killed her or the French king who insouciantly let it happen. George Bernard Shaw summed things up in his wittily irksome way in the preface to his play *Saint Joan* (1924) by calling her 'the first Protestant martyr.' In 1936, Shaw squabbled with the Legion of Decency and Breen regarding a possible film of his play, wherein he complained of 'meddling amateur busybodies who do not know that the work of censorship requires any qualification beyond Catholic baptism.' Two years earlier there had been talk of Katharine Hepburn in the role, although the Legion had reportedly found Joan's life too controversial for the screen, and Hepburn's announcement in May of that year that she had filed for divorce rendered her unsuitable for the part.[40]

If Shaw was out of the question, a reprise of Carl Dreyer's *Passion de Jeanne d'Arc* (1928), with its faithfulness to the trial transcript, its hyperbrutal capturing of Cauchon's cross-examination, its hypocritical bishops and uncouth Englishmen, a film banned in England and denounced by the archbishop of Paris, was unthinkable, even without the expressionist 'artiness' that few Americans could comprehend, much less enjoy. In July 1947, Breen was pleased to tell Father Lord that the new Joan project would derive from Maxwell Anderson's play *Joan of Lorraine*, then on Broadway, and that the film's producer, Walter Wanger, had invited from France a Jesuit priest who would 'serve as a combination French-Catholic Technical Adviser,' alongside Father Devlin. With both Catholic and French interests thus covered, the British market was less important, and the resulting film so pleased another of the priests hired as a consultant on the film, Catholic University's William Lallou, that he wrote: 'Hollywood, whose standards of morality once fell so low that a Legion of Decency had to be organized to protect Catholics from ... vicious influence ... has given us ... a story which priests may confidently recommend to their people, of whatever age,' the production being 'in perfect consonance with the life of Saint Joan as summarized in the decree of her canonization' in 1920, that is, the film took no liberties with the 'official' Catholic version of her life and death. Father Devlin called it 'as historically accurate as possible,' while Wanger dared promote the film as not just a 'commercial' but a 'spiritual' success.[41]

Ingrid Bergman had starred in Anderson's play on Broadway, the reviews of her performance being nothing short of reverential, yielding cover stories in *Life* and *Newsweek*. What made the play interesting was the added dimension of having Bergman play a modern actress struggling with the role, trying to understand Joan's faith as a predicate for her own performance. The movie deleted this extra dimension, leaving a costume drama which invites us to venerate Joan's faith while giving us no cogent reason for doing so. While the various clerical consultants kept themselves busy avoiding anti-Catholic elements, apparently no one thought to include in the film anything establishing a positive story of the power and/or virtue of Catholic belief. Although all hands endeavoured to replicate the 'feel' of Olivier's brilliant and lucrative *Henry V*, in the years since Murnau's *Sunrise* (1927), Hollywood had seldom captured the integrity and genius of the European tradition, and *Joan of Arc* is left with the hollow form of 'Art,' relieved only by the crackling American accents of the Virgin Warrior's soldiers, instilling the sense that perhaps the film was about medieval knights laying siege to the fort at Cedar Rapids. Although there was some self-gratulatory banter about the industry's having made an 'important' film and it garnered Academy Awards for colour cinematography and colour costume design, the project was a box-office disaster. Bergman and her husband, Dr Petter Lindstrom, lost their entire investment, while Walter Wanger, who as the film's producer was awarded a special Oscar 'for distinguished service to the industry in adding to its moral stature in the world community,' had staked his entire personal fortune and went bankrupt. Director Victor Fleming had a heart attack and died.[42]

In 1946, Sam Wanamaker, who had co-starred with Bergman in the Broadway play, told her she was wasting her time in Hollywood and had her see *Open City* at the World Theater. When Bergman two years later saw *Paisan*, she proceeded to ask Rossellini for work. Hollywood had always been willing to buy foreign talent, and at the time he received Bergman's letter, Rossellini was already negotiating with Selznick to make a film with Jennifer Jones. Arriving in Hollywood in January 1949, Rossellini discussed with Bergman a film he wished to make on the volcanic island of Stromboli, near Sicily, the story to be derived from Rossellini's chance meeting with a Latvian refugee whose part Bergman would play. Rossano Brazzi arranged for a gala luncheon at the Beverley Hills Hotel and served as interpreter between Bergman and Rossellini, although as the meal progressed he commented to Jean Negulesco that soon the two would need no translator. In April, Bergman flew to Italy to begin location shooting on Stromboli, leaving Dr Lindstrom and their daughter Pia in Los Angeles. Federico Fellini said of Bergman's arrival in Rome: 'She gave this feeling of being a fairy queen,' more a Disney character than an actress, one 'who could make little miracles ... For Italians, who are so deeply touched by the Catholic Church and the figure of the Virgin Mary, she was someone who reminded you of an American saint.'[43]

At the time Rossellini first took up with Anna Magnani during the filming of *Open City*, he had exchanged his failed marriage for two serious affairs as well as a variety of other encounters. Although Hearst gossip columnist Louella Parsons had advised readers just a few months earlier that she had never before been so impressed by Bergman as 'Mrs Peter Lindstrom,' the domesticated wife and mother, now Italian newspapers began carrying stories about an affair with Rossellini. When on 13 April 1949 Hearst society columnist Igor Cassini predicted that Bergman and Rossellini would divorce their respective spouses and marry, Lindstrom flew to Italy for a confrontation. On 5 August, Bergman announced that she would file for divorce. The next day, a Roman newspaper alleged pregnancy. Gossip columnist Hedda Hopper flew over for an interview, and, when the question was posed, Bergman said nothing other than: 'Oh, my goodness, Hedda. Do I look it?' Hopper took that as a denial, accepted it, and allayed her readers' concerns by declaring that the rumours were false.[44]

While her talent, work ethic, professional bravery, and beauty positioned Bergman for the lifetime adulation available to only a handful of entertainers, public tastes were fickle. Even before the allegation of pregnancy, Joe Breen wrote to her on the *Stromboli* set to say that the newspaper accounts 'are the cause of great consternation among large numbers of our people who have come to look upon you as the first lady of the screen – both individually and artistically ... Such stories ... may result in the American public becoming so thoroughly enraged that your pictures will be ignored, and your box-office value ruined.'[45] Although most of Hollywood's inevitable mischief was kept from the public eye, not everything could be suppressed. In 1942, Errol Flynn was charged with having violated an underage girl, and in 1943 a paternity suit was filed against Charlie Chaplin, whose reputation was already tarnished because of his propensity to marry teenagers. Although both cases were dismissed, the publicity damaged both actors. Flynn became a subject of ribald jokes (including the serviceable assonance 'In Like Flynn'), while Chaplin would eventually be drummed out of America. And here Ingrid Bergman's reputation seemed to be in tatters, the shock being that much greater because of the public's collective fantasy about her 'Palmolive' qualities, just as Chaplin's fall – like Arbuckle's two decades earlier – was the more dramatic because people had once thought him funny.

Bergman arrived back in the United States and commenced divorce proceedings. Dr Lindstrom, whom Louella Parsons described as so cold that at a party he could look at you as if you were an object for laboratory dissection, made the ungallant decision to contest the divorce. Someone came to know that the pregnancy rumour was true, and told Parsons, on the condition that Parsons could never reveal her source. She honoured that, other than referring to the source as a significant person in the media. The obvious choices would be Howard Hughes or the aging William Randolph Hearst himself. Hughes had financed *Stromboli* because Bergman was in it. After watching the publicist Birdwell parlay tawdry publicity about the unknown Jane Russell into an ongoing public interest in seeing Russell's breasts heave in a film with nothing else to recommend it, Hughes undoubtedly guessed that millions of people who would never otherwise buy a ticket to an 'art' film, might nevertheless pay money to see *Stromboli* in order to gawk at Bergman's belly. Hearst, too, had much to gain by generating a scandal, since his tabloids would fly off the newsstands with such an exclusive. Neither man would think twice about such exploitation. Hughes had been utterly shameless in his promotions of *The Outlaw*, while Hearst was widely believed to have cobbled up the Spanish-American War just to sell newspapers. Whatever the trail of information, on 12 December 1949 Parsons broke the story, complete with an analogy to everyone's favourite royal fairy tale, that of Edward VIII throwing away a kingdom for the love of Mrs Simpson. Hearst's *Los Angeles Examiner* set up Parsons's account with huge type across page one announcing that Bergman was pregnant.[46]

In the Birdwell tradition, Hughes's promotion of *Stromboli* included posters proclaiming, 'Raging Island ... Raging Passions!' against an erupting and phallic Stromboli volcano, a treatment grossly inappropriate for this sombre and astringent film. Rossellini broke his press silence to describe Hughes's efforts as 'practically pornographic,' and when Hughes meddled with the version of the film released in the United States, Rossellini disavowed the picture.[47] With *Bells of St Mary's* of recent happy memory and Bergman now also portraying the virgin warrior of Orléans, the tabloid scandal-mongering, along with Hughes's exploitative advertising, forced upon the public a collective cognitive dissonance.

Although Ohio had already granted *Stromboli* a licence, that state's superintendent of public instruction asked his attorney general whether the Bergman/Rossellini scandal justified revoking it. Ohio's film censorship statute provided that 'only such films as are in the judgment and discretion of the Department of Education of a moral, educational or amusing and harmless character shall be passed and approved,' another provision authorizing the Department to revoke any licence 'whenever in [its] judgment ... the public welfare requires it.' Despite the open-endedness of this second provision, Ohio's attorney general concluded that the first provision limited the censors to consider only the content of the film before them, not the off-screen headlines about those who made it. A law-review writer disagreed, urging that 'the educational and moral value of a film is a joint product of (a) the content of the film and (b) the situation in which it is to be shown.'[48]

Political and religious figures elsewhere similarly tried to rescind the licences previously issued for *Stromboli*, Memphis censor Lloyd Binford going so far as to ban *all* of Bergman's films, her soul being as 'black as the soot of hell.' Senator Edwin Johnson (D-CO), alleging a personal betrayal in that he was a Swedish American, introduced a bill to require a federal licence not only for films but for those who make them, its stated object being 'to insure wholesome motion pictures for the people and to eliminate persons of low character from making and appearing in films.' 'Out of the ashes of Ingrid Bergman,' he asserted, 'will arise a better Hollywood.' He smeared the MPAA's Eric Johnston as a 'front for the money changers' who should have summarily banished Bergman as Hays had once banished Arbuckle, characterized Rossellini as 'a money-mad home-wrecker' and a 'swine,' and Bergman herself as 'our most popular but pregnant Hollywood movie queen' as well as a 'cheap, chiseling female' because she would profit from the increase in *Stromboli*'s box office occasioned by the scandal.[49] While undoubtedly such allegations played well among constituents, in fact, Bergman had long since turned her back on the typical studio fare that would have made her the richest woman in Hollywood, in favour of the failed independents *Arch of Triumph* and *Joan of Arc*, before volunteering for Rossellini's on-location project next to a spewing volcano, the earth tremors from which nearly killed her.

Louella Parsons – unlike Senator Johnson – could legitimately claim a bit part in the *mise en scène*, if only as the messenger people now wanted to shoot. 'It appeared that ... if Ingrid had sinned,' she wrote, 'the fault was mine for revealing it.' The public, protected by Hollywood and the Church from filmic portrayals of life as it is actually lived, seemed utterly incapable of dealing with the Rossellini/Bergman matter in anything like a reasonable way. In the early 1920s, just after Will Hays purged Arbuckle in order to establish Hollywood's collective innocence, John Cowper Powys wrote in *Psychoanalysis and Morality*:

> The repulsive and odious vulgarity of our modern American attitude to sex-pleasure is flagrantly illustrated by the tone of our popular newspapers when any social lapse ... is dragged forth into the light. A queer torrent of emotion seems just then released wherein a half-comic, half-obscene sentimentality, gloating over its victims, mingles with a positive orgy of ethical vengeance, the brutality of which rises to the sadism of the pillory.
>
> ... Psychoanalysis will deserve the gratitude of all sensitive and generous spirits if ... it reveals the complicated wickedness of these persecutors of sex-delinquents. It will show how in the bursts of blind moral anger displayed by the average man and woman when confronted by some sex-lapse in another person, there surges up a boiling flood of suppressed envy and jealousy and thwarted lust ...

Powys hoped for a time when 'the particular inhibitions which have always been the ambiguous and questionable element in Christianity will relax their hold.' Louella Parsons, a professional dealer in gossip about movie stars, well understood the 'boiling flood' of 'suppressed envy' and 'thwarted lust' of which her readers were capable. 'It is a curious commentary on both motion pictures and the public,' she wrote, 'that when Ingrid sinned she should have to be the scapegoat for the sins of all; either committed or contemplated. Millions of persons reacted as if they had been the victims of a personal betrayal. Every husband felt wronged. Every wife felt guilty.'[50] Although psychoanalysts, psychologists, and sociologists periodically attempted to explain how such collective syndromes operate, they never improved on Tocqueville's off-hand observation that America is a nation of 'decent and ordinary' people who live 'in the perpetual practice of self-applause.' By placing all of their sins – committed or contemplated – on their favourite movie star, Americans could once more affirm their collective innocence. Unable to face and scrutinize any lapses in their own behaviour, they would have no interest in the irony that their scapegoating of Bergman in some sense replicated what the villagers had done to Nanni in *Il miracolo*. Amidst blaring accusations that *Il miracolo* was sacrilegious, blasphemous, insulting, disgusting, etc., no one seemed to notice its penetrating insight into human hypocrisy.

Europe indulged itself in no similar paroxysm of moral outrage. Felix Morlion, a French Dominican whose colourful background included intelligence work for the United States, had witnessed first-hand the human turmoil Rossellini captured in *Open City*. One of those who popularized the term 'neo-realism,' he became a clerical consultant on *Francesco, giullare di Dio* (*Francis, Jester of God* a.k.a. *The Little Flowers of St Francis*, 1950), the film Rossellini was directing in the final months of Bergman's pregnancy. Installed as president of Rome's Università Internazionale 'Pro Deo,' Morlion in January 1950 wrote to Joe Breen: 'I must tell you confidentially, because as a Catholic you can understand, that precisely the same courage in accepting the responsibility of motherhood (so often avoided in the film world) is bringing [Rossellini and Bergman] nearer to God.' Bergman, that is, rejected the tactic followed by an untold number of starlets: that of quietly choosing the easy way out. On 2 February a child was born. Rossellini, on location for *Francis*, received from local peasant women a basket of ricotta cheese, a traditional gift to the father of a new son.[51] The issue of a divorce decree hung in limbo. Then, on 9 February a mail-order decree was issued in Mexico, followed on 24 May by a certificate of marriage for Bergman and Rossellini.

Misunderstanding

The day after Spellman's denunciation, Joseph Burstyn held a press conference at which he presented photostatic copies of documents indicating that Italian authorities did not consider *Il miracolo* sacrilegious. Informed about what was happening in New York, Rossellini on 10 January sent Spellman a cable stating that he had made *The Miracle* 'with the humble spirit of brotherhood to show that the absence of charity in the hearts of men had given way to an immense darkness and sorrow,' adding that in the film 'men are still without pity, because they still have not come back to God, but God is already present in the faith, however confused, of that poor, persecuted woman, and since God is wherever a human being suffers and is misunderstood, "The Miracle" occurs when at the birth of the child the poor, demented woman regains sanity in her maternal love.' The better to convince Spellman of his earnestness, Rossellini closed with 'humillime provolutus ad sacram purpuram,' 'most humbly prostrated before the sacred [cardinal's] purple,' suggesting that perhaps Father Morlion had helped him with the drafting.[52]

Although Spellman had had no compunction about publicly calling Rossellini satanic, Philip T. Hartung in the 12 January issue of *The Commonweal* showed more restraint, suggesting that Rossellini 'may have had the most sincere intentions ... but the finished result is so dangerously close to being sacrilegious that it would have been better to leave this material alone,' since 'not all subjects are grist for the movie camera.' Three days later, *Life* magazine described the film's final scene in language Rossellini would have embraced: 'In a deserted church on a mountaintop [Nanni] brings forth a child in solitary agony, and here the true miracle takes place: the mother's transfiguring love for the newborn child, which turns a dirty, ignorant, thieving girl into a holier person than all the proper people who spat on her.' But neither Rossellini's cable, nor Hartung's suggestion that Rossellini's intentions might have been bona fide, nor *Life*'s published description of the film, gave Spellman pause. Meanwhile, although each blue licence form issued by the Motion Picture Division provided that 'the Division reserves the right to revoke this license,' Dr Flick had no intention of doing so in this instance. In a formal memorandum submitted to the State deputy education commissioner, James E. Allen, just after Spellman's denunciation, Flick indicated that four members of his staff had seen *The Miracle*, and that three had approved it. 'It was the majority opinion,' he reported to his superior, 'that the principal theme was the portrayal of inhumanity of man to man' and that Nanni's 'hallucination concerning the paternity of her child was a figment of her unbalanced mind and was based on a deep and sincere love of God.' Thus, the majority did not consider the film 'as sacrilegious but rather as the delineation of the cold cruelty of a community toward a misguided and mentally disturbed member of such community.' Flick added that although he was open to amending the statute so that the Regents could overturn any 'honest error' made by his staff, those who had already been granted licences had property rights in them, and for the Regents suddenly to negate those rights violated due process.[53]

On 19 January Fr. Masterson told Breen that *The Miracle* was objectionable because it would be seen by 'those who are not familiar with the facts concerning the birth of Christ' and who might believe that Jesus could have been the offspring of a liaison similar to the one portrayed in the film. Mary, 'a simple obscure girl' and the 'sanest and greatest of God's creatures,' he wrote, 'conceived a child by the direct intervention of God,' while the heroine of Rossellini's film, 'a half-demented peasant girl' and 'goat tender,' conceived a child 'because she was seduced ... by a man who was addressed as Saint Joseph, who looked like Saint Joseph, and who was guilty of this despicable act.' In Masterson's view, 'the implications are clear ... St. Joseph, the foster-father of Christ and guardian of Mary, his Immaculate spouse, was a casual seducer and betrayer of a half-wit woman. Mary, the Mother of God, recognized by the non-Catholic poet [Wordsworth] as "our tainted nature's solitary boast" is a dolt who, plied with wine or other blandishments, is easy prey to the lusts of an ordinary passer-by.'[54]

Because the Gospel account of the Virgin Birth involves a woman found to be pregnant but not by her husband, in Christianity's early days a convenient way to deride Christian faith was by vulgar suggestions of cuckoldry, as when Celsus, a second-century anti-Christian pagan, asserted that Mary was impregnated by a Roman soldier.[55] Enlightenment scholars, their programmatic task being to dispel credulity, thought the Virgin Birth must be assigned some rational explanation, as when K.H. Venturini suggested that some seducer might have told Mary he was a messenger from God. By 1951, however, scientific, rationalist, empiricist attacks on faith were old hat, and such books were seen as having proven nothing. In any event, the various 'natural' explanations of Christ's birth in such books would be of no interest to Rossellini, nor does an objective viewing of *The Miracle* support Masterson's argument that in Nanni's seduction by a stranger, Rossellini is suggesting that this is what 'really' happened to Mary.

Beyond all this, it would have been difficult to find anyone so ignorant of the biblical tradition that, having wandered into Manhattan's Paris Theatre to see a triad of European art films, he could come away – as Masterson suggests – with the erroneous belief that Christ was born in the circumstances portrayed in *The Miracle*. Masterson's whole sense of the film is not just inept but obtuse. That a delusional woman has faith is not to suggest that faith is delusional. The stranger in *The Miracle* does in one sense resemble Saint Joseph in that, like the image of Joseph in honourific Italian paintings that rendered him as a northerner, the stranger has blond hair. Perhaps it is this fact that causes Nanni to 'recognize' him as Joseph, but that is hardly enough for the audience to accept that she must be correct, particularly since he is wearing modern clothes. Since she tells the stranger that Jesus fought demons but is not going to return to earth, she understands on some level that Jesus lived and died, and that therefore she cannot be Mary and cannot be carrying the infant Jesus, even if a woman who is both deluded and devout may believe both that Jesus once lived and that He lives again within her.[56] But whatever Nanni believes, in carrying a child, she is carrying the key to her own salvation. This is ultimately what the film is about, and Masterson misses it completely.

Given American Catholicism's hypersensitivity, around this time, to purported slights, it would be reasonable to assume that any film dealing with religious miracles – in particular, that of the Virgin Birth – would have triggered similar anger. Yet one could hardly say that Rossellini's film received even-handed treatment. In Dore Schary's and William Wellman's *The Next Voice You Hear*, following God's miraculous interventions on earth, the character Joe peeks into a delivery room where a baby's crying is heard. Mary is suddenly wheeled out on a gurney, as an onlooker proclaims: 'Talk about miracles!' The American bishops did not find this sacrilegious, nor did they protest the film's larger motif: that God might choose to reveal Himself via such miraculous techniques as speaking to Joe, Mary, and the rest of the post-war world on prime-time radio, and by such cheap gimmicks as secretly fixing the worn-out starter on Joe's old car.[57]

Churchmen commonly refer to a newborn as a 'gift of God,' and in that sense the onlooker in *The Next Voice You Hear* (who clearly is *not* suggesting that God – not Joe – is the father of Mary's baby) is accurate when he describes the birth of their baby as a 'miracle.' But is the birth of a child to Nanni less miraculous? The Vatican's young reviewer, Piero Regnoli, concluded that the 'carnality' of *Il miracolo* made it morally objectionable, since the non-marital birth 'is not mitigated by Nanni's faith; rather, this psychopathic and pseudo-religious coloring remains, unfortunately, an important negative element.'[58] In *The Next Voice You Hear*, Joe and Mary are married, already have another child, and are pursuing the American Dream. Until the moment Nanni gives birth, she had nothing in the world and had wished only to die. Perhaps the archangel Michael has provided Nanni with healing water and has fought and killed her demons. Even if we reject that interpretation, we have no reason to challenge Rossellini's comment that the birth brings her 'sanity,' in the sense that it brings her back to the world and gives her something to live for in the world. But by a less compassionate logic, the birth of a child to Nanni cannot be a 'miracle,' not just because she is unmarried, but because of who she is. In the rush to declare and avenge Rossellini's 'subversion' of the Virgin Birth, it occurred neither to Masterson nor to Spellman that Nanni might evoke, not disdain, but compassion. To dismiss her as 'half-demented,' a 'half-wit,' and a 'dolt' (Masterson's terms) or an 'idiot-woman' (Spellman's) is utterly inappropriate, indicating a coarse failure of sympathy that is disappointing in men presumably trained for a pastoral commitment, while investing Spellman's Christian names – 'Francis Joseph' – with an unfortunate irony. Rossellini captured the innocence of a religious faith shorn of everything: of adequate bonds with the community, even of the everyday, two-dimensional 'sanity' by which we claim superiority over the likes of Nanni.

Neither in *The Miracle* nor in Rossellini's other works is there anything like the satanic spirit of mockery Masterson and Spellman purported to find; that is, they did not understand the film intellectually or aesthetically, much less spiritually. A more accurate sense of the film comes from Rossellini himself, both in his cable to Spellman and in his later comments to Eric Rohmer and François Truffaut: 'Here we have a mad woman afflicted by some sort of religious fixation. However, besides her fixation, she also has a real deep faith [mais, en plus de cette manie, la foi, vraie, profonde] ... Some of the things she believes in, I admit, may seem blasphemous, but her faith is so huge that it rewards her. Her action is absolutely normal and human: she nurses her child.' Nanni's faith is not only more true and more profound than that of the villagers, but it is as capable of miracle-working – in its way – as a faith that was mistakenly focused on the bones of a dog. Rossellini prefaced his comments to Rohmer and Truffaut with an unequivocal declaration: 'Selon moi, *Le Miracle* est une œuvre absolument catholique.'[59]

Thoughtful critics would agree. In 1953, Rohmer and Fereydoun Hoveyda found Rossellini's films 'profoundly infused with Christian symbolism,' describing *The Miracle*, *Francis*, and *Europa '51* as 'new stones in this cathedral which Christianity never stops building to the glory of God.' Rohmer characterized *The Miracle*, *Stromboli*, and Fellini's *La strada* (1954) as all having the same moral – 'that the being closest to God is the most humble, the most disgraced' – while Raymond Borde, reviewing *The Miracle* in Jean-Paul Sartre's *Les Temps Modernes*, described Rossellini and Fellini as 'believ[ing] in God, through a Franciscan lens.' Andrew Sarris in 1961 went so far as to call Rossellini 'the most

Catholic of all directors,' and Martin Scorsese has commented that in *The Miracle* Rossellini proposes that Christianity is meaningless if it cannot accept sin and allow for its redemption.[60]

Masterson's allegations against *The Miracle* might have been more appropriately aimed at Preston Sturges's *Miracle of Morgan's Creek* (1944), a plot summary of which sounds like something submitted to Breen as a prank. Trudy Kockenlocker (Betty Hutton) seems to have been impregnated by a soldier at an Army dance but can't remember who – except his name might have been 'Ratskywatsky, or was it Zitzikiwitzky?' Her male friend, Norval (Eddie Bracken), is too oafish for her to have gone to bed with, no matter how drunk she was that night. When Brian Donlevy, playing the crooked Irish governor audiences had grown to love in Sturges's *The Great McGinty* (1940), finds out that the result of Trudy's evening out is sextuplets, he grasps the unique public-relations potential and pulls all the strings necessary to make things right. Paul Gallico called Sturges's film one of the 'most daring pictures of all time' as well as one of the 'funniest,' while James Agee, who analogized watching it to 'taking a nun on a roller coaster,' commented: 'the Hays Office has been either hypnotized into a liberality for which it should be thanked, or has been raped in its sleep.' The awarding of a PCA seal in 1943 to a wartime comedy about an underage girl who gets pregnant after an Army dance is unusual enough. But as Richard Corliss has noted, the film is also sacrilegious. Since Trudy gets her first labour pains in a farmhouse, as a cow watches, then gives birth to sextuplets on Christmas morning, the film was intentionally (Corliss writes) 'a blasphemous ... retelling of the Nativity story – with the Virgin Mary as a fun-loving World War II party girl, Saint Joseph as the adenoidal 4-F stuck on the home front, [and] God (or the Angel Gabriel) as an unseen soldier' whose name may be Ratzkiwatzki.[61]

Such inconsistencies in the enforcement of the censorship regime derived ultimately from the inadequacies of those the Church assigned to monitor films, rendering them incapable either of spotting the subtle sacrilege in Sturges's rapid-fire work, or of understanding Rossellini's Franciscan sensibility. Intent on ferreting out and suppressing ideas it supposed to be anti-Catholic, the hierarchy granted internal preferment to those who vigorously enforced that suppression. Inevitably, such men would lack aesthetic sophistication, expending great energy tracking one supposed slight while remaining oblivious to another, and utterly misapprehending pro-Catholic messages which lay outside a constricted range of 'approved' ideas. But by this point a certain myopia, resulting in uneven and unfair treatment, was not the only problem with the Church's role as Hollywood's moral overseer. The Church's close relationship with Hollywood, launched in the mid-1930s not by shared ideals or shared concerns but rather via the stranglehold of a boycott threat, by the late 1940s had evolved into a symbiotic arrangement whereby the Church continued to hold substantial power over what Hollywood produced – no longer exercised by threats because threats were no longer required – but in which Hollywood had also become the Church's publicist, representing it to America and the world. It did so, not out of admiration, but as an extra form of consideration in the ongoing bargain. *Boys Town*, *The Song of Bernadette*, the two McCarey films, and *Fighting Father Dunne* all demonstrated that Hollywood now 'sold' the Church much as it had once 'sold' sumptuous bathtubs, getaway cars, and fallen women. If a film was to be made about Joan of Arc, or if Cardinal Richelieu was to have a walk-on part, only the Catholic version of history would do. As André Bazin wryly remarked: so much for Hollywood decadence.[62]

In a sense, Hollywood (with a few exceptions like Stanley Kramer and Joseph L. Mankiewicz, who were willing to speak 'on the record') had lost its collective will. Although frayed by television and *Paramount*, it retained its business sense. Clare Boothe Luce, author of the story behind *Come to the Stable*, told C.S. Lewis that Hollywood was 'Christian' only in the sense that Christmas cards and Easter bonnets are Christian, 'in short, wherever it is box office to be Christian.'[63] Since neither Hollywood nor the Church wanted artistic or intellectual freedom, Hollywood 'sold' the Church in the artistically and intellectually limited way the moguls and the bishops could all understand: by warm, pro-Catholic messages about how faith can save the parish church from becoming a parking lot, can cause the construction of a boys' school, or of a children's hospital, etc. *Come to the Stable* is one such filmic Christmas card. It is supposedly about the faith of two nuns, but they succeed in getting the hospital built only because of the succession of coincidences that drive the plot forward: (a) the racketeer who owns the tentative building site had a son who died in France near the nuns' original hospital; (b) a local songwriter who wants to block the project finds out that the great melody he has just written is actually a Gregorian chant he had heard in France; (c) one of the nuns trying to raise money also happens to have played in the French Open, etc.

Film-makers are entitled to sentimental bargains with the audience. *Going My Way* is a well-disciplined work in this vein, and De Sica's

Bicycle Thief and *Umberto D* are noble achievements. But the sentimentality of *Come to the Stable* derives from an unsatisfactory ambiguity. Because mere coincidence is as un-Catholic as is blind Hegelian inevitability, the film would have us accept that something beyond coincidence is at work. But we have no idea what it is. Is the film suggesting that coincidences are caused by God? By faith in God? If so, it gives us no more articulable reason for accepting such notions than it does for accepting that God made all this happen because (like Mrs Luce) He happens to be an avowed Francophile. Ultimately, *Come to the Stable* is not an exposition of Catholic faith but a cloying attempt to manipulate us into warm feelings about Catholic faith and its efficacy in accomplishing good works. *The Miracle*, in contrast, is about natural events, pain, love, isolation, faith, sin, and – as Martin Scorsese has noted – the possibility of redemption. Detesting Hollywood sentiment, Rossellini pulls no punches.

The Santa Claus known to most Americans derives from a series of paintings done for Coca-Cola by the brilliant commercial artist Haddon Sundblom. This is a secularized, commercialized pseudo-deity on whose lap children may sit in order to list for their parents what they want from among the thousands of items available in the store paying Santa's salary. He is not recognized by the Church as one of its saints, being too distant and too transmogrified a descendant of Saint Nicholas. Nevertheless, only half-heartedly did the Legion protest the Oscar-winning *Miracle on 34th Street* (dir. George Seaton; 1947), a movie positing that a broken-down Macy's Santa is in fact the 'real' Santa Claus. While hypersensitive about Cardinal Richelieu and Joan of Arc, the Legion and the hierarchy let the Santa question drop; none of the memos and correspondence in Breen's office even recognize that a film in which Santa is found to be 'real' might pose a Catholic issue. To trigger such headlines as 'Church Does Not Believe in Santa Claus' was to court a public-relations disaster, and public relations now seemed to count for everything. The Church had so unreservedly embraced the 'feel-good' sentimentality that Hollywood could generate on its behalf, that it had lost the will to stand up for doctrines which might be deemed inconsistent with the image Hollywood had created for it. At the apex of their respective powers, the studios and the hierarchy – once sworn enemies – had drawn closer and now saw things the same way.[64]

The symbiotic relationship is amply demonstrated in *The Miracle of the Bells*. Its premise, British critic Richard Winnington noted, is fundamentally sacrilegious: we are invited to accept the legitimacy of a religious revival even though it grows out of the demonstrably erroneous belief that God has caused statues of the Virgin Mary and Saint Michael to move, that belief deriving from the refusal of the parish priest to declare that this was only the floor shifting under the weight of a capacity crowd. The Church had rigorously cross-examined Bernadette Soubirous because – to guarantee that the faithful would never be defrauded – it wanted the term 'miracle' confined to phenomena which could not be otherwise explained. But *The Miracle of the Bells* approves a situation in which a Hollywood publicity man convinces a priest to remain silent about what has really happened, merely so that a maudlin revival (initiated by the publicist's own Birdwell-like scheme) will not lose momentum. What difference does it make, Fred MacMurray's character says, whether God is speaking from 'up there' or only through people's hearts? This would have been the moment for Father Paul (Frank Sinatra) to reply that since God did not cause the statues of Mary and Michael to move, the Church cannot allow people to believe that He did, no matter how good it makes them feel. But instead he goes along with the fraud. Winnington, characterizing the film as 'Hollywood's latest and crudest act of publicity on behalf of the Roman Catholic Church,' found its sacrilegious 'pay-off message' to be that 'anything that brings hope to the people is an act of God. Conclusion – even God needs a good press agent.' And if this were not enough of a public-relations bargain between Hollywood and the Church, the film's 'happy ending' – the construction of a hospital for black-lung disease – is underwritten by the Jewish mogul, Marcus Harris (Lee J. Cobb), exemplifying that the days of salaciousness are long gone and that Hollywood has become the Church's working partner in achieving worthy ends. James Agee was sufficiently appalled to threaten starting a 'Society for the Prevention of Cruelty to God.' *Time*'s review said the film's box-office gross 'should be a fair measure of the depths of U.S. pseudo-religious depravity.' [65]

Rossellini as Communist

The 6 January 1951 number of Quigley's *Motion Picture Herald* proclaimed:

An essential bulwark of the Western World against Communism – and the chief hope of millions reduced to slavery behind the Iron Curtain – is religious belief and practice ... 'The Miracle' is blasphemous ... Its thinly veiled symbolism is an attack not only on Christian faith but all religion ... Its logical birthplace ... is Soviet Russia, though it is to be doubted whether even the Communists in Russia would dare make a film so offensive to many of their own citizens who still keep religious faith alive within their hearts ... With Americans dying daily in Korea and the nation girding for total war if necessary to preserve our way of life, which is based on belief in God and the inalienable rights of man, it is intolerable that a film such as 'The Miracle' should be shown in an American theatre.

Bosley Crowther, on the other hand, rhetorically asked readers whether the nation in fact wanted a free screen. Protesters at the Paris Theatre now numbered one thousand, spilling over to the small park in front of the Plaza Hotel. Some of the pickets were from the Holy Name Society; a fraternal order of New York City policemen, with a larger contingent representing the New York Catholic War Veterans, of which McCaffrey had been an official. When Rossellini's film was released in Italy two years earlier, a rumour had circulated that Pius XII was allegedly pleased that even a Communist could do a modern rendition of the miracle of the Virgin Birth. During a tumultuous period in Italian politics, the label 'Communist' derived, not from any political affiliation or creed declared by Rossellini, but from his neo-realist subject matter and tone, which Italian leftists warmly approved, while the Church preferred the stylish 'white telephone' musicals and romances of the 1930s. The Italian Communist Party had applauded *Open City*, but did so despite the fact that its hero is a priest. Then it lost faith in Rossellini, characterizing *Stromboli* as a retreat from neo-realism and a feeding at the capitalist trough, as demonstrated by its rich American star and the financial backing of Howard Hughes.[66] Reports circulated that Soviet authorities denounced *The Miracle* as pro-Catholic propaganda.

A protestor outside the Paris Theatre seized upon a phrase deemed likeliest to intimidate or dissuade potential patrons, and put it on a poster: 'Don't be a Communist – all the Communists are inside.' In the atmosphere of the time, any deemed attack on the Virgin Birth was *ipse dixit* a Communist scheme. A Brooklyn-based Catholic diocesan newspaper, *The Tablet*, quoted Quigley's *Motion Picture Herald*: 'Friends of Communism, at home and abroad, pledged to the abolition of all faiths, must now be smiling' at what was happening in New York, adding that if Hollywood had no Production Code, those 'of the Rossellini stamp ... would not hesitate to make films every bit as deliberately designed to belittle Christian principles and advance the crawling cause of Atheistic

Communism.' In his polemic against *The Miracle*, Spellman urged that 'producers of racial [i.e., anti-Italian] and religious [i.e., anti-Catholic] mockeries' were out to 'divide and demoralize Americans so that the minions of Moscow might enslave this land of liberty.' In his movie column in the February *Sign*, a national Catholic magazine, Jerry Cotter called *The Miracle* a 'vile and offensive mockery' of Catholicism which justified McCaffrey's ban, even if 'the immediate reaction from the self-appointed guardians of "civil liberty" was much as you would expect. These self-styled liberals set in motion a campaign of vilification, distortion, and lies that could have come from a Kremlin handbook. The pattern was clear and so was the objective, just as clear as Rossellini's purpose in filming such a perverse and antireligious vignette ... If we have reached the stage where depravity and outright mockery of religion are to be excused as artistic and defended in the name of freedom, then we are indeed in a sorry mess.' William H. O'Neill, vice-commander of the New York Catholic War Veterans, stated that although *The Miracle* 'was reputed to be a piece of art from Italy,' it 'reflected the writings of Moscow.' The collective voice of 167 American Legion posts, few of whose members could have seen the film, said it 'ridicules the American principles that we fought for in two world wars,' a statement geared to trigger patriotic anger, even if *The Miracle* mentions no American principles, either for purposes of ridicule or otherwise.[67]

Although the pickets outside the Paris Theatre neither knew nor cared that Rossellini was being bruited as the post-war world's greatest director, if they had subjected his prior career to scrutiny, they would have found absolutely nothing either attacking Christianity or praising Communism. He had been trained in and made his first films in the great Cinecittà studios, built by Mussolini's son Vittorio, who was unlikely to have accommodated a committed Communist. Rossellini's *L'uomo dalla croce* (*Man of the Cross*, 1943), based on the life of a real priest, is not just a stirringly nationalistic war film but ranks as one of the most pro-Catholic films ever made.[68] Its hero, like the priest in *Open City*, is no sentimentalized Hollywood archetype. A handsome, bespectacled intellectual wearing an Italian officer's uniform, he gathers a collection of Soviet peasants, Italian soldiers, and a pair of doctrinaire Communists in the remains of a peasant's hovel in the middle of a raging battle, where he teaches the children how to cross themselves. One of the Communist ideologues (she also happens to be an adulteress) rejects religion because she does not want to be 'weak' like her mother. The priest quietly instructs her in the difference between 'weak-

ness' and 'humility.' Converted by his pure verbal power, she embraces
a baby just born to one of the peasants. The film ends with the priest's
heroic death, followed by the caption: 'This Film Is Dedicated to the
Memory of the Military Chaplains Who Died ... on Foreign Soil Fighting
the Barbarous Enemy.'

For all the loose talk of Rossellini's Communism after *Open City*, he let
the films reveal their own messages and ambiguities, leading
filmographer Peter Brunette to call him 'this religious atheist and bourgeois revolutionary.' While collectivism and class struggle are obvious
in Giuseppe De Santis's *Riso amaro* (*Bitter Rice*, 1948), Rossellini's post-
war films are self-consciously anti-ideological, revealing his only real
'ism': humanism. Although he told readers of the February 1951 *Sight
and Sound* that his films deal with the 'problem' of faith, faith as a
human issue to be analysed, they do not simply 'analyse' faith, but
embrace it as the central human virtue. Clare Boothe Luce once called
Saint Francis 'the most Christlike character in Christendom ... His ador-
able gaiety in the dreariest hours, his brisk and bubbling gratitude to
God for the mere sight of a feather wafted across the sky, or a flower
blowing in a field ... are clad by God in far more glory than Solomon's.'
Rossellini, discussing *Francis, Jester of God*, said he found in Saint Francis
and sought to portray in the film 'the most accomplished form of the
Christian ideal.' Inviting Bergman to participate in *Stromboli*, he describes her character as Franciscan, one who comes to understand 'the
mighty power of he who possesses nothing' and thus 'procures complete freedom.' In Rossellini's view, he was just as much a 'realist' in
portraying Francis's world, 'full of simple joy and serene happiness,' as
he had been in the films by which others had labelled him 'pessimistic.'
Francis, its production aided by two Franciscans (Felix Morlion and
Alberto Maisano) and a Dominican (Antonio Lisandrini), is a brilliant
affirmation of Christian faith and fortitude.[69]

In Rossellini's *Europa '51* a.k.a. *The Greatest Love* (1952), Bergman
plays a bourgeoise who, following her young son's suicide, commits
herself to helping the poor, becoming a female Saint Francis with no
agenda other than to take personal charity seriously. She rejects her
industrialist husband's capitalist ideology and finds conditions in his
factory to be dehumanizing. Although her husband originally attributes
her frequent absences from home to her having an affair with a Communist journalist, soon he decides instead that she has simply gone
mad. Her mink-cloaked mother agrees, and they have her institutionalized, the husband's smooth-tongued lawyer making clear to the au-

thorities that the wife's conduct is injuring her husband's business reputation. The psychiatrists, the priest, the judge, the Communist, all of them intelligent, none of them really evil, are all tainted by the same materialist mentality which cannot recognize a true saint. Despite their many ideological and social differences, they all conspire to have a selfless woman declared insane and locked up, dealing with her with no more understanding or compassion than the villagers in *The Miracle* could summon in dealing with Nanni. Ingrid Bergman noted the message of *Europa '51* to be that if Saint Francis reappeared, he would be labelled a Communist.[70]

Shortly after Spellman's pulpit speech in January 1951, Republican assemblyman Samuel Roman telegrammed New York governor Thomas E. Dewey 'in behalf of Roman Catholic and Protestant faiths' in his Manhattan district, requesting that Dewey intervene to revoke the two permits previously issued for *The Miracle*. Hundreds of letters making that same demand were now arriving at the offices of the state's Board of Regents and of its education commissioner, Lewis A. Wilson, although letters urging the Regents *not* to close the film arrived from Richard Rodgers, Moss Hart, Frederick Lewis Allen, Russel Crouse, Howard Lindsay, John Mason Brown, Rex Stout, and Howard Barnes.

Back in December, shortly after Commissioner McCaffrey had first banned the film, New York mayor Vincent Impellitteri had attempted to defuse the controversy by appointing a priest, a rabbi, and a Protestant minister to decide *The Miracle*'s fate. That plan never reached fruition. Now the Regents, comprised of six Protestants, two Catholics, and two Jews, announced a similar idea, delegating from among their members a three-person subcommittee representing each of the three faiths.

The Board of Regents had been formed in 1784 to secure public education 'from all danger of clerical control,' albeit this was to be achieved not via non-denominational management but by giving each major religious group one seat on the Board.[71] That the subcommittee assigned to the *Miracle* controversy represented New York's three most populous faiths was consistent (whether knowingly or not) with that original philosophy, although undoubtedly someone must have voiced a concern as to what would happen if the Protestant and Jew disagreed with the Catholic regarding whether *The Miracle* was sacrilegious. After all, most Protestants and virtually all Jews rejected the idea that Mary was the Mother of God.[72]

The three saw the film on 15 January and unanimously declared it sacrilegious, the Regents thereafter issuing an order-to-show-cause requiring distributor Joe Burstyn to explain to the subcommittee on 30 January why the two licences previously issued for the film should not be revoked. With all the attendant publicity, the Paris Theatre was filled to capacity. On 20 January it began receiving anonymous bomb threats, which twice cleared the theatre. Fire Commissioner George F. Monoghan, a Legion of Decency member, closed the theatre for a day, alleging violations of the city fire code.[73]

17 'A Sense of Decency and Good Morals'

The New York Film Critics Circle announced that it would give Joseph Burstyn its award for *The Miracle* and the other two films constituting *Ways of Love* at a dinner to be held at Radio City Music Hall on 28 January 1951. Martin Quigley told Radio City's manager that if he chose to honour the Film Critics' reservation, he would incur Cardinal Spellman's wrath and could expect pickets. When the archdiocese confirmed its displeasure, the Film Critics switched their dinner to the picket-proof heights of Rockefeller Center's Rainbow Room.

Joe Burstyn's background was one with which the old-time Hollywood moguls might have felt kinship. Born in Poland in 1900, he immigrated to New York as a young man, worked as a diamond polisher, and did publicity for the Yiddish Theatre, before partnering with Paramount publicity director Arthur L. Mayer in the 1930s in the then marginal business of importing foreign films. While Hollywood was willing to recognize *Henry V* and *Hamlet* (Laurence Olivier was, after all, an adopted Hollywood star), Burstyn was an outsider. With *Open City* and *The Bicycle Thief*, he had flouted Breen's seal-giving power, and in doing so had introduced a small wedge of competition into Hollywood's domestic monopoly. Nor was Burstyn cowed by Catholic authorities, who so far had been incapable either of getting *The Miracle* banned legally, or of intimidating the Paris Theatre into cancelling its exhibition. Hollywood, meanwhile, content with its own arrangements with the Church and with government censors, was not going to lift a finger to help Burstyn try to establish freedom for this film, or for films in general. On 11 January, responding to MPAA executive Kenneth Clark's comment that 'Burstyn's troubles cause me no anguish,' Breen referred to the *Miracle* controversy as 'Burstyn's latest attempt to stir up trouble' that might result in demands for tougher film regulation in New York.[1]

In his speech at the Rainbow Room accepting the Film Critics' award, Burstyn addressed an audience whose luminaries included Bette Davis, Gregory Peck, and Joseph Mankiewicz. Choosing neither to ask for the studios' help nor to lambaste them for having offered none, he acknowledged that he had stirred up things that Hollywood had wanted left alone. 'Perhaps I should apologize,' he began. 'Perhaps I brought some embarrassment to some of you. I'm not sorry, but I apologize anyhow. I accept the award as a tribute to the integrity of people who really care about films, as a symbol of the truth cherished by all Americans.'[2] Having won Film Critics Circle awards for *Open City*, *Paisan*, *The Bicycle Thief*, and now *Ways of Love*, Burstyn was addressing these comments, not to the New York journalists who had shown such loyalty, but to the Hollywood contingent. Though the tone was dignified, the message was unambiguous: you don't really have integrity, and you don't really care about serious films. I pity you that you don't care, but others do care, and I will fight this fight for them, and for American audiences.

Hollywood and Southern Prejudice

Although Hollywood had no interest in helping Burstyn, there were rumours that the industry was contemplating its own assault on *Mutual Film*, by challenging one or more municipal censors in the American South. But this was bad for business. The hero of Richard Brooks's novel *The Producer* (1951) 'was always being told by self-appointed authorities ... that movies had to start showing how American Life really was, which meant it was wonderful ... [with] happy Americans ... stuffed with Turkey, God, and new models of automobiles.' Novelist Budd Schulberg, having grown up in Hollywood, observed that even in the muckraking years of Lincoln Steffens, Theodore Dreiser, Upton Sinclair, and Frank Norris, few people wanted to see 'message' films, what some called 'silver bullet' films. If you want to send a message, Sam Goldwyn said, call Western Union. Revenues were optimized and disruptions minimized by embracing the status quo.

Innumerable Southern whites deeply resented any kind of criticism, seeing it as somehow a resurgence of the Reconstruction regime imposed from outside, as portrayed in *The Birth of a Nation*. Griffith's film, with its vile racism, was warmly embraced by many, as it told the story of Reconstruction as they – like Griffith – wanted to believe it. In the Hollywood of Breen's hegemony, race was to be avoided because it would cause censorship, controversy, and economic sanctions. In 1937, Mervyn LeRoy released *They Won't Forget*, based on the infamous anti-Semitic lynching of Leo Frank in 1915.[3] Even two decades after Frank's murder, there was substantial sentiment in Georgia that the mob had done justice, and *They Won't Forget*, like LeRoy's previous exposé of Southern justice, *I Am a Fugitive from a Chain Gang*, was banned in several Southern states. Not that the film was self-consciously provocative: it never mentions its protagonist's religion, leaving audiences who did not know the underlying facts to accept that he is disliked by everyone in a local Southern town simply because he is from the North.

For the film industry, there was no virtue in spoiling a significant market, and every reason to placate it. Lost in the heavy sentiment of Norman Taurog's *Boys Town* (1938) is the fact that the hundreds of boys Father Flanagan has taken off the streets include not one African American. Hollywood chose to premiere *Gone with the Wind* in Atlanta even though Hattie McDaniel, Butterfly McQueen, and others were not permitted to attend the whites-only performance, and – adding insult to injury – some would later whisper that McDaniel's Oscar for that film was only the industry's way of tacitly apologizing. After the war, most in Hollywood still wanted to avoid the issue of race, since it was a pressing, unresolved American problem, at a time when everyone felt duty-bound to portray America's superiority to Sovietism. Under the specter of HUAC, as in similarly parlous times before the war, Hollywood experienced the immense pressures that could be brought to bear insofar as it abandoned its 'entertainment' function in favour of 'propaganda.' Having a film characterized as race propaganda was particularly dangerous, since the primary source of protest about America's race problem had been the Communist Party USA. The foul-mouthed Harry Cohn told Garson Kanin to write a script that was 'somethin' good, somethin' I can use and nothin' controversial – like niggers or God!'[4]

Despite men like Cohn and other executives who were more polite but held similar views, and despite HUAC and other pressures, the 1940s proved to be for Hollywood a watershed regarding race. To begin with, in keeping with the wartime mentality that 'we're all in this together,' the typical army platoon portrayed in Hollywood films was a spectrum of ethnicity, albeit white ethnicity, the armed forces having not yet been integrated. Frank Sinatra's eleven-minute colour short, *The*

House I Live In (1945), co-produced by LeRoy, pled for ethnic tolerance at the neighbourhood level, while ethnic hatred could be portrayed as characteristic of America's enemies. In Leslie Fenton's *Tomorrow the World* (1944), a young German boy, adopted by a decent American family as an act of charity, complains that on his way to their house he 'was forced to sit next to a big fat Jew,' a piece of dialogue that would have been unthinkable in any other context. And Edward Dmytryk's *Till the End of Time* (1946), contrary to the unspoken Hollywood rule requiring that every GI be portrayed as an honest Joe, features a fascist, racist organization of U.S. veterans who proselytize for new members in a bar, while Dmytryk's *Crossfire* (1947) centres on a returning veteran who is a pathological anti-Semite.[5] To a character who does not seem to care about anti-Semitism, the Irish-American detective explains that his grandfather, having escaped the potato famine, was killed by a Philadelphia mob in 1848.

Under the leadership of John Rankin (D-MS), HUAC targeted industry personnel who had in one way or another challenged American anti-Semitism. *The House I Live In* had been scripted by HUAC victim Albert Maltz, while Ring Lardner, Jr, had co-scripted *Tomorrow the World*. Dmytryk and producer Adrian Scott were reportedly targeted by HUAC because of their respective involvements in *Crossfire*. They prophesized (accurately) that their film 'will stand as a testament to our Americanism' long after Rankin and the other HUAC leader, J. Parnell Thomas, were dead. Terminated by RKO, Dmytryk and Scott were barred from accepting a civic award for *Crossfire*'s contribution to tolerance, and Dore Schary, who had consistently tried to help them, refused to cooperate with their ouster by accepting the award as a stand-in. Thus the tolerance award was accepted by Eric Johnston, who had made promises to help them, then chaired the Waldorf meeting that had sealed their fate. But some grim satisfaction was soon to be had when Parnell Thomas, convicted in a kickback scheme, was sent to the federal prison in Danbury, Connecticut, where two of his victims – Lardner and Lester Cole – would soon join him. In the federal proceedings against him, Thomas had opted to 'take the Fifth,' although that strategy availed him nothing. Thomas's job was in the chicken coop, collecting eggs and scraping droppings, thus prompting Cole to comment, as he passed by: 'I see just like in Congress, you're still picking up chicken shit.'[6]

Rankin may unwittingly have helped prompt Hollywood to segue its wartime protest against anti-Semitism into a protest against racism, in that Rankin was not only anti-Semitic but anti-black, announcing on the floor of the House in February 1947: 'It is not a disgrace to be a real Negro ... If I were a Negro, I would want to be as black as the ace of Spades. I would then go out with Negroes and have a real good time.' In the prepared statement Lardner had drafted but HUAC would not let him recite, he asserted that if Rankin and HUAC succeeded, 'the really important effect would be that the producers ... would lose control over their pictures, and that the same shackling of education, labour, radio, and newspapers would follow. We are already subject in Hollywood to a censorship that makes most pictures empty and childish. Under the kind of censorship which this inquisition threatens, a leading man wouldn't even be able to blurt out the words "I love you" unless he had first secured a notarized affidavit providing that his leading lady was a pure white, Protestant gentile of old Confederate stock.'[7]

In films made by whites for whites, the few parts for blacks were caricatures. When a Negro is cast as a maid, Richard Brooks wrote in his novel, it is thought anti-Negro. When the role is thus altered and given to a white woman, the African American who auditioned for the part complains that to cut her out is worse than casting her as a maid. It is then decided to make her a friend of the family, until it is realized that censors in Southern states would not allow such a friendship. 'Let Zanuck and Schary make pictures about Jews and Negroes,' the fictional producer bellows in Brooks's novel, Brooks having cleaned up Harry Cohn's actual words. The Code cared nothing about racial stereotyping, but would not tolerate interracial romance. The National Association for the Advancement of Colored People, having for decades concentrated much of its energy on protesting *The Birth of a Nation*, eventually adopted the more militant strategies of Italian Americans, Mexican Americans, and other ethnic groups by lobbying Hollywood to stop its prejudicial caricatures. Not until 1942 did Hollywood agree to avoid reprises of such glaring personae as Stepin Fetchit, Butterfly McQueen's 'Prissy' in *Gone with the Wind*, and Willie Best's ghost-ridden character in the Charlie Chan series. But the tendency to caricature died hard, and well-meaning whites were baffled when African Americans picketed *Song of the South* (1946; dir. Harve Foster and Wilfred Jackson), an adaptation of Joel Chandler Harris's *Uncle Remus* stories. Vincente Minnelli's *Cabin in the Sky* (1943), with its African-American woman lovin' and prayin' for her no-'count man, was the kind of fare whites thought appropriate and even endearing entertainment. Thus, to the degree one's understanding of the world derived from movies, Hollywood contributed substantially to a damaging image and thus, with some African-American children, a damaging self-image.[8]

Pure screen presence, such as Dooley Wilson in *Casablanca*, suggested that the regime of stereotyping had not only wasted talent but cheated audiences. The shared experience of a war against virulently racist enemies, coupled with the achievements of blacks in that war and the liberal predisposition of some Hollywood executives, suggested moving forward. It was said that Dore Schary deliberately waited until a script of *Bataan* was drafted before he cast an African-American actor, Kenneth Spencer, in a significant role, so that the part would contain no built-in stereotyping. Allan Dwan's remake of *Brewster's Millions* (1945) gives the raspy-voiced Eddy Anderson ('Rochester' on the *Jack Benny Program*) the standard role of the African-American Scapino, but in a sense puts him on the same level as the film's three white war buddies, by pointing out that he has just returned from Saipan. In 1947, Jackie Robinson's gallant breaking of the colour barrier in major league baseball, introducing millions of white people to a handsome athletic genius, provided Hollywood liberals with a powerful precedent for committing themselves to everyday race themes in mainstream films. Two of the films made in this quickly changing environment are remarkable. In 1949, Juano Hernandez in Clarence Brown's film of Faulkner's *Intruder in the Dust* provided a convincing portrayal of a smart, tough, poor, dignified black man on trial for murder in the South. In the same year, Stanley Kramer, Carl Foreman, and George Glass produced *Home of the Brave*. The underlying play by Arthur Laurents, produced on Broadway during the war, dealt with the psychological problems of a returned Jewish veteran, but because *Crossfire* and Kazan's *Gentleman's Agreement* had mooted the novelty of dealing with anti-Semitism, the play was reworked to make the protagonist African American. Kramer later noted that he so feared trouble from racist groups that the production went forward in secrecy. When the film opened in Georgia, an observer of a white audience sensed a negative reaction as the subject matter unfolded, then noted a collective relaxation, followed by a sympathetic discomfort, as the white psychiatrist (Jeff Corey) hurls epithets at his black patient in order to snap him out of his psychogenic paralysis.[9] The film ended up doing very well, grossing $2 million domestically. Then, as a mainstay of television movie fare in the years just prior to the civil-rights movement, it introduced a new generation of whites to African Americans as intelligent, complicated, courageous, deeply human, subject to the same brutal stresses of war as their white comrades, and fully qualified to be called war heroes.

The infamous Memphis Board of Censors was essentially a one-man show operating out of a ten-foot by ten-foot cubicle off a dentist's waiting room. Lloyd T. Binford, born during Reconstruction, proud to have left school in the fifth grade, ruled arbitrarily, by fiat. He banned train robbery films because as a rail clerk he had once been robbed. He banned *Dead End* because 'there is no need of showing a picture that might influence boys how to be gangsters.' He banned DeMille's *King of Kings* even after it had been seen by 600 million people in twenty-seven languages, because in it Christ is whipped and crucified. Sharing with D.W. Griffith a sick vision of the 'redeemed' South, Binford in August 1945 banned Jean Renoir's *The Southerner* (1945), despite hearty endorsements by the Daughters of the Confederacy, because in his view it depicted Southerners as 'common, lowdown, ignorant white trash.' When the film started playing just beyond his town jurisdiction, he had the state legislature invest him with county-wide power in order to close it down. When Charlie Chaplin refused to cooperate with HUAC's investigation, Binford not only banned all of Chaplin's work but called him a 'former London guttersnipe' as well as 'a traitor to the Christian American way of life, an enemy of decency, virtue, holy matrimony and godliness in all of its forms.'[10]

With regard to the treatment of African Americans in films, Binford was all that one might expect. He banned *Brewster's Millions* because Eddie Anderson's character was too significant in the plot and 'too familiar' with the white characters. He cut Lena Horne's scenes from major white musicals because 'there are plenty of good white singers.' In 1945 he deleted a scene showing Cab Calloway and his band because he thought them 'inimical to public health, safety, morals, and welfare,' words found in the Memphis film censorship ordinance. *New Orleans* (1947; dir. Arthur Lubin) never played in Memphis because there was no way to cut Louis Armstrong out of the picture. He banned *Annie Get Your Gun* because in it a railroad conductor is black. In Roy Chanslor's novel *Hazard* (1947), the main female character, a compulsive gambler, asks a black porter for a racing tip. He replies politely that since he is a Sunday-school teacher he does not know about gambling. Paramount in October 1947 told Chanslor and co-scenarist Arthur Sheekman that in drafting a script, the porter should be white, presumably because Binford would find intolerable a conversation between a beautiful white gambling addict and a respectful, Christian black man. In 1949, Binford padlocked a local theatre so that a group of forty clergymen could not have a private viewing of Louis de Rochemont's *Lost Boundaries*, a film based upon a true story, concerning an African-American family who for years live as respected members of a New Hampshire town because they 'pass' for white, only to face prejudice when their race is revealed. 'We don't take that kind of picture here,' Binford reportedly commented. And when Binford later suppressed Richard Brooks's path-breaking *Blackboard Jungle* (1955), Dore Schary told Congress it was undoubtedly because the actor in the starring role, Sidney Poitier, was African American.[11] Although Binford's absolute monarchy was a very small domain, he evidently enjoyed the national news coverage his vile rhetoric afforded him, and pointed with pride to *Variety*'s offhandedly referring to sliced-up movies as having been 'Binfordized,' as if it were some patented process of moral and racial dry-cleaning.

Some in Hollywood excused the industry's collective refusal to help Joe Burstyn by suggesting that better odds for overturning *Mutual Film* lay in either of two pending court cases concerning race. One involved Binford's banning of *Curley* (1947; dir. Bernard Carr), a Hal Roach film in an 'Our Gang' format, because it portrayed 'little negroes' in a predominantly white school, and 'the south does not permit negroes in white schools nor recognize social equality between the races even in children.' On appeal, the Tennessee Supreme Court professed to be 'in no wise in disagreement' with the view that a film should not be banned on that basis. It then held, however, that neither of the two plaintiffs in the case, producer Hal Roach Studios, Inc. and distributor United Artists Corporation, had legal standing to make any free-speech argument concerning the film, since the court would have entertained that argument only if it had come from one of the Memphis movie theatres under Binford's control. The court could thus comfortably be all things to all people, saying that the portrayal of an integrated school was not a valid basis for banning a film, while also finding a technical basis for not actually enforcing what it professed to believe. United Artists appealed, but in May 1950 the Supreme Court refused the case.[12]

Atlanta's municipal film censor, Christine Smith, a former college teacher and director of the League of Women Voters, banned *Lost Boundaries* because its exhibition would 'adversely affect [Atlanta's] peace, morals and good order,' language appearing in the city's film censorship ordinance. De Rochemont appealed to Smith's superiors, the trustees of Atlanta's public library. Losing there, he went to federal court, arguing that because of Justice Douglas's comment in *Paramount*, *Mutual Film* was no longer the law. In March 1950 the court rejected that argument, concluding that Douglas had merely made an offhand comment. De Rochemont appealed to the Fifth federal Circuit Court, also in Atlanta. In an amicus brief, Morris Ernst and the ACLU pressed the argument that *Mutual Film* – in effect – had been abandoned. The Fifth Circuit responded that it was not its duty 'to consult crystal ball gazers or diviners ... in order to base a decision on a prophesy' of what the Supreme Court might do. Further, the court 'particularly disagree[d] ... that moving pictures have now emerged from the business of amusement into instruments for the propagation of ideas,' thus subjecting them, like newspapers, to the First Amendment. De Rochemont then squarely asked the U.S. Supreme Court to decide whether *Mutual Film* was still the law. On 16 October 1950 the Court rejected his petition.[13] Only Justice Douglas had wanted to accept the case, suggesting that perhaps Douglas's comment in *Paramount* represented only his opinion, and that *Mutual Film* still represented the Supreme Court's collective view.

Another of de Rochemont's responses to the bans by Memphis and Atlanta was to announce that he would play *Lost Boundaries* on television in those cities. A state could not censor films shown on its local television stations, since the federal Communications Act of 1934 gave Congress exclusive authority to regulate television content.[14] Thus, in states with strict film censorship laws, theoretically one could see on television a film that was outlawed in local theatres. Nevertheless, television stations tended to be no braver than exhibitors, since local 'watchdog' groups and even disgruntled individuals commonly sent complaint letters to the Federal Communications Commission, which reviewed them at licence-renewal time. A television licensee thus ran a risk by playing a film that had been banned from theatres.

With the studios showing little interest in getting involved with Burstyn, and with the Supreme Court having declined review of the *Lost Boundaries* and *Curley* cases, some in Hollywood said the industry was putting its collective conscience behind another movie about race, *Pinky* (1949), a story about an African-American woman who 'passes' for a Caucasian. Ethel Waters plays an Alabama washerwoman who sends her granddaughter to Massachusetts to train as a nurse. The granddaughter, who has passed for white in Boston for some years, returns to care for the dying town matriarch, played by Ethel Barrymore. Although the underlying novel ends with 'low-down white trash' torching the matriarch's grand home so that it cannot be converted into a hospital for African Americans, the film omits this in favour of Pinky's decision to eschew the pleasant life of 'passing' far from home in favour of dedicating her nursing skills to help her own people. Breen advised, 'Avoid physical contact between Negroes and whites, throughout this picture' so as to avoid 'audience offence in a number of sections of this country,' a problem that was alleviated (or dodged) by the simple expedient of casting a white actress, Jeanne Crain, as the nurse. In Atlanta, Christine Smith required the deletion of several scenes but did not – to the surprise of some – ban *Pinky* altogether. It opened without incident at the downtown Roxy Theatre, where the huge balcony could accommodate a substantial number of African Americans.[15]

In 1949 the population of Marshall, Texas, was about twenty-two thousand. When the operator of the local Paramount theatre, W.L. Gelling, showed *Pinky* without first obtaining a town licence, he ended up spending a night in jail, prompting Darryl Zanuck to dispatch an MPAA lawyer to help get Marshall's film ordinance declared unconstitutional. Although *Pinky*'s controversial race theme had already yielded substantial national press coverage, the Texas Court of Criminal Appeals held:

> We cannot concede that the motion picture industry has emerged from the business of amusement and become propagators of ideas entitling it to freedom of speech. If in fact circumstances have developed surrounding the industry whereby television can bring to the youth of our cities, and even of rural areas, matters which are improper and even though magazines of a type are circulated through the U.S. Mails which present ideas derogatory to the proper development of good citizens, yet we cannot concede that this has divested the municipal authorities of the right to regulate such subjects ... The desire of a great industry to reap greater fruits from its operations should not be indulged at the expense of Christian character, upon which America must rely for its future existence.[16]

The court thus believed that while it could not block television and magazines from introducing the youth of East Texas to cosmopolitan ideas, *Mutual Film*, with its doctrine that movies are not protected by free-speech principles because movies do not contain ideas, still stood as a bulwark against Hollywood's making money at the expense of the 'Christian character' protecting America against its atheist enemies. The Supreme Court, having already turned down de Rochemont's petition, received a petition from Gelling's lawyers to review the Texas court's decision.

Opposition

The day after Burstyn's speech at the Rainbow Room, his lawyers filed a motion to stop the Board of Regents' three-person subcommittee from holding its scheduled hearing to consider the revocation of *The Miracle*'s licence. They argued that while New York's film statute expressly permitted *an applicant* to appeal to the Regents when the Motion Picture Division has *denied* a licence, it included no provision authorizing the Regents to cancel a licence the Division had already issued. In the absence of any such provision – they urged – neither the Board of Regents nor a subcommittee thereof could revoke a film licence previously issued by the Division. As historical support, they pointed out that at no time since the Regents assumed jurisdiction of film censorship in 1927 had such a revocation occurred.[17] Burstyn's motion was denied, and the hearing went forward the following afternoon at the City Bar Association on West 44th Street.

Burstyn and his lawyers might profitably have used the hearing as a forum to argue that the subcommittee had misconstrued the film, that it in fact carried a strongly Christian message, and that the Film Critics Circle would never have given its prestigious award to a sacrilegious work. Even if those arguments might not win the day before the particular panel assembled to hear them, they certainly warranted greater exposure than Burstyn and his lawyers had given them thus far, and would have garnered significant support among millions who knew nothing about the film other than what Spellman and McCaffrey had said. Instead, one of Burstyn's attorneys, John C. Farber, reasserted that the Regents had no statutory authority to overrule the Division, adding that since the subcommittee had already unanimously found the film to be sacrilegious, it would be not just humiliating but procedurally unfair and even futile for his client now to take on the burden of persuading the subcommittee that it had been wrong. The *Catholic Standard* noted that Hollywood was taking no interest in the case because it was 'smart enough to know' when it 'hasn't a leg to stand on,' that is, the industry was staying away not because it disliked Burstyn, nor because it feared Catholic retaliation, but merely because it knew Burstyn would lose.[18]

On 1 February the *New York Times* published a letter by Allen Tate, prominent poet and former editor of the *Sewanee Review*, who just a few months earlier had converted to Catholicism. Noting that Pius XII had not himself seen fit to ban *The Miracle*, Tate questioned how Spellman could have a better idea than the Holy See of what is and is not sacrilegious. 'When we remember,' Tate added, 'that the works of Dante Alighieri were publicly burned by a fourteenth-century Pope, the weapon of suppression begins to look ridiculous.' On 3 February, the reviewer for the periodical *Ave Maria*, under the heading 'New Low in Pictures,' suggested that if the deranged woman were portrayed as having had 'an imagined illicit relationship with, say, Washington or Lincoln,' *The Miracle* would never have received a licence, that is, by originally issuing it a licence, New York State had discriminated against the Church. Jerry Cotter in *The Sign* called the film 'sacrilegious and blasphemous.' Then on 11 February, Msgr Albino Galletto, head of the Centro Cattolico Cinematografico, issued a variant on the idea voiced earlier by Masterson: that in the United States, where most people do not understand the tenets of Catholicism, they would be unable to distinguish the film – a misguided attempt to portray a religious subject in good faith – from an intended ridicule of the Church. *Time* magazine, reporting his comment, noted that such confusion was more likely because of the pope's recent declaration of the Assumption of Mary as Church dogma (perhaps because the Assumption was one more thing non-Catholics found hard to understand).[19] Although Galletto tacitly contradicted Spellman's position that *The Miracle* was intentionally satanic, he did seem to answer Tate: what the Vatican thinks about the film is irrelevant since the problem is that it will prejudice America's Catholic minority in the eyes of an ignorant Protestant majority.

In its issue hitting the newsstands on 15 February, *Time* asserted what had been widely assumed but not previously stated as fact: that Spellman had demanded that the Regents revoke *The Miracle*'s licence. That day the thirteen people comprising the entire Board of Regents (two of them Catholic) saw the film, unanimously confirmed the subcommittee's conclusion that it was 'sacrilegious,' and revoked the two licences issued previously by the Motion Picture Division, stating: 'In this country where we enjoy the priceless heritage of religious freedom, the law recognizes that men and women of all faiths respect the religious beliefs held by others. The mockery or profaning of these beliefs that are sacred to any portion of our citizenship is abhorrent to the laws of this great State. To millions of our people the Bible has been held sacred ... This picture takes the concept so sacred to them ... and associates it with drunkenness, seduction, mockery and lewdness.' More specifically, *The Miracle* was sacrilegious because 'there are millions of citizens in the

State of New York to whom it is a matter of sacred religious belief and of Truth related in the Holy Gospels that Jesus Christ is the son of God, born of the Virgin Mary, who is referred to as the Blessed Virgin; that she was married to Saint Joseph; that she conceived Jesus through direct intervention of God, the Holy Ghost, and that she remained, before and after conception, a Virgin.'[20] *The Miracle*, they were saying, was a mockery of these beliefs.

Burstyn's lawyers immediately filed an appeal, which in short order was rejected by a judge in Albany. In that proceeding, they had submitted a letter from the director of Biennale di Venezia, indicating that if *Il miracolo* had been blasphemous, the festival committee would have rejected it. The Société Nouvelle Pathé Cinéma, the French owner of the Paris Theatre, ceased playing *The Miracle* and substituted Jean Delannoy's *God Needs Men* (*Dieu a besoin des hommes*, 1950). In that film, a layman reluctantly assumes the role of a priest on an isolated island, admitting sacraments and granting absolution. Originally chosen to represent France at the 1950 Venice Film Festival, it was withdrawn because Catholic doctrine forbids unordained persons from hearing confession, although a public showing yielded such a positive response that the Festival accepted the film anyway. The producer, Paul Graetz, noted that he had no interest in approaching religious issues – as Hollywood typically did – by such techniques as placing nuns on bicycles. Following a Vatican directive that priests and nuns should not attend the Festival nor sit on its juries, a lay jury of the International Catholic Film Office, fully apprised of the doctrinal problem of the unordained *confesseur*, awarded Delannoy's film a prize as 'homage to one of the most remarkable efforts to show on the screen, through the medium of a particularly delicate case, belief in a living Faith and in the vital necessity of religious practices based on the Sacraments.' The jury noted that if one did not issue awards to such pro-Catholic films – despite their objectionable aspects – then the Communists would lay claim to them for their allegedly anti-Catholic viewpoint. They had already made such claims for *Roma città aperta*, despite its strong Christian themes. Dr Flick had issued *God Needs Men* a licence without any protest from local Church officials, nor did they now demand that its licence be revoked. After the film had played for a few days, Masterson asked Graetz to eliminate the scene in which the unordained person grants absolution, and Graetz complied. Masterson told Breen that it was 'necessary to do something' about the International Catholic Film Office and similar groups in Italy and France.[21]

The Miracle violated the Code in several respects. Moreover, although the Code barred films solely because of their content, Breen announced that *no* film directed by Rossellini and starring Bergman would get a PCA seal. On the evening of Sunday, 7 January, following Spellman's diatribe against the film, his friend Louella Parsons mentioned it in her radio broadcast from Los Angeles, later promising Spellman to do everything in her power to keep the film from being shown there. As Archbishop Cantwell's successor in Los Angeles, the Vatican had installed Spellman's preferred candidate, James Francis McIntyre. On 5 March, McIntyre told Spellman that he had conferred with Hollywood's most powerful lawyer, Mendel Silverberg, with a view to ensuring that the film not be exhibited in Los Angeles. 'The big people [i.e., studio-owned theatres and large circuits], of course, would not touch it,' McIntyre reported. Regarding the independent theatres, 'Mr. Silverberg called a luncheon meeting ... at the Hotel Ambassador here, and conferred with them, at his own expense. He got a promise from them that they would not bid for the picture if all agreed to do the same thing. This they did, and none of them bought the picture.' Silverberg told the *New York Times*, 'My only interest is that I hate the kind of controversy this film has provoked.' On 13 March, Louella Parsons reported to Spellman that, following a meeting with Breen, she prevailed upon the *Los Angeles Examiner*, the home base for her six-hundred-newspaper column, not to carry 'any review or make any mention of the picture.' A week later, McIntyre told Spellman that Burstyn was threatening to sue because of a conspiracy to keep the film from opening. Thus, although Los Angeles was an 'industry town' free of government censorship, no studio-owned theatre or independent circuit would play it because of the Code, and Silverberg had successfully convinced the non-seal houses to block it from appearing anywhere else. In desperation, Burstyn finally opened the film by renting the Monica in West Hollywood, one of the many second-run theatres marginalized by television,[22] Since McIntyre, Breen, Silverberg, Louella Parsons, the studios, the theatres they owned, the circuits, the independent theatres, and major newspapers, had all reacted to the film's arrival in town with uncanny silence, it had little publicity, but did attrack an audience.

Following its ban on *The Miracle*, the New York Board of Regents received a telegram from thirty Protestant clergymen saying that the Catholic Church had no right 'to attempt to force its view on [the] state as a whole.' The Paris-based *Herald Tribune* ran a *Louisville Courier-Journal* editorial to the effect that the Church, whatever its authority with regard to its own communicants, had no right to bar others from seeing the film. The Rev. Donald Harrington of the Community Church on East 35th Street publicly called the Catholics' handling of the controversy 'dangerous and subversive of our civil liberties,' while Dr Paul Austin Wolfe of Brick Presbyterian Church on Park Avenue argued that *The Miracle* simply was not sacrilegious. This was also the consensus of Protestant theologians who gathered to view the film at special screenings in Boston and Princeton, some of whom called it reverent. Karl M.C. Chworowsky, minister of the Flatbush Unitarian Church in Brooklyn, vociferously criticized Spellman in the *Churchman* for 'the arrogance of his presumption that only they who agree with him are "decent."' 'I find it difficult to imagine,' Chworowsky wrote, 'any person of culture and esthetic appreciation leaving a showing of *The Miracle* with anything but a quickened sense of ... emotions of pity, compassion, and understanding not only for the poor, mentally deranged woman who is the chief figure of the story, but for all poor, ignorant, superstitious and mistreated souls that fall easy prey to the ridicule and contempt of their misguided neighbors. I cannot conceive of any intelligent member of *The Miracle* audience even remotely gaining the impression that in this picture Catholicism was being attacked.' Thus, Chworowsky added, 'only a person "with a chip on his shoulder" could have found anything insulting to Italian womanhood, to motherhood, or to Catholicism' in the film. On 1 March, *Library Journal* said no one had the right to block anyone else from seeing Rossellini's film. In the March number of the periodical *Tomorrow*, Harold Clurman, a towering figure in New York legitimate theatre, called *The Miracle* 'strangely impersonal and unsentimental' (two Rossellini hallmarks) yet 'deeply religious.' In London, these words were echoed in Vernon Jarratt's book-length study of Italian cinema.[23]

Most Catholic publications either agreed with Spellman or had no appetite for contradicting him. Nothing was to be expected from *American Ecclesiastical Review*, an august periodical founded in 1889, which had survived the attacks on free inquiry by Leo XIII and Pius X only to come under the editorship in 1944 of Father Joseph C. Fenton, who had made it 'the mouthpiece of Catholic theological intransigence in the United States.' Some Catholics who, like Allen Tate, chose to violate Spellman's prohibition by seeing the film, sided with the Protestant view. An editorial in the 2 March *Commonweal* held that perhaps the net result of the *Miracle* 'whoopdedoo' was a perception of the Church by outsiders as 'an alien force that didn't give two cents for their personal liberty' and which 'reduce[s] the struggle for the hearts and minds of men to a contest between picket lines and pressure groups,' thus slighting 'the emphasis Catholic doctrine puts on free consent and reasoned morality.' In the 22 March 1951 number of the *Catholic Messenger*, the diocesan newspaper of Davenport, Iowa, movie reviewer Frank Getlein wrote that in the controversy 'the Church has been viciously misrepresented' by its own spokesmen, who issue 'public statements ... almost all on the edge of hysteria.' Getlein proceeded to cite the staunchly moral and recognizably Catholic themes in Rossellini's other films, contrasting them with what passed for religious subject matter in Hollywood. He complimented Burstyn as the importer of good films from Catholic countries, and criticized the Knights of Columbus for intimidating a theatre in Queens into closing *The Bicycle Thief* because – the Knights had told the theatre manager on 13 February – that film 'glorifies a thief.' He described the last scene of *The Miracle* as one of 'a profound and profoundly sane maternal love,' and then noted that 'Rossellini's real crime, of course, has nothing to do with *The Miracle*,' but with impregnating 'an American star whom American Catholics ... had just finished canonizing as a popular saint. She had played a nun a couple of times, and she had played a saint. She had become, for the American Catholic fan, the symbol of feminine sanctity. Attending her movies was practically accepted as a devotional act. For these innocents, and their number was legion, the affair was sacrilege indeed, and the arrival of *The Miracle*, with its ambiguous sounding story, provided a splendid opportunity to strike back at the man who had debauched a saint.'[24]

On 14 April 1951, Spellman wrote to Ralph Leo Hayes, bishop of Davenport, demanding that Hayes respond to comments among Catholics that Spellman was the unnamed target of Getlein's article. On 18 April, Hayes sent a brief reply, indicating (disingenuously, no doubt) that he did not think Getlein was referring to Spellman. On 31 May, Spellman responded: 'I am in complete disagreement with you ... Many Bishops with whom I have talked as well as clergy and laity were scandalized by this article.' Hayes on 9 June reiterated that there was no reason for concern. But suddenly Getlein was fired from his teaching position at Fairfield University, a Catholic institution in Connecticut. He believed Spellman was behind it.[25]

In the 16 March issue of *Commonweal*, William P. Clancy, an instructor in Notre Dame University's English Department, published an article subtitled 'The Catholic as Philistine,' suggesting that Spellman's position vis-à-vis *The Miracle* suggested 'the specter of McCarthyism':

Even should we accept the hypothesis that, despite Rossellini's intention (and charity surely demands that we accept his word as the artist) the film is finally blasphemous, who is competent to decide this? Surely no one has ever claimed that along with the sacramental powers conferred by Holy Orders every cleric received the intuitive insights of a competent literary and art critic. Still less can we look for such subtle judgments on the nature and intent of art to the sensitivities of veterans' organizations, or Police Commissioners, be they Catholic or not ... If art and the integrity of the artist mean anything at all they mean that final judgment on them must be reached quietly, prayerfully and intelligently by those who are morally, intellectually, and aesthetically qualified.

On 17 April, *People's World*, a Communist daily published in San Francisco, saw a chance to stir up trouble and published an article entitled 'The Catholic Opinion Splits on Rossellini's "The Miracle,"' mentioning that two Catholic writers, Getlein and Clancy, had challenged Spellman regarding the film. Among Spellman's close friends was Rev. John Francis O'Hara, who served as Spellman's auxiliary before Spellman consecrated him as bishop of Buffalo in 1945. In the 1930s, O'Hara had been president of Notre Dame. On 18 April 1951, Rev. Theodore Hesburgh, executive vice-president of Notre Dame, wrote to O'Hara: 'I have been checking into the *Commonweal* article by Professor Clancy. We can all recognize the imprudence of one of our professors trying to criticize the Archbishop for his care in the matter of faith and morals in the Archdiocese. From all indications, Professor Clancy will not be with us next year. Perhaps this is the most permanent answer to the difficulty. I thought you would like to know this, and perhaps communicate it to his Eminence [Spellman]. Thanks once more for bringing this to our attention.' Clancy was fired. On 23 April, O'Hara replied to Hesburgh: 'Your letter of April 18th indicates a very satisfactory solution of the problem I proposed. I am happy to share your letter with His Eminence.' Five weeks later, Cardinal Dougherty of Philadelphia died, and O'Hara was chosen to replace him.[26] Several months after that, Hesburgh assumed Notre Dame's presidency.

The Miracle on Appeal

On appeal from the Regents' decision, a three-judge panel of the Appellate Division of the New York Supreme Court, sitting in Albany, viewed *The Miracle* and was favoured with off-setting amicus briefs by the New

York State Catholic Welfare Committee and the New York City Civil Liberties Committee, as well as a deluge of letters offered by Burstyn's lawyers from prominent Baptists, Evangelicals, Presbyterians, Methodists, rabbis, and professors, their collective views encapsulated by art historian H.W. Janson's comment that it was 'inconceivable' that *The Miracle* 'could possibly be interpreted as blasphemous or in any sense anti-religious.' Catholic lay leader Otto L. Spaeth, director of the American Federation of the Arts, stated that he had arranged for a group of Catholic intellectuals to see the film, and they unanimously approved it. Spaeth himself opined: 'There was indeed "blasphemy" in the picture – but it was the blasphemy of the villagers, who stopped at nothing, not even the mock singing of a hymn to the Virgin, in their brutal badgering of the tragic woman.' In the uproar over the film, Spaeth added, Rossellini's 'scathing indictment of their evil behavior ... was seemingly overlooked.' On the other hand, Msgr Raymond P. Etteldorf wrote that although Protestant ministers were urging that the *Miracle* controversy presented an issue of free speech, the real issue was whether civil authorities were empowered 'to guarantee to citizens the *right* to violate the moral law.'[27]

On 12 March 1951 the three-judge panel heard three hours of oral argument. Among the points raised by Burstyn's lawyers was one that had been put forward by Mutual Film's lawyers in 1915: that film censorship constitutes a prior restraint and thus violates the First Amendment, applicable to the states via the Fourteenth Amendment. While in *Mutual Film* that argument had been flatly rejected, in the 1920s and '30s the Supreme Court repeatedly held that the First Amendment's free-speech and free-press clauses did afford protection against actions by a state, and in *Paramount*, Justice Douglas had intimated that the First Amendment might also protect a film. Nevertheless, on 9 May 1951 the three judges affirmed the Regents' ban.[28] By now the record showed that some found *The Miracle* to be projecting an anti-Catholic, anti-Christian, and/or pro-Communist message, while others found its message to be Christian, Catholic, and reverential. Having presumably reviewed all these conflicting comments about what the film meant, the judges nevertheless reiterated almost verbatim what Justice McKenna had said in *Mutual Film*: that motion pictures are not protected by free-speech principles because they are exhibited 'for entertainment purposes alone' and 'are not within the category of inquiry and discussion.'

Burstyn now appealed to the New York Court of Appeals, whose members had a private screening in Albany and on 1 June 1951 heard oral argument. An amicus brief by the American Jewish Congress asserted that 'governmental intervention in religious affairs has inexorably resulted in violent and bloody ... religious persecution,' adding that the Regents' ban 'threaten[s] ... the private right of the individual to address himself to matters of philosophic and artistic importance.'[29] The Regents' response was as sibilant as Spellman's had been: 'What is meant by the title "Miracle"? No miracle appears in the picture. The picture itself is a sadistic presentation of the most sordid character. The insane heroine, the unprincipled hero, the drunkenness, seduction, crass imitations of Biblical events, labour, childbirth – where is the miracle?' Christ's nativity is 'deliberately lampooned with no foreseeable purpose other than [to] hold it up to scorn, – in other words, to establish for the amusement of the audience a "miracle" which is thus proved not a miracle.' In short, 'the direct imitation of the Bible story caricatured as it is in the picture and the calling the event a "miracle" when the audience knows ... that no miracle has occurred ... is the worst kind of sacrilege.'[30]

The New York Court of Appeals issued its decision on 18 October 1951. Since the issue was whether *The Miracle* was 'sacrilegious,' the court deemed it appropriate to state what the word means, turning to the definition of 'sacrilege' in the authoritative *Funk & Wagnalls New Standard Dictionary* (1913): 'The act of violating or profaning anything sacred.' Like Spellman and the Regents, the court construed *The Miracle* to be a 'gratuitous insult to recognized religious beliefs,' rendering it 'sacrilegious' and thus violative of the film censorship statute in which that word was used. The court concluded both that *The Miracle* could be banned because *Mutual Film* was still the law, and that the Regents had intrinsic power to reverse the several licences issued by the Motion Picture Division. Although this would have been enough to dispose of the case, the court further characterized the film as 'an infringement of the freedom of others to worship and believe as they choose' – as if Rossellini, like some totalitarian *apparatchik*, had padlocked the doors of New York's Catholic churches.

Judge Stanley Fuld, joined by another judge, dissented. In a bravura exercise of statutory interpretation, Fuld wrote that because the New York statute *expressly* authorized the Regents to overturn the Motion Picture Division's *denial* of a licence, it should not be interpreted as having also *impliedly* authorized them to overturn the Division's *granting* of a licence. This would itself have been a cogent and complete reason to dissent, having nothing to do with the First Amendment or the film. However, Fuld did not stop there. It is sometimes observed that the law of the land is not what the U.S. Supreme Court *has* said, but what it is *about* to say. In the *Lost Boundaries* case, the Fifth federal Circuit would have none of that. Fuld, however, dared suggest that *Mutual Film* was no longer the law, that is, he inferred from what the Supreme Court had said in several recent decisions that if the Court had before it a case where the viability of *Mutual Film* was squarely in issue, it would overrule its own precedent and find films to be protected by the First Amendment. Given Fuld's confident belief regarding what the Supreme Court was likely to do if presented with an appropriate case, he wrote his dissenting opinion as if the Court had already done so. Well aware that the *Miracle* controversy was highly charged politically, he added that New York's film censorship statute constituted a prior restraint as well as an attempt to 'legislate orthodoxy in matters of religious belief,' a practice which Fuld took to be barred by the clause of the First Amendment disallowing an established religion.

While *Thornhill* (1940) and *Barnette* (1943) had substantially advanced First Amendment jurisprudence, several subsequent decisions were even more remarkable. When James Farley resigned as postmaster general, FDR awarded the job to Frank Walker, another of the President's links with his crucial Catholic constituency. Walker, who had worked closely with Bishop Noll on censorship issues, disliked *Esquire* magazine, which combined articles by top writers of fiction and non-fiction with racy cartoons by Alberto Vargas. Just months after Walker took office, he forced *Esquire* to black out an already-printed poem in the December 1940 issue because it portrayed Santa Claus as a randy nocturnal lover. Soon *Esquire*'s editor, Arnold Gingrich, was travelling to Washington every month to negotiate the changes necessary to keep Walker from carrying out his ongoing threat to ban the magazine from the mails under the Comstock Act. In May 1942 the Post Office refused to have further meetings with Gingrich, indicating that it was not obliged to provide such an accommodation to borderline publications and that any publisher who entertained doubts about a given item should resolve them by applying 'a sense of decency and good morals.'[31]

A full-blown administrative hearing within the Post Office concluded with a finding that *Esquire* was not 'obscene,' the only relevant basis for declaring such a magazine non-mailable under the Comstock Act. This did not satisfy Walker. He had previously managed to destroy Father Charles Coughlin's anti-Roosevelt, anti-interventionist periodical, *Social Justice*, by an indirect method first used by Will Hays's predecessor in the Post Office to stop anti-war sentiments during the First World

War, that is, by withdrawing the beneficial second-class mail rate, a form of federal subsidy enjoyed by newspapers and magazines because of their value in enhancing public awareness and knowledge. Walker had asserted that *Social Justice* interfered with the war effort, a clear violation of federal law. Since *Esquire's* popularity among troops conclusively demonstrated that it was a *positive* factor in wartime morale, Walker could not again use that rationale. Instead, he asserted that the relevant statute designated the beneficial mailing rate only for newspapers and magazines which disseminated 'information of a public character' or were 'devoted to literature, the sciences, [or] arts,' and in his view *Esquire* failed to comply with these statutory requirements.[32] Walker thought *Esquire* should be closed down (the inevitable result of denying the second-class rate to a subscription-based magazine) because in his view it and certain other magazines inhabited 'that obscure and treacherous borderland zone where the average person hesitates to find them technically obscene, but still may see ample proof that they are morally improper and not for the public welfare and the public good.' When – he claimed – racy cartoons and men's-club humour become a publication's 'dominant and systemic feature,' it 'most certainly cannot be said to be for the public good.'

The case went to court. Thurman Arnold, having become a justice of the District of Columbia Court of Appeals, held that a postmaster general has no authority to decide what periodicals are and are not in the public interest. Walker appealed, but in February 1946 the Supreme Court, in an opinion by Justice Douglas, affirmed Arnold's decision. 'Under our system of government,' Douglas wrote, 'there is an accommodation for the widest varieties of tastes and ideas. What is good literature, what has educational value, what is refined public information, what is good art, varies with individuals as it does from one generation to another. There doubtless would be a contrariety of views concerning Cervantes' *Don Quixote*, Shakespeare's *Venus & Adonis*, or Zola's *Nana*. But a requirement that literature or art conform to some norm prescribed by an official smacks of an ideology foreign to our system.'[33] Justice Frankfurter added that since Congress had used the words 'devoted to literature, the sciences, [or] arts' without also qualifying these terms 'by any standards of taste or edification or public elevation,' Walker had no authority to invoke his own standards, much less to destroy a magazine he did not think complied with them.

In 1943, New York City prosecutors charged a magazine vendor named Murray Winters with selling *Headquarters Detective – True Cases from the Police Blotter,* in violation of a New York statute prohibiting publications 'principally made up of criminal news, police reports, or accounts of criminal deeds, or pictures, or stories of deeds of bloodshed, lust or crime.' If the stories in *Headquarters Detective* were in fact 'True Cases from the Police Blotter,' all purse-snatchings and lost dogs had been deleted, leaving only such fare as 'Girl Slave to a Love Cult,' 'Girls' Reformatory,' and 'Bargains in Bodies,' exactly the stuff that New York's statute and similar laws in twenty-four other states had been enacted to suppress. Although principles of free speech applied to 'news,' few observers were so unabashed as to apply that term to the increasingly vulgar amalgam of sex and violence that had characterized such magazines since the *National Police Gazette* initiated the genre in the 1840s.

The New York Court of Appeals confirmed Winters's conviction, construing the statute as prohibiting only magazines and paperbacks containing enough bad stuff that they became stimulants for 'inciting violent and depraved crimes,' assuming (and the court did assume) that some critical mass of such material did in fact stimulate some readers to 'act out.' In March 1948, however, the Supreme Court reversed, Justice Reed observing that since no publisher, news dealer, or jury could reasonably know when a publication contained a sufficient number of stories of lust and bloodshed so as to become a stimulus for depraved and violent crimes, such a statute was unconstitutionally vague. The due process clause of the Fourteenth Amendment requires that criminal statutes adequately inform people of what conduct is forbidden. Since there was nothing illegal about any one story, there was no way to predict how many stories were necessary to trigger illegality. New York argued that although these stories were not obscene, not one of them was legally protected, since the First Amendment protects 'only ... the exposition of ideas' and not the witless material found in *Headquarters Detective*. Reed flatly rejected that argument, observing: 'The line between the informing and the entertaining is too elusive for the protection of that basic right ... What is one man's amusement, teaches another's doctrine.'[34]

This was radically new. In *Mutual Film,* Justice McKenna had deemed movies unprotected by free-speech principles because they were only 'entertainment,' yet here Justice Reed refused to draw a line between information and entertainment – even sleazy entertainment. Nor could Reed's pronouncement possibly be construed, like Douglas's aside about free speech in *Paramount,* to be a mere will-o'-the-wisp. Reed could hardly have been clearer: 'Though we can see nothing of any possible value to society in these magazines, they are as much entitled to the protection of free speech as the best of literature.' Although the rationale for a free press had traditionally been its value in keeping citizens informed, the Court would now protect material whose informational value was not readily apparent. Reed was indicating that stuff like 'Bargains in Bodies' – just short of obscene – was entitled to as much First Amendment protection as Locke's *Second Treatise of Civil Government*. Since Reed's language was so sweeping and categorical in extending the First Amendment to published 'entertainment,' Judge Fuld in his dissent in the *Miracle* litigation concluded that the Supreme Court, when presented with an appropriate case, would abandon *Mutual Film*'s contrary conclusion regarding films.

Not that the legal walls against obscenity itself were about to fall. In October 1948, the Supreme Court had before it yet another case from the New York Court of Appeals. Edmund Wilson, author of such classics in criticism as *Axel's Castle* (1931) and *To the Finland Station* (1940), had written *Memoirs of Hecate County* (1946), an extraordinary set of short stories about life in a rich New York suburb, providing a cold-hearted, cynical, and at times graphic depiction of sexual morality among the 'swells.' The litigation centred on one of the stories, 'The Princess with the Golden Hair,' which included an explicit depiction of a sexual encounter by a character who is fully capable of capturing everything about the experience in the finest detail, yet who is utterly incapable of real psychological involvement, much less 'love.' The result is a literary tour-de-force of ironic distance. The book's publisher, Doubleday, had argued that the traditional *Hicklin* standard should not be applied because Wilson's book would be read only by the sophisticated readers for whom it was intended, that is, it would not fall into the hands of the children and low-lifes whom the *Hicklin* court sought to protect from immoral influences. That being so, Doubleday further argued that Wilson's book was protected by the First Amendment because, under the test first articulated by Justice Holmes thirty years before, it presented no 'clear and present danger' of any wrong which New York had authority to stop.[35] The New York Court of Appeals unanimously rejected both arguments, while choosing not to issue an opinion articulating its rationale. Doubleday appealed to the Supreme Court, where four judges voted to affirm, four dissented, and one (Justice Frankfurter) did not participate. The resulting tie, announced without substantive written opinions pro or con, comprised an unexplained 'draw' concerning the constitutional validity of the New York

Court of Appeals' unexplained decision that Edmund Wilson had written an obscene book that was properly prohibited from sale.[36] Thus could the Supreme Court give its affirmative blessing to the big-bosomed 'dumb blondes' in *Esquire* and the 'bloodshed and lust' of 'Girl Slave to a Love Cult' because they were just this side of obscene, while allowing New York to ban a serious work of fiction by America's premiere man of letters because it had gone over the line.

18 'The Law Knows No Heresy'

Joe Burstyn, having suffered an unbroken string of five defeats in New York – the Regents' subcommittee, the entire Board of Regents, an individual judge, a panel of the Appellate Division, and then the Court of Appeals – remained undaunted. Not that any bookmaker would have laid odds in his favour. If the Court could allow New York to outlaw a major work of fiction by Edmund Wilson without so much as a brief articulation of why, what interest would it take in a film judicially determined to mock the Virgin Birth, by an Italian director most people knew of only because he had seduced a married American movie star? While Justice Reed in *Winters* had greatly expanded the First Amendment, Justice Frankfurter, joined by Justices Jackson and Burton, had written a stinging dissent in that case, voicing a strong judicial deference to state legislation, particularly to laws which (like the several state film censorship statutes) had been in place for a long time and had been repeatedly enforced in a variety of circumstances. Frankfurter had also written: 'Free speech is not so absolute or irrational a conception as to imply paralysis of the means for effective protection of *all* freedoms secured by the Bill of Rights.' Freedom of religious practice was one of those rights, and the New York Court of Appeals had specifically concluded that Rossellini's film infringed 'the freedom of others to worship and believe as they choose.'[1]

Nor were Frankfurter, Jackson, and Burton the only justices who seemed unlikely to apply the First Amendment to strike down New York's long-standing film censorship law. Two liberals, Frank Murphy and Wiley Rutledge, were dead, replaced by two conservatives, Sherman Minton and Tom Clark. Minton was a Catholic, while Clark's views on civil liberties might be gleaned from his prior service as civilian coordinator for the internment of American citizens of Japanese descent in California. On 10 April 1950 the Supreme Court refused the petitions of the Hollywood Ten, thus reaffirming that the First Amendment provides no blanket protection against government interference. Only Douglas and Black thought the Hollywood Ten's case worth examining.

Given these facts, when considered alongside Douglas's comment in *Paramount* and Reed's language in *Winters*, it appeared that only Douglas, Black, and Reed might even consider Burstyn's case. As for the other justices, many observers saw the Court as a rubber-stamp for the general post-war trend against civil liberties. Nor did Burstyn's case elicit any real groundswell of public support. Carey McWilliams, co-author of one of the briefs filed on behalf of the Hollywood Ten, wrote that the more people became upset with Communism's insults to freedom abroad, the greater became their 'indifference to clear and flagrant violations' of civil rights at home, indicating a desire for uniformity of belief which in some sense paralleled the Communist totalitarianism they so despised.[2] With all of these factors at work, Burstyn's lawyers had two problematic tasks: to get five of nine justices to leverage Douglas's passing comment about freedom of the screen into the demise of *Mutual Film*, and then to have those five apply the First Amendment in such a way as to negate everything that the Regents and the New York courts had done.

On the other hand, Burstyn's case was not hopeless. If Douglas, Black, and Reed could be convinced, only two more votes would be needed. Although precedent suggested that Frankfurter, Minton, Jackson, Clark, and Vinson would themselves probably form a five-vote phalanx against overturning New York's ban, an additional ray of light was the *Associated Press* decision, with its emphasis on the public's right to obtain multiple perspectives on matters of importance. While numerous New York officials had found Rossellini's film to be a mockery of the Virgin Birth, some competent observers had disagreed, and although the Supreme Court seldom overturned factual findings, this was a film, and the justices could see it for themselves and make up their own minds.

And then there were *Cantwell v. Connecticut* (1940) and *Kunz v. New York* (1951). In *Cantwell*, a Jehovah's Witness ventured into a Catholic neighbourhood in New Haven, Connecticut, where he asked people to listen to a phonograph record setting forth 'a general attack on all organized religious systems as instruments of Satan,' while 'singl[ing] out the Roman Catholic Church for strictures couched in terms which naturally would offend not only persons of that persuasion, but all others who respect the honestly held religious faith of their fellows. The hearers were in fact highly offended. One of them said he felt like hitting Cantwell,' while another 'told Cantwell he had better get off the street before something happened to him.' Cantwell took that advice and left the neighbourhood, although he was subsequently arrested, tried, and convicted for inciting a breach of the peace. The Supreme Court reversed, Justice Owen J. Roberts stating:

> In the realm of religious faith, and in that of political belief, sharp differences arise. In both fields the tenets of one man may seem the rankest error to his neighbor. To persuade others to his own point of view, the pleader, as we know, at times, resorts to exaggeration, to vilification of men who have been, or are, prominent in church or state, and even to false statement. But the people of this nation have ordained in the light of history, that, in spite of the probability of excesses and abuses, these liberties are, in the long view, essential to enlightened opinion and right conduct on the part of the citizens of a democracy.

The Court concluded that discordant religious beliefs must be permitted to develop 'unmolested and unobstructed,' even if most people view them as 'the rankest error.' Thus, the free-exercise clause of the First Amendment, applied to the states via the Fourteenth Amendment, protected Cantwell's right to voice his religious views, even in neighbourhoods where those views were anathema.[3]

In *Kunz*, decided in January 1951, a New York City ordinance barred gathering on the street 'for public worship or exhortation, or to ridicule or denounce any form of religious belief, service or reverence, or to preach or expound atheism or agnosticism,' while allowing clergymen, lay preachers, atheists, and agnostics to hold assemblies if they first obtained a police permit. Hardly a model of drafting clarity, the ordinance seemed intended to allow street gatherings for collective worship and even for the renunciation of worship, so long as police permission was obtained, while not allowing the street to become a venue for the public ridicule or denunciation of any particular religion. Carl Jacob Kunz, a Baptist minister, applied for and obtained a permit, only to have it revoked in November 1946, on evidence that in his street gatherings he ridiculed other people's religious beliefs. He did not appeal that revocation, and his new applications for permits in 1947 and 1948 were both denied. At 9:00 p.m. on 11 September 1948, speaking to a gathering of twenty people at New York's Columbus Circle, Kunz referred to the pope as 'the anti-Christ,' to Catholicism as 'a religion of the devil,' and to Jews as 'Christ-killers,' adding: 'All the garbage that didn't believe in Christ should have been burnt in the incinerators. It's a shame they all weren't.' He was arrested for speaking without the requisite police permit and was tried, convicted, and fined $10. In December 1949 the New York Court of Appeals affirmed the conviction, Judge Charles S. Desmond observing that New York City was invested with the power to prohibit people 'from starting religious wars on [its] teeming thoroughfares.'

The Supreme Court reversed. An ordinance investing the police with unbridled discretion to decide in advance who should be permitted to speak on religious matters, the Court held, comprised a prior restraint of Kunz's First Amendment rights. Although one of the traditional rationales for suppressing speech deemed vile and/or blasphemous was that it tends to incite public disorder, the Court stated that government may not delegate to administrative officials broad discretion to suppress speech solely because it might provoke a breach of the peace. This was a surprisingly expansive view of civil liberties, particularly so because the majority opinion came from the conservative Chief Justice Fred Vinson himself.[4] Justice Jackson, recently returned from duty as chief American prosecutor in the Nuremberg trials, wrote a harsh dissent, citing a long line of cases going back to Holmes in support of the idea that no one may expound rhetoric likely to incite violence. While Joe Burstyn's lawyers might have found *Kunz*'s expansive reading of the First Amendment to be encouraging, it also showed unequivocally that Justice Jackson, following his experience at Nuremberg, was no free-speech liberal when scrutinizing utterances that might be offensive to a religious group.[5]

Blasphemy

Exodus 20:7 and Deuteronomy 5:11 provide: 'Thou shalt not take the name of the Lord thy God in vain.' There was power – even magic – in the deity's name, enough to suggest great care in its use. In Leviticus 24:16, the punishment for blasphemy is death. In the Plymouth colony, where the statutes for some capital crimes were taken verbatim from the Old Testament, execution awaited those who rebelled against the sovereignty of the colony, of Great Britain, or of Jesus Christ, while Article 2 of Virginia's 'Lawes Divine, Morall, and Martiall' (1612) declared: 'That no man speake impiously or maliciously ... against God the Father, God the Son, and God the holy Ghost ... ypon paine of death.'[6]

In *Rex v. Taylor* (1676), a Surrey yeoman claimed to be Jesus' brother yet called Jesus 'a whoremaster' and 'a bastard' and characterized religion as 'a cheat.' By affirming the man's conviction, Sir Matthew Hale established that blasphemy was no longer to be referred to an ecclesiastical panel of the kind that had convicted Joan of Arc of heresy 250 years before, but was instead a crime cognizable in court. In the following century, the influential British treatise writer William Hawkins cited common-law authorities for such 'offences ... against God' as 'denying his being or providence' and making 'contumelious reproaches of Jesus Christ,' while a nineteenth-century criminal-law treatise defined blasphemy as 'any oral or written reproach maliciously cast upon God, his name, attributes, or religion.'[7]

Several separate rationales emerged for prosecuting blasphemy as a crime. First, since a form of Christianity was Britain's state religion, attacks on Christianity were a sort of seditious slander against the state. God could be 'injured' by insult much as the King could be, the injury being to the entire national enterprise of which God and King were the two sovereigns.[8] Those convicted of blasphemy included not just deluded Surrey yeomen but sober and committed scientists, nonconformists, sceptics, and atheists. As stated in *Rex v. Woolston* (1729): 'the Christian religion is established in this kingdom; and therefore [the court] would not allow any books to be writ, which should tend to alter that establishment.' When in the late eighteenth century a resident of Northampton, Massachusetts, ordered from a Boston bookseller a collection of David Hume's essays as well as John Leland's *A View of the Principal Deistical Writers* (1754/55), 'he arranged their delivery with all the surreptitiousness attaching to contraband traffic.' In the case brought against Thomas Paine's deistical *Age of Reason*, Lord Kenyon told the jury: 'I sincerely wish that [Paine] ... may become a partaker of that faith in revealed religion, which he has so grossly defamed, and may be enabled to make his peace with God, for that disorder which he has endeavoured, to the utmost of his power, to introduce into society.'[9] In 1823, Lord Chancellor Eldon refused to enforce the copyright of Sir William Lawrence's *Lectures on Physiology, Zoology, and the Natural History of Man* (1822) on the ground that English law 'does not give protection to those who contradict the Scriptures.'[10]

A related rationale for criminalizing blasphemy was that protecting

God from insult not only maintained a societal fear of God but was also a sound way for society to protect itself from wrongdoers, since some people who think they can evade constables will nevertheless refrain from mischief insofar as they fear punishment by an omniscient and omnipotent deity. Moreover, a collective fear of God helps make a justice system fair and efficient in a society where witnesses tend to testify truthfully once they have sworn on a Bible to do so. While it was absurd (treatise writer Thomas Starkie observed) for human judges and juries to 'attempt to redress or avenge insults to a supreme and omnipotent Creator,' impieties nevertheless 'tend to weaken and undermine the very foundation on which all human laws must rest, and to dissolve those moral and religious obligations, without the aid of which mere positive laws and penal restraints would be inefficacious.' Starkie added one additional rationale for prosecuting blasphemy. In a society that respects God, blasphemous utterances comprise 'gross insults to those who believe in the doctrines which are held up to scorn and contempt,' and thus such utterances 'immediately tend to acts of outrage and violence.'[11] Under this rationale, to prosecute blasphemy was to minimize public disturbances.

An adjunct to prosecuting those who would insult God's dignity was to prosecute those who would satirize God's human representatives. A 1711 Massachusetts statute concerning the licensing of inns provided: 'whosoever shall be convicted of composing ... any filthy, obscene, or profane song, pamphlet, libel or mock sermon, in imitation or in mimicking of preaching, or any other part of divine worship ... shall be punished by fine ... not exceeding twenty pounds, or by standing on the pillory once or oftener, with an inscription of his crime in capital letters affixed over his head, according to the discretion of the justice in quarter sessions.'[12] Despite such strictures, in any free society, clerics and others who hold themselves up as moral authorities will inevitably be subjected to parody. The form of indictment approved for prosecuting obscene libels came from a case involving a London print portraying 'The Parson receiving Tithes in Kind,' purporting to show 'a man in the habit of a clergyman, in an obscene, impudent, and indecent posture with a woman.'[13]

The new government of the United States, unlike that of Great Britain, sponsored no religion, nor did it wish to deal with most religious issues. In 1783 the papal nuncio at Versailles told Ben Franklin that since Catholics in Franklin's new nation were no longer colonials overseen by the Vicar Apostolic in London, the pope proposed that the

Continental Congress designate in what city an American bishopric could be established. Franklin forwarded the communication to Jefferson, who with two other members of the Continental Congress responded that since choosing a place for Catholic headquarters in the United States pertained to matters 'purely spiritual,' federal lawmakers had 'no authority to permit or refuse it, these powers being reserved to the several states individually.'[14] Just where the Catholic Church might locate its national headquarters, that is, was thought none of the federal government's business.

Freedom of religious belief entailed freedom of speech regarding religious issues. As Frances Wright declared in the 1820s, 'Where no law says what is orthodoxy, no man is entitled to say what is heresy.' The Supreme Court in *Watson v. Jones* (1871) noted a universal concurrence in 'the full and free right to entertain any religious belief, to practice any religious principle, and to teach any religious doctrine which does not violate the laws of morality ... The law knows no heresy, and is committed to the support of no dogma, the establishment of no sect.' Thus, the federal government could not prohibit words or conduct which a nation with an endorsed religion might deem heretical or blasphemous. Nevertheless, the language of *Watson v. Jones* was not absolute, and in the federal Utah Territory, the Mormon practice of polygyny, which many thought a glaring sin against fundamental Christian principles, could be construed as 'violat[ing] the laws of morality,' thus taking that practice, or anything else found offensive to 'laws of morality,' outside the protections of the First Amendment.[15]

Since the First Amendment forbade a national religion, British blasphemy law presumably would have nothing to which to apply federally, even if many thought that as part of the common law it was still viable among the states. While Jefferson and Madison stopped the establishment of a state religion in Virginia, Congregationalism remained the established, tax-supported religion in Connecticut until 1818, and in Massachusetts until 1833. As a federal judge noted in 1891, as far as the federal Constitution was concerned, each state retained 'absolute power,' if it so chose, to 'establish a Church or Creed' and to maintain it as such.[16] Principles of British blasphemy law could thus be applied to vindicate a state's established religion, or its citizens' collective desire to protect their several Christian traditions against such powerful new threats as deism, atheism, agnosticism, free-thinking, even Unitarianism. Thus in Connecticut, 'blasphemy against God, or ... the persons of the Holy Trinity, or the christian religion, or the holy scriptures,' carried a penalty of up to a year in jail and a $100 fine. Even in Pennsylvania, with no state religion and a remarkable history of religious freedom, officials were prepared to prosecute material deemed offensive to faith. When in 1813 Jefferson ordered from his Philadelphia bookseller a copy of Regnault de Bécourt's *Sur la création du monde, ou Système d'organisation primitive*, local authorities, upon getting wind of the transaction, charged the bookseller with trafficking in blasphemous matter. Jefferson was 'mortified to be told that, in the United States of America,' the sale of a book could be carried before a civil magistrate. 'Is this then our freedom of religion? And are we to have a censor whose imprimatur shall say what books may be sold, and what we may buy? And who is thus to dogmatize religious opinions for our citizens? ... Is a priest to be our inquisitor? Or shall a layman, simple as ourselves, set up his reason as the rule for what we are to read, and what we must believe?' In 1844 the U.S. Supreme Court concluded that Christianity was part of Pennsylvania common law in that the divine origin of Scripture was not to be reviled, and in 1870 a Pennsylvania court refused to enforce a will's devise of land to an 'Infidel Society in Philadelphia' because its intended purpose was to build a hall for the untrammelled discussion of religious questions.[17]

Article VI of the federal Constitution provides, in part: 'no religious Test shall ever be required as a Qualification to any Office or public Trust under the United States.' Although this applied on the federal level, in 1892 Supreme Court justice David Brewer saw no legal impediment to Delaware's requiring that state officials declare their 'faith in God the Father, and in Jesus Christ His only Son, and in the Holy Ghost, one God, blessed for evermore; and ... acknowledge the Holy Scriptures of the Old and New Testament to be given by divine inspiration.' After all, Justice Brewer noted, 'this is a religious people' and 'a Christian nation.' Although the Fourteenth Amendment had been ratified some years before, not until the 1940s was its due-process provision construed to cause the First Amendment ban on an established religion to apply to the states.[18]

Among the objections to Congress's proposed purchase of Jefferson's library was that it contained works by 'French infidel philosophers.' Enlightenment writings had already caused many impressionable readers to reject the stricter forms of Calvinism, and many young intellectuals abandoned Christianity itself. Yale president Ezra Stiles bemoaned the college's inability to attract enough interested students to staff the dozens of New England parishes requiring Congregational ministers.

Between 1775 and 1815, Yale graduated a mere nine clergymen a year, and at one time its student body reportedly included only four professing Christians. Among the ninety-three graduates of Williams College in its first seven years (1793–1800) could be counted but five Christians. So disdained was religion that some wags conducted a mock Last Supper. Jonathan Edwards's grandson, Timothy Dwight, was appalled to see students become 'disciples of Voltaire, Rousseau, d'Alembert, and Diderot,' the French 'dregs of infidelity ... vomited upon us':

> The Frenchman knows *a priori* that there is nothing beyond the grave. The Englishman usually admits the distinction between right and wrong, and acknowledges that men are under some obligation to do that which is right, and to abstain from that which is wrong. The Frenchman, when you express your belief of these doctrines, looks at you with a stare made up of pity, surprise, and contempt, as an ignorant rustic entering for the first time ... the world's great metropolis of science ... The Frenchman knows intuitively ... that God exercises no moral government over man, that moral obligation is a chimera, that animal pleasure is the only good, and that man is merely a brute upon two legs.

Lyman Beecher, Dwight's prize student in the mid-1790s, noted that the literati of Yale's senior class called each other Voltaire, D'Alembert, etc. Nor was Beecher surprised to find that with irreligion came liquor hidden in students' rooms, followed by 'profanity, gambling and licentiousness.'[19]

Nor was the problem confined to New England, an Episcopal divine travelling in Virginia finding 'every educated young man ... a skeptic, if not an avowed unbeliever.' A minister visiting the frontier town of Cleveland, Ohio, in 1802 observed a general habit of 'Infidelity and profaning the Sabbath,' with the people 'bid[ding] fair to grow into a hardened corrupt society.' In 1812 in Kentucky, Joseph Buchanan, a twenty-four-year-old polymath deeply influenced by David Hume, urged that while many philosophers believed in 'an independent spiritual existence, mysteriously connected with the human body,' he could accept only 'an organic state of matter, such as constitutes the human brain.'[20] Not that such notions were widely embraced outside the colleges. When Buchanan tried to market a book-length manuscript setting forth his materialist ideas, he met general resistance. Back in the mountains of western Massachusetts, Dr Charles Knowlton, failing to build a medical practice with which to support his family, immersed himself in studying the infidel writers in preparation to 'astonish the world, and become even far more famous than John Locke ever was.' Accosting Williams College president Edward Dorr Griffin, D.D., on the town common, Knowlton said he would desist from publishing his treatise if Griffin could refute it. 'Why, as for refuting materialism by philosophy,' Griffin retorted, 'no mortal man can ever do it. It is only by scripture that it can be done.' Finding that refutation philosophically inadequate, Knowlton paid to have his text, *Elements of Modern Materialism*, set in type and proceeded to New York City with thoughts of wealth and fame. But there he found that 'the bare title was enough to satisfy every bookseller ... [t]hey wanted nothing to do with it.' A perusal of the first pages reveals such passages as: 'The sentiment that a being exists which never commenced existence, or, what is the same thing, that a being exists which has existed from all eternity, appears to us to favour atheism.' Knowlton was now not only $1,000 in debt but 'regarded as ... [an] infidel, "bad man," &c.'

While less dogged or more reasonable men would have given up, Knowlton instead went wandering about upstate New York and Vermont trying to peddle his tome. Stopping for the night in Amherst on his way home from this fruitless quest, he tried to interest some students in buying the book and, failing in that effort, called upon Amherst College president Heman Humphrey. At the dedication of the college's chapel a year before, Humphrey had said: 'No one is so independent, as not to need God's help ... Let the men of active business and honest gains, write it upon their ships, upon their manufactories, and in their counting-rooms, at the corner of every street ... Let the student ... record it upon every blank leaf of his classics.' Skimming through Knowlton's work, Amherst's president was as negative as Williams's had been, advising Knowlton that he 'ought to be in better business than in carrying such a book about the country.' Within minutes, Knowlton was arrested for peddling. Upon trying to set up a medical practice in Ashfield, Massachusetts, he observed that while the townspeople said of another local doctor that he was a 'Quack' and 'Don't know nothing,' Knowlton had 'No principles' or 'Bad principles,' that is, 'Don't believe a man has got any soul.' Apparently undaunted by the trouble stirred up by his radical challenges to scriptural revelation, he proceeded to become a radical physician and to write the nineteenth century's most famous book on contraceptive techniques, for which he went to jail.[21]

In the 1830s Abner Kneeland, owner of the *Boston Investigator* and the probable (although safely anonymous) publisher of Dr Knowlton's pioneering birth-control book, published a periodical in which he asserted that he believed in neither God, nor Christ, nor the Resurrection. Charged under Massachusetts's blasphemy statute, he was brought to trial before Herman Melville's father-in-law, Chief Justice Lemuel Shaw. Although Congregationalism was no longer the Commonwealth's official sect, the prosecutor proclaimed what few in the courtroom would have denied: that Massachusetts' statutory, constitutional, and common law all agree that 'Government depends upon ... the Christian Religion as its basis, and as the strong foundations of morality, duty and Law.' Further, 'there have been other infidels – Hume, Gibbon, Voltaire, Volney, &c. but the works of those persons were read only by men of literary habits – necessarily a few – and to men of sound understanding they carried their antidote with them. But here is a Journal, a Newspaper, cheap – and sent into a thousand families, &c. Where one man should be injured by Hume, Gibbon, or Volney, a thousand may be injured by this Newspaper.' Thus, Kneeland's crime was not that he espoused certain views, but that he wanted to communicate them to the general public. His conviction demonstrated that in Massachusetts, blasphemy, 'either by wilful or obstinate denying the true God, or his creation, or government of the world,' was still a crime. In 1849, Richard Hildreth wrote that while the conviction in fact contravened a provision of the Massachusetts constitution mandating religious freedom, constitutions 'go for very little when in conflict with the hereditary sentiments of their expositors.'[22]

Insults to Mary

In several of the reported American blasphemy cases, the words uttered closely mimic those for which the deranged Surrey yeoman was convicted in *Rex v. Taylor*. In 1811, for instance, the great New York jurist James Kent was presented with language to the effect that Jesus 'was a bastard, and his mother must be a whore,' epithets repeated in another case brought twenty-six years later in Delaware. In 1923 a prosecution was brought in New York against a man who declaimed that 'God almighty is a whoremaster, the Virgin Mary a damned whore, and Jesus Christ is a bastard.'[23] These cases, so distant in time and place from seventeenth-century Surrey, indicate that blasphemers entertained some thoroughly perverse and bellicose need to sully fundamental articles of faith by attacking Jesus' legitimacy, from there moving to meretricious inferences regarding Mary. No one publicly utters such things unless his psychological profile is of one hell-bent to say the worst imaginable thing, the similarity of expression over the course of two centuries suggesting not simple godlessness or diabolism but perhaps coprolalia (compulsive swearing), a symptom of Tourette's syndrome.

Such utterances might well trigger violent reactions among otherwise law-abiding citizens, thus vindicating the notion that blasphemy could constitute a crime even in the absence of an established religion. Kent, however, saw blasphemy not as a subset of disturbing the peace but as akin to obscenity, in that both 'corrupt moral sentiment.' The drafters of the federal Comstock Act of 1873 criminalized sending 'obscene' and 'lascivious' material through the U.S. mail, although they did not also include blasphemous or sacrilegious matter. In 1884 the rector of Grace Church in Jersey City, New Jersey, demanded that Postmaster General A.A. Freeman suppress as 'blasphemous' a pamphlet entitled 'The Deistic Pestilence and Religious Plague of Man.' Freeman refused, noting that since the pamphlet was neither obscene nor lascivious, federal law provided no statutory basis to bar it from the mails, adding that the Comstock Act leaves undisturbed 'the liberty of the press and the freedom of conscience, subject alone to the condition that the rights thus secured shall not be exercised in such manner as to interfere with the rights of others.' In 1900 a postmaster in Kentucky refused to mail an article entitled 'The Virgin Mary' which 'questions the chastity of Mary ... and ridicules in coarse fashion the idea of the supernatural origin' of Jesus. A federal judge concluded that the defendant would have violated the Comstock Act's ban on obscenity and lasciviousness if he had questioned the chastity of the girl-next-door, or of all the women in town. In fact, many ill-starred defendants in prosecutions under the Comstock Act were sent to prison for mailing just such material. Yet the court reasoned that a tawdry suggestion regarding Mary was categorically different, in that it did not – like obscene or lascivious matter – cause sexual arousal. That is, 'to mail a paper which ... contends that even such a woman as Mary had actually been unchaste in the remote past is not, and cannot be, an offence under the statute ... To allege ... however falsely, that a woman, the most honoured among men, was in fact unchaste thousands of years ago, cannot naturally or justly be said to have a tendency to allure men now to such immorality as relates to sexual impurity.' Thus – the court reasoned – 'unless infidelity and atheism are to be proscribed as beyond the bounds of the rule of the freedom of religious thought and speech ... it cannot be justly said that the man who believes that the child Jesus came in the ordinary way of humanity may not advocate that belief, and thus attempt to establish his contention that the Christian religion is not the true one, or, indeed, that there is no true religion at all.'[24]

While allegedly blasphemous matter thus could not be prosecuted under the federal Comstock Act unless it also happened to be sexually stimulating, the state common law of blasphemy carried no such limitation. In September 1919, at the height of the Red Scare, an itinerant socialist named Mykolas Mockus gave three lectures in Lithuanian to an audience of predominantly Catholic Lithuanian immigrants in Rumford, Maine, hoping to convince them that religion was a tool of the capitalist state. Among the translated passages: 'Mary had a beau. When her beau called one evening (both being young) he seduced her. He brought her a flower and put her in a family way. No woman can give birth to a child without a man ... The father of Christ was a young Jew and was no Angel Gabriel. Any girl who wants a child can call a Gabriel or some John ... Religion, capitalism, and government are all damned humbugs, liars, and thieves. Those three classes combine into one organization ... There is no truth in the Bible; it is monkey business.' The jury found Mockus guilty, accepting the prosecution's argument that although he was undermining religion, his ultimate goal was 'to destroy the government.' The court sentenced him to one to two years in prison, declaring: 'there is no community and no society that can tolerate a willful and a spiteful attempt to subvert its religion.'[25]

Although in and after the First World War, dozens of state and federal courts found ways to convict syndicalists, socialists, and anarchists, *Mockus* was unusual in that it did so by employing the vestigial common law of blasphemy. While a vast array of evangelical Protestants had just scored their greatest triumph with Prohibition, and the Scopes 'monkey trial' would soon reveal to the nation its own deep impulse of religious fundamentalism, blasphemy prosecutions, because they raised free-speech and church/state questions, were on the wane, particularly after the Supreme Court in *Gitlow v. New York* (1925) began the process of broadening federal free-speech rights and protecting them against intrusions by states. A year earlier, *People v. Baylinson* presented a dispute over a painting which portrayed Jesus as opposing Prohibition. The Eighteenth Amendment banning alcohol had been duly ratified by all but two states, and Rep. Andrew Volstead's National Prohibition Act was enacted thereunder with substantial moral fervour. The quasi-evangelist William Jennings Bryan would soon be defending scripture against evolution in the Scopes trial. As secretary of state under Woodrow

Wilson in the years before Prohibition, Bryan had directed that grape juice be served at diplomatic receptions, a reminder to European diplomats that theirs was an exotic posting.

Among eight hundred works at the 1923 annual exhibition of the Society of Independent Artists at New York's Waldorf-Astoria was A.S. Baylinson's pictorial parody of the wedding feast at Cana (John 2:1–11). In the painting, Jesus has just performed the miracle of turning water into wine, and Bryan and Volstead are shown dumping it out, as Jesus comments: 'Father, Forgive Them, for They Know Not What They Do.' A complaining police officer told the Society's president, artist John Sloan, to remove the painting, and Sloan refused. New York, like most states, had a general-purpose statute which outlawed obscenity but said nothing about blasphemy or sacrilege. Undeterred by this lack of statutory authority for banning the painting, the trial judge chose to characterize it as an outrage to public decency and ordered it removed from the exhibition. New York's Appellate Division, however, while calling the picture both 'sacrilegious' and 'in bad taste' by portraying the God-fearing Bryan and Volstead as acting in direct contravention of Jesus' own wishes, came to the common-sense conclusion that since the complaining police officer was the only person out of ten thousand attendees who had voiced any objection, the picture could not reasonably be characterized as an outrage to public decency.[26]

In 1928, Massachusetts prosecutors had a warrant issued against the educator Horace Kallen because he said of Sacco and Vanzetti: 'If [they] were anarchists, so also were Socrates and Jesus Christ.' In the end, the Commonwealth decided not to serve the warrant, Kallen later quipping: 'The story is as comic as it is Catholic.' In March 1933 several Detroit clergymen decried as a 'sacrilegious parody' Diego Rivera's mural 'Vaccination Panel' in the Detroit Institute of Art, part of a set of murals commissioned by the city's arts council, chaired by Edsel Ford. Rivera, endowed with the modern artist's desire to shock the bourgeois, portrayed serum-providing animals surrounding a newborn who has the face of the Lindbergh baby, kidnapped and murdered a year before. As three scientists / wise men look on, the attending nurse, wearing a halo-like white cap, has the face of 'blonde bombshell' star Jean Harlow, while the physician resembles the Art Institute's director. Although the particular mural was called 'sacrilegious,' the entire set of murals was deemed Communistic, an odd allegation since they repeatedly show labour and management working in harmony, and Rivera had been thrown out of Mexico's Communist Party four years before. Some would-be detractors chose to remain silent because they did not wish to be associated with Father Charles Coughlin, who had excoriated Rivera's mural on his radio program. Rivera stated: 'The religious are attacking me because I am religious. I paint what I see.' It was later suggested that the museum and/or Edsel Ford had intentionally provoked the controversy in order to stimulate public interest in the museum.[27] In any event, allegations of blasphemy – it seemed – were no longer being fought out in the courts.

19 In the Supreme Court

On 4 February 1952, the Supreme Court announced that it would review Joseph Burstyn's case.[1] Several weeks later, the Regents and the New York State Catholic Welfare Committee filed briefs urging that since the ongoing viability of *Mutual Film* was the only Constitutional issue, it was all the Court needed to consider, so that a simple reaffirmation of *Mutual Film* would leave in place all that had been decided in New York. Burstyn's lawyer, free-speech specialist Ephraim London, argued that in the years since 1915, so many films had dealt with so many serious social issues that *Mutual Film* should 'be relegated to the history shelf,' a rather flip way to dismiss what had been for almost four decades the Constitutional authority for all state and municipal film censorship. Keying on the issues of statutory vagueness that had carried the day in *Winters* and *Kunz*, London further asserted that the word 'sacrilegious' in New York's statute failed to specify what conduct was and was not unlawful, the word being so vague as to violate the First and Fourteenth Amendments. In addition, he urged that if a state could ban a film as 'sacrilegious,' it could in effect dictate what was and was not appropriate commentary on religious matters, thus not only contravening the rationales of *Cantwell* and *Kunst*, but breaching the 'wall of separation' between church and state posited by Jefferson.[2] The Court was also favoured with a history of blasphemy law in an amicus brief submitted on behalf of the American Civil Liberties Union and the American Jewish Congress by lawyers Arthur Garfield Hays and Morris Ernst, the latter having already achieved substantial fame by – among other things – winning the *Ulysses* case. (He also happened to be the cousin of Burstyn's partner, Arthur Mayer.)

Oral argument took place on 24 April 1952. Ephraim London, alluding to *Winters*, asserted that *Mutual Film*'s refusal to recognize free-speech protections for 'entertainment' should be overruled because every serious work of fiction from Harriet Beecher Stowe's *Uncle Tom's Cabin* (1850/52) to Akira Kurosawa's film *Rashomon* (1951) both entertains and informs.[3] New York State solicitor general Wendell Brown, appearing for the Regents, repeated the argument that the Regents had used successfully thus far: that no one has a Constitutional right 'to lampoon and vilify' or to throw 'gratuitous insults' either at religion generally or at a particular faith. Responding to Vinson's question about Douglas's comment in *Paramount*, Brown stated that it was dictum, to which the chief justice ambiguously replied, 'It shows what it shows.'

In 1915, just prior to the release of the Supreme Court's decision in *Mutual Film*, several members of the Supreme Court had had a special screening of D.W. Griffith's *Birth of a Nation*. For most people who saw it, whether in the North, South, or around the world, it came to be everything they knew – or thought they knew – about a crucial moment in American history. Yet seeing that film apparently had no impact on the Court's conclusion in *Mutual Film* that movies were mere entertainment, conveying neither information nor opinion. Thirty-seven years later, with regard to *The Miracle*, on the day before oral argument, the Court for the first time in its history (with three members absent) watched a film as a piece of evidence in a controversy regarding the legality of its contents. Afterwards it was rumoured that 'at least some of the Justices' thought the film 'very poor entertainment.' But whether they 'liked it' or not (the immediate and the *only* question most viewers ever consider when exiting a Hollywood movie) was simply irrelevant to the task before them.[4]

Among those submitting amicus briefs in the case, Hollywood was notable for its absence. The Regents' counsel, Wendell Brown, saw fit to inform the Court that Burstyn had asked the studios to support his cause but they had declined, Brown's implication being that whether Burstyn had free-speech rights worth protecting was somehow to be gauged by whether Hollywood thought he did. Brown, that is, hoped to plant in the justices' minds the notion that it would be illogical or even unseemly for the Court to give films the protections of the First Amendment if America's film industry had no interest in the Court's doing so. Brown also read extensively from Hollywood's Production Code, asserting that *The Miracle* had violated several of its provisions. Yet, as Brown spoke, some of the justices may have recalled the ACLU's brief in *Paramount*, which characterized the self-censorship of the Production Code as a means to exclude outsiders. Or they might have noticed an editorial in *The Nation* commenting that American producers were 'so afraid of offending the Legion of Decency and incurring its blackmail in the form of denunciation and pressure – which were so effective in suppressing *"The Miracle"* – that they long ago submitted abjectly to prior censorship in the Production Code and have never challenged the manifest unfairness of denying films the protection of the First Amendment.'[5]

'Sacrilegious'

Wendell Brown repeated the argument that no one had a legal right to mock either a specific religion or religion in general. Brown's co-counsel, Charles A. Brind, Jr, lawyer for the State Education Department, argued that Rossellini's film was not 'sacrilegious' vis-à-vis any specifically Catholic doctrine, but instead offended the general Christian belief in Jesus' divinity. This position, responding to a question by Justice Frankfurter, was new, undoubtedly intended to blunt any suggestion that the Regents had overruled their own film experts and banned *The Miracle* solely in response to Catholic pressure. The best support for Brind's argument was that the Regents' subcommittee and the Board of Regents itself were multi-religious, although a reading of the entire record would reveal that Spellman had not enlisted Protestant or Jewish support in his campaign against the film, and that the letters and affidavits submitted in the case by Protestants stated that *The Miracle* presented no challenge to Christ's divinity.[6]

Just four days after oral argument, Burstyn's lawyers must have been disheartened to see the Court's decision in *Zorach v. Clausen*, affirming a New York statute that permitted students to leave school for religious instruction. 'We are a religious people,' the Court declared,

> whose institutions presuppose a Supreme Being ... When the state ... cooperates with religious authorities by adjusting the schedule of public events to sectarian needs, it follows the best of our traditions. For it then respects the religious nature of our people and accommodates the public service to their spiritual needs. To hold that it may not would be to find in the Constitution a requirement that the government show a callous indifference to religious groups. That would be preferring those who believe in no religion over those who do believe ... [W]e find no constitutional requirement which makes it necessary for government to be hostile to

religion and to throw its weight against efforts to widen the effective scope of religious influence.[7]

This must have been particularly worrisome since the opinion was written by Justice Douglas, to whom Burstyn's lawyers looked not just to overturn *Mutual Film* but to take an action which would be widely perceived as showing a 'callous indifference' to 'sectarian needs' and 'religious influence' by approving a film that had been judicially characterized as a mockery of Christian beliefs. Although comfort could be derived from the dissents of Justices Black, Jackson, and Frankfurter, the particular differentiation of views in *Zorach*, when compared with the splits in other recent cases, seemed to make further augury impossible.

A month later, on 26 May 1952, the Supreme Court issued its decision in *Burstyn*. In a unanimous decision (9–0), it reversed the New York Court of Appeals and lifted the ban on *The Miracle*. Associate Justice Tom Clark, in an opinion joined by five others, held that the First Amendment applied to film, that New York's film censorship statute constituted a prior restraint on free speech, and that while the First Amendment does not bar all prior restraints, a state may not repress speech in order to protect a religious group from viewpoints it dislikes. Alternative rationales were provided in concurrences submitted by Justices Reed and Frankfurter.

Justice Clark first dealt with *Mutual Film*. The Court seldom repudiates one of its own decisions as merely 'wrong,' and Clark strove mightily to distinguish the earlier case. First, he pointed out that *Mutual Film* had not involved the First Amendment, which in 1915 had not yet been declared available as a protection against state laws. While true, this was not a substantive distinction. Although the issue in *Mutual Film* was whether Ohio's film censorship statute violated the free-speech provision of Ohio's constitution, Justice McKenna would have reached the same result if he had applied the First Amendment, that is, he asserted unequivocally that film-making, 'a business pure and simple' and not an 'organ of opinion,' did not enjoy *any* kind of free-speech privileges.

Nor had any changes in the film medium justified a new legal standard. While Justice Clark noted that *Mutual Film* predated 'talkies,' he did not go so far as to urge that the invention of sound justified a change in free-speech law. The intertitles in the melodramatic silent films of 1910–1915 – offering significant viewpoints on such major issues as wrongful imprisonment and venereal disease – had provided clear similarities with newspapers and other 'organs of public opinion' protected by free-speech principles. Yet Justice McKenna had apparently found nothing in intertitles – even those in newsreels – to justify protecting them from censorship. Nor could anyone familiar with the great silent films say that sound had brought more significant content; indeed, knowledgeable observers argued the contrary. And if the invention of sound were legally significant, why would it take almost a quarter of a century for a relevant case to reach the Supreme Court?[8] In fact, the only change since *Mutual Film* was the Supreme Court's own expanding array of free-speech decisions.

While prudentially declining to criticize McKenna directly, Clark nevertheless contradicted almost everything McKenna had said. Although McKenna had strained to avoid admitting any similarities between film-making, 'a business pure and simple,' and the publication of books, magazines, and newspapers, Clark offhandedly suggested that these other forms of communication are no less commercial than movies. Nor could one doubt, Clark added, 'that motion pictures are a significant medium for the communication of ideas' and 'may affect public attitudes and behavior in a variety of ways, ranging from direct espousal of a political or social doctrine to the subtle shaping of thought which characterizes all artistic expression.' This sentence, in effect 're-placing' McKenna's oft-quoted conclusions and thus dispatching them to history, was a logical extension of what Justice Reed had written in *Winters*: that the line between 'informing' and 'entertaining' is 'too elusive' for the Court to declare that the First Amendment protects one but not the other.

Clark was not obliged to refute *everything* written in *Mutual Film*, since the only present issue was whether New York could ban *The Miracle* as 'sacrilegious,' and Clark had no interest in inviting lawsuits to test whether the First Amendment now barred states and municipalities from censoring films (or other media, for that matter) for any other reason.[9] In the case involving Edmund Wilson, the Court's tenuous 4/4 tie, unadorned by any commentary, left unsettled whether the First Amendment might provide *some* kind of protection for *some* works alleged to be 'obscene.' But Clark now stressed that the First Amendment would hobble censors only insofar as they attempted to ban material as 'sacrilegious,' and only because government may not engage in prior restraints of 'real or imagined attacks upon a particular religious doctrine.' Obscenity, that is, remained categorically outside

Constitutional protection. Clark then concluded: 'To the extent that ... *Mutual Film* ... is out of harmony with the views here set forth, we no longer adhere to it.' The sole legal authority he cited to support this was Justice Douglas's offhand comment about freedom of the screen in *Paramount*, thus lifting that comment above the status of mere dictum by making it legal authority for a secular change in the history of free speech. This must have pleased Judge Fuld in New York, who had accurately construed Douglas's words as prophecy of what was now positive law.

Persons with an abiding faith in art and its prerogatives might have been looking to the Court to vindicate Rossellini's film as a *bona fide* comment on human prejudice and spiritual redemption, a work which merits legal protection because of its moral and aesthetic contributions to the culture. Three federal judges – Learned Hand, Augustus Hand, and John Monroe Woolsey – had shown years before that courts might *protect* a work of art by *approving* it as a medium for conveying 'innocent' ideas. In the proceedings involving Edmund Wilson's book, Lionel Trilling, second in eminence only to Wilson himself, had joined other major literary authorities in declaring Wilson's earnestness and good faith.[10] Yet the Supreme Court did not accept Wilson's case, and now Clark and those who joined him did not address whether *The Miracle* was 'innocent.' Finding the relevant word in New York's statute, 'sacrilegious,' to violate the First Amendment when used as authority for the prior restraint of *any* work, there was no reason to discuss the content of Rossellini's film, much less to say whether it was – in *any* sense – 'sacrilegious.'[11] Having disaffirmed one hoary precedent, *Mutual Film*, in order to expand the reach of the First Amendment to films, and having concluded that the Regents and the New York courts had no business protecting religious groups from 'real or imagined attacks' upon their beliefs, the controversy was disposed of, even if one accepted that Rossellini *did* mock the Virgin Birth. After all, *Kunz*, one of the First Amendment cases in which the Court had recently found speech to be protected, involved language at its most disgusting, while another recent case, *Winters*, concerned writing whose sole purpose was the cheap thrill to be derived from reading 'Girl Slave of a Love Cult' and 'Bargains in Bodies.' The combined logic of *Kunz* and *Winters* – once Clark embraced it – would lead him to repudiate *Mutual Film* and to protect *The Miracle*, even if Rossellini's work had been as tawdry as 'Girls' Reformatory' or as vile as Kunz's comment that the Holocaust did not go far enough.

Justice Reed concurred in the result but chose not to embrace Justice Clark's narrow rationale that the word 'sacrilegious' was an inadequate premise for a prior restraint of First Amendment rights. Instead, Reed broadly and ambiguously declared that *The Miracle* 'does not seem to me to be of a character that the First Amendment permits a state to exclude from public view.'[12] Reed, author of the new First Amendment protection articulated in *Winters*, was perhaps suggesting what Learned Hand, Augustus Hand, and Judge Woolsey had written about the free-speech rights to be accorded artists and their 'innocent' ideas. But Reed did not see fit to explain himself, leaving readers to guess what it was in the 'character' of *The Miracle* that might exempt it from censorship laws.

Justice Frankfurter's Concurrence

Forty years earlier, Giorgio La Piana, a young priest travelling from his native Sicily to Rome, had divulged his pro-Modernist sympathies to another priest he met on the train, and soon found himself blocked from further advancement in the Church. Sent back home, he received a doctorate from the University of Palermo, then in 1913 sailed from Naples to America. He stayed long enough in Milwaukee to write an account of the Italian immigrants there, then abandoned the priest-hood, gave up church attendance, and enrolled in the Harvard Divinity School, where he was soon teaching a course on Catholic moral theology and writing on a variety of subjects, including the primitive Church, the schisms within Protestantism, and (not surprisingly) Catholic Modernism. Eventually he became J.H. Morison Professor of Church History. Reaching emeritus status in 1947, he delivered a series of lectures on American Catholicism entitled 'A Totalitarian Church in a Democratic State' (1949), while giving Paul Blanshard assistance with the series of articles that would lead to the Board of Superintendents' getting *The Nation* banned from New York City's public schools. A 1971 obituary in the *Catholic Historical Review* would remember La Piana as 'the last survivor of the priest-scholars ... involved in the Modernist controversy.'[13]

Among La Piana's friends at Harvard was Felix Frankfurter, who started teaching there shortly before La Piana arrived. Frankfurter's extraordinary career combined scholarship with co-founding the ACLU, advising the NAACP, writing numerous pieces (signed and unsigned) for the *New Republic*, advising Al Smith, consulting on such high-profile matters as the Sacco/Vanzetti and Scopes cases, and leading 'Frankfurter's happy hot dogs,' a brilliant phalanx of ex-students like Thomas G. Corcoran, Dean Acheson, and Alger Hiss, in shaping FDR's various melioration programs. His intellectual circle included Holmes, Brandeis, Learned Hand, and Benjamin Cardozo. Married to the daughter of a Congregationalist minister, he counted himself a non-observant, agnostic Jew who enjoyed discussing theological issues with friends like Reinhold Niebuhr. When FDR nominated Frankfurter to the Supreme Court in 1939, anti-Semitic remarks by Catholic journals were sufficiently numerous that *Commonweal*'s George Shuster said they could be collected in 'a rather harrowing little anthology.'[14]

As the 'scholar' on the Court, Frankfurter occasionally drafted deeply researched and sometimes discursive concurring opinions on matters he found interesting. Although Frankfurter might simply have joined in Clark's conclusion that 'sacrilegious' was an inappropriate legislative premise for a prior restraint of free-speech rights, he chose instead to write such a concurrence. The statute under scrutiny in *Winters* had prohibited any and all publications 'principally made up of criminal news, police reports, or accounts of criminal deeds, or pictures, or stories of deeds of bloodshed, lust or crime.' In that case, Justice Reed had written that such a statute, 'so vague and indefinite' that it permits 'the punishment of incidents fairly within the protection of the guarantee of free speech,' must fall, because it fails to comply with the Fourteenth Amendment requirement of due process.[15] Frankfurter obviously felt the same way about New York's film censorship statute, particularly regarding its use of the undefined word 'sacrilegious,' even though the New York Court of Appeals had attempted to 'save' the statute by giving the word a dictionary definition.[16] The New York court had issued its opinion in *Burstyn* on 18 October 1951. Several days later, Burstyn let it be known that he would try to take the case to the Supreme Court. A few days after that, Frankfurter wrote to Professor La Piana asking for a list of books and articles indicating what 'sacrilegious' meant in Catholic usage, while candidly acknowledging to his friend a strong predisposition to find in the word no fixed meaning. He then sent a law clerk to the Library of Congress and Catholic University library to gather further definitions. On 25 April 1952, one day after oral argument in *Burstyn* and just before the Court's internal post-argument conference, Frankfurter submitted to the other justices a list of definitions of 'sacrilege.' In a cover memo he wrote:

On first reading of *The Miracle* opinion, way back in November, in antici-
pation of the case coming here, I got under way, with my law clerks, lines
of inquiry without which, I was confident, the case could not reasonably
be decided. I did so because I knew that the studies that had to be made
were labourious and time-consuming. I could not wait until after the case
was argued because I knew that that would be more or less near the
home-stretch [of the Court's judicial year]. I wanted neither to skimp the
work nor run the risk of being responsible for delaying the adjournment
of the Court.[17]

Thus, long before Burstyn actually filed his papers with the Court,
Frankfurter had been scouting for authorities by which he might show
that the relevant operative word in New York's film censorship statute
was too vague to survive Constitutional scrutiny.

Nothing in Professor La Piana's several responses or in the volumi-
nous research generated by Frankfurter's clerks suggested that his original sense about 'sacrilegious' had been wrong. His concurring opinion
declares that 'sacrilegious' is such a vague word that it tramps on First
Amendment rights, and that the New York Court of Appeals, by applying the *Funk & Wagnalls* definition ('The act of violating or profaning
anything sacred'), failed to 'save' the word by giving it a clearer meaning, since 'profaning' and 'sacred' were themselves so vague. Burstyn's
counsel, Ephraim London, who had made the 'vagueness' argument a
central tenet of his case, must have been gratified to see it accepted by
the justice who had taken such an interest in it during oral argument,
although London could not have known just how much work Frankfurter, his clerks, and Professor La Piana had already done. London
must have been particularly gratified since Frankfurter was here voting
to strike down a state statutory provision that had been in place for
thirty years and had been employed by other states. After all, Frankfurter had dissented in *Winters*, there urging his brethren to give due
respect to state statutory provisions that had been on the books for
some time. Even more remarkably, the two justices (Jackson and Burton)
who had joined Frankfurter in that dissent now switched with him.
Perhaps the difference was that there had been a number of prosecutions under the statutory language at issue in *Winters*, while none of the
several states that had used 'sacrilegious' in their respective film statutes had ever tested the word in court.

In his original letter to Professor La Piana many months before,
Frankfurter had specifically asked not to be shown authorities in Latin

or Greek, since he counted himself 'semi-educated' with a 'linguistic illiteracy.' These were rhetorical self-abasements a man of Frankfurter's substantial achievements could well indulge, having arrived in New York as a steerage passenger at age twelve, learning English (in six weeks, rumour had it) at P.S. 25 on East 5th Street, while his father struggled to build a retail fur business of the kind with which so many Jewish immigrants got their start.[18] The list of definitions Frankfurter distributed to his brethren was subsequently published as an appendix to his concurring opinion.

'Sacrilege' combines the Latin *sacer* or *sacrum*, a sacred object, observance, or person, with *legere*, to gather, remove, or steal, while two related terms, *sacrilegium* and *sacrilegus*, concern an impious act with respect to consecrated objects, observances, or persons.[19] Following the research done on his behalf, Frankfurter concluded that 'sacrilegious' could be defined narrowly enough to survive due-process scrutiny if it were limited to mean a *physical* injury to sacred objects or persons, and he presumed to find authority for this restricted meaning in Aquinas's *Summa Theologica* and subsequent Catholic usages. If, he suggested, the New York Court of Appeals in dealing with *The Miracle* had only embraced this Thomist/Catholic definition (he does not mention the awkward issues that might have raised), the word would have been clear and definite enough to survive any constitutional challenge.[20] In his view, the New York court had instead confused 'sacrilege' with such non-physical wrongs as 'heresy,' 'apostasy,' 'profanation,' and – in particular – 'blasphemy,' which Frankfurter describes as a 'treacherous' word even when it is used in a nation with an official religion, since what was considered blasphemous in seventeenth-century England shifted radically, depending on whether a Catholic or Protestant was in power. (Under the Test Act of 1678, one could not hold a Crown office without first declaring 'the invocation of the virgin Mary' to be 'superstitious and idolatrous.') And in the United States, with multiple religions, each holding a variety of things 'sacred,' what might be deemed 'sacrilegious' is multiplied, leading censors to enforce the dictates of whatever religious sect happens to wield political strength.

Statutory language that is so vague as to be unconstitutional may be the product of poor draftsmanship, or it may represent a legislative compromise when neither side has the votes to support a more definite statement of principle. On the other hand, draftsmen commonly employ broad and undefined words on the assumption that 'everyone knows' what they mean, and in the thirty-plus years since New York and several other states had employed the word 'sacrilegious' in their respective film censorship laws, no one other than Burstyn's lawyer had claimed an inability to know what the word meant. Nor was the New York Court of Appeals doing anything unusual in trying to immunize the word from Constitutional attack by endowing it with a dictionary definition. Indeed, the gist of that definition had been in place for several centuries. Everyone knew that 'sacrilege' was 'the act of violating or profaning anything sacred,' and if in the abstract one could not explain just what kinds of acts did and did not qualify, one could at least say regarding 'sacrilege' what Justice Potter Stewart said in a later film censorship case about 'hard-core pornography': that while he could not articulate just what it entailed, 'I know it when I see it.'[21] Most people had little hesitation identifying sacrilege when they saw it. For millions of citizen/voters, if mocking the Virgin Birth was not sacrilegious, what was? But in a pluralistic society with no state religion, there could be no real consensus on what was 'sacrilegious' because there was no real consensus on what was 'sacred.'

Although Frankfurter, in effect, told New York's highest court that it should have given the relevant statutory word a Catholic definition, he also freely admitted that this would have rendered the word utterly useless as a statutory basis for censoring films. In choosing the word 'sacrilegious,' legislative draftsmen simply could not have meant a physical injury to sacred things, since movies, whatever else they do, cannot break into churches and smash sacred objects. Thus, in the end, Frankfurter's inquiries to Professor La Piana and his extended 'scholarly' discussion led him up a blind alley: to a conclusion that New York's highest court could have saved its statutory provision from Constitutional attack by rendering it incapable of performing the censorship function it was intended to perform.

Frankfurter, like Clark, found it unnecessary to discuss – much less to approve – the contents of Rossellini's film, although he did go so far as to observe that such 'vague, undefinable powers of censorship' as found in New York's 'sacrilege' provision were 'bound to have stultifying consequences on the creative process of literature and art.' Various notes in Frankfurter's file indicate that he closely monitored newspaper accounts of the Church's involvement, and while Clark had alluded to the church/state ramifications of how the *Miracle* controversy had started in New York, Frankfurter went so far as to take judicial notice of what Catholic power had done to free speech in Hollywood:

To stop short of proscribing all subjects that might conceivably be interpreted to be religious, inevitably creates a situation whereby the censor bans only that against which there is a substantial outcry from a religious group. And that is the fair inference to be drawn ... from what has been happening under New York censorship. Consequently the film industry, normally not guided by creative artists, and cautious in putting large capital to the hazards of courage, would be governed by its notions of the feelings likely to be aroused by diverse religious sects, certainly the powerful ones.

While noting that 'the effect of such demands upon art and upon those whose function is to enhance the culture of a society need not be laboured' (presumably because it is obvious and/or not directly relevant), Frankfurter could not resist alluding to an item he had seen in the newspaper, the infamous Richelieu incident, exemplifying what he called the Church's 'distorting influence' on history.[22]

We might quibble with Frankfurter's odd choice of Aquinas as the authority by which to interpret a film censorship statute, and in a controversy in which some were accusing the Church of high-handedness. But Frankfurter was undoubtedly correct that in a nation with no state religion, the word 'sacrilegious' could not be defined broadly enough to include *all* 'profanations' of *all* things held 'sacred' by *all* religions, and still be definite enough in its meaning to pass due-process scrutiny. Meanwhile, Professor La Piana, whose brilliant career as a priest had abruptly ended because on a train in southern Italy he had admitted Modernist views to a Vatican prelate, had now helped a justice of the U.S. Supreme Court derail a cardinal's efforts to suppress as 'sacrilegious' a work by the greatest exponent of Italian neo-realism. If, following his abandonment of the priesthood and his long career of achievement in secular America, La Piana still harboured any bitterness for the treatment he had received, that incident on an Italian train over forty years earlier was now in some large sense avenged.

Movie critic Ezra Goodman commented that Joe Burstyn 'knew more about the movies – both as art and commerce – and he had more guts than all the Hollywood nabobs combined.' Although Goodman saw Burstyn's victory as meaning 'more for Hollywood than for Burstyn himself,' when *Time* magazine told its Beverly Hills bureau to collect industry reactions to this extraordinary victory for freedom of the screen, studio executives 'were either so afraid that they refused to give out a statement, or they made meaningless, innocuous remarks ... still fearful of speaking up against censorship.' Martin Quigley commented that 'in face of the confusion precipitated by the court's decision,' the American film industry 'may well find cause for renewed rejoicing in its commitment to its own Production Code,' through which Hollywood can protect both 'the public interest and its own, irrespective of how the winds blow in the troubled area of political censorship and judicial pronouncement.'[1]

The appeal of the Texas case involving *Pinky*, on which some had placed Hollywood's faint interest in overturning *Mutual Film*, had been submitted and on file in the Supreme Court for some time. On 2 June 1952, one week after *Burstyn*, the Court issued a decision reversing the Texas state court's decision and striking down the relevant ordinance, thus clearing the way for the re-release of *Pinky* in the town of Marshall. Most of the justices saw no reason to draft an opinion, and instead simply cited to the opinions in *Burstyn* and *Winters* as sufficient authority to dispose of the *Pinky* controversy. Justice Frankfurter in a brief concurrence noted that Marshall's ordinance, allowing municipal censors to ban any film they thought 'prejudicial to the best interests' of local citizens, was as vague and thus as unconstitutional as the 'sacrilegious' provision struck down in *Burstyn*. Justice Douglas chose briefly to reprise the rationale of Justice Clark's majority opinion in *Burstyn*, finding Marshall's ordinance a flagrant prior restraint.[2]

Priests are fond of quoting Augustine: *Roma locuta est, causa finita est* ('Rome has spoken, the case is closed'). Lawyers are fond of quoting Justice Jackson's candid admission in 1953: '[R]eversal by a higher court is not proof that justice is thereby better done. There is no doubt that if there were a super–Supreme Court, a substantial portion of our reversals of state courts would also be reversed. We are not final because we are infallible, but we are infallible only because we are final.' A number of Catholic leaders considered the Supreme Court's unanimous decision in *Burstyn* grossly fallible and rued that it was final. The *Catholic Lawyer* called it 'unfortunate,' while Fr. Robert C. Harnett, editor of the Jesuit magazine *America*, said it 'has just about emptied our law of respect for Almighty God.' The *St John's Law Review* commented: 'This nation is founded upon a belief and trust in God. He is the ultimate sanction of our laws. We recognized our dependence upon Him in our organic documents and utterances, on our coins and through our public prayers. Our philosophy of government is entirely consonant with a jealous respect for His Name and Person ... The statute in the instant case is a legitimate effort of the duly-chosen officials of the State of New York to prevent the offensive reviling of the Deity.' John Courtney Murray, S.J., editor of the prestigious Jesuit quarterly *Theological Studies* as well as religious editor of *America*, concluded that the Court's underlying theory was that of Holmes's free marketplace of ideas, the law's sole function being to protect the openness of the market, with no vested interest in approving or criticizing the ideas and opinions being promoted in that marketplace. While many would call this a governmental guarantee of political, moral, intellectual, and spiritual freedom, Murray characterized it as 'a false and disastrous philosophical relativism,' in that government should decide which moral and religious ideas are correct, and enforce them against those that are incorrect. Quigley noted: 'Happily ... for the purposes of a decent society there are but few persons who wish to produce, exhibit or even patronize a film which is offensive to any man's religious sensibilities.'[3]

Charles Whelan, S.J., argued in the *Georgetown Law Journal* for a 'constitutional concept of morality,' proclaiming that *Mutual Film* had been correctly decided and should not have been overturned, that 'freedom of speech, press, assembly and religion ... was never meant to protect public indulgence in harmful or immoral entertainment,' and that 'it is no longer merely the constitutionality of censorship which is in issue, but the very existence of the power of government to regulate the morals of the people.' Judge Charles Desmond of the New York Court of Appeals, a Catholic who in *Burstyn* had voted to uphold the word 'sacrilegious' against First Amendment challenge, wrote in the *Notre Dame Lawyer*: 'It all comes down to questions of public order and decency, and the power of democratic governments to protect order and decency from the harm done by greedy men.' Cardinal Spellman's official biographer, former Fordham president Robert I. Gannon, S.J., wrote that while a left-wing publication described the *Burstyn* decision as 'a humiliating defeat' for Spellman, in Gannon's view it instead showed 'how through technicalities our precious safeguards of liberty can be used to protect the very forces that are working against the best interests of the country.'[4]

The *Miracle* controversy exposed a wide gulf between what had become quasi-official Catholic culture, enforceable through pressure exerted on Hollywood, on publishers and bookstores, and on government, and a work of art at variance with that culture. As against such mawkish fare as *The Miracle of the Bells* and *Come to the Stable*, the re-release of *The Miracle* allowed any curious person to contemplate a Catholic message delivered, not via moving statues and tennis-playing nuns, but through a serious exploration of faith, prejudice, and religious hypocrisy. Although *The Miracle* would not prove 'popular' and the Supreme Court's imprimatur did not cause Spellman to lift his own ban, the film's second run fostered the recognition that perhaps it was time for immigrant Catholicism to move forward. New voices emerged. William F. Lynch, S.J., having written a book about media, said his purpose had been to dissuade Catholics from considering the 'miracles' portrayed in Hollywood's various pro-Catholic films as significant or meaningful. In 1953, Walter Kerr, *New York Herald Tribune* critic and formerly in the drama department at Catholic University, told the readers of *Commonweal*: 'The sort of judgment which at best reveals an alarming innocence of the very texture of art, and which at worst smacks suspiciously of cant, has pretty much become rule-of-thumb for the American Catholic moviegoer. A film featuring a saint is a film of majestic technical excellence. A film showing a nun driving a jeep is a superbly made comedy. A film embracing a jolly priest, a self-sacrificing Catholic mother, and an anti-Communist message must be defended in the diocesan press from those irresponsible esthetes and conspiratorial leftists – and even worse, those maverick Catholics –

who have had the meanness and the malice to question it.' Allen Tate asserted that since imaginative writers deal with people as they are rather than as they ought to be, the Church has had a 'standing quarrel' with writers, although Christianity itself will have 'reality' only insofar as writers seek 'that reality in the depths, as well as the heights, of the human situation as it is.' He dared add that 'it is not loyalty to the Church to condone the secular ignorance and the vulgarity' of a novel like *The Foundling*, just because its author, Cardinal Spellman, is a high church official.[5]

Those monitoring the Supreme Court wondered whether the serial expansion of the First Amendment, culminating in *Burstyn*, might presage a similar expansion to protect the growing number of HUAC's victims. In October 1952, Learned Hand, eighty years old and retired as chief judge of the Second federal Circuit, accepted an honourary degree from the New York Board of Regents. Regarding the atmosphere of anti-Communist paranoia he had witnessed for several years, he forcefully observed that a community is 'already in the process of dissolution where each man begins to eye his neighbor as a possible enemy, where nonconformity with the accepted creed, political as well as religious, is a mark of disaffection; where denunciation, without specification or backing, takes the place of evidence; where orthodoxy chokes freedom of dissent; where faith in the eventual supremacy of reason has become so timid that we dare not enter our convictions in the open lists to win or lose.'[6] The Regents had suspended the medical licence of Edward K. Barsky, pursuant to a provision of the New York Education Law which granted them discretionary authority to suspend the licence of anyone 'convicted ... of a crime.' Dr Barsky had been convicted for contempt of Congress following his refusal to turn over to HUAC a list of those connected with the Loyalist cause in Spain. He had been a prominent surgeon, trained at Columbia and holding a senior position at New York's Beth Israel Hospital. His colleagues warranted that his conviction for this particular crime – given the circumstances – in no way affected his fitness to practise medicine. On appeal, his lawyers argued that the phrase 'convicted ... of a crime' was so vague a predicate for suspending someone's medical licence as to violate the due-process clause of the Fourteenth Amendment, particularly where the 'evidence' considered by the Regents included mere allegations that Dr Barsky's Joint Anti-Fascist Committee was 'subversive' and 'Communist.' In April 1953, Judge Charles Desmond concluded for the New York Court of Appeals that although the Regents may have considered such stuff in their decision to suspend Dr Barsky's licence, the Court of Appeals was powerless to reverse them.

As with the Court of Appeals' decision in *Burstyn*, Judge Stanley Fuld dissented. While in *Burstyn* the Supreme Court in effect sided with Judge Fuld, here it affirmed the decision of Judge Desmond's majority, over the dissents of Justices Frankfurter, Black, and Douglas. Douglas commented: 'When a doctor cannot save lives in America because he is opposed to Franco in Spain, it is time to call a halt and look critically at the neurosis that has possessed us.'[7] Shortly thereafter, in 1957, the theory that the First Amendment protects citizens from inquiries into their political affiliations, considered novel when first argued a decade earlier by Dr Barsky and the Hollywood Ten, would finally get some traction with the Supreme Court.[8]

The Hollywood Ten, meanwhile, had served out their time. Dalton Trumbo, like Fatty Arbuckle thirty years before, dealt with his forced exile from the industry by using pseudonyms and/or collabourators and 'fronts.' When in 1957 the Motion Picture Academy announced that the Best Original Story award went to one 'Robert Rich' for *The Brave One*, no one stepped forward. It would be some years before the Oscar statuette awarded that night would find its way into Trumbo's hands, although in 1960 Trumbo would be the first of the Ten to have his screen credit restored.[9]

Although the *Burstyn* decision automatically nullified the word 'sacrilegious' in the film censorship laws of the several states where it had been on the books, Maryland, as a matter of legislative housecleaning, formally struck the word from its statute.[10] Neo-realism's direct influence on American cinema quickly waned, with the exception of *The Little Fugitive* (1953), the story of a boy from a Brooklyn tenement alone in Coney Island. Produced and directed by Ruth Orkin, Ray Ashley, and still photographer Morris Engel, it employed some of the Italians' conscious techniques, while perforce replicating their shoestring budgets. Joseph Burstyn distributed it into the venues where Rossellini's films had made their mark, while also helping a struggling young filmmaker, Stanley Kubrick, by booking his first feature, *Fear and Desire* (1953), at New York's Guild Theatre. In March 1953, Burstyn was named president of a new Independent Motion Picture Distributors Association of America. Eight months later, while flying to Europe, he died of a heart attack, at age fifty-three.

Justice Clark had urged that the new First Amendment right to exhibit a 'sacrilegious' film entailed no similar right to exhibit an 'obscene' one, while Justice Reed seemed to say that Rossellini's film could not be banned on *any* basis. The legal community, pondering these utterances, wondered what other censorship criteria might now fall.[11] In 1953, Judge Desmond concurred in the affirmance of the Regents' ban on Max Ophüls's film *La Ronde* (1950) because it was 'immoral' and would 'tend to corrupt morals' within the meaning of New York's film censorship law, elsewhere noting that the Supreme Court – despite its holding in *Burstyn* – had not yet forged an obstacle 'to keep such evil' as Ophüls's work 'from our people.' But in January 1954 the Supreme Court held that *Burstyn* would not allow New York to ban this Ophüls masterwork.[12] The Court issued no opinion, as if telling Desmond and his brethren that if they had given *Burstyn* a fair reading, they would have come to this result on their own, thus saving the Supreme Court the trouble of reversing them.

In 1954, Ohio's Supreme Court construed *Burstyn* broadly as standing for the proposition that no film censorship statute could stand First-Amendment scrutiny unless it was 'clearly drawn.' Under that test, it held that Ohio's statute, authorizing censors to ban any film they thought not 'of a moral educational, or amusing and harmless character,' was not 'clearly drawn' and therefore violated the First Amendment. Five members of the Ohio court agreed, thus striking down the state law that the U.S. Supreme Court itself had approved in *Mutual Film*.[13] The Illinois Supreme Court, on the other hand, held that Chicago's film censors could ban *The Miracle* under a city ordinance prohibiting 'immoral and obscene' films, since in its view 'obscene,' unlike 'sacrilegious,' had been given a clear and enforceable meaning in *Hicklin* and other judicial glosses over the years, while 'immoral' could reasonably be construed as merely a synonym for 'obscene.' The U.S. Supreme Court (with Justices Black, Harlan, and Douglas dissenting) refused to review that decision, but only on the technical ground that the Illinois court had not issued a 'final judgment.' Eventually the case came before an intermediate Illinois court.[14] It concluded that even if one applies the old *Hicklin* test, a 'salaciously inclined' person would not be stimulated by *The Miracle*, a film containing 'no gloss of glamour' and whose central character 'is clothed only in rags and whose personality is devoid of any charm.' Further, to assert that *The Miracle's* 'predominant effect ... is to arouse sexual passion' would be 'to deny [Rossellini's] intent and his artistry,' while to emphasize the seduction scene with which the film opens would be contrary to its central theme as well as its 'aesthetic and ... dramatic merit.'[15] *The Miracle*, its artistic integrity finally noted by an appellate tribunal, now reopened in Chicago.

While Catholic parishioners continued to receive notices indicating what they could and could not see, the majoritarian culture no longer wanted Catholic bishops to protect it from what movie producers were willing to provide. As it became clear that television was going to cut deeply and permanently into Hollywood's bottom line, the studios experimented not only with enhanced visual and sound techniques which television technology could not replicate, but also new content which television – federally regulated – dared not offer. In Otto Preminger's *The Moon Is Blue* (1953), the ingénue offhandedly and repeatedly refers to herself as a 'virgin,' a term theretofore unheard of in Hollywood films. In the *Catholic World*, a Jesuit wrote that the industry's system of self-censorship no longer worked and that whenever 'private organizations prove ineffectual,' government 'has a duty to step in and safeguard the common good.' Kansas's film censors demanded that Preminger make sixty-five deletions, under a statute proscribing films 'such as are cruel, obscene, indecent or immoral, or such as tend to debase or corrupt morals.' The Kansas Supreme Court, although citing *Burstyn*, affirmed the censors' authority to ban *The Moon Is Blue* if the changes were not made. The U.S. Supreme Court summarily reversed, while leaving to Kansas the task of figuring out what was wrong with its statute. As authority, the Supreme Court merely cited to its own decisions in *Burstyn* and in the *La Ronde* case, which was itself only a citation to *Burstyn*.[16]

Lloyd Bacon's *The French Line* (1954) re-enlisted Jane Russell's bosoms, this time in 3-D, a visual experience one could not find at home. Joe Breen retired. Preminger's *The Man with the Golden Arm* (1955) dealt with drug addiction, while Elia Kazan's *Baby Doll* (1956) spares none of the seething sexual energy Tennessee Williams had brought to the New York stage. Although Breen had been appalled by a child's killing his father in *Germany Year Zero*, Mervyn LeRoy's *The Bad Seed* (1956) features a little girl so diabolical that her own mother tries to poison her, while Charles Laughton's *The Night of the Hunter* (1955) features a psychotic preacher, and in Vincente Minnelli's *Tea and Sympathy* (1956) a married prep school housemother takes a student to bed to rid him of his incipient homosexuality. Each of these films flagrantly ignored the Code and all proved lucrative at the box office. Since the industry now saw television as a more immediate and palpable threat than the Legion and the bishops, it substantially liberalized the Code to accommodate this new frankness. As each former barrier of taste was breached, the public became marginally more 'sophisticated,' that is, better prepared for the next assault on the next obstacle to sexual candour. As Learned Hand had understood back in 1913, the 'critical point in the compromise between candor and shame' was constantly moving.

Since the Hays Office, a private enforcement organization funded and run by the studios, was under no obligation to adjust the Code's language to conform with what the Supreme Court might say, in its 1956 revision it retained its decades-long prohibition on 'blasphemy.' Rep. Edward H. Rees (R-KS), chairman of the House Post Office and Civil Service Committee, either to garner votes back home or perhaps out of plain pique, introduced a bill to have the word 'blasphemous' inserted into the list of grounds upon which the federal Post Office could ban material from the mails.[17] (The bill died in committee.) Traditional, Hollywood-style Christianity had a resurgence in *The Robe* (1953; dir. Henry Koster), Darryl Zanuck's attempt to take back market-share from television via 'CinemaScope.' DeMille responded in 1956 with a remake of his own *The Ten Commandments* (1923), this time establishing the gold standard in the genre of sumptuous biblical epics.

In his concurring opinion in *Burstyn*, Justice Frankfurter noted a newspaper item announcing that a film was to be made about Martin Luther. Frankfurter speculated that, whether the portrayal was handled sympathetically or unsympathetically, someone was bound to find the film sacrilegious. The project was financed by six Lutheran groups, who in their collective wisdom hired director Irving Pichel. Best known for *The Miracle of the Bells*, Pichel had been working steadily since first arriving in Hollywood in 1927 and apparently understood – from his early days at Republic – what might be achieved on a less than Croesan budget. Frankfurter had been prophetic, in that *Martin Luther*, produced with the prospect of showing it only in church basements, portrays Catholic prelates, not as Spellman, Breen, and Father Devlin would have them, but as Luther saw them. Its cast of brilliant British actors, coupled with the understated black-and-white settings Pichel put together, made it the kind of art film that Hollywood could never make, yielding extraordinary popularity and critical acclaim upon its release in 1953, capped off by two Oscar nominations. In 1956, Chicago television station WGN announced that it would air the film, then backed out. Although it was widely assumed that the station had capitulated to pressure from the Chicago Archdiocese, the latter denied any involvement.[18]

Redemption American-Style

In her last film with Rossellini, *Giovanna d'Arco al Rogo* (*Joan of Arc at the Stake*, 1954), Bergman reprised her portrayal of the Virgin Warrior, backed by the music of Arthur Honegger and a text by Paul Claudel. Anna Magnani came to the United States and played in Daniel Mann's screen version (1955) of Tennessee Williams's *The Rose Tattoo*, for which she won an Academy Award. That just a few years before she had participated in a 'satanic' parody of the Virgin Birth was now utterly forgotten. In 1956 Twentieth Century-Fox, after seeking and obtaining the approval of the Legion of Decency and the Daughters of the American Revolution, reintroduced Bergman to American audiences in Anatole Litvak's *Anastasia* (1956), a project whose comfort level was optimized by being produced outside the United States, thus eliminating the possibility of any unpleasant confrontations between disgruntled American citizens and their erstwhile idol. Fans who had opted to consider the whole Rossellini episode as a bad dream must have taken heart to see Bergman (in John Kobal's words) as the 'much put-upon and suffering' Anastasia, a refugee with amnesia, tricked by a foreign man into assuming an identity not her own. Thus was Bergman redeemed from what Tallulah Bankhead deftly called the public's 'shocking kettle of stewed moral inconsistencies.' Bergman, maintaining her dignity and honesty, refused to participate in this evolution of public perceptions, even if her purported rehabilitation was to be completed by the fairy-tale climax of receiving an Academy Award. In the event that she won, Cary Grant later noted, he was under instruction to move forward quickly and accept the award on her behalf, so that no one else 'could get up and say, "Dear Ingrid, we forgive you." All that crap.' And when the Price-Waterhouse envelope was opened (Louella Parsons wrote) and revealed Bergman's name, bedlam erupted, 'as if all those people in that theatre felt that they had somehow undone harm, cleansed themselves of viciousness and prudery and prejudice.' Shortly thereafter, the Bergman/Rossellini marriage ended. For each, as for Magnani as well, a lifelong quest for artistic achievement continued. When Magnani died in 1973, Bergman placed roses on her casket.[19]

Community Standards

In 1957 the Supreme Court in *Roth v. United States* commenced an exploration of obscenity which over the next sixteen years would consume a sizeable portion of the justices' time. In deciding how putatively 'obscene' something could be without losing First Amendment protection, the Court found no role for *Hicklin*. Instead, the first of the Court's evolving obscenity tests was 'whether to the average person, applying contemporary community standards, the dominant theme of the material taken as a whole appeals to prurient interest,' the latter defined as 'material having a tendency to excite lustful thoughts.' Articulated in another way, the test was whether an average juror thought his community would find that the most significant thing about the book or film under scrutiny was that it was sexually arousing. This was a sort of formula for locating – regarding any given work at any given moment – Learned Hand's 'critical point in the compromise between candor and shame.' In *Roth* and another case decided in the same year, *Butler v. Michigan*, the Court began expanding protection for various kinds of commercialized sex and violence, usually relying upon *Winters'* perspective that government could not suppress a work simply because it had no articulable value. As people read news reports of the famous case involving *Lady Chatterley's Lover*, they began not only to buy and read copies of Lawrence's theretofore expurgated novel, but to expect free expression for novelists, film-makers, and artists as a matter of course.[20] A succession of progressively liberal decisions issuing from the Supreme Court in these years resulted in increasingly explicit films, books, photographs, and magazines dealing with an increasingly variegated list of sexual themes and orientations, their appearance both reflecting and fostering what would soon be recognized as a Sexual Revolution.

In 1970, Protestant theologian James M. Gustafson of Yale Divinity School wrote: 'God and man both know that Christians,' by 'identifying sin with sexuality,' have 'committed a mistake of the highest order of magnitude' and in doing so 'have perpetrated untold anguish, pain and suffering on the world.' The issue of sex ethics, he urged, should no longer be viewed negatively in terms of 'puritanical restraints,' but rather in terms of 'how to conduct life in freedom,' an argument proposed by D.H. Lawrence, Bertrand Russell, and others over forty years before, only to be met with censorship and general disapproval. For years, numerous communities tried to define the line between 'candor' and 'shame' under the Supreme Court's various tests. Then, in 1973, in addressing an appeal from Marvin Miller's conviction under California's obscenity statute for mailing unsolicited, sexually explicit advertising brochures for a film and several books, Chief Justice Warren Burger structured a three-part test for obscenity:

– 'whether "the average person, applying contemporary community standards," would find that the work, taken as a whole, appeals to the prurient interest';
– 'whether the work depicts or describes, in a patently offensive way, sexual conduct specifically defined by the applicable state law'; and
– 'whether the work, taken as a whole, lacks serious literary, artistic, political, or scientific value.'

Miller's three-part test, culminating the sixteen years of tinkering that had begun with *Roth*, remained the law, allowing the *status quaestionis* on obscenity finally to come to rest. Some states, the better to abide by the new *Miller* standard, simply wrote Justice Burger's operative language into their respective obscenity statutes, thus immunizing them from any claim that their censorship laws did not comport exactly with what the Supreme Court required.[21] The regime lasted, even though the emergence of cable television and then the Internet rendered irrelevant the whole idea of a geographical community.

Hard cases, it is said, make bad law. The U.S. Supreme Court must often accept and decide extremely hard cases, their difficulty commonly revealed in advance by the contrary results already reached by lower courts. In *Texas v. Johnson* (1989), a Texas criminal statute forbade the 'Desecration of [a] Venerated Object.' The defendant did indeed desecrate a venerated object – under any fair-minded definition of these words – in that he publicly burned an American flag, a secular example of what Justice Frankfurter had described as a good definition of 'sacrilege': physical injury to a sacred thing. Many believe that flag-burning – deemed a flagrant insult to the memory of those who gave the last full measure of devotion to their nation – is a crime of sufficient viciousness to justify a capital penalty. But to burn a sacred symbol is to make some kind of statement, and so the case presented a significant problem under the First Amendment. With a clarity Cicero would have applauded, Justice William Brennan, a major contributor to the expanded First Amendment jurisprudence between *Roth* and *Miller*, now declared:

'We do not consecrate the flag by punishing its desecration, for in doing so we dilute the freedom that this cherished emblem represents.'[22] But Justice Brennan was writing for a narrow, five/four majority. The following years would see constant pressure to put flag desecration outside the First Amendment's protection by the only means the Supreme Court could not touch: a Constitutional amendment.

Catholicism Transformed

In September 1953, Pius XII proclaimed a Marian year to commemorate the centenary of the dogma of the Immaculate Conception. Mary, he said, 'wished to confirm by some special sign' the legitimacy of the 1854 announcement, and did so by describing herself to Bernadette as 'the Immaculate Conception,' a statement 'properly interpreted by the faithful' to mean the Blessed Virgin Mary, whose 'miraculous favours ... excite the admiration of all, and confirm that the Catholic religion is the only one given approval by God.' In October, Pius XII declared: 'Let all Christians ... glory in being subjects of the Virgin Mother of God, who, while wielding royal power, is on fire with a mother's love.' The number of yearly pilgrims to Lourdes passed the two-million mark. In the United States, churches named in Mary's honour now numbered more than 4,200, including 588 invoking the Immaculate Conception, another 149 called 'Mary Immaculate of Lourdes,' and sixty named 'Our Lady of Fátima.' Marian names were also found on more than 70 colleges, 500 high schools, 2,000 elementary schools, and 280 hospitals and clinics, as well as 2,200 convents and 100 seminaries.[23]

The Marian year of 1953–4 would be seen in retrospect as an apex of Marian devotionalism, a sense emerging thereafter that interest in Mary had been over-indulged. The 'Our Lady of Television' statue, positively and intimately associated with Fulton Sheen's popular broadcast, was soon gone, along with Sheen's brilliant prime-time conversation. In 1957, Cardinal Spellman demanded reimbursement for a supply of powdered milk he had forwarded to Sheen as American director of the World Mission Society for the Propagation of the Faith. Aware that Spellman had obtained the powdered milk *gratis* from the U.S. Government, Sheen refused to pay. Their dispute came before Pius XII, who – despite his decades-long friendship with Spellman – accepted Sheen's proffered evidence that he owed Spellman nothing. Spellman had Sheen's television program cancelled and eventually exiled him to the bishopric of Rochester, New York, an assignment which in effect assured that Sheen, despite his intellectual productivity, his extraordinary popularity, and his proven fund-raising ability, would never be Spellman's successor as archbishop. The liberalizations instituted by the Second Vatican Council in the mid-1960s included a collective retreat from what was now deemed an excessive Mariolatry, and innumerable parish churches began putting their ubiquitous Marian statues in storage. Pope Paul VI's *Lumen Gentium* (1964) advised 'that true devotion [to Mary] consists neither in sterile or transitory affection, nor in a certain vain credulity, but proceeds from true faith, by which we are led to know the excellence of the Mother of God, and we are moved to a filial love toward our mother and to the imitation of her virtues.'[24]

On 12 December 1960, a month after John F. Kennedy, a Catholic, was elected to the U.S. presidency, *Time*'s cover featured John Courtney Murray, S.J., whose new book, *We Hold These Truths*, renewed the argument for the compatibility of Catholic and American ideals. Frank Getlein, who had been fired from his teaching position at Fairfield University for questioning the intellectual, moral, and aesthetic premises of Spellman's attack on *The Miracle*, became a nationally recognized art critic, writing innumerable articles and several dozen books, including *Movies, Morals, and Art* (1961), co-authored by critic and censorship expert Harold Gardner, S.J. William Clancy, who had been fired from his teaching position at Notre Dame following his criticism of Spellman in the March 1951 *Commonweal*, moved to New York and continued contributing to that magazine. He became affiliated with the 'Study of Religious Institutions in a Democratic Society,' a unit of the Fund for the Republic sponsored by the Ford Foundation to 'support activities directed toward the elimination of restrictions on freedom of thought, inquiry and expression,' also becoming education director of the Church Peace Union, later renamed the Carnegie Council on Ethics and International Affairs. In 1958, Clancy had a drink with Notre Dame writing professor Frank O'Malley, who confirmed Clancy's suspicion that Spellman had been behind his termination, recounting that Spellman had telephoned Notre Dame president John J. Cavanaugh, CSC, and demanded that Clancy be fired because of his 'anti-Catholic attitudes.' In 1961, Clancy and seven others co-authored *Religion and American Society: A Statement of Principles*, published by the Center for the Study of Democratic Institutions and containing the following passage: 'Persuasion is a long, painful process and not always successful. A picket-line outside a theatre or a skillful power-play in a local community – the "right" telephone call or the "word" passed along to a librarian, a bookstore salesman, or a theatre-owner – can often do what the arts of oratory have failed to do; a political officeholder arbitrarily declaring a policy ban at the behest of one or another religious group ... can accomplish in an hour what may take years to bring about by the conscious use of pulpit or podium.' Clancy was ordained in 1964, becoming provost of the Oratory of the University of Pittsburgh. He died in 1982. A convert to Catholicism saluted him as 'a scholar and a gentleman' with 'a deep and sympathetic insight' into the hearts of the university community under his pastoral care.[25]

Among the radical pronouncements of Vatican II was *Dignitatis Humanae* (7 Dec. 1965), characterized as an American contribution, which recommended a formal separation of church and state. Vatican II's many revolutionary changes were followed by Paul VI's decision in 1968 to retain the Church's conservative position on contraception, thus rejecting the majority report of those he had called upon to study the issue. The quick succession of Vatican II's initiatives, followed by the conservative papal dictate regarding contraception, whiplashed many Catholics into a personalized, pick-and-choose, 'do-it-yourself' Catholicism, which undermined the absolute moral authority that had been the Church's franchise for two millennia. While the salaries of American Catholics rose substantially between 1960 and 1990, their average rate of giving to the Church dropped from 2.2 per cent of income to 1.1 per cent. Between 1963 and 1977 the percentage of Catholics who attended Mass every week dropped from 72 per cent to 42 per cent. Although Spellman remained head of the American Church until his death in 1967, in 1963 Cardinal Cushing had said of him, 'He's lost his power,' perhaps alluding to the death of Spellman's friend, Pope Pius XII in 1958, or perhaps sensing a slippage in what had been the hierarchy's formerly adamantine control of a passive laity. Upon Spellman's death, national leadership passed momentarily to Notre Dame president Theodore Hesburgh, who dared disagree with Paul VI on contraception and other issues. Andrew Greeley noted: 'The curia sent two apostolic delegates to the United States who were determined to punish the American Church for its progressive contributions' to Vatican II. '[B]etween 1963 and 1973, virtually all the men raised to major archdioceses in the country were incompetent nonentities. That Hesburgh did not become an archbishop and a cardinal ... was not an accident but a matter of deliberate curial policy. Rome did not want to have to deal with a passionate, charismatic, influential pragmatist.'[26]

In 1973 a somewhat world-weary Caryl Rivers wrote of her happy childhood, with Jesus looking down from the wall of her third-grade classroom while Mary, 'his mother, was a porcelain statue with the skin of a Revlon, streaming God-grace from down-turned hands':

> As I look back from a distance of some twenty years, I see a world of changeless truth, simple moral choices, and nodding assent that seems as distant from contemporary reality as the age when cross-breasted crusaders whacked heathen skulls in the name of Jesus Christ. I cannot imagine that it has vanished so utterly; it seemed so durable ... Fulton Sheen surely should have outlasted Ed Sullivan, with his laser-beam eyes and that small, pleased smile that crept across his finely cut face when he made a point particularly well ... Sheen, so daring then, seems small potatoes. Today's priests get hunted by the FBI, agitate to get married and disagree with the Pope.[27]

Catholicism had lost its hold as the dominant force over popular morality, except insofar as it followed the agenda now set by the headline-grabbing 'Moral Majority,' a movement quickly associated with a variety of conservative, media-savvy Protestants. Although the mainstream Protestantism of the 1930s had been inadequate to meet the hard times, by 1980 various denominations had been revivified, with the most dramatic success among evangelical, Fundamentalist, and Pentecostalist groups. Protestant radio programs proliferated, in which conservative political ideas were mixed with explications of scriptural passages to which the Church had paid scant attention, exegesis having never been a highlight of the Catholic service. As innumerable people declared themselves Christians and studied their Bibles on the bus going to work, it could be said that Protestantism, like its increasingly voluble adherents, had been 'born again.'

By 1975, a survey of American family incomes by religious and ethnic background showed Italian Catholics third, behind Jews and Irish Catholics, with Protestant groups arrayed below. Meanwhile, the Catholic Church, John Tracy Ellis noted in 1982, was 'no longer in fashion with many of her own members.' While ordination had once been the highest indicium of personal achievement, between 1962 and 1985 the number of Catholic seminaries dropped from 545 to 318.[28] Someone said all the Church had left was 'the Blessed Mother and the parochial schools,' while Father Greeley observed that among feminists, Mary 'simply won't do.' Although Pope Paul VI in *Marialis Cultus* (1974) found it necessary to explain that one could venerate Mary even though she did not follow the 'life-style' of a modern woman, many thought that the Church's projection of Mary was out of step with feminist progress.[29] The number of new nuns in 1985 was 15 per cent of what it had been in 1966. While in 1976 the General Convention of the Protestant Episcopal Church, meeting in Minneapolis, voted in favour of the ordination of women into its priesthood and episcopate, Pope John Paul II in the apostolic letter *Ordinatio Sacerdotalis* (1994) denied women ordination as Catholic priests, reasoning that Christ chose only men as his twelve apostles, excluding even Mary herself.[30] Between 1966 and 2006, the number of American nuns dropped from 180,000 to 70,000, with only 6,000 of these under age fifty.

As the 'Sexual Revolution' matured in stride with feminism, it became unfashionable to call Mary 'the Virgin,' virginity itself having – for many – lost its perennial power as a symbol of purity and innocence, some seeing it merely as a 'hang-up' from an outdated time, others as a means of traditional anti-feminist repression. In 1993 sociologist David Halle went so far as to suggest that most Catholics no longer considered premarital chastity significant.[31] Then, over a period of years, the Church was rocked by numerous trials of priests for the sexual abuse of young boys in their charge, resulting in – among other things – dramatic declines in contributions just as diocesan endowments were being drained by multi-million dollar judgments and settlements. In 2004 the palazzo built by Cardinal O'Connell in a Boston suburb had to be sold to pay a $90-million disposition. When in 2005 a seventy-three-year-old priest in the west of Ireland fathered a child with a thirty-one-year-old special-needs teacher with whom he had been having a long affair, a Dublin cleric quipped that he found news of a heterosexual priest refreshing. Locals in the rural Galway parish closed ranks to protect the couple, resisting fierce media attention. When several newspapers snidely referred to the woman as 'Madonna' followed by her name, numerous readers throughout Ireland objected, not because the allusion to Mary was blasphemous, but because the press, by publishing the woman's name, had invaded her right to privacy. The lay chairman of the local pastoral council noted: 'At the end of the day, they're two consenting adults. A child has been born, and that's something to be celebrated, not scorned.'[32]

Halle noted a decline in devotional images of saints, their presumed efficacy in miraculous healing having been eclipsed by medical advances. But even if Vatican II had discouraged Mariolatry, and even if some could not reconcile Mary with feminism and the Sexual Revolution, Mary was too strong an element in Catholic faith, answered too many deeply felt human needs, to be brushed aside in favour of scientific breakthroughs, changing political priorities, and a growing ethos of secular humanism, driven by the advertising of commercial products to consumers, and summed up by the expression: 'Who says you can't have it all?' The new devotion to personal consumption did not make everyone materialists. A 1989 Gallup poll revealed that 82 per cent of Americans believed that 'even today, miracles are performed by the power of God.' Although Catholicism had suffered dramatic declines in priests, nuns, parishioners, and funds, visions of Mary in the United States multiplied from 21 between 1945 and 1979 to 150 between 1980 and 2002, leading some proudly to declare America as the new home of Marian apparitions.[33]

In 1993 a theology professor in Ohio began a movement to have Pope John Paul II infallibly declare as dogma that Mary was Christ's Co-Redemptrix, making her a participant with Him in humankind's salvation. But this was the kind of development that Pope Paul VI in *Lumen Gentium* had discouraged, and in 1997, despite petitions containing a reported 4.3 million signatures, John Paul II chose not to declare this a third Marian dogma. A housewife on a farm outside Atlanta reported to a crowd of thirty thousand that Mary, appearing to her as a light on a wall, warned that if people continued to offend God, He would instigate a great war. This Marian event, like most, failed to receive Church recognition. In 1999, Fátima received slightly more pilgrims (5.3 million) than Lourdes (5.2 million).[34] In 2002, Thomas S. Monaghan, former owner of the Domino's pizza chain and the Detroit Tigers baseball team, announced plans to build an Ave Maria University near Naples, Florida, to combine conservative, pre–Vatican II Catholic doctrine and practice with an evangelizing aspect more commonly associated with contemporary Protestant groups. Next to the university a town began, also called Ave Maria.

The Freedom to Reveal All

In 1966, Pier Paolo Pasolini, a Marxist, directed *The Gospel According to St Matthew*, using such neo-realist techniques as employing amateurs and a hyper-flat acting style. Although the film met with protest in several American cities, it was not banned. Neither the 1976 film based on Hugh Schonfield's book *The Passover Plot*, nor the airing on television of Franco Zeffirelli's *Jesus of Nazareth* in 1977, nor (even) Monty

Python's *Life of Brian* (1979), a farce based on the life of Jesus, resulted in injunctive lawsuits. The exhibition of Jean-Luc Godard's *Hail Mary* at the New York Film Festival at Lincoln Center in October 1985 drew five thousand demonstrators. Two generations before, many had feared that the Soviets' denial of God's existence would so anger Him that He would destroy not just Russia but the entire world. In reaction to *Hail Mary*, the rector of the St Thomas Aquinas Seminary in Richfield, Connecticut, suggested that God might enlist the Soviets as his agents, that is, 'when the bombs fall on Manhattan, one will especially fall on the cinema where this film is being shown ... God does not allow His Mother to be insulted with impunity.'[35] But the film was not banned.

The opposition to *The Miracle* had included the notion that it constituted an obstacle to Catholic worship, as if a film playing on 58th and Fifth could impede services at St Patrick's, seven blocks to the south. In 1989 an individual sued to enjoin Martin Scorsese's controversial film *The Last Temptation of Christ* at a Houston theatre, on the ground that its dream sequence, in which Jesus marries Mary Magdalene, was 'a defamatory interpretation of the life of Jesus Christ' which infringed on the Constitutional right of believers 'to freedom of worship and religion.' The court held, on the authority of *Burstyn*, that this was not a justiciable question, that is, not the kind of complaint for which courts could provide relief. The Oklahoma State University Board of Regents temporarily stopped the Student Union from showing Scorsese's film, pending advice from counsel regarding what the Board described as a 'tension' in the First Amendment between free speech and the separation of church and state. Upon obtaining that advice, the Board decided that the film could be shown.[36]

In 1961, the same year Frank Getlein co-authored *Movies, Morals, and Art*, he and his wife wrote *Christianity in Modern Art*. It begins: 'The first thing to be said about contemporary Christian art is that such an art is possible,' a proposition which might have struck many experts as counter-intuitive. It seemed that most American artists who were 'recognized' as 'serious' tended to consider themselves avant-gardist atheists or materialists, offering 'realistic' 'alternatives' to faith rather than capturing or fostering faith itself. Since many artists – and writers as well – considered it their solemn duty to challenge majoritarian ideas and traditional institutions and/or to disavow and deride their respective upbringings, their work inevitably raised questions of blasphemy and sacrilege. Seldom were such artists challenged in court, however, *Burstyn* having rendered such cases hopeless.[37]

In 1972 pornography, what D.H. Lawrence had called doing dirt on sex, became a middle-class entertainment, as the World Theatre (where *Open City* had once triumphed) and the Monica in West Hollywood (where *The Miracle* had played to a full house) both now featured *Deep Throat*. In the other arts, meanwhile, the standard now seemed to be: the more insulting to traditional religious beliefs, the better. The new *Miller* standards for obscenity, it has been said, came 'at a radical turning point' in American culture, when post-modern art rebelled against the idea that a work 'be serious, or that it have any traditional "value" at all.' Thus, the *Miller* test, Amy Adler has written, 'evaluates contemporary art by the very standard which that art seeks to defy,' protecting works of art from censorship because of their 'value,' even when made by artists who purport not to believe in 'value.'[38] With Dada passé, one artist proffered as a work of art having someone shoot him in the arm. Another showed the audience her cervix.

Constitutional church/state disputes proliferated as cities experimented with providing school buses, remedial specialists, second-hand textbooks, and other benefits to local religious schools. In 1962 the so-called 'Regents' prayer' – 'Almighty God, we acknowledge our dependence upon Thee, and we beg Thy blessings upon us, our parents, our teachers and our Country' – drafted by the New York Board of Regents for recitation in each public classroom in New York State at the start of each school day, was held to violate the Establishment clause, Justice Black thinking it 'neither sacrilegious nor antireligious' to conclude that government had no business drafting official prayers. Then in 1963 the Court struck down a Pennsylvania statute requiring the recitation of the Lord's Prayer or other Bible readings each morning, thus ending what had been an almost universal tradition.[39] Many believed such decisions to be signs of increasing atheist and/or Communist influence on the Court, until in 1989 what many thought the most disturbing of the Court's decisions – that a Nativity scene displayed in a government building violates the Establishment clause – happened to coincide with the collapse of the Soviet Union.[40] When in 2006 for the first time a majority of Supreme Court justices were Catholic, observers wondered whether perhaps new interpretations of the Establishment clause were in prospect.

When in the spring of 1986 Godard's *Hail Mary* was advertised to be shown at the Sheldon Memorial Art Gallery at the University of Nebraska, state senator Bernice Labedz announced that she wanted the film stopped because 'it blasphemed the Blessed Virgin Mary and the birth of Christ' and might give rise to demonstrations. Gallery director George Neubert cancelled the film because it was 'offensive to a segment of society and did not merit the efforts it would take to defend it,' telling gallery supporters: 'I determined that a screening of this particular movie at this time could surely be used by politicians and some segments of the community for their personal or political gain' by trying to diminish the gallery's budget. But some people wanted to see the film, and sued to force Neubert to show it. U.S. District Court judge Warren K. Urbom adopted a line of thought going back to *Burstyn* and *Kunz*, reasoning that 'action taken by an arm of the state merely to avoid controversy from the expression of ideas is an insufficient basis for interfering with the right to receive information.' Echoing what Judge Woolsey had written about Joyce's *Ulysses* over five decades earlier, Judge Urbom noted that he had seen Godard's film and found it 'dull, beautiful, incomprehensible, brave, shallow, penetrating, vulgar, demeaning and, no doubt, blasphemous for some and inspirational for others.' Robert Kiely, a humanities professor at Harvard and a practising Catholic, dismissed *Hail Mary* as 'in perfect keeping with the long line of vulgar artifacts' associated with the Blessed Mother, albeit the film was less accessible than a plaster statue.[41]

In John Pielmeier's play *Agnes of God*, opening in New York in 1980, a mentally challenged and stigmatic nun gives birth, seemingly in the absence of any natural father. Since times had changed, there was no moral uproar, although critic and philosophy professor Robert Lauder of the Cathedral College of the Immaculate Conception faulted Pielmeier for suggesting that a miracle might be responsible for Agnes's pregnancy, while failing first to set the appropriate tone of religious mystery. In Father Lauder's view, this made the pregnancy seem less like a miracle than a 'magic trick.' Nor, several months earlier, did pickets or injunctions meet Christopher Durang's play *Sister Mary Ignatius Explains It All for You*, a satiric exposition of the simplistic but adamantine Catholic ethos drummed in at the parochial schools of Durang's youth. When a performer from Michigan named Madonna Louise Ciccone became 'Madonna' and used rosaries and crucifixes as costume jewellery, Professor Joseph A. Varacalli suggested that for some, this pop star had temporarily replaced the Virgin Mother as their 'most central mediator' with the Ultimate. In 1992, Frank McEntire took a plastic reproduction of the famous Mormon Salt Lake City Temple, covered it with glue, and scattered over it pieces of his own hair. One viewer commented: 'I found it offensive because it came across as mocking people's religious views.' But another said: 'What a wonderful reminder that all we must do is look inside & see God.'[42]

Politicians had a feeding frenzy upon discovering that the federally funded National Endowment for the Arts had underwritten Andres Serrano's photograph *Piss Christ* (1987), a minor relict of Dadaism whose 'value' seemed to be that it caused controversy. U.S. Senator Jesse Helms (R-NC), noting that Serrano 'went out of his way to insult the Christian community,' sponsored a bill disqualifying from taxpayer largesse all works that 'denigrate the objects or beliefs of the adherents of a particular religion.' That amendment was rejected in favour of language requiring the NEA, in awarding grants, to consider 'general standards of decency and respect for the diverse beliefs and values of the American public.'[43]

In 1997, Robert Gober's installation at Geffen Contemporary in Los Angeles featured a life-sized cement Mary with a piece of culvert pipe driven through her abdomen. Although it was allusive, ambiguous, complicated, the product of several years' hard work, many visitors could see in it no 'value' other than its being 'controversial.' Although criticized by the Los Angeles Archdiocese, it was protected by *Burstyn*. In 1999 the Brooklyn Museum of Art exhibited *The Holy Virgin Mary* (1996), a six-foot-by-eight-foot stylized depiction of an African Mary, along with a chunk of shellacked elephant dung and surrounded by collaged cut-outs of female genitalia from pornographic magazines. The artist, Chris Ofili, British and of Nigerian descent, was reportedly a Catholic. New York mayor Rudolph Giuliani reacted to Ofili's work by withholding the city's $7.2-million annual subsidy and suing to eject the museum and its collections from its city-owned building, declaring: 'You don't have a right to a government subsidy to desecrate someone else's religion ... [and] most personal and deeply held views.' Federal judge Nina Gershon, citing *Burstyn*, the *Esquire* case, the *Barnette* case involving the refusal of Jehovah's Witnesses to salute the American flag, and the more recent Texas flag-burning case, ruled that the First Amendment barred Giuliani from punishing a municipal museum for what it chose to exhibit.[44] Several weeks later, a devout Catholic managed to get behind a Plexiglas shield to spread white paint on Ofili's painting, in an apparent effort to purify what he described as a blasphemous image.[45] The new edition of H.W. Janson's standard history of art included Ofili's painting.

In 2001 the Brooklyn Museum again provoked Giuliani when it exhibited Renée Cox's *Yo Mama's Last Supper*, a five-panel photographic work featuring Christ as a nude black woman. Giuliani called for a decency panel to set standards for art in publicly funded museums. On Ash Wednesday 2004, Mel Gibson released *The Passion of the Christ*, a film notable primarily for its graphic depictions of Jesus' scourging and crucifixion, based on the descriptions set forth by the stigmatic visionary Anna Emmerich in 1833. Some observers found the film blasphemous, while some considered it anti-Semitic. Others thought it cut through centuries of polite overlay to place them in the presence their suffering Saviour.

Rossellini's Legacy

Rossellini's career, like his personal life, was nothing if not self-directed. Once he was labelled 'neo-realist,' the Communists expected him to repeat ad infinitum the gritty realism of *Open City* and *Paisan*, to tell the truth of the streets, to continue exposing the decadence of the bourgeoisie, etc. Instead he moved in various directions, eventually directing films for television in which he returned to Christian themes. While a commercialized, degraded international pop culture identified a market for a 'relevant' Jesus by repackaging Him as a rock'n'roller in *Godspell* (1973) and *Jesus Christ, Superstar* (1973), Rossellini made films which, like *Francis*, might have been – from all appearances – the work of a gifted seminarian. These extraordinary works included *Atti degli Apostoli* (*Acts of the Apostles*, 1969), *Blaise Pascal* (1972), *Agostino di Ippona* (*Augustine of Hippo*, 1972), and *Il Messia* (*The Messiah*, 1975).[46] When aired on television, *Blaise Pascal* was seen by a reported 10 million people, bringing the proportion of Italians who had heard of Pascal from under 1 per cent to 45 per cent.[47] Pascal's writings, providing much of the film's dialogue, sold briskly. This was an extraordinary introduction of a major Catholic thinker into Italian homes, all the more amazing when accomplished by a film-maker with no tolerance for the sentimentality, simplifications, and pyrotechnics Hollywood had thought necessary to attract a wide audience to a significant historical figure.

Upon seeing Rossellini's films about Paul, Augustine, and Pascal, critics pestered him about his personal religious convictions. His various answers were as 'consistently evasive' as the various versions of how *The Miracle* had come to be made. Although the religious content of Rossellini's work had long been recognized, he steadfastly ducked all labels, telling an interviewer in 1973 that he was tied to no orthodoxy. A year later, he denied that his films were fundamentally religious, adding that while perhaps other people thought so, he found the idea absolute 'nonsense.'[48] Having tired of the designation 'neo-realist,' he understood that insofar as he admitted to having any 'viewpoint' – religious or otherwise – he would be tagged with it and interpreted by it, something he desired neither for himself nor for his audience.

In 1948 a British review of *The Miracle* criticized Rossellini for 'effac[ing]' himself from the film, leaving Magnani to do everything. In 1950 it was said of Rossellini: 'His puritanism, his studied incoherence, his achievement of pathos by methods related rather to Picasso's war paintings than to the ordinary technique of cinema, have made it difficult to see Rossellini's achievement easily, let alone assess it.' His daughter Isabella recalled that he would refer to self-consciously artistic camera work as 'immoral.' During his two years as film-maker-in-residence at Rice University, he proclaimed: 'I want to be as objective as possible. I'm afraid to do any sort of propagandizing. I don't want to convey any message. I have no point of view.' Summing up his portrayals of Augustine, the apostles, Pascal, and Louis XIV, he wrote: 'I show the customs, prejudices, fears, aspirations, ideas and agonies of an epoch and a place. I show a man – an innovator – confront[ing] these. And I have a drama equal to any other drama ever conceived, or ever to be conceived. I always avoid the temptation to exalt his personality; I limit myself to observing him. Confronting a man with his age gives me enough material to construct action and incite curiosity.' In an interview at New York's Algonquin Hotel in 1974, he proclaimed: 'I am looking at people who believe in God. Should I superimpose my own thoughts?'[49]

Thus, in an era when it had become fashionable to invest each major director with *auteur* status and then to trace how each film succeeded or failed to exhibit his presumed *auteurist* preoccupations, Rossellini had an abiding desire to avoid treating his works as the products of a unified philosophy and/or aesthetic, instead calling them 'objective' and forcing people to react accordingly, without preconceptions. He hated what was predictable, sentimental, programmatic. Closing down the set of *Acts of the Apostles* one day, he jokingly told the young actor playing Saint Paul, 'Perform us a miracle,' then commented to an onlooker: 'I will not show any real miracle in the film. On the screen, they are banal.' Yet no one could deny that the exploration of religious faith was a prominent – perhaps the most prominent – feature of his work. In 1995, on the centenary of the invention of cinema, the Vatican's Pontifical Council for Social Communications compiled a list of forty-five 'great films,' the fifteen films of specifically 'religious' merit including

Rossellini's *Francis, Jester of God*. In the separate fifteen-film category of 'Values' appeared *Open City*, alongside *Bicycle Thief* as well as *It's a Wonderful Life*, *On the Waterfront*, *The Seventh Seal*, and *Intolerance*.[50]

Father Patrick C. Peyton, CSC, grew up in County Mayo. What impressed him most about his early life 'was the voice of my mother talking to Mary: "Holy Mary, Mother of God, pray for us sinners now and at the hour of our death."' He was a frequent visitor to the shrine at Cnoc Mhuire, the Mayo village where Mary had appeared in 1879. As a boy, he emigrated to work in the Pennsylvania coal mines, and became the janitor at a church called St Joseph's. In 1939, seriously ill with tuberculosis, he promised the Blessed Mother that if she cured him so he could be ordained the same day as his brother, he would 'spend the rest of my life promotin' the Holy Rosary.' And because on the ninth day of his nine-day novena the doctors found him miraculously cured, he spent his life fulfilling his promise. It is the story of a miracle in the Pennsylvania coal country that is far more touching than *The Miracle of the Bells*, while bearing the singular virtue of being true. Peyton's lovely, self-effacing autobiography is entitled *All for Her*.

On Good Friday, 20 April 1945, Father Peyton picked up the telephone and told the operator: 'I'd like to speak to Mr. Bing Crosby in Hollywood, California.' Several days later, Crosby, on the set of *The Bells of St Mary's*, returned Peyton's call and agreed to do a national radio show 'promotin' the Holy Rosary.' For over a decade, the International Federation of Catholic Alumnae had told the faithful to treat Mother's Day as Mary's Day as well. In 1945 it happened to fall on 13 May, which was also Our Lady of Fátima Day. The show was broadcast nationally, with Peyton, Spellman, and others in a studio in New York, tied in with Crosby at an affiliate station in Hollywood. The show was well received, and some well-wisher gave Peyton a train ticket for California so he might continue his good work. As he emerged from Union Station in downtown Los Angeles, the first priest he could find arranged for him to outline his media plans to Archbishop Cantwell. Upon Cantwell's approval, Peyton proceeded to ask Loretta Young to gather some movie stars to say the rosary together on the radio on 15 August, the Feast of Mary's Assumption. Participants included Crosby, Irene Dunne, Ann Blyth, Pat O'Brien, Ethel Barrymore, Don Ameche, Jane Wyatt, and Rosalind Russell.[51]

These events, comprising a story more beautiful than *Come to the Stable*, were recounted by Peyton without syrupy touches. In 1947 he founded the Family Rosary Crusade, arranging huge communal rosaries at baseball parks and other large venues. Every inch the charismatic Irish priest, more handsome than the clerics played by Crosby, Spencer Tracy, and Pat O'Brien, he soon expanded his evangelical work into television and film, the signature line for his popular *Family Theater* radio program being a million-dollar slogan: 'The Family that Prays Together Stays Together.' Featuring Hollywood stars in moral dramas, the show ran from 1947 to 1969, and when a complimentary letter about it arrived from Pope Pius XII, Peyton took it as 'an assurance from Mary through her Son's vicar that I was doing what she wanted.'[52]

Peyton asked Rossellini to make a film about Jesus. A film contract was drawn up and signed, solemnized by being read aloud to Michelangelo's *Pietà* at St Peter's, followed by Peyton's leading Rossellini in praying the rosary, a scene memorialized in the snapshots of Japanese tourists. Although Peyton proceeded to issue a $2 million letter of credit for the production costs, at first no bank would lend against it. Then (at least by one account) Rossellini himself wrote to Pope Paul VI, declaring himself a non-believer who wanted to make a film about Jesus for non-believers. The Vatican's bank accepted the letter of credit, and the project went forward.[53]

Much of the script for the resulting film, called *The Messiah*, is the text of the Gospels, particularly the Gospel of John. While Hollywood was not averse to using biblical language from time to time, it did so with a DeMillean, sugared pseudo-holiness, exactly what Rossellini detested. Rossellini instead presents Jesus as an intelligent carpenter, in contact with God but less the Son of God than the Perfect Man. The film – as per Rossellini's method – is shot 'objectively' and includes no miracles. For the role of Mary, he cast an adolescent, Mita Ungaro, who without make-up played the Blessed Mother both in youth and at the time of Jesus' death, Rossellini having borrowed from the *Pietà* and from Catholic tradition the concept of a Mary who never aged. During the forty-two-day shoot in the blistering heat of Tunisia in the summer of 1975, Rossellini was reportedly seen weeping. 'I got very emotional,' he admitted. 'I don't need miracles to know that Jesus is God incarnated so that we can love him. Certainly he conquered me, I'm in love with him.' But this was but a momentary lapse in the director's persona of detached objectivity, and when an interviewer suggested that *The Messiah* seemed to support the miracle of the Resurrection, Rossellini bristled: 'I try to resist any kind of propaganda or interpretation in my work. I'm obsessed with not preaching anything, because I believe it's wrong, a violation of the personalities of the people watching. It's best to offer material and let each human being take from it what he wants. People should be given data to work with, to elabourate upon, and then – who knows? – perhaps they will be able to come up with something new. Anyway, I'm not religious at all. I'm the product of a society that is religious among other things, and I deal with religion as a reality.' Following the picture's completion, Rossellini said that if someone had asked him, 'Let's see, Mr. Rossellini, what do you think of Christ? That's what we want to know,' he would have responded: 'I think nothing of Christ. I am content to restore what Christ thought.' By such dramatic locutions, he could so flummox interviewers that they would forget to ask the more relevant questions: Why the preoccupation with Christ, Augustine, Francis, Pascal? Why not a series on several of the world's sociopaths? Eric Rohmer and Fereydoun Hoveyda had hit the mark back in 1953 by describing Rossellini's films as new stones in the cathedral Christians never stop building to the glory of God.

In the end, *The Messiah* was withheld from release in the United States. Father Peyton's producer and others deemed its 'objective' concentration on Jesus' everyday life to be too 'boring,' its lack of miracles adding to that boredom while tending (some said) to undercut Jesus' divinity. Apparently Rossellini's anti-DeMillean approach was not what most people wanted. It seemed they wished not only to believe in miracles but to see miracles performed on screen, and a film about Jesus that included no miraculous pyrotechnics was not thought worth releasing.

Of how Father Peyton and Rossellini had first joined forces in the project there are several versions.[54] By one account, Peyton had asked prominent Hollywood Catholics like Gene Kelly to name the best director for a film about Jesus. Peyton told other versions, however. In one, he decided to make a movie about Jesus that would 'make people love him,' and was visited in his sleep by the Virgin Mary, who instructed him to 'get the best film-maker in the world: Roberto Rossellini.' Peyton sought out the director at Rice University and, entering Rossellini's hotel room, asked him to kneel, touched his head, and said that in a dream the Madonna had told him: 'You must make a film on the Messiah and the director has to be Rossellini.' Since no Rossellini film could be depended upon to get back its costs, raising capital was the threshold issue. Once it was clear that the project could be financed to completion, Rossellini reportedly declared: 'Well, if it's the Madonna who says so ...'

Notes

Newspaper references are to section, page, and column, for instance, § 3:6/4.

Abbreviations

ABP: Alvah C. Bessie Papers, U.S. Mss 59An, Wisconsin Hist. Soc., Madison, WI.

ACLUP: American Civil Liberties Union Papers, Seeley G. Mudd Manuscript Library, Princeton University.

AHBP: Alfred H. Barr, Jr, Papers (microform), Museum of Modern Art, New York.

AMP: Albert Maltz Papers, U.S. Mss 14N, Wisconsin Hist. Soc., Madison, WI.

BCP: Bosley Crowther Papers, Mss 1491, L. Tom Perry Special Collections, Brigham Young University, Provo, UT.

DALP: Daniel A. Lord, S.J., Papers, Midwest Jesuit Archives, St Louis University (noted by file name).

EBP: Erik Barnouw Papers, Butler Library, Columbia University, New York.

FFP: Felix Frankfurter Papers (microform), Harvard Law School.

FSP: Francis Spellman Papers, s/c33, folders 1–3, Archives, Archdiocese of New York, Saint Joseph's Seminary, Dunwoodie, Yonkers, NY.

GLPP: George La Piana Papers, Harvard Divinity School Collection, Cambridge, MA.

HUAC/1: U.S. Cong. H.R. Committee on Un-American Activities, Hearings Regarding the Communist Infiltration of the Motion Picture Industry, 80th Cong. 1st Sess. (Oct. 1947).

HUAC/2: U.S. Cong. H.R. Communist Infiltration of Hollywood Motion-Picture Industry – Parts 1–5, Hearings before the Committee on Un-American Activities, 82d Cong. 1st Sess. (March–Sept. 1951).

ICORP: Industrial Commission of Ohio, Records of Proceedings, State Archives Series 757, BV3408, Columbus, OH.

JBC: Joseph Burstyn, Inc. Collection, Museum of Modern Art, New York.

JDMP: U.S. Cong. Sen. Juvenile Delinquency (Motion Pictures): Hearings before the Subcommittee to Investigate Juvenile Delinquency of the Committee on the Judiciary Pursuant to S. Res. 62, 84th Cong. 1st Sess. (15 June 1955).

LGP: Lillian Gerard Papers, L. Tom Perry Special Collections, Brigham Young University, Provo, Utah.

MI: *Miracolo, Il*, file 52695, box 2561, New York State Archives, Albany, NY.

MLEP: Morris L. Ernst Papers, Harry Ransom Humanities Research Center, University of Texas, Austin.

MQP: Martin Quigley Papers, Georgetown University Library (noted by box and file).

PCA: Production Code Administration Records, Motion Picture Association of America, Inc., Margaret Herrick Library, Academy of Motion Picture Arts and Sciences, Beverly Hills.

PMP: U.S. Cong. Sen. Propaganda in Motion Pictures: Hearings before a Subcommittee of the Committee on Interstate Commerce on S. Res. 152, 77th Cong. 1st Sess. (9 Sept. 1941).

RKP: Robert W. Kenny and Robert S. Morris Papers, U.S. Mss 29AN, Wisconsin Hist. Soc., Madison, WI.

RRSB: Roberto Rossellini scrapbook, Call no. 81.5 R734, Museum of Modern Art, New York.

USBB: United States v. Ballaban, boxes 1767–68, Dep't of Justice case files 60-6-17 to 60-6-30, location 230/27/17/7, National Archives and Records Administration, College Park, MD.

WHP: Papers of Will Hays (microform), ed. Douglas Gomery, Pt. II, Arts Library, UCLA (noted by reel and page).

WOL: *Ways of Love*, file 55250, box 2561, New York State Archives, Albany, NY.

WOLR: *Ways of Love* (Revised), file 55627, box 2562, New York State Archives, Albany, NY.

WPP: Papers of Wilfrid Parsons, Georgetown University Library (noted by box and file).

Other authorities cited in shortened form in the Notes are also listed in the Bibliography.

Introduction

1 The speech does not appear in the underlying novel by Russell Janney.

2 United States v. Hiss, 185 F.2d 822 (2d Cir. 1950), *cert. denied*, 340 U.S. 948 (1951); Massa 58–9; Robert Griffith, *The Politics of Fear* (Lexington, KY 1970) 48–51; Crosby 43; McWilliams 13–15; Chambers, *Witness* (NY 1952) 542.

1 'A Business Pure and Simple'

1 *Bleistein v. Donaldson Litho. Co.*, 188 U.S. 239, 251 (1903).
2 Chicago Code § 1627 (1911): '*Immoral Pictures – Permit Not to be Granted. –* If a picture ... is immoral or obscene, or portrays any riotous, disorderly, or other unlawful scene, or has a tendency to disturb the public peace, it shall be the duty of the general superintendent of police to refuse such permit.' Cod. and rev. Edward J. Brundage (Chicago 1911). See also Robert Armour, 'Effects of Censorship Pressure on the New York Nickelodeon Market, 1907–1909,' *Film Hist.* 4/2:113 (1990); Nancy Rosenbloom, 'Between Reform and Regulation: The Struggle over Film Censorship in Progressive America, 1909–1922,' *Film Hist.* 1:307 (1987); Daniel Czitrom, 'The Politics of Performance: Theater Licensing and the Origins of Movie Censorship in New York,' in Couvares 16; Robert Fisher, 'Film Censorship and Progressive Reform,' *J. Pop. Film* 4/2:143 (1975).
3 *Sociological Research Film Corp. v. New York City*, 83 Misc. 605, 145 N.Y.S. 492 (Sp. T. 1914); Howe, 'What to Do with the Motion-Picture Show,' *Outlook* 107:412 (20 June 1914); Cocks/Shaw, 16 Oct. 1914, NYPL/Lincoln Ctr. MFL n.c. 3; 'The White Slave Films: A Review,' *Outlook* 106:345, 347 (14 Feb. 1914); Harmon Stephens, 'The Relation of the Motion Picture to Changing Moral Standards,' *AAAP&SS* 128:151, 153 (Nov. 1926); Shelley Stamp, 'Moral Coercion, or The National Board of Censorship Ponders the Vice Films,' in Bernstein (1999) 41.
4 *Independent* 77:432, 433 (30 March 1914); U.S. Cong. H.R. Motion Picture Comm'n: Hearings before the Comm. on Educ., 63d Cong. 2d Sess. (20 March–5 May 1914) 3; Lindsay, *The Art of the Moving Picture* (NY 1915) 225; Lawson, 'The Miracle of the Movie,' *Harper's Weekly* 60:7, 8–9 (2 Jan. 1915). Psychologist Carl Seashore stated: 'No person can look at a lewd picture, hear debasing words, or think depraved thoughts without having this tinge the attitudes of his life' (*Psychology in Daily Life* [NY 1913] 140). But neither Seashore, nor anyone else, explained how a 'lewd picture' tinged attitudes.
5 See 7 July 1913, ICORP. The idea of a state censorship board appears to have had the backing of the motion-picture trade organization in Ohio, which thought it could in this way wrest censorship responsibilities away from Cleveland and other municipalities. U.S. Cong. H.R., Federal Motion

Picture Comm'n, Hearings before the Committee on Education on H.R. 456, 64th Cong. 1st Sess. (15 Jan. 1916) 134–5; Motion Picture Theater Owners of America, *The Case against Censorship* (NY April 1921) 5–6.

6 See 19 Aug. 1913, ICORP; Wirt 200–3.

7 'Morals and Movies,' *Harper's Weekly* 59:577 (19 Dec. 1914); W.P. Lawson, 'Do You Believe in Censors?' *Harper's Weekly* 60:86, 87 (23 Jan. 1915).

8 *Mutual Film Corp. v. Industrial Comm'n of Ohio*, 236 U.S. 230 (1915); Jowett (1989); Wertheimer 171–6. Mutual also challenged the Kansas statute. *Mutual Film Corp. v. Kansas*, 236 U.S. 230 (1915); Butters 24–51.

9 Federalist no. 84 in B. Schwartz 3:578. See also Noah Webster, 'An Examination into the Leading Principles of the Federal Constitution' (1787), in *Pamphlets on the Constitution of the United States Published during Its Discussion by the People 1787–1788*, comp. Paul Leicester Ford (Brooklyn 1888) 48; James Wilson, 'Substance of an Address to a Meeting of the Citizens of Philadelphia' (1787), in *id.*156; Amar (1998) 36–7, 40; Amar (2005) 102–3, 319–20; Pfeffer 125–31; Emerson (1977) 751–4; Tocqueville (1960) 301; Oliver Wendell Holmes, *The Common Law* (Boston 1881). Regarding whether British common law was thought appropriate for the new United States, see, for example, P. Miller Bk. 2

10 Blackstone 4.4.2 pp. 151–2; James Madison in B. Schwartz 5:1026; Emerson (1955) 651–2.

11 U.S. Const. amend. I. See D. Mayer 145–8. Compare U.S. Const. Art VI § 3.

12 See *Grosjean v. American Press Co.*, 297 U.S. 233, 245–9 (1936).

13 Between 1791 and 1889, the Supreme Court entertained only twelve First Amendment cases, noting that the provision neither laid down 'novel principles of government' nor protected those who libelled government officials or issued 'indecent articles' and 'publications injurious to public morals.' *Robertson v. Baldwin*, 165 U.S. 275, 281 (1897). See Rabban (1981); Rabban (1997); Alexis J. Anderson, 'The Formative Period of First Amendment Theory,' *Am. J. Leg. Hist.* 24:56 (1980).

14 *People ex rel. Attorney General v. News-Times Publishing Co.*, 35 Col. 253, 84 P. 912 (1906).

15 32 U.S. (7 Pet.) 243, 246 (1833). Although the House of Representatives in 1789 approved Madison's language providing that 'no State shall infringe the equal rights of conscience, nor the freedom of speech or of the press,' the amendment did not pass the Senate. Warren 434–5; Amar (1998) 22–3; Amar (2005) 316–17, 386; William J. Brennan, Jr, 'State Constitutions and the Protection of Individual Rights,' *Harv. L. Rev.* 90:489, 503–4 (1977). On 11 Sept. 1804, Jefferson wrote to Abigail Adams: 'While we deny that Congress have a right to controul the freedom of the press, we have ever

asserted the right of the states, and their exclusive right, to do so.' Quoted in *Dennis v. United States*, 341 U.S. 494, 522n4 (1951) (Frankfurter, J. concurring). See also Berger 6, 13, 87–89.

16 U.S. Const. amend. XIV; *Adamson v. California*, 332 U.S. 46, 71–2 (1947) (Black, J. dissenting); Warren 438–9; Berger 31–36, 91–104; Amar (1998) chs. 8–10; Amar (2005) 387–8; Fairman 134–8; Morrison.

17 *Smyth v. Ames*, 169 U.S. 466, 522 (1898); National Bankruptcy Act of 1898 § 1, 30 Stat. 544, 11 U.S.C. § 1; *J.D.L. Corp. v. Bruckman*, 171 Misc. 3, 7, 11 N.Y.S.2d 741, 746–7 (Sp. T. Albany 1939); Amar (2005) 388.

18 See *Grosjean v. American Press Co.*, 297 U.S. 233, 244 (1936) (citing authorities); *Palko v. Connecticut*, 302 U.S. 319, 324–5 (1937) (citing authorities); Warren 463; Berger 12–14, 21–2.

19 See, for example, *Twining v. New Jersey*, 211 U.S. 78, 99–114 (1908). Justice Frankfurter later described due process as something beyond the Constitution's enumerated rights, immunities, and privileges, that is, something comprising 'standards of justice ... not authoritatively formulated anywhere as though they were prescriptions in a pharmacopoeia,' but comprising 'those canons of decency and fairness which express the notions of justice of English-speaking peoples.' *Malinski v. New York*, 324 U.S. 401, 414–17 (1945) (Frankfurter, J. concurring). See also *Beauharnais v. Illinois*, 343 U.S. 250, 287 (1952) (Jackson, J. dissenting); *Powell v. Alabama*, 287 U.S. 45, 68 (1932); David A.J. Richards, *Conscience and the Constitution* (Princeton 1993) ch. 6; Berger 9–11; Pfeffer 143–5; Kurland ch. 11; Warren; Morrison 163–4; Murphy 261–70.

20 *Allgeyer v. Louisiana*, 165 U.S. 578, 589 (1897). See also Warren 439–55.

21 See *Adamson v. California*, 332 U.S. 46, 78–82 and App. (1947) (Black, J. dissenting); Fairman.

22 *Patterson v. Colorado*, 205 U.S. 454, 461–2 (1907). Cf. *Davis v. Massachusetts*, 167 U.S. 43 (1897) (delivering speech without permission); *Fox v. Washington*, 236 U.S. 273 (1915) (speech 'tend[ing] to discourage disrespect for law');*Toledo Newspaper Co. v. United States*, 247 U.S. 402 (1918); Rabban (1997) 30–7; Schofield (1914) 69–71. *New York Times Co. v. Sullivan*, 376 U.S. 254 (1964), comprised a Constitutional revolution in the law of seditious libel and First Amendment jurisprudence.

23 103 Ohio L. 399 (1913), *codified* at Ohio Gen. Code § 871–49 (1913) *and* Ohio Gen. Code §§ 871–48, 871–53d (1920). See also Wirt 55–80.

24 Ohio Const. Art. I § 11; Brief of Appellants 15, *Mutual Film Co. v. Industrial Comm'n of Ohio*, 236 U.S. 230 (1915). See also *Beauharnais v. Illinois*, 343 U.S. 250, 296–7 (1952) (Jackson, J. dissenting).

25 Complaint ¶¶ 5, 6, J.E. Hennesey aff. exh. A, Transcript of Record 3–4, 19–

39, *Mutual Film Co. v. Industrial Comm'n of Ohio*, 236 U.S. 230 (1915); *Kalem Co. v. Harper Bros.*, 222 U.S. 55 (1911).

26 See *Biograph Bulletins*, comp. Kemp R. Niver (Los Angeles 1971) 12–13; Dan Schiller, *Objectivity and the News: The Public and the Rise of Commercial Journalism* (Philadelphia 1981) 88–95.

27 In March 1899, the guileless audience at New York's Union Square Theatre thrilled to see 'genuine pictures of the British naval guns in action' in South Africa's Boer War, although the action had in fact been cobbled up locally. See Robert C. Allen, *Vaudeville and Film, 1895–1915* (1977; NY 1980) 138–47.

28 Emanuel Cohen, 'The Business of International News by Motion Picture,' *AAAP&SS* 128:74 (Nov. 1926) 74; Eileen Bowser, *The Transformation of Cinema, 1907–1915* (Berkeley 1990) 185; Winifred Johnson, *Memo on the Movies: War Propaganda* (Norman, OK 1939) 10–11; Porter, 'Evolution of the Motion Picture' (1914), in *Film Makers on Film Making*, ed. Harry M. Geduld (Bloomington, IN 1967) 33.

29 Gaynor, 27 Dec. 1912 in *Some of Mayor Gaynor's Letters* (NY 1913) 131–2; *Col. L. Rev.* 15:546 (1915).

30 *Mutual Film Co. v. Indus. Comm'n of Ohio*, 215 Fed. 138, 142 (N.D. Ohio 1914), *aff'd*, 236 U.S. 230 (1915); Trans. Rec. 65, *Mutual Film Co. v. Indus. Comm'n of Ohio*, 236 U.S. 230 (1915). But see *Dailey v. Superior Court*, 112 Cal. 94, 44 P. 458 (1896), involving 'The Crime of the Century,' a play derived from evidence in a pending case, positing that the defendant was guilty. The court indicated that under the California equivalent of Ohio's free-speech law, one 'may speak freely,' in a play as well as a newspaper.

31 *Jacob Hall's Case*, 1 Mod. 76, 86 Eng. Rep. 115, 744 (K.B. 1683); Conn. Pub. Stat. L. tit. 22 §§ 87–8 (1821); Vermont v. Fox, 15 Vt. 22 (1843). See Vt. Comp. Stat. tit. 28 ch. 110 § 15 (1851). Fox's conviction was reversed on appeal because, as an individual, he did not constitute a 'company of players or persons.' See also 1819 N.Y. Laws 240 § 1 *codified at* 1 N.Y. Rev. Stats. 660 (Albany 1829); *Downing v. Blanchard*, 12 Wend. [N.Y.] 383, 384–5 (Sup. Ct. Jud. 1834); Wertheimer 162–4.

32 Bartholomew 10, 12; Louise de Koven Bowen, 'Five and Ten Cent Thea-tres' (Chicago n.d.) [1]-[2]; Smith, *The Three Gifts of Life* (NY 1913) 103–4; Foster in *The Social Emergency*, ed. Foster (Boston 1914) 13, 19.

33 1 Boyce (24 Del.) 330, 76 Atl. 479 (Gen. Sess. 1910).

34 119 Minn. 145, 137 N.W. 417 (1912). See also Henry Schofield, *Essays on Constitutional Law and Equity, and Other Subjects* (Boston 1921) 2:529–30; 'Stat. Reg. of Motion Pictures,' Am. and Eng. Annot. Cases 30 (1913E) 1306.

35 236 U.S. 242. See also Wertheimer; Matthew McDevitt, *Joseph McKenna* (1946; NY 1974) 1–3, 227; James F. Watts, Jr, 'Joseph McKenna,' in *The Justices of the United States Supreme Court*, ed. Leon Friedman and Fred Israel (NY 1980) 3:1717.

2 The Church, 'Modernism,' and 'Americanism'

1 Beecher wrote: 'If the potentates of Europe have no design upon our liberties, what means the paying of the passage and emptying out upon our shores such floods of pauper emigrants – the contents of the poorhouse and the sweepings of the streets?' *A Plea for the West*, 2d ed. (Cincinnati 1835) 54–60. Harriet Martineau was told in the 1830s 'that the Catholics of America were employed by the Pope, in league with the Emperor of Austria and the Irish, to explode the Union.' *Society in America*, ed. Seymour Martin Lipset (1962; re-ed. New Brunswick, NJ 1981) 335. Morse in 1834 warned readers 'to watch the Protean shapes of Popery, to suspect and fear it most when it allies itself to our interests in the guise of a friend.' 'Prefatory Remarks,' *Foreign Conspiracy against the Liberties of the United States*, 7th ed. (NY 1847) 29, 32. As a small boy growing up in Boston in the 1870s, Arthur Train was told by his mother never to use the words 'Irish' or 'Roman Catholic,' in front of the servants (Big Bridget, Little Bridget, Old Bridget, and Young Bridget), since doing so would somehow trigger baneful consequences vis-à-vis the conspiracy between Romanists and Russians to make America subservient to the Pope. *Puritan's Progress* (NY 1931) 326–7. See also Hennesey (1981) 119; Ray Allen Billington, *The Protestant Crusade, 1800–1860* (NY 1938) 123; Diner 85–93; Gabriel ch. 5.

2 See Hamburger ch. 11; Alfred W. Meyer, 'The Blaine Amendment,' *Harv. L. Rev.* 64:939 (1951); Gaustad xiv; Feldman ch. 2. So-called Blaine Amendments did pass in various states.

3 Tocqueville (2000) 275–6; Hamburger 226n89; Stokes 1:285, 324–33, 787–812; Dolan (1985) ch. 4; Marraro 58; Brownson (1852) 373; Brownson (1853) 3–5; Garrison (1928) 106–7; Reher ch. 2; R.W.B. Lewis, *The American Adam* (Chicago 1955) 183–93; Gleason (1992) 272–8; McGreevy 43–9.

4 Robert Swierenga, 'Ethnorelgious Political Behavior in the Mid-Nineteenth Century,' in Noll (1990) 146, 158–60; Guilday 246–7; Tocqueville (1960) 33, 82; Spalding, 'The Higher Education' (1884), in *Means and Ends of Education* (Chicago 1895) 181, 222–4; Spalding, 'Patriotism' (1899), in John A. Ryan and Moorhouse Millar, *The State and the Church* (NY 1922) 299, 301; Lilley 107; Merle Curti, *The Social Ideas of American Educators* (1935; 2d ed. Totowa, NJ 1959) ch. 10; Reher ch. 4.

5 Ireland, 'Catholicism and Americanism' (1913), in John A. Ryan and Francis J. Boland, *Catholic Principles of Politics* (NY 1940) 343, 357; Ireland, 'The Mission of Catholics in America' (1889), in Ireland 1:71, 88; Marvin O'Connell, 'John Ireland,' in Fogarty (1989A) 138; Dorothy Dohen, *Nationalism and American Catholicism* (NY 1967) 104–15, 142–6; Shannon 123; Fogarty (1985) 39–44; D. O'Brien (1989) 98–9; Callahan (1963) 65–72; Leo XIII, 16 July 1892; Will 1:553–7.

6 Giles ch. 3; Reher ch. 3; Gabriel 61–9; Farley 154–6; Seldes (1934) 300–2; E.H. Russell, 'A Bit of Unpublished Correspondence between Henry Thoreau and Isaac Hecker,' *Atl. Monthly* (Sept. 1902) 370; Guilday 249; Amanda Porterfield, *The Transformation of American Religion* (NY 2001) 62–72.

7 *Quanta Cura*, in Carlen 1:381; D'Agostino 42–4; D. O'Brien (1989) 102; Hennesey (1970) 39; *De Fide Catholica* (24 April 1870); Bacon; Cogley 262–3; Ellis (1963) 162, 170–1; Bury 1–2; Paul Collins, *Upon This Rock* (Melbourne 2000) 238; Küng (2001) 162; Marshall 81; Daniel-Rops 252–3, 283–5.

8 Sullivan 68–9; M.E. Hussey, 'John Baptist Purcell,' in Fogarty (1989A) 89, 100. Another who thought the declaration inexpedient was John Henry Newman. Sparrow-Simpson 130–2, 246, 280–8.

9 Hennesey (1983) 123–4, 174, 230–5; Hasler; Allitt 8; Cross 19–21; Hales 293–319; Warner (1983) chs. 6 and 16; Zimdars-Swartz 43–67; Reher 52–3; Hennesey (1981) 168–71; Hennesey (1970) 41; Farley 285–6; Butler 206–7, 405–11; McAvoy (1969) 211–17; Zwierlein 2:57, 63; Fogarty (1985) 1–9. The decree, *De Romani Pontificis Infallibili Magisterio*, more commonly known by its incipit, *Pastor Aeternus*, states: 'When the Roman Pontiff speaks *ex cathedra* – that is, when he is using his office as Pastor Doctor of all Christians – and in virtue of his apostolic office defines a doctrine of faith and morals to be accepted by the whole church, he, by the divine help promised him by the Blessed Peter, possesses that infallibility with which the Divine Redeemer was pleased to invest his church in definition of the doctrine on faith or morals, and therefore such definitions of the Roman Pontiff are irreformable in their own nature and not because of the consent of the church.' See Küng (2001) 113; Ellis (1952) 1:99; Marshall ch. 4; Hunter 1:442; Hughes; Manning ch. 5; O'Neill (1952) ch. 11. Although the declaration was thought to be unnecessary by those who already assumed that any formal papal statement regarding matters of faith and morals was infallible, the bull *Qui Quorundam* (1324) issued by the Avignon pope, John XXII, expressly denied such infallibility. Archbishop Peter Kenrick published the speech he had been barred from giving, arguing that while it was entirely proper for a pontiff, acting alone, to declare an article-of-

faith such as Mary's Immaculate Conception (as Pius had done in 1854) to be a dogma of the Church, declaring papal infallibility to be dogma was categorically different, since papal infallibility was neither recognized by early Church sources nor accepted as an article of faith in the English-speaking countries where Catholicism was a minority religion. 'Speech of Peter Richard Kenrick' (1870), in Bacon 94, 137–43.

10 Sparrow-Simpson 268–74; Raymond J. Clancy, 'American Prelates in the Vatican Council,' in Meehan 65–70; Daniel-Rops 296; Hales 309–10; Garrison (1928) 49–54; Butler 412–16.

11 Ellis (1963) 162, 174–87; Ellis (1952) 1:100; Hennesey (1963) 9; Hennesey (1983) 279–84; Zwierlein 2:59–60.

12 J. Paul Williams, *What Americans Believe and How They Worship* (NY 1952) 18; Hennesey (1963) 77, 230, 281–2; Ellis (1952) 1:95; Shannon 120. Gibbons's anecdote was said to be apocryphal. When Kenrick chose eventually to submit to the doctrine of papal infallibility, the Holy See determined that this ended the matter and thus did not ask him to repudiate the substance of his speech. See 'The "Concio" of Archbishop Kenrick,' in Meehan 93; Hennesey (1983) 244–51, 315–26; Butler 424–5; Ellis (1952) 1:99; Fogarty (1985) 2–9; Farley 287; Luis Bermejo, *Infallibility on Trial* (Westminster, MD 1992) 192. Over two decades later, Gibbons, by then a seasoned veteran of both Church and American politics, saw no reason in his published reminiscences to accent the partisanship of the debates. Gibbons (1916) 19–20, 32, 177–84; Will 1:116–39.

13 Sparrow-Simpson 276. By 1876, all Prussian bishops had been either exiled or imprisoned. Reventlow/Farmer 26, 31.

14 Jemolo ch. 2; D'Agostino 46–52. In 1907 it was rumoured that Richard Kerens, an Irish-born railroad tycoon from St Louis, was raising $40 million among American Catholics so that the pope could purchase as sovereign territory a narrow strip of land extending west from Rome to the sea, on which Kerens would build a railroad affording the pope access to international travel without ever having to set foot in 'Liberal' Italy. The scheme never reached fruition. Schneider 188–9.

15 'Modernism' in this context has been defined as the generic name for 'varied attempts to reconcile the Christian religion with the findings of agnostic philosophy, rationalistic science of history, and ... with all those cultural movements which in their development have progressively become estranged from religion or have set themselves in hostile opposition to it.' Neuner/Dupuis 48. See also Rhodes (1983) 193–6.

16 *Immortale Dei*, in Carlen 2:107, 112, 114; *Longinqua Oceani*, in *id*. 2:211, 218; Marshall 88–147; Ellis (1952) 1:603.

17 Zwierlein 2:172, 178–82, 3: ch. 31; Ellis (1952) 1:600–1; Ellis (1971) 58–9;
    Ellis (1983) 147–8; Barry 70–1, 217–25; Hennesey (1970) 28, 43–4; Fogarty
    (1985) 80–5, 107–42; Kurtz 45–8; McAvoy (1969) 284; D. O'Brien (1989) 124.
18 D. O'Brien (1992) 376–7; D. O'Brien (1989) 118; Hennesey (1963) 27–31;
    Dolan (1985) 315–17; Schultenover ch. 2; Ireland, Introduction to Walter
    Elliott's *Life of Father Hecker* (NY 1891), reprinted in Klein; Fogarty (1985)
    151–76; Reilly ch. 5; Fogarty (1989B) 65–6; Fogarty (1985) 161–4;
    Messbarger (1971) 12; Reher 80–1.
19 Sparrow-Simpson 293–5; Butler 116–19, 308; Barry 239–41; Garrison (1933)
    69; Walburg 39, 46; Ellis (1971) 511, 513; M. Gannon 325; Messbarger
    (1971); Schneider 35–7; Barry 221–2.
20 Reher 73–4; Barry 226–30, ch. 6; Sullivan 57–63; Will 1:553–7; Ellis (1952)
    ch. 16; Samuel Thomas, 'The American Periodical Press and the Apostolic
    Letter *Testem Benevolentiae*,' *Cath. Hist. Rev.* 62/3:408 (July 1976); Gustave
    Weigel, 'The Church and the Democratic State,' *Thought* 27:165, 177–80
    (Summer 1952); Fogarty (1985) 177–88; Cross 20–1; Gleason (1992) 291–2;
    Maynard (1953) 86–97; Messbarger (1971) 8; McKeown 14–16; Merwick
    148–61; Rhodes (1983) 137–9; D. O'Brien (1992) 391; J.E.E. Dalberg Acton,
    'The Vatican Council' (1870), in *The History of Freedom and Other Essays*
    (London 1907) 492, 495–6; Butler 468. Denis O'Connell subsequently re-
    established his orthodoxy and in 1903 himself became rector of Catholic
    University. Reher 164nn40, 46; Barry 247–9.
21 Ellis (1952) 2:70–1; Barry 240–1; Fogarty (1985) 188–9; Rhodes (1983) 139.
22 Ireland 2:221, 246; Fogarty (1985) 190; Greeley (1977) 34; D. O'Brien (1989)
    128–9; Gaffey 242–3; Handy (1977) 325; Joseph Chinnici, *Living Stones: The
    History and Structure of Catholic Spiritual Life in the U.S.* (NY 1989) ch. 11;
    Gleason (1992) 278–82; McAvoy (1957) 290; Cross ch. 10; Cuneo 7–8; David
    Killen, 'Americanism Revisited,' *Harv. Theol. Rev.* 66/4:413 (Oct. 1973);
    McCann 4–5.
23 Washington Gladden, *Who Wrote the Bible?* (Boston 1891); Thomas
    Schlereth, 'John Zahm,' in *Evolution and Dogma*, by Zahm (NY 1978); Reher
    73–80; Pernicone 52–3; Rhodes (1983) 177–8; McAvoy (1957) 263–74;
    McAvoy (1969) 320–1; Handy (1977) 325; M. Gannon 314–18; Ronald L.
    Numbers, *Darwinism Comes to America* (Cambridge, MA 1998) 2; Ahlstrom
    840; John Gmeiner, *Modern Scientific Views and Christian Doctrines Compared*
    (Milwaukee 1884) 73–81.
24 Sabatier 39, App. 3; Lilley 247–57; Butler 469–70; Kurtz 153–7; Paul
    Collins, *Papal Power* (London 1997) 23–7; Maynard (1953) 94, 173–5; C.A.
    Campbell, 'The Authority and the Authorship of Scripture,' *Am. Eccles.
    Rev.* 38/2:166 (Feb. 1908); Zwierlein 3:240–5; Fogarty (1985) 141; Fogarty

(1982) 173; Barry 241; Handy (1977) 323; Gunther Scholtz, 'The Notion of Historicism and 19th Century Theology,' in Reventlow/Farmer 149. See also *Praestantia Scripturae* (18 Nov. 1907).

25 *Pascendi* in Carlen 3:82–3; Victor Consemius, 'The Condemnation of Modernism and the Survival of Catholic Theology,' trans. Robert R. Barr, in *The Twentieth Century: A Theological Overview,* ed. Gregory Baum (Maryknoll, NY 1999) 14; Lilley 205–12, 258; Schultenover ch. 1; Butler 470–1; *Editae Saepe Dei,* 26 May 1910; Rhodes (1983) 196; Sabatier 39; Vidler 1–11, 217–18; Falconi 60–9; Anon. [John Ireland?], 'Three Years and a Half of Pius X,' *North. Am. Rev.* 184:35 (Jan. 1907).

26 Fogarty (1985) 191; Barry 244–5n13; G. Williams 122–5; Anthony Viéban, 'Who Are the Modernists of the Encyclical?' *Am. Eccles. Rev.* 38/5:489, 507 (May 1908).

27 www.fisheaters.com/sacrorum.html; C. Brown 140; *Pieni L'Animo* (28 July 1906), in Carlen 3:57; 'Modernism in the Church in America,' *Am. Eccles. Rev.* 38/1:1 (Jan. 1908); 'Modernism,' *Catholic Encyclopedia* (1913); Canon 1393, in Bachofen (1921) 6:450; Ellis (1971) 63–8; Garrison (1928) 243; McAvoy (1957) viii; Reher 99–101.

28 O'Toole (1989) 172, 178; O'Toole (1992) 82, 90, 196–204, 217–19; Gaffey 226; Ellis (1983) 70–7; Fogarty (1989B) 173–80; Fogarty (1985) 204–6; Dorothy Wayman, *Cardinal O'Connell of Boston* (NY 1954) 215; Robert Trisco, 'Bishops and Their Priests in the United States,' in Ellis (1971).

29 Greeley (1977) 33–5, 57; Laura Wittman, '*Omnes velut aqua dilabimur,*' in Somigli/Moroni 130; Falconi 25–6; M. Williams (1934) 163–5; O'Toole (1992) 83–4; Merwick xii, 185–96; Dolan (1985) 259; Barry 7–11.

30 McAvoy (1963) 300, 317; Callahan (1966) 35, 41; E.B. Barrett vii-viii; John McKenzie, 'Problems of Hermeneutics in Roman Catholic Exegesis' (1958), in Smith/Handy/Loetscher 2:484; Shelley 583–4; M. Gannon 326–50; Fogarty (1985) 190–3, 346; Fogarty (1989B) 132–9, 163–7; Ellis (1971) 66–8; Reher 95–8; Dolan (1985) 318–19; Ellis, 'The U.S.A.,' in Aubert 253, 276–7; D. O'Brien (1989) 99; Ellis (1971) 65–74; Vaillancourt 41; Komonchak 35, 36.

31 Maude Dominica Petre, *Modernism: Its Failure and Its Fruits* (London 1918) 194–7; Allitt 8–9; Küng (2001) 173–4; Falconi 35–6, 41, 71; Merwick 180–2; Rhodes (1983) 196–7; G. Williams 126–7; P. Johnson 473; Atkin/Tallett 163.

32 Gleason (1995) 12–13, 128–9, ch. 5, 297–304; Gleason (1987) chs. 3 and 4; *Aeterni Patris,* in Carlen 2:17, 23–6; Pius XI, *Studiorum Ducem* (29 June 1923); McCool 226–40; Kurtz 39–43; Anon., 'The Study of the Christian Fathers,' *Am Eccles. Rev.* 3/1:28, 31 (July 1890); Ellis (1971) 39–42; Falconi 5; Hennesey (1981) 203, 215–16; Hennesey (1990) 304; Hasler 245–50; Ong

541; McGreevy 127–8, 139–42; Halsey chs. 8 and 9; René Fülöp-Miller, *Leo XIII and Our Times*, trans. Conrad M.R. Bonacina (London 1937) 152–4; Cross 215–16; Cuneo 9–10; Marsden (1994) 273–4; Mark D. Jordan, *The Invention of Sodomy in Christian Theology* (Chicago 1997) 136–7.

33 Pius X, *Vehementer Nos* (11 Feb. 1906) ¶ 8; Benedict XV, *Ad beatissimi apostolorum principis* (1 Nov. 1914) ¶¶ 22–7; Falconi 31–2, 210–11.

3 A Church of Immigrants

1 Patrick J. Blessing, 'Irish Emigration to the United States, 1800–1920,' in Drudy 11, 12; Gibbons (1916) 249; Liptak 7; D. O'Brien (1989) 20; Ellis, 'Foreword' to Hennesey (1981) viii-ix; Tocqueville (1958) 149–50, 164–5, 174–5; Tocqueville (2000) 275; O'Neill (1952) ch. 1; Herberg 151; Beaumont 83; Bayor/Meagher Pt. 1; www.law.umn.edu/irishlaw/chron.html; Cavour, *Thoughts on Ireland* (1844), trans. H.B. Hodgson (London 1868) 10. See also T. Brown 28–9: 'Of all the Catholic peoples of Western Europe, the Irish alone were without a stake in perpetuating the anti-democratic governments and aristocratic societies of the past.'

2 Shannon 29–31, 134–5; *The Times* (1848) quoted in Fisher (2002) 44; Farley 3–7; Mill quoted in Brody 57n; K. Miller (1985) chs. 5–7; K. Miller (1999) 186; J. O'Brien 21; Akenson 111–16, 145; Connolly 7–11; Foster 324–31; Morris 33; Mulcrone 219, 235n2; Larkin (1967) 852–4, 876–8; Connell (1950) 27–9; Greeley (1981A) 54–5; Edwards/Williams xiii-xv; T.P. O'Neill, 'The Organisation and Administration of Relief, 1845–52,' in *id*. 207; MacDonagh 376–84; McHugh 410–11; Wittke chs. 15–17; Connolly (1982) 7–11; McCaffrey (1976) 56–8; Kenny (2000) 92–6; Beckett 293–4, 336–53; Irene Whelan, 'The Stigma of Souperism,' in *The Great Irish Famine*, ed. Cathal Póirtéir (Cork 1995).

3 Jones 104–12; Morris ch. 2; K. Miller (1985) 4–5, 455–90, 582; MacDonagh 322–3; Hasia R. Diner, '"The Most Irish City in the Union": The Era of the Great Migration 1844–1877,' in Bayor/Meagher 87, 104; T. Brown 17–19; Comerford; Terry Coleman, *Going to America* (Baltimore 1987) ch. 9; Akenson 102; Loomis, *Modern Cities and Their Religious Problems* (1886; NY 1887) 73–83; Biever 533; Barnard 20; Glazer/Moynihan 219–20; Ravitch 27; Wittke ch. 5; Hughes quoted in Dolan (1975) 32–5.

4 Strong, *Diary*, ed. Allan Nevins and Milton Thomas (NY 1952) 2:348; Hale quoted in Potter 161; Waugh 652. See also Daniel Patrick Moynihan's foreword to Greeley (1972) xiv.

5 Larkin (1972) 639, 648–9; Connell (1968) 86, 127–9; Kerby Miller, 'Class, Culture, and Immigrant Group Identity in the U.S.,' in *Immigration Recon-*

sidered, ed. Virginia Yans-McLaughlin (NY 1990) 96, 101; K. Miller (1985) 10, 109–10, 116–28, and ch. 7; K. Miller (1999) 181–2; Shannon 8–9, 21–3; Wittke 7–8; Beaumont 59–72; Cogley 147–8; Bowen 259; Humphreys 26; Potter 75–7; Stahl 41–3, 54; Ruth Clark, *Strangers and Sojourners at Port Royal* (Cambridge 1932) chs. 13–14; Connolly (1982) 45–7, 93–4, 185, 284–6; Connolly (1985) 11–12; Keenan 59; Arland Ussher, *The Face and Mind of Ireland* (NY 1950) 109, 122–41; Ussher 161–2; Michael Sheehy, *Is Ireland Dying? Culture and the Church in Modern Ireland* (NY 1969) 17–18; Corish, *The Catholic Community in the Seventeenth and Eighteenth Centuries* (Dublin 1981) 87–8; Corish, *Maynooth College, 1795–1995* (Dublin 1995) 122–3; J. O'Brien 105; D. Vincent Twomey, *The End of Irish Catholicism?* (Dublin 2003) 47–8, 180n14; LaGumina; Varbero 35; Greeley (1972) 82; McDowell 66; Küng (2001) 72, 93; T.W. Moody and J.C. Beckett, *Queen's, Belfast, 1845–1949* (London 1959) 1:xxxix–xliv; Reinhardt, *The Theological Novel of Modern Europe* (NY 1969) 17.

6 Beaumont 201–2, 233; Larkin (1972); Larkin (1980); K. Miller (1985) 73, 80–4; Staunton 153, 161; D. Miller (1975) 88–93; Thackeray 50–1, 59, 83; Tocqueville (1958) 145, 169–72, 187–9. See also Brown/Miller 177; Akenson 139–40; McDowell 69; S.J. Connolly, *Religion, Law, and Power: The Making of Protestant Ireland, 1660–1760* (Oxford 1992) ch. 7; Connolly, 'Religion and History,' *Irish Econ. Soc. Hist.* 10:66, 71 (1983); Ellis (1971) 20–1; Connolly (1982) 33–7, 101–20; Potter 82–4; Foster 207, 338–9.

7 See Connell (1968) 79–86, 119; Beaumont 201; Brody 60 (quoting Connell); Connolly (1982) 187–9; Foster 218–19; Akenson 30–4; Tocqueville (1958) 142, 179, 191.

8 Morris 30; Hynes 148–50; D. Miller (1975) 82 and n8; Greeley (1981A) 61–2; Connell (1968) 113–18; Connell (1950) 37–61, 79–80, 161–83; Connell (1962); Connell (1957) 77, 80, 85; Kennedy 12–15, 139–72; Connolly 217; Akenson 26–7; McDowell 5; Stahl; Diner 6–23, 46–52; Potter 38; Humphreys 19–20; Foster 334–5; Michael Drake, 'Marriage and Population Growth in Ireland, 1750–1845,' *Econ. Hist. Rev.* 16 (2d ser.) 301 (1962); James J. Walsh, M.D., 'Shy Irish Bachelors,' *America* (29 March 1930) 592; Connolly (1982) 217; Biever 254; McCaffrey 76. For a very different experience in rural Italy, see Bell ch. 5 and App. C. In the 1890s, despite the Irish tradition of late marriage and the high proportion of permanently unmarried, Ireland's ratio of non-marital to total births was the lowest in Europe.

9 See, for example, Connell (1968) 86, 140n4; Potter 83; Edmund W. Majewski, S.J., review of Twomey, *The End of Irish Catholicism?* in *Hom. and Past. Rev.* 105/5:74 (Feb. 2005).

10 Sullivan 36.

11 Diner 9, 15–16; Dolan (1985) 229; Dolan (1975) 62–7; Hennesey (1981) 187, 284, 300–1; Skinner 25–7.

12 Mary 'has been ... a mechanism of sex sublimation for all who adore her. She shows no vestige of earthly love, for this was from the first repressed and spiritualized; and she has always stood forth in doctrine and in art as the embodiment of the ideal of virginity, both of her own and for our sake.' Hall 1:56. See also Besant 65–6; Margaret Culkin Banning, 'There Is Still Hope,' in J. O'Brien 123, 130–1.

13 See Condren 48–58, 74, 103–10, 160–82; O'Dwyer (1988) 124–5, 217–18, 293–5; O'Dwyer (1981) 8–48; Peter O'Dwyer, 'A Fresh Look at *Versiculi Familiae Benchuir*' (1975), in O'Dwyer, *Devotion to Mary in Ireland 700–1100* (Dublin 1976) 1–13; W. Sherlock, *Some Account of St Brigid* (Dublin 1896) 16–19. See also Kim McCone, *Pagan Past and Christian Present in Early Irish Literature* (Maynooth 1990).

14 Beaumont 80; Cornelius A. Bouman, 'The Immaculate Conception in the Liturgy' (1954), in O'Connor 113, 125–7; Foster 340. It was to a thirteenth-century Englishman, Simon Stock, that Mary reportedly gave the brown scapular.

15 Larkin (1980) 3–4; Rhodes (1983) ch. 1; Staunton 153, 161; Comerford 30–1; John Murphy, 'Priests and People in Modern Irish History,' *Christus Rex* 23/4:235, 252 (1969); Norman 4–20; Kenny (2000) 136, 164; Keenan 148–52, 243; Connolly (1985) 12–15, 26–7, 47–60; Akenson 36; Bowen x, chs. 3–4. At Vatican I, Cullen's arguments for infallibilism drew the ire of an American anti-infallibilist, the French-born Augustin Verot, bishop of St Augustine: 'It is true that the Irish believe in the Pope's infallibility,' Verot argued, 'but they also believe in their priests' infallibility – and not only do they believe it, but they beat with sticks any who deny it. But will the Cardinal of Dublin say that they believe Hadrian IV was infallible when he handed over Ireland to the King of England?' Butler 109, 286, 307–13, 323, 355, 382–4. When, in 1873, Cullen sidestepped St Patrick by dedicating Ireland to the Sacred Heart of Mary, the *Dublin Evening Mail* stated, 'Absurdities suited to the latitude of Rome and Naples are sadly out of place in Ireland.' Bowen 139–41, 288–9.

16 Humphreys 20–1; Larkin (1972); Larkin (1962) 298–301; D. Miller in Brown/Miller 159; K. Miller (1985) 73, 526; Connell (1968) 113–14, 121, 160 App.; Connell (1962); John A. Murphy, 'Religion and Irish Identity,' in *Irishness in a Changing Society*, ed. Princess Grace Library (Gerrards Cross 1988) 132, 134–6; Connolly (1985) 49–50; Máire MacNeill, *The Festival of Lughnasa* (London 1962) 21–2, 34, 43–70; Elizabeth Fitzpatrick, 'The

Gathering Place of Tír Fhiachrach?' *Proc. Royal Irish Acad.* 101C:67, 70 (2001); Foster 207–8, 340–1, 371; McHugh 395; MacDonagh 324, 329; Diner ch. 1; Donnelly 282. England's first notable Marian vision occurred in Walsingham, 818 years before An Cnoc.

17 Dolan (1975) 22; Morris 49; Beaumont 238–9; Ellis (1971) 75; Ellis (1963) 100; Potter 348–50; Morris ch. 1; Ravitch 36–57; Shelley 580; Greeley (1972) 84–5. As a surprising exception to a well-proven trend, in 1894, with ninety-seven pastors in English-speaking Boston parishes, only thirty-nine were Irish-born, and of these only seven had reached America before ordination. Merwick x–xi; Dolan (1975) 7–8, 56–60. See also Keenan 245.

18 See Marsden (1990) 87; Dolan (1985) 128; Gillis 60–1; Handy (1977) 196; Robert Baird, *Religion in America* (NY 1856) 543; K. Miller (1985) 346, 350, 569; Kennedy 22; Edmund M. Hogan, *The Irish Missionary Movement* (Dublin 1990) 205; Timothy L. Smith, *Revivalism and Social Reform in Mid-Nineteenth-Century America* (NY 1957) 22; Russel Blaine Nye, *Society and Culture in America 1830–1860* (NY 1974) 308–10; Smith ch. 1; Kenny (2000) 55. Between 1846 and 1911, Ireland's population dropped from 8.2 million to 4.4 million. Foster 323, 331, 345.

19 McCaffrey (1996) 218–19; J.J. Lee in Lee/Casey 20; Kenny (2000) 76–7; Keenan 27; Connell (1957) 87; Yeats, 'Dedication to a Book of Stories Selected from the Irish Novelists' (1891); Dever 20; Jay P. Dolan, *Catholic Revivalism: The American Experience, 1830–1900* (Notre Dame, IN 1978) 195–6; John C. Messenger, *Inis Beag: Isle of Ireland* (NY 1969) 88–9; Clarence Darrow, *Verdicts out of Court* (Chicago 1963) 317.

20 Wakin/Scheuer 39; Greeley (1981A) 122 and ch. 10; Beaumont 196; Besant 14–15; Greeley, *Priests in the United States* (Garden City 1972) 51–2; Greeley (1981A) 122; Greeley (1972) 104–15, 129–43; Greeley (1971) 139–40; Potter 88; Keenan 69; Kenny (2000) 200–3; Desmond Fennell, *The Changing Face of Catholic Ireland* (Washington, DC 1968) 121–34; McCaffrey (1996) 213–14; J. O'Brien 88; Seán Ó Faoláin, 'Love among the Irish,' in J. O'Brien 111, 121; Mary Frances Keating, 'Marriage-Shy Irishmen,' in *id.* 170; Ussher 156; Kennedy ch. 7; Nuala Fennell, *Irish Marriage – How Are You!* (Dublin 1974) 43–5. See also Diner 19–23 and ch. 5; Akenson 27, 202–3n33; Nancy Scheper-Hughes, *Saints, Scholars, and Schizophrenics* (Berkeley 1979) 70–3, 104–22, 193; James J. Gill, S.J., M.D., 'Despondence – Why We See It in Priests,' *Med. Insight* 1/3:21 (Dec. 1969); Ruether, 'Beginnings: An Intellectual Autobiography,' in *Journeys*, ed. Gregory Baum (NY 1975) 34, 35–6. Father Greeley, in a moment of surprising harshness, describes the Irish as 'a cold, frustrated, sexless, repressed people with little emotional flexibility, and practically no capacity to give themselves in intimate

relations,' adding that the Great Hunger caused the Irish and Irish Americans to have 'a much harder time' than before 'being affectionate.'

21 Farley 327; R.L. Moore 70; Marty (1959) 3; Staunton 176; Dolan (1985) 257–8; Dale B. Light, Jr, 'The Role of Irish-American Organisations in Assimilation and Community Formation,' in Drudy 113.

22 Rhodes (1983) 131; K. Miller (1999) 495–6; Greeley (1981A) 115–16; Liptak 61–3; B. Lynch 67.

23 Carroll (1989) 164–5. During 1820–60, a mere 13,792 Italians emigrated to the United States. Marraro ix. Regarding the substantial contribution of Italian intellectuals to the nation's founding, see Philip diFranco, *The Italian American Experience* (NY 1988) ch. 3.

24 Of 3,505 priests in the United States as of 1869, 1,160 were of Germanic heritage. Ellis (1971) 31. German-American Catholics predominated in some regions, particularly in the so-called 'German Triangle' formed by Cincinnati, Milwaukee, and St Louis. Barry ch. 2; Liptak ch. 6; J.T. Fisher (2002) 51; Fogarty (1985) 45–61; Dolan (1975) ch. 4; M. Gannon 300; D. O'Brien (1972) 105–6. Bismarck's *Kulturkampf* against the Church during 1865–80 made German-American priests more strident in defence of their prerogatives in the United States, believing that once their Catholicism was separated from its traditional German roots, it would inevitably become a mere backwash in an English-speaking, multicultural amalgam dominated by the Irish. Despite their long, rearguard battle, their power did decline. By 1900, 62 per cent of U.S. bishops claimed an Irish heritage. In St Louis, although German priests outnumbered Irish priests, eleven of twelve bishops appointed between 1854 and 1922 were Irish. Dolan (1985) 143–4, 302; Alba 21–3; Barry ch. 1; Walburg 43; Gleason (1992) 281–2; Shannon 136; Handy (1977) 318–19; Rhodes (1983) ch. 6; Shane Leslie, *The Irish Issue in Its American Aspect* (NY 1917) 162–4.

25 Glazer/Moynihan 204. Of one hundred American bishops in 1940, most were Irish-born or of Irish ancestry. Maynard (1953) 117–18; Ellis (1963) 50–1.

26 Palmieri 128–9; McNicholas (1908) 681–2; Liptak 151–4; DeConde 92–4; Vecoli (1969) 240–7, 260–1; Schiavo 243; Avella 16–17; Villari 156–7; Zarrilli 71–3; Stephen M. DiGiovanni, 'Michael Augustine Corrigan and the Italian Immigrants,' in L. Tomasi 302, 307–15; Rose 100–4, 132–3. Boston nevertheless established two Italian parishes by 1900, rising to fourteen by 1935, Cardinal O'Connell having somehow found Italian-speaking priests to staff them. O'Toole 146; LaGumina 53–5.

27 Shaughnessy 220–1; Palmieri 136–8; D'Agostino 135–8; H. Brown 58, 67–9; Glazer/Moynihan 202–3; J. Briggs 245–52; Nelli 127–8; S. Tomasi 95–7;

Sarah Gertrude Pomeroy, *The Italians* (NY 1914) 35–7. In 1918, with over
three million people of Italian heritage living in the United States, there
were only 710 Italian priests. Vecoli (1969) 266. A condescending contributor to *Ecclesiastical Review* wrote that the Italian Catholic, 'whatever his
misconceptions in matters of religious observance, still clings – and often
in an admirable spirit of self-sacrifice – to the principles, doctrines, and
traditions of the Church in which he was reared. Accordingly, the one
person whom he is disposed to trust under all circumstances ... is the
priest ... of his own nationality or race, unless the same prove himself
unworthy of such trust and leadership.' 'Pastoral Care of Foreign Catholics,' *Eccles. Rev.* 70:178 (Feb. 1924).

28 Casillo 3–36; S. Tomasi 47–50, 76–104, 154–9; Irma B. Jaffe, 'Joseph Stella:
Madonnas and Related Work' (1993), in http://www.nd.edu/~sniteart/;
Stella, 'Discovery of America: Autobiographical Notes,' *Art News* 59/7:41,
66 (Nov. 1960).

29 O'Toole 154; DeConde 78–82; Sanders 166; Rose 99; McNicholas (1908)
678; Orsi 54–61, 164, 172; Hynes 141–5; Villari 151–4; P. Williams 149–58;
Hooker 30, 97–9; Child 34–5; Carroll (1989) 158–60; Carroll (1992) 133–6;
Vecoli in Miller/Marzick 32–3; Vecoli (1969) 264; Palmieri 127–8; Cogley
156; Nelli 128; Gambino 169; S. Tomasi 34, 37, 61, 123–8, 143–4; Lucia
Chiavola Birnbaum, 'On the Significance of Italian Folklore for Italian-
Americans,' in *Italian Americans in Transition*, ed. Joseph V. Scelsa et al.
(Staten Island, NY 1990) 105, 106–7; Denise Mangieri DiCarolo, 'The
Italian Festa in the United States as an Expression of Ethnic Pride,' in *The
Columbus People: Perspectives in Italian Immigration to the Americas and
Australia*, ed. Lydio F. Tomasi, Piero Gastaldo, and Thomas Row (Staten
Island, NY 1994) 79, 85–6.

30 Moe 165; Joseph Sciorra, 'The Black Madonna of East Thirteenth Street,'
Voices 30 (Spring/Summer 2004); Levi 3–4, 39–43, 102, 117–21; Lucia
Chiavola Birnbaum, *Black Madonnas: Feminism, Religion, and Politics in Italy*
(Boston 1993) 39–40, 102–4, and ch. 4; Hooker 87; Bagot 135–6; John F.
Murphy, 'Origin and Nature of Marian Cult,' in Carol 3:1, 4–6; H.S.
Hughes 34.

31 Neuner/Dupuis 359–62; Astarita 124–5, 144–5, and ch. 5; Carroll (1992)
112–28; Carroll (1996) 3, 200–6; Bagot 56; Weinstein/Bell 193; P. Williams
135, 139; Gambino 194–216; Moe 50–3; Martin Shaw Briggs, *In the Heel of
Italy* (NY 1911) 280; Bagot 55–6; Bell 1–2, 60.

32 Carroll (1992) 15–17; Hennesey (1983) 281; Hennesey (1963) 46n59; Butler
413–14; Vecoli in Miller/Marzick 27; Gambino 212–13; Glazer/Moynihan
204–5.

33 Douglas ch. 31; Covello, *The Social Background of the Italo-American School Child* (1944; Totowa, NJ 1972) 103–6, 119–28; Vecoli in Miller/Marzick 28; Mangione/Morreale 41; P. Williams 136–8; C.T. Ramage, *The Nooks and Byways of Italy* (1828; London 1965) 59–60, 82–4. During an eruption of Vesuvius, Neapolitans took to the streets with relics of their patron saint, San Gennaro. When the wind changed, sparing the city from volcanic ash, one woman observed: 'Well, our saint has saved us again,' to which another replied: 'He'd better have. It would have been worse for him if he hadn't.' Salvatore Primeggia, 'The Social Contexts of Religious Devotion: How Saint Worship Expresses Popular Religiosity,' in Varacalli 68, 73–4; Mary Elizabeth Brown, 'Italian Americans and Their Saints: Historical Considerations,' in *id.* 35; Joseph Varacalli, 'The Saints in the Lives of Italian American Catholics,' in *id.* 231, 232–6; Varacalli, 'As the Saints (Apparently) Go Marching Out: Why Study Them?' in *id.* 3, 7; Mario B. Mignone, 'Foreword,' in *id.* iv, vii. See also Carroll (1992); Carroll (1996) ch. 1; Carroll (1989) 160–1; Villari 157–9; Mircea Eliade, *A History of Religious Ideas* (1978), trans. Willard R. Trask, vol. 2 (Chicago 1982) 293–4, 410; Bagot 58–61; Peter Brown, *The Cult of the Saints* (Chicago 1981) 20–30; Edward C. Banfield, *The Moral Basis of a Backward Society* (Glencoe, IL 1958); Rose 46–7. Recently, John Paul Russo and other scholars have pointed to a 'paganizing,' anti-clerical bias in writers like Douglas and Covello.

34 Alba 21–30 and 41n4; Ravitch 175–6; Astarita 289; V.W. Brooks (1915) 8; Foerster 423; Orsi; S. Tomasi; Donald J. D'Elia, 'People of the Festa: The Incarnational Realism of the Italian Americans,' in Varacalli 203, 212. Local Marian influences were also significant among immigrants from Poland, Germany, and Russia. The Black Madonna of Czestochowa, Poland, in particular, is said to have been responsible for many miracles.

35 Dolan (1975) 23–7; D'Agostino; Vecoli (1969) 221–5; Marraro ch. 6; J. Briggs 126; Rose 42–4, 51; B. Lynch; Rhodes (1983) 126; Liptak 143; Bagot 8–9; J. Briggs ch. 1 and 75–94; Comerford 60–2; Schiavo 151; Mangione/ Morreale 33, 101; Child 21–2 and ch. 3; Alba 29–31;Villari 4, 14; Astarita 285–8; Gambino 39–79; S. Tomasi 23–4, 65–6, 118–22; David A.J. Richards, *Italian American* (NY 1999) ch. 3; Bowen 200–4; H.S. Hughes 46–53; Norman 45–52; Harold J. Abramson, 'Ethnic Diversity within Catholicism: A Comparative Analysis of Contemporary and Historical Religion,' *J. Soc. Hist.* 4/4:359, 372–6 (Summer 1971); Murphy 29; Nelli 22–31.

36 Ginder 16; Vecoli in Miller/Marzick 34–7; M.E. Brown, 'Italian Americans and Their Saints,' in Varacalli 35, 48; Robert J. Batule, 'From Ethnicity to Ideology,' in *id.* 172, 175–80; J.F. Quinn, 'Saints over Sacraments?' in *id.* 93,

100–2; H. Brown 58; Kelley, 'The Church and the Immigrant,' *Catholic Mind* 13/17:471, 479, 481 (8 Sept. 1915); Casillo 82–5; McNicholas (1908) 685.

37 Silvano M. Tomasi, 'The Ethnic Church and the Integration of Italian Immigrants in the United States,' in Tomasi/Engel 163, 167; S. Tomasi 18–22; B. Lynch 68–72; K. Miller (1999) 582; Elizabeth Ewen, *Immigrant Women in the Land of Dollars* (NY 1985) 50–1; Dolan (1985) 131–2, 280; Hooker 13; Diner 31–3; Howard B. Grose, *Aliens or Americans?* (NY 1906) 306; H. Brown 47–8; Levi 103–4; Burns 107–10; Mangione/Morreale 89–98, 159–60; J. Briggs 35; Foerster 30; Muredach 36; Vecoli (1969) 238, 248–50; *Eccles. Rev.* 70:178 (Feb. 1924); Zarrilli 70; Sanders 166; Kantowicz (1983) 70–1; J. Briggs chs. 9 and 10; Rose 100, 128; Alba 91; DeConde 92–3.

38 Nicholas John Russo, 'Three Generations of Italians in New York City: Their Religious Acculturation,' in Tomasi/Engel 195, 203–5; Sartorio 76, 81, 89, 99, 104; Vecoli (1969) 266–7; Richard Renoff, 'Church Dedications of Italian American National Parishes,' in Varacalli 107, 117; Rose 100–28; Wakin/Scheuer 29; Child 34; Schneider 88–94; Shaughnessy 223 and chs. 13–15; Garrison (1928) 95–7; M. Williams (1934) 57; Lourdeaux 17, 48, 66–81.

4 A New Catholic-American Culture

1 Akenson 116–28; Zwierlein vol. 2 ch. 19; Feldman ch. 2; Hamburger 223–4; D. O'Brien (1989) 44–54; Reilly 18–20; Ravitch 51; David B. Tyack, *The One Best System* (Cambridge, MA 1974) 84–6; Dolan (1985) 263–4.

2 Robert Emmett Curran, 'Michael Corrigan,' in Fogarty (1989B) 150, 153; Fogarty (1989A) chs. 1 and 2; Stokes 1:822–3; Dolan (1975) ch. 6; Dolan (1985) 242 and ch. 10; Smith/Handy/Loetscher 2:84–8, 106; D. O'Brien (1989) 104, 110–11; Farley 1; Holifield ch. 20; McAvoy (1969) 259–60; Guilday 238; McGreevy ch. 1; Wakin/Scheuer 57–8; Burns 17–20, 123–45, 191–293; Pierce v. Society of Sisters, 268 U.S. 510 (1925).

3 'Reflections of a Priest on the School Question,' *Am Eccles. Rev.* 3/4:277, 279 (Oct. 1890); H.L. Richards, 'An Ideal School Bill,' *id.* 7/1:1 (July 1892); P.R., 'Trend of Modern Educational Legislation,' *id.* 22/1:4, 27 (Jan. 1900); Reilly 34–6, 48–9, 143–7; Oates 61; Zwierlein 2:142; Satolli 31–2; Callahan (1963) 58–9, 74; Schneider 62–4; Dolan (1985) 264; Sanders 134–54; Gleason (1995) 98; Morris 123; John F. McClymer, 'Of "Mornin' Glories" and "Fine Old Oaks,"' in Bayor/Meagher 374; Merton 26; Lawrence McCaffrey, 'Irish-American Politics,' in Drudy 169.

4 Dolan (1985) 277, 288–93; Mary J. Oates, '"The Good Sisters": The Work

and Position of Catholic Churchwomen in Boston, 1870–1940,' in Sullivan/O'Toole 171, 184; Oates 61–9; Sargent ch. 10; Massa 181–2; Maynard (1953) 227; McLoughlin 35; Gleason (1979) 197–9; M. Gannon 355–6; Burns; 'The Catholic Church and the Modern Mind,' *Atlantic Monthly* 141/1:12, 17 (Jan. 1928).

5 Cogley 178; William P. Clancy, *Time's Covenant: The Essays and Sermons of William Clancy*, ed. Eugene Green (Pittsburgh 1987) 53; Reher 126; Burns 346–54.

6 E.B. Barrett 28–9; Carroll (1989) ch. 7; C.P. Ceroke, 'The Scapular Devotion,' in Carol 3:128; Callahan (1963) 83.

7 Greeley (1981A) 112; Gleason (1995) 96–7, 171–7; Gleason (1979) 193; Hennesey (1981) 238; Joseph A. Tetlow, S.J., 'In Oratione Directa,' in *Jesuit Higher Education*, ed. Rolando E. Bonachea (Pittsburgh 1989) 105, 112–13; McLoughlin 186–7; Gleason (1979) 195–6; M. Williams (1934) 281; Burns 371–4; Marshall ch. 16. In Matt. 28:19, quoted by Pius XI in *Divini illius magistri* (31 Dec. 1929), teaching ($\mu\alpha\theta\eta\tau\epsilon\acute{\upsilon}\omega$) refers not to explaining a subject matter but to making disciples for one's doctrine.

8 Cogley 149, 203; Gleason (1979) 195–6; Bull, 'The Function of a Catholic Graduate School,' *Thought* 13:364, 366 (Sept. 1938); J. Moore 225–9.

9 Halsey 50; Allitt ix; Hofstadter (1963) 138–9; Francis L. Broderick, *Right Reverend New Dealer* (NY 1963) 31–2; McGuire 4:117; Shuster 172; Callahan (1963) 84–5; Messbarger (1985); Arnold J. Sparr, 'From Self-Congratulation to Self-Criticism: Main Currents in American Catholic Fiction, 1900–1960,' *U.S. Cath. Historian* 6:213, 215–20 (1987); Waugh 644, 654; Cicognani, *Sanctity in America* (1939), 3d ed. (Paterson, NJ 1945) chs. 14 and 15; Maynard (1941) 579–80; Brogan 66; McGreevy ch. 7; McCool 251–5; O'Dea 10.

10 Loisy 251; Lilley 61–94, 185–94; Falconi 36; Kurtz ch. 4; P. Johnson 472; Bachofen (1924) 353; Newman Smyth, *Passing Protestantism and Coming Catholicism* (NY 1908) ch. 2; Halsey; Gleason (1995) ch. 5; Gleason (1979) 194–5; Inge 448; Reher 116–18; A.C. McGiffert, 'Modernism and Catholicism,' *Harv. Theol. Rev.* 3:24, 29 (Jan. 1910). A new era for biblical scholarship was announced on 30 September 1943, in Pope Pius XII's *Divino Afflante Spiritu*. R. Brown (1973) 4–5.

11 Shuster 14–15; McAvoy (1967) 108; Brogan 66; Avella 19–20, 24n33; Reher 116; Fogarty (1985) 346; Sperry 137, 218; Cushing quoted in Glazer/Moynihan 238; Ahlstrom 1007; M. Gannon 294.

12 Dolan (1985) 392; Ellis (1963) 54, 61–2; B. Kelly in McGuire 4:103, 115; Cram, *The Catholic Church and Art* (NY 1930) 120; Belloc in *id.* 7; Biever 671; Sylvester, *Moon Gaffney* (NY 1947) 43–4.

13 Pick in *The Catholic Renascence*, ed. Norman Weyand (Chicago 1951) 161;
   Ong 523–6; Ellis, 'American Catholics and the Intellectual Life' (1955), in
   Gleason (1970) 115; McCaffrey (1976) 167; Garrison (1928) 40; Helene,
   'American Catholics and Art since 1900,' in Ward 230, 232; Arnold J. Sparr,
   'From Self-Congratulation to Self-Criticism: Main Currents in American
   Catholic Fiction, 1900–1960,' *U.S. Cath. Historian* 6:213 (1987); Sheed; Ellis,
   'The U.S.A.,' in Aubert 253, 295; Morris 266–81; McDonald 83–94, 247–57;
   O'Dea 42–3; Maynard (1953) 251.

14 Fred Lewis Pattee, *The New American Literature, 1890–1930* (NY 1930) 183–
   4; Giles chs. 5–7; Messbarger (1985) 147, 152–3; Bloom, introduction to
   Long Day's Journey into Night (New Haven 2002); Edward Shaughnessy,
   Down the Nights and Down the Days (Notre Dame, IN 1996) 40; John H.
   Raleigh, 'O'Neill's Long Day's Journey into Night and New England Irish
   Catholicism,' *Partisan Rev.* 26:573 (1959); Greeley (1981A) 184; McLoughlin
   183; Cogley 234.

15 Chesterton, 'Introduction' to Sheen, *God and Intelligence in Modern
   Philosophy* (London 1925) vii; Sheen in *id.* 62; Weigel 47; Reeves 43–59;
   Avella 17–18.

16 Maynard in *Sat. Rev. Lit.* 4/29:588 (11 Feb. 1928); Richard J. Regan, *American Pluralism and the Catholic Conscience* (NY 1963) 38; Fisher (1989) 51;
   Stringfellow Barr, 'American Catholics and Their Intellectual Heritage,' in
   American Catholics, ed. Philip Sharper (NY 1959) 5, 7; Joseph Fichter in
   McDonald 34.

17 Leo XIII's encyclical *Rerum Novarum* (1891) invited progressive labour
   policies and sparked Catholic Social Justice Teaching, a distinctly Catholic
   and ongoing mode of Progressive thought. ¶¶ 4, 8–10. On the other hand,
   the encyclical was widely construed as anti-socialist rather than pro-
   union. When Fr. Edward McGlynn embraced Henry George's argument in
   Progress and Poverty (1879) for a heavy tax on the rich to offset their oppression of the poor, Michael Corrigan, New York's conservative
   archbishop, had him excommunicated, albeit Satolli later reversed that
   punishment. Fogarty (1985) 92, 105–6; Ellis (1952) ch. 13; Fisher (2002) 79–
   80; Morris 93–6; Messbarger (1971) 9; D. O'Brien (1989) 84–8; Reilly 43;
   Rhodes (1983) 143–4.

18 Gibbons in *Our Bishops Speak* (Milwaukee 1952) 173, 174; Liptak 73;
   D'Agostino 110–13; Gleason (1995) 74; Thomas Beer quoted in Glazer/
   Moynihan 247; McAvoy (1967) 113–14; Humbert S. Nelli, *Italians in Chicago
   1880–1930: A Study in Ethnic Mobility* (NY 1970) 202–3; Rose 97.

19 J. Ryan (1920) ch. 2; Ryan, *A Living Wage* (NY 1906); Ryan, *Distributive
   Justice* (NY 1916); W.F. Montavon, 'National Catholic Welfare Conference,'

in Ward 242; McKeown 22–3 and chs. 3–5; 'Pastoral Letter (1919),' in Nolan 212, 230–2; McNicholas quoted in Handy (1977) 330. See also H.J. Ford 1:100–1; Ed Marciniak, 'Catholics and Social Reform,' in Commonweal 123; Reher 107–12; Dolan (1985) 334–46; Ahlstrom 1004; Fisher (2002) 95–8; McCann 21–2; Reeves 40–1; Falconi 4; Parker T. Moon, 'Catholic Social Action,' in McGuire 2:209.

20 Marty (1991) 26; Handy (1977) 326; Reuter, *Population Problems* (Philadelphia 1923) 297; Callahan (1963) 80–1; Mangione/Morreale 33; David J. Rothman, *Strangers at the Bedside* (NY 1991) 123; Kantowicz (1989) 204–5; S. Tomasi 15; Fogarty (1985) 228–30; Ellis (1983) 18; Kantowicz (1983) 166–8.

21 M. Williams (1928) 39, 102–7, 120–5, 347; Williams quoted in Garrison (1933) 203–4.

22 Talbott, 'Catholicism in America,' in Stearns 528–42; Black (1998) 18; Halsey 108–10; Hennesey (1981) 221; Gleason (1979) 189–90.

23 Walter Lippmann, 'The Catholic Issue in Politics,' *Vanity Fair* 28/5:31 (July 1927); Michael Williams, *The Shadow of the Pope* (NY 1932) vii; Marty (1991) 245–6; Marouf Arif Hasian, Jr, *The Rhetoric of Eugenics in Anglo-American Thought* (Athens, GA 1996) 93.

24 Shuster, *The Catholic Spirit in America* (NY 1927) 166; Garrison (1928) 16, 144–58; Siegfried, *America Comes of Age* (1927), trans. H.H. Hemming and Doris Hemming (NY 1929) 33; Keyser/Keyser 41–3.

25 Chief among those opposing Smith's candidacy on the ground that a Catholic president would inevitably have divided loyalties, was an Episcopalian attorney, Charles Marshall, who proclaimed that 'a civic community or state motivated in moral matters through a Roman Catholic solidarity by an ecclesiastical government at Rome differs radically from one motivated by the civic primacy of its people within the state.' *Governor Smith's American Catholicism* (NY 1928) 17. See also R.M. Miller 59; M. Williams (1928) ch. 6; Robert C. Fuller, *Naming the AntiChrist: The History of an American Obsession* (NY 1995) 146–8; Hennesey (1981) 252–3; Marty (1991) ch. 3. Protestant fears of Smith's being a doctrinaire Romanist were unfounded. When someone asked whether Smith could govern the nation and still abide by Leo XIII's encyclical *Immortale Dei* (1885), Smith reportedly commented: 'Will somebody please tell me what in hell an encyclical is?' Hennesey (1990) 313.

26 Gleason (1992) 208; Maynard (1941) 588; D. O'Brien (1971) 443–4.

27 J. Moore 5–6; George P. West, 'The Catholic Issue,' *New Republic* 278 (1 March 1943); M. Williams (1928) ch. 6.

28 'Lateran,' in *New Catholic Enclyclopedia* (1966); Rhodes (1973) 27 and ch. 3;

D'Agostino chs. 6–7; Pius XI, *Divini illius magistri* (31 Dec. 1929) ¶ 26; H.S. Hughes 94–5.

29 See M. Williams (1934) 324; J. Carroll-Abbing, 'Catholic Action in Italy,' in *Restoring All Things*, ed. John Fitzsimons and Paul McGuire (NY 1938) 98, 119–20; Gleason (1995) 152–8; Gleason (1979) 191; Garrison (1928) 194; Kantowicz (1983) 174–202.

30 Fisher (1989) chs. 1–3; Morris 142–3; Cogley 98–103; Massa ch. 5; Fisher (2002) 105–13. Day recounted starting the Catholic Worker movement following prayer at Washington's Shrine of the Immaculate Conception on 8 December, the Feast of the Immaculate Conception. McDonald 102.

31 W.A. Brown, *Church and State in Contemporary America* (NY 1936) 183; Flynn xix-xx; Ahlstrom 925; Reeves 165; Morris 151–2; Greeley (1959) xv; Greeley (1981A) ch. 6; J. Moore 240 and ch. 3.

32 See *Quadragesimo Anno* (15 May 1931) and *Non Abbiamo Bisogno* (29 June 1931), in Carlen 3:415, 445; J. Ryan (1931); Rev. Joseph Reiner, S.J., 'A Program for Catholic Social Action' (St Louis 1935); Halsey; Gleason (1987) ch. 9; McGreevy 150–2; Michael Kazin, *The Populist Persuasion: An American History* (NY 1995) ch. 5; Abell 257; H.S. Hughes 98.

33 See Abell 235; J. Ryan quoted in Horace M. Kallen, *Individualism* (NY 1933) 23–4.

34 J. Ryan (1941) ch. 16; Fogarty (1985) 246–7; George Seldes, *Witch Hunt: The Techniques and Profits of Redbaiting* (NY 1940) 169; D. O'Brien (1972) 121–8; D. O'Brien (1989) 171–4; George Seldes, 'Father Coughlin: Anti-Semite,' *New Republic* 47:353 (2 Nov. 1938); Massa 90; Reeves 6, 107–8; Jeffrey M. Burns, *American Catholics and the Family Crisis 1930–1962* (NY 1988) 5–7.

5 Protestantism Balkanized

1 Hamburger ch. 1, 194–5, 204–5; *Creeds and Platforms of Congregationalism*, ed. Williston Walker (NY 1893) 194, 199–209, 222; Dwight 4:279–83; V.W. Brooks (1915) 8; Brooks, *The Wine of the Puritans* (London 1908) 13–15, 47–9; Atkins/Fagley 82–5.

2 Laski, *The American Democracy* (NY 1948) 266–7; Christopher Lasch, *The True and Only Heaven* (NY 1991) 247–61; Handy (1977) 86–92; Hatch 170–83; R. Niebuhr (1952) 24–6, 71; Mark A. Noll, 'Jonathan Edwards and Nineteenth-Century Theology,' in *Jonathan Edwards and the American Experience*, ed. Nathan O. Hatch and Harry S. Stout (NY 1988) 205, 279–80; Henry F. May, 'Jonathan Edwards and America,' in *id.* 19, 30; James Hoopes, 'Calvinism and Consciousness from Edwards to Beecher,' in *id.* 205, 221–2; Boyd Hilton, *The Age of Atonement* (Oxford 1988) 83.

3 Hatch 3, 195–9; Hein/Shattuck 71; Abbott (1898) 45–7, 68–9; Handy (1977) 192–4, 266–7; Ahlstrom ch. 40; Tocqueville (1960) 197–8; Smith ch. 1.

4 Hatch ch. 2; H.W. Schneider, *Religion in 20th Century America* (Cambridge, MA 1952) 16; Daniel Walker Howe, 'Religion and Politics in the Antebellum North,' in Noll 121, 131–2.

5 Lucy Mack Smith quoted in Hatch 43; *id.* 199; D.H. Meyer 83 (quoting Charles C. Cole, Jr), 92, and chs. 5 and 14.

6 Douglas, *The Feminization of American Culture* (NY 1977) 21–43; Daniel Walker Howe, *The Unitarian Conscience* (Cambridge, MA 1970) 7; Handy (1977) 198–200; R.L. Moore 52; Cogley 46–8; Comm'n of Appraisal to the Am. Unitarian Ass'n, *Unitarians Face a New Age* (Boston 1936) 16.

7 Paul A. Carter, *The Spiritual Crisis of the Gilded Age* (DeKalb, IL 1971) 179–90; Grant Wacker, *Religion in Nineteenth Century America* (NY 2000) 63–5; Marsden (1980) 109–110; Washington Gladden, *Social Facts and Forces* (1897), excerpted in *The Church and the City, 1865–1910*, ed. Robert D. Cross (Indianapolis 1967) 40, 46–7.

8 Jefferson (11 April 1823); Sidney Warren, *American Freethought, 1860–1914* (NY 1943) 70–4; Herbst 92; Royce, *The Problem of Christianity* (NY 1913) 2:9.

9 See Ahlstrom ch. 46. The translation of Albert Schweitzer's *The Quest of the Historical Jesus* proved a useful aid to the anglophone world. Trans. W. Montgomery and F.C. Burkitt (London 1910).

10 *De Fide Catholica* (24 April 1870), ch. 4 ¶¶ 12–14, www.ewtn.com/library/COUNCILS/V1.HTM#4; Fogarty (1989A) chs. 4–8; Charles A. Briggs and Friedrich von Hügel, *The Papal Commission and the Pentateuch* (London 1906); Sean Kopcynski, 'Rediscovering the Decrees of the Pontifical Biblical Commission,' in *Living Tradition: Organ of the Roman Theological Forum*, no. 94 (July 2001), www.rtforum.org/lt/lt94.html; Hans Rollman, 'Baron Friedrich von Hügel and the Conveyance of German Protestant Biblical Criticism in Roman Catholic Modernism,' in Reventlow/Farmer 197, 203.

11 See Meier 2:525n6; 2:633nn5, 6; Acts 2:22, 14:3 (δύναμις, τέρας); Acts 14:3 (σημεῖον); John 5:20, 36; 10:32 (ἔργον). Regarding miracles in the New Testament, see Meier 2:507–1038 and the authorities cited in *id.* 2:522–4n4.

12 C. Brown 3–12; Meier 2:665–6n18; Darrow 109–11; Neander, *The Life of Jesus Christ* (1837; 4th ed. 1847), trans. John M'Clintock and Charles Blumenthal (London 1851) 146.

13 Goodenough 26–7; Crapanzano 37; Hall 1:vii, xiii, 198, 2:592–676; Orr 4–8.

14 Eliot excerpted in Smith/Handy/Loetscher 2:233, 235; G. Gordon ix, xlvi, 29–30, 84–5, 118–41. See also Rom. 7:18, 13:11–14; 1 Cor. 6, 7; Lears 185; Meier 2:632n2; Prothero 23–6; Palmer (1954) 529; Orr 17; J.W. Buckham, *Progressive Religious Thought in America* (Boston 1919) ch. 3; Smith 95–6; Atkins (1932) 29–32; Sheen (1952) 54–6.

15 'Miracles' [review of Paul Schanz, *A Christian Apology*], *Am Eccles. Rev.* 6/ 1:48, 49–50 (Jan. 1892).

16 Cauthen 19; Goodenough 12–15; Prothero 93–4; Hatch 215; Noll (2002) ch. 5.

17 See Smith/Handy/Loetscher 2:67–8; Darrow 7, 51.

18 William Adams Brown, *The Church in America* (NY 1922) 99, 249–57, and ch. 13; Cauthen ch. 3; John M. Murrin, 'Religion and Politics in America from the First Settlements to the Civil War,' in Noll (1990) 19, 26; Garrison (1933) chs. 12 and 14; Sperry 232 and ch. 12; Edgar Young Mulllins, *Baptists Beliefs* (1912; 4th ed. Philadelphia 1925) 8–10; R.M. Miller 157; Marty (1991) 164–76; Handy (1977) 210–13, 383; Bruce Barton, *What Can a Man Believe?* (Indianapolis 1927) 182–6, 215–17.

19 Crapanzano 47; H.R. Niebuhr (1937) xiii–xiv, 2–3; R.A. Schneider, 'Voice of Many Waters: Church Federation in the Twentieth Century,' in Hutchison (1989) 95, 102–10; Handy (1977) 305–6; Hein/Shattuck 111–12; Ahlstrom 897–8; Robert Lee, *The Social Sources of Church Unity* (NY 1960) 28–30; Handy, 'Protestant Theological Tensions and Political Styles in the Progressive Period' (1990), in Noll 281, 286–7; Handy (1953) 15; Handy (1977) 193–4.

20 Prothero chs. 2 and 3; H.J. Ford 90, 91; Gleason (1979) 193–4; Lundén 31, 57; Hein/Shattuck 116; Putney 123–4; Roy Wood Sellers, *Religion Coming of Age* (NY 1928) 93; Luke 7:36–50; Maltby (1990); Prothero 98–109; Joel A. Carpenter, 'From Fundamentalism to the New Evangelical Coalition,' in *Evangelicalism and Modern America*, ed. George Marsden (Grand Rapids, MI 1984) 3, 6.

21 Gaustad, 'The Pulpit and the Pews,' in Hutchison (1989) 21, 30; Sperry 10.

22 R.M. Miller 119–23, and chs. 5–7, 9–10; D.G. Hart, *Defending the Faith: J. Gresham Machen and the Crisis of Conservative Protestantism in America* (Baltimore 1996).

23 R. Niebuhr (1935) 4. Writing in 1940, Halford Luccock observed that there was new talk about a God of Judgment, something that would have been unthinkable in the years just prior to the Depression. Luccock (1971) 241. See also Ahlstrom 947; Bernard M. Loomer, 'Neo-Naturalism and Neo-Orthodoxy,' *J. of Rel.* 27/2:79, 88–90 (April 1948); Deane William Ferm, 'American Protestant Theology, 1900–1970,' in *Protestantism*, ed. Hugh T. Kerr (Woodbury, NY 1979) 134, 140–4.

24 Luccock (1936) 179, 186; R.M. Miller 3–4; Kathleen N. Nyberg, *The New Eve* (Nashville 1967) 43.

25 Felix Frankfurter, 'Mr. Justice Holmes' (1944), in Frankfurter (1956) 158, 159; Harvey Wickham, *The Impuritans* (NY 1929) 21, 33.

26 (NY 1944) 59. The era also saw the beginning of the Puritans' rehabilita-

tion. Kenneth B. Murdock, *Increase Mather* (Cambridge, MA 1925); Perry Miller, *The New England Mind* (NY 1939); Edmund S. Morgan, 'The Puritans and Sex,' *New Eng. Quart.* 15/4:591 (Dec. 1942); Morgan, *The Puritan Family* (1942–3; 2d rev. ed. NY 1966) 64; Henry F. May, 'The Recovery of American Religious History' (1964), in *Ideas, Faiths, and Feelings* (NY 1983) 65, 72–3.

27 G.C. Homans, *The Human Group* (NY 1950) 352; Jaroslav Pelikan, 'Foreword' to Cauthen vii-viii; H.R. Niebuhr (1929) 25; Weigel 52–67; B.M. Loomer, 'Neo-Naturalism and Neo-Orthodoxy,' *J. Rel.* 27:85–91 (1948).

28 Dewey, *A Common Faith* (New Haven 1934) 9; Aubrey, *Religion and the Next Generation* (NY 1931) 170–7.

29 Handy (1960) 14; Noll 432–3. Even as he spoke, Protestant ecumenism was underway, only to be delayed by the war. The World Council of Churches was not formed until 1948.

30 M. Williams (1934) 2; A.C. McGiffert, *Christianity as History and Faith,* ed. A.C. McGiffert, Jr (NY 1934) 43; Merton 6, 211–12; Massa ch. 2; Fisher (1989) 213–15.

31 Fogarty (1985) 204–6; James M. O'Toole, 'Prelates and Politicos: Catholics and Politics in Massachusetts, 1900–1970,' in Sullivan/O'Toole 15, 16, 24; O'Toole (1989) 178; Robert Trisco, 'Bishops and Their Priests in the United States,' in Ellis (1971).

6 Reining In Hollywood

1 *Moving Picture World* (8 Oct. 1921) 626; Inglis (1947) 83–4; *Survey* 46/8:231 (21 May 1921); Wertheimer 188–9n169.

2 Joseph Cook, 'Introduction' to *Practical Christian Sociology,* by Crafts, 4th ed. (NY 1907) 9; *Moving Picture World* (1 April 1916) 57; International Reform Federation, *History of the International Reform Bureau, 1895–1911* (Washington, DC 1910); S. Carr 68–9; *NYT* (15 March 1921) 11/1.

3 *NYT* (3 Jan. 1922) 32/1; Edward G. Lowry, *Washington Close-Ups* (Boston 1921); *The Masses, Inc. v. United States,* 244 Fed. 535 (S.D.N.Y.) (Hand, D.J.), rev'd, 246 Fed. 24 (2d Cir. 1917), on remand, 252 Fed. 232 (S.D.N.Y. 1918); Stone 146–70; D. Johnson 47.

4 NYPL/Linc. Ctr. MFL n.c. 1, 5; *Boston Sunday Globe* (9 April 1922) 8/1.

5 See *Federal Trade Comm'n v. Paramount Famous-Lasky Corp.,* 57 F.2d 152 (2d Cir. 1932).

6 Lorentz, 'Moral Racketeering in the Movies,' *Scribner's* 88/3:256 (Sept. 1930); Krock 21; clipping ca. March 1931, NYPL/Linc. MWEZ + n.c. 6791. See also Adolph Zukor, *The Public Is Never Wrong* (NY 1953) 205; Redman (1938A) 71; Fritz Lang, 'Freedom of the Screen' (1947), in Koszarski 135, 140.

7 Adler 192–4. See also Allene Talmey, *Doug and Mary and Others* (NY 1927) 10.

8 Israel 203; Charles A. Beard and Mary R. Beard, *America in Midpassage* (NY 1939) 2:608; Albert Shaw, 'Will Hays: A Ten-Year Record,' *Rev. of Revs.* (March 1932) 30; Krock 21, 22.

9 Jowett (1976) 178; Joseph Levenson, 'Censorship of the Movies' (1923), in Rutland 81, 86; Alison Parker, 'Mothering the Movies,' in Couvares 73.

10 Federal Council of Churches of Christ in America, Dep't of Research and Education, *The Public Relations of the Motion Picture Industry* (1931) ch. 9 and 113–14, 148–9; Ruth Vasey, 'Beyond Sex and Violence: "Industry Policy" and the Regulation of Hollywood Movies, 1922–1939'(1995), in Bernstein (1999); Jacobs (1989); Jowett (1976) 176; Eastman 52. Mrs Winter subsequently became the public-relations person for the Association of Motion Picture Producers, Inc., headed by Louis B. Mayer.

11 Garrison (1933) 69; William Warren Sweet, *Methodism in American History* (NY 1933) 325; Susan Curtis, *A Consuming Faith: The Social Gospel and Modern American Culture* (Baltimore 1991) 36–8. Out of these interdenominational discussions in 1925 came the Federal Motion Picture Council in America, first headed by Charles Scanlon, general director of the Presbyterian Church's Department of Moral Welfare.

12 'Is the Federal Council Retained?' *Churchman* 141/1:8 (4 Jan. 1930); 'The Federal Council of Churches WAS Retained,' *Churchman* 141/14:8 (5 April 1930); Brooklyn *Eagle* (23 Dec. 1933). See also Maltby (1990).

13 Federal Motion Picture Council in America, Inc., *Broken Promises of the Motion Picture Industry* (Brooklyn [ca. 1928]); Gilman; Seabury (1926) 158–70, 181–93, 290; Seabury, *Motion Picture Problems: The Cinema and the League of Nations* (NY 1929) 184; U.S. Cong. Sen. Motion Picture Films: Hearing before the Committee on Interstate Commerce on S. 1667, 70th Cong. 1st Sess. (2 March 1928) 247; Albert F. McLean, Jr, *American Vaudeville as Ritual* (Louisville 1965) 73.

14 *Churchman* 140/14:14 (5 Oct. 1929); Welford Beaton, 'Will H. Hays Is Done,' *id.* 11; Shipler, 'The Camouflagers,' *id.* 140/2:8 (13 July 1929); 'The Movie Masqueraders,' *id.* 140/12:14 (21 Sept. 1929).

15 See *American Mercury, Inc. v. Chase*, 13 F.2d 224 (D. Mass 1926); Arthur Garfield Hays, *Let Freedom Ring* (NY 1928) 160–85.

16 Lynd/Lynd 332, 348; McCabe (1927) 5; Stewart, 'Deflating the Movies,' *Christian Century* 47:987, 988 (13 Aug. 1930); *Cong. Rec.* 71:4463 (11 Oct. 1929); *New Haven* [CT] *Journal-Courier-Times* (6 Nov. 1933).

17 Herbert F. Sherwood, 'Democracy and the Movies,' *Bookman* 47/3:235 (May 1918) 237; *Moving Picture World* (8 Oct. 1921) 626; 'Censorship of Motion Pictures,' *Yale L.J.* 49:87, 91–2 (1939).

18 Wirt 163–5, 237; Cleveland Recreation Survey, *Commercial Recreation* (Cleveland 1920) 37. Between the inception of Ohio's law in April 1913 and November 1919, Ohio made cuts in 27 per cent of the films submitted, banning another 5 per cent outright.

19 McCabe (1926) 25–6; William H. Short, *A Generation of Motion Pictures: A Review of Social Values in Recreational Films* (NY 1928) 67; *Moving Picture World* (4 Dec. 1920) 597; 'State Censorship of Motion Pictures Opposed by New York State Conference of Mayors and Other City Officials,' undated sheet, MFL + nc 2125, NYPL/Lincoln Ctr.; Ernst/Lorentz 82–4. Kansas and Ohio both deleted any scene showing a woman smoking, thus enforcing a widely acknowledged cultural prohibition even well after it had been abandoned by Jazz Age flappers. Pennsylvania did not *per se* outlaw scenes of women smoking, but only 'when women are shown in suggestive positions or their manner of smoking is suggestive or degrading.' Oberholtzer 215; Henry MacMahon, 'Big Shears – or Common Sense?' *Independent* 105:662, 680 (25 June 1921); Nathan, *Art of the Night* (NY 1928) 106–7; Nathan, *Passing Judgments* (NY 1935) 199.

20 Inglis (1947) 112; Francis G. Couvares, 'Hollywood, Main Street, and the Church,' in Couvares 129; Richard Maltby, '"To Prevent the Prevalent Type of Book"' (1992), in *id.* 77, 97, 105; *United States v. Paramount Famous Lasky Corp.*, 34 F.2d 984, 986–7 (S.D.N.Y. 1929), *aff'd*, 282 U.S. 30 (1930); Vieira 214; Jowett (1976) 238; Douglas Fairbanks, Jr, *The Salad Days* (NY 1988) 129; Doherty (2007) 35–7; Edwin E. Hullinger, 'Free Speech for Talkies?' *North Amer. Rev.* 227/6:737 (June 1929) 740.

21 Douglas Gomery, 'The Coming of Sound,' in Balio (1985) 229.

22 *Summa Theologiae* [1267–73] vol. 25 Sin Ia2ae Q. 77,5, trans. John Fearon (London 1969) 170–3.

23 Pernicone 54–60; http://users.pandora.be/leopold.winckelmans/bull/sollicit.htm.

24 Putnam 2:67, 194; Henri de Courcy, *The Catholic Church in the United States*, trans. John Gilmary Shea (NY 1856) 227–36; Dolan (1985) 167–72; Pernicone 49, and chs. 2 and 7.

25 ¶ 15, www.papalencylcicals.net/Greg16/g16mirar.htm; Hamburger 231–4; Hales 45–9.

26 Leo XIII, *Officiorum ac munerum* (25 Jan. 1897); Pius X, *Dilecta in Christo Filia* (1904), in Eliza Lummis, *Daughters of the Faith* (NY 1905) xvii-xxi; McCann 20.

27 See Bachofen (1921) 6:428–9, 431n7, 454, 460, 467, 475 (italics in original); Pernicone 181–7; Stanislaus Woywod, *A Practical Commentary on the Code of Canon Law* (NY 1926) 2:129–30; Leo XIII, *Officiorum ac munerum* (25 Jan. 1897) ch. 6 ¶ 15.

28 Canon 1399(9); Bachofen (1921) 6:467, 474; *Canon Law Digest*, ed. T. Lincoln Bouscaren (Milwaukee 1934) 687–9; Pernicone 166–74; M. Williams (1934) 105–12.

29 Pernicone 3, 21,167–8; *Index of Prohibited Books* viii–ix.

30 *Divini illius magistri* (31 Dec. 1929) ¶ 90. Gerald Kelly, S.J., writing for Father Daniel Lord's Jesuit publishing house, argued that since the law of God barring adultery and sexual stimulation is attainable by reason, that is, by considering the relevant organs and the purpose for which God made them, Church teachers saw no reason to confine its moral teachings regarding such matters to Catholics. Gerald Kelly, *Modern Youth and Chastity* (St Louis 1945) 64–73; Gladden 388–9.

31 See *The Drive for Decency in Print*, vol. 2 (Huntington, IN 1940); NODL *Newsletter* (March 1957); James Rorty, 'The Harassed Pocket-Book Publishers,' *Antioch Rev.* 15:411 (1956); William J. Hempel and Patrick M. Wall, 'Extralegal Censorship of Literature,' *N.Y.U. L. Rev.* 33:989, 994–8, and App. I (1958); James E. Harpster, 'Obscene Literature,' *Marq. L. Rev.* 34:301, 302 (1951); Cadegan.

32 *NYT* (15 Dec. 1898) 5/3; Musser 208–21; Musser, 'Passions and the Passion Play,' in Couvares 43; Musser, 'The Passion Play of Oberammergau (Select Scenes),' in *Before Hollywood: Turn-of-the-Century American Film* (NY 1987) 51; Brooks McNamara, 'Scene Design and the Early Film,' in *id.* 92; Terry Ramsaye, *A Million and One Nights: A History of the Motion Picture* (NY 1926) ch. 33.

33 G.B. Donnelly, 'An Open Letter to Dr Wingate,' *America* 48/1:84, 85 (29 Oct. 1932); Schmiedeler, *An Introductory Study of the Family* (NY 1930) 168–9; M. Williams (1928) ch. 6; AP wire (24 April 1927); Gibbs reprinted in U.S. Cong. H.R. Federal Motion Picture Comm'n: Hearing before the Committee on Interstate and Foreign Commerce on H.R. 6097, 73d Cong. 2d Sess. (19 March 1934) 44, and in W.S. Chase, *The Case for the Federal Supervision of Motion Pictures* (Washington 1927) 11.

34 Garesché (1927) 472; Slattery, 'The Catholic Woman in Modern Times,' *Catholic Mind* 28:124 (22 March 1930), reprinted in Ruether/Keller 3:187. In February 1934, Mrs Slattery would be among those calling for a Catholic boycott of films. WHP 10:1155.

7 The Production Code

1 Kantowicz (1983) 5–8, 72–83; Kantowicz (1989) 205; Hennesey (1990) 313.

2 Kantowicz (1989) 38, 46; Kantowicz, 'Foreword' to *This Confident Church*, by Steven M. Avella (Notre Dame 1992) x; Lord memo [1954], 'Movie Prod. Code Found with Sodality Papers,' DALP; Lord (1956) 296–7; Heins

n32; Halsey, Stuart and Co., 'The Motion Picture Industry as a Basis for Bond Financing,' in Balio (1985) 195. Stuart later helped engineer the famous ouster of William Fox.

3 Vaughn (1990) 57–9; Kantowicz (1983) 208–9; C.H. Metzger/Lord, 3 Nov. 1941, 'Movie Prod. Code – Re-writing the Code 1941–54–56,' DALP.

4 Lord (1956) 287; Dinneen/'Martin' [Quigley], 24 July 1930, WPP 10.16; Dinneen/Parsons, 2 Jan. 1932, WPP 10.18; Quigley/Breen, 5 June 1930 and 21 Feb. 1938, MQP 1.3; Black (1991) 100; Doherty (2007) 19–40; Kenneth Anger, *Hollywood Babylon* (San Francisco 1975) 18. Dinneen had influence with two of the five Catholics on Chicago's six-member censorship board. Anon. memo to J.J. McCarthy, 14 Aug. 1934, WHP 11:646.

5 Quigley to editor of the *Brooklyn Tablet*, 1 Sept. 1936, 'Movie Prod. Code Quigley, Martin to Lord 1932 1949,' DALP; Lord (1956) 301; Walsh (1996) ch. 3; Lord to [probably] Charles Cloud, 17 Feb. 1930, 'Movie Prod. Code 1929–1956,' DALP; Janes ii, 4–5.

6 See 'Movie Prod. Code 1929–1930,' 'Movie Prod. Code Quigley, Martin to Lord 1927–1932,' and 'Movie Prod. Code 1929–1956' files, DALP.

7 Father Lord would author some 350 pamphlets, his combined total circulation of 25 million copies making him a best-selling author, what Alfred Barrett would call 'God's super-salesman.' Among Father Lord's hymns were 'Mother Beloved' and 'For Christ the King,' the latter chosen as the anthem of Seton Hall University. Parsons/Arthur D. Maguire, 14 June 1934, WPP 10.17; Lord (1956) 277–85; Black (1989) 170–2; Black (1994) 37–8; Maltby (1995A) 16–17.

8 Lord, *My Mother: The Study of an Uneventful Life* (St Louis 1934) 148; Gleason (1995) 152; 'The Film Evangel' (1930), in Potamkin 158, 159.

9 Arthur Knight, *The Liveliest Art* (NY 1957) 118; Ruth Schwartz Cowan, 'Two Washes in the Morning and a Bridge Party at Night,' in *Our American Sisters*, 4th ed. (Lexington, MA 1987) 447, 459–60; Vieira 17; Maltby (1995A) 33; Black (1998) App. The Boston *Post* (1 Jan. 1934) quoted popular writer Walter P. Eaton: 'I don't believe the movies ever had any influence on my morals or anyone else's.'

10 Krows, 'Literature and the Motion Picture,' *AAAP&SS* 128:70 (Nov. 1926); Bates, 'We Americans,' in *Our Neurotic Age*, ed. Samuel D. Schmalhausen (NY 1932) 434, 439; Pitkin, 'The Crisis in the Movies,' *Parents' Mag.* 5/2:11 (Feb. 1930); Barrows, 'Motion Pictures: Success through Self-Regulation,' *Rev. of Revs.* 85/3:32, 35 (March 1932); Pettijohn, 16 May 1934, WHP 11:636.

11 Gordon/Gordon 82; Wilk 3; *Upton Sinclair Presents William Fox* (Los Angeles 1933) 15–17.

12 Kevin Starr, *Inventing the Dream: California through the Progressive Era* (NY 1985) 315; Griffith, *The Man Who Invented Hollywood*, ed. James Hart (Louisville, KY 1972) 88; Jim Tully (attributed), 'Erich von Stroheim,' *Vanity Fair* 26/1:50 (March 1926); Johnston 13, 15, 34, 38.

13 Quigley to *Brooklyn Tablet*, 1 Sept. 1936, 'Movie Prod. Code Quigley, Martin to Lord 1932–1949,' DALP; C.H. Metzger/Lord, 3 Nov. 1941, 'Movie Prod. Code – Re-writing the Code 1941–54–56,' DALP; Vaughn (1990); 'Statement of Cardinal Mundelein Re Motion Picture Code,' Dinneen/Quigley, WPP 10.16. Cf. Black (1991) 128n55.

14 Conflicting accounts of the respective contributions of Lord and Quigley are gleaned from Parsons/Lord, 15 March 1930, WPP 10.16; WHP 11:247; Hays/Lord, 4 March 1930, Lord/Breen 29 June 1954, 'Movie Prod. Code 1929–1956,' Lord/Breen, 12 Sept. 1945, 'Breen, Joseph, MPC 1933–1954,' 'Movie Prod. Code 1929–1930,' DALP; NY Pub. Lib. * C p.v. 369.r.

15 Lord wittily told Quigley that Hays's praising him to Mundelein 'isn't going to get me a Cardinal's hat.' 30 April 1931, 'Movie Prod. Code Quigley, Martin – Corresp Various 1927–1932,' DALP.

16 Moley Apps. E and F; Ernst/Lindey App. C; Vieira 17–18, 214; U.S. Cong. H.R. Investigation of Communist Propaganda, Hearings on H. Res. 220 before a Special Committee to Investigate Communist Activities, 71st Cong. 2d Sess., Pt. 5 vol. 3 (8 Oct. 1930) 279–81; H. Lewis 385–8; Jowett (1976) 241; *Movies and Mass Culture*, ed. John Belton (New Brunswick, NJ 1996) 138. A variant version is in Martin and in Doherty (1999) App. 1.

17 'Movie Prod. Code 1929–1930' file; Lord to [probably] Charles Cloud, S.J., 17 Feb. 1930, 'Movie Prod. Code Quigley, Martin – Corresp Various 1927–1932,' DALP.

18 Moley App. F 244–7; Terry Ramsaye, 'What the Production Code Really Says,' *Motion Picture Herald* (11 Aug. 1934).

19 Quigley 9–15. See also Leo H. Lehmann, 'The Catholic Church in Politics II: Censorship by the Church,' *New Republic* 47:64 (9 Nov. 1938); Messbarger (1985) 155.

20 Farrell, *Literature and Morality* (NY 1947) 92–4; *NYT* (13 July 1934) 1/1.

21 *The Motion Picture in a Changing World* (NY 1940) 15, 17, 28; Richard Koszarski, *An Evening's Entertainment: The Age of the Silent Picture, 1915–1923* (Berkeley 1990) 208–10.

22 W. Parsons (1930); W. Parsons (1931). Lord told the *Hollywood Reporter* (8 Nov. 1946): 'No move of any kind toward a Code was made by the Catholic Church ... This Code was not to be an expression of the Catholic point of view ... The Catholic Church was not "back of me."'

23 Parsons/Lord, 15 March 1930, WPP 10.16; Maltby (1995A); Maltby (1995B)

46–52; Inglis (1947) 116–17; Quigley 51; Hays 439–40; Lord/ECMP, 'Dinneen, Fr. George S.J. Corresp., etc. 1934,' DALP.

24   WHP 11:249; Moley 74; *NYT* (15 May 1938) § 10:4/1; Hays 446; J. Mankiewicz in Hodgins (1949B); Maltby (1995B) 52.

25   Moley 64–5; Jacobs (1991) 27–9; Joy/William LeBaron, 29 June 1931; Beetson/LeBaron, 12 Oct. 1931; Joy/Trotti, 28 Oct. 1931; Trotti/Joy, 28 Oct. 1931; Maurice McKenzie/J.V. Wilson, 5 Nov. 1931; *Are These Our Children?* PCA; Ruth Vasey, *The World According to Hollywood, 1918–1939* (Madison, WI 1997) 114.

26   Vieira 27; Lotti/Thalberg, 27 April and 16 May 1932, Richardson/ Milliken, 22 [June] 1932, Milliken/ Joy, 11 July 1932, Joy/Milliken, 7 July 1932, Zanuck/Joy, 17 Aug. 1932, *Red-Headed Woman*, PCA; Charles Higham, *Merchant of Dreams: Louis B. Mayer* (NY 1993) 113; Jacobs (1991).

27   Howard T. Lewis, 'Motion Pictures,' in *Encyclopaedia of the Social Sciences* 11:58, 61 (1933); Doherty (2007) 49;Pizzitola 330; J.P. McEvoy, 'The Back of Me Hand to You,' *Sat. Evening Post* 211:8, 47–8 (24 Dec. 1938).

28   Breen/Quigley, 1 May 1932, MQP 1.3; Vizzard 36; Breen/Parsons, in Leff 444n3; Koppes 265; Morris 203; Doherty (2007) 55, 198–203; Buhle/ Wagner (2002) 12; S. Carr 128–31; *Am. Eccles. Rev.* 90:136 (Feb. 1934) 142–3. Fox was, in fact, Jewish, born Wilhelm Fried in Hungary.

29   Dinneen/Parsons, Jan. 1932, WPP 10.8; Lord (1934) 36–7; Lord (1956) 309; Montavon 253; Lord/Breen, 25 Feb. 1933, 'Breen, Joseph, MPC 1933 to 1942,' Lord/Hays, 26 May 1933, 'Quigley, Martin – Corres 1933 to 1934,' DALP.

30   Quigley 32–6; H.J. McCord/Wingate, 19 May 1933, enc. [4], Wingate/ Hays, 16 May 1933, enc. [1], *Baby Face*, PCA; George F. Custen, *Twentieth Century's Fox: Darryl F. Zanuck and the Culture of Hollywood* (NY 1997) 142– 7; Dawn B. Sova, *Forbidden Films: Censorship Histories of 125 Motion Pictures* (NY 2001) 29–33; Vieira 50–62, 148–9; Maltby (1986) 22; Jacobs (1991) 71–2.

31   Schulberg (1941) 66; Wingate/Hays, 2 March 1933, Wingate/ Hays, 20 May 1933, McCord/Wingate, 19 May 1933, enc. p [1], *Baby Face*, PCA; Quigley 32–6; Breen/Wingate, 17 July 1933, Wingate/Howson, 29 Sept. 1933, *Female*, PCA; Lord/Breen, 22 May 1933, 'Breen, Joseph, MPC 1933 to 1942,' DALP.

32   Ramona Curry, *Too Much of a Good Thing: Mae West as Cultural Icon* (Minneapolis 1996) 47; Breen/Johnston, 10 March 1949, MQP 1.4; Vieira 149–51; Jacobs (1989); J.E. Williams, review of Moley, *The Hays Office*, in *Hollywood Quart.* 1:120–1 (1945–6); Lord/Hays, 26 May 1933, WPP 10.18.

33   Dinneen/Parsons, 12 July 1933, WPP 10.18; Giannini 49; Quigley/Breen, 30 March 1934, MQP 1.3; Breen/Johnston, 10 March 1949, MQP 1.4;

Breen/Lord, 21 Aug. 1933, 'Breen, Joseph, MPC 1933–1954,' DALP; Maltby (1995B) 54–60.

34 Cicognani, *Canon Law* (1925; 2d ed. Philadelphia 1935); *NYT* (2 Oct. 1933) 5/7; Parsons/Maguire, 22 June 1934, WPP 10.17; Facey; Richard Corliss, 'The Legion of Decency,' *Film Comment* 14:25 (Summer 1968) 26–7; Cooney 67, 112; Breen/Cicognani, 2 Oct. 1933, MQP 1.3.

35 Cantwell, 'Priests and the Motion Picture Industry,' *Am. Eccles. Rev.* 90:136 (Feb. 1934); *Cath. Educ. Rev.* 32:238 (April 1934); Weber 240–1; Walsh (1996) chs. 4, 5; Vieira 153; Janes 48; K.L. Russell/Hays, 3 Nov. 1933, 13 Nov. 1933, WHP 10:215, 285–6; Cadegan.

36 12 Jan. 1934, 'Breen, Joseph, MPC 1933–1954,' DALP; Beetson/Hays, 15 Feb. 1934, WHP 10:972.

37 U.S. Cong. Sen. Motion Picture Films: Hearing before the Committee on Interstate Commerce on S. 1667, 70th Cong. 1st Sess. (27 Feb. 1928) 65–7 (testimony of Mrs Morey V. Kerns); House Committee on Interstate and Foreign Commerce (19 March 1934) 58; Pettijohn debate w/ Walter B. Littlefield, Worcester Board of Motion Pictures and Theatre Review (27 March 1934), Remarks to Women's Republican Club of Boston (16 May 1934), WHP 11:42, 149–53, 178–80, 634–5; W.W. Marsh in *Cleveland Plain Dealer* (14 Oct. 1933) 18/3; 'Support Good Films,' *The Truth* [Elkhart, IN] (6 Nov. 1933); *Trenton* [NJ] *Sunday Times-Advertiser* (7 Jan. 1934) 6; Couvares 140.

8 The Legion of Decency

1 Breen/Lord, 19 Jan. 1934, 'Breen, Joseph, MPC 1933 to 1942,' DALP; Weber; McNicholas/Dinneen, 3 March 1934, Dinneen/Parsons, 8 March 1934, J.A. Luther/Parsons, 14 June 1934, WPP 10.17; AP wire, 12 March 1934; 'Legion of Decency Pledge,' *Catholic Action* (May 1934), reprinted in *Catholic Mind* 32/15:281 (8 Aug. 1934); *Cath. Educ. Rev.* 32:304 (May 1934); 'The Legion of Decency,' *Commonweal* 20/3:57 (18 May 1934); A.D. Maguire/Parsons, 11 June 1934, WPP 10.17.

2 Forman 158; Jowett/Jarvie/Fuller 2–5, 101–8; Jowett (1976) ch. 9. See also Forman, 'To the Movies – but Not to Sleep!' *McCall's* 59/12:12 (Sept. 1932); 'Movie Madness,' *McCall's* 60/1:14 (Oct. 1932); Forman, 'Molded by the Movies,' *McCall's* 60/2:17 (Nov. 1932). Among social scientists who excoriated Forman's book was sociologist Kimball Young. *Am. J. Sociol.* 41/2:249 (Sept. 1935).

3 'The Screen's Contribution to the Prevention of Crime,' *Proc. Att'y General's Conf. on Crime Held December 10–13, 1934* (Washington, DC [n.d.])

119,121–3; Milliken, 'Proposal for a National Crime Research Institute' (23 Nov. 1933), WHP 10:497, 498; Michael Jerome and Mortimer J. Adler, *Crime, Law and Social Science* (NY 1933) 169.

4 Lord/Hays, 28 May 1934, 'Movie Prod. Code Hays, Will,' DALP; Lord (1934) 3, 7–12, 36, 44, 48.

5 In 'Pastorals and Statements,' *Catholic Mind* 32/15:282, 283 (8 Aug. 1934).

6 Lord/Breen, 29 May 1934, 'Breen, Joseph, MPC 1933 to 1942,' DALP; *NYT* (9 June 1934) 3/2; 'Fair Is Fair,' *Variety* (10 July 1934) 3/1. Dougherty was one of American Catholicism's most powerful leaders, so successful in building schools and churches that he referred to himself as 'God's brick-layer.' Morris ch. 7; Dolan (1985) 350; Dennis Clark, 'The Irish Catholics: A Postponed Perspective,' in Miller/Marzik 48, 60. Like Mundelein and O'Connell, Dougherty did not deprive himself of creature comforts. Reeves 124.

7 *NYT* (19 June 1934) 24/4; *NYT* (20 June 1934) 23/3; WHP 12:2, 145, 163; Janes 50; Vieira 172; McAvoy (1969) 419; Varbero 45–52; Huettig 78–9; Maltby (1983) 101. 'The Legion of Decency is not a private organization. It was organized and is supported by the Hierarchy ... It represents the Hierarchy in one particular limited field of activity namely, to criticize entertainment films solely and exclusively on their moral qualities. To this end, the Legion of Decency operates under policies set up by a Committee of five bishops.' P.J. Masterson/L.M. Boye, 30 April 1951, FSP/sc33/2.

8 *NYT* (3 July 1934) 18/1; *NYT* (6 July 1934) 13/4; Morris 166–7.

9 Maguire/Boyle, 15 June 1934, WPP 10.17; McNicholas (1934); WHP 12:473; R. Whelan 658; Janes 50; Inglis (1947) 122–5; 'How to Judge the Morality of Motion Pictures' (Washington [1939]), National Catholic Office for Motion Pictures clippings file, NYPL/Lincoln Center; *Motion Pictures Classified by National Legion of Decency February, 1936–November, 1950* (NY 1951).

10 Tocqueville (2000) 235–49; F.W. Allport/Hays, 6 July 1934, WHP 12:146–62; *NY Herald Tribune* (24 Aug. 1934); Kantowicz (1983) 210.

11 'The Movies['] Last Chance,' *Christian Century* 51:822 (20 June 1934); Rorty (1934) 125; *NYT* (8 July 1934) 1/4; Israel 200; *NY Herald Tribune* (22 July 1934) § 5:1/6; Sklar 162–5; Howard/Hays, 29 June 1934, WHP 12:20.

12 Olasky 169; Quigley/Lord, 'Breen, Joseph, MPC 1933 to 1942,' DALP; *NY Evening J.* (13 July 1934) 3/1; *St Louis Star-Times* (11 June 1934) 14; *Boston Herald* (15 June 1934) 1/4.

13 Seldes (1939) 216; Janes 20; Lennig 36, 62; *NYT* (18 June 1934); *Cleveland Plain Dealer* (11 June 1934).

14 Adamic, *My America 1928–1938* (NY 1938) 543–5; Seldes (1939) 233.

15 ACLU press release, 16 July 1934, WHP 12:184–8; Allen 159; Cooke 28; Luccock (1971) 44–5; Quigley 9–15.
16 Gilbert Seldes, *The Movies Come from America* (1937; NY 1978) 133.
17 Hays 452–3; Dinneen/Parsons, 8 March 1934, Parsons/J.T. McCormick, 14 June 1934, WPP 10.17; Doherty (2007) 51, 61–3, 180–1.
18 Press releases by Bishops' Committee on Motion Pictures (21 June 1934) and by MPPDA (22 June 1934 and 12 July 1934), WHP 12:47–50, 66, 280; Appendix C to Ernst/Lindey and Appendixes E and F to Moley; Vieira 219; Patricia White, *unInvited: Classical Hollywood Cinema and Lesbian Representability* (Bloomington, IN 1999) 10; LaSalle 193–201; Janes 52–3.

9 The Breen Office

1 Facey 16; Vizzard 46–8; Doherty (2007) 48–9; Black (1991) 128n55.
2 *NYT* (23 Sept. 1934) 32/8; Parsons/Dinneen, 13 March 1934, WPP 10.17; Walsh (1996) chs. 5 and 6; Janes 18–19; G.B. Donnelly, '"Definitely Cleaner" Films,' *America* 53/16:5 (27 July 1935); *NYT* (22 July 1934) § 6:1/1. Breen had earlier written articles in *America* under the pseudonym 'Eugene Weare.' Parsons/Z.J. Maher, 7 Jan. 1932, WPP 10.18.
3 Vizzard 14, 30; Stewart 236; Leff; Dunne (1987) 8.
4 Breen/Atlantic Pictures Corp., 19 April 1935, *Scarface*, PCA; Thorp 206; Black (1991) 106–8; Mast 427, 431; Vieira 196, 211.
5 Breen/Merian Cooper, 8 April and 14 April 1936, Breen/S.J. Briskin, 11 Jan. 1937, *Coquette*, PCA; Robert Ardrey, 'Hollywood's Fall into Virtue,' *The Reporter* 16:13, 16–17 (21 Feb. 1957); Dunne (1987) 10; Korda 161.
6 Breen/S.J. Briskin, 10 Feb. 1937, *Are These Our Children?* PCA; *Self-Regulation in the Motion Picture Industry: Annual Report of the MPPDA* (28 March 1938) 9–10; Redman (1938A) 68, 72; Redman (1938B) 4; Hays 485; J.J. McCarthy, 'Man of Decency,' *Esquire* 4/3:64 (Sept. 1935); Brief of Appellee 15, Superior Films, Inc. v. Ohio Dep't of Educ., 346 U.S. 587 (1954); William C. De Mille, *Hollywood Saga* (NY 1939) 254–5.
7 Vieira 175; Breen/ Warner, 12 Nov. 1940, *The Great Lie*, PCA; Breen/ Warner, 19 Jan. 1938, *Angels with Dirty Faces*, PCA; Breen/J.J. Nolan, 15 July 1940, *Kitty Foyle*, PCA; Breen/Cohen, 4 March 1949, *And Baby Makes Three*, PCA.
8 Breen/William Gordon, 9 March 1944, *None but the Lonely Heart*, PCA; S. Graham 90; Graham/Frank 214–16; Shurlock memo, 10 June 1938, Milliken/N.M. Schenck, 18 Jan. 1938, *Fidelity*, PCA; 'Infidelity: A Screen-play,' *Esquire* 80/6:193 (Dec. 1973); *NYT* (23 June 1939) 15/1; *Good Girls Go*

to Paris, PCA; Raoul de Roussy de Sales, 'Love in America,' *Atlantic* 161/
5:645, 646 (May 1938); Breen/David Selznick, 15 Feb. 1937, *Prisoner of
Zenda*, PCA; Stewart 235–6.

9 Eastman/Ouellette 3; Milliken 4–5; *NYT* (13 Oct. 1934) 15/6; Redman
(1938B); George Bernard Shaw, 'Film Censorship in the United States,'
London Mercury 34:490 (1936); Yeaman; Thorp 208–9.

10 Leff/Simmons 104–5; Doherty (2007) 134–5; Walsh (1996) 149.

11 Ames, 'The Screen Enters Politics,' *Harpers* (March 1935) 473; Martin 5,
53–60; Rorty (1934) 126; Dunne (1987) 8.

12 *Vigilanti Cura*, in Carlen 3:517; Atkin/Tallett 243; 'Movie Prod. Code Papal
Encyclical on Movies,' DALP; Cornwell 176; 'Motion Pictures: Encyclical
Letter of His Holiness, Pope Pius XI' (Washington, DC 1936); 'The Pope
and the Films,' *America* 51/11:242 (23 June 1934); Leff/Simmons 58–9;
Skinner 48; Vaughn (1990); *NY Post* (2 July 1936); Gardiner 92; Weber.

13 Yeaman; Jowett (1990) 17; Weber; National Legion of Decency List, 1/1 (6
Feb. 1936); Skinner 57–8; 'National Catholic Office for Motion Pictures,'
New Cath. Encyc. 10:222 (1967); W.J. Nagle, 'Professor Says Competent
Artistic Criticism of Drama Covers Its Moral Aspects,' *Catholic Messenger*
(5 April 1951) 5; Black (1991) 125.

14 Seldes (1939) 237; 'Is Hollywood on the Spot?' *Liberty* 15:18 (10 Sept. 1938);
Bernstein (1994) 134–7; Kanfer 83–4; Greg M. Smith, 'Blocking *Blockade*,'
Cinema J. 36/1:18 (Fall 1996) 23–4; Roffman/Purdy 205–7; W. Goodman
215; Janes 58; Kempton 195; R. Whelan.

15 McClafferty quoted in Seldes (1939) 233.

10 The *Paramount* Case

1 Bordwell/Staiger/Thompson 401; Ralph Cassady, 'Monopoly in Motion
Picture Production and Distribution,' *S. Cal. L. Rev.* 32:325, 329–50 (1959);
Jeanne Allen, 'Afterword,' in Kindem (1982) 68; Reese V. Jenkins, *Images
and Enterprise* (Baltimore 1975) ch. 13; Balio (1985) 103; Tom Gunning,
D.W. Griffith and the Origins of American Narrative Film (Urbana, IL 1991)
61–5; Bertrand; Izod 18.

2 Bordwell 402; Seabury 12–102; *United States v. Motion Picture Patents Co.*,
225 Fed. 800, 811 (E.D. Pa. 1915); *Film Hist.* 1/3:187 (1987) (Gov't brief);
Motion Picture Patents Co. v. Ullman, 186 Fed. 174 (Cir. S.D.N.Y. 1910);
Motion Picture Patents Co. v. Laemmle, 178 Fed. 104 (Cir. S.D.N.Y. 1910);
Conant 20; Izod ch. 4; Jeanne Allen, 'The Decay of the Motion Picture
Patents Company,' in Balio (1976) 119; Robert Anderson, 'The Motion
Picture Patents Company' (1983), in Balio (1985) 133, 152; W. Hamilton 39.

3 Brief for Petitioner [FTC] 7, Order Directing a Revision and Condensation of the Evidence 7, *Federal Trade Comm'n v. Paramount Famous-Lasky Corp.*, 57 F.2d 152 (2d Cir. 1932); Huettig 116–31; Moley 194; U.S. Cong. Sen. Motion Picture Films: Hearing before the Committee on Interstate Commerce on S. 1667, 70th Cong. 1st Sess. (27 Feb.–2 March 1928); John Eugene Harley, *World-Wide Influences of the Cinema*, U.S.C. Cin. Ser. no. 2 (Los Angeles 1940) 58–60, 303; Hawley 365–7; *Ivan Film Prods. v. Bell*, 167 N.Y.S. 123 (Sp. T. N.Y. Co. 1916); Pizzitola 119–20, 254–6.

4 Bordwell/Staiger/Thompson 401–3; Richard Maltby, 'The Political Economy of Hollywood,' in *Cinema, Politics and Society in America*, ed. Philip Davies and Brian Neve (NY 1981) 42; 334 U.S. 131nn9, 18.

5 Donald Slesinger, 'The Film and Public Opinion,' in *Print, Radio, and Film in a Democracy*, ed. Douglas Waples (Chicago 1942) 79, 83; 'Decent Films and Block-Booking,' *St Louis Star-Times* (11 June 1934) 14.

6 U.S. Cong. H.R., Motion-Picture Films, Hearing before the Committee on Interstate and Foreign Commerce on S. 280, 76th Cong. 3d Sess. (13–21 May, 3–4 June 1940); WHP 11:791; Doherty (2007) 61–3; Sklar 169–71. Although Art. V/F/6 of the NRA rule allowed exhibitors to reject only 10 per cent of any block, it provoked little acrimony. Reproduced in Louis Nizer, *New Courts of Industry* (NY 1935) 290–1.

7 Randall (1968) 200; McDonough/Winslow 386–90; Bertrand 9–14; Huettig 78–9; Schatz 16; *Interstate Circuit, Inc. v. United States*, 306 U.S. 208 (1939); 'Restraint of Trade,' *U. Va. L. Rev.* 25:736 (1939); 'Trade Regulation,' *U. Pa. L. Rev.* 87:750 (1939); 'Monopolies,' *Minn. L. Rev.* 23:689 (1939); 'Legislation by Consent in the Motion Picture Industry,' *Yale L.J.* 50:854 (1941); *Motion Picture Herald* (8 June 1940) 12; Robert A. Brady, 'The Problem of Monopoly,' *AAAP&SS* 254:126 (Nov. 1947); *NYT* (4 June 1939) 17 col. 1; Littlefield/Pettijohn debate, 27 March 1934, WHP 11:160–1.

8 Arnold, *The Folklore of Capitalism* (New Haven 1937). Arnold hired dozens of lawyers for the Division and more than tripled the number of complaints filed, his five years in office accounting for 44 per cent of all antitrust litigations brought in the fifty-three years since the Sherman Anti-trust Act had been enacted. See Report of Ass't Att'y Gen. in Charge of Antitrust Div. [Wash., DC 1939] 6; 'Antitrust Law Enforcement, Past and Future,' *L. and Contemp. Prob.* 7:5, 12 (1940); Arnold (1940) 170–3; Arnold (1977) 276, 292–3, 341; Hofstadter (1965) 194; Edwards 339.

9 In 1936, independent producer Harry Webb complained to a Justice Department official that the major studios, by forcing the independents to get pre-approval from the PCA, were dictating the content of their competitors' films. In June 1940, independent producer Phil Goldstone

complained to the same official that Breen refused a seal to Goldstone's 1937 remake of Eugène Brieux's *Damaged Goods* (1914) because it dealt with syphilis, but then granted a seal to Warner Brothers' *Dr Ehrlich's Magic Bullet* (dir. William Dieterle, 1940). Two months later, J. Edgar Hoover forwarded to Arnold information indicating that a disaffected ex-PCA employee would be willing to testify that Breen aggressively used the Code to ban or eviscerate an Australian film, Charles Chauvel's *Uncivilised* (1936), while granting seals to studio films containing similar material, and that Breen's office planted news items to dissuade Code-regulated theatres from carrying Chauvel's film. Collins/Webb (11 Aug. 1936); Collins/Goldstone (15 June 1940), Hoover/Arnold (27 Aug. 1940), file 60-6-30-5 § 8, USBB. See also Leff 433–4, 443; Giuliana Muscio, *Hollywood's New Deal* (Philadelphia 1997) 144–58; Schatz 15, 160–4; Roffman/Purdy 1–9.

10 *United States v. Paramount Pictures, Inc.*, 66 F. Supp. 323, 331–3 (S.D.N.Y. 1946), *modified*, 70 F. Supp. 53 (S.D.N.Y. 1947); Bertrand 59–62, 73–85; Schatz 19–21; Izod 120–1.

11 *United States v. Associated Press*, 52 F. Supp. 362, 366 (S.D.N.Y. 1944), *aff'd*, 326 U.S. 1 (1945); Brief of Gov't 32–4, 59, Brief of AP 53, *Associated Press v. United States*, 326 U.S. 1 (1945).

12 Spencer Waller, 'The Antitrust Legacy of Thurman Arnold' 38n126, www.luc.edu/law/academics/special/center/antitrust/arnold_rev.pdf; Arnold (1977) 450–51. Cf. Oswald Garrison Villard, *The Disappearing Daily* (NY 1944) 68.

13 *United States v. Associated Press*, 52 F. Supp. 362 (S.D.N.Y. 1944), *aff'd*, 326 U.S. 1 (1945).

14 [1868] L.R. 3 Q.B. 360, 371. See Norman St John-Stevas, *Obscenity and the Law* (London 1956) 126–9.

15 See Nancy Lusignan Schultz, 'Introduction,' in *Veil of Fear: Nineteenth-Century Convent Tales*, by Rebecca Reed et al. (West Lafayette, IN 1999) vii. Lyman Beecher wrote that pauper immigrants will vote as dictated by their priests, 'who at the confessional learn all the private concerns of their people, and have almost unlimited power over the conscience as it respects the performance of every civil or social duty.' *Plea for the West*, 2d ed. (Cincinnati 1835) 54–60. Anti-Catholicism, Richard Hofstadter observed, 'has always been the pornography of the Puritan.' Hofstadter (1965) 21.

16 Op. no. 1411 of R.P. Goodwin, 18 May 1906, *Official Opinions of the Ass't Attorneys-General for the Post-Office Dep't* (Washington, DC 1909) 4:161–2.

17 *United States v. Kennerley*, 209 Fed. 119 (S.D.N.Y. 1913); Frankfurter, 'Judge Learned Hand' (1947), in Frankfurter (1956) 213, 214; Frankfurter (1965); Ernst 316, 324.

18 249 U.S. 47, 51–2 (1919). See also *Dennis v. United States*, 341 U.S. 494, 503,

509–10 (1951); Stone 192–210, 395–411; Murphy 249–51; R. Carr (1952) 8–10; Frankfurter, *Mr. Justice Holmes and the Supreme Court* (Cambridge, MA 1938) 60–2.

19 *Gitlow v. NY*, 268 U.S. 652 (1925); Murphy ch. 13; Warren 432–3, 455–8; Morrison 169–70; Fairman; Pfeffer 142–5; Hamburger 447–8n137; *Stromberg v. California*, 283 U.S. 359, 369 (1931).

20 5 F. Supp. 183 (S.D.N.Y. 1933), *aff'd*, 72 F.2d 705 (2d Cir. 1934); 'Too Busy Snooping' (15 March 1934), reprinted in Moscato/LeBlanc 13.

21 *Near v. Minnesota*, 283 U.S. 697, 716 (1931); Paul Vanderham, *James Joyce and Censorship: The Trials of 'Ulysses'* (NY 1998) 147–52.

22 Grosjean, 297 U.S. 233, 248–50 (1936). See also *Near v. Minnesota*, 283 U.S. 697, 716–17 (1931); Bridges v. California, 314 U.S. 252, 264 (1941) (Black, J. *quoting* Schofield [1914]).

23 *Lovell*, 303 U.S. 444, 452 (1938) (emphasis supplied); *Thornhill*, 310 U.S. 88, 101–2 (1940) (emphasis supplied); *Schneider v. New Jersey*, 308 U.S. 147 (1939); *Marsh v. Alabama*, 317 U.S. 519 (1946). As discussed in chapter 1, courts had been slow in settling whether the Fourteenth Amendment caused any parts of the Bill of Rights to apply to the states, and – if it did – whether it did so via its 'privileges or immunities' clause or its 'liberty/ due process' clause. While Justices Owen J. Roberts and Hugo Black urged the 'privileges and immunities' approach, Justice Stone, with the concurrence of Justice Reed, claimed that the rights of speech and assembly were enforceable against the states via the 'liberty' / 'due process' clause. *Hague v. CIO*, 307 U.S. 496 (1939). Stone's position ultimately prevailed. See, e.g., *McIntyre v. Ohio Elections Comm'n*, 514 U.S. 334, 336n1 (1995) (citing *Whitney v. California*, 274 U.S. 357, 373 (1927) (Brandeis, J. concurring)).

24 *Barnette*, 319 U.S. 624, 634–6, 642 (1943); Feldman 150–63. While the Court has been repeatedly asked to decide whether the words 'under God,' added to the pledge in 1954, violate the First Amendment separation of church and state, it has not yet done so. See *Newdow v. United States Congress*, 542 U.S. 1 (2004).

25 Thoreau, *Resistance to Civil Government* ¶ 4; Feldman ch. 1; *Whitney v. California*, 274 U.S. 357, 375 (1927) (Brandeis, J. concurring) (the founders 'believed that freedom to think as you will and to speak as you think are means indispensable to the discovery and spread of political truth'). Jefferson's *Virginia Statute for Religious Freedom* (1777; 1786) provided that attempts by government to coerce religious conformity 'tend only to beget habits of hypocrisy and meanness.' See also *Olmstead v. United States*, 277 U.S. 438, 478 (1928) (Brandeis, J. dissenting); Stephen Goode, *The Right to Privacy* (NY 1983) 6–25.

26 The flag salute commonly used before the war, an upturned right arm (with palm either up or down), was rejected because of its resemblance to the Nazi salute. Compare *Minersville School Dist. v. Gobitis*, 310 U.S. 586 (1940) (per Frankfurter, J.); H. Thomas ch. 2; Hirsch 171–6.

27 52 F. Supp. 362, 372 (S.D.N.Y. 1944), *aff'd*, 326 U.S. 1 (1945).

28 *Associated Press v. United States*, 326 U.S. 1, 20, 28–9 (1945); Lewin; 'Press Associations and Restraint of Trade'; Cooper, *The Right to Know* (NY 1956) xiii.

29 'Movie Crisis,' *Bus. Week* (29 Sept. 1945) 83; *United States v. Paramount Pictures, Inc.*, 66 F. Supp. 323 (S.D.N.Y. 1946), *modified*, 70 F. Supp. 53 (S.D.N.Y. 1947), *aff'd in part, rev'd in part and remanded*, 334 U.S. 131, 166 (1948), *on remand*, 85 F. Supp. 881 (1949), *aff'd per curiam*, 339 U.S. 974 (1950). See also *United States v. Griffith*, 334 U.S. 100 (1948); *Schine Theatres, Inc. v. United States*, 334 U.S. 110 (1948); Ernest Borneman, 'United States versus Hollywood: The Case Study of an Antitrust Suit' (1951), in Balio (1985) 449; Kindem (1997) 323–8; Ralph Cassady, 'Impact of the *Paramount* Decision on Motion Picture Distribution and Price Making,' *S. Cal. L. Rev.* 31:150 (1958); Michael Conant 'The *Paramount* Decrees Reconsidered,' *L. and Contemp. Prob.* 44:79 (1981); *NYT* (7 Nov. 1948) X5; Izod 122–8.

30 See *United States v. Paramount Pictures, Inc.*, 334 U.S. 131, 166 (1948). See also J. Lewis 63–5; Doherty (2007) 274–6, 305–7.

31 Motion for Leave to File Brief as Amicus Curiae and Brief in Support Thereof 3–6, *United States v. Paramount Pictures, Inc.*, 334 U.S. 131 (1948).

32 334 U.S. 166 (1948); *Yale L.J.* 60:696, 702n16 (1951); *Kovacs v. Cooper*, 336 U.S. 77 (1949) (Frankfurter, J. concurring).

33 Wanger [Grover Jones], '120,000 American Ambassadors,' *Foreign Affairs* 17 (Oct. 1939); Inglis (1947); Chafee, *Government and Mass Communications* (Chicago 1947) 1:vii, 35, and ch. 11; Chafee, *Free Speech in the United States*, 2d ed. (Cambridge, MA 1941) 545–6; Hodgins (1949B) 90, 91, 104–8. In 1945 the *American Mercury* had similarly called the Legion a 'pressure group' which the producers would never challenge 'so long as the dollar is more important than principle in Hollywood.' R. Whelan; Rotha 449.

34 H. Levy 2.

11 Cocktails and Communism

1 Frank S. Nugent quoted in Rosten 156; Ronald Brownstein, *The Power and the Glitter* (NY 1990) ch. 3; Kempton 189–91; Horne xx, 274n78; Richard H. Pells, *Radical Visions and American Dreams* (NY 1973) 296; Josephson 449–53; Keats 193–4; Hamilton 106–8; Radosh/Radosh 49–51.

2 Montagu 50–1; Hamilton ch. 3; Mencken, 'Interlude in the Socratic Manner' (1927), in Mast 228, 231–2.

3 Schulberg (1950) 47; Johnston 60–4; Hamilton 17–20; Gordon/Gordon 91; Rorty (1936) 293; John O'Hara, *Hope of Heaven* (NY 1938).

4 Rorty (1936) 298; Mildred Cram, 'Author in Hollywood,' in *The American Spectator Year Book*, ed. George Jean Nathan et al. (NY 1934) 175, 176; David Robinson, *Hollywood in the Twenties* (London 1968) 42–3; Hecht, 'Elegy for Wonderland,' in McClure 357; Horne 57. In 1941, of two hundred people in Hollywood making over $75,000 per year, only five were screenwriters. Ceplair/Englund 3–4.

5 Montagu 11; Keats 178; Schulberg (1950) 29–30; Kempton 190; Stewart 223; Graham/Frank 187.

6 N.L. Schwartz 10, 82–3; Hamilton ch. 6; Caute 487; Fariello 255; Ceplair/Englund 104–12, 186–94; Kempton 191, 195–6; Buhle/Wagner (2001) 50. The semi-documentary *Native Land* (dir. Leo Hurwitz and Paul Strand), released in 1942, amply demonstrated how a well-made film could tell a pro-worker, anti-government story. But this was the only film of its kind.

7 Seldes (1939) 234; Buhle/Wagner (2002); Quigley/Breen, 10 Jan. 1939, 30 Jan. 1939, MQP 1.3.

8 Ceplair/Englund 323–4; Hamilton 126–7; Mussolini in Birdwell 84; Schulberg (1941) 68; 'A Patriotic Short' (1940), in *The Stories of F. Scott Fitzgerald*, ed. Malcolm Cowley (NY [n.d.]) 469, 470; Roffman/Purdy ch. 8; Allen 277; L.B. Reid, 'Amusement: Radio and Movies,' in Stearns 33.

9 Moser 738; Thorp 285, 298–9; Birdwell ch. 3; Hamilton 211–14; JDMP 127; S. Carr 193; Doherty (1993) 39–40; Editors of 'Look,' *Movie Lot to Beachhead* (Garden City 1945) 27.

10 Dies, *Martin Dies's Story* (NY 1963); Dies, *The Trojan Horse in America* (NY 1940); Robert Vaughn, *Only Victims* (NY 1972) 15; S.A. Diamond, *The Nazi Movement in the United States* (Ithaca, NY 1974) 280; Michael Wreszin, 'The Dies Committee 1938,' in Schlesinger/Bruns 287, 289; 'Constitutional Limitations' 417–18; Stone 244–8; Dunne (1980) 130. The film that made Temple a star, Hamilton MacFadden's *Stand Up and Cheer* (1934), could be described either as aggressively pro-Roosevelt or as more 'anti-American' than any of the films targeted by Dies's successors after the Second World War.

11 Stewart in N.L. Schwartz 138–9; E.L. Barrett 224; August Ogden, *The Dies Committee* (Washington 1943) 212–13; Dunne (1980) 130–1; Radosh/Radosh 32–5, 61; Schatz 34; Rosten 141–51; Ceplair/Englund 150–7; Friedrich 52–3; Pizzitola 376–8; Kempton 202.

12 George Seldes, 'The New Propaganda for War,' *Harper's* 169:540, 553 (Oct. 1934); 87 Cong. Rec. A3736, A3740; J.E. Wiltz, 'The Nye Munitions Committee 1934,' in Schlesinger/Bruns 249; PMP 48; Black (1994) ch. 2; Wayne S. Cole, *Roosevelt and the Isolationists* (Lincoln, NE 1983) 475–6.

13 Dunne (1980) 116; Roffman/Purdy 74–7; Donald S. Strong, *Organized Anti-Semitism in America* (Washington 1941); *America* 59/5:98 (7 May 1938); *Life* (6 March 1939) 28, 59; S. Carr 112; Buhle/Wagner (2002) 57; *Fortune* 13/1:67 (Jan. 1936).

14 Birdwell ch. 6; S. Carr ch. 8; Moser; Kanfer 20; PMP 11–20, 486; *Motion Picture Herald* (11 Oct. 1941) 17; Wayne S. Cole, *Senator Gerald P. Nye and American Foreign Relations* (Minneapolis 1962) 185–90; Doherty (1993) 41–2; Rosten 267 (cf. Hamilton 181).

15 Nicholas John Cull, *Selling War* (NY 1995) 18, 48–9, 80–1, 179; Roy Hoopes, *When the Stars Went to War* (NY 1994) 70; Hamilton 127–31; Korda 154–63 (cf. Friedrich 51).

16 R.R. Lingeman, *Don't You Know There's a War On?* (NY 1970) 172; Pizzitola 384–5; Adler 193; Thomas Cripps, *Hollywood's High Noon* (Baltimore 1997) 80.

17 Dunne (1980) 107–14, 132–3; Cooke 55–6; Dorothy B. Jones, 'Communism and the Movies,' in John Cogley, *Report on Blacklisting I. Movies* (NY 1956) 214 and App. III-D; McDonald 71–3; Ottanelli 206–7.

18 For example: Gregory Ratoff's *Public Deb Number One* (1940) and Ernst Lubitsch's *Ninotchka* (1939).

19 Allan Winkler, *The Politics of Propaganda* (New Haven 1978) 58; cf. C.R. Koppes and G.D. Black, 'What to Show the World' (1977), in Staiger 279; R. Carr (1952) 58–75.

20 Radosh/Radosh 90–1; Brett Westbrook, 'Fighting for What's Good,' *Film Hist.* 4/2:165 (1990); Hamilton 227–8; Koch ch. 10; David Thaxton, 'Mission to Moscow,' in *The American Film Heritage* (Washington, DC 1972) 40; Radosh/Radosh ch. 5; R. Carr (1952) 62–3; Lewis Jacobs, 'World War II and the American Film' (1968), in McClure 153, 171–2; Hamilton 130–1, 225–7; Kanfer 45. British reviewer Richard Winnington described *Song of Russia*'s 'message' to be 'that the Russians are brave, simple, musical, lovable and above all quaint.' Winnington 39–40.

21 R. Carr (1952) 214–25; Dalton Trumbo, 'The Time of the Toad' (1949), in Trumbo 11; Stone 352–66.

22 Joseph R. Starobin, *American Communism in Crisis, 1943–1957* (Cambridge, MA 1972) 122–6; Fariello 199–204; R. Carr (1952) 56. See also Oliver Carlson, 'The Communist Record in Hollywood,' *Am. Mercury* 66:135 (Feb. 1948).

23 R. Carr (1952) 21–2, 57; L. Cole 279–83, 291; Dunne (1980) 193–204; Dmytryk 55.

24 Fariello 255; Houseman (1950); Horne 177–9.

25 Dick 3; Ring Lardner, Jr, in McGilligan/Buhle 409; N.L. Schwartz 260; Ceplair/Englund 289; Kanfer 73; Pizzitola 415; Roffman/Purdy 235–42.

26 In *Loew's, Inc. v. Cole*, 185 F.2d 641, 651 (9th Cir. 1950), *cert. denied*, 340 U.S. 954 (1951).
27 Kanfer 42–3, 50–1; HUAC/1 (20 Oct.) (Warner) 11, (23 Oct.) (Reagan) 214, (30 Oct.) (Brecht) 494; Dick 7–8; Dmytryk 69–71; Hamilton 246–52, 291–2. Regarding leftist elements in *Hangmen Also Die* (1943), co-written by Brecht and director Fritz Lang, see Radosh/Radosh 87–8.
28 Schickel 108; McWilliams 72; Koch 167; Dmytryk 36–54; Richard English, 'What Makes a Hollywood Communist,' *Sat. Ev. Post* (19 May 1951) 30, 148; Bosworth 226–44; Horne 186, 195; Schrecker 322–30; J. Lewis 34–5.
29 Dalton Trumbo, 'The Devil in the Book' (1956), in Trumbo; N.L. Schwartz 269; Dmytryk 53; L. Cole 268; 18 U.S.C. § 2385 (2006); *De Jonge v. Oregon*, 299 U.S. 353, 363–6 (1937); *Herndon v. Lowry*, 301 U.S. 242, 258–61 (1937). But see *Dennis v. United States*, 341 U.S. 494 (1951).
30 Lardner in McGilligan/Buhle 404, 409; *NYT* (18 March 1978) 23; R. Carr (1951) 308–15.
31 Dunne (1980) 199, 212; *Barnette*, 319 U.S. 642; *Lawson v. United States*, 176 F.2d 49, 51 (D.C. Cir. 1949), *cert. denied*, 339 U.S. 934 (1950); McWilliams 68; 'Congressional Investigations and the First Amendment Restrictions on the Compulsion of Testimony,' *Indiana L.J.* 29:162 (1954); Victor S. Navasky, *Naming Names* (1980; Harmondsworth 1981) 82; Ceplair/ Englund xiii, 267–71; Dunne (1980) 130; 'First Amendment Does Not Justify Refusal to Answer Pertinent Question of Congressional Commit- tee,' *Col. L. Rev.* 56:798 (1956); R. Lardner 10–11; Bosworth 231, 240; Maltz/ Morgolis, 19 March 1973, Margolis/Maltz, 6 April 1973, Margolis/ Lardner, 19 Dec. 1977, Lardner/Margolis, 27 Dec. 1977, AMP 17/1.
32 See *Barsky v. United States*, 167 F.2d 241, 244–5 (D.C. Cir.), *cert. denied*, 334 U.S. 843 (1948); R. Carr (1952) 32–47; *Selections from the Letters ... of Thurman Arnold* (Washington 1961) 64. Dr Barsky's committee included Bessie, Maltz, Trumbo, and Bartley Crum, as well as Pablo Picasso, Albert Einstein, and Dorothy Parker.
33 *Kilbourn v. Thompson*, 103 U.S. 168, 190 (1880); Margolis/Kenny, 8 Dec. 1947, RKP 1/4; Memo. in Support of Motion to Quash Subpoenas (19 Oct. 1947), In re Investigation by the Committee on Un-American Activities; Horne 269n2, 321n97; 'Contempt of Congress,' *Va. L. Rev.* 39:532 (1953); 'Applicability of Privilege against Self-Incrimination to Legislative Investigations,' *Col. L. Rev.* 49:87, 88 (1949); Stamps 31–2, 44–7; R. Carr (1951) 291–308; *United States v. Josephson*, 165 F.2d 82, 90–1 (2d Cir. 1947), *cert. denied*, 333 U.S. 838 (1948); *Barsky v. United States*, 167 F.2d 241, 246 (D.C. Cir.), *cert. denied*, 334 U.S. 843 (1948); Dick 9; 'Constitutional Limitations' 424–7. See also *McCulloch v. Maryland*, 17 U.S. (4 Wheat.) 316, 423 (1819) (Marshall, C.J.); *Dennis v. United States*, 341 U.S. 494 (1951).

34 Frank (1958) 190; Herman Pritchett, 'Libertarian Motivations on the Vinson Court,' *Am. Pol. Sci. Rev.* 47/2:321, 322 (June 1953); Caute 144; I.F. Stone, 'The New Chief Justice' (1953), in *The Haunted Fifties* (NY 1963) 58; *Dennis v. United States*, 341 U.S. 494 (1951); Stamps 47–51; Ceplair/ Englund 264. Leon Josephson, a lawyer and Communist activist, was convicted for contempt of Congress just as the HUAC hearings began. *United States v. Josephson*, 165 F.2d 88–9, 92 (2d Cir. 1947), *cert. denied*, 333 U.S. 838 (1948).

35 Ring Lardner, Jr, in McGilligan/Buhle 409–10; R. Lardner 119; Robert Lees in *id.* 432; W. Goodman 210; L. Cole 267; Horne 211–13.

36 Kahn v, chs. 16 and 17; Breen/L.B. Mayer, 16 March 1943, *Song of Russia*, PCA; HUAC/1 (22 Oct. 1947) 166; HUAC/2 (12 April 1951) 238.

37 HUAC/1 (27 Oct. 1947) 293–4; Radosh/Radosh 25–30; Kanfer 63–5; Buhle/Wagner (2001) 92; *U.S. v. Josephson*, 165 F.2d 87–8; Hamilton 104–6; Horne 269n2, 321n97; Dunne (1980) 200.

38 Although Charlie Chaplin aggressively tweaked HUAC, the committee chose not to subpoena him, perhaps believing that his quick wit and acting skills would make him too winsome. See Kenneth S. Lynn, *Charlie Chaplin and His Times* (NY 1997) 461–2. While *It's a Wonderful Life* had been publicly faulted for depicting a banker's unsympathetic handling of a veteran's loan application, it is unlikely that Trumbo, one of several leftists who did uncredited work on the picture, would have lost a give-and-take with HUAC about whether the film was 'un-American.'

39 HUAC/1 (20 Oct. 1947) (J.L. Warner) 13–15, 43–4, (23 Oct.) (Gary Cooper) 220, (24 Oct.) (Lela Rogers) 231, 233; Dmytryk 46; L. Cole 275; Koch 101, 169; Fariello 273; L. Cole 274; Harmetz 243. Koch ran an ad in the 26 November 1947 *Variety*, swearing, 'I am not and have never been a member of the Communist Party,' while defending his prior decision to stand mute before HUAC.

40 See Maltz, 'What Shall We Ask of the Writers?' *New Masses* (12 Feb. 1946) 19; Buhle/Wagner (2001) 92–6; Hamilton 278–9; Judy Kutulas, 'Becoming "More Liberal,"' *J. Am. Culture* 13:71, 75 (Spring 1990); Maltz notes, AMP 17/5; Horne 213–16; Norma Barzman, *The Red and the Blacklist* (NY 2003) 70–3; Walter Bernstein, *Inside Out* (NY 1996) 138–9.

41 Caute 457, 491; Granville Hicks, *Where We Came Out* (NY 1954) 57; R. Carr (1952) 74–5; Horne 199; Buhle/Wagner (2003). L.B. Mayer later testified that Communism 'can't get into our pictures' because 'too many of us are reading the scripts and we would throw it out if it was there.' Trans. of Rec. 1:325–6, *Loew's, Inc. v. Cole*, 185 F.2d 641 (9th Cir. 1950), *cert. denied*, 340 U.S. 954 (1951).

42 Harold W. Horowitz, 'Loyalty Tests for Employment in the Motion Picture Industry,' *Stanford L. Rev.* 6:438, 443n21 (1954); *Additional Dialogue: Letters of Dalton Trumbo, 1942–1962*, ed. Helen Manfull (NY 1970) 58–9, 493, 498; Ceplair/Englund 275–7, 329; Alvah C. Bessie, *Inquisition in Eden* (NY 1965) 189, 193, 221–9; *NYT* (22 Nov. 1947) 10/2; Ring Lardner, Jr, in Fariello 262; Dmytryk 90; U.S. Cong. H.R., Investigation of So-Called 'Blacklisting,' Entertainment Industry – Report of the Fund for the Republic, Inc. – Part 1, Hearings before the Committee on Un-American Activities, 84th Cong. 2nd Sess. (10 July 1956) 5185–6 (John Cogley); Dunne (1980) 204, 212, 257; Kahn chs. 23–5; L. Cole 289–90; Kanfer 76–7; Hellman 67; Schatz 310.

43 *Photoplay* 32/4:52 (March 1948). See also Barbas 267–8; Horne 194; N.L. Schwartz 281; Kenneth Lloyd Billingsley, *Hollywood Party* (Rocklin, CA 1998) 192–6; Radosh/Radosh 161–2.

44 *United States v. Josephson*, 165 F.2d 82 (2d Cir. 1947), *cert. denied*, 333 U.S. 838 (1948); *Barsky v. United States*, 167 F.2d 241 (D.C. Cir.), *cert. denied*, 334 U.S. 843 (1948); *Lawson v. United States, Trumbo v. United States*, 339 U.S. 934 (1950) (*denying cert.*), *rehearing denied*, 339 U.S. 972 (1950). Dr Barsky's subsequent petition for a rehearing was denied, over the objection of Justices Black and Douglas. *Barsky v. United States*, 339 U.S. 971 (1950). Josephson had the cold comfort of knowing that Justices Douglas, Murphy, and Rutledge had wanted to accept his petition.

45 Ceplair/Englund 329, 350–4; N.L. Schwartz 256–7; Caute 514–15; Ralph S. Brown, *Loyalty and Security: Employment Tests in the United States* (New Haven 1958) 150–7; *Twentieth-Century Fox Film Corp. v. Lardner*, 216 F.2d 844 (9th Cir. 1954), *reh. denied*, 348 U.S. 944 (1955); Scott v. RKO Radio Pictures, Inc., 240 F.2d 87, 88, 91 (9th Cir. 1956), *cert. denied*, 353 U.S. 939 (1957); *NYT* (29 April 1952) 32; RKP 7/2; Audience Research, Inc., 'Congressional Investigation of Communism in Hollywood: What the Public Thinks,' RKP 8/1. Thurman Arnold, although not representing any of the Ten, suggested to Kenny that he bring a Sherman Act claim against the studios, characterizing the Waldorf agreement to blacklist as an antitrust conspiracy. Kenny replied that while he well understood the value of scaring the studios with antitrust charges, the only case in which a court had accepted that blacklisting professional employees constituted a Sherman Act violation was a case Arnold had himself brought, *American Med. Ass'n v. United States*, 317 U.S. 519 (1943). Milton Freeman/Kenny, 1 Dec. 1947, Kenny/Freeman, 17 Dec. 1947, RKP 1/4. Rather than retry the question of whether Zanuck had corporate authority, Lardner settled, netting $4,867. Kenny/Bessie, 31 Aug. 1955, ABP 26/1; C.J. Katz/Martin

Popper, 6 July 1951, RKP 1/6. Schary, RKO's executive vice-president in charge of production, admitted telling Scott that in his view 'a man's employment' was 'based on his ability to perform a service' and that his politics were irrelevant. Tr. of Rec. 2:688, 703–4, *Twentieth-Century Fox Film Corp. v. Lardner*. Lardner subsequently settled out of court. See also Joan LaCour Scott in McGilligan/Buhle 593.

46 E.L. Barrett 246–55; L. Cole 300–1; *Loew's, Inc. v. Cole*, 8 F.R.D. 508 (S.D. Ca.1948), *rev'd*, 185 F.2d 641 (9th Cir. 1950), *cert. denied*, 340 U.S. 954 (1951); Biberman[?]/Bessie, 2 Nov. 1951, ABP 26/1.

47 McGilligan/Buhle 411; L. Cole 273; McWilliams 80–1; Trumbo 19–22; Bosworth 233–4; N.L. Schwartz 85.

48 *Loew's, Inc. v. Cole*, 185 F.2d 641, 653 (9th Cir. 1950), *cert. denied*, 340 U.S. 954 (1951). The First Amendment argument having failed, Bessie in his parole application wrote that his refusal to answer had been based on 'the Bill of Rights,' and that, since he was not a lawyer, that expression should be construed to mean that he meant to have pled the Fifth Amendment as well as the First. Bessie/Kenny, 18 Dec. 1950, RKP 1/1. See also Biberman, 'Petition for Executive Clemency' (20 June 1950), RKP 1/3; Albert Maltz notes, AMP 17/4.

49 HUAC/2 (21 March 1951) 107, (25 April 1951) 410–11, (24 Sept. 1951) 476–7; Caute 511; Kashner/MacNair 76–80; Wilk 236; Buhle/Wagner (2001) 89–90; *Wilson v. Loew's Inc.*, 142 Cal. App.2d 183, 298 P.2d 152 (1956).

50 Geoffrey Wagner, *Parade of Pleasure: A Study of Popular Iconography in the USA* (NY 1955) 31–2.

51 Robin Wood, *Sexual Politics and Narrative Film: Hollywood and Beyond* (NY 1998) 141–2.

12 New Realities

1 Thompson quoted in Peter Kurth, *American Cassandra: The Life of Dorothy Thompson* (Boston 1990) 387; *New Yorker* (6 Dec. 1947) 33/2; Schneider, 'Probing Writers' Problems,' *New Masses* (23 Oct. 1945) 22; Houseman (1947A) 161–3; Houseman (1947B); Hodgins (1949A) 100; Hodgins (1949B) 90; Hellinger quoted in E. Goodman 421; Knight/Alpert in *Playboy* 13/11:162, 165; Goldwyn, 'Hollywood in the Television Age' (1949/50), in Mast 634; Schulberg, 'Movies in America,' *Atlantic* 180:116, 119 (Nov. 1947); ACLU 10 Oct. 1945 discussion points re: getting the studios to go to court 'when some local board – Memphis, for example, cracks down on one of their pictures.' BCP 6/6.

2 Doob, *Public Opinion and Propaganda* (NY 1948) 502–4; Bernstein, 'A Tale of Three Cities,' *Cinema J.* 35/1:27 (1995), in Bernstein (1999) 157. The per-

centage of films listed as 'B' went from 11.5 in 1945 to 22.44 in 1950. The percentage of 'C' films went from 0 in 1945 to 2.78 in 1949. *Legion of Decency Films Reviewed, November 1949–November 1950* (NY 1951) 25; *Motion Pictures Classified by National Legion of Decency, February, 1936–November, 1950* (1951) 25.

3 Gerald Mast, *A Short History of the Movies*, 3d ed. (Chicago 1981) 219–20; Robert Ray, *A Certain Tendency of the Hollywood Cinema* (Princeton 1985) 129, 132. In a film market (i.e., excluding those neither too old, young, or infirm to attend) of 81 million people, 56 million attended at least once every three weeks. Inglis (1947) 45; Andrew Dowdy, *'Movies Are Better than Ever'* (NY 1973) 1; Conant 4.

4 Black (1998) 67–9; J.R. Oakley, *God's Country* (NY 1986) 10–14, 97; Anderson 432–44; Fredric Stuart, 'The Effects of Television on the Motion Picture Industry' (1975), in Kindem (1982) 257.

5 Raymond Borde and Etienne Chaumeton, *A Panorama of American Film Noir, 1941–1953* (1955), trans. Paul Hammond (San Francisco 2002) 127–8; Naremore 13–18; Harmetz 169, 285–6.

6 Bordwell in Bordwell/Staiger/Thompson 1, 75–6; Naremore 15, 68; John Belton, *American Cinema / American Culture* (NY 1994) 184–6; Nicholas Christopher, *Somewhere in the Night* (NY 1997) 14; Robert Corber, *Homosexuality in Cold War America* (Durham, NC 1997) 55, 210–11.

7 Koch 77–8; Harmetz 30, 93.

8 See James Harvey, *Movie Love in the Fifties* (NY 2001) 7.

9 Farber, 'Fight Films' (1949), in Farber, *Negative Space* (NY 1971) 64, 66. Breen repeatedly rejected early scripts of *Pitfall* because the adultery theme did not include compensating moral values. While he rejected the initial *Champion* script for the same reason, presumably the boxer's death resolved that issue. *Pitfall*, PCA; Breen/George Glass, 21 Oct. 1948, *Champion*, PCA.

10 *NYT* (20 Nov. 1949) § 2:5/1; Breen/Quigley, 29 November 1949, *Beyond the Forest*, PCA.

11 Kracauer (1946).

12 Houseman (1947B) 125; Howe, 'Notes on Mass Culture' (1948), in Rosenberg/White 496, 498, 502; Kracauer (1949) 259, 275–6.

13 Liehm 35–8, 52–9; R. Rossellini (1955A) 4; Stephen Gundle, 'From Neorealism to *Luci Rosse*,' in *Culture and Conflict in Postwar Italy*, ed. Zygmunt G. Barañski and Robert Lumley (NY 1990) 209; Gallagher (1998) 168–221.

14 Elena Agarossi, *A Nation Collapses: The Italian Surrender of September 1943*, trans. Harvey Fergusson II (Cambridge 2000) 91–138; Trevelyan 24–5; Katz 5, 189, 317; Jane Scrivener [pseud., Mother Mary Saint Luke], *Inside Rome with the Germans* (NY 1945) 193–5; Tittmann 148–57; Fogarty (1985) 288–

305; Fogarty (1989B) 227–8; Reeve 153; Rhodes (1973) 276–9; H.S. Hughes 119–40.

15 Wilson 202; Gallagher (1998) 156–7; Liehm 61–65; Rossellini (1972) xvi; Ennio Di Nolfo, 'Intimations of Neorealism in the Fascist *Ventennio*,' in Reich/Garofalo 83; Marcel Oms,'Du fascisme à la démocratie chrétienne,' *Positif* no. 28 12 (1958), trans. in Don Ranvaud, 'Critical Trajectory I,' in Ranvaud 38, 40; H.S. Hughes 237–40. In her filmic salute, Isabella Rossellini has her father's character observe that when in 1939 he read that a woman was shot in a poor neighbourhood, 'I went there and asked how it happened,' thus providing verisimilitude to the scene in *Open City*. I. Rossellini (2006) 36.

16 R. Rossellini (1955A) 4; Rossellini interview (ca. 1962), in R. Rossellini (1992) 114; Rossellini, 'Sur une boîte en argent' (1977), in R. Rossellini (1987) 129, 134–5; Gallagher (1998) 217–22; Rossellini interview with Henri Hell (1954), excerpted in *Sighting Rossellini*, comp. David Degner (Berkeley [1973]) [16]; Alpert 56; Lauren Rabinovitz, 'Experimental and Avant-Garde Cinema in the 1940s,' in Schatz 445, 448.

17 Crowther, *Vintage Films* (NY 1977) 79; *NY Herald Trib.* (26 Feb. 1946); *NYT Mag.* (5 May 1946) 18; Gallagher (1998) 176–7; Leprohon 92; Peter Ordway, 'Prophet with Honor,' *Theatre Arts* 33 (Jan. 1949) 49, 50; Dmytryk 97; R. Rossellini (1955A) 4; Zeffirelli 77; Wilson 79; E. Goodman 202.

18 Zeffirelli 78–9, 270–1; Jarratt 59; Liehm 64; Rossellini interview (1948) with Georges Sadoul, in R. Rossellini (1992) 17, 18; Alpert 40–2; Gallagher (1998) 121–33, 159; Serceau 148–50. Magnani was in fact the non-marital child of a Roman mother and a Calabrian father.

19 Agee in *The Nation* 162:443 (13 April 1946), 162:354 (23 March 1946); Ruth Ben-Ghiat, *Fascist Modernities: Italy, 1922–1945* (Berkeley 2001) 202–3; Bondanella (1983) 38; Black (1998) 73–8.

20 *General Education in a Free Society* (Cambridge, MA 1945) 30; Houseman (1947B); Kracauer (1946).

21 A.H. DeBra/Burstyn, 6 May 1946, G.S. White memos, 14 July and 17 July 1947, *Open City*, PCA; A. Mayer 221; Marcus ch. 2.

22 Kracauer, 'Those Movies with a Message,' *Harpers* 196:567, 571 (June 1948); *Rosselliniana*, ed. Adriano Aprà (Rome 1987) 90; Jarratt 63; Gallagher (1998) ch. 8; Derek Monsey, 'Letter from Rome,' *World Rev.* 58, 60 (Jan. 1949); Zeffirelli 79–80; R. Rossellini (1955A) 9; I. Rossellini 84; DeConde 265–8. In *Il miracolo*, Rossellini chose a local beggar to play the role of Magnani's would-be boyfriend. When the man became so immersed in the jealousy his character was supposed to display that he began to 'act out,' Rossellini let the camera roll, the resulting scene demonstrating –

Massimo Mida has noted – that 'reality is enough by itself to express an artistic fiction in its fullness.' *Roberto Rossellini* (Parma 1953) 26.

23 Breen/DeBra, 28 March 1949, *Paisan*, PCA; *NYT* (7 March 1948) X5; Black (1998) 78–81; *Daily Variety* (6 Dec. 1948) 14; Breen/F.N. Levenstein, 12 Oct. 1948, Vizzard/Breen, 25 Jan. 1950, *Germany – Year Zero*, PCA; Gallagher (1998) 313; Liehm 71; Bur. 9, JBC.

24 Rossellini in Marcus 14n34; Zinnemann, 'Different Perspective' (1948), in Koszarski 144, 145. See also *Time* (29 March 1948) 101.

25 French 59–60; 'Unkindest Cut,' *NYT* (2 April 1950) § 2:1; Gardner 174–5.

26 Breen/Arthur Mayer and Jos. Burstyn, Inc., 31 Jan. 1950, De Sica/J.D. Proctor [n.d.], *Bicycle Thief*, PCA.

27 Breen/G.S. White, 9 Aug. 1950, Burstyn/ Breen, 27 Feb. 1950, MPAA press releases, 3 and 29 March 1950, *Bicycle Thief*, PCA; *Daily Variety* (23 Oct. 1950); F. Miller 142; Leonard J. Leff and Jerold L. Simmons, 'No Trollopes, No Tomcats,' *Am. Film* 15:40, 52 (Dec. 1989).

28 Houseman (1950); Rotha 25–6; Schatz 462, 465; Inglis (1946) 481; U.S. Cong. Sen. Subcommittee to Investigate Juvenile Delinquency, 'Television and Juvenile Delinquency,' Rpt. no. 1466, 84th Cong. 2nd Sess. (31 Jan. 1956) 6.

29 Houseman (1950); Robert Sklar, '"The Lost Audience,"' in *Identifying Hollywood's Audiences: Cultural Identity and the Movies*, ed. Melvyn Stokes and Richard Maltby (London 1999) 81, 82; Richard Maltby, 'Sticks, Hicks and Flaps,' in *id.* 23; Doherty (1993) 300; Schatz 68–71; E. Goodman 177; Peter Biskind, *Easy Riders, Raging Bulls* (NY 1998) 35; *Daily Variety* (15 Dec. 1948) 3; Goldwyn, 'Hollywood in the Television Age,' *NYT Mag.* 15 (13 Feb. 1949); Inglis (1946) 478. In 1947 some theatres installed crude audience-reaction meters.

30 Lewis Milestone, 'First Aid for a Sick Giant' (1949), in Koszarski 148, 149, 152; McDonough/Winslow 404–5; W.P. Armstrong, 'Sherman Act and the Movies,' *Temple L.Q.* 26:1, 17 (1952); Robert H. Stanley, *The Celluloid Empire* (NY 1978) 135–7; Robert Coughlan, 'Now It Is Trouble That Is Supercolossal in Hollywood,' *Life* (13 Aug. 1951) 102.

13 Visions of Mary

1 Luke 1:32–3; Ashe 62–3; www.newadvent.org/cathen/15464b.htm; M.J. Gruenthaner, 'Mary in the New Testament,' in Carol 1:81, 83; Paul Maier, 'New Light on the Nativity,' *Lutheran Witness* (Dec. 1999); E. Johnson 226; Hall 1:249; Hines 20; Boff 139; R. Brown (1993) 67–90, 134–9, 287–8n27, 320–1, 519, 540; R. Brown (1973) 55, 64. On whether the biological heritage

of Jesus, maternally or paternally, is significant in deciding the Davidic question, see Vermes 26–45, 72–3 and Meier 1:217–19.

2 Matt. 1:18–25, 2:20, 10:35–7, 12:46–50, 13:55; Mark 3:31–5, 6:3; Luke 2:41–52, 8:19–21, 11:27–8; John 2:1–12, 6:42, 19:25–7, 20:1–18; Acts 1:14; Gal. 4:4; 2 Tim. 2–8. See also Gospel of Thomas 114:1n, in R.J. Miller 322; Revelation 12; Miegge ch. 1; Gambero 19, 59; E. Johnson 217–20; Donald Senior, 'Gospel Portrait of Mary,' in Donnelly 92; Lawrence Cunningham, *Mother of God* (San Francisco 1982) 25–30; Ashe ch. 3, and 105–14; Jelly chs. 3 and 4; Laurentin (1991C) 1–46; Haskins 3–9; Carroll (1986) 4–8.

3 Some translate the Hebrew *'almâh* and its Greek equivalent in the pre-Christian Septuagint, παρθένος, not as 'virgin' but as 'young woman,' 'maiden,' or 'girl.' See, for example, Meier 1:222; Vermes 67–72; Eric May, 'Mary in the Old Testament,' in Carol 1:51, 63; Machen 287–325; J. Reumann et al., 'Mary in the Gospel of Luke and the Acts of the Apostles,' in *Mary in the New Testament*, ed. R.E. Brown et al. (Philadelphia 1978) 105; Guitton 19, 28–38; E. Johnson 26, 232–3; Pope Pius XII, *Mediator Dei* (20 Nov. 1947) ¶ 169; O'Dwyer (1988) 23. Some Catholic scholars suggest that there is no reason to discount the Bible's textual evidence for a virginal conception, while others suggest that Catholics need not accept it as a literal event. See R. Brown (1993) 124–6, 527–30; R. Brown (1973) 16; Meier 1:244–5n76.

4 Jelly 17; E. Johnson 258–74; Journet 25–8.

5 Augustine, *De sancta Virginitate*, 'On Holy Virginity' (ca. 401 C.E.), in *Seventeen Short Treatises of Augustine* (Oxford 1847) 308; Pius IX, *Ineffabilis Deus* (8 Dec. 1854); 'Virgin Birth of Christ,' *Cath. Encycl.* (1910); Warner (1983) chs. 1–4; R. Brown (1993) 288n27; Cunneen 31–57; Weinstein/Bell 37–45; E. Johnson 138–9, 191–2; Gambero 33–42; Jouassard 58–9; Ashe 122, 124, and chs. 7 and 8.

6 Jerome, Letter 21, *Select Letters of St Jerome*, trans. F.A. Wright, Loeb Classical Library (Cambridge, MA 1991), 92–3, 98–9; 'Jerome to Eustochium on Guarding Virginity,' in *Collected Works of Erasmus*, vol. 61, ed. and trans. J.F. Brady and J.C. Olin (Toronto 1992) 155; Ashe 143–8.

7 That Mary remained a virgin is supported by translating ἀδελφός not as 'brother' but 'cousin,' 'relative,' 'kinsman,' 'comrade,' or 'community of the faithful.' See Matt. 12:46–7, 13:55–6; Mark 3:31–5, 6:3; Luke 8:19–21; Gal. 1:19; Acts 1:14; John 7:3. Cf. the Hebrew *'Ach* in Gen. 19:7, 29:12, 15; Num. 20:14. See also Gambero 104; E. Johnson 195–9; Boff 56–7; Ashe 65–73; Pelikan (1959) 131; P.J. Donnelly, 'The Perpetual Virginity of the Mother of God,' in Carol 2:228; Harold Bloom, *Jesus and Yahweh* (NY 2005) 19. In the Douay version, Matthew's comment that Joseph 'knew her not till she brought forth her firstborn son' (1:25), essentially the same in the

King James version, implies that Mary's virginity did not outlast Jesus' birth, although Catholic scholars have asserted that the underlying Semitic idiom typically translated as 'till' did not mean that the situation changed once the object of the 'till' was reached, and that 'firstborn,' a technical term establishing certain legal rights, did not necessarily suggest subsequent births. 'Virgin Birth of Christ,' *New Catholic Dictionary* (1929). The *New Jerusalem Bible* uses only 'son' rather than the literally translated 'son and firstborn,' and rejects 'till,' in favour of 'when,' thus omitting any suggestion that Mary had additional children after Jesus. The *New American Bible* notes: 'The Greek word translated "until" does not imply normal marital conduct after Jesus' birth, nor does it exclude it.'

8 As Pope Leo I declared in the fifth century, Mary's virginity was 'as untouched in giving [Christ] birth as it was in conceiving him.' Tanner 1:73, 77, 84; Boff 146–7.

9 *Cum quorumdam hominum* (5 Aug. 1555) excerpted in Neuner/Dupuis 203; *Catechism of the Catholic Church*, nos. 499, 510 (1994; NY 1995); Pelikan (1996) 29; R. Brown (1993) 518n2; Joseph Wilhelm and T.B. Scannell, *Manual of Catholic Theology Based on Scheeben's 'Dogmatik'* (London 1898) 2:209–10; Jouassard 62.

10 Not that the issue went unaddressed earlier. The *Interrogatory Creed of Hippolytus* (ca. 215 C.E.) asked: 'Dost thou believe in Christ Jesus, the Son of God, who was born by the Holy Spirit from the Virgin Mary?' Tanner 1:35, 44, 58; J.R. Shinners, 'Mary and the People,' in Donnelly 161, 164; Jelly ch. 7. Cyril of Jerusalem (ca. 348–50 C.E.) asked: 'O ye Jews, what is more difficult, for a virgin to bear a child, or for a rod to be quickened into a living creature [i.e., a serpent]? ... From whom was Eve begotten at the start? What mother conceived her who was without mother? Do not the Scriptures say that she was formed from the side of a man? So why cannot a child be born without a father from the womb of a virgin?' Catechetical Lecture 12 ¶¶ 28–9, www.newadvent.org/fathers/310112.htm. Gregory of Nazianzus (ca. 382 C.E.) proclaimed: 'If anyone does not accept holy Mary as Mother of God, he is cut off from the Deity. If anyone should say that Christ passed through the Virgin as through a channel, and was not fashioned in a way that is divine as well as human ... he is equally godless. If anyone should say that the man was fashioned and only afterwards did God steal in, he also is to be condemned.' In Palmer (1952) 4–9; E. Johnson 117–18; Machen ch. 1. See also Pope Pius XI, *Lux Veritatis* (25 Dec. 1931); Doheny/Kelly 155.

11 Baliæ 164–212; Nicolas 332; Sebastian 260; Jouassard 64–84; Carr/Williams 364–6; Laurentin (1956) 292–3. Regarding Aquinas's position, see *Am. Eccles. Rev.* 31/6:566 (Dec. 1904); Baliæ 191–5; Journet 45n76; Carr/

Williams 366. Cf. Pope Pius XII, *Fulgens Corona* ¶ 14 (8 Sept. 1953); Karl Rahner, *Mary, Mother of the Lord* (NY 1963) 42–52; Edward D. O'Connor, 'Modern Theories of Original Sin, and the Dogma of the Immaculate Conception,' *Marian Studies* 20:112 (1969).

12 Gatta ch. 1; Carr/Williams 328–9.

13 Laurentin (1963) 298–9; Baliæ 204–12; Carr/Williams 331–2, 366–9; Sullivan 75–6. Cf. Tanner 1:35, 58.

14 Sebastian 228–32, 248–53; Baliæ; Neuner/Dupuis 202; G.W. Shea, 'Outline History of Mariology in the Middle Ages and Modern Times,' in Carol 1:281, 309; Putnam 2:141–6; Jelly ch. 6; Laurentin (1963) 301–2.

15 1 Tim. 2:14; Ephrem in Palmer (1952) 16–17. See also 'Dialogue with Trypho,' *Saint Justin Martyr*, ed. T.B. Falls (NY 1949) 304–5; *Irenaeus against Heresies* [*Adversus haereses*], in *The Ante-Nicene Fathers*, ed. Alexander Roberts and James Donaldson (1885; Edinburgh 1993) 1:309, 547; Jelly 70–5; Gambero 44–8, 106, and ch. 4; National Conference of Catholic Bishops, *Behold Your Mother* (Washington, DC 1973) 15–18.

16 Hales 65–8; Brownson (1853); DeConde 45–55; Trevelyan in Raffaele De Cesare, *The Last Days of Papal Rome 1850–1870* (Boston 1909) xvi; Crawford, *Ave Roma Immortalis* (NY 1898) 2:222.

17 Atkin/Tallett 121–3; Nielsen 2:160; Hales 89–98; Marraro chs. 2–4; Jemolo ch. 1; Daniel-Rops 252–3; D'Agostino 26–31.

18 Hales 68, 82–100, 229, and ch. 6; Gilley 166, 185; Atkin/Tallett 133–5; D'Agostino 38; Marraro ch. 8; George Martin, *The Red Shirt and the Cross of Savoy* (NY 1969) 260–2, 335–67, 401–5; Marshall 76–80; Aubert 26; McAvoy (1969) 163; *The Holy Rosary*, trans. Paul J. Oligny (Boston 1980) 35–41; Taves 27–39; Jelly ch. 8; Ellis (1971) 38–9; Daniel-Rops 236.

19 Graef 2:79; Nielsen 2:188; Doheny/Kelly 1–5; Laurentin (1956) 308–11; 'Pastoral Letter' (1849), in Nolan 121, 123–6.

20 Bury 48–9; McCool 37–40; Butler 33–47; Hales 41–2; Sparrow-Simpson 149–51. For biblical and early authority for the doctrine of the Immaculate Conception, see Carr/Williams. For an earlier defence of infallibility, see Joseph de Maistre, *Du Pape* (1819), trans. Aeneas M. Dawson (London 1850) xxxi-9.

21 Brownson (1853) 25; Hennesey (1964) 410n7, 414–19; Hennesey (1981) 164; Hennesey (1970) 40; Hales 148–9; Bury 50, 52; Carroll (1992) 70; Sparrow-Simpson 363; Nielsen 2:192–4; Doheny/Kelly 9–27; Palmer (1952) 81–9; Daniel-Rops 256, 276–7; Callahan (1966) 35, 42–3.

22 Lasserre 35; Nowak 96; Laurentin (1957) 48, 80, 233nn3–5, 282, 285n5, 298n7; Laurentin (1979) 75–6, 242–3; Keyes 23–45; Ruth Harris, *Lourdes: Body and Spirit in the Secular Age* (NY 1999); Alan Neame, *The Happening at*

Lourdes: The Sociology of the Grotto (NY 1967) 64, 114, chs. 11–12; Eamon R. Carroll, 'Survey of Recent Mariology,' *Marian Studies* 20:137, 163–5 (1969); Carroll (1986) 156; Peter Eicher, *Visions of Mary* (NY 1996) 193–201.

23 Peter, *Studies in the History of the Renaissance* (London 1873) 47–50; Guitton viii; Max Thurian, *Mary: Mother of All Christians* (1962; NY 1963) ch. 3.

24 Zimdars-Swartz 46; J.-K. Huysmans, *The Crowds of Lourdes* (1906), trans. W.H. Mitchell (London 1925) 201–2; Nowak 121–3; Werfel 99; L.J.M Cros, S.J., *Lourdes 1858: témoins de l'événement* (Paris 1957) 213, 214; Georges Bertrin, *Histoire critique des événements de Lourdes* (Lourdes 1906) 9–10; Laurentin (1957) 131–5; Laurentin (1979) 14.

25 Mariá de Jesús, de Agreda, *Mystical City of God,* trans. Fiscar Marison, 4 vols. (1902; Washington, NJ 1971); Keyes 37–43; Laurentin (1957) 89–128, 141–3, 158–60; Laurentin (1979) 41–50; Odile De Montfort and John O'Meara, *Ordeal at Lourdes* (London 1958) ch. 4; Kselman 180–3; Lasserre 63–96.

26 Victor and Edith Turner, 'Postindustrial Marian Pilgrimage,' in *Mother Worship: Theme and Variations,* ed. James Preston (Chapel Hill 1982) 145, 168; Matt. 11:25; Luke 10:21 (Confrat.); David Blackbourn, *Marpingen: Apparitions of the Virgin Mary in Bismarckian Germany* (NY 1993) 9–10.

27 See A.J.F. Brierre de Boismont, M.D., *Hallucinations,* 2d ed. (trans. 1853; NY 1976) 403–4; Claude-François Michéa, *Du délire des sensations* (Paris 1846) 27–8n; Leuret 28.

28 'Brief of His Holiness Pius IX,' in Lasserre 4; Cunneen 228, 235; Cross ch. 1; Butler 455–75; Kselman 141; Pernicone 61; Leo XIII, *Decreta Generalia de Prohibitione et Censura Librorum* (1897) ch. 5 ¶ 13.

29 Pelikan (1996) 179; Atkin/Tallett 183; Salvatore J. Bonano, 'Marian Shrines and Apparitions,' in Carol 3:326.

30 Durham 10–11, 94–5; Pelikan (1996) 179; Atkin/Tallett 183; S.J. Bonano, 'Marian Shrines and Apparitions,' in Carol 3:326; Foster 219–20, 319–20; Membership Booklet, The Central Association of the Miraculous Medal (Philadelphia 1957) 7; Graef 2:85–8; Taves 37; Spretnak 7; B.C. Pope, 'Immaculate and Powerful,' in Atkinson/Buchanan/Miles 173, 178–9; Kselman 62–5; Connell (1950) ch. 5.

31 Pius X, *Ad Diem Illum Laetissimum* (2 Feb. 1904), in Carlen 4:175; Doheny/Kelly 134; Manuel Cardozo, 'Preface,' in Costa Broachado, *Fátima,* trans. and ed. G.C.A. Boehrer (Milwaukee 1955) 60–76; Avella/Kselman 407–10.

32 Leuret 96; McDannell 139–40, and ch. 5; Fisher (2002) 61–2; E. Ryan 369–71; Taves 98–100; Laurentin (1973) 144; Benjamin B. Warfield, *Counterfeit Miracles* (NY 1918) 275–6; www.udayton.edu/mary/resources/shrines/us.html.

14 Mary or Communism

1 Macleod 2, 4, 28–9; E. Ryan 365; Sargent chs. 1–4.
2 Sperry 201–2; Handy (1977) 21–47; Atkins/Fagley 82–5; Liguori, *The Glories of Mary*, trans. John Chapin (1962–3; Liguori, MO 2000); Liguori, *The Mission Book: A Manual of Instructions and Prayers* (NY 1863); Home; Astarita 153–5; 'Pastoral Letter' (1846), in Nolan 115, 119; Palmer (1952) 79–80; E. Ryan 361–2; Guilday 148–51; 'Pastoral Letter' (1919), in Nolan 212, 220; O'Dwyer (1988) 28.
3 *Elizabeth Cady Stanton*, ed. Theodore Stanton and Harriot Stanton Blatch (NY 1922) 1:73; Lears chs. 5 and 7; Giles ch. 4; Santayana in Wilson 50; Newman (1836–42); Newman (1850); Brownson (1853) 20–1; Colleen McDannell and Bernhard Lang, *Heaven: A History* (New Haven 1988) 160; Rosetti, *Ave* (1847). When, as a Union soldier stationed in Florida during the Civil War, Anthony Comstock wandered into a Catholic midnight mass one Christmas Eve, he came away (he wrote in his diary) 'disgusted ... Seemed much like Theater.' Quoted in Heywood Broun and Margaret Leech, *Anthony Comstock: Roundsman of the Lord* (NY 1927) 38.
4 Mackay, 'Protestantism,' in *Great Religions of the Modern World*, ed. E.J. Jurji (Princeton 1946) 337, 355; Spalding, 'The Virgin Mother,' in *Lectures and Discourses* (1882; NY 1890) 208, 212–13; Brownson (1853) 10–11, 22–3; J. Spencer Northcote, *Mary in the Gospels*, 2d ed. (London 1885) 1–3; Palmer (1954) 526–7, 533n52. Thomas Smyth, a South Carolina Presbyterian, complained in 1846 'that the worship of the Virgin Mary is practically the religion and the only real worship of a large portion of Romanists throughout the world.' *Mary Not a Perpetual Virgin nor the Mother of God: But Only a Sinner Saved by Grace* (Charleston 1846) 5; Dougherty; Guitton vii. And the 670 pages of *History of Christianity in the Apostolic Age* (1897) by another prominent Presbyterian, A.C. McGiffert, include next to nothing about Mary.
5 Ruth Fox Hume, *Our Lady Came to Fatima* (NY 1957) 61–3; Laurentin (1991A) 138; Laurentin (1991B) 137–41; J.F. Murphy, 'The Immaculate Heart,' in Carol 3:168; Carroll (1989) 143–5.
6 Pius XI, *Ingravescentibus malis* (29 Sept. 1937); Werfel 8–9, 162–71.
7 Laurentin (1978) l:21, 2:139; Breen/Lord, 1 March 1943, 'Breen, Joseph, MPC 1933–1954,' DALP; Florence Rounds/Breen, 16 Aug. 1942, *Song of Bernadette*, PCA; Thomson 366–9, 391, 410–11; Beverly Linet, *Star-Crossed: The Story of Robert Walker and Jennifer Jones* (NY 1986) 85–139.
8 Pius XI, *Mit Brennender Sorge* ¶ 8; *Divini Redemptoris* ¶ 8; Falconi 207–8, 228–9; George Weigel, *The Final Revolution* (NY 1992) 64; Rhodes (1973)

258–71; *Wartime Correspondence between President Roosevelt and Pope Pius XII*
(NY 1947) 61–4; István Deák, 'The Pope, the Nazis and the Jews,' *NY Rev.
of Books* 47/5:44, 49 (23 March 2000); Tittmann 57–68; Babiuch/Luxmoore
chs. 3–5; Guenter Lewy, *The Catholic Church and Nazi Germany* (NY 1964) 6–
7, 272; A.D. Morse, *While Six Million Died* (NY 1967) 168–9; Cornwell 61,
272–3, 283–5, 296; Susan Zuccotti, *Under His Very Windows* (New Haven
2000) ch. 1; P. Johnson 490–3; Trevelyan 26–9; Atkin/Tallett 255–60;
Georges Passelecq and Bernard Suchecky, *The Hidden Encyclical of Pius XI*
(1995), trans. Steven Rendall (NY 1997); Phayer 221; Falconi 257–62;
www.holycross.edu/departments/history/vlapomar/hiatt/piusXII.htm.

9 *Principles for Peace: Selections from Papal Documents*, ed. Harry C. Koenig
(Washington 1943) 785; Doheny/Kelly 202; Tittmann 116–27; Donnelly
259–62; R. Graham ch. 10; Phayer 219–20.

10 Spellman, *The Foundling* (NY 1951) 279; Pius XII, *Superiore Anno* (15 April
1940), *Quamvis Plane* (20 April 1941), *Dum Saeculum* (15 April 1942);
Doheny/Kelly 191, 195, 198; Sheen (1948) 216; Spellman, *Prayers and Poems*
(NY 1946).

11 Nowak 10, 28, 32. On the dramatic rise in church membership, see Martin
E. Marty, *The New Shape of American Religion* (NY 1959) 15–16.

12 *NYT* (7 Feb. 1949) 3/2; Atkin/Tallett 270–1; Babiuch/Luxmoore 42–4;
Crosby 11–12; Dever 135–6; Simone Pelizza, 'The 1948 Italian Elections,'
www.geocities.com/iturks/html/the_1948_italian_elections.html;
DeConde 276–308; Vittorio Ivella, 'Party Rule in the Democratic State,'
Foreign Affairs 28/1:75 (Oct. 1949); Miller, *Timebends* (NY 1987) 162. In the
failed 1956 uprising against the Soviet-backed regime, Mindszenty found
sanctuary in the American legation, where he lived until 1971. In 1998,
Pope John Paul II, whose staunch anti-Communism was a crucial component of the defeat of Communism in Poland and ultimately in the Soviet
Union, beatified Stepinac.

13 Vaillancourt 53–4; Falconi 265–73; Cornwell 328–30; Blanshard (1951) 19;
'Ingruentium Malorum,' in Carlen 3:213, 215; 'Orientales Ecclesias,' in *id.*
3:217.

14 Cooke 37; Ceplair/Englund xiii, 255–7; Crosby 9–10; Carlo Sforza, 'Italy,
the Marshall Plan and the "Third Force,"' *Foreign Affairs* 26/3:451 (April
1948).

15 P.R. Kenrick, *The New Month of Mary* (Victorhill, NY 1904); João De Marchi,
The Immaculate Heart: The True Story of Our Lady of Fatima (NY 1952) 261–6;
Sheen (1948) 216; Sheen, *Life Is Worth Living*, 2d ser. (NY 1954) 84; Massa
98; McGrath, *Fatima or World Suicide* (Scarboro Bluffs, ON 1950);
Revelations and Messages as Given through Mary Ann Van Hoof (Necedah

1971) xxxix, xlvii; *NYT* (16 Aug. 1950) 19/5; Zimdars-Swartz 222–3, 259–67; *The Tablet* 42/25:4 (12 Aug. 1950); Avella/Kselman.

16 Spellman, *'What America Means to Me' and Other Poems and Prayers* (NY 1953) 4, 16–18; Reeves 181; Colgan, 'The Blue Army of Our Lady,' *The Marian Era* 6:47 (1965); Cuneo 135; Cunneen 243–4; Avella/Kselman; Raphael Brown (pseud., Beverly Holladay Brown), *The Life of Mary as Seen by the Mystics* (Milwaukee 1951); Massa 30; Carroll (1989) ch. 1; Meier 2:528n22. Modern Marian 'armies' include St Maximillian Kolbe's Pious Union of the Militia of the Immaculate Conception (1917) and Frank Duff's Legion of Mary (1921). A book about Marian organizations published by the Marianum Center in Rome in 1954 ran to 625 pages. R.M. Charest, 'The Legion of Mary,' in Carol 3:257; W.F. Keegan, 'Marian Associations,' in *id.* 3:235; Fisher (1989) 157; Elder Mullan, 'History of the Sodality of Our Lady,' *Am. Eccles. Rev.* 34/5:480 (May 1906), 39/6:618 (Dec. 1908); Laurentin (1965) 10; E. Ryan 373; Congregation for Divine Worship and the Discipline of the Sacraments, *Directory of Popular Piety and the Liturgy* (Vatican City 2001).

17 Ruth Cranston, *The Miracle of Lourdes* (NY 1955); D.J. West, *Eleven Lourdes Miracles* (London 1957) 4; Laurentin (1973) 144, 153n; Patrick Marnham, *Lourdes* (NY 1981) 187–90; Leuret 31.

18 G.W. Shea, 'The Dominican Rosary,' in Carol 3:88, 99–103; Jelly 186; Beverly Donofrio, *Looking for Mary; or, The Blessed Mother and Me* (NY 2000) 55–6; Spretnak 7; Dolan (1985) 384–5; Fisher (1989) 90; Peyton 121; Hardon (1952) 254; *Auspicia Quaedam* (1 May 1948); E.R. Carroll, 'Marian Congresses,' in Carol 3:295; Hardon (1952) 254.

19 Reeve 136; Peyton 164; Waugh 648; Pius XII, *Ingruentium Malorum* in Carlen 3:213, 214, Doheny/Kelly 249; Membership Booklet / The Central Association of the Miraculous Medal 10–13.

20 W.G. Most, 'Marian Centers, Libraries, and Publications,' in Carol 3:283, 287–8; Eric May, 'Mariological Societies,' in *id.* 3:272, 277–9; Laurentin (1965) 10–11; Eamon R. Carroll, 'A Survey of Recent Mariology,' *Marian Studies* 22:91, 94 (1971); E. Ryan 377.

21 Hasler 262–7; Carroll (1996) ch. 8; Edmund Schlink et al., 'Evangelical Opinion on the Proclamation of the Dogma of the Bodily Assumption of Mary,' *Lutheran Quart.* 3:123, 126–8 (1951); *NYT* (15 Aug. 1950) 31/5; *The Tablet* 42/26:1 (19 Aug. 1950); Pelikan (1959) 83; Hardon (1952) 253; Winch/Bennett 2–3; E.R. Carroll, 'Mary in the Documents of the Magisterium,' in Carol 1:28. Because the Assumption had no textual basis in Scripture, Cynthia Pearl Maus omitted works portraying it in her substantial anthology of works depicting the Madonna. *The World's Greatest Madonnas* (NY 1947).

22 Carlen 4:109; Doheny/Kelly 220; *id.* 101; *Nostis Profecto* (30 Oct. 1950), *id.*
    208; Jacques Bur, *How to Understand the Virgin Mary* (1992), trans. John
    Bowden and Margaret Lydamore (NY 1996) 79, and ch. 5; Hardon (1952)
    254–6; Winch/Bennett; Spretnak 36–7; Hardon (1959) 206–7; Pohle 105–19;
    NYT (2 Nov. 1950) 1/2; *Tablet* 42/37:1, 14–15 (4 Nov. 1950); Jelly ch. 9.
23 Donnelly 255; 'Assumption,' in *New Catholic Encyclopedia* (1967); L.P.
    Everett, 'Mary's Death and Bodily Assumption,' in Carol 2:461; Warner
    (1983) 92; Hardon (1952) 249; Hardon (1959) 205.
24 Pelikan (1996) 183; Pelikan (1959) 71; Falconi 289. Pius XII thought the two
    dogmas 'intimately connected, 'for the greatest possible glorification of
    [Mary's] virgin body is the complement, at once appropriate and
    marvelous, of the absolute innocence of her soul.' *Fulgens Corona* ¶¶ 20–1
    (8 Sept. 1953).
25 Dennis Barton, 'Apparitions of Our Lady in Their Historical Context,'
    www.church-in-history.org/pages/booklets/apparitions(n)-2.htm; Falconi
    42–55, 283, 290; Hardon (1952); *Tablet* 42/27:1 (26 Aug. 1950). Pius X was
    beatified in June 1951 and canonized in May 1954. Among priestly organi-
    zations disavowing Vatican II as a capitulation to modernism is the
    Society of St Pius X. Pius IX was beatified in 2000.
26 Hardon (1959) 207; Blanshard (1951) 6–7; Fisher (2002) 123; Sheen (1952)
    141–2; Anne Carr, 'Mary: Model of Faith,' in Donnelly 7, 9.

15 The Priest as Public Figure

1 Reeves 119, 211, 286; Ellis (1983) 80; Luce, 'The Real Reason,' *McCalls* 88:17
   (April 1947); Wilfrid Sheed, *Clare Boothe Luce* (NY 1982) ch. 6; Shadegg
   209–11; Massa 82, 93.
2 Breen/J.L. Warner, 20 May 1938, *Angels with Dirty Faces*, PCA; Breen/
   Luigi Luraschi, 12 Aug. 1943, *Going My Way*, PCA; Breen/Lord, 12 Nov.
   1945, 'Movie Prod. Code – Re-writing the Code 1941–54–56,' DALP; *NYT*
   (16 Feb. 1947) § 2:5/5; Brochure, 1 Nov. 1947, Breen/Ford, 21 Oct. 1946,
   The Fugitive, PCA; Greeley (2000) 149–52; Lourdeaux 115.
3 McAvoy (1969) 259–60, 420; Morris ch. 7; D. O'Brien (1989) 22–7; Farley
   184–94; Potter 359–61; Cogley 256; M. Williams (1934) 216–18, 335.
4 Fisher (2002) 86; Ellis, 'St Patrick in North America' (1961), in Ellis (1963)
   39, 48–9.
5 Breen memo, 27 Feb. 1945, Breen/Earl Rettig, 7 March 1945, W.F. Higby/
   Breen, 25 March 1946, Howard Strong/Joyce O'Hara, 8 March 1946, *Bells
   of St Mary's*, PCA. McCarey later said he patterned Fitzgerald's character
   on a priest he knew in Santa Monica. In Bogdanovich 421.
6 Greeley (1959) 71; HUAC/1 (23 Oct. 1947) 225. Cf. Getlein in Getlein/

Gardiner 98: 'The message of all these films is that religion can be fun. It can't ... To most nonreligious observers of this successful venture, it is clear that, to some degree, the Catholics are being "bought off" by the jolly priest movies.'

7 O'Toole 96, and ch. 4; D. O'Brien (1989) 129; Dever 159.

8 Gaffey 244; Ellis (1983) 72–3, 141–2; Fogarty (1989B) 217; Fogarty (1985) 246–8; Dever ch. 5.

9 Fogarty (1989B) 221–2; Fogarty (1985) 240–1, 256; Wakin/Scheuer 18; Ellis (1983) 81.

10 J. Ryan (1928) 31, 39–40; Maynard (1941) 613; Cooney 108–9; R. Gannon 331–2. The Methodist director of the New England Watch and Ward Society, on the eve of that organization's decline, noted that the Irish 'make notable Puritans.' A.L.S. Wood, 'Keeping the Puritans Pure,' *Am. Mercury* (Sept. 1925) 74, 76; Biever 720–1; Doherty (2007) 143–5.

11 Spellman, *The Road to Victory* (NY 1942) 4–5, 15–16; D. O'Brien (1989) 204, 220.

12 *McCollum v. Bd. of Ed.*, 333 U.S. 203 (1948); Hirsch 167, 180; Frankfurter, *From the Diaries of Felix Frankfurter* (NY 1975) 344; *Martin v. Struthers*, 319 U.S. 141 (1943) (ops. of Frankfurter and Murphy, JJ.).

13 La Piana 124, 125; *Everson v. Bd. of Educ.*, 330 U.S. 1, 16 (1947); Baker 230–1; Hamburger 1–17, 155–62, 219–40, 259; Gaustad 73–112; McBrien 63–5; Thomas 135–6; Pfeffer 131–6, 150–3; D. Mayer 158–66; Feldman 23–5, 53–4.

14 *Nat'l Cath. Almanac* (Paterson, NJ 1949) 90; Parsons (1948) chs. 2 and 6; Reeves 166–7; Drinan, 'The Novel "Liberty" Created by *McCollum*,' *Georgetown L.J.* 39:216 (1951); O'Neill (1949) 4, and ch. 12.

15 William Jansen, *Should Religious Beliefs Be Studied and Criticized in an American Public High School?* (1948), Box 756, folder 11, ACLUP; McGreevy ch. 6; Cooney 180–1; Jeanette Hopkins, 'Paul Blanshard and Mary Hilyer Blanshard,' www.harvardsquarelibrary.org/unitarians/blanshard.html; 'School Boards, Schoolbooks and the Freedom to Learn,' *Yale L.J.* 59:928, 932–9 (April 1950); O'Neill (1952) 119–21; Blanshard (1958); *NYT* (20 Nov. 1949) 11; La Piana 9. See also W. Russell Bowie, 'Protestant Concern over Catholicism,' *American Mercury* 69: 261, 269 (Sept. 1949).

16 Wilson 50; Brogan 67; Sweet, *The American Churches: An Interpretation* (London 1947) 30–1; *New Republic* (1 March 1943); Gleason (1992) 209; D'Agostino 308. Growing polarization was evidenced by an increased number of anti-Catholic articles in a prominent Protestant magazine, coupled with a similar rise in anti-Protestant articles in a prominent Catholic magazine. *NYT* (29 Dec. 1950) 21.

17 *NYT* (7 Dec. 1947) X9/1; Breen/L.B. Mayer, 31 Jan. 1947, *Three Musketeers,*

PCA; *NYT* (20 Nov. 1949) § 2:5/1; Wade, 'Catholicism and Puritanism,' *Commonweal* 48/3:650 (23 April 1948).

18 Crosby 134. See also Cogley 234–5. Spellman, doubting his own abilities as a public speaker, often had Sheen speak at St Patrick's. Ellis (1983) 89.

19 *NYT* (23 July 1949) 1/4, 26/2; *NYT* (28 July 1949) 1/2, 16 cols. 4–5; Cooney 176–8; Hennesey (1981) 297–8; Stokes 2:744–58; File 190.4, 'Pacific Trip 1943,' 31–2, Eleanor Roosevelt Papers, Franklin D. Roosevelt Library, Hyde Park, NY; Eleanor Roosevelt, *This I Remember* (NY 1949) 295–310; Timothy P. Maga, 'Humanism and Peace,' *Maryland Historian* 19/2:34, 38–46 (1988).

20 Willis Rudy, *Schools in an Age of Mass Culture* (Englewood Cliffs, NJ 1965) 217; Stokes 2:747; Ellis (1983) 93; Cogley 236; Jerry Tallmer, 'The Silent Treatment II,' *The Nation* 170/6: 22 (11 Feb. 1950).

21 Crosby 134; Cogley 112–13; Vincent P. De Santis, 'American Catholics and McCarthyism,' *Cath. Hist. Rev.* 51/1:1, 5 (April 1965); Reeves 232–5; Anthony Nugent, 'Introduction,' in *The Catholic Church and Politics* (Cambridge, MA 1950) 5.

16 'Woman Further Defamed'

1 *In re* 'Harvest,' Ed. Dep't Case no. 4324 (15 Sept. 1939), NY Dep't Rpts 62:42; *NYT* (3 Oct. 1939) 19/4. On appeal, the Board of Regents reversed the ban. See also *In re* 'The Last Will of Dr Mabuse,' Ed. Dep't Case no. 3121 (20 June 1935), NY Dep't Rpts 52:71. The Division banned *The Forgotten Village*, the John Steinbeck/Herbert Kline documentary distributed by Burstyn and Mayer, because it showed the face of a mother during childbirth. After respectable organizations protested the ban, the Regents reversed the Division's action. *NYT* (22 Aug. 1941) 19; *NYT* (18 Nov. 1941) 33.

2 Fewer than 1 per cent of films processed were refused a licence. Flick/ Arthur D. Goldstein, 28 Feb. 1952, Box 1274, ACLUP. The Division was a self-perpetuating profit center, netting in 1935–40 $1.1 million in licence fees. *Administrative Adjudication in the State of New York* 4:170 (1942); *NY Evening J.* (13 July 1934) 6/1.

3 The arrangement between Lopert and Burstyn is discussed in *Variety* (27 Dec. 1950). U.S. distribution of *A Human Voice* may have been barred by an unresolved copyright issue, or possibly by Rossellini's having sold 'exclusive' rights to more than one distributor. Alpert 67; Baxter 82.

4 Westin 7–8. The owner of world distribution rights to *Il miracolo*, Tania Film, arranged for a screening of the film for Mrs Looram and several priests from the Netherlands, Belgium, and England, after they missed its

first, official showing. Rodolphe Solmsen affidavit, reel 2175, AHBP.

5 Gillis 225.

6 'Anna Magnani dans *Le miracle*,' *Revue du Cinéma* 3/14:15, 16 (June 1948); Truffaut; Gallagher (1998) 252. Burstyn's U.S. print gives Fellini story credit, although his collaborator, Tullio Pinelli, has received secondary credit. Baldelli 307. Their respective contributions are discussed in Baxter 79; Fellini 31–2; Spoto 261; Brunette 92–3.

7 Alpert 66–7; Baxter 79; Charlotte Chandler, *I, Fellini* (NY 1995) 62–4; Claude Mauriac, 'L'écran prémonitoire,' *Le Figaro Litteraire* (7 April 1956) 12; Bergala/Narboni 22–3; R. Rossellini (1992) 117; Hovald 105. In 1955, Rossellini told *Cahiers du Cinéma* that Fellini had falsely told him it was a Russian story whose author he had forgotten. Rossellini (1955B) 7. Italo Calvino's *Italian Folktales* (1956), trans. George Martin (NY 1980) reveals nothing similar.

8 Piero Regnoli in *L'Osservatore Romano* (25 Aug. 1948) 2/1, in reel 2175, AHBP; *Commonweal* (March 1951) 592; Arturo Lanocita, '"Amore" di Rossellini film per la Magnani,' *Corriere della Sera* (22 Aug. 1948) 3/2. See D'Annunzio, *Tales of My Native Town*, trans. Rafael Mantellini (1920; NY 1968); Gallagher (1998) 289–90 (re: negative Italian reviews).

9 Madrid, 'Rossellini ha llevado a la pantalla una novela de Valle-Inclán,' *El Hogar* [Buenos Aires] no. 2029 (3 Sept. 1948) 6; Madrid, *La Vida Altiva de Valle-Inclán* (Buenos Aires 1943) 211–16. That the novella was Fellini's source was mentioned in the U.S. litigation regarding *The Miracle*, and is repeated in, for example, Masi 38; Michelone 212; Guarner; Di Giammatteo 48; Rossi 8. Fellini later conjured an alternative derivation from an alleged incident in Gambettola, although undoubtedly he did so only to deflect Madrid's allegation of plagiarism. Adriano Aprà's filmography credits Valle-Inclán. In Edward Knoblock's play *Marie-Odile* (1915), a novice in a convent has intercourse with a soldier, whom she takes to be Saint Michael. Totally ignorant of such matters, she treats the birth as an immaculate conception.

10 *Cahiers du Cinéma* 37:4–5 (July 1954), trans. in R. Rossellini (1992) 47, 51; Bergala/Narboni 22–3, R. Rossellini (1992) 117; Iris Origo, *The World of San Bernardino* (London 1963) 178.

11 Interview (1970), in R. Rossellini (1992) 179, 197–8.

12 Matt. 26:17; Leviticus 14: 1 Cor. 5:7; 1 Peter 1:19; Amédéé Ayfre, 'Sens et non-sens de la Passion dans l'univers de Rossellini,' *La passion du Christ comme thème cinématographique* ed. Michel Estève (Paris 1961) 169, 180, 183. Regarding Christ's ability to drive out demons, see Mark 5:7–13; Matt. 8:28–32; Luke 8:27–39, 11:14–26; Meier 2:650–3, 664–5n15.

13 *Il Popolo* (3 Nov. 1948), reel 2175, AHBP; Bur. 21, JBC; Record on Appeal
     72–8, *Joseph Burstyn, Inc. v. Wilson*, 303 N.Y. 242, 101 N.E.2d 665 (1951);
     FSC Box H #210, JBC; Baxter 82; Renoli, *L'Osservatore Romano* (25 Aug.
     1948) 2/1; *Commoweal* (March 1951) 592; *NYT* (11 Feb. 1951) § 2:4/4–5;
     Jacqueline Reich, 'Mussolini at the Movies,' in Reich/Garofalo 3, 14–15;
     David Forgacs, 'Sex in the Cinema,' in *id.* 141, 146; Liehm 6.
14 Skinner 89, 97–8; *Newsweek* (18 Dec. 1950) 93–4; *NY Daily News* (13 Dec.
     1950) 82/3; *Time* (18 Dec. 1950) 60; *Time* (19 Feb. 1951) 96; *NYT* (13 Dec.
     1950); *NYT* (17 Dec. 1950); *NY Journal-American* (13 Dec. 1950) 22; Archer
     Winsten, *NY Post* (13 Dec. 1950) 80; Max Lerner, 'The Shadow of the
     Screen,' *NY Post* (26 Dec. 1950) 26. Elmer Rice stated that thirteen of New
     York's sixteen newspaper film critics had signed a protest against
     McCaffrey's actions. Rice / Elsa B. Valentine, 8 Jan. 1951, Box1274,
     ACLUP.
15 W.P. Lawson, 'Standards of Censorship,' *Harper's Weekly* 60:63, 64 (16 Jan.
     1915); Kan. L. ch. 294 §§ 2, 5 (1913), *codified* Gen. Stats. Kan. §§ 10775,
     10778 (1915). See *Mutual Film Corp. of Missouri v. Hodges*, 236 U.S. 248
     (1915); *Mutual Film Corp. v. Kansas*, 236 U.S. 230 (1915); *Kansas ex rel.
     Brewster v. Ross*, 101 Kan. 377, 166 Pac. 505 (1917). See also Pa. Pub. L.
     (1911) 1067 (effective 1 April 1913); *Buffalo Branch, Mutual Film Corp. v.
     Breitinger*, 250 Pa. 225, 95 A. 433 (1915); Act of 15 May 1915, Pa. P.L. 534;
     Neville March Hunnings, *Film Censors and the Law* (London 1967) 164–92.
     In 1917 Kansas deleted 'sacrilegious' from its statute. Kan. L. ch. 608 § 6
     (1917). Kansas disbanded its censorship organization in 1956, the same
     year Pennsylvania's statute was declared unconstitutional in *Hallmark
     Prods., Inc. v. Carroll*, 384 Pa. 348, 121 A.2d 584 (1956). Pennsylvania's
     legislature then enacted a substitute, although it was struck down in
     William Goldman Theatres, Inc. v. Dana, 405 Pa. 83, 173 A.2d 59 (1961).
16 1921 N.Y. Laws ch. 715 *codified* N.Y. Ed. L. Art. 43 §§ 1080–1092; 1927 N.Y.
     Laws ch. 153, art. 43 § 1090; *Moving Picture World* 8:58, 141, 227, 234 (April
     1916), 8:1490 (27 May 1916).
17 'Reason for Regulation' (1922), in Rutland 63, 68. Of 1,793 deletions
     demanded by the Division in the first six months of 1934, only seven were
     on grounds of sacrilege. *NY Evening J.* (13 July 1934) 6/1. In 1935 the
     Division, then headed by Irwin Esmond, denied a licence to Mexican
     director Juan Bustillo Oro's *Monja y Casada,Virgen y Mártir* ('Nun and
     Married, Virgin and Martyr,' 1935) because, among other things, it was
     'sacrilegious.' See also *In re Appeal of Mariano Viamonte*, Ed. Dep't Case
     no. 3370 (9 Oct. 1935), NYS Dep't Rpts 52:488; *In re Appeal ... 'The Puritan'
     (Le Puritan)*, Ed. Dep't Case no. 4140 (24 Feb. 1939), NYS Dep't Rpts

60:163; *In re 'The Egomaniac,'* Ed. Dep't Case no. 4760 (19 June 1942), NYS Dep't Rpts 64:253 (same film); *In re Appeal ... 'Polygamy,'* Ed. Dep't Case no. 4179 (16 June 1939), NYS Dep't Rpts 60:217.

18 Wirt 193; Joseph Burstyn aff. ¶ 3 ca. Feb. 1951, *'In re Proceeding for the Rescinding ... N.Y. State Dep't of Ed.,'* FSC Box H, #208, JBC.

19 *NYT* (24 Dec. 1950) 1/2; *Joseph Burstyn, Inc. v. McCaffrey*, 198 Misc. 884, 101 N.Y.S.2d 892, 894 (Sp. T. N.Y. Co. 1951); Driggs 25–32. In *Silverman v. Gilchrist*, 260 Fed. 564, 565 (2d Cir. 1919), a case predating the New York State film statute, the court concluded that when reasonable people disagree about whether a film about venereal disease should be shown, the New York City commissioner of licences acts reasonably when he concludes that it should not be, that is, a film may be banned because it is controversial. A press release of 10 January 1951 by Glenn L. Archer, executive director of Protestants and Other Americans United for Separation of Church and State, alleged that Spellman was behind McCaffrey's actions. Box 1274, ACLUP.

20 *N.Y. Herald-Tribune* (28 Dec. 1950); Glazer/Moynihan 208–12; Spellman/Parsons, 1 Feb. 1951, FSP sc/33/1; *Life* (15 Jan. 1951) 59; Gerard (1977A) 26, 30; Barbas 31, 270–1; Isabella Taves, 'Louella Parsons,' *Look* (10 Oct. 1950) 60, 64; *France Amérique* (31 Dec. 1950); BCP 6/6. The young writer Clancy Sigal wrote to McCaffrey, with a copy to Impellitteri, stating that Rossellini 'has created in this film a very moving, powerfully poignant indictment of intolerance and bigotry, of those who in a modern world cannot or will not abide by the ones who choose to believe with a simple, fervent faith. While it is true that the full meaning of the film is open to interpretation, only a bigot, a fool or a philistine could interpret "The Miracle" as blasphemous, immoral or a slight on the Mother Church. If we condemn the picture because it uses as its basic material the symbols and appurtenances of the Church, then we must also attack some of the great literature, theatre and cinema of our era, including that which has been created by eminent Catholic artists ... It is rather ironic that you should ban this film, when you pass without a whisper of protest, the profoundly immoral garbage of Hollywood which fills our New York screens with its stench arising from leeringly coy sex, irrational and glamorized brutality and aesthetic monumentalization of social immorality' (24 Dec. 1950, BCP 6/6). A post card mailed to the *New York Times* stated: 'if [McCaffrey] can get away with this, you might as well start bringing your books to City Hall for a bonfire' (BCP 7/2).

21 *Weber v. Freed*, 239 U.S. 325 (1915); Petition, Order of Cert. and Return 4–5, *In re Eureka Prods., Inc. v. Byrne*, 252 App. Div. 355, 300 N.Y.S. 218 (3d Dep't

1937), *leave denied*, 276 N.Y. 688 (1938); Knight/Alpert in *Playboy* 13/4:204–5; Hedy Lamarr, *Ecstasy and Me* ([n.p.] Bartholomew House 1966) 19–34; *United States v. Two Tin Boxes*, 79 F.2d 1017 (2d Cir. 1935); *Eureka Prods., Inc. v. Mulligan*, 108 F.2d 760 (2d Cir. 1940); *NYT* (8 Aug. 1935).

22 *Eureka Prods., Inc. v. Lehman*, 17 F. Supp. 259 (S.D.N.Y. 1936) (Manton, J.), *aff'd*, 302 U.S. 634 (1937). See *License Cases*, 46 U.S. (5 How.) 504 (1847); *Gibbons v. Ogden*, 22 U.S. (9 Wheat.) 1 (1824); *Mutual Film Corp. v. Industrial Comm'n of Ohio*, 236 U.S. 230 (1915); *Mutual Film Corp. of Missouri v. Hodges*, 236 U.S. 248, 258 (1915); *Caldwell v. North Carolina*, 187 U.S. 622 (1903); *Blumenstock Bros. Advertising Agency v. Curtis Publishing Co.*, 252 U.S. 436 (1920); *Crenshaw v. Arkansas*, 227 U.S. 388, 397 (1912); *Savage v. Jones*, 225 U.S. 501 (1912); *Alexander Film Co. v. Alabama*, 44 So.2d 581, 584 (Ala. 1950).

23 1935 La. Acts (3d extra sess.) no. 16 § 3 *codified* 1939 La. Gen. Stats. comp. B.W. Dart § 9594.13. Cf. 1914 La. Acts no. 180 *codified* 1939 La. Gen. Stats. §§ 5843–45; *City of Lynchburg v. Dominion Theatres, Inc.*, 175 Va. 35, 7 S.E.2d 157 (1940); 'Film Censorship / Administrative Analysis,' *Col. L. Rev.* 39:1383, 1386n (1939).

24 *Look* 18/5:96 (9 March 1954); Jane Russell interview in 'Hollywood Uncensored' (video; Castle Hill Productions 1988); Tony Thomas, *Howard Hughes in Hollywood* (Secaucus, NJ 1985) 80–5; Doherty (2007) 252–63.

25 Schumach 146; Marilyn Yalom, *A History of the Breast* (NY 1998) 49–50, 137–8; Wini Breines, *Young, White, and Miserable: Growing Up Female in the Fifties* (Boston 1992) 99–100; David White and Robert S. Albert, 'Hollywood's Newspaper Advertising,' in Rosenberg/White 257, 450 n2.

26 *In re 'The Outlaw*,' Ed. Dep't Case no. 4754 (15 May 1942), NYS Dep't Rpts 64:246; Skinner 73–8; Black (1998) ch. 2; Knight/Alpert in *Playboy* 13/10:172, 160, 164.

27 *Hughes Tool Co. v. Motion Picture Ass'n of America, Inc.*, 66 F. Supp. 1006 (S.D.N.Y. 1946); *NYT* (12 April 1946) 22/6; Walsh (1996) 196–201.

28 Thomson 469; Black (1998) 54; Selznick 260–1; Lord/Breen, 11 March 1947, 'Breen, Joseph, corresp. 1943–1954,' DALP; Breen/Lord, 26 March 1947, 'Breen, Joseph, MPC 1933–1954,' DALP; Masterson/Breen, 18 Feb. 1947, Breen/Masterson, 21 Feb. 1947, *Duel in the Sun*, PCA; *Cong. Rec.* (19 June 1947) 7456–9; Velie 12. See also 'Cleavage and the Code,' *Time* (5 Aug. 1946) 98.

29 *NYT* (23 Oct. 1947) 36/4; *NYT* (1 Nov. 1947) 11/5; Negley Teeters and John Reinemann, *The Challenge of Delinquency* (Englewood Cliffs, NJ 1950) 183; *NYT* (6 Nov. 1947) 36/5; *NYT* (7 Nov. 1947) 20/3; *NYT* (12 Nov. 1947) 35/4; *NYT* (22 Nov. 1947) 10/5; *NYT* (5 Dec. 1947) 33/1; Box 755, folder 12,

ACLUP; Willi Frischauer, *Behind the Scenes of Otto Preminger* (NY 1974) 115–16; *NYT Mag.* (25 July 1948) 14; Otto Preminger, *Preminger* (Garden City 1977) 105–6; Black (1998) 61. The film's co-scenarist, Ring Lardner, Jr, returned from the HUAC hearings to resume work with Preminger on the script, only to be fired by Darryl F. Zanuck.

30 *United Artists Corp. v. Amity Amusement Corp.*, 188 Misc. 146, 66 N.Y.S.2d 299 (Sp. T. 1946), *aff'd*, 271 App. Div. 825, 66 N.Y.S.2d 621 (1st Dep't 1946) (mem.), *legislatively overruled by* 1950 N.Y. Laws ch. 624(1) *amending* Penal Law § 1141; *Hughes Tool Co. v. Fielding*, 188 Misc. 947, 73 N.Y.S.2d 98 (1947) (Shientag, J.), *aff'd*, 272 App. Div. 1048, 75 N.Y.S.2d 287 (1st Dep't 1947), *aff'd*, 297 N.Y. 1024, 80 N.E.2d 540 (1948).

31 Greenberg, J., unofficial transcript, FSC Box H, #208, JBC; *NY Post* (29 Dec. 1950); *NYT* (31 Dec. 1950) 23/4; *The Tablet* [Brooklyn] 42/46:7 (6 Jan. 1951); Winnington 108.

32 198 Misc. 884, 101 N.Y.S.2d 892 (Sp. T. N.Y. Co. 1951); *The Tablet* 42/47:4 (13 Jan. 1951); Papers on Appeal, *Joseph Burstyn, Inc. v. McCaffrey* (App. Div. 1st Dep't 1951).

33 Crowther 36; *NYT* (8 Jan. 1951) 1/2. When another of *The Times'* film critics, Thomas M. Pryor, a Catholic, visited the Archdiocese in an attempt to attain some kind of resolution, he was told that if he publicly stated that the film had merit, he would be excommunicated. Driggs 47.

34 Harmetz 228–37; Chandler 65–90; Smit 240, 249–50; Sarris (1998) 416; Knight/Alpert in *Playboy* 13/10:172; *Time* (2 Aug. 1943) 55; Selznick 225; Kanin 173–4.

35 With cameras rolling, Bergman played a joke on Father Devlin by engaging in a long, erotic kiss with Crosby. Charles Thompson, *Bing: The Authorized Biography* (NY 1975) 111–12; Chandler 113.

36 *NYT Magazine* (16 Dec. 1945) 45; James Damico, 'Ingrid from Lorraine to Stromboli: Analyzing the Public's Perception of a Film Star,' *J. of Pop. Film* 4/1:11 (1975); Sarris (1998) 416.

37 Victoria Sackville-West, *Saint Joan of Arc* (Garden City 1936) 288, 292, 307, 363–8; Michael Monahan, *My Jeanne D'Arc* (NY 1928) 182; Sven Stolpe, *The Maid of Orleans*, trans. Eric Lewenhaupt (NY 1956) 278.

38 Warner (1981) 256–63; Evelyn Acomb, *The French Laic Laws (1879–1889)* (NY 1941) ch. 1; D'Agostino 55; Rhodes (1983) chs. 8 and 15; Lilley 221–31; Leo XIII, *Au Milieu des Sollicitudes* (16 Feb. 1892); D. Lynch 333.

39 Rhodes (1973) 80–7; Canons 1991–41, 2117–20, 2138 (1917); Bachofen (1921) 7:385–402; Woyzod 2:352–82; Warner (1981) 264. In the year of Joan's canonization, Denis Lynch, S.J., characterized as a 'slur' the frequent allegation that 'the Church burned Joan.' D. Lynch 21, 342–9. Joan

was executed on 30 May 1431. The Council of Basel, headed by Cardinal Giuliano Caesarini under approvals of Pope Martin V and his successor, Pope Eugene IV, did not open until 25 July, the Council's schism with Rome commencing only later. Better evidence for the argument that it was not 'the Church' that burned Joan would be that the several priests participating in her trial refused her request to contact the pope.

40 Shaw, *Selected Plays* (NY 1949) 2:265, 308; Seldes (1939) 222; *NY Herald Tribune* (22 July 1934) § 5:1/6; *Baltimore Sun* (1 May 1934) 1/4; Twain xiii; Doherty (2007) 185–5; Chandler 72, 76.

41 Breen/Lord, 22 July 1947, 'Breen, Joseph, MPC 1933–1954,' DALP; Leamer 138; 'Saint Joan on the Screen' 2, 7–8, *Joan of Arc*, PCA; Bernstein (1986) 104; Bernstein (1994) 242; Gallagher (1998) 314–15; E.V.R. Wyatt, review, *Cath. World* 168:321 (Jan 1949) ('one must be very grateful for the [film's] rightful emphasis on [Joan's] appeal to the Pope').

42 Bernstein (1986); Leamer 147; Elizabeth Treadway, review, *Collier's* 121 (26 June 1948) 24; Steele 28–9, 105, 127–8.

43 Steele 92, 161–2; Leamer 3, 151–4, 158; R. Rossellini (1955B) 8; R. Rossellini (1992) 17, 20, 129, 140–3; I. Rossellini 75–9; Dmytryk ch. 13; Gallagher (1998) 257, 309; Roberto Rossellini, 'Perchè ho scelto Ingrid Bergman,' *L'Elefante* (24–31 March 1949), RRSB.

44 Gallagher (1998) 154, 235–6, 325–6, 676–7; L. Parsons (1948); Steele 104, 171, 233–6; Pizzitola 427; Leamer 175–84; Kanin 177–8; Adela Rogers St Johns, *Love, Laughter and Tears* (Garden City 1978) 289; Eells 249; Leamer 191–2; Gundle 64.

45 Spoto 278; Vizzard 146; Brunette 112.

46 L. Parsons (1961) 70, 74, 173–88; Steele 259–64; Barbas 137, 292–3; Leamer 199; Eells 248–50.

47 *Collier's* 125/8:58–9 (25 Feb. 1950); Dore Schary, *Heyday* (Boston 1979) 270–1; Roberto Rossellini interview with Edgardo Maorini, in *Les Lettres Françaises* (2 March 1950), RRSB; R. Rossellini (1992) 24, 26.

48 Herbert Duffy, 1950 Op. Att'y Gen. no. 1463 (8 Feb. 1950) 80; Ohio Gen. Code 154–47b; Ivan Brychta, 'The Ohio Film Censorship Law,' *Ohio State L.J.* 13:350 (1952).

49 Thomas Leary and J.R. Noall, 'Entertainment,' *Harv. L. Rev.* 71:326, 338 (1957); Sen. 3237, 81st Cong. 2d Sess. (1950); *Cong. Rec.* 96:3262, 3281–8, 3353, 3396–9; Bergman/Burgess 273–4; Kupferman/O'Brien 294–6; Vizzard 149–50; Bernstein (1986) 91.

50 L. Parsons (1961) 68; Powys, *Psychoanalysis and Morality* (San Francisco 1923) 13–14.

51 Morlion/Breen, 26 Jan. 1950, *Joan of Arc*, PCA; 'How the Rossellini Film

"Stromboli" Became "God's Earth,"' in *id*; Mario Arosio, 'Il figliol pro-digo,' *Rivista del cinematografo* (July 1977) 305; Gallagher (1998) 268, 274; *Time* (13 Feb. 1950) 86; Steele 269–98. Pundits said that Bergman's pregnancy was the most publicized pregnancy in 1,950 years. 'Final Draft' 44, LGP.

52 *Kingsport* [TN] *News* (14 Jan. 1951) 14A; Burstyn statement at 8 Jan. press conf., box 2561, file 55250, WOL; Mildred F. Citron/Alfred H. Barr, 18 Jan. 1951, and enclosure, reel 2175, AHBP.

53 Hartung, 'The Screen,' *Commonweal* 53/14:350 (12 Jan. 1951); *Life* (15 Jan. 1951) 59; Flick/Allen (10 Jan. 1951) 5, WOL. Dr Flick did not identify which member of his staff objected, or on what basis. Two years later, he told Hollis Alpert that all of his examiners had seen *Ways of Love* and that of the three films, only the Renoir film, translated as *A Day in the Country*, had caused any concern. Alpert, 'Talk with a Movie Censor,' *Sat. Rev.* (22 Nov. 1952) 21, 50.

54 Masterson/Breen, 19 Jan. 1951, *Miracle*, PCA.

55 Machen 10, 272–3; Origen, *Contra Celsum*, trans. Henry Chadwick (Cambridge 1953) Bk. 1 ¶¶ 28, 29, 32, 33; www.come-and-hear.com/sanhedrin/sanhedrin_67.html, note 12; Gospel of Thomas 105n, in R.J. Miller 321; Meier 1:222–4; Vermes 82–4; R. Brown (1993) 523, 530–42; Walter Burghardt, 'Mary in Western Patristic Thought,' in Carol 1:109, 137–8; George Herbert Box, *The Virgin Birth of Jesus* (London 1916) 201–3; E. Johnson 228–32. See also Palmer (1954) 520–2.

56 See Jackson Thomas, 'Fragments of a Schizophrenic's "Virgin Mary" Delusions,' *Am. J. Psychiat.* 12/2:285 (Sept. 1932); William Fielding, *Love and the Sex Emotions* (NY 1932) 308, 315, 318; Eugen Bleuler, *Dementia Praecox* (1911), trans. Joseph Zinkin (NY 1950) 121, 427; Charles Féré, *Scientific and Esoteric Studies in Sexual Degeneration in Mankind and in Animals*, trans. Ulrich Van Der Horst (1917; NY 1932) 84; Ernest Jones, *On the Nightmare* (London 1931) 92; Edward C. Spitzka, *Insanity* (NY 1883) 318; J.É.D. Esquirol, *Mental Maladies* [1838], trans. E.K. Hunt (Philadelphia 1845) 322, 328, 333.

57 The PCA file on the film includes a 9 Feb. 1950 letter from Breen to L.B. Mayer indicating that he should consult with clerics to ensure that the film was free of irreverence or blasphemy.

58 *Osservatore Romano* (12 Nov. 1948) 2/3. Cf. *Johnny Belinda* (1948).

59 *Cahiers du Cinéma* 37:4–5 (July 1954), trans. in R. Rossellini (1992) 47, 51; R. Rossellini (1955B) 7–8 ('C'est une folle mais, au milieu de sa confusion mentale, elle a une foi, hallucinée si l'on veut *mais une foi*'); Giorgio Garrè in Menon 33.

60 Rohmer and Hoveyda in *Cahiers du Cinéma* 25:2 (July 1953), reproduced in
    Verdone 187, 188–9; Rohmer, 'Les deux images de la solitude,' *Cahiers du
    Cinéma* 10:38, 40 (May 1956); Borde in *Les Temps Modernes* 13/139:566
    (Sept. 1957); Sarris (1970) 36, 37, 40; *Interviews with Film Directors*, ed.
    Sarris (Indianapolis 1967) 405; Leprohon 118; Mario Arosio, 'Il cristiane-
    simo di Rossellini,' *Riv. del Cine.* 326 (Aug. 1977); Henri Agel, *Le cinéma et
    le sacré*, 2d ed. (Paris 1961); Scorsese disc 1. Rudolf Thome finds *The
    Miracle* free of parody. Peter Bondanella sees it as a meditation on the
    meaning of Christian faith. Thome; Bondanella (1993) 16; Bondanella
    (1983) 38, 48–9. See also Ferrara 19, 36; Liehm 3; Hillier 192, 201; Serceau
    154; Baldelli 94; Gallagher (1988) 332; Leo Braudy, *The World in a Frame*
    (Garden City 1976) 69.
61 Gallico, 'What We Talked About,' in *While You Were Gone: A Report on
    Wartime Life in the United States*, ed. Jack Goodman (NY 1946) 46; Agee, *The
    Nation* 158/6 (5 Feb. 1944); Richard Corliss, *Talking Pictures: Screenwriters
    in the American Cinema* (1974; Woodstock, NY 1985) 47–8; Knight/Alpert in
    Playboy 13/8:120, 149; Friedrich 210–12; Doherty (1993) ch. 8. Breen issued
    innumerable complaints about the film during production, but then
    awarded it a seal. *Miracle of Morgan's Creek*, PCA.
62 'Cinema and Theology' (1951), in *Bazin at Work* (NY 1997) 61, 63.
63 Shadegg 218.
64 L.B. Mayer planned to make a film of Spellman's 'The Risen Soldier' (1944),
    a sentimentalized account of a letter by an airman to his parents who
    correctly sensed that his next mission would be his last. (The film was never
    produced.) Spellman, *The Risen Soldier* (NY 1944) 35; *Life* (21 Jan. 1946) 102.
    Spellman's novel *The Foundling* (1951), with its kindly priest and blinded
    solider, reads like the novelization of a typical studio film.
65 Winnington 86–7; Agee in *The Nation* 166/17 (24 April 1948); *Time* 51/
    13:101 (29 March 1948).
66 Quigley, Jr; Crowther, *NYT* (14 Jan. 1951) § 2:1/8; Baxter 82; Gallagher
    (1998) 65–6, 112, 119, 148, 166–71; Gundle 74–5.
67 *Tablet* 42/48:17 (20 Jan. 1951); Quigley, Jr; Cotter, 'Stage and Screen,' *The
    Sign* 30/7:45 (Feb. 1951); NY County American Legion press release, 29
    Jan. 1951, FSP/sc33/1; Charles B. McGroddy / Patrick Murphy Malin (8
    Jan. 1951), box 1274, ACLUP. Another sign read: 'Europe you need our
    help. We don't need your filth.' 'Final Draft,' Pt. II, p. 3, LGP. A customer
    later commented that when picketers yelled at him and his wife, 'No
    decent man would take a decent woman to that filth!' it 'reminded me of
    Magnani's getting pelted by vegetables in the film.' Booton Herndon/
    Crowther (8 Jan. 1951), BCP 7/2.

68 Quentin Reynolds, *Leave It to the People* (NY 1949) 145–6; Rotha 41–2, 596–601; Brunette 355; Mario Cannella, 'Ideology and Aesthetic Hypotheses in the Criticism of Neo-Realism,' *Screen* 14/4:5 (Winter 1973–4) 14–15; Marcus 26–7; Gallagher (1988) 83–93; R. Rossellini (1992) 33, 41; Guarner; Liehm 45–6; Hay 71–2; Landy 13–15; Enrique Seknadje-Askénazi, *Roberto Rossellini et la Seconde Guerre mondiale* (Paris 2000) 47.

69 R. Rossellini (1992) 31, 179, 196–8; Luce, 'Saints,' in *Saints for Now*, ed. Luce (NY 1952) 8; I. Rossellini (2006) 78; Liehm 109; Thome; *Sight and Sound* 19/10:393, 394 (Feb. 1951); Brunette 129–30. In an article about *Stromboli*, George Weller quoted Rossellini to the effect that in Europe, 'nobody believes in anything. Fascism has failed. The role of Communism is not yet clear. What is necessary is a film that can transcend both politics and economics, and give man back faith in himself and also a new apprehension of God.' 'Ingrid's Rossellini,' *Collier's* 124: 14, 15 (12 Nov. 1949). Introducing Criterion's DVD of *La strada*, Martin Scorsese links Rossellini with Fellini by a common Franciscan preoccupation.

70 Kobal 475; Chandler 176–8.

71 Sidney Sherwood, 'University of the State of New York: Origin, History and Present Organization,' *Regents' Bulletin* no. 11 (Jan. 1893) 222; Ravitch 6–7. In 1894 conservative Rochester bishop Bernard McQuaid, former president of Seton Hall University, campaigned for a seat on the Board. Two years earlier, he had vigorously opposed Archbishop John Ireland's daring arrangement for a partnership between the Church and public education in two Minnesota towns, and now Ireland campaigned to defeat McQuaid's candidacy. The battle between these two prelates, fought out in the arena of American civic politics, dramatized for Curial officials that they would have to intervene to end 'Americanist' ideas. They did, in Leo XIII's 'anti-Americanist' letter to Gibbons, a signal defeat for Archbishop Ireland and liberalism, a victory for McQuaid and conservatism. Aaron J. Massey, 'The Phantom Heresy?' http://are.as.wvu.edu/massey.htm; Hennesey (1990) 309–10; Reilly ch. 4; Barry ch. 5.

72 Of 100 Protestant ministers replying in 1954 to the question 'Do you believe that Mary is the Mother of God?' 63 said no and 22 yes, with 15 unsure. Kenneth Dougherty, 'Contemporary American Protestant Attitudes toward the Divine Maternity,' *Marian Studies* 6:137, 143 (1955); Dougherty 427. Regarding Mayor Impellitteri's plan, see *NY Post* (29 Dec. 1950) 4.

73 *NY Post* (29 Dec. 1950); *NYT* (9 Jan. 1951); *NY World Telegram* (9 Jan. 1951); *NYT* (20 Jan. 1951) 1/2; *NYT* (29 Jan. 1951) 14/3; Gerard (1977B) 28; Gilbert Seldes, 'Pressures and Pictures,' *The Nation* 172:104, 132 (3, 10 Feb.

1951); Crowther 36; Westin 12; Turner 124–5; Skinner 98; Cooney 197; *NY Herald Trib.* (10 Feb. 1951). Burstyn's lawyer, Ephraim London, later said that one member of the Regents' committee, Jacob Holtzman, had initially dissented, but then became convinced that the decision should be unanimous. Driggs 85–9.

17 'A Sense of Decency and Good Morals'

1 De Grazia/Newman 77; Clark/Breen, 4 Jan. 1951, Breen/Clark, 11 Jan. 1951, *The Miracle*, PCA; Herbert Mitgang, 'Transatlantic "Miracle Man,"' *Park East* (Aug. 1952) 32, 34; *NYT* (3 Dec. 1950) X5; Clifford Forster/Morris Ernst, 25 Sept. 1946, MLEP.

2 *NYT* (29 Jan. 1951) 14/1. Regarding the change of venue to the Rainbow Room, see Crowther/R.F. Holzmann (29 Jan. 1951) BCP 7/1.

3 See Frank v. Magnum, 237 U.S. 309 (1915); *The Crisis* 10:276 (Oct. 1915); Leonard Dinnerstein, *The Leo Frank Case* (1968; Athens, GA 1987); Robert Seitz Frey and Nancy Thompson-Frey, *The Silent and the Damned* (Lanham, MD 1988); Steve Oney, 'The Lynching of Leo Frank,' *Esquire* 104/3:90 (Sept. 1985); C. Vann Woodward, *Tom Watson* (NY 1938) 434–50.

4 R. Brooks 17–18; Budd Schulberg, 'Movies in America,' *Atlantic Monthly* 180:115, 116–17 (Nov. 1947); Kanin 185. When Ingrid Bergman protested that African Americans could not attend her Washington, DC, run of *Joan of Lorraine*, some Washingtonian shouted 'nigger lover' at her on the street. Steele 122.

5 See Cripps (1993) 89–92.

6 Radosh/Radosh ch. 7; N.L. Schwartz 260, 273; Darryl Fox, 'CROSSFIRE and HUAC,' *Film Hist.* 3/1:29 (1989); Kahn 192; Naremore 117–23; Kanfer 81; Trumbo 10n, 21; W. Goodman 219; Cole 320; R. Lardner 9–10, 135–6; Fariello 263; McGilligan/Buhle 414; Eric Bentley, *Are You Now or Have You Ever Been* (NY 1972) 15–16.

7 R. Carr (1952) 214–25; Stone 352–66; R. Lardner 197.

8 R. Brooks 131–2; Thomas Cripps, *Slow Fade to Black: The Negro in American Film, 1900–1942* (NY 1977) 3, 6, 67, 94, 349; Cripps, 'The Reaction of the Negro to the Motion Picture Birth of a Nation,' *The Historian.* 25/3:344 (May 1963); John McManus and Louis Kronenberger, 'Motion Pictures, the Theater, and Race Relations,' *AAAP&SS* 244:152 (1946); Black/Koppes (1986). The self-image problem of African-American children, supported by psychological studies, would be one of the issues presented to the Supreme Court in *Brown v. Board of Education*, 347 U.S. 483 (1954).

9 Hardwick; Dorothy Jones, 'Tomorrow the Movies IV,' *New Republic* 123 (3

Feb. 1945); Donald Spoto, *Stanley Kramer: Filmmaker* (NY 1978); Kramer, *A Mad, Mad, Mad, Mad World* (NY 1997) 36–7; Gerald Weales, 'Pro-Negro Films in Atlanta,' *Films in Review* 3:455 (1952) 460; Joseph Klapper, *The Effects of Mass Communication* (Glencoe, IL 1960) 23, 42, 48.

10　Velie; Jane M. Friedman, 'The Motion Picture Rating System of 1968: A Constitutional Analysis of Self-Regulation in the Film Industry,' *Col. L. Rev.* 73:185 (1973); Richard Lord, 'Film Is a Four Letter Word,' *Memphis St. L. Rev.* 5:41, 46n47 (1974); Leab 134; Cripps (1993) 93, 178, 231; Fleener-Marzec 72–6; 'Higher Criticism in Memphis,' *Time* 46/7:20 (13 Aug. 1945); Ira H. Carmen, *Movies, Censorship, and the Law* (Ann Arbor 1966) 206–12; Collie Small, 'Rock of Hollywood,' *Collier's* 125/8:13, 66 (25 Feb. 1950); *NYT* (4 May 1947) § 2:5/5; *Cong. Rec.* 93/6:7308 (19 June 1947); Ralph Ellison, 'The Shadow and the Act,' *Reporter* 1:17 (6 Dec. 1949); Max Lerner, *Actions and Passions* (NY 1949) 70.

11　Ephraim London, 'The Freedom to See,' *The Nation* (19 Dec. 1953) 545; Philip T. Hartung, 'Trillions for Brewster,' *Commonweal* 62/4:94 (11 May 1945); Collie Small, 'What Censorship Keeps You from Knowing,' *Redbook* 97/3:24, 82 (July 1951); David Halberstam, *The Fifties* (NY 1993) 467; *NYT* (26 Oct. 1947) § 2:4/4; Velie; *NYT* (21 Aug. 1949) 61/3; JDMP 113. Binford called John M. Stahl's *Imitation of Life* (1934) 'the worst case of racial equality' he had ever seen.

12　*United Artists Corp. v. Board of Censors*, 189 Tenn. 397, 225 S.W.2d 550 (1949), *cert. denied*, 339 U.S. 952 (1950). See box 755, folder 11, and box 756, folders 21 and 25, ACLUP; Curley De Grazia/Newman 230–1.

13　Murdock 70, 76–7; Donald Bogle, *Toms, Coons, Mulattoes, Mammies, and Bucks* (NY 1974) 202–14; *RD-DR Corp. v. Smith*, 89 F. Supp. 596, 597 (N.D. Ga.), *aff'd*, 183 F.2d 562 (5th Cir.), *cert. denied*, 340 U.S. 853 (1950); Brief for Appellants in RD-DR Corp. v. Smith, 183 F.2d 562 (5th Cir.); *NYT* (21 Aug. 1949) 61/3; *NYT* (11 Oct. 1950) § 2:1/1; *NYT* (15 Oct. 1950) X5/1. The Atlanta ordinance was declared unconstitutional in *K. Gordon Murray Productions, Inc. v. Floyd*, 217 Ga. 784, 125 S.E.2d 207 (1962).

14　*Allen B. Dumont Labs, Inc. v. Carroll*, 184 F.2d 153, 155–6 (3d Cir. 1950), *cert. denied*, 340 U.S. 929 (1951) (*construing* 47 U.S.C. § 301).

15　Mary Ann Doane, *Femmes Fatales: Feminism, Film Theory, Psychoanalysis* (NY 1991) 232–45; Cid Ricketts Sumner, *Quality* (Indianapolis 1946) 270–86; Dunne (1980) 60–2; Breen/Joy, 28 Feb. 1949, Zanuck/Harmon, 30 March 1949, *Pinky*, PCA; Mel Gussow, *Don't Say Yes until I Finish Talking* (Garden City 1971) 151; Winnington 110; Roffman/Purdy 248–50; *NYT* (29 Oct. 1949) 8/8; *Time* 54/22:82 (28 Nov. 1949).

16　*Gelling v. Texas*, 157 Tex. Crim. App. 516, 247 S.W.2d 95 (30 Jan. 1952).

Reportedly, the ordinance had not been enforced for many years, prior to the town's decision to use it against *Pinky*. Eric Johnston, "Blue-Pencil Freedom," box 758, folder 9, ACLUP; *Motion Picture Daily* (14 March 1952) 1. See also box 763, folder 9, ACLUP; *Film Daily* (21 Feb. 1950) 1; *Variety* (9 May 1951) 3; *Hollywood Reporter* (3 March 1952) 3.

17 In a previous case, after the public complained about the content of a film licensed by the Motion Picture Division, the Division *itself* served upon the distributor an order to show cause why the licence should not be revoked. See *In re* 'He,' Ed. Dep't Case no. 4626 (20 June 1941), NYS Dep't Rpts 64:117. See also *In re* 'The Virtuous Zizi,' Ed. Dep't Case no. 5067 (18 Jan. 1946), NYS Dep't Rpts 66:37, 38.

18 'Meeting of a Subcommittee of the New York Board of Regents,' in 'Record of Proceedings to Review a Determination Pursuant to Article 78 of the Civil Practice Act,' *Joseph Burstyn, Inc. v. Wilson* (App. Div. 3d Dep't 1951), and in FSC Box H, #208, JBC; *NYT* (27 Feb. 1951); *Cath. Standard* (2 March 1951).

19 *NYT* (1 Feb. 1951) 24/7; *Ave Maria* 73:133 (3 Feb. 1951); Giles ch. 8; Cotter, 'Stage and Screen,' *The Sign* 30/7:45 (Feb. 1951); *NYT* (11 Feb. 1951) § 2:4/4; *Time* (19 Feb. 1951) 61.

20 *Time* (19 Feb. 1951) 61; Record on Appeal 18, *Joseph Burstyn, Inc. v. Wilson*, 303 N.Y. 242, 101 N.E.2d 665 (1951); *NYT* (17 Feb. 1951) 1/1, 9/2; Transc. Rec. 10, 19, 55, *Joseph Burstyn, Inc. v. Wilson*, 343 U.S. 495 (1952); Pfeffer 668.

21 Back in December, the Paris added to Burstyn's trilogy an animated short, Robert Cannon's *Gerald McBoing Boing* (1950). When *Riders to the Sea* proved unpopular, the Paris substituted for it a second Cannon short, *Brotherhood of Man* (1945), and began featuring *Gerald McBoing Boing* in newspaper ads, before adding *God Needs Men*. See 'Final Draft' 33, LGP; Graetz/Crowther, 30 Jan. 1951, BCP 18/5; *NYT* (1 April 1951) § 2:l/8; *NYT* (8 April 1951) § 2:5/5; 'Record of Proceedings to Review a Determination Pursuant to Article 78 of the Civil Practice Act,' in *Joseph Burstyn, Inc. v. Wilson* (App. Div. 3d Dep't 1951) 78; Masterson/ Breen, 15 Feb. 1951, *God Needs Men*, PCA. In William Wellman's *The Ox-Bow Incident* (1943), one of the characters, about to be hanged by a posse, confesses to a layman, a serious violation of Catholic doctrine apparently overlooked by Breen, although Masterson called the film 'most objectionable' on that basis. Masterson/Connors, 9 March 1943, *Ox-Bow Incident*, PCA.

22 *Variety* 181/3:1, 47 (27 Dec. 1950); Parsons/Spellman, 22 Jan. 1951, 13 March 1951, FSP/33/1; McIntyre/Spellman, 2, 5, and 21 March 1951, FSP/33/2; *NYT* (4 March 1951) 101/3; Fogarty (1985) 314; Walsh (1996) 253.

23 *Joseph Burstyn, Inc. v. Wilson*, 343 U.S. 495, 514n20 (Frankfurter, J. concurring); Transcript of Record 15–17, 30, 44, 48–52, 96, 122–7, *id.*; Record 103, Joseph Burstyn, Inc. v. Wilson, 303 N.Y. 242, 101 N.E.2d 665 (1951); FSC Box H #211, 5–11, JBC; Earle F. Walbridge, *Library Journal* 76:418 (1 March 1951); Draper 69; Jarratt 68.

24 '"*The Miracle*" and Related Matters,' *Commonweal* 53/21:507 (2 March 1951); *NYT* (16 Feb. 1951) 25/4; Getlein 4; McLean 163. Philip O'Brien, the MPAA lawyer who had been assigned the *Pinky* litigation, was seen in the gallery during oral argument in *Burstyn*, but did not participate. *Film Daily* (25 April 1952) 4.

25 FSP/sc33/2; Cooney 199.

26 Clancy, 'Prudence and the Picket: The Catholic as Philistine,' *Commonweal* 53/23:567 (16 March 1951); Hesburgh/O'Hara, 18 April 1951, O'Hara/ Hesburgh, 23 April 1951, FSP/sc33/2; J.A. Nelson/Spellman, 2 Nov. 1951, FSP/sc33/3; Cooney 199; Thomas J. Reese, *Archbishop* (San Francisco 1989) ch. 1.

27 Spaeth, "Fogged Screen," *Magazine of Art* 44/2:44 (Feb. 1951); 'Record of Proceedings to Review a Determination Pursuant to Article 78 of the Civil Practice Act,' *Joseph Burstyn, Inc. v. Wilson* (App. Div. 3d Dep't 1951); Rec. 72, 100, *Joseph Burstyn, Inc. v. Wilson*, 303 N.Y. 242, 101 N.E.2d 665 (1951); Cooney 199–200; *Commonweal* (23 March 1951) 590–1.

28 278 App. Div. 253, 104 N.Y.S.2d 740 (3d Dep't), *aff'd*, 303 N.Y. 212, 101 N.E.2d 665 (1951), *rev'd*, 343 U.S. 495 (1952). See *Gitlow v. New York*, 268 U.S. 652 (1925); *Near v. Minnesota*, 283 U.S. 697, 707–8 (1931); *Grosjean v. American Press Co.*, 297 U.S. 233, 243–51 (1936); *De Jonge v. Oregon*, 299 U.S. 353 (1937); *Palko v. Connecticut*, 302 U.S. 319, 324–5 (1937); *Herndon v. Lowry*, 301 U.S. 242 (1937); *United States v. Paramount Pictures, Inc.*, 334 U.S. 131, 166 (1948).

29 Despite that position, a number of Jewish groups had protested the character of Fagan in David Lean's *Oliver Twist* (1948), doing so with sufficient vehemence that while *The Miracle* was in the courts, Lean's film, although passed by New York's censors, failed to open for over a year. See Crowther. Dore Schary applauded the censorship, observing: 'We are still in a war – a war against prejudice and venal intolerance. During such a state of siege we owe some obligations to minority groups.' Schary, 'Censorship and Stereotypes,' *Sat. Rev. Lit.* (30 April 1949) 9, 10. Cf. John Haynes Holmes, 'Sensitivity as Censor,' *Sat. Rev. Lit.* (26 Feb. 1949) 9, 10. Concern about *Oliver Twist* had also played some part in Mendel Silverberg's decision to play an active role in blocking *The Miracle* from exhibition in Los Angeles. *NYT* (4 March 1951) 101/3.

30 Brief of Respondents 9, *Joseph Burstyn, Inc. v. Wilson*, 303 N.Y. 242, 101 N.E.2d 665 (1951).

31 Jean Preer, 'Esquire v. Walker,' *Prologue* 23/1 (Spring 1990); Cadegan. While the cabinet position of postmaster general was commonly described as a political sinecure for political services rendered, Gershon Legman in 1945 characterized it as 'the price the Democratic party pays for the political support of the Catholic Church.' Jay Gertzman, *Bookleggers and Smuthounds* (Philadelphia 1999) 205.

32 39 U.S.C. § 226 (1940). See *The Masses, Inc. v. United States*, 246 Fed. 24 (2d Cir. 1917), *rev'ing* 244 Fed. 535 (S.D.N.Y.) (L. Hand, D.J.), *on remand*, 252 Fed. 232 (S.D.N.Y. 1918); Felix Frankfurter, 'Press Censorship by Judicial Construction' (1921), in *Law and Politics*, ed. Archibald MacLeish and E.F. Pritchard, Jr (NY 1939).

33 *Hannegan v. Esquire, Inc.*, 327 U.S. 146 (1946), *aff'ing* 151 F.2d 49 (D.C. Cir. 1945); Thurman Arnold, *Fair Fights and Foul* (NY 1965) chs. 17–18.

34 *People v. Winters*, 294 N.Y. 545, 63 N.E.2d 98 (1945), *rev'd*, 333 U.S. 507 (1948). See also Abood v. Detroit Bd. of Educ., 431 U.S. 209, 231 and n28 (1977); *In re Banks*, 56 Kan. 242 (1895) (enforcing similar statute). Although the 'bloodshed' provision struck down in *Winters* was part of a larger New York criminal statute entitled 'Obscene prints and articles,' the Court did not strike the entire statute, nor did it find the crime magazines under scrutiny to be 'obscene.'

35 See *Schenck v. United States*, 249 U.S. 47, 51–2 (1919).

36 *Doubleday & Co. v. NY*, 335 U.S. 848 (1948), *aff'ing per curiam by equally divided Court* 297 N.Y. 687, 77 N.E.2d 6 (1947), *aff'ing* 272 App. Div. 799, 71 N.Y.S.2d 736 (1st Dep't); Lockhart/McClure (1954) 294–301. Wilson's book would not be in print again for another decade.

18 'The Law Knows No Heresy'

1 *Bridges v. California*, 314 U.S. 252, 282 (1941) (Frankfurter, J. dissenting) (emphasis supplied). Frankfurter had learned from Holmes and from the writings of James Bradley Thayer that statutes enacted by elected legislatures are to be afforded great judicial deference. See *West Virginia St. Bd. of Educ. v. Barnette*, 319 U.S. 624, 667–70 (1943) (Frankfurter, J. dissenting); Frankfurter (1960) 299–300; Kurland ch. 2; Hirsch 128–9, 174, 180–1; Alexander Bickel, 'Applied Politics and the Science of Law,' in Mendelson 164, 179–81; Baker 223–4; Thomas 5–7.

2 *Lawson v. United States*, 339 U.S. 934 (*denying cert.*), *rehearing denied*, 339 U.S. 972 (1950); Frank (1958) 190; Herman Pritchett, 'Libertarian

Motivations on the Vinson Court,' *Am. Pol. Sci. Rev.* 47/2:321, 322 (June 1953); Caute 144; I.F. Stone, 'The New Chief Justice' (1953), in *The Haunted Fifties* (NY 1963) 58; McWilliams 74–6.

3 310 U.S. 296, 303, 310 (1940). See also *Thomas v. Collins*, 323 U.S. 516, 537 (1945) ('"Free trade in ideas" means free trade in the opportunity to persuade to action, not merely to describe facts') (citing authority); *Chaplinsky v. New Hampshire*, 315 U.S. 568, 569–70 (1942); *United States v. Ballard*, 322 U.S. 78, 87 (1944) (per Douglas, J.).

4 *Kunz*, 340 U.S. 290, 294 (1951), *rev'ing* 300 N.Y. 273, 278, 90 N.E.2d 455 (1949), *citing Saia v. New York*, 334 U.S. 558 (1948); Frank (1958) 191. See also *Niemotko v. Maryland*, 340 U.S. 268 (1951); *Chaplinski v. New Hampshire*, 315 U.S. 568, 571–2 (1942).

5 Before Nuremberg, Jackson had written: 'The very purpose of the First Amendment is to foreclose public authority from assuming guardianship of the public mind through regulating the press, speech, and religion. In this field every person must be his own watchman for truth, because the forefathers did not trust any government to separate the true from the false for us.' *Thomas v. Collins*, 323 U.S. 516, 545 (1945) (Jackson, J. concurring) (citing *Barnette*). See also *Terminiello v. Chicago*, 337 U.S. 1, 32 (1949) (Jackson, J. dissenting).

6 Gen. 32:29; *Records of the Colony of New Plymouth*, vol. 11, *Laws 1623–1682*, ed. David Pulsifier (Boston 1861) 172; James Deetz and Patricia Scott Deetz, *The Times of Their Lives: Life, Love, and Death in Plymouth Colony* (NY 2000) 133; *For the Colony in Virginea Britannia*, comp. William Strachey (ca. 1611), ed. David Flaherty (Charlottesville 1969).

7 *Rex v. Taylor*, 3 Keble 608, 84 E.R. 906 (1676); Lawton 25–8; Hawkins, *Treatise of the Pleas of the Crown*, 7th ed. (London 1795) 1:12; Joel Bishop, *Bishop on Criminal Law*, 9th ed. (Chicago 1923) 2:54.

8 *Rex v. Taylor*; *State v. Chandler*, 2 Harr. 553, 556 (Del. 1837); James Fitzjames Stephen, *History of the Criminal Law of England* (London 1883) 2:469–76; Lindsey Middleton Aspland, *The Law of Blasphemy* (London 1884) 6–7; L. Levy 219–22; Nokes 56, 59. In Part VI of the *Reflections on the Revolution in France* (1790), Burke wrote that the English, 'far from thinking a religious national establishment unlawful, hardly think it lawful to be without one,' the established church being 'the foundation of their whole Constitution.' Blackstone characterized reviling the ordinances of the Church of England as a 'crime of a much grosser nature than ... mere non-conformity.' Blackstone 4.4.4 pp. 50–9.

9 *Rex v. Woolston*, 2 Str. 820, Fitzg. 64, 1 Barn. K.B. 162, 266, 94 Eng. Rep. 112, 181 (1729); James D. Hart, *The Popular Book* (NY 1950) 36; *Rex v. Williams*,

26 How. St Tr. 653, 703 (1797). See also *Regina v. Moxon*, 2 Mod. St Tr. 356 (Q.B. 1841) (prosecution of Shelley's *Queen Mab*).

10 *Lawrence v. Smith*, Jacob 471, 37 Eng. Rpts. 928 (Ch. 1822). See also *Southey v. Sherwood*, 2 Mer. 435, 35 Eng. Rpts. 1006 (Ch. 1817).

11 Francis Ludlow Holt, *Law of Libel* (NY 1818) 80n, quoting *Rex v. Williams*; Starkie, *Treatise on the Law of Slander and Libel* [abridgment of 2d London ed. of 1830] (Hartford, CT 1858) 2:127–31.

12 Province Laws ch. CV §§ 7, 8, *Charters and General Laws of the Colony and Province of Massachusetts Bay* (Boston 1814) 399.

13 William Bruce, *Archbold's Pleading and Evidence in Criminal Cases*, 20th ed. (London 1886) 892; *Crown Circuit Companion*, 8th ed. (London 1811) 260–1; *Crown Circuit Companion* (NY 1816) 260–1. See also *Hustler Magazine, Inc. v. Falwell*, 485 U.S. 46 (1988).

14 'Report on Letters from the Ministers in Paris' (20 Dec. 1783), in *Works of Thomas Jefferson*, ed. Paul Leicester Ford (NY 1904–5) 4:189, 197–8; Hamburger chs. 4–5, 7.

15 Wright, *Views of Society and Manners in America* (1821), ed. Paul R. Baker (Cambridge, MA 1963) 224–5; *Watson v. Jones*, 80 U.S. 679, 728 (1871). See also *Davis v. Beason*, 133 U.S. 333, 341–2 (1890) (per Field, J.) (polygamy is a crime tending 'to destroy the purity of the marriage relation, to disturb the peace of families, to degrade woman, and to debase man. Few crimes are more pernicious to the best interests of society ... To call [its] advocacy a tenet of religion is to offend the common sense of mankind'); Feldman 99–108; Gaustad 44–9.

16 *Updegraph v. Commonwealth*, 11 Serg. and Rawle 394, 409 (Pa. 1824); Madison, 'Memorial and Remonstrance against Religious Assessments' (20 June 1785), in *Papers of James Madison*, ed. William T. Hutchinson and William M.E. Rachal (Chicago 1962–91) 8:298; *In re King*, 46 Fed. 912 (W.D. Tenn. 1891); Curry 204–22. See also 'Constitution or Form of Government for the Commonwealth of Massachusetts – 1780,' Pt. I Art. III, in *Federal and State Constitutions[,] Colonial Charters, and other Organic Laws of the States, Territories and Colonies*, comp. Francis Newton Thorpe (Washington 1909) 3:1889; 'Constitution of New Hampshire – 1792, Bill of Rights Art. VI,' in *id.* 4:2471–2; *Engel v. Vitale*, 370 U.S. 421, 428n10 (1962); Amar (1998) 32–3; Amar (2005) 390; Stokes 1:408–66; Hamburger 213. When Connecticut's church/state connection was dissolved, Jefferson professed to Adams his pleasure 'that a Protestant popedom is no longer to disgrace the American history and character.' Quoted in Gaustad 38.

17 Conn. Pub. Stat. L. tit. 22 § 67 (1821); Md. Rev. L. (1859) Art. 30 § 12; Jefferson/Dufief, 19 April 1814, in *Writings of Thomas Jefferson*, ed. Andrew

A. Lipscomb and Albert Ellery Bergh (Washington 1903–7) 14:127; *Vidal v. Mayor of Philadelphia*, 43 U.S. (2 How.) 127, 198 (1844); *Zeisweiss v. James*, 63 Pa. 465, 470–1 (1870).

18 *Church of the Holy Trinity v. United States*, 143 U.S. 457, 465–6, 471 (1892); Hamburger 273–5; *Cantwell v. Connecticut*, 310 U.S. 296, 303 (1940); *Everson v. Bd. of Educ.*, 330 U.S. 1, 15–16 (1947); Amar (1998) 33, 41–5; McBrien 68; Berger 6–7.

19 Hatch 59–60; Dwight 4:260, 269; Handy (1977) ch. 5; Tocqueville (1960) 62.

20 James Turner, *Without God, without Creed: The Origins of Unbelief in America* (Baltimore 1985) 53, 74–5, 101; Rand B. Evans, 'The Origins of American Academic Psychology,' in *Explorations in the History of Psychology in the United States*, ed. Josef Brozek (Lewisburg, PA 1984) 17, 35; Post 21–2; Daniel Dorchester, *Christianity in the United States*, rev. ed. (Cincinnati 1895) 349; Buchanan, *The Philosophy of Human Nature* (1812; re-ed. Gainesville, FL 1969) 3–4; J. Woodbridge Riley, *American Philosophy: The Early Schools* (1907; NY 1958) 373–95.

21 Knowlton, *Elements of Modern Materialism* (Adams, MA 1829); Humphrey, *Miscellaneous Discourses and Reviews* (Amherst 1834) 257, 258; Smith 50; S.J.W. Tabor, 'The Late Charles Knowlton, M.D.,' *Boston Med. and Surg. J.* 45:153–7 (1851); Knowlton, *A History of the Recent Excitement in Ashfield* (Ashfield, MA 1834) 2; Knowlton, *Fruits of Philosophy* (1836), in Sripati Chandrasekhar, *'A Dirty Filthy Book': The Writings of Charles Knowlton and Annie Besant on Reproductive Physiology* (Berkeley 1981).

22 *Commonwealth v. Kneeland*, 37 Mass. 206 (1838); *Report of the Arguments of the Attorney of the Commonwealth* [S.D. Parker], *at the Trials of Abner Kneeland, for Blasphemy* (Boston 1834) 12, 13; Andrew Dunlap, *Speech Delivered before the Municipal Court of the City of Boston in Defence of Abner Kneeland* (Boston 1834); A Cosmopolite [David Henshaw], *Review of the Prosecution against Abner Kneeland, for Blasphemy* (Boston 1835); Post 52–7; Hamburger 188–9; Norman Himes, *Medical History of Contraception* (1936; NY 1970) 226; Himes, 'Introductory Note,' in Knowlton, *Fruits of Philosophy*, ed. Himes (Mount Vernon, NY 1937) v, ix; Helen Lefkowitz Horowitz, *Rereading Sex: Battles over Sexual Knowledge and Suppression in Nineteenth-Century America* (NY 2002) 70–3; L. Levy 413–23; 'The Legality of Atheism,' *Harv. L. Rev.* 31:289 (1917); P. Miller 195; Hildreth, *History of the United States*, vol. 1 (1849) 369.

23 *People v. Ruggles*, 8 Johnson's [NY] Rep. 290, 291 (1811); L. Levy 401–7; *State v. Chandler*, 2 Harr. 553, 555 (Del. 1837); *Ex parte Delaney*, 43 Cal. 478, 481 (1872); Joel Bishop, *Commentaries on the Criminal Law*, 7th ed. (Boston 1882) 1:309–10; *People v. Porter*, 2 Park Crim. Rep. [NY] 14 (1923).

24 Opinion no. 377, 8 Feb. 1884, *Official Opinions of the Assistant Attorneys-*

General for the Post-Office Department, vol. 1 (Washington, DC 1905) 899; *United States v. Moore,* 104 Fed. 78, 79 (D. KY 1900).

25 State v. Mockus, 120 Me. 84, 113 A. 39 (1921); William Wolkovich-Valkavicius, 'Two Lithuanian Immigrants' Blasphemy Trials during the Red Scare,' *Hist. J. of Mass.* 145–57 (Summer 1998).

26 *People v. Baylinson,* 211 App. Div. 40, 206 N.Y.S. 809 (1st Dep't 1924); Walter E. Edge, 'The Non-Effectiveness of the Volstead Act,' *AAAP&SS* 109:67, 82–4 (1923).

27 Kallen, *The Liberal Spirit* (Ithaca, NY 1948); Pfeffer 788n; Jane Clapp, *Art Censorship* (Metuchen, NJ 1972) 240–2; Linda Bank Downs, *Diego Rivera* (NY 1999) 111–12, 173–9; http://xroads.virginia.edu/~MA04/hess/RockRivera/newspapers.html.

19 In the Supreme Court

1 *Joseph Burstyn, Inc. v. Wilson,* 342 U.S. 930 (1952) (*per curiam*).

2 Statement as to Jurisdiction 12, Brief for Appellant 25–46, *Joseph Burstyn, Inc. v. Wilson,* 343 U.S. 495 (1952).

3 Transcript 4, *Joseph Burstyn, Inc. v. Wilson,* 343 U.S. 495 (1952). A transcript of the oral argument is in Bur. 19, JBC. It is summarized by Leo Pfeffer of the Commission on Law and Social Action of the American Jewish Congress in *CLSA Reports* (28 April 1952).

4 Frank (1952–3) 30n90.

5 *Nation* (24 Nov. 1951) 451–2; *Box Office* (8 March 1952) 1. Yale law professor John Frank later wrote that if *The Miracle* had been a U.S. production, 'the Legion of Decency and private censorship within the industry would have strangled [it]' long before it reached New York's censors, since 'the industry shivers under attack from anyone with a loud voice.' Frank (1952–3) 30.

6 See Transcript of Record 15–17, 30, 48–52, *Joseph Burstyn, Inc. v. Wilson,* 343 U.S. 495 (1952).

7 343 U.S. 306, 313–14 (1952).

8 343 U.S. 502n12; Pfeffer 674; Thomas ch. 8. The onset of sound stimulated a few deluded optimists to argue that talkies comprised a new medium to which *Mutual Film* did not apply. Fox, for instance, argued that it was not obliged to present its sound films to Pennsylvania's censors, since in enacting its film censorship statute back in 1915, the state's legislature could not have had the censorship of the human voice in mind. In 1929, Pennsylvania's highest court flatly rejected that argument. *In re Fox Film Corp.,* 295 Pa. 461, 145 A. 514 (1929). See also *In re Vitagraph, Inc.,* 295 Pa. 471, 145 A. 518 (1929).

9   343 U.S. 506n20.

10 Trilling and others testified that Wilson's book was painful, even 'cynical,' perhaps in the end a failure, but strictly literary, even astringent, and not sexy or tawdry in the mode of Kathleen Winsor's best-seller *Forever Amber* (1944). Record on Appeal 49–54, *People v. Doubleday and Co.*, 297 N.Y. 687, 77 N.E.2d 6 (1947), *aff'd per curiam by equally divided Court*, 335 U.S. 848 (1948).

11 The closest Clark came to acknowledging the content of Rossellini's film was to quote in a footnote Judge Fuld's comment that 'the film in question makes no direct attack on, or criticism of, any religious dogma or principle, and it is not claimed to be obscene, scurrilous, intemperate or abusive.' 343 U.S. 504n15, *quoting* 303 N.Y. 271–2, 101 N.E.2d 680 (Fuld, J. dissenting).

12 343 U.S. 506–7 (Reed, J. concurring).

13 G. Williams 117. Cf. La Piana's several autobiographical musings, at age ninety-one, when he was apparently seeking a reconciliation with the Church. GLPP.

14 Frankfurter (1960) 291; Shuster 6; Baker 40. When conservative Chief Justice Fred Vinson died before oral argument in the civil-rights cases collectively known as *Brown v. Board of Education*, Frankfurter reportedly remarked: 'This is the first indication that I have ever had that there is a God.'

15 *Winters*, 333 U.S. 509 citing *Stromberg v. California*, 283 U.S. 359, 369 (1931). The Supreme Court believed that a state statute relating to, for example, utility regulation, may satisfy the Fourteenth Amendment's due-process requirement on a mere showing that there was a 'rational basis' for enacting it, but that a more rigorous standard must be applied to any statute touching on the more sensitive civil-rights questions involved in the First Amendment. Such statutes would be held valid 'only to prevent grave and immediate danger to interests which the state may lawfully protect.' *Barnette*, 319 U.S. 639 (Jackson, J.). See also *Herndon v. Lowry*, 301 U.S. 242, 258 (1937); *Schenck v. United States*, 249 U.S. 47, 51–2 (1919) (per Holmes, J.); *Connally v. Gen. Const. Co.*, 269 U.S. 385, 390–4 (1926). As Justice Clark indicated in *Burstyn*, suppressing speech in order to protect religious groups from feeling offended is not something a state may lawfully do. See also *Adamson v. California*, 332 U.S. 46, 67–8 (1947) (Frankfurter, J. concurring); Davis 262–3; Thomas ch. 7.

16 303 N.Y. 242, 101 N.E.2d 665 (1951). See also *Winters*, 333 U.S. 510 *citing Fox v. Washington*, 236 U.S. 273, 277 (1915). At oral argument, in response to a question by Frankfurter, Brind averred that in deciding that legislative

use of the word 'sacrilegious' complied with due process, the New York Court of Appeals had used only the dictionary and its own collective experience.

17 bMS 104, GLPP; La Piana 11; Frankfurter memo, 25 April 1951, Reel 58, Part One, 01, 05, FFP; *NYT* (28 Oct. 1951) 93. See also Herbert Monte Levy / Charles A. Brind, 5 Nov. 1951, Box 1274, ACLUP.

18 Frankfurter (1960) 4; Hirsch 13; Garson Kanin, 'Trips to Felix,' in Mendelson 34, 41.

19 Mark 13:14 and Matt. 23:15 allude to the 'abomination' or 'devastating desecration' ($\beta\delta\acute{\epsilon}\lambda\upsilon\gamma\mu\alpha$) predicted in Daniel 9:27 and 10:31 of attempting to place an image, idol, or altar of Zeus in the Temple in order to convert it into a shrine to the Greek god. Such a thing was attempted by Antiochus IV Epiphanes in 167 B.C.E., one of the acts triggering the Maccabean revolt. The Hebrew word used in Daniel and in 1 Macc. 1:57 for such an 'abomination' or 'idol' was *shiqqūts*. The physicality of blasphemy also inheres in the Hebrew used in Leviticus 24:16, *nāqav*, which can mean to deface God's name by, for example, piercing a piece of paper with His name on it. Tractate Sanhedrin 56a.

20 343 U.S. 522–4 (Frankfurter, J. concurring). While Aquinas defines 'the sin of sacrilege' as 'the irreverent treatment of a sacred thing,' he does not really limit sacrilege to the violation of physical objects, stating that 'any injury inflicted on the Christian people, for instance, that unbelievers should be put in authority over it, is an irreverence for a sacred thing, and is reasonably called a sacrilege.' Further: 'Those are said to sin against the sanctity of divine law who assail God's law, as heretics and blasphemers do. These are guilty of unbelief, through not believing in God; and of sacrilege, through perverting the words of the divine law.' *Summa Theologica*, trans. Fathers of the English Dominican Province (NY 1947–8), Second Part of the Second Part, Question 99, Arts. 1–2; *id.* Art. 3; La Piana, 'Sacrilege,' undated MS, GLPP. As the quoted passage indicates, Aquinas finds blasphemy and sacrilege to be similar, since assailing divine law is also the perversion of the words of that law. An overlap between the two terms is noted by Samuel Johnson, whose *Dictionary of the English Language* (1755) quotes John Ayliffe's *Parergon Juris Canonici Anglicani* (London 1726): 'Blasphemy is a malediction, and a sacrilegious distraction from the Godhead.'

21 *Jacobellis v. Ohio*, 378 U.S. 184, 197 (1964) (Stewart, J. concurring). Among the sources of *Funk and Wagnalls New Standard Dictionary* was Samuel Johnson's *Dictionary*, defining sacrilege as 'the crime of appropriating ... what is devoted to religion ... the crime of violating or profaning things

sacred,' although Johnson wittily placed between these two phrases his own dramatic locution: 'the crime of robbing heaven.' In 1632, Sir Henry Spelman had defined 'sacrilege' as 'an invading, stealing, or purloining from God, any Sacred thing, either belonging to the majesty of his Person, or appropriate to the celebration of his Divine Service.' *The History and Fate of Sacrilege* (1632; London 1698) 1. The *Oxford English Dictionary* (1884–1928) includes among its definitions: 'The profanation of anything sacred,' although it characterizes this as only a 'figurative' and 'transferred' sense. In 1918 an appellate court refused to allow a jury to hear expert testimony on the issue of whether a film called *Sins of the Sons* was obscene, since 'the average person of healthy and wholesome mind knows well enough what the words "immoral" and "obscene" mean and can intelligently apply the test to any picture presented to him.' *People ex rel. Guggenheim v. Chicago*, 209 Ill. App. 582, 583 (1918) quoting *Block v. Chicago*, 239 Ill. 251, 87 N.E. 1011 (1909). See also *United States v. Limehouse*, 285 U.S. 424, 425 (1932) (Comstock Act amendment proscribing 'filthy' letters was violated by a man who sent letters that were 'unquestionably filthy within the popular meaning of that term').

22 343 U.S. 531–2 and n56 (Frankfurter, J., concurring). Frankfurter had thought it inappropriate to see the film. De Grazia/Newman 81.

20 Candour and Shame

1 E. Goodman 424; *Motion Picture Herald* 187/9:7 (31 May 1952). The MPAA's official reaction was positive. *Motion Picture Bulletin* (17 June 1952). Newspaper reactions, predominantly positive, are collected in Box 1274, ACLUP.

2 *Gelling v. Texas*, 343 U.S. 960 (1952), *rev'ing per curiam* 157 Tex. Crim. App. 516, 247 S.W.2d 95; Frankfurter, 'Memorandum for the Conference,' 28 May 1952, Frankfurter/Vinson, 29 May 1952, reel 57, FFP.

3 *Brown v. Allen*, 344 U.S. 443, 540 (1953); Marshall 63–4; 'New York Motion Picture Censorship Law,' *Catholic Lawyer* 1/1:58, 59 (Jan. 1955); Note, *St John's L. Rev.* 27:131, 134–5 (1952); Murray 54, 60; Couvares 267; Driggs 131–3.

4 Whelan, 'Censorship and the Constitutional Concept of Morality,' *Georgetown L.J.* 43:547, 548–9, 567 (1955); Desmond 35; R. Gannon 332–4.

5 Turner 109, 134; Lynch, *The Image Industries* (NY 1959) 49; Kerr in *Commonweal* 209, 210–11; McDonald 186; Tate, 'Orthodoxy and the Standard of Literature,' *New Republic* 128:24 (5 Jan. 1953).

6 *NYT* (25 Oct. 1952) 1/2; partially quoted in *Wieman v. UpDegraff*, 344 U.S. 183, 191n4 (1952).

7 *Barsky v. Bd. of Regents*, 305 N.Y. 89, 111 N.E.2d 222 (1953), *aff'd*, 347 U.S. 442 (1954).

8 *Watkins v. United States*, 354 U.S. 178, 187–99 (1957) (Congress is not a 'law enforcement or trial agency' and has 'no general authority to expose the private affairs of individuals without justification in terms of [its] functions ... [n]or can the First Amendment freedoms of speech, press, religion, or political belief and association be abridged'); *Sweezy v. New Hampshire*, 354 U.S. 234 (1957).

9 Dmytryk 118–19; Jeff Smith, '"A Good Business Proposition,"' *Velvet Light Trap* 23:75 (1989); R. Lardner 146–8; Fariello 63–5.

10 Art. 66A § 6(a), Md. Ann. Code (1955 Cum. Supp.) 449; *United Artists Corp. v. Maryland State Bd. of Censors*, 210 Md. 586, 124 A.2d 292 (1956).

11 Stanley Wiener, 'Final Curtain Call for the Motion Picture Censor,' *Western Res. L. Rev.* 4:148 (1953); T. Lewis; Jack Siegal, Note, *Temple L. Rev.* 26:192 (1952/53); John Sanders, Note, *N.C. L. Rev.* 31:103 (1952); Note, *Minn. L. Rev.* 37:209 (1953).

12 *In re Commercial Pictures Corp. v. Bd. of Regents*, 305 N.Y. 336, 113 N.E.2d 502 (1953), *rev'd*, 346 U.S. 587 (1954); Desmond 27. Although New York's legislature subsequently attempted to revive 'immoral' as a statutory term by giving it a definition, the U.S. Supreme Court struck the new statute. See *Kingsley Int'l Pictures Corp.* v. *Regents of the Univ. of the State of N.Y.*, 360 U.S. 684 (1959).

13 *R.K.O. Radio Pictures, Inc. v. Dep't of Educ.*, 162 Ohio St 263, 122 N.E.2d 769 (1954); *Superior Films, Inc. v. Dep't of Educ. of Ohio*, 346 U.S. 587 (1954), *rev'ing* 159 Ohio St 315, 329, 112 N.E.2d 311, 318 (1953). The Ohio case involved Joseph Losey's 1951 remake of Fritz Lang's *M*.

14 *American Civ. Lib. Union v. Chicago*, 3 Ill.2d 334, 348, 121 N.E.2d 585, 592 (1954), *app. dism'd*, 348 U.S. 979 (1955). See also Box 1275, folder 1, ACLUP.

15 *American Civ. Lib. Union v. Chicago*, 13 Ill. App.2d 278, 288, 141 N.E.2d 56, 61 (1st Dist. 1957).

16 *Catholic World* 180:24, 26 (Oct. 1954); *Holmby Prods., Inc. v. Vaughn*, 350 U.S. 870 (1955) (*per curiam*) *rev'ing* 177 Kan. 728, 282 P.2d 412 (1955); Butters 252–62; Leff/Simmons ch. 9; Black (1998) 120–8; *Superior Films, Inc. v. Dep't of Educ.*, 346 U.S. 587 (1954).

17 Kashner/MacNair ch. 6; Paul Blanshard, *The Right to Read* (Boston 1955) 208.

18 343 U.S. 531–2n56 (Frankfurter, J., concurring); Bob Pondillo, 'The Chicago Television "Holy War" of 1956–1957' (speech, Aug. 1998), Ass'n for Education in Journalism and Mass Communication Archives, AEJ 98 PondillB HIS (21 Dec. 1998) .

19 Kanin 178; *Esquire* 48/1:31, 32 (July 1957); Leamer 250–3; Steele 321–31; McLean 179–80; L. Parsons (1961) 80; Kobal 466n; Zeffirelli 271.

20 *Roth*, 354 U.S. 476 (1957); *United States v. Kennerley*, 209 Fed. 119 (S.D.N.Y. 1913) (L. Hand, D.J.); *Butler*, 352 U.S. 380 (1957); Lockhart/McClure (1960); Louis B. Schwartz, 'Criminal Obscenity Law: Portents from Recent Supreme Court Decisions and Proposals of the American Law Institute in the Model Penal Code,' *Pa. Bar Ass'n Q.* 29:8 (1957).

21 Gustafson in *Sexuality on the Island Earth* (NY 1970) 28, 34–5; *Miller*, 413 U.S. 15, 24 (1973); David A.J. Richards, 'Free Speech and Obscenity Law: Toward a Moral Theory of the First Amendment,' *U. Pa. L. Rev.* 123:45 (1974–5); Randall (1968) ch. 4; 1974 N.Y.L. ch. 989 § 1 *codified* N.Y. Penal Code § 235.00(1) (McKinney 2000).

22 491 U.S. 397 (1989).

23 *Fulgens Corona Gloriae*, in Carlen 3:231; *Ad Caeli Reginam*, in *id.* 3:271; Hardon (1959) 208–9; E. Ryan 365–7.

24 Edward Schillebeeckx and Catharina Halkes, *Mary* (1992) trans. John Bowden (NY 1993) 1; Pelikan (1959) 138–41; Neuner/Dupuis 199; Guitton 1; Carroll (1989) 41–2; Reeves 253–7, 286–90, 364–6; E. Johnson 125–31; Francis Simons, 'The Catholic Church and the New Morality,' *Cross Currents* 16/4:429, 430–1n (Fall 1966); Hines 7, 47; Spretnak 50, 55; *Lumen Gentium* (21 Nov. 1964) ¶ 67.

25 D. O'Brien (1972) 66–79; McDonald 171; Clancy et al. (Santa Barbara 1961) 63–4; Clancy, 'Freedom of the Screen,' *Commonweal* 59/20:500, 501 (19 Feb. 1954); *Time's Covenant: The Essays and Sermons of William Clancy*, ed. Eugene Green (Pittsburgh 1987) vii, viii; www.faithquest.com/modules.php?name=Sectionsandop=viewarticleandartid=76.

26 Avery R. Dulles, *The Reshaping of Catholicism* (San Francisco 1988) 8; Cogley 121–3; Dever 69; Greeley (1986) 367; Greeley (2004) chs. 2–5; D. O'Brien (1972) 156–61; Paul VI, *Humanae Vitae* (25 July 1968); Greeley (1990) 6, 11; Greeley (1981A) 131; Biever 537–9.

27 Rivers, *Aphrodite at Mid-Century* (Garden City 1973) 38–40. See also D. O'Brien (1972) ch. 8.

28 Humbert S. Nelli, 'Italian Americans in Contemporary America,' in L. Tomasi 78, 83–4; Foreword to Fogarty (1985) xi; Reher 140. See also Greeley (1971) ch. 6. By 1970, of 47.8 million Catholics in the United States, 10 million were of Italian background, 8.3 million Irish, 7.6 million German, 5.3 million Polish. Harold J. Abramson, *Ethnic Diversity in Catholic America* (NY 1973) 19.

29 Bill McCready quoted in Greeley (1986) 364; Greeley, *Crisis in the Church* (Chicago 1979) 10; Greeley (2000) 100; Cogley 136–9; *Marialis Cultus* (2 Feb. 1974) ¶ 34. See also Ellen Chesler, *Women and Madness* (Garden City, NY 1972) 26, 230–1, 268–73; Susie Bright, *Susie Bright's Sexual State of the Union* (NY 1997) 11–12; Biever 585–8; Marianne Hirsch, *The Mother/*

Daughter Plot: Narrative, Psychoanalysis, Feminism (Bloomington, IN 1989) 7, 34–6.

30 Regarding women's extensive leadership in the early Church, see Elisabeth Schüssler Fiorenza, *In Memory of Her: Some Feminist Concerns and the Relevance of the New Testament* (NY 1983).

31 Halle, *Inside Culture* (Chicago 1993) 182–4; Greeley (2004) ch. 8; R. Brown (1973) 24–34; E. Johnson 9–11.

32 *Times* [London], 20 Jan. 2006; *Irish Independent*, 19 Jan. 2006; *NYT*, 22 Jan. 2006.

33 Meier 2:520–1, 533nn41–2; Crapanzano 30; Apolito 5, 23–32.

34 Pelikan (1959) 137–8; Spretnak 614; Otto Semmelroth, *Mary, Archetype of the Church* (NY 1963) ch. 3.

35 Richard C. Stern, Clayton N. Jefford, and Guerric DeBona, *Savior on the Silver Screen* (NY 1999) 95–125; Locke/Warren 1, 7.

36 *Nayak v. MCA, Inc.*, 911 F.2d 1082 (5th Cir. 1990), *cert. denied*, 498 U.S. 1087 (1991); Charles Lyons, *The New Censors: Movies and the Culture Wars* (Philadelphia 1997) ch. 5; *Cummins v. Campbell*, 44 F.3d 847 (10th Cir. 1994); L. Levy 531–3; Haskins 360–1.

37 Pfeffer 675.

38 'Post-Modern Art and the Death of Obscenity Law,' *Yale L.J.* 99:1359 (1990).

39 *Engel v. Vitale*, 370 U.S. 421, 425 (1962); *Abington Township School District v. Schempp*, 374 U.S. 203 (1963).

40 *Allegheny County v. ACLU*, 492 U.S. 573 (1989). But see *Lynch v. Donnelly*, 465 U.S. 668 (1984).

41 *Brown v. Board of Regents*, 640 F. Supp. 674, 679 (D. Neb. 1986) (citing authority); Locke/Warren 75, 76.

42 *NYT* (1 Aug. 1982) H5; Varacalli 3, 5; Apolito 14; McDannell 37; Richard N. Ostling et al., 'Why Believers Are Outraged,' *Time* 133/9:30, 31 (27 Feb. 1989).

43 See *National Endowment for the Arts v. Finley*, 524 U.S. 569 (1998).

44 *Brooklyn Inst. Of Arts v. City of New York*, 64 F. Supp.2d 184 (E.D.N.Y. 1999).

45 *NYT* (17 Dec. 1999) 1/3.

46 See Trasatti 47–61, 95–104, 161–7, 227–77; R. Rossellini (1977) 33; Richard Walsh, *Reading the Gospels in the Dark: Portrayals of Jesus in Film* (Harrisburg, PA 2003).

47 R. Rossellini (1971) 15; J. Hughes 89; Brunette 307; Gallagher (1998) 593; Trasatti 85–94.

48 Forgacs/Lutton/Nowell-Smith 80, 89; Bergala/Narboni 11, 15; R. Rossellini (1992) 230; J. Hughes 89.

49 *Monthly Film Bull.* 194/17:24–5 (Feb.-March 1950); Venturi; *Sight and Sound*

19/2:86 (April 1950); I. Rossellini 39; *Corpus Christy Times* (*NYT* News Service) (22 June 1971); Gallagher (1998) 600–602; Forgacs/Lutton/ Nowell-Smith 161, 162; R. Rossellini (1992) 230.

50 Renata Adler, *Year in the Dark* (NY 1969) 224; www.usccb.org/fb/ vaticanfilms.htm.

51 Peyton 57–64, 87–9; Donnelly 262; Joan Wester Anderson, *Forever Young* (Allen, TX 2000) ch. 6; Lord (1953) 313.

52 Peyton 118–19.

53 Kathleen Carroll, 'Christ and the Odd Couple,' *NY Daily News* (14 Oct. 1975) 52/1; Gallagher (1998) 665; Brunette ch. 38.

54 R. Rossellini (1987) 29, 45–6; Gallagher (1998) 664–74; *Chicago Tribune* (14 Sept. 1975) 25; *NY Daily News* (14 Oct. 1975) 52; Virgilio Fantuzzi, *Cinema sacro e profano* (Rome 1983) 92. In an interview appended to the Multi-media San Paolo DVD (2000) of *Il messia*, writer/producer Silvia D'Amico Bendico stated that for several years Rossellini had rejected Peyton's entreaties to do a film about the Madonna, but that when Peyton caught up with him at Rice University, Rossellini suggested doing a film about Jesus instead.

Bibliography

Abbott, Lyman. 'The New Puritanism.' In *The New Puritanism*, by Abbott et al. NY 1898.

Abell, Aaron I. *American Catholicism and Social Action: A Search for Social Justice, 1865–1950*. Garden City 1960.

– ed. *American Catholic Thought on Social Questions*. Indianapolis 1968.

Abrahamson, Harold J. 'Ethnic Diversity within Catholicism.' *J. Soc. Hist.* 4/4:359 (1971).

Adler, Mortimer J. *Philosopher at Large: An Intellectual Biography*. NY 1977.

Agee, James. *Agee on Film*. 2 vols. NY 1958–60.

Ahlstrom, Sydney E. *A Religious History of the American People*. New Haven 1972.

Akenson, Donald Harman. *Small Differences: Irish Catholics and Irish Protestants, 1815–1922*. Kingston, ON 1988.

Alba, Richard D. *Italian Americans: Into the Twilight of Ethnicity*. Englewood Cliffs, NJ 1985.

Allen, Frederick Allen. *Since Yesterday: The Nineteen-Thirties in America*. NY 1940.

Allitt, Patrick. *Catholic Converts: British and American Intellectuals Return to Rome*. Ithaca, NY 1997.

Alpert, Hollis. *Fellini: A Life*. NY 1986.

Amar, Akhil Reed. *America's Constitution: A Biography*. NY 2005.

– *The Bill of Rights: Creation and Reconstruction*. New Haven 1998.

Anderson, Christopher. 'Television and Hollywood in the 1940s.' In Schatz 422.

Apolito, Paolo. *The Internet and the Madonna*. 2002. Trans. Antony Shugaar. Chicago 2005.

Arensberg, Conrad M., and Solon T. Kimball. *Family and Community in Ireland*. Cambridge, MA 1940.

Arnold, Thurman. *Bottlenecks of Business*. NY 1940.

– *Voltaire and the Cowboy: The Letters of Thurman Arnold*. Boulder 1977.

Ashe, Geoffrey. *The Virgin: Mary's Cult and the Re-emergence of the Goddess*. London 1976.

Astarita, Tommaso. *Between Salt Water and Holy Water: A History of Southern Italy*. NY 2005.

Atkin, Nicholas, and Frank Tallett. *Priests, Prelates and People: A History of European Catholicism*. NY 2003.

Atkins, Gaius Glenn. 'Craftsmen of the Soul.' In *'Craftsmen of the Soul' and Other Addresses*. NY 1925.

– *Religion in Our Times*. NY 1932.

Atkins, Gaius Glenn, and Frederick L. Fagley. *History of American Congregationalism*. Boston 1942.

Atkinson, Clarissa W., Constance H. Buchanan, and Margaret R. Miles, eds. *Immaculate and Powerful*. Boston 1985.

Aubert, Roger, et al. *The Church in a Secularised Society*. NY 1978.

Austin, Bruce A., ed. *Current Research in Film: Audiences, Economics, and Law*. Vol. 4. Norwood, NJ 1988.

Avella, Steven M. 'J.T. McNicholas in the Age of Practical Thomism.' *Rec. Am. Cath. Hist. Soc. Phil.* 97:15 (1986).

Avella, Steven M., and Thomas A. Kselman. 'Marian Piety and the Cold War in the U.S.' *Cath. Hist. Rev.* 72/3:403 (July 1986).

Ayer, Douglas, Roy E. Bates, and Peter J. Herman. 'Self-Censorship in the Movie Industry' (1970). In Kindem 215.

Babiuch, Jolanta, and Jonathan Luxmoore. *The Vatican and the Red Flag*. London 1999.

[Bachofen, Charles Augustine.] *Commentary on the New Code of Canon Law*. 6 vols. St Louis 1921.

– *The Pastor According to the New Code of Canon Law*. 1923; 3d ed. St Louis 1926.

– *The Rights and Duties of Ordinaries According to the Code and Apostolic Faculties*. St Louis 1924.

Bacon, Leonard Woolsey. *An Inside View of the Vatican Council*. NY [1870?].

Bagot, Richard. *The Italians of Today*. 1912; Chicago 1913.

Baker, Liva. *Felix Frankfurter*. NY 1969.

Baldelli, Pio. *Roberto Rossellini*. Rome 1972.

Baliæ, Carolo. 'The Mediaeval Controversy over the Immaculate Conception' (1955). In O'Connor 161.

Balio, Tino, ed. *The American Film Industry*. 1976; 2d ed. Madison, WI 1985.

– *Grand Design: Hollywood as a Modern Business Enterprise 1930–1939*. 1993; Berkeley 1995.

Barbas, Samantha. *The First Lady of Hollywood: A Biography of Louella Parsons.* Berkeley 2005.

Barnard, Toby. *A New Anatomy of Ireland: The Irish Protestants, 1649–1770.* New Haven 2003.

Barrett, Alfred. 'Father Lord – Citizen of Two Worlds.' *Catholic World.* 180:418 (March 1955).

Barrett, E. Boyd. *While Peter Sleeps.* NY 1929.

Barrett, Edward L., Jr. *The Tenney Committee: Legislative Investigation of Subsersive Activities.* Ithaca, NY 1951.

Barrows, J.H., ed. *The World's Parliament of Religions.* 2 vols. Chicago 1893.

Barry, Colman. *The Catholic Church and German Americans.* Milwaukee 1953.

Bartholomew, Robert O. *Report of Censorship of Motion Pictures ... of Cleveland.* Cleveland 1913.

Bates, Ernest Sutherland. *American Faith: Its Religious, Political, and Economic Foundations.* NY 1940.

Baxter, John. *Fellini.* NY 1993.

Bayor, Ronald H., and Timothy J. Meagher, eds. *The New York Irish.* Baltimore 1996.

Beaumont, Gustave de. *Ireland: Social, Political, and Religious.* 1839. Trans. W.C. Taylor. Cambridge, MA 2006.

Beckett, J.C. *The Making of Modern Ireland.* NY 1966.

Bell, Rudolph M. *Fate and Honor, Family and Village.* Chicago 1979.

Bergala, Alain, and Jean Narboni, eds. *Roberto Rossellini.* Paris 1990.

Berger, Raoul. *The Fourteenth Amendment and the Bill of Rights.* Norman, OK 1989.

Bergman, Ingrid, and Alan Burgess. *My Story.* NY 1980.

Bernstein, Matthew. 'Hollywood Martyrdoms: *Joan of Arc* and Independent Production' (1986). In Austin 89.

– *Walter Wanger: Hollywood Independent.* Berkeley 1994.

– ed. *Controlling Hollywood: Censorship and Regulation in the Studio Era.* New Brunswick, NJ 1999.

Bertrand, Daniel, et al. *The Motion Picture Industry – a Pattern of Control.* 1941; NY 1978.

Besant, Annie. *Annie Besant: An Autobiography.* London 1893.

Biever, Bruce Francis. *Religion, Culture, and Values.* 1965; NY 1976.

Birdwell, Michael E. *Celluloid Soldiers: The Warner Bros. Campaign against Nazism.* NY 1999.

Black, Gregory D. *The Catholic Crusade against the Movies, 1940–1975.* Cambridge 1998.

– 'Hollywood Censored.' *Film History* 3/3:167 (1989).

– *Hollywood Censored: Morality Codes, Catholics and the Movies.* Cambridge 1994.

– 'Movies, Politics, and Censorship.' *J. Policy Hist.* 3:95 (1991).

Black, Gregory D., and Clayton R. Koppes. 'Blacks, Loyalty, and Motion Picture Propaganda in World War II.' *J. Am. Hist.* 73/2:383 (1986). Reprinted in Bernstein (1999) 130.

– *Hollywood Goes to War.* NY 1987.

Blackstone, William, Sir. *Commentaries on the Laws of England.* 4 vols. Oxford 1769.

Blanshard, Paul. *American Freedom and Catholic Power.* 1949; 2d ed. Boston 1958.

– *Communism, Democracy, and Catholic Power.* Boston 1951.

Boff, Leonardo. *The Maternal Face of God.* 1979. Trans. R.R. Barr and John W. Diercksmeier. San Francisco 1987.

Bogdanovich, Peter. *Who the Devil Made It.* NY 1997.

Bondanella, Peter. *The Films of Roberto Rossellini.* Cambridge 1993.

– *Italian Cinema: From Neorealism to the Present.* NY 1983.

Borde, Raymond. Review of *Amore. Les Temps Moderns* 13/139:566 (Sept. 1957).

Borde, Raymond, and Chaumeton Etienne. *A Panorama of American Film Noir, 1941–1953.* 1955; San Francisco 2002.

Bordwell, David, Janet Staiger, and Kristin Thomspon. *The Classical Hollywood Cinema.* NY 1985.

Bosworth, Patricia. *Anything Your Little Heart Desires.* NY 1997.

Bowen, Desmond. *Paul, Cardinal, Cullen and the Shaping of Modern Irish Catholicism.* Dublin 1983.

Briggs, Charles Augustus. 'Criticism and the Dogma of the Virgin Birth.' *North Am. Rev.* 182/6:861 (June 1906).

Briggs, John W. *An Italian Passage: Immigrants in Three American Cities 1890– 1930.* New Haven 1978.

Brody, Hugh. *Inishkillane: Change and Decline in the West of Ireland.* NY 1974.

Brogan, Denis W. *U.S.A.: An Outline of the Country, Its People and Institutions.* London 1941.

Brooks, Richard. *The Producer.* NY 1951.

Brooks, Van Wyck. *America's Coming-of-Age.* NY 1915.

Brown, Colin. *Miracles and the Critical Mind.* Grand Rapids, MI 1984.

Brown, Henry J. 'The "Italian Problem" in the Catholic Church of the United States, 1880–1900.' *Historical Records and Studies* [United States Catholic Historical Society] 35:46 (1946).

Brown, Raymond Edward. *The Birth of the Messiah.* 2d ed. NY 1993.

– *The Virginal Conception and Bodily Resurrection of Jesus.* NY 1973.

Brown, Stewart J., and David W. Miller, eds. *Piety and Power in Ireland 1760– 1960.* Belfast 2000.

Brown, Thomas N. *Irish-American Nationalism 1870–1890*. Philadelphia 1966.

Brownson, Orestes A. 'Catholicity Necessary to Sustain Popular Liberty' (1845). In *Essays and Reviews Chiefly on Theology, Politics, and Socialism*. NY 1852.

– 'Moral and Social Influence of Devotion to Mary' (1866) and 'Our Lady of Lourdes' (1875). In *Works of Orestes A. Brownson*. Vol. 8. 1883; NY 1966.

– 'The Worship of Mary.' *Brownson's Quarterly Review* 10:1 (Jan. 1853).

Brownstein, Ronald. *The Power and the Glitter: The Hollywood-Washington Connection*. NY 1990.

Brunette, Peter. *Rossellini*. NY 1987.

Buhle, Paul, and Dave Wagner. *Blacklisted: The Film Lover's Guide to the Hollywood Blacklist*. NY 2003.

– *Radical Hollywood: The Untold Story behind America's Favorite Movies*. NY 2002.

– *A Very Dangerous Citizen: Abraham Lincoln Polonsky and the Hollywood Left*. Berkeley 2001.

Burns, James A. *The Growth and Development of the Catholic School System in the United States*. NY 1912.

Bury, J.B. *History of the Papacy in the 19th Century (1864–1878)*. Ed. R.H. Murray. London 1930.

Butler, Edward Cuthbert. *The Vatican Council 1869–1870*. 1930; Westminster, MD 1962.

Butters, Gerald R., Jr. *Banned in Kansas: Motion Picture Censorship, 1915–1966*. Columbia, MO 2007.

Cadegan, Una M. 'Guardians of Democracy or Cultural Storm Troopers?' *Cath. Hist. Rev.* 87/2:252 (April 2001).

Callahan, Daniel. 'The Legacy of Pio Nono' (1965). In *The New Church: Essays in Catholic Reform*. NY 1966.

– *The Mind of the Catholic Layman*. NY 1963.

Carlen, Claudia, ed. *The Papal Encyclicals*. 5 vols. [Wilmington, NC] 1981.

Carol, Juniper B., ed. *Mariology*. 3 vols. Milwaukee 1955–61.

Carr, Aidan, and German Williams. 'Mary's Immaculate Conception.' In Carol 1:328.

Carr, Robert K. *The House Committee on Un-American Activities 1945–1950*. Ithaca, NY 1952.

– 'The Un-American Activities Committee and the Courts.' *La. L. Rev.* 11:282 (1951).

Carr, Steven Alan. *Hollywood and Anti-Semitism*. NY 2001.

Carroll, Michael. *Catholic Cults and Devotions*. Kingston, ON 1989.

– *The Cult of the Virgin Mary: Psychological Origins*. Princeton 1986.

– *Madonnas That Maim: Popular Catholicism in Italy since the Fifteenth Century*. Baltimore 1992.

– *Veiled Threats: The Logic of Popular Catholicism in Italy*. Baltimore 1996.

Casillo, Robert. *Gangster Priest: The Italian American Cinema of Martin Scorsese.* Toronto 2006.

Caute, David. *The Great Fear: The Anti-Communist Purge under Truman and Eisenhower.* NY 1978.

Cauthen, Kenneth. *The Impact of American Religious Liberalism.* NY 1962.

Ceplair, Larry, and Steven Englund. *The Inquisition in Hollywood.* Garden City 1980.

Chandler, Charlotte. *Ingrid: Ingrid Bergman, a Personal Biography.* NY 2007.

Child, Irvin L. *Italian or American? The Second Generation in Conflict.* New Haven 1943.

Cogley, John. *Catholic America.* NY 1973.

Cole, Lester. *Hollywood Red: The Autobiography of Lester Cole.* Palo Alto, CA 1981.

Comerford, R.V. *The Fenians in Context: Irish Politics and Society, 1848–82.* Dublin 1985.

Commonweal. *Catholicism in America.* NY 1954.

Conant, Michael. *Antitrust in the Motion Picture Industry: Economic and Legal Analysis.* Berkeley 1960.

Condren, Mary. *The Serpent and the Goddess.* San Francisco 1989.

Connell, K.H. *Irish Peasant Society: Four Historical Essays.* Oxford 1968.

– 'Peasant Marriage in Ireland after the Great Famine.' *Past and Present* 12:76 (1957).

– 'Peasant Marriage in Ireland: Its Structure and Development since the Famine.' *Econ. Hist. Rev.* 14:510 (1962).

– *The Population of Ireland, 1750–1845.* Oxford 1950.

Connolly, S.J. *Priests and People in Pre-famine Ireland, 1780–1845.* NY 1982.

– *Religion and Society in Nineteenth-Century Ireland.* Dublin 1985.

'Constitutional Limitations on the Un-American Activities Committee.' *Col. L. Rev.* 47:416 (1947).

Cooke, Alistair. *A Generation on Trial: U.S.A. v. Alger Hiss.* NY 1950.

Cooney, John. *The American Pope: The Life and Times of Cardinal Francis Spellman.* NY 1984.

Cornwell, John. *Hitler's Pope: The Secret History of Pius XII.* NY 1999.

Couvares, Francis G., ed. *Movie Censorship and American Culture.* Washington, DC 1996.

Crapanzano, Vincent. *Serving the Word: Literalism in America from the Pulpit to the Bench.* NY 2000.

Cripps, Thomas. *Making Movies Black.* NY 1993.

Crosby, Donald F. *God, Church, and Flag: Senator Joseph R. McCarthy and the Catholic Church.* Chapel Hill, NC 1978.

Cross, Robert D. *The Emergence of Liberal Catholicism.* Cambridge, MA 1958.

Crowther, Bosley. 'The Strange Case of "The Miracle."' *Atlantic* 187:35 (April 1951).

Cuneo, Michael W. *The Smoke of Satan.* NY 1997.

Cunneen, Sally. *In Search of Mary: The Woman and the Symbol.* NY 1996.

Curry, Thomas J. *The First Freedoms: Church and State in America to the Passage of the First Amendment.* NY 1986.

D'Agostino, Peter R. *Rome in America: Transnational Catholic Ideology from the Risorgimento to Fascism.* Chapel Hill, NC 2004.

Daniel-Rops, Henri. *The Church in an Age of Revolution, 1789–1870.* 1960. Trans. John Warrington. London 1965.

Darrow, Floyd L. *Miracles: A Modern View.* NY 1926.

'Decision ... the Constitution.' TV program, Center for Mass Communications, Columbia Univ. 1959.

DeConde, Alexander. *Half Bitter, Half Sweet: An Excursion into Italian-American History.* NY 1971.

De Grazia, Edward, and Roger K. Newman. *Banned Films: Movies, Censors, and the First Amendment.* NY 1982.

De Rosa, Gabriele. *Chiesa e religione popolare nel Mezzogiorno.* Rome 1978.

Desmond, Charles S. 'Censoring the Movies.' *Notre Dame Lawyer* 29:27 (1953).

Dever, Joseph. *Cushing of Boston: A Candid Portrait.* Boston 1965.

Dick, Bernard F. *Radical Innocence: A Critical Study of the Hollywood Ten.* Lexington, KY 1989.

Di Giammatteo, Fernaldo. *Roberto Rossellini.* Florence 1990.

Diner, Hacia R. *Erin's Daughters in America: Irish Immigrant Women in the 19th Century.* Baltimore 1983.

Dmytryk, Edward. *Odd Man Out: A Memoir of the Hollywood Ten.* Carbondale, IL 1996.

Doheny, William J., and Joseph P. Kelly, eds. *Papal Documents on Mary.* Milwaukee 1954.

Doherty, Thomas. *Hollywood's Censor: Joseph I. Breen & the Production Code Administration.* NY 2007.

– *Pre-Code Hollywood: Sex, Immorality, and Insurrection in American Cinema, 1930–1934.* NY 1999.

– *Projections of War: Hollywood, American Culture, and World War II.* NY 1993.

Dolan, Jay P. *The American Catholic Experience: A History from Colonial Times to the Present.* Garden City 1985.

– *The Immigrant Church: New York's Irish and German Catholics, 1815–1865.* Baltimore 1975.

Donnelly, James S., Jr. 'The Peak of Marianism in Ireland, 1930–60.' In Brown/ Miller 252.

Dougherty, Kenneth F. 'Our Lady and the Protestants.' In Carol 3:422.

Douglas, Norman. *Old Calabria*. London 1915.

Doyle, David Noel. 'The Remaking of Irish America, 1845–1880.' In Lee/ Casey 213.

Doyle, David Noel, and Owen Dudley Edwards, eds. *America and Ireland, 1776–1976*. Westport, CT 1980.

Draper, Ellen. '"Controversy Has Probably Destroyed Forever the Context": *The Miracle* and Movie Censorship in America in the Fifties.' *Velvet Light Trap* 25:69 (Spring 1990). Reprinted in Bernstein (1999) 186.

Driggs, Andrew J. '"The Miracle": The Controversy and the Constitution.' M.A. thesis, Brig. Young Univ. 1986.

Drudy, P.J.; ed. *The Irish in America: Emigration, Assimilation and Impact*. Cambridge 1985.

Dunne, Philip. 'Blast It All.' *Harvard Magazine* (Sept./Oct. 1987) 8.

– *Take Two: A Life in the Movies*. NY 1980.

Durham, Michael S. *Miracles of Mary: Apparitions, Legends, and Miraculous Works of the Blessed Virgin Mary*. San Francisco 1995.

Dwight, Timothy. *Travels in New England and New York*. Ed. Barbara M. Solomon. 4 vols. Cambridge, MA 1969.

Eastman, Fred. 'What Can We Do about the Movies?' *Parents' Magazine*. 6/ 11:19 (Nov. 1931).

Eastman, Fred, and Edward Ouellette. *Better Motion Pictures*. Boston 1936.

Edwards, C.D. 'Thurman Arnold and the Antitrust Laws.' *Pol. Sci. Quart.* 58/ 3:338 (Sept. 1943).

Edwards, R. Dudley, and T. Desmond Williams, eds. *The Great Famine*. NY 1957.

Eells, George. *Hedda and Louella*. NY 1972.

Ellis, John Tracy. *Catholic Bishops: A Memoir*. Wilmington, DE 1983.

– 'The Formation of the American Priest: An Historical Perspective.' In *The Catholic Priest in the United States: Historical Investigations*. Ed. John Tracy Ellis. Collegeville, MN 1971.

– *The Life of James Cardinal Gibbons: Archbishop of Baltimore*. 2 vols. Milwaukee 1952.

– *Perspectives in American Catholicism*. Baltimore 1963.

– ed. *Documents of American Catholic History*. Milwaukee 1956.

Emerson, T.I. 'Colonial Intentions and Current Realities in the First Amendment.' *U. Pa. L. Rev.* 125:737 (1977).

– 'The Doctrine of Prior Restraint.' *L. and Contemp. Prob.* 20:648 (1955).

Ernst, Morris L. 'Sex and Censorship.' In *Sex in the Arts*. Ed. John Francis McDermott and Kendall B. Taft. NY 1932.

Ernst, Morris L., and Alexander Lindey. *The Censor Marches On*. NY 1940.

Ernst, Morris L., and Pare Lorentz. *Censored: The Private Life of the Movie*. NY 1930.

Facey, Paul W. *The Legion of Decency*. 1945; NY 1974.

Fairman, Charles. 'Does the Fourteenth Amendment Incorporate the Bill of Rights?' *Stan. L. Rev.* 2:5 (1949).

Falconi, Carlo. *The Popes in the Twentieth Century*. Trans. Muriel Grindrod. Boston 1967.

Fariello, Griffin. *Red Scare: Memories of the American Inquisition*. NY 1995.

Farley, John. *The Life of John Cardinal McCloskey*. NY 1918.

Feldman, Noah. *Divided by God: America's Church-State Problem – and What We Should Do about It*. NY 2005.

Fellini, Federico. *Fellini on Fellini*. Ed. Costanzo Costantini. Trans. Sohrab Sorooshian. London 1995.

Ferrara, Giuseppe. 'L'Opera di Roberto Rossellni' (1967). In *Rossellini/ Antonioni/Bunuel*. Ed. Piero Mechini and Roberto Salvadori. Padua 1973.

Fisher, James Terence. *The Catholic Counterculture in America, 1933–1962*. Chapel Hill, NC 1989.

– *Communion of Immigrants: A History of Catholics in America*. NY 2002.

Fitzgerald, F. Scott. *The Last Tycoon*. NY 1941.

Fleener-Marzec, Nickieann. *D.W. Griffith's 'The Birth of a Nation': Controversy, Suppression, and the First Amendment as It Applies to Filmic Expression, 1915–1973*. 1977; NY 1980.

Fleming, Pierce J. 'Moving Pictures as a Factor in Education.' *Pedagogical Seminary* 18:336 (1921).

Flynn, George Q. *Roosevelt and Romanism: Catholics and American Diplomacy, 1937–1945*. Westport, CT 1976.

Foerster, Robert F. *The Italian Emigration of Our Times*. Cambridge, MA 1919.

Fogarty, Gerald P. *American Catholic Biblical Scholarship*. San Francisco 1989 ['A'].

– 'Francis J. Spellman: American and Roman' (1989). In Fogarty (1989B).

– 'The Quest for a Catholic Vernacular Bible in America.' In *The Bible in America: Essays in Cultural History*. Ed. Nathan O. Hatch and Mark A. Noll. NY 1982.

– *The Vatican and the American Hierarchy from 1870 to 1965*. 1982; Wilmington, DE 1985.

– ed. *Patterns of Episcopal Leadership*. NY 1989 ['B'].

Ford, Henry Jones. 'The Application of Catholic Principles to Contemporary Social Problems.' In McGuire 1:90.

Ford, John C., and Gerald Kelly. *Contemporary Moral Theology*. Vol. 2. *Marriage Questions*. Westminster, MD 1964.

Forgacs, David, Sarah Lutton, and Geoffrey Nowell-Smith. *Roberto Rossellini: Magician of the Real*. London 2000.

Forman, Henry James. *Our Movie Made Children*. NY 1933.

Fosdick, Harry Emerson. 'Beyond Modernism: A Sermon.' *Christian Century* 52/49:1549 (4 Dec. 1935).

Foster, R.F. *Modern Ireland, 1600–1972*. London 1988.

Frank, John P. *Marble Palace: The Supreme Court in American Life*. NY 1958.

– 'The United States Supreme Court: 1951–52.' *U. Chicago L. Rev.* 20:1 (1952–5).

Frankfurter, Felix. *Of Law and Life and Other Things That Matter*. Ed. Philip B. Kurland. Cambridge, MA 1965.

– *Of Law and Men: Papers and Addresses ... 1939–1956*. Ed. Philip Elman. NY 1956.

– *Reminiscences*. Comp. Harlan B. Phillips. NY 1960.

Freedman, Max, comp. *Roosevelt and Frankfurter: Their Correspondence, 1928–1945*. Boston 1967.

French, Brandon. 'The Continuity of the Italian Cinema.' *Yale Italian Studies* 2/1:59 (Winter 1978).

Friedrich, Otto. *City of Nets: A Portrait of Hollywood in the 1940's*. 1986; Berkeley 1997.

Gabriel, Ralph Henry. *The Course of American Democratic Thought*. 3d ed. Westport, CT 1986.

Gaffey, James. 'The Changing of the Guard: The Rise of Cardinal O'Connell.' *Cath. Hist. Rev.* 59:225 (July 1973).

Gallagher, Tag. *The Adventures of Roberto Rossellini*. NY 1998.

– 'NR = MC2: Rossellini, "Neo-realism," and Croce.' *Film History* 2/1:87 (1988).

Gambero, Luigi. *Mary and the Fathers of the Church*. 1991. Trans. Thomas Buffer. San Francisco 1999.

Gambino, Richard. *Blood of My Blood: The Dilemma of the Italian-Americans*. Garden City, NY 1974.

Gannon, M.V. 'Before and after Modernism: The Intellectual Isolation of the American Priest.' In J.T. Ellis (1971).

Gannon, Robert I. *The Cardinal Spellman Story*. Garden City, NY 1962.

Gansera, Rainer, ed. *Roberto Rossellini*. Munich 1978.

Gardella, Peter. *Innocent Ecstasy: How Christianity Gave America an Ethic of Sexual Pleasure*. NY 1985.

Gardiner, Harold C. *The Catholic Viewpoint on Censorship*. Garden City, NY 1958.

Gardner, Gerald. *The Censorship Papers: Movie Censorship Letters from the Hays Office, 1934 to 1968*. NY 1987.

Garesché, Edward. *The Most Beloved Woman: The Prerogatives and Glories of the Blessed Mother of God*. NY 1919.

– 'The Parish Priest and the Moving-Pictures.' *Am. Ecces. Rev.* 76/5:465 (May 1927).

Garrison, Winfred Ernest. *Catholicism and the American Mind.* Chicago 1928.

– *The March of Faith: The Story of Religion in America since 1865.* NY 1933.

Gatta, John. *American Madonna: Images of the Divine Woman in Literary Culture.* NY 1997.

Gaustad, Edwin S. *Proclaim Liberty throughout the Land: A History of Church and State in America.* NY 1999.

Gerard, Lillian. 'The Miracle in Court.' *American Film* (July-Aug. 1977 ['B']).

– '"Withdraw the Picture!" the Commissioner Ordered.' *American Film* (June 1977 ['A']).

Getlein, Frank. 'Film Critic Gives Some Aspects of "The Miracle" Story.' *Cath. Messenger* (22 March 1951) 4.

Getlein, Frank, and Harold S. Gardner, S.J. *Movies, Morals, and Art.* NY 1961.

Giannini, A.H. 'Financing the Production and Distribution of Motion Pictures.' *AAAP&SS* 128:46 (Nov. 1926).

Gibbons, James. *Faith of Our Fathers.* 1876; [n.p.] 1895.

– *A Retrospect of Fifty Years.* Baltimore 1916.

Giglio, Ernest David. 'The Decade of the Miracle, 1952–1962.' D.S.S. diss., Syracuse Univ., 1962.

Giles, Paul. *American Catholic Arts and Fictions: Culture, Ideology, Aesthetics.* NY 1992.

Gilley, Sheridan. 'The Emergence of the Modern Papacy, 1721–1878.' In *The Papacy,* by Paul Johnson. Ed. Michael Walsh. London 1997.

Gillis, Chester. *Roman Catholicism in America.* NY 1999.

Gilman, Catheryne Cooke. *Responsibility for Better Motion Pictures.* Minneapolis 1929.

Ginder, Richard. *Binding with Briars: Sex and Sin in the Catholic Church.* Englewood Cliffs, NJ 1975.

Gladden, Washington. 'Christianity and Popular Amusements.' *Century Illus. Mag.* 29/3:384 (Jan. 1885).

Glazer, Nathan, Daniel Patrick Moynihan. *Beyond the Melting Pot.* 1963; 2d ed. Cambridge, MA 1970.

Gleason, Philip. *Contending with Modernity: Catholic Higher Education in the Twentieth Century.* NY 1995.

– 'In Search of Unity.' *Cath. Hist. Rev.* 65/2:185 (April 1979).

– *Keeping the Faith: American Catholicism Past and Present.* Notre Dame, IN 1987.

– *Speaking of Diversity: Language and Ethnicity in Twentieth-Century America.* Baltimore 1992.

– comp. *Catholicism in America.* NY 1970.

Goodenough, Erwin R. *Toward a Mature Faith*. NY 1955.

Goodman, Ezra. *The Fifty-Year Decline and Fall of Hollywood*. NY 1959.

Goodman, Walter. *The Committee*. NY 1968.

Gordon, George A. *Religion and Miracle*. 2d ed. Boston 1910.

Gordon, Jan, and Cora Gordon. *Star-Dust in Hollywood*. London 1930.

Graef, Hilda. *Mary: A History of Doctrine and Devotion*. NY 1965.

Graham, Robert A. *The Vatican and Communism in World War II: What Really Happened?* San Francisco 1996.

Graham, Sheilah. *Hollywood Revisited: A Fiftieth Anniversary Celebration*. 1984; NY 1985.

Graham, Sheilah, and Gerold Frank. *Beloved Infidel: The Education of a Woman*. NY 1958.

Greeley, Andrew M. *The American Catholic: A Social Portrait*. NY 1977.

– *The Catholic Imagination*. Berkeley 2000.

– *The Catholic Myth: The Behavior and Beliefs of American Catholics*. NY 1990.

– *The Catholic Revolution*. Berkeley 2004.

– *The Church and the Suburbs*. NY 1959.

– *Confessions of a Parish Priest*. NY 1986.

– *The Irish Americans: The Rise to Money and Power*. NY 1981['A'].

– *The Mary Myth: On the Femininity of God*. NY 1977.

– *The Religious Imagination*. Los Angeles 1981['B'].

– *That Most Distressful Nation: The Taming of the American Irish*. Chicago 1972.

– *Why Can't They Be like Us? America's White Ethnic Groups*. NY 1971.

Gribben, Arthur, ed. *The Great Famine and the Irish Diaspora in America*. Amherst, MA 1999.

Guarner, José Luis. *Roberto Rossellini*. Trans. Elisabeth Cameron. NY 1970.

Guilday, Peter. *A History of the Councils of Baltimore (1791–1884)*. NY 1932.

Guitton, Jean. *The Virgin Mary*. 1949. Trans. A. Gordon Smith. NY 1952.

Gundle, Stephen. *Between Hollywood and Moscow: The Italian Communists and the Challenge of Mass Culture, 1943–1991*. Durham, NC 2000.

Hales, E.E.Y. *Pio Nono: A Study in European Politics and Religion in the Nineteenth Century*. 2d ed. London 1956.

Hall, G. Stanley. *Jesus, The Christ, in the Light of Psychology*. 2 vols. Garden City 1917.

Halsey, William M. *The Survival of American Innocence: Catholicism in an Era of Disillusionment, 1920–1940*. Notre Dame, IN 1980.

Hamburger, Philip. *Separation of Church and State*. Cambridge, MA 2002.

Hamilton, Ian. *Writers in Hollywood 1915–1951*. NY 1990.

Handel, Leo A. *Hollywood Looks at Its Audience: A Report of Film Audience Research*. Urbana, IL 1950.

Handlin, Oscar. *Boston's Immigrants: A Study in Acculturation*. 3d ed. Cambridge, MA 1979.

Handy, Robert T. 'The American Religious Depression, 1925–1935.' *Church Hist*. 29:3 (March 1960).

– *History of the Churches in the United States and Canada*. NY 1977.

– 'The Protestant Quest for a Christian American 1830–1930.' *Church Hist*. 22:8 (March 1953).

– ed. *The Social Gospel in America, 1870–1920*. NY 1966.

Hardon, John A., S.J. 'The Mariology of Pope Pius XII.' *Rev. for Religious* 205 (July 1959).

– 'Pope Pius XII and Our Lady.' *Rev. for Religious* 11:249 (Sept. 1952).

Hardwick, Leon H. 'Negro Stereotypes on the Screen.' *Hollywood Quart*. 1:236 (1945–6).

Harmetz, Aljean. *Round Up the Usual Suspects: The Making of 'Casablanca.'* NY 1992.

Harrigan, William M. 'Pius XI and Nazi Germany, 1937–1939.' *Cath. Hist. Rev*. 51/4:457 (Jan. 1966).

Haskell, Thomas L. *The Emergence of Professional Social Science*. Urbana, IL 1977.

Haskins, Susan. *Mary Magdalen: Myth and Metaphor*. NY 1993.

Hasler, August Bernhard. *How the Pope Became Infallible*. Garden City 1981.

Hatch, Nathan O. *The Democratization of American Christianity*. New Haven 1989.

Hawley, Ellis W. *The New Deal and the Problem of Monopoly*. Princeton 1966.

Hay, James. *Popular Film Culture in Fascist Italy: The Passing of the Rex*. Bloomington, IN 1987.

Hays, Will H. *Memoirs of Will H. Hays*. Garden City 1955.

Hein, David, and Gardiner H. Shattuck, Jr. *The Episcopalians*. Westport, CT 2004.

Heins, Marjorie. 'The Miracle: Film Censorship and the Entanglement of Church and State.' *Univ. Va. Forum for Contemporary Thought* (28 Oct. 2002).

Hellman, Lillian. *Scoundrel Time*. Boston 1976.

Hennesey, James, S.J.. *American Catholics: A History of the Roman Catholic Community*. NY 1981.

– 'The Distinctive Tradition of American Catholicism' (1966). In Gleason (1970) 28.

– *The First Council of the Vatican: The American Experience*. NY 1963.

– 'Prelude to Vatican I: American Bishops and the Definition of the Immaculate Conception.' *Theol. Studies* 25/3:409 (Sept. 1964).

– 'Roman Catholics and American Politics, 1900–1960' (1990). In Noll 302.

Herberg, Will. *Protestant-Catholic-Jew: An Essay in American Religious Sociology.* Garden City 1955.

Herbst, Jurgen. *The German Historical School in American Scholarship.* Ithaca, NY 1965.

Higham, John. *Strangers in the Land: Patterns of American Nativism 1860–1925.* 1963; 2d ed. NY 1990.

Hillier, Jim, ed. *Cahiers du Cinéma: The 1950s: Neo-Realism, Hollywood, New Wave.* Cambridge, MA 1985.

Hines, Mary E. *What Ever Happened to Mary?* Notre Dame, IN 2001.

Hirsch, H.N. *The Enigma of Felix Frankfurter.* NY 1981.

Hodgins, Eric. 'A Round Table on the Movies.' *Life* (27 June 1949 ['B']) 90.

– 'What's with the Movies?' *Life* (16 May 1949['A']) 98.

Hofstadter, Richard. *Anti-intellectualism in American Life.* NY 1963.

– *The Paranoid Style in American Politics.* NY 1965.

Holifield, E. Brooks. *Theology in America.* New Haven 2003.

Hooker, Katharine. *Through the Heel of Italy.* NY 1927.

Horne, Gerald. *The Final Victim of the Blacklist: John Howard Lawson, Dean of the Hollywood Ten.* Berkeley 2006.

Houseman, John. 'Hollywood Faces the Fifties.' *Harper's* 200:50 (April 1950).

– 'Today's Hero: A Review.' *Hollywood Quart.* 2:161 (Jan. 1947 ['A']).

– 'What Makes American Movies Tough?' *Vogue* 109:88 (15 Jan. 1947 ['B']).

Hovald, Patrice G. *Le néo-réalisme italien et ses créateurs.* Paris 1959.

Huettig, Mae D. *Economic Control of the Motion Picture Industry.* Philadelphia 1944.

Hughes, H.G. 'Some Thoughts on Papal Infallibility.' *Am. Eccles. Rev.* 36/5:501 (May 1907).

Hughes, H. Stuart. *The United States and Italy.* 3d ed. Cambridge, MA 1979.

Hughes, John W. 'In Search of the "Essential Image."' *Village Voice* (10 May 1973) 89.

Hughes, Kathleen. *The Church in Early Irish Society.* Ithaca, NY 1966.

Humphreys, Alexander J. *New Dubliners: Urbanization and the Irish Family.* London 1966.

Hunter, Sylvester Joseph. *Outlines of Dogmatic Theology.* 2 vols. NY 1895–6.

Hutchison, William R. *The Modernist Impulse in American Protestantism.* Cambridge, MA 1976.

– ed. *Between the Times: The Travail of the Protestant Establishment in America, 1900–1960.* Cambridge 1989.

Hynes, Eugene. 'The Great Hunger and Irish Catholicism.' *Societas* 8:137 (Spring 1978).

Index of Prohibited Books, Revised and Published by Order of His Holiness Pope Pius XI. 1929; trans. Vatican City 1930.

Inge, William R. 'Catholic Church and Anglo-Saxon Mind.' *Atlantic Monthly* 131/4:440 (April 1923).

Inglis, Ruth A. *Freedom of the Movies: A Report on Self-Regulation*. Chicago 1947.

– 'Freedom to See and Hear: Movies.' *Survey Graphic* 35:477 (Dec. 1946).

Ireland, John. *The Church and Modern Society*. 2 vols. St Paul, MN 1905.

Israel, Edward L. 'Morals and the Movies.' *Forum and Century* 200 (1934).

Izod, John. *Hollywood and the Box Office, 1895–1986*. NY 1988.

Jacobs, Lea. 'The Censorship of *Blonde Venus*: Textual Analysis and Historical Method.' *Cinema J.* 27/3:21 (1988).

– 'Industry Self-Regulation and the Problem of Textual Determination.' *Velvet Light Trap* 23:4 (1989).

– *The Wages of Sin: Censorship and the Fallen Woman Film, 1928–1942*. 1991; Berkeley 1997.

Jacobs, Lea, and Richard Maltby. 'Rethinking the Production Code.' *Quart. J. Film and Video* 15/4:1 (1995).

Janes, Robert William. 'The Legion of Decency and the Motion Picture Industry.' M.A. thesis, Univ. of Chicago, 1939.

Jarratt, Vernon. *The Italian Cinema*. London 1951.

Jelly, Frederick. *Madonna*. Huntington, IN 1986.

Jemolo, A.C. *Church and State in Italy, 1850–1950*. Trans. David Moore. Oxford 1960.

Johnson, Donald. 'Wilson, Burleson, and Censorship in the First World War.' *J. South. Hist.* 28/1:46 (Feb. 1962).

Johnson, Elizabeth A. *Truly Our Sister: A Theology of Mary in the Communion of Saints*. NY 2003.

Johnson, Paul. *A History of Christianity*. NY 1976.

Johnston, Alva. *The Great Goldwyn*. 1937; NY 1978.

Jones, Maldwyn Allen. *American Immigration*. 2d ed. Chicago 1992.

Josephson, Matthew. *Infidel in the Temple: A Memoir of the Nineteen-Thirties*. NY 1967.

Jouassard, Georges. 'The Fathers of the Church and the Immaculate Conception' (1954). In O'Connor 51.

Journet, Charles. 'Scripture and the Immaculate Conception' (1954). In O'Connor 3.

Jowett, Garth S. '"A Capacity for Evil": The 1915 Supreme Court *Mutual* Decision.' *His. J. of Film, Radio and Television* 9/1:59 (1989). Reprinted in Bernstein (1999) 16.

– *Film: The Democratic Art*. Boston 1976.

– 'Moral Responsibility and Commercial Entertainment: Social Control in the United States Film Industry, 1907–1968.' *Hist. J. of Film, Radio and Television* 10/1:3 (1990).

– '"A Significant Medium for the Communication of Ideas": *The Miracle Decision and the Decline of Motion Picture Censorship, 1952–1968.*' In Couvares 258.

Jowett, Garth S., Ian C. Jarvie, and Kathryn H. Fuller. *Children and the Movies: Media Influence and the Payne Fund Controversy*. NY 1996.

Kadin, Theodore. 'Administrative Censorship: A Study of the Mails, Motion Pictures and Radio Broadcasting.' *Boston U. L. Rev.* 19:533 (1939).

Kael, Pauline. *I Lost It at the Movies*. Boston 1965.

Kahn, Gordon. *Hollywood on Trial: The Story of the 10 Who Were Indicted*. NY 1948.

Kallen, Horace M. *Indecency and the Seven Arts*. NY 1930.

Kanfer, Stefan. *A Journal of the Plague Years*. NY 1973.

Kanin, Garson. *Hollywood: Stars and Starlets, Tycoons and Flesh-Peddlers*. NY 1974.

Kantowicz, Edward R. 'The Beginning and End of an Era: George William Mundelein and John Patrick Cody in Chicago' (1989). In Fogarty (1989B) 202.

– *Corporation Sole: Cardinal Mundelein and Chicago Catholicism*. Notre Dame, IN 1983.

Kashner, Sam, and Jennifer MacNair. *The Bad and the Beautiful: Hollywood in the Fifties*. NY 2002.

Katz, Robert. *The Battle for Rome: The Germans, the Allies, the Partisans, and the Pope*. NY 2003.

Keats, John. *You Might as Well Live: The Life and Times of Dorothy Parker*. NY 1970.

Keenan, Desmond J. *The Catholic Church in Nineteenth-Century Ireland*. Totowa, NJ 1983.

Kempton, Murray. *Part of Our Time: Some Ruins and Monuments of the Thirties*. NY 1955.

Kennedy, Robert E., Jr. *The Irish: Emigration, Marriage, and Fertility*. Berkeley 1973.

Kenny, Kevin. *The American Irish: A History*. Harlow, Essex 2000.

– 'Race, Violence, – and Anti-Irish Sentiment in the Nineteenth Century.' In Lee/Casey 364.

Keyes, Frances Parkinson. *Bernadette of Lourdes: Shepherdess, Sister and Saint*. NY 1953.

Keyser, Les, and Barbara Keyser. *Hollywood and the Catholic Church*. Chicago 1984.

Kindem Gorham A. 'SAG, HUAC, and Postwar Hollywood.' In Schatz 313.

– ed. *The American Movie Industry: The Business of Motion Pictures*. Carbondale, IL 1982.

Klein, Félix. *Americanism: A Phantom Heresy.* 1949; Atchison, KS 1951.

Knight, Arthur. 'The Negro in Films Today: Hollywood's New Cycle.' *Films in Review* 1/1:14 (Feb. 1950).

Knight, Arthur, and Hollis Alpert. 'The History of Sex in Cinema.' *Playboy* 13 (April–Nov. 1966).

Kobal, John. *People Will Talk.* NY 1986.

Koch, Howard. *As Time Goes By: Memoirs of a Writer.* NY 1979.

– *'Casablanca': Script and Legend.* Woodstock, NY 1973.

Kolmacic, Joseph M. 'Prior Restraints on Motion Pictures.' *Cath. U. L. Rev.* 4:112 (1954).

Komonchak, Joseph A. 'Returning from Exile: Catholic Theology in the 1930s.' In *The Twentieth Century: A Theological Overview.* Ed. Gregory Baum. Maryknoll, NY 1999.

Koppes, Clayton R. 'Regulating the Screen.' In Schatz 262.

Korda, Michael. *Charmed Lives: A Family Romance.* 1979; NY 1981.

Koszarski, Richard, ed. *Hollywood Directors, 1941–1976.* Oxford 1977.

Kotre, John N. *The Best of Times, the Worst of Times: Andrew Greeley and American Catholicism, 1950–1975.* Chicago 1978.

Kracauer, Siegfried. 'Hollywood's Terror Films.' *Commentary* 2/2:132 (Aug. 1946).

– 'National Types as Hollywood Presents Them' (1949). In Rosenberg/White 257.

Krock, Arthur. 'Doctor of Movies.' *New Yorker* (8 May 1926) 21.

Kselman, Thomas A. *Miracles and Prophecies in Nineteenth-Century France.* New Brunswick, NJ 1983.

Kuhn, Annette. *Cinema, Censorship and Sexuality.* NY 1988.

Küng, Hans. *The Catholic Church: A Short History.* Trans. John Bowden. NY 2001.

– *Infallible? An Inquiry.* Trans. Edward Quinn. Garden City 1971.

Kupferman, Theodore R., and Philip J. O'Brien, Jr. 'Motion Picture Censorship – The Memphis Blues.' *Cornell L.Q.* 36:273 (1951).

Kurland, Philip B. *Mr. Justice Frankfurter and the Constitution.* Chicago 1971.

Kurtz, Lester R. *The Politics of Heresy: The Modernist Crisis in Roman Catholicism.* Berkeley 1986.

LaGumina, Salvatore J. 'Italian American and Irish American Interaction.' In *Models and Images of Catholicism in Italian Americana.* Ed. Joseph A. Varacalli et al. Stony Brook, NY 2004.

Landy, Marcia. *Fascism in Film: The Italian Commercial Cinema, 1931–1943.* Princeton 1986.

La Piana, George. 'A Totalitarian Church in a Democratic State' (1949). In *Catholic Power vs. American Freedom: George La Piana and John W. Swomley.* Ed. Herbert F. Vetter. Amherst, NY 2002.

Lardner, Lynford A. 'How Far Does the Constitution Separate Church and State?' *Am. Pol. Sci. Rev.* 45/1:110 (Jan. 1951).

Lardner, Ring, Jr. *I'd Hate Myself in the Morning.* NY 2000.

Larkin, Emmet. 'Church and State in Ireland in the 19th Century.' *Church History* 31:295 (1962).

– 'The Devotional Literature in Ireland, 1850–75.' *Am. Hist. Rev.* 77/3:625 (June 1972).

– 'Economic Growth, Capital Investment, and the Roman Catholic Church in Nineteenth-Century Ireland.' *Am. Hist. Rev.* 72/3:852 (April 1967).

– *The Making of the Roman Catholic Church in Ireland, 1850–1860.* Chapel Hill, NC 1980.

– *The Roman Catholic Church and the Creation of the Modern Irish State, 1878–1886.* Philadelphia 1975.

LaSalle, Mick. *Complicated Women: Sex and Power in Pre-Code Hollywood.* NY 2000.

Lasserre, Henri. *Our Lady of Lourdes.* 1869. Trans. 1870; NY 1874.

Latham, Aaron. *Crazy Sundays: F. Scott Fitzgerald in Hollywood.* NY 1971.

Laurentin, René. *Bernadette of Lourdes: A Life Based on Authenticated Documents.* 1978. Trans. John Drury. Minneapolis 1979.

– *Comment la Vierge Marie leur a rendu la liberté.* Paris 1991 ['A'].

– *Lourdes: dossier des documents authentiques.* Vol. 1. *Au temps des seize premières apparitions.* 2d ed. Paris 1957.

– *Multiplications des apparitions de la Vierge aujourd'hui: Est-ce elle? Que veut-elle dire?* 3d ed. Paris 1991 ['B'].

– 'The Persistence of Popular Piety.' In *The Persistence of Religion.* Ed. Andrew Greeley and Gregory Baum. NY 1973.

– *The Question of Mary.* 1963. Trans. I.G. Pidoux. NY 1965.

– 'The Role of the Papal Magisterium in the Development of the Dogma of the Immaculate Conception' (1956). Abridged in O'Connor 271.

– *A Short Treatise on the Virgin Mary.* Trans. Charles Neumann. Washington, NJ 1991 ['C'].

– *Visage de Bernadette.* Paris 1978.

Lawton, David. *Blasphemy.* Philadelphia 1993.

Leab, Daniel J. *From Sambo to Superspade: The Black Experience in Motion Pictures.* Boston 1975.

Leamer, Laurence. *As Time Goes By: The Life of Ingrid Bergman.* NY 1986.

Lears, T.J. Jackson. *No Place of Grace: Antimodernism and the Transformation of American Culture.* NY 1981.

Lee, J.J., and Marion R. Casey, eds. *Making the Irish American.* NY 2006.

Leff, Leonard J. 'The Breening of America.' *PMLA* 106:432 (1991).

Leff, Leoard J., and Jerold L. Simmons. *The Dame in the Kimono: Hollywood, Censorship, and the Production Code from the 1920s to the 1960s.* NY 1990.

Lennig, Arthur. 'A History of Censorship in the American Film.' In *Sexuality in the Movies.* Ed. Thomas R. Atkins. Bloomington, IN 1975.

Leprohon, Pierre. *The Italian Cinema.* 1966. Trans. Roger Greaves and Oliver Stallybrass. NY 1972.

Leuret, François, M.D. *Modern Miraculous Cures.* Trans. A.T. MacQueen and John C. Barry. NY 1957.

Levi, Carlo. *Christ Stopped at Eboli.* Trans. Frances Frenaye. NY 1947.

Levy, Herbert M. 'The Case against Film Censorship.' *Films in Review* 1/3:1 (April 1950).

Levy, Leonard W. *Blasphemy: Verbal Offence against the Sacred, from Moses to Salman Rushdie.* NY 1993.

Lewin, John Henry. 'The Associated Press Decision – an Extension of the Sherman Act?' *U. Chi. L. Rev.* 13:247 (1946).

Lewis, C.S. *Miracles: A Preliminary Study.* 1947; NY 1996.

Lewis, Howard T. *The Motion Picture Industry.* NY 1933.

Lewis, Jon. *Hollywood v. Hard Core.* NY 2000.

Lewis, Thomas P. 'Freedom of Speech and Motion Pictures – the "Miracle" Decision.' *Ky. L.J.* 41:257 (1953).

Liehm, Mira. *Passion and Defiance: Film in Italy from 1942 to the Present.* Berkeley 1984.

Lilley, Alfred Leslie. *Modernism: A Record and Review.* London 1908.

Liptak, Dolores Ann. *Immigrants and Their Church.* NY 1989.

Locke, Maryel, and Charles Warren, eds. *Jean-Luc Godard's 'Hail Mary': Women and the Sacred in Film.* Carbondale, IL 1993.

Lockhart, William B., and Robert C. McClure. 'Censorship of Obscenity: The Developing Constitutional Standards.' *Minn. L. Rev.* 45:5 (1960).

– 'Literature, the Law of Obscenity, and the Constitution.' *Minn. L. Rev.* 38:294 (1954).

Loisy, Alfred. *Quelques lettres sur des questions actuelles et sur des événements récents.* Ceffonds, Haute-Marne 1908.

Lord, Daniel A. *I Can Read Anything / All Right Then Read This.* 1930; rev. ed. St Louis 1956.

– *The Motion Pictures Betray America.* St Louis 1934.

– 'Our Lady in the United States.' *Lumen Vitae* 8:311 (1953).

– *Our Part in the Mystical Body.* St Louis 1935.

– *Played by Ear.* Chicago 1956.

– *Speaking of Birth Control.* St Louis 1931.

Lourdeaux, Lee. *Italian and Irish Filmmakers in America.* Philadelphia 1990.

Luccock, Halford Edward. *American Mirror*. 1940; NY 1971.

– *Christian Faith and Economic Change*. NY 1936.

– *Contemporary American Literature and Religion*. Chicago 1934.

– *Jesus and the American Mind*. NY 1930.

Lundén, Rolf. *Business and Religion in the American 1920s*. Westport, CT 1988.

Lynch, Bernard J. 'The Italians in New York.' *Cath. World* 46:67 (April 1888).

Lynch, Denis. *St. Joan of Arc: The Life-Story of the Maid of Orleans*. NY 1920.

Lynd, Robert S., and Helen Merrell Lynd. *Middletown: A Study in Contemporary American Culture*. NY 1929.

McAvoy, Thomas T. *The Americanist Heresy in Roman Catholicism, 1895–1900*. Notre Dame, IN 1963.

– *Father O'Hara of Notre Dame: The Cardinal-Archbishop of Philadelphia*. Notre Dame, IN 1967.

– *The Great Crisis in American Catholic History, 1895–1900*. Chicago 1957.

– *A History of the Catholic Church in the United States*. Notre Dame, IN 1969.

McBrien, Richard P. *Caesar's Coin: Religion and Politics in America*. NY 1987.

McCabe, George P. *Control of Motion Pictures by Federal Law*. Washington, DC 1927.

– *Forces Molding and Muddling the Movies*. Washington, DC 1926.

McCaffrey, Lawrence J. 'Forging Forward and Looking Back.' In Bayor/Meagher 213.

– *The Irish Diaspora in America*. Bloomington, IN 1976.

McCann, Dennis P. *New Experiment in Democracy: The Challenge for American Catholicism*. Kansas City 1987.

McClure, Arthur F., ed. *The Movies: An American Idiom*. Rutherford, NJ 1971.

McCool, Gerald A. *Catholic Theology in the Nineteenth Century*. NY 1977.

McDannell, Colleen. *Material Christianity: Religion and Popular Culture in America*. New Haven 1995.

MacDonagh, Oliver. 'Irish Emigration to the United States ... during the Famine.' In Edwards/Williams 317.

McDonald, Donald. *Catholics in Conversation: Seventeen Interviews*. Philadelphia 1960.

McDonough, John R., Jr., and Robert L. Winslow. 'The Motion Picture Industry.' *Stanford L. Rev.* 1:385 (1949).

McDowell, R.B. 'Ireland on the Eve of the Famine.' In Edwards/Williams 3.

McGilligan, Patrick, and Paul Buhle. *Tender Comrades: A Backstory of the Hollywood Blacklist*. NY 1997.

McGreevy, John T. *Catholicism and American Freedom: A History*. NY 2003.

McGuire, C.E., ed. *Catholic Builders of the Nation: A Symposium*. 5 vols. Boston 1923.

Machen, J. Gresham. *The Virgin Birth of Christ*. London 1930.

McHugh, Roger J. 'The Famine in Irish Oral Tradition.' In Edwards/Williams 389.

McKeown, Elizabeth. *War and Welfare: American Catholics and World War I*. NY 1988.

McLean, Adrienne L. 'The Cinderella Princess and the Instrument of Evil.' In *Headline Hollywood*. Ed. Adrienne L. McLean and David A. Cook. New Brunswick, NJ 2001.

Macleod, Xavier Donald. *Devotion to the Blessed Virgin Mary in North America*. NY 1866.

McLoughlin, Emmett. *American Culture and Catholic Schools*. NY 1960.

McNicholas, John T. 'The Episcopal Committee and the Problem of Evil Motion Pictures.' *Eccles. Rev.* 91/2:113 (Aug. 1934).

– 'The Need of American Priests for the Italian Missions.' *Eccles. Rev.* 39:677 (Dec. 1908).

McWilliams, Carey. *Witch Hunt: The Revival of Heresy*. Boston 1950.

Maltby, Richard. '"Baby Face" or How Joe Breen Made Barbara Stanwyck Atone for Causing the Wall Street Crash.' *Screen* 27/2 (March-April 1986).

– 'The Genesis of the Production Code.' *Quart. Rev. of Film and Video* 15/4:5 (1995) ['A'].

– *Harmless Entertainment: Hollywood and the Ideology of Consensus*. Metuchen, NJ 1983.

– 'The *King of Kings* and the Czar of All the Rushes: The Propriety of the Christ Story.' *Screen* 31/2:188 (1990). Reprinted in Bernstein (1999) 60.

– 'The Production Code and the Hays Office.' In Balio (1995) 46 ['B'].

Mangione, Jerre, and Ben Morreale. *La Storia: Five Centuries of the Italian American Experience*. NY 1992.

Manning, Henry Edward. *The True Story of the Vatican Council*. 2d ed. London n.d.

Marcus, Millicent. *Italian Film in the Light of Neorealism*. Princeton 1986.

Marraro, Howard R. *American Opinion on the Unification of Italy 1846–1861*. NY 1932.

Marsden, George M. *Fundamentalism and American Culture*. NY 1980.

– *Religion and American Culture*. San Diego 1990.

– *The Soul of the American University: From Protestant Establishment to Established Nonbelief*. NY 1994.

Marshall, Charles C. *The Roman Catholic Church in the Modern State*. 1928; rev. ed. NY 1931.

Martin, Olga J. *Hollywood's Movie Commandments*. NY 1937.

Marty, Martin E. *Modern American Religion*. Vol. 2. *The Noise of Conflict 1919–1941*. Chicago 1991.

– *The New Shape of American Religion*. NY 1959.

– *Second Chance for American Protestants*. NY 1963.

Masi, Stefano. *I film di Roberto Rossellini*. Rome 1987.

Massa, Mark S. *Catholics and American Culture: Fulton Sheen, Dorothy Day, and the Notre Dame Football Team*. NY 1999.

Mast, Gerald, ed. *The Movies in Our Midst: Documents in the Cultural History of Film in America*. Chicago 1982.

Mathews, Shailer. *The Faith of Modernism*. NY 1924.

Mayer, Arthur. *Merely Colossal: The Story of the Movies from the Long Chase to the Chaise Lounge*. NY 1953.

Mayer, David N. *The Constitutional Thought of Thomas Jefferson*. Charlottesville, VA 1994.

Maynard, Theodore. *The Catholic Church and the American Idea*. NY 1953.

– *The Story of American Catholicism*. NY 1941.

Meade, Emily Fogg. 'The Italian on the Land.' *Bulletin of the Bureau of Labor* 70:473 (May 1907).

Meehan, Thomas, ed. *Hist. Records and Studies*. Vol. 28 (NY 1937).

Meier, John P. *A Marginal Jew: Rethinking the Historical Jesus*. 3 vols. NY 1991–2001.

Mendelson, Wallace, ed. *Felix Frankfurter: A Tribute*. NY 1964.

Menon, Gianni, ed. *Dibattito su Rossellini*. Rome 1972.

Merton, Thomas. *The Seven Storey Mountain*. NY 1948.

Merwick, Donna. *Boston Priests, 1848–1910*. Cambridge, MA 1973.

Messbarger, Paul R. 'The Failed Promise of Catholic Literature.' *U.S. Cath. Historian* 4:153 (1985).

– *Fiction with a Parochial Purpose*. Boston 1971.

Messenger, John C. 'Sex and Repression in an Irish Folk Community.' In *Human Sexual Behavior*. Ed. Donald S. Marshall and Robert C. Suggs. NY 1970.

Meyer, Donald B. *The Protestant Search for Political Realism, 1919–1941*. Berkeley 1960.

Meyer, Donald H. *The Instructed Conscience: The Shaping of the American National Ethic*. Philadelphia 1972.

Michelone, Guido. *Invito al cinema di Roberto Rossellini*. Milan 1996.

Miegge, Giovanni. *The Virgin Mary: The Roman Catholic Marian Doctrine*. 1950. Trans. Waldo Smith. London 1955.

Miller, David W. 'Irish Catholicism and the Great Famine.' *J. Soc. Hist.* 9:81 (Fall 1975).

– 'Mass Attendance in Ireland in 1834.' In Brown/Miller 158.

Miller, Frank. *Censored Hollywood: Sex, Sin and Violence on Screen*. Atlanta, GA 1994.

Miller, Kerby A. *Emigrants and Exiles: Ireland and the Irish Exodus to North America*. NY 1985.

– '"Revenge for Skibbereen": Irish Emigration and the Meaning of the Great Famine' (1999). In Gribben 180.

Miller, Perry. *The Life of the Mind in America from the Revolution to the Civil War*. NY 1965.

Miller, Randall M., and Thomas D. Marzik, eds. *Immigrants and Religion in Urban America*. Philadelphia 1977.

Miller, Robert J., ed. *The Complete Gospels: Annotated Scholars Version*. 3d ed. San Francisco 1994.

Miller, Robert Moats. *American Protestantism and Social Issues 1919–1939*. Chapel Hill, NC 1958.

Milliken, Carl E. *Who Selects America's Movies?* NY 1937.

Moe, Nelson. *The View from Vesuvius: Italian Culture and the Southern Question*. Berkeley 2002.

Moley, Raymond. *The Hays Office*. Indianapolis 1945.

Montagu, Ivor. *With Eisenstein in Hollywood*. NY 1969.

Moore, John F. *Will America Become Catholic?* NY 1931.

Moore, R. Laurence. *Religious Outsiders and the Making of Americans*. NY 1986.

Morris, Charles R. *American Catholic*. NY 1997.

Morrison, Stanley. 'Does the Fourteenth Amendment Incorporate the Bill of Rights?' *Stan. L. Rev.* 2:140 (1949).

Moscato, Michael, and Leslie LeBlanc, eds. *The United States of America v. One Book Entitled 'Ulysses' by James Joyce: Documents and Commentary – A 50-Year Retrospective*. Frederick, MD 1984.

Moser, John E. '"Gigantic Engines of Propaganda": The 1941 Senate Investigation of Hollywood.' *Historian* 63/4:731 (Summer 2001).

Mosley, Leonard. *Zanuck: The Rise and Fall of Hollywood's Last Tycoon*. Boston 1984.

'Motion Pictures and the First Amendment.' *Yale L.J.* 60:696 (1951).

Moule, C.F.D., ed. *Miracles: Cambridge Studies in Their Philosophy and History*. London 1965.

'The Movies['] Last Chance.' *Christian Century* 51:822 (20 June 1934).

Mulcrone, Mick. 'The Famine and Collective Memory.' In *America and Ireland, 1776–1976*. Ed. David Noel Doyle and Owen Dudley Edwards. Westport, CT 1980.

Murdock, Pat. 'The Lone "Lady Censor": Christine Smith Gilliam and the Demise of Film Censorship in Atlanta.' *Atlanta Hist.* 43/2:68 (Summer 1999).

Muredach, Myles. 'An Experiment in City Home Missions.' *Extension Mag.* (April 1923) 35.

Murphy, Paul L. *The Meaning of Freedom of Speech.* Westport, CT 1972.

Murray, Gilbert. 'The Crisis in Morals.' *Harpers* 160:133 (Jan. 1930).

Murray, John Courtney. 'The Problem of Free Speech' (1953). In *Bridging the Sacred and the Secular: Selected Writings of John Courtney Murray, S.J.* Washington, DC 1994.

Musser, Charles. *The Emergence of Cinema: The American Screen to 1907.* Berkeley 1990.

Naremore, James. *More than Night: Film Noir in Its Contexts.* Berkeley 1998.

Nelli, Humbert S. *From Immigrants to Ethnics: The Italian Americans.* Oxford 1983.

Neuner, Josef, and Jacques Dupuis. *The Christian Faith in the Doctrinal Documents of the Catholic Church.* Rev. ed. Staten Island, NY 1982.

Newman, John Henry. 'The Glories of Mary for the Sake of Her Son' (1849). In *Discourses Addressed to Mixed Congregations.* 2d ed. London 1850.

– 'The Reverence Due to Her.' In *Parochial Sermons.* 2d ed. London 1836–42.

Nicolas, Marie-Joseph. 'The Meaning of the Immaculate Conception in ... St Thomas' (1955). In O'Connor 327.

Niebuhr, H. Richard. *The Kingdom of God in America.* Chicago 1937.

– *The Social Sources of Denominationalism.* NY 1929.

Niebuhr, Reinhold. *An Interpretation of Christian Ethics.* NY 1935.

– *The Irony of American History.* NY 1952.

Nielsen, Fredrik K. *The History of the Papacy in the XIXth Century.* Trans. A.J. Mason et al. 2 vols. London 1906.

Nokes, G.D. *A History of the Crime of Blasphemy.* London 1928.

Nolan, Hugh J., ed. *Pastoral Letters of the American Hierarchy, 1792–1970.* Huntington, IN 1971.

Noll, Mark A. *A History of Christianity in the United States and Canada.* Grand Rapids, MI 1992.

– *The Work We Have to Do: A History of Protestants in America.* 2000; NY 2002.

– ed. *Religion and American Politics from the Colonial Period to the 1980s.* NY 1990.

Norman, E.R. *The Catholic Church and Ireland in the Age of Rebellion.* London 1965.

Nowak, Andrew T.F. *American Ambassadors to Lourdes.* NY 1955.

Oates, Mary J. 'Professional Preparation of Parochial School Teachers.' *Hist. J. Mass.* 12/1:60 (Jan. 1984).

Oberholtzer, Ellis Paxson. *The Morals of the Movie.* Philadelphia 1922.

O'Brien, David J. *American Catholics and Social Reform: The New Deal Years.* NY 1968.

– 'The American Priest and Social Action.' In Ellis (1971) 423.

– *Isaac Hecker: An American Catholic*. NY 1992.

– *Public Catholicism*. NY 1989.

– *The Renewal of American Catholicism*. NY 1972.

O'Brien, John A., et al. *The Vanishing Irish: The Enigma of the Modern World*. Ed. John A. O'Brien. NY 1953.

O'Connor, Edward Dennis, ed. *The Dogma of the Immaculate Conception*. Notre Dame, IN 1958.

O'Dea, Thomas F. *American Catholic Dilemma: An Inquiry into the Intellectual Life*. NY 1958.

O'Dwyer, Peter. *Highlights in Devotion to Mary in Ireland from 1600*. Dublin 1981.

– *Mary: A History of Devotion in Ireland*. Dublin 1988.

Olasky, Marvin N. 'The Failure of Movie Industry Public Relations, 1921–1934.' *J. Pop. Film and Television* 12:163 (Winter 1984–5).

O'Neill, James M. *Catholicism and American Freedom*. NY 1952.

– *Religion and Education under the Constitution*. NY 1949.

Ong, Walter J. 'American Catholicism and America.' *Thought* 27:521 (Winter 1952).

Orr, James. *The Virgin Birth of Christ*. 1907; NY 1924.

Orsi, Robert A. *The Madonna of 115th Street: Faith and Community in Italian Harlem, 1880–1950*. New Haven 1985.

O'Toole, James M. *Militant and Triumphant: William Henry O'Connell and the Catholic Church in Boston, 1859–1944*. Notre Dame, IN 1992.

– 'The Name That Stood for Rome: William O'Connell and the Modern Episcopal Style' (1989). In Fogarty (1989B) 171.

Ottanelli, Fraser M. *The Communist Party of the United States: From the Depression to World War II*. New Brunswick, NJ 1991.

Palmer, Paul F. *Mary in the Documents of the Church*. Westminster, MD 1952.

– 'Mary in Protestant Theology and Worship.' *Theological Studies* 15:519 (Dec. 1954).

Palmieri, Aurelio. 'The Contribution of the Italian Clergy to the United States.' In McGuire 2:127.

Parrish, Michael E. *Felix Frankfurter and His Times: The Reform Years*. NY 1982.

Parsons, Louella. 'Ingrid – The Story of Bergman as a Woman.' *Photoplay* 32/3:42 (Feb. 1948).

– *Tell It to Louella*. NY 1961.

Parsons, Wilfrid. 'A Code for Motion Pictures.' *America* 43/1:32 (19 April 1930).

– 'Federal Film Censorship.' *America* 45/1:7 (11 April 1931).

– *The First Freedom: Considerations on Church and State in the United States*. NY 1948.

Paul, James C.N., and Murray L. Schwartz. *Federal Censorship: Obscenity in the Mail*. Glencoe, IL 1961.

Pelikan, Jaroslav. *Mary through the Centuries: Her Place in the History of Culture*. New Haven 1996.

– *The Riddle of Roman Catholicism*. NY 1959.

Pernicone, Joseph M. *The Ecclesiastical Prohibition of Books*. Catholic U. of America Studies in Canon Law no. 72. Washington, DC 1932.

Peyton, Patrick. *All for Her*. Hollywood, CA 1973.

Pfeffer, Leo. *Church[,] State and Freedom*. Rev. ed. Boston 1967.

Phayer, Michael. *The Catholic Church and the Holocaust, 1930–1965*. Bloomington, IN 2000.

Pizzitola, Louis. *Hearst over Hollywood: Power, Passion, and Propaganda in the Movies*. NY 2002.

Pohle, Joseph. *Mariology*. 5th ed. Trans. and ed. Arthur Preuss. St Louis 1914.

Post, Albert. *Popular Freethought in America, 1825–1850*. NY 1943.

Potamkin, Harry Alan. *The Compound Cinema*. Ed. Lewis Jacobs. NY 1977.

Potter, George. *To the Golden Door: The Story of the Irish in Ireland and America*. Boston 1960.

'Press Associations and Restraint of Trade.' *Yale L.J.* 55:428 (1946).

Prothero, Stephen R. *American Jesus: How the Son of God Became a National Icon*. NY 2003.

Putnam, George Haven. *The Censorship of the Church of Rome and Its Influence upon the Production and Distribution of Literature*. 2 vols. NY 1906–7.

Putney, Clifford. *Muscular Christianity*. Cambridge, MA 2001.

Quigley, Martin. *Decency in Motion Pictures*. NY 1937.

Quigley, Martin, Jr. '"The Miracle": An Outrage.' *Motion Picture Herald* 182/1:1 (6 Jan. 1951).

Rabban, David M. 'The First Amendment in the Forgotten Years.' *Yale L.J.* 90:516 (1981).

– *Free Speech in Its Forgotten Years*. Cambridge 1997.

Radosh, Ronald, and Allis Radosh. *Red Star over Hollywood*. San Francisco 2005.

Randall, Richard. 'Censorship: From *The Miracle* to *Deep Throat*.' In Balio (1985).

– *Censorship of the Movies: The Social and Political Control of a Mass Medium*. Madison, WI 1968.

Ranvaud, Don, ed. *Roberto Rossellini*. BFI Dossier no. 8. London 1981.

Ravitch, Diane. *The Great School Wars: New York City, 1805–1973*. NY 1974.

Redman, Ben Ray. 'The Hays Office.' *Fortune* 18:68 (Dec. 1938 ['A']).

– 'Pictures and Censorship.' *Sat. Rev.* 10:3 (31 Dec. 1938 ['B']).

Reeves, Thomas C. *America's Bishop: The Life and Times of Fulton J. Sheen.* San Francisco 2001.

Reher, Margaret Mary. *Catholic Intellectual Life in America.* NY 1989.

Reich, Jacqueline, and Piero Garofalo, eds. *Re-Viewing Fascism: Italian Cinema.* Bloomington, IN 2002.

Reilly, Daniel F. *The School Controversy (1891–1893).* Washington, DC 1943.

Reventlow, Henning Graf, and William Farmer. *Biblical Studies and the Shifting of Paradigms, 1850–1914.* J. Study of the Old Test. Supp. Ser. 192. Sheffield 1995.

Rhodes, Anthony. *The Power of Rome in the Twentieth Century.* NY 1983.

– *The Vatican in the Age of the Dictators 1922–1945.* NY 1973.

Roffman, Peter, and Jim Purdy. *The Hollywood Social Problem Film.* Bloomington, IN 1981.

Rohmer, Eric, 'Les deux images de la solitude.' *Cahiers du Cinéma* 10:38 (May 1956).

Rondolino, Gianni. *Rossellini: Roberto Rossellini di Gianni Rondolino.* Florence 1974.

Rorty, James. '"It Ain't No Sin."' *The Nation* 139:124 (1 Aug. 1934).

– *Where Life Is Better: An Unsentimental American Journey.* NY 1936.

Rose, Philip M. *The Italians in America.* NY 1922.

Rosenberg, Bernard, and David Manning White, eds. *Mass Culture.* Glencoe, IL 1957.

Rossellini, Isabella. *In the Name of the Father, the Daughter and the Holy Spirits: Remembering Roberto Rossellini.* Munich 2006.

– Script for *My Dad Is 100 Years Old.* Dir. Guy Maddin. 2005.

Rossellini, Roberto. 'De "Rome, Ville Ouverte" à "India," conversations télévisées.' In Bergala/Narboni 22. Trans. in R. Rossellini (1992) 114.

– 'Dix ans de cinéma.' *Cahiers du Cinéma* 50:3 (Aug. 1955) ['A'], 52:3 (Nov. 1955) ['B'], 55:9 (Jan. 1956) ['C'].

– *Roberto Rossellini.* Paris 1987.

– 'Roberto Rossellini by Roberto Rossellini.' *Cinema* 7/1:14 (Autumn 1971)

– *Roberto Rossellini, My Method.* Ed. Adriano Aprà. Trans. Annapaola Cancogni. NY 1992.

– 'Roberto Rossellini Talks about Marx, Freud and Jesus.' *Cineaste* 8/1:32 (Summer 1977).

– *The War Trilogy.* 1972. Trans. Judith Green. NY 1973.

Rossi, Patrizio. *Roberto Rossellini: A Guide to References and Resources.* Boston 1988.

Rosten, Leo C. *Hollywood: The Movie Colony / The Movie Makers.* NY 1941.

Rostron, Allen. '"No War, No Hate, No Propaganda": Promoting Films about European War and Fascism during the Period of American Isolationism.' *J. Pop. Film and Television* (Summer 2002).

Rotha, Paul. *The Film till Now.* 1930; 4th ed. Feltham, Middlesex 1967.

Russo, John Paul. 'DeLillo: Italian American Catholic Writer.' *Altreitalie* 25:4 (2002).

Rutland, J.R., comp. *State Censorship of Motion Pictures.* NY 1923.

Ryan, Edward A. 'Devotion to Our Lady in the United States.' In Carol 3:353.

Ryan, John A. *The Catholic Church and the Citizen.* NY 1928.

– *Distributive Justice: The Right and Wrong of Our Present Distribution of Wealth.* NY 1916.

– 'The Papal Encyclical on Labor.' *Survey* 66/6:307 (15 June 1931).

– *Social Doctrine in Action: A Personal History.* NY 1941.

– *Social Reconstruction.* NY 1920.

Sabatier, Paul. *Modernism: The Jowett Lectures, 1908.* Trans. C.A. Miles. NY 1908.

Sanders, James W. 'Catholics and the School Question in Boston.' In Sullivan/ O'Toole 121.

Sargent, Daniel. *Our Land and Our Lady.* NY 1939.

Sarris, Andrew. 'Rossellini, Renoir, and Ford' (1961). In *Confessions of a Cultis.* NY 1970.

– *You Ain't Heard Nothin' Yet.* NY 1998.

Sartorio, Enrico C. *Social and Religious Life of Italians in America.* 1918; Clifton, NJ 1974.

Satolli, Francis. *Loyalty to Church and State.* Baltimore 1895.

Schatz, Thomas, et al. *Boom and Bust: The American Cinema in the 1940s.* NY 1997.

Schiavo, Giovanni. *Four Centuries of Italian American History.* NY 1992.

Schickel, Richard. *Schickel on Film: Encounters – Critical and Personal – with Movie Immortals.* NY 1989.

Schlesinger, Arthur Meier, Jr, and Roger Bruns, eds. *Congress Investigates, 1792–1974.* NY 1975.

Schneider, Nicholas. *The Life of John Cardinal Glennon.* Liguori, MO 1971.

Schofield, Henry. 'Freedom of the Press in the United States.' *Am. Sociol. Soc. Papers and Proc.* 9:67 (1914).

Schrecker, Ellen. *Many Are the Crimes: McCarthyism in America.* Boston 1998.

Schulberg, Budd. *The Disenchanted.* NY 1950.

– *What Makes Sammy Run?* NY 1941.

Schultenover, David G. *A View from Rome: On the Eve of the Modernist Crisis.* NY 1993.

Schumach, Murray. *The Face on the Cutting Room Floor: The Story of Movie and Television Censorship.* NY 1964.

Schwartz, Bernard. *The Roots of the Bill of Rights.* 5 vols. 1971; NY 1980.

Schwartz, Nancy Lynn. *The Hollywood Writers' Wars.* NY 1982.

Scorsese, Martin. *My Voyage to Italy.* Buena Vista Home Entertainment DVD. 1999.

Seabury, William Marston. *The Public and the Motion Picture Industry.* NY 1926.

Sebastian, Wenceslaus. 'The Controversy over the Immaculate Conception from after Scotus to the End of the Eighteenth Century' (1954). In O'Connor 213.

Seldes, George. *The Catholic Crisis.* NY 1939.

– *The Vatican: Yesterday – Today/Tomorrow.* NY 1934.

Selznick, Irene Mayer. *A Private View.* NY 1983.

Serceau, Michel. *Roberto Rossellini.* Paris 1986.

Shadegg, Stephen. *Clare Boothe Luce: A Biography.* NY 1970.

Shannon, William V. *The American Irish.* NY 1963.

Shaughnessy, Gerald. *Has the Immigrant Kept the Faith?* NY 1925.

Sheen, Fulton J. *Communism and the Conscience of the West.* Indianapolis 1948.

– *The World's First Love.* NY 1952.

Shelley, Thomas J. 'Twentieth-Century American Catholicism and Irish Americans.' In Lee/Casey 574.

Shuster, George N. 'The Conflict among Catholics.' *Am. Scholar* 10:5 (Winter 1940).

Skinner, James M. *The Cross and the Cinema.* Westport, CT 1993.

Sklar, Robert. *Movie-Made America: A Cultural History of American Movies.* NY 1975.

Smit, David W. 'Marketing Ingrid Bergman.' *Quart. Rev. of Film and Video* 22:237 (July–Sept. 2005).

Smith, H. Shelton, Robert T. Handy, and Lefferts A. Loetscher. *American Christianity: An Historical Interpretation with Representative Documents.* 2 vols. NY 1960–3.

Smith, Timothy L. *Revivalism and Social Reform in Mid-Nineteenth-Century America.* NY 1957.

Somigli, Luca, and Mario Moroni, eds. *Italian Modernism: Italian Culture between Decadentism and Avant-Garde.* Toronto 2004.

Sparrow-Simpson, W.J. *Roman Catholic Opposition to Papal Infallibility.* London 1909.

Sperry, William L. *Religion in America.* NY 1946.

Spoto, Donald. *Notorious: The Life of Ingrid Bergman.* NY 1997.

Spretnak, Charlene. *Missing Mary: The Queen of Heaven and Her Re-emergence in the Modern Church.* NY 2005.

Stahl, Ellen J. 'A New Explanation of Sexual Repression in Ireland.' *Central Issues in Anthropology* 1/1:37 (March 1979).

Staiger, Janet, ed. *The Studio System.* New Brunswick, NJ 1995.

Stamps, Norman L. 'The Power of Congress to Inquire and Punish for Contempt.' *Baylor L. Rev.* 4:29 (1951).

Staunton, Michael. *The Voice of the Irish: The Story of Christian Ireland.* 2001; Mahway, NJ 2003.

Stearns, Harold E., ed. *America Now: An Inquiry into Civilization in the United States.* NY 1938.

Steele, Joseph H. *Ingrid Bergman: An Intimate Portrait.* NY 1959.

Stewart, Donald Ogden. *By a Stroke of Luck! An Autobiography.* NY 1975.

Stokes, Anson Phelps. *Church and State in the United States.* 3 vols. NY 1950.

Stone, Geoffrey R. *Perilous Times: Free Speech in Wartime.* NY 2004.

Sullivan, Robert E., and James M. O'Toole, eds. *Catholic Boston.* Boston 1985.

Sullivan, William Laurence. *Under Orders.* 1944; Boston 1966.

Tanner, Norman P., ed. *Decrees of the Ecumenical Councils.* 2 vols. London 1990.

Taves, Ann. *The Household of Faith: Roman Catholic Devotions in Mid-Nineteenth Century America.* Notre Dame, IN 1986.

Thackeray, William Makepeace. *The Irish Sketch Book.* 1842; Oxford 1925.

Thomas, Helen Shirley. *Felix Frankfurter: Scholar on the Bench.* Baltimore 1960.

Thome, Rudolf. 'Kommentierte Filmografie.' In Gansara 143. Trans. Dominique Petit as 'Filmographie commentée.' In Bergala/Narboni 111.

Thomson, David. *Showman: The Life of David O. Selznick.* NY 1992.

Thorp, Margaret Farrand. *America at the Movies.* New Haven 1939.

Tittmann, Harold H., Jr. *Inside the Vatican of Pius XII.* NY 2004.

Tocqueville, Alexis de. *Democracy in America.* Trans. and ed. Harvey C. Mansfield and Delba Winthrop. Chicago 2000.

– *Journey to America.* Trans. George Lawrence. Ed. J.P. Mayer. New Haven 1960.

– *Journeys to England and Ireland.* Trans. George Lawrence and K.P. Mayer. New Haven 1958.

Tomasi, Lydio F., ed. *Italian Americans: New Perspectives in Italian Immigration and Ethnicity.* Staten Island, NY 1985.

Tomasi, Silvano M. *Piety and Power.* Staten Island, NY 1975.

Tomasi, Silvano M., and Madeline H. Engel, eds. *The Italian Experience in the United States.* Staten Island, NY 1970.

Tomasi, Silvano M., and Edward C. Stibili. *Italian Americans and Religion: An Annotated Bibliography.* NY 1978.

Trasatti, Sergio. *Rossellini è la televisione*. Rome 1978.

Trevelyan, Raleigh. *Rome '44: The Battle for the Eternal City*. NY 1981.

Truffaut, François. 'Amore de Roberto Rossellini.' *Arts* (4–10 April 1956) 5.

Trumbo, Dalton. *The Time of the Toad: A Study of Inquisition in America*. NY 1972.

Turner, Jay Craig. 'Public Reaction to the National Legion of Decency as Reflected in the Popular Press, 1934–1952.' M.A. thesis, Univ. of Texas, 1984.

Twain, Mark. *Saint Joan of Arc*. 1904; NY 1919.

Ussher, Arland. 'The Boundary between the Sexes.' In J. O'Brien 156.

Vaillancourt, Jean-Guy. *Papal Power: A Study of Vatican Control over Lay Catholic Elites*. Berkeley 1980.

Varacalli, Joseph A., et al., eds. *The Saints in the Lives of Italian Americans*. Stony Brook, NY 1999.

Varbero, Richard A. 'Philadelphia's South Italians and the Irish Church: A History of Cultural Conflict.' In *The Religious Experience of Italian Americans*. Proceedings of the Sixth Annual Conference of the American Italian Historical Association. Ed. Silvano M. Tomasi. NY 1975.

Vaughn, Stephen. 'Financiers, Movie Producers and the Churches' (1986). In Austin 201.

– 'Morality and Entertainment: The Origins of the Motion Picture Production Code.' *J. Am. Hist.* 77/1:39 (June 1990).

Vecoli, Rudolph J. 'Cult and Occult in Italian American Culture.' In Miller/Marzik 25.

– 'Prelates and Peasants: Italian Immigrants and the Catholic Church.' *J. Soc. Hist.* 2:217 (Spring 1969).

Velie, Lester. 'You Can't See That Movie: Censorship in Action.' *Collier's* 125/18:11 (6 May 1950).

Ventresca, Robert A. 'The Virgin and the Bear.' *J. Soc. Hist.* 37/2:439 (Winter 2003).

Venturi, Lauro. 'Roberto Rossellini.' *Hollywood Quart.* 4/1:1 (Fall 1949).

Verdone, Mario. *Roberto Rossellini*. Paris 1963.

Vermes, Geza. *The Nativity: History and Legend*. London 2006.

Vidler, A.R. *The Modernist Movement in the Roman Church: Its Origins and Outcome*. Cambridge 1934.

Vieira, Mark A. *Sin in Soft Focus: Pre-Code Hollywood*. NY 1999.

Villari, Luigi. *Italian Life in Town and Country*. NY 1903.

Vizzard, Jack. *See No Evil: Life inside a Hollywood Censor*. NY 1970.

Wakin, Edward, and Joseph F. Scheuer. *The De-Romanization of the American Catholic Church*. NY 1966.

Walburg, Anthony. *The Question of Nationality in Its Relation to the Catholic Church in the U.S.* Cincinnati 1889.

Walsh, Frank. '"The Callahans and the Murphys" (MGM, 1927): A Case Study of Irish American and Catholic Church Censorship.' *Hist. J. of Film, Radio and Television* 10/1:33 (1990).

– *Sin and Censorship: The Catholic Church and the Motion Picture Industry.* New Haven 1996.

Ward, Leo Richard, ed. *The American Apostolate.* Westminster, MD 1952.

Warner, Marina. *Alone of All Her Sex: The Myth and the Cult of the Virgin Mary.* 1976; NY 1983.

– *Joan of Arc: The Image of Female Heroism.* NY 1981.

Warren, Charles. 'The New "Liberty" under the Fourteenth Amendment.' *Harv. L. Rev.* 39:431 (1926).

Waugh, Eveyln. 'The American Epoch in the Catholic Church' (1949). In *A Treasury of Catholic Reading.* Ed. John Chapin. NY 1957.

Weber, Francis J. 'John J. Cantwell and the Legion of Decency.' *Am. Eccles. Rev.* 151/4:237 (Oct. 1964).

Weigel, Gustave. 'Survey of Protestant Theology in Our Day.' *Proc. Cath. Theol. Soc. of America* (1953) 43.

Weinstein, Donald, and Rudolph M. Bell. *Saints and Society: The Two Worlds of Western Christendom.* Chicago 1982.

Werfel, Franz. *The Song of Bernadette.* Trans. Ludwig Lewisohn. NY 1942.

Wertheimer, John. 'Mutual Film Reviewed: The Movies, Censorship, and Free Speech in Progressive America.' *Am. J. Legal Hist.* 37/2:158 (April 1993).

Westin, Alan F. *The Miracle Case: The Supreme Court and the Movies.* Inter-University Case Program no. 64. Indianapolis 1961.

Whelan, Irene. 'Religious Rivalry and the Making of Irish-American Identity.' In Lee/Casey 271.

Whelan, Russell. 'The Legion of Decency.' *Am. Mercury* 60:655 (June 1945).

Whitney, Simon N. 'Antitrust Policies and the Motion Picture Industry' (1958). In Kindem 161.

Wilinsky, Barbara. *Sure Seaters: The Emergence of Art House Cinema.* Minneapolis 2001.

Wilk, Max. *The Wit and Wisdom of Hollywood.* NY 1971.

Will, Allen S. *Life of Cardinal Gibbons, Archbishop of Baltimore.* 2 vols. NY 1922.

Williams, George H. 'Professor George La Piana (1878–1971) Catholic Modernist at Harvard.' *Harvard Lib. Bull.* (April 1973) 117.

Williams, Michael. *The Catholic Church in Action.* NY 1934.

– *Catholicism and the Modern Mind.* NY 1928.

Williams, Phyllis H. *South Italian Folkways in Europe and America.* 1938; NY 1969.

Wilson, Edmund. *Europe without Baedeker*. 2d ed. NY 1966.

Winch, Raymond, and Victor Bennett. *The Assumption of Our Lady and Catholic Theology*. London 1950.

Winnington, Richard. *Film: Criticism and Caricatures 1943–53*. Ed. Paul Rotha. London 1975.

Wirt, Frederick M. 'State Film Censorship with Particular Reference to Ohio.' Ph.D. diss., Ohio State Univ., 1956.

Wittern-Keller, Laura. "Fighting for Freedom of the Screen: The Legal Battle over State Film Censorship, 1930–1965." www.oah.org/meetings/2004/papers/wittern-keller.doc.

Wittke, Carl. *The Irish in America*. Baton Rouge 1956.

Wohlforth, Robert. 'People and Pickets.' *New Republic* (5 Feb. 1951) 13.

Wood, Robin. 'Ingrid Bergman on Rossellini.' *Film Comment* 10/4:12 (July/Aug. 1974).

Yeaman, Elizabeth. 'The Catholic Movie Censorship.' *New Republic* 96:233 (5 Oct. 1938).

Zarrilli, John. 'A Suggestion for the Solution of the Italian Problem.' *Eccles. Rev.* 76:70 (Jan. 1924).

Zeffirelli, Franco. *Zeffirelli: The Autobiography of Franco Zeffirelli*. NY 1986.

Zimdars-Swartz, Sandra. *Encountering Mary*. Princeton 1991.

Zwierlein, Frederick J. *The Life and Letters of Bishop McQuaid*. 3 vols. Rome 1925–7.1.

Index